THE ROUTLEDGE COMPANION TO MEDIA AND HUMANITARIAN ACTION

In this moment of unprecedented humanitarian crises, the representations of global disasters are increasingly common media themes around the world. *The Routledge Companion to Media and Humanitarian Action* explores the interconnections between media, old and new, and the humanitarian challenges that have come to define the twenty-first century. Contributors, including media professionals and experts in humanitarian affairs, grapple with what kinds of media language, discourse, terms, and campaigns can offer enough context and background knowledge to nurture informed global citizens. Case studies of media practices, content analysis and evaluation of media coverage, and representations of humanitarian emergencies and affairs offer further insight into the ways in which strategic communications are designed and implemented in the field of humanitarian action.

Contributors: Tamara Alrifai, Irene Amuron, Klas Backholm, Adrian Bergmann, Aregawi Berhe, Heather Bourbeau, Garrett M. Broad, Kenzie Burchell, Meinrad Bürer, Richard Choularton, Simona Cruciani, Henia Dakkak, Mathieu Destrooper, Pamela DeLargy, Rudelmar Bueno de Faria, Erin Coughlan de Perez, Adama Dieng, Ivar Evensmo, Pat Fast, Laura Fontaine, Pierre-Olivier François, Suzanne Franks, Elsebeth Frey, Yehia Ghanem, Elke Grittmann, DeeDee Halleck, Linda M. Hartling, Emma Heywood, Harald Hornmoen, Konstanze Kampfer, Azza Karam, Epp Lauk, Evelin Gerda Lindner, Maria Konow Lund, Heather McIntosh, Rebecca Miller, Pierluigi Musarò, Ulrich Nitschke, Dorothy Njoroge, Fadwa Ahmed Obaid, Eva-Karin Olsson, Rune Ottosen, Hajime Ozaki, Shawn Powers, Gudrun Reimerth, Piers Robinson, Alexandra Rüth, Kim Scipes, Anne Skjelmerud, Nadia Sraieb-Koepp, Steen Steensen, Peter Sutherland, Jordi Torrent, Turo Uskali, Priti Vaishnav, Alexander van Tulleken, Heike Wülfing, Kevin Wyjad

Robin Andersen is Professor of Communication and Media Studies at Fordham University in New York. She is the author of four books, dozens of book chapters, journal articles, and writes media criticism for a variety of publications. Her book *A Century of Media: A Century of War* won the 2007 Alpha Sigma Nu Book Award, the honor society of Jesuit colleges and universities. She helped develop the curriculum for Fordham University's MA Program on Humanitarian Action.

Purnaka L. de Silva is Director at the Institute for Strategic Studies and Democracy Malta. He was previously Senior Advisor at the United Nations Global Compact in the Executive Office of Secretary-General Kofi Annan and served as a Lecturer in the School of Politics and the Centre for the Study of Ethnic Conflict at Queen's University Belfast in Northern Ireland. He has over thirty years of experience in conflict and peace studies with special focus on political violence, paramilitaries, counter-terrorism, and transnational security, as well as the role of diplomacy within the United Nations system.

THE ROUTLEDGE COMPANION TO MEDIA AND HUMANITARIAN ACTION

Edited by
Robin Andersen and
Purnaka L. de Silva

Routledge
Taylor & Francis Group

NEW YORK AND LONDON

First published 2018
by Routledge
711 Third Avenue, New York, NY 10017

and by Routledge
2 Park Square, Milton Park, Abingdon, Oxon OX14 4RN

Routledge is an imprint of the Taylor & Francis Group, an informa business

Library of Congress Cataloging in Publication Data
Names: Andersen, Robin, editor. |
De Silva, Purnaka L., editor.
Title: The Routledge companion to media and humanitarian action /
edited by Robin Andersen and Purnaka L. de Silva.
Other titles: Companion to media and humanitarian action.
Description: New York and London : Routledge,
Taylor & Francis Group, [2017]
Identifiers: LCCN 2017004171| ISBN 9781138688575 (hardback) |
ISBN 9781315538129 (ebk)
Subjects: LCSH: Humanitarian intervention. | Mass media.
Classification: LCC JZ6369 .R677 2017 | DDC 363.34/9856—dc23
LC record available at https://lccn.loc.gov/2017004171

ISBN: 978-1-138-68857-5 (hbk)
ISBN: 978-1-315-53812-9 (ebk)

Typeset in Bembo
by Florence Production Limited, Stoodleigh, Devon, UK

CONTENTS

CONTENTS

CONTENTS

CONTRIBUTORS

Tamara Alrifai is the Regional Advocacy and Communications Advisor for the Arab States at the United Nations Population Fund and based in Cairo, Egypt. She was previously the Advocacy and Communications Director for Middle East and North Africa at Human Rights Watch, and the International Committee of the Red Cross Delegate and Spokesperson at the United Nations in New York. She contributes to Arab media on human rights, the Syrian civil war, power politics, press freedoms, population issues, refugees, and democracy. She writes regular Op-ed articles/blogs, and is followed on Twitter @TamaraAlrifai.

Irene Amuron is the Disaster Risk Reduction Coordinator at the Uganda Red Cross Society. She has a professional background in public health and many years of experience working within the Red Cross and Red Crescent Movement. She is now the main focal point for Forecast-based Financing within the Uganda Red Cross. In 2015, she coordinated groundbreaking humanitarian action in Uganda that was triggered by scientific forecasts of flood risks.

Robin Andersen is Professor of Communication and Media Studies at Fordham University in New York. She is the author of four books, dozens of book chapters, journal articles and writes media criticism for a variety of publications. Her book *A Century of Media: A Century of War* won the 2007 Alpha Sigma Nu Book Award, the honor society of Jesuit colleges and universities. She helped develop the curriculum for Fordham University's MA Program on Humanitarian Action.

Klas Backholm is a Postdoctoral Researcher at the Åbo Akademi University in Vasa, Finland. His interests include investigating how social media platforms are used in crisis journalism and how covering crises affects journalists psychologically. He is currently the leader of a work package in the research project RESCUE in which he investigates the usability of a web-based social media information verification toolset for journalists and crisis communicators.

Adrian Bergmann is a Research Fellow at the Central American University in El Salvador. His research interests are in Qualitative Social Research, Social Theory and Conflict processes, focusing on the crossroads of peace-building, conflict transformation, and non-violent struggle. He has broad multicultural work experience in Central America, Europe and the Middle East. He received a Master's degree in Peace and Reconciliation Studies, with Distinction, from Coventry University in the United Kingdom. He was previously, Adjunct Professor in Peace and Conflict Studies at the World Peace Academy—Swiss Centre for Peace in Basel, Switzerland, and Director and Chair of Peace Culture at the Universidad Don Bosco.

Aregawi Berhe is one of the co-founders and former military commander of the Tigrayan People's Liberation Front. He received his PhD from Vrije Universiteit Amsterdam in the Netherlands. He is a humanitarian analyst who focuses on political and multicultural affairs in Ethiopia and the Horn of Africa. His writings include the book (2009) *A Political History of the Tigray People's Liberation Front (1975–1991): Revolt, Ideology and Mobilization in Ethiopia*, a number of articles on Ethiopian colonial history and politics, and the chapter (2000) "Ethiopia: A Success Story or State of Chaos" in Munck, Ronaldo and Purnaka L. de Silva (eds) *Postmodern Insurgencies: Political Violence, Identity Formation and Peacemaking in Comparative Perspective*, London and New York: Macmillan and St. Martin's Press.

Heather Bourbeau's journalism has appeared in *The Economist, The Financial Times, Foreign Affairs, Foreign Policy*, and *The New York Times*. She was a contributing writer to the *New York Times* bestseller, *Not On Our Watch: A Mission to End Genocide in Darfur and Beyond* with Don Cheadle and John Prendergast. She has worked with various United Nations agencies, including the World Food Programme, UN peacekeeping mission in Liberia, and UNICEF Somalia.

Garrett M. Broad is an Assistant Professor in the Department of Communication and Media Studies at Fordham University. His research investigates how media and storytelling shape contemporary communities and networked movements for social and environmental justice. He is author of the book *More Than Just Food: Food Justice and Community Change* (University of California Press, 2016).

Kenzie Burchell is Assistant Professor of Journalism at the University of Toronto Department of Arts, Culture and Media (UTSC) and the Faculty of Information (iSchool). He received his PhD in 2012 from Goldsmiths, University of London, where he also worked as a Lecturer and Visiting Tutor. He was previously a Research Associate of European Media Studies at the University of Manchester.

Meinrad Bürer is Senior Officer Climate Change Mitigation at the International Federation of Red Cross and Red Crescent Societies in Geneva. Prior to joining the Red Cross and Red Crescent Movement he was Technical Director for The Gold Standard Foundation, which has an internationally recognized certification standard for climate change mitigation projects, with a focus on stakeholder consultation and environmental and socio-economic benefits.

Richard Choularton is Chief for Climate and Disaster Risk Reduction Programmes at the World Food Programme in Rome. His academic background lies within risk, crises and disaster management, with a strong focus on climate risks and food security. Before working for the World Food Programme, he reformed the early warning activities of the Famine Early Warning Systems Network, and was the Director of the Humanitarian Assistance Office of Global Communities.

Simona Cruciani is Political Affairs Officer at the UN Office on Genocide Prevention and the Responsibility to Protect. She is responsible for issues related to religious violence and the role of religious leaders and actors in preventing atrocity crimes and their incitement, human security, democratization, human rights in conflict and post-conflict situations, and, recently, on combating human trafficking. She has worked extensively in United Nations field operations, including as an Electoral and Civil Affairs Officer for the ONUB Peacekeeping Operations in Burundi, and a Civil Affairs Officer for UNMIS in Sudan.

Henia Dakkak is an MD and MPH and the Senior Humanitarian Technical Advisor at the United Nations Population Fund, providing support to Country Offices dealing with emergencies that involve reproductive and mental health issues, during the crisis and in the post-crisis phase. She was previously the Director of Relief and Development Programs at the International Medical Corps, covering HIV/AIDS epidemic and reproductive health needs. She currently has eleven projects in nine conflict and post-conflict countries in Africa, Central Asia, Middle East and North Africa, and South East Asia. She has also worked in war-affected Kosovo, and founded a multispecialty medical center in Jerusalem. She conducted postdoctoral research at Columbia University on a Fulbright scholarship.

Mathieu Destrooper is the German Red Cross Delegate for the Forecast-based Financing pilot project in Peru. He has broad experience in disaster risk management, disaster response and development cooperation. He holds a Master's degree in Development and International Politics. Before joining the German Red Cross, he worked in different coordination functions, as Country Representative for the Belgian Red Cross in Africa, and Project Manager for Disaster Risk Management at the United Nations Development Programme.

Pamela DeLargy is Senior Advisor at the Office of the United Nations Special Representative of the Secretary-General on International Migration. She is responsible for issues dealing with refugees, migration, humanitarian action, and youth, with special interest in women, health, and war in the Horn of Africa. She worked previously at the United Nations Population Fund where she held a number of important portfolios, including, Country Representative in Sudan, Senior Advisor Arab States Special Programmes, Chief Humanitarian Response and Country Representative in Eritrea. She is followed on Twitter @umasalam.

Rudelmar Bueno de Faria is the Representative of the World Council of Churches to the United Nation in New York, and is Coordinator of United Nations Ecumenical Office. He has over 20 years of experience working with national and international NGOs on program development, planning, management, hands-on-advocacy, mediation and negotiation, and on training that covers humanitarian intervention, peace-building, sustainable development and environmental issues. He has served in Brazil, El Salvador, Guatemala, Honduras, Nicaragua, Colombia, Switzerland, and the United States. On mission, he has traveled to over 80 countries in Africa, Americas, Asia, Europe, and Australasia. He worked previously in Department for World Service at the Lutheran World Federation, where he held several important portfolios.

Erin Coughlan de Perez is the Senior Climate Specialist of the Red Cross Red Crescent Climate Centre. She provides technical support to enable the interpretation and use of climate information by disaster managers worldwide. She is the Climate Centre's liaison at the International Research Institute for Climate and Society, delivering real-time decision-making support in response to climate-related questions from humanitarian actors. She also designs participatory games for capacity building and climate change awareness.

Purnaka L. de Silva is Director at the Institute for Strategic Studies and Democracy Malta. He was previously Senior Advisor at the United Nations Global Compact in the Executive Office of Secretary-General Kofi Annan. He has taught Political Science and International Relations at a number of universities in the United States and served as a Lecturer in the School of Politics and the Centre for the Study of Ethnic Conflict at Queen's University Belfast in Northern Ireland. He has over thirty years' experience in conflict and peace studies with special focus on political violence, paramilitaries, counter-terrorism, and transnational security, as well as the role of diplomacy within the United Nations system. His current research focuses on human trafficking, forced migration and terrorism in Libya, Iraq, and Syria. He is co-editor, with Ronaldo Munck, of *Postmodern Insurgencies: Political Violence, Identity Formation and Peacemaking in Comparative Perspective*, 2000.

Adama Dieng is the Under-Secretary-General/Special Advisor of the Secretary-General on Prevention of Genocide. He is mandated by the United Nations Security Council to collect and assess information on genocide and related crimes. His responsibilities include advising the United Nations Secretary-General and the Security Council, making recommendations to prevent and halt genocide, and liaising with the United Nations system on preventive measures. He is a legal and human rights expert with a distinguished career in contributing to the strengthening of the rule of law, fighting impunity, and promoting capacity building in the area of judicial and democratic institutions, including through fact-finding missions, publications and media. He served for ten years as the Secretary-General of the International Commission of Jurists, based in Geneva. He was previously the Registrar of the International Criminal Tribunal for Rwanda. He has held a number of important portfolios, including United Nations Independent Expert for Haiti (1995–2000), Envoy of the United Nations Secretary-General to Malawi (1993), Registrar of the Supreme Court of Senegal (six years), and Registrar of the Regional and Labour Courts in Senegal. He is credited with being the driving force behind the establishment of the African Court on Human and Peoples' Rights, as well as the draft of the African Union Convention on Preventing and Combating Corruption.

Ivar Evensmo is Senior Advisor for Media and Civil Society in the Section for Human Rights and Gender Equality at the Norwegian Agency for Development Cooperation. His work focuses on exploring linkages between freedom of expression, sustainable development, democracy, conflict resolution, civil society, and media development. He has extensive professional experience in donor support to civil society and media in transitional and post-conflict societies. He received his PhD in Social Anthropology from the University of Oslo, Norway. He was previously the Nansen Dialogue Project Manager and Advisor at the International Peace Research Institute Oslo.

Pat Fast is an MD, PhD, and the Senior Technical Advisor at the International AIDS Vaccine Initiative. She is an immunologist and pediatrician who worked in biotech on the influenza vaccine, both at the National Institutes of Health at the US Department of Health and Human Services. Currently she works at the nonprofit International AIDS Vaccine Initiative to help test preventive HIV vaccine for candidates in the US, Africa, and Europe. During the Ebola virus epidemic she helped the World Health Organization establish the first trials of the successful vaccine. She is an Adjunct Clinical Associate Professor of Pediatric Infectious Diseases at Stanford University School of Medicine in California.

Laura Fontaine is a Consultant for the German Red Cross and other humanitarian and development organizations with a special focus on climate change and broader environmental issues. She holds a Master's degree in Geography. She works as Associate Director for Natural Environment and Climate Issues for World Vision International, and is Consultant on Humanitarian Action and Climate Change for the United Nations Office for the Coordination of Humanitarian Affairs. Her research focus is on policy implications within the context of Forecast-based Financing.

Pierre-Olivier François is a French-German TV reporter and documentary filmmaker who studied Political Science and Journalism at the *Institut d'Etudes Politiques* in Paris, and at the *Freie Universität* Berlin. His work covers French and European politics, foreign affairs, culture and the arts. He started making documentary films in 2000 for European public television network ARTE and international channels. His documentary films include, in cooperation with PBS *Cyberwar: A Secret History of the NSA* (2015), with Alegria in coproduction with ARTE and other public broadcasters *UN: Last Station Before Hell* (2014) about peacekeeping for the 70th anniversary of the United Nations, *Korea Divided* (2013) the first documentary in which North and South Korean high-ranking witnesses appear in the same film, and *A Barrel Full of Dreams* (2009), which dealt with power and oil in Putin's Russia. He worked previously for the German press, the *Economist* and briefly for the United Nations in New York, as a French-speaking press attaché covering the General Assembly and Security Council.

Suzanne Franks is Professor and Head of the Department of Journalism at City University London. She is a former BBC TV journalist and has written widely on the history of broadcasting, the coverage of international news and humanitarian communication. Her recent publications include (2013) *Reporting Disasters. Famine, Aid, Politics and the Media*, London: Hurst, and the co-edited book, (2016) *Africa's Media Image in the Twenty-first Century*, London and New York: Routledge.

Elsebeth Frey is Associate Professor of Journalism at the Department of Journalism and Media Studies Oslo and Akershus University College of Applied Sciences in Oslo, Norway. Her research focuses on crisis journalism, journalistic core values, and online journalism.

Yehia Ghanem is a professional journalist who has worked for Egypt's largest newspaper, Al Ahram, since 1988. As a war correspondent he spent his first nineteen years covering conflicts in Serbia, Croatia, Bosnia, Yemen, Afghanistan, Rwanda, and the Democratic Republic of Congo. He received an award for his coverage of Bosnia. He contributes to *Huffington Post* and *Al Jazeera*, among other news media outlets. He was previously an International Journalist in Residence at the CUNY Graduate School of Journalism. In 2012, he became Chairman of the Board of Al Hilal Media, a subsidiary of Al Ahram, and in 2008 the Managing Director of Al Ahram. He has a BA in Journalism from the University of Cairo. His publications include *A True Account of the Arab Israeli Arms Reduction Negotiations* (1999, Cairo: Dar Al-Khayel); *What is Going On in Asia? The Impact of Nuclear Tests by Pakistan and India on the Strategic Balance* (1997, Cairo: Al Ahram); *Media Disinformation: A Study on Iraq, Libya, Egypt and Bosnia* (1995, Cairo: Dar Al-Khayel); *I Was There: A Journal of a War Correspondent in Bosnia* (1993, Cairo: Dar Al-l'tisam). He is followed on yehiaghanem.com and Twitter @Ghanem3.

Elke Grittmann is Visiting Professor at the Institute of Culture and Aesthetics of Digital Media, Leuphana University Lueneburg, Germany. Her research interests include media and migration, visual communication (especially photography), transcultural media communication, gender media studies and journalism and memory. Her recent publications include, "DasUnwort erklärt die Untat." *Die Berichterstattung über die NSU-Morde—eine Medienkritik* ("The un-word explains the Misdeeds." *Media Coverage of the NSU Crimes—a Media Critique*, Otto Brenner Stiftung, 2015).

DeeDee Halleck is Co-founder of the alternative media production and distribution collectives, Paper Tiger Television and Deep Dish Television, and author of *Hand-Held*

Visions: The Impossible Possibilities of Community Media (2002, New York: Fordham University Press). She is Professor Emeritus at the University of California, San Diego, and has worked around globe as consultant for community and independent media development. She holds numerous awards for her pioneering work in media development, such as the Dallas Smyth Award for Lifetime Achievement from the Union for Democratic Communications.

Linda M. Hartling is the Director of Human Dignity and Humiliation Studies, and co-founder of the World Dignity University initiative and the Dignity Press. She received her PhD in Clinical and Community Psychology from the Union Institute Graduate School in Cincinnati, Ohio. She was previously Associate Director of the Jean Baker Miller Training Institute at the Stone Center, part of the Wellesley Centers for Women at Wellesley College. She is author of numerous papers and chapters, and co-editor of *The Complexity of Connection: Writings from the Stone Center's Jean Baker Miller Training Institute* (2004, New York: Guilford Press), and creator of the Humiliation Inventory, a scale to assess the internal experience of derision and degradation. She is the recipient of the 2010 Research Award presented by the Association for Creativity in Counseling, American Counseling Association.

Emma Heywood is a Lecturer in French at the School of Humanities and a Researcher with the Centre for Trust, Peace and Social Relations at Coventry University in the United Kingdom. She received her PhD in Russian Studies from the University of Manchester. She conducts research into foreign conflict reporting, the media and war-affected areas, and European reporting of the Middle East conflict in the post-Cold war and 9/11 era. She has recently been awarded British Academy funding to investigate the role of local media in NGO activities in conflict-affected areas. Fieldwork for this project took place in 2016. She is currently investigating the interaction between local media, particularly radio, and NGOs in the West Bank in Palestine.

Harald Hornmoen is Professor of Journalism at the Department of Journalism and Media Studies, Oslo and Akershus University College of Applied Sciences in Oslo, Norway. His research interests include risk and environmental communication, science journalism, and literary journalism. He currently coordinates RESCUE, which is a multidisciplinary research project that seeks to develop knowledge about, and tools and recommendations for, the use of social media during crises.

Konstanze Kampfer is the German Red Cross Delegate of the Forecast-based Financing pilot project in Mozambique. She holds a Master's degree in Geography and provides consulting services in the field of risk reduction project management, project development, monitoring and evaluation for the Mozambican National Institute for Disaster Management, as well as GIZ, IP-Consult, the Brazilian Agency for Cooperation, the Swedish Civil Contingencies Agency, and Munich Re Foundation.

Azza Karam is Senior Advisor, Multilateral Affairs Branch at the United Nations Population Fund. She is also Coordinator of the United Nations Interagency Task Force on Religion and Development. Her work focuses on population, youth, health, human rights, religion, gender, political economy, and democracy. She received a PhD, *Summa Cum Laude*, from the University of Amsterdam in the Netherlands. She was previously Senior Policy Advisor in the Regional Bureau for Arab States United at the Nations Development Programme, and Coordinator of the *Arab Human Development Reports*. She founded the first Global Women of Faith Network, and was President of the Committee of Religious NGOs at the United Nations. She also served as Senior Program Officer at the International Institute for Democracy and Electoral Assistance in Stockholm, Sweden, and as a Consultant to the Organization for Security and Cooperation in Europe. She has lectured in post-graduate and graduate studies programs including at the School of Politics and the Centre for the Study of Ethnic Conflict at Queen's University Belfast, Northern Ireland. Her books publications include, *Transnational Political Islam* (2004, London: Pluto), *A Woman's Place: Religious Women as Public Actors* (2001, New York: WCRP), *Islamisms, Women and the State* (1998, London and New York: Macmillan and St. Martin's Press), *Women in Parliament: Beyond Numbers* (1998, Stockholm: IIDEA) and *Islam in a Non-Pillarized Society* (1996, Amsterdam: Trans-National Institute).

Epp Lauk is Professor of Journalism and Head of the Department of Communication at the University of Jyväskylä in Finland. Her research interests include media development in Eastern and Central European new democracies, and the history and culture of journalism and its professionalization in national and international perspective. More recently, she has focused on the interaction of journalism and social media, including innovations in media, such as drone journalism.

Evelin Gerda Lindner holds an MD and two PhDs, and is Founding President of the Human Dignity and Humiliation Studies, an emerging academic field. She is Co-Founder World Dignity University, WDU Press, and was a Nominee for the Nobel Peace Prize in 2015 and 2016. Her affiliations are with Columbia University's Morton Deutsch International Center for Cooperation and Conflict Resolution, New York; the Maison des Sciences de l'Homme, Paris; University of Oslo Department of Psychology; and Norwegian Centre for Human Rights. She has written *Honor, Humiliation, and Terror* (2016), *A Dignity Economy* (2012). She is the recipient of the 2009 Prisoner's Testament Peace Award, given in Norway, and the (2006) Applied Psychology Award, Swiss Association of Applied Psychology.

Maria Konow Lund holds a PhD and is Associate Professor in the Faculty of Social Sciences, Department of Journalism and Media Studies at Oslo, and Akershus University College of Applied Sciences. Her research interests include crises and communication studies, ethnographic news production, studies on journalism and entrepreneurship, media management, and media innovation.

Heather McIntosh is Assistant Professor of Mass Media at Minnesota State University, Mankato. She is co-editor of *Documenting Gendered Violence: Representations, Collaborations, and Movements* (Bloomsbury, 2015). She is also a blogger for PBS's POV series.

Rebecca Miller is a Research Assistant at the German Red Cross, and supports the coordination of the Federal Foreign Office Action Plan for Humanitarian Adaptation to Climate Change. She has a Bachelor's degree in Business Engineering and Environmental Science from the Berlin School of Economic and Law. She is currently enrolled for her Master's degree in Environmental and Resource Management at the Brandenburg University of Technology Cottbus, Germany.

Pierluigi Musarò is Associate Professor of Sociology at the University of Bologna. He is also Visiting Fellow at the London School of Economics and Political Science, and at the Institute for Public Knowledge, New York University. His primary research interest focuses on the relationship between social justice and humanitarianism in contemporary mediated communication. He has recently edited: "The Banality of Goodness: Humanitarianism

Between the Ethics of Showing and the Ethics of Seeing," *Humanity Journal*, 6.2, 2015, pp. 317–335; 'Africans' vs. 'Europeans': Humanitarian Narratives and the Moral Geography of the World, in Beyond Humanitarian Narratives," *Sociologia della Comunicazione*, 45, Milano, 2013, pp. 37–59.

Ulrich Nitschke is the Sector Program Head for "Values, Religion and Development," Deutsche Gesellschaft für Internationale Zusammenarbeit, and Coordinator of "International Secretariat on Religion and Sustainable Development." He is a former GIZ Head directing the unit, Local Governance and Civil Society Development Program, Future for Palestine. He also held the position of Chairperson, GIZ Sector Network Governance for MENA, GTZ Director Programme for Decentralization and Communal Development in Benin, and managed the Municipal Development (Eine-Welt) for Cooperation with Countries from the South. He is Licentiate in Theology and Philosophy, Fribourg University, Switzerland.

Dorothy Njoroge is Senior Lecturer of Journalism at United States International University-Africa (USIU-A). She obtained her PhD in Mass Communication and Media Arts from Southern Illinois University, Carbondale and has taught in Africa and the USA. Her research interests include issues of social justice, and global justice campaigns for Africa focusing on the Make Poverty History campaign fronted by Bono and, most recently, the Bring Back our Girls Campaign. Dorothy developed the curriculum for Master in Communication Studies at USIU-A. She has also co-authored *An Introduction to Communication* (Oxford University Press, East Africa).

Fadwa Ahmed Obaid is a Consultant for Communication, Media and Outreach, and a Strategist for Saudi Arabia, Gulf Cooperation Council countries, and international organizations. She works with TV broadcasters, government organizations, NGOs and foundations, as well as educational institutions. Her focus is on designing and implementing online-offline communications and media outreach strategies for TV and radio, print and social media campaigns, and digital production. She also does community outreach with media workshops and social development initiatives in Egypt and Lebanon. She has over 20 years of TV and media experience including, Head of Audience Research and Programme Development Abu Dhabi TV, and Head of Programme Content MBC TV. She is also a UK-qualified life-coach and mentor.

Eva-Karin Olsson is Associate Professor of Political Science at the Swedish Defence University. Her research interests include crisis management, political communication, and international organizations. She has published her work in journals such as *Journalism*, *International Journal of Press/Politics*, *Public Administration*, and *Media, War and Conflict*.

Rune Ottosen is Professor of Journalism at Oslo and Akershus University College of Applied Sciences. He has written extensively on press history and media coverage of war and conflicts. Ottosen is Deputy President of the Norwegian Association of Press History and was President of The Norwegian Non-Fiction Writers and Translators Association 2001–2005. He has been Guest Lecturer at a number of universities in Norway, Sweden, Denmark, Belgium, Estonia, USA, South Africa, Nepal, and Pakistan.

Hajime Ozaki is a 36-year veteran of *Kyodo News* and since 2014 has served as the New York Bureau Chief for *Kyodo News*. With 50 million subscribers, *Kyodo News* distributes reports to almost all newspapers, radio, and television networks in Japan. He oversees media-production and contributes to special interest reports and conducts in-studio interviews. He was the Geneva Bureau Chief from 2003 to 2007 for Kyodo News, and the UN Correspondent in New York from 1996 to 1999, and the Tel Aviv Jerusalem Bureau Chief from 1990 to 1994.

Shawn Powers PhD Directs the Center for Global Information Studies and is an Associate Professor in the Department of Communication at Georgia State University (GSU). Powers routinely speaks to media, policymakers, and international organizations on the geopolitics of information and technology policy. He is a faculty affiliate of GSU's Transcultural Violence and Conflict initiative and co-leads its British Council and European Commission funded project, "Civic Approaches to Religious Conflict and Violence." Powers serves on the Board of Advisors for the State Department's Advisory Commission on Public Diplomacy and has received fellowships from the London School of Economics, the University of Pennsylvania's Center for Global Communication Studies, Oxford's Programme in Comparative Media Law and Policy, and Central European University's Center for Media, Data and Society, and the Institute for Advanced Studies. Powers recently published, with Michael Jablonski, *The Real Cyber War: A Political Economy of Internet Freedom* (2015, The University of Illinois Press).

Gudrun Reimerth is Lecturer of Communications at the Institute of Journalism and Public Relations, FH Joanneum, and at the University of Applied Sciences, Graz, Austria. Her research focuses on organizational communication and public relations in the digital world.

Piers Robinson is Chair in Politics, Society and Political Journalism at the Department of Journalism Studies, School of Social Sciences, University of Sheffield. He researches media and conflict and is currently working on propaganda and Organized Persuasive Communication (OPC). He has published extensively in international journals and is on the editorial boards of *Media, War and Conflict* and *Critical Studies on Terrorism.*

Alexandra Rüth is the Coordinator for Climate Change Adaptation for the German Red Cross. She has a background in agricultural engineering, development studies, and multiple years of experience working on international development cooperation projects and emergency relief operations for different organizations. She now coordinates the German Federal Foreign Office Action Plan for Humanitarian Adaptation to Climate Change.

Kim Scipes PhD, is an Associate Professor of Sociology at the Purdue University Northwest, Westville Indiana. He is a Global Labor scholar and has worked to build solidarity with workers around the world for over 30 years. He is editor of *Building Global Labor Solidarity in a Time of Accelerating Globalization* (2016, Chicago: Haymarket Books).

Anne Skjelmerud is a Senior Advisor and Team Coordinator for the Department for Global Health, Education and Research at the Norwegian Agency for Development Cooperation, NORAD. Her focus is on global HIV/AIDS epidemic, gender, and sexual and reproductive health and rights. She employs participatory methodologies that focus on marginalized groups. She has extensive professional experience involving cooperation between governments, the UN, and civil society. She is a registered Social Worker and did postgraduate studies in Sociology at the University of Oslo.

Nadia Sraieb-Koepp has been a Press Officer at the United Nations since 1977. She is Co-founder of Engagement Citoyen, a not-for-profit organization dedicated to facilitating the democratic transition process in Tunisia through communication and media campaigns, as well as grassroots level advocacy initiatives. Previously she was Marketing Director for the French media conglomerate Canal Plus in Tunisia. She has a Master's degree in Middle Eastern Studies from New York University and an MBA from l'Institut d'Administration des Entreprises in Aix en Provence, France.

Steen Steensen is Professor of Journalism and Head of the Department of Journalism and Media Studies, Oslo and Akershus University College of Applied Sciences (Oslo, Norway). His research interests include social media, digital journalism, and meta-research on journalism studies. He has been editor-in-chief of *Norsk medietidsskrift* (the Norwegian journal of media and communication research) and the co-editor of a volume on *Theories of Journalism in a Digital Age* (2016, Routledge).

Sir Peter Denis Sutherland GCIH KCMG SC is a former Attorney General of Ireland associated with the Fine Gael Party. He is a barrister by profession and Senior Counsel of the Irish Bar. Sir Peter Sutherland was the United Nations Special Representative of the Secretary-General (SRSG) for International Migration and Development from January 2006 to March 2017. He is responsible for the creation of the Global Forum on Migration and Development, which addresses the challenges of refugees, migrants and internally displaced persons. He is President of the International Catholic Migration Commission, as well as Member of the Migration Advisory Board of the International Organization for Migration (IOM). He has received numerous awards including European Person of the Year in 1988.

Jordi Torrent studied Philosophy at the University of Barcelona and did graduate work in Anthropology and Cinema at the Sorbonne University, Paris. He was Media Educator Consultant for the Department of Education of New York City from 1990 to 2007. In 2004 he co-founded "Overseas Conversations," an annual series of international conferences in New York focusing on youth, media, and education. He has co-edited, among other publications, *Mapping Media Education Policies in the World*, *Youth Media Visions: Conversations Across Cultures* and *New Opportunities for Media and Information Literacy in the MENA Region*. Since 2007 Torrent has been Project Manager of Media and Information Literacy initiatives at the United Nations Alliance of Civilizations (UNAOC).

Turo Uskali is the Head of Journalism, Senior Research Scholar, and Adjunct Professor at the Department of Communication/University of Jyväskylä, Finland. He is also Associate Professor II at the Department of Information Science and Media Studies, University of Bergen, Norway. Uskali heads several research projects focusing on innovations in journalism, the newest ones on mobile data journalism, smartwatches in journalism, and journalism research news service (JRN). Uskali has worked as a visiting researcher at the University of Oxford and as a visiting scholar at the Stanford University. His research has been published in *Digital Journalism*, *Innovation Journalism*, *Journalism and Mass Communication Educator*, *Central European Journal of Communication*, and *The Journal of Media Innovations*.

Priti Vaishnav serves as a Consultant and is the former Child Protection Project Coordinator, Nonviolent Peaceforce working with UNICEF. She received a PhD in International Relations from the Jawaharlal Nehru University in New Delhi. She has experience and expertise in Program Management and Leadership, and Provision of Civilian Protection in Complex Emergencies. Her special focus is on Child Protection in Armed Conflict. In Mindanao, the Philippines, she dealt with insurgencies and civilian displacement and peace negotiations, and was part of a ceasefire mechanisms between Government of the

Philippines and Moro Islamic Liberation Front. She has published in *Journal of Contemporary Central Asia, Russian International Affairs Council.*

Alexander van Tulleken is MD and the Helen Hamlyn Senior Fellow at the Institute of International Humanitarian Affairs (IIHA). He is directly responsible for teaching all undergraduate courses that comprise the International Humanitarian Affairs Minor, and serves as the Academic Director for the Master's in International Humanitarian Action. Dr. van Tulleken has worked for Médecins du Monde (MDM), Merlin, and the World Health Organization (WHO) in humanitarian crises around the world. His most recent mission was in 2010 in Darfur running health clinics in the embattled Jebel Marra Region. He has a diploma in Tropical Medicine and a Master's in Public Health from Harvard. He is an Honorary Lecturer in Conflict and Migration at University College London and is currently editing the first edition of the *Oxford Handbook of Humanitarian Medicine.*

Heike Wülfing is a Consultant for Sector Program Values, Religion and Development for the German Corporation for International Development Cooperation, and for the International Secretariat on Religion and Sustainable Development. He is also the online Press Editor for *Engagement Global gGmbH, Deutsche Welthungerhilfe e.V., Edition Lempertz— Brandenburgisches Verlagshaus.* He graduated in Political Science, Spanish and Italian Language and Literature in Bonn. He also studied in Spain and Italy. Previously he was a consultant for NGO/GOs in cooperation and municipal development and education, and Head Clerk for German Parliament members compiling political statements and analysis.

Kevin Wyjad is the German Red Cross delegate of the Forecast-based Financing pilot project in Bangladesh. He holds a Master's degree in International Affairs and has worked as Senior Risk Analyst and Deputy Head of the Analysis and Early Warning Unit of the World Food Programme in Rome. He was responsible for the technical coordination of contextual risk analysis and early warning, including links to emergency preparedness and resource allocation.

xxi

PREFACE

Sir Peter Sutherland

UN Special Representative of the Secretary-General
on International Migration

**Opening Remarks at "Bearing Witness: Combating
Human Trafficking and Forced Migration," Side Event,
United Nations General Assembly, September 23, 2016**

Our world is a world on the move. With over 240 million migrants every year and with almost 20 million people forced from their countries by conflict and disasters, we urgently need a better global consensus on sharing responsibility for people in need of protection and better policies for assisting refugees and migrants to find ways to live normal lives—lives where they can not only feel safe but where they can work to care for their families, where they can send their children to school, where they can be part of productive and peaceful communities.

The current situation, in which the responsibilities are all borne by the frontline states to a conflict or by the first countries of asylum a refugee might reach, has led to a very inequitable sharing of responsibility and has also led to the sort of unmanaged, unsafe (often deadly) movements of migrants and refugees onward, as they seek, in place after place, simply to live a life of dignity. Ironically, it is this very human quest for security that makes so many of them vulnerable to exploitation, including human trafficking.

In this important panel, you are focusing on the very worst of migration related challenges—on the horrific patterns of human trafficking that have devastated so many lives all over the world. Even this minute, as we sit comfortably in this room in New York, there are men, women, and children who are being bought, sold, held against their will, abused, and exploited. And this is happening everywhere in the world—from a few blocks from here in the Lower East Side and throughout Asia, Africa, and Europe. Later today you will hear from people who have been victims of trafficking and also those who work daily to help prevent trafficking. It is their voices that should be heard, not mine. Because they are the only ones who understand exactly what should be done to help survivors and what can be done to end this scourge. But all of us here can contribute to their cause, to the cause of human decency.

Although there were some successes this week in the UN—a recommitment by member states to recognizing the rights of migrants and refugees, the current policies responding to large population movements have been erratic, inconsistent, ineffective, and unenforceable. And, unfortunately, protection has been a very low priority for many states. We have seen a pattern of "global intolerance" as the Pope called it—with many countries reacting to migrants with fences and walls, draconian detention policies, xenophobia and even violence. We must recognize that trafficking and exploitation are often a *result* of these policies, as well.

Let me give an example: Many of the European responses to the so-called migration crisis have been reactive and ill thought out. They have been fraught with unintended consequences. Measures designed to deter sea crossings have made the journey much more dangerous. Increasingly, sophisticated measures to intercept migrant boats have shifted the trips from the hands of amateurs and pushed them ever more firmly into the purview of organized crime. It seems that the more the attention and resources are devoted to security, the more dangerous the journeys become. Something is very wrong.

In the European region, this has contributed to the ever increasing loss of life in the Mediterranean. There was one day this summer when over 400 people died in that sea when a ship sank off the coast of Egypt. But even today, we do not know who they all were. It took days to get any details about the accident at all. This is a horrible indicator of how little those poor souls meant to the rest of the world.

Think about a comparison: When the same number were lost in an airline crash last year, millions of hours and millions of dollars were spent searching for the wreckage, partly in an attempt to give the families of the victims some closure. The whole world seemed to accept that those grieving families deserved to know what happened to their loved ones. And that no cost should be spared to achieve this. But most of the families of those who perished on that rickety boat in the Mediterranean will never know what happened to their loved ones. We do not even know the names of many of the almost 4000 souls who have perished this year in that same sea. The 41 people who survived that shipwreck were labelled as "lucky" by the few sympathetic European media. Yet, those 41 had not only experienced horrors in their homelands and dangerous initial flights as refugees but then also had the trauma of seeing their friends or family members drown—and now, in a xenophobic Europe, also face very uncertain asylum fates. It is a sick world where they could possibly be considered lucky.

Colleagues, none of this—neither the invisibility of suffering migrants and refugees and trafficking victims nor the impunity for the cruelty of traffickers—should be happening in the twenty-first century. We have the knowledge, the resources, the ingenuity to protect our brothers and sisters and ensure that their human rights are protected.

Those of you here today are the champions for protection of basic human rights and dignity for the most vulnerable among us. You are the advocates for those who are often not in a position to make their voices heard. I wish you all courage and strength in your quest to make a better, fairer, and kinder world.

INTRODUCTION

The Power of Media in Times of Humanitarian Crisis: Global Challenges, Constraints, and Consequences

Robin Andersen and Purnaka L. De Silva

We live in a time of unprecedented humanitarian crises, and representations of global disasters are increasingly common media themes around the world. This volume explores the interconnections between media, old and new, and the humanitarian challenges that have come to define the twenty-first century. According to the United Nations, there are currently more crises around the globe than at any other time in human history, and the number of people affected by complex emergencies and humanitarian crises has more than doubled in the last decade. Crisis communication is now intimately connected to the international humanitarian community—global publics, first responders, and all who provide sustained humanitarian assistance during complex emergencies and their aftermath. Currently, over 1000 languages are spoken in the 18 countries that have ongoing appeals for humanitarian assistance, a situation that underscores the challenges of communicating across boundaries, language, culture and borders, and between the beneficiaries of aid and the complex web of relief organizations. As the ground seems to shift beneath the people and communities affected by disasters—either human, natural, environmental or conflict generated—a newly emergent 24/7 media landscape reports, disseminates and ultimately interprets news of human suffering worldwide. In doing so, global publics are also affected by the information, appeals for aid, images, and narratives of crises that they receive on a proliferating number of screens, outlets, devices, and platforms.

Unquestionably, since the end of the Second World War, the intensity and humanitarian impacts of global crises and their geographical spread are unprecedented. In the aftermath of conflicts and environmental disasters, the disruption of everyday life and communities create continuing humanitarian needs, sometimes over many decades that frequently reverberate across international borders. Millions of internally displaced persons (IDPs) and refugees, as a result of forced migrations, all create new challenges. The multiple ways in which media interact with these new global parameters will have their effects on everything from the delivery of support, aid, and resources, to the perceptions of local and global publics, to the influences on public opinion and humanitarian policies and actions.

1

The current migration crisis in Europe has turned the Mediterranean into a watery cemetery. The world has watched as thousands of refugees and migrants—men, women, newborns, children, the elderly and infirm—from many countries have drowned. So many of these tragedies have been recorded, filmed, and broadcast to global publics. The dangers the migrants face along their journey, and the assistance being offered by agencies and individuals, often sit uncomfortably beside official reports from government leaders about the demands for European security and the need to stop the flow of unwelcome migrants into fortress Europe.

While some countries, including Italy, Malta, Ireland, and Britain among others, engaged in rescue missions in the Mediterranean, there was mounting anti-immigration sentiment, racism, and xenophobia across Europe and the United States. Political discourse in the United States continued to descend throughout 2016, with xenophobia increasing steadily across Europe as well. Early in the crisis, the British tabloid newspaper *The Sun* featured an article by Katie Hopkins titled, "Rescue Boats? I'd use gunships to stop migrants." Comparing the migrants to "cockroaches," she went on to say, "They might look like 'Bob Geldof's Ethiopia circa 1984' but they are built to survive a nuclear bomb. . . . Some of our towns are festering sores, plagued by swarms of migrants and asylum seekers, shelling out benefits like Monopoly money." Such language harks back to the Rhawandan genocide, when Hutu leaders incited the paramilitary militia to massacre minority Tutsis by repeatedly referring to them as "cockroaches" over radio broadcasts. Though her comments evoked criticism, Heaven Crawley, a professor of International Migration at Coventry University in the UK, argued that the publication had opened the door to similar invective." Even a few years ago you could not have imagined this particular newspaper allowing this columnist to say something like this."[1] As the situation worsens, US and European press reports emphasizing security concerns are far more frequent than media coverage of the causes for migration and the needs of refugees.

Throughout 2016 United States republican presidential candidates demonized refugees in terms rarely repeated in legitimate public utterances, some barely coherent, others outright falsities. Republican primary candidate Ben Carson explained, "If there is a rabid dog running around your neighborhood, you're probably not going to assume something good about that dog. And you're probably going to put your children out of the way." New Jersey governor Chris Chistie in his presidential bid made policy statements asserting, "we need appropriate vetting, and I don't think orphans under 5 should be admitted into the United States at this point." Indeed, as the Republican candidate, Donald Trump made numerous false claims crafted to brand all refugees as terrorists and block them from entering the US with these words: "I watched when the World Trade Center came tumbling down, and I watched in Jersey City, New Jersey, where thousands of people were cheering as the building was coming down."[2] Now President Trump, who characterized migrants from Mexico as criminals, murderers, and rapists, currently seeks to ban all Muslims from entering the country and is planning to build a wall between Mexico and the United States. One journalist summarized Trump's message as a generalized hostility toward all non-white, non-conventional persons, which he sees as the *Other* (Conn 2016). Such linguistic strategies place refugees outside of the boundaries of humanitarian communities, creating a division between us and them, good and evil, those who can be trusted and those who are irredeemable deviants who don't belong.

The language of demonization and the superficial narratives of current media, contribute to policies—and in turn justify the policies—that corral migrants in places like "the Jungle" in Calais, France, or close off the borders of Europe and send refugees back across the

Mediterranean. Current discourse and actions have come to challenge what were once considered fundamental humanitarian assertions in play until only a few years ago. Calhoun (2002, 2010) has written extensively on what he identifies as the cosmopolitan disposition defined as a global community in which its members are able to express empathy and caring towards vulnerable others, and act on their behalf. We do this without any request or anticipation of reciprocity. Indeed, the idea of humanitarianism finds its roots in a variety of religious and secular traditions; the religious tradition of agape or care towards the stranger in need, to mention only one. As late as 2009, Riflin's assertion that in late modernity we enjoy a relatively coherent moral order defined generally as "an empathetic civilization." Alexander Van Tulleken (2007, 46) articulated such a humanitarian imperative now firmly established in international circles. He asserted a "simple set of beliefs" that needed no "lengthy philosophical justification," that "all lives are equally valuable." Such fundamental norms were "accepted" and "widespread," he argued, evident "in the Genocide Convention, in human rights legislation, and in the widespread public support for NGOs and governments that champion human rights." And Chouliaraki (2013) has identified what she calls the humanitarian imagination defined as the imperative to act when we are confronted with the vulnerability of strangers by taking action to alleviate their suffering. Indeed, the great migrations across Europe beginning in 2015, termed significantly a "crisis," have shaken the very foundations of humanitarianism, so often lauded as a uniquely Western, indeed European, value and practice.

Our exploration of media and humanitarian action takes place within this context, and underscores the urgency of the task. As we explore the history, formats, visuals, language, and media framing of humanitarian narratives, we seek to understand the interconnections between representation and action. Humanitarian communication then encompasses all of the different ways in which global publics encounter vulnerable others, through the mediations of visual language and storytelling, through the witness of journalists, documentaries, the appeals of aid agencies, including sadly, the demonization of migrants, immigrants, and refugees in political discourse. Humanitarianism depends on the affirmation that when confronted by the representations of the suffering of those in need, we are compelled to act in solidarity with them. But the process of communicating their suffering invariably influences our responses to it. The ways in which the conditions of their stress are narrated, the visual depictions of those who suffer, the language and storytelling of media coverage complicate and alter our responses. The "aesthetic logic" of communicating humanitarian concerns through media presents tensions and pitfalls that ultimately transform the humanitarian imagination.

The humanitarian imperative has always been based on assumptions that "all lives are valuable," and that all human beings by nature are ultimately good, and entitled to human rights no matter their race, religion, gender, nationality, or cultural differences. Indeed, the Principle of Humanity mandates that all humankind shall be treated impartially and humanely irrespective of nationality, race, ethnicity, caste, gender, sexual orientation, creed and culture. These definitions provide the common basis for engagement. Current political language and media discourses that demonize entire groups of people challenge these foundations. The articulation of stereotypes that lump all Muslims together as terrorists, equated them with rapid dogs and cockroaches, claim that they "cheer for terrorists," or that children under five are dangerous, are not ones that compelled publics to act in solidarity with them. In this way the changing landscapes and visual fields of humanitarian communication have indeed come to challenge the "ethics of solidarity" (Chouliaraki 2013) and the very foundations of humanitarianism.

In addition to confronting what Calhoun (2002) has conceptualized as a cosmopolitan sensibility of empathy toward global others, the current refugee crisis in Europe challenges another fundamental definition of the humanitarian imaginary. As Chouliaraki (2013) has defined it, Western humanitarianism has been anchored on the conditions of difference and separation. Undergirding the concept is a West/South divide. Though recognizing that not all publics in the West are affluent, and those in the South impoverished, there is nevertheless a division of power and prosperity that resides along those lines. We do after all, live with the consequences of colonialism, in an era of extreme wealth inequality, and at the apex of neoliberalism globally, punctuated by the brutality of ever escalating war and conflict. In addition, the unequal distribution of "resources along the West/South axis, reproduces the prosperity of the former whilst perpetuating the poverty of the latter." Western affluent publics do not experience the same extremes of poverty that those of the global South endure. Therefore, the humanitarian imagination identifies the moral imperative to act in solidarity with vulnerable others, not only on those close to us, but also on *distant others*, the "strangers we will never meet."

The second decade of the twenty-first century has posed the greatest threat to conceptions of Western humanitarianism—as it is being dismantled on a number of fronts. The refugee crisis in Europe has sent migrants from battered and bombed societies across borders and into the communities, regions and countries of the North. Those in need are no longer distant others, the strangers we will never meet. They are demanding entrance into our lives and cultures and societies. The distance seemingly essential to the humanitarian imagination has collapsed, and with it so too has much, but certainly not all, of the solidarity with, and the moral imperative to help, those in need.

As we will find in the pages of this volume, the humanitarian West/South divide is a distinction whose boundaries are breaking down. A distinctly Western European humanism is challenged by the current migrations, indicated by refugee camps in Greece and France, among others, that do not meet even the minimum of humanitarian standards that are provided in countries with many fewer resources such as the camps in Jordan, Sudan, and Thailand. In addition, after Hurricane Katrina hit the US Gulf Coast in 2005, Japanese government donations surpassed $1 million, with $200,000 given to the American Red Cross to provide aid to hurricane victims. Private businessman Takashi Endo alone donated $1 million to Katrina relief efforts.[3] In addition, other important new donors to the United Nations have emerged on the global scene, and China is the largest non-traditional donor at country level. China's "average financial contribution . . . surpasses that of any other emerging donor (like Brazil, India, and South Africa)."[4] The Chinese model of "official financial assistance" to countries in need is arguably driven by geopolitical considerations and access to sources of raw materials. But in an age of philanthrocapitalism, Special Economic Zones and micro-financing—all of which offer the neoliberal market models defined by global capitalism for development—we also ask, whether less than altruistic motivations seep into the humanitarian programs provided by many Western countries as well. Are these new developments discussed in the global media, and if so how?

Additionally, in the highly competitive field of funding streams, aid agencies are often compelled to adopt corporate strategies to compete. Throughout the 1980s and 1990s, the growth of aid agencies and INGOs rapidly increased, and over the decades since has resulted in numerous organizations that now find themselves competing for funding, regional coverage and prestige. In responding to these circumstances, much of the field of humanitarian communication has adopted managerial strategies aligned with market forces that have transformed the way media and messages are designed. In a highly competitive market, tactics that target audiences with strategic messages now present many aid agencies as brands, and in doing so, set in motion the same psychosocial dynamic that defines consumer culture. According to Chouliaraki (2013) these changes in humanitarian communication have also transformed the "ethics of solidarity." Her formulation of the ironic spectator posits that Western publics no longer respond to the vulnerability of others through compassion or the moral imperative to act without need of receiving anything in return. On the contrary, like consumers invited to choose products through emotional gratifications, through charismatic performers and celebrities, or construct personal identities through consumer brands, spectators of those in need now seek an individual emotional experience, a "feel good" moment when acting on the behalf of others. Thus are the ethics of solidarity transformed by communication strategies, from acting on a sense of compassion based on public witness, to a privatized emotional motivation that offers in return a sense of identity based on brand, the equivalent of purchasing a stylish product.

Even as the global crisis escalates, and political and media discourses shift, people in communities, villages, towns, and islands struggle to support and help the migrants flooding into Europe, and the small number that has been accepted in the United States. Humanitarian actors—amateur and professional—seek to provide aid, shelter, and medical care to refugees, as in Turkey, Lebanon, Jordan, Libya, Sicily, Italy, and Greece among countries in the direct path of migratory routes. In the United States, faith-based communities, inspired by media imagery of the struggles of migrants, have worked to help refugees adjust to their new lives. After the election of Donald Trump, "sanctuary cities" are being designed to counter the growing US xenophobia. Global publics protest on refugees' behalves, and defy authorities that criminalize their solidarity. Under these circumstances media coverage and alternative technologies of online social media campaigns become essential in communicating across boundaries and divides.

As this book goes into production, the majority of the American public and the global community struggle to come to terms with the newly elected 45th President of the United States, Donald J. Trump. Trump rode to power on a wave of anti-immigrant sentiment and promises to deport, block, and wall off the country, using campaign language that has posed the greatest challenges to humanitarianism than we have seen in decades. This volume addresses these prescient times, the challenges faced by humanitarian actors, and the overall need for more complete knowledge and less sensational representations in order to better involve publics, and deepen their understanding of international humanitarian efforts. As Hammock and Charney (1996) point out, "myths and stereotypes" make "long term change and development more difficult if not impossible." In this volume we look back at the history of humanitarian communication, from its beginnings to the present day, to better understand the power and limits of media, from the public responses to humanitarian communication to the historical conventions that shape it. We grapple with media language, discourses, coverage and campaigns to identify those that have and have not nurtured informed global citizens in the past and into the present day. We offer analysis that seeks to document the power of social media in contradictory and often disturbing ways, from online organizing on behalf of victims, to the propagandized anti-immigrant fake news that spins across social media platforms.

As we identify the problems with humanitarianism and humanitarian communication in this twenty-first century of global disorder, we view these contradictions as productive tensions, not as immutable realities unable to be overcome. We seek to find examples from case studies and identify best practices for humanitarian communication including visual storytelling that works to undergird the foundations of the humanitarian imagination. We explore the ways in which media technologies, online and social media facilitate care and concern for those in need. We look to ethical media depictions and standards in gathering and disseminating humanitarian communication.

In providing an overview of an entire subject area or sub-discipline, this volume examines the role the media play in complex humanitarian emergencies from the relevant points of view. We survey the global media response to the escalation of suffering. We include multidisciplinary perspectives by a variety of distinct international voices and experts representing the varied aspects of media and humanitarian action, taking into consideration the complex partnerships involved in humanitarian crises.

We expand our view to include the positive and negative impact of legacy media from documentary to fictional representations and beyond. Included herein are the new terrains of technology and social media, and discussions of the ways in which social media platforms are interacting and changing the management and implementation of relief efforts in complex emergencies, and the ongoing instability affecting civilians across the globe.

Through the contributions of professional media specialists, this volume features unique insights and analysis of the ways in which humanitarian communications are designed and implemented in the field of humanitarian action. These contributions are particularly important given the difficulties of carrying out academic fieldwork in crisis situations, and the often-difficult task of acquiring data on the topic. This study also includes case studies of media practices, and content analysis and evaluation of media coverage and representations of humanitarian emergencies and affairs. We offer critical perspectives on discourses that discourage fundamental humanistic assumptions formulated in the aftermath of the brutality of the twentieth century. In addition, the volume includes critiques of the sometimes competing needs of relief organizations, their communication practices, and the beneficiaries they serve.

This volume is timely and essential. In response to the current global crises, a World Humanitarian Summit, the first of its kind, took place in Istanbul, Turkey on May 23–24, 2016. The World Humanitarian Summit was an initiative of the United Nations Secretary-General and spearheaded by the United Nations Office for the Coordination of Humanitarian Affairs (UN-OCHA) in New York. UN-OCHA is the part of the United Nations Secretariat responsible for bringing together humanitarian actors to ensure a coherent response to emergencies. The World Humanitarian Summit's primary goal was to draw the global community together to commit to new ways of working collaboratively and more effectively. We offer assessment of the summit, which includes the drawbacks of its organization and the hurdles yet to be undertaken in the field of humanitarian communications.

In our concluding essay, we grapple with what has become a central question, possibly the most significant one for the humanitarian community as well as for the global public. In an age of terrorism, perpetual war, environmental crises and grinding global inequality, how do we narrate the causes of, and solutions to, global suffering, and how do those stories affect our ability to perpetuate a humanitarian imagination? How do we formulate a new vision and discourse that transforms the need for relief into humanitarian practices based on justice, equality, and solidarity, and in accordance with the principle of humanity?

Notes

1. On the Media, National Public Radio: April 24, 2015, available at: www.onthemedia.org/story/narratives-migration/transcript/
2. For a discussion of this language see *The Nation*: www.thenation.com/article/an-illustrated-guide-to-the-dumbest-things-republicans-have-said-about-refugees/

3. The Editorial Board, "Japan's Tsunami is a Time for Repaying Their Generosity after Katrina: Here's How," *Times-Picayune* (March 11, 2011), available at: www.nola.com/opinions/index.ssf/2011/03/time_to_repay_japan.html

4. Overseas Development Institute (ODI), (2016) *An Age of Choice for Development Finance,* published by the ODI reports at: www.odi.org/sites/odi.org.uk/files/resource-documents/10450.pdf www.odi.org/hpg/remake-aid/

References

Calhoun, C. (2002) *Nations Matter: Culture, History and the Cosmopolitan Dream*, Abingdon, UK and New York: Routledge.

Calhoun, C. (2010) "The Idea of Emergency: Humanitarian Action and Global (Dis)order," in D. Fassin and M. Pandolfi (Eds.), *Contemporary States of Emergency*, New York: Zone Books, pp. 29–58.

Chouliaraki, L. (2013) *The Ironic Spectator: Solidarity in the Age of Post-Humanitarianism*, Cambridge, UK: Polity.

Conn, J. (2016) "In Search of a National Dialogue on Race," Salon.com, September 27, available at: www.alternet.org/culture/search-national-dialogue-race?akid=14690.19806.G4PgoV&rd=1&src=newsletter1064390&t=14

Hammock, J., and Charny, J. (1996) "Emergency Response as Morality Play," in R. I. Rotberg and T. G. Weiss (Eds.), *Massacres to Genocide: The Media, Public Policy, and Humanitarian Crises*, Cambridge, MA: World Peace Foundation and the Brookings Institution.

Van Tullenken, A. (2007) "No Justice without Power: The Case for Humanitarian Intervention," in K. Cahill (Ed.), *The Pulse of Humanitarian Assistance*, New York: Fordham University Press, p. 41–76.

Part 1

THEORIES AND PRACTICE OF MEDIA AND THEIR IMPACT ON HUMANITARIAN ACTION

INTRODUCTION
TO PART 1

These essays open the discussion of media and humanitarian action by detailing key theoretical perspectives that continue to shape the discourse of analysis in the field of humanitarian action. The perspectives presented here have been used as guideposts for many photojournalists, the news media, and aid agencies as well. They span the field of humanitarian action, from news reporting of famines, disasters, and conflicts, to the role played by communication discourses designed for relief agencies and human rights conventions, and the way language is shaped in hate speech that can lead to violence and even atrocity crimes.

In Chapter 1, "Media, Politics, Compassion, and Citizenship in the Post-Humanitarian Debate", Robin Andersen explores the definition of humanitarian communication, its history, language, visual renderings, and narrative structures. Building on the historical effects of media depictions and their relationship to aid appeals and public response, the chapter engages the concepts of empathy and compassion, post-humanitarianism, the formulation of an ironic spectator, the contentious notion of compassion fatigue, the ethics of solidarity, and the articulation of global citizenship. She discusses the challenges that complex emergencies and human suffering pose to journalists, media organizations, and aid agencies, and addresses the media pitfalls and dominant critiques of crisis representation. From early-published photographs of starving children, to contemporary aid appeals for Syrian Refugees, issues of stereotypes and narrative exclusions are understood along a trajectory of historical development and context.

In "Communicating for Impact, The Voice of the Victims: The Role of Media Design in Humanitarian and Human Rights Organizations", Tamara Alrifai discusses the hard work, planning and strategic design required to communicate humanitarian crises to global publics. During her long professional career she has helped news media understand the needs of aid agencies and their beneficiaries, and communicated humanitarian attitudes and actions on a global scale. With the number and severity of complex emergencies, human rights violations, and global conflicts escalating, informing and moving the public to act is now understood as an intrinsic part of any operation, and not an "accessory" added at the end of the planning process. Designing effective communication with the ability to mobilize public opinion and help release additional funds from government treasuries is a dynamic and evolving field.

Yehia Ghanem tracks the rise of Al-Jazeera on the global stage. In the "Al-Jazeera Effect, News Media Coverage of Global Humanitarian Emergencies", he maps out the network's development into a full-fledged journalism organization dedicated to covering the humanitarian consequences of war and conflict, and later its partnerships with aid agencies and the network's on-going commitment to covering humanitarian emergencies. At a time when other international broadcast media—especially the corporate-owned profit-minded networks in the United States—were cutting operating funds, firing staff, and closing international news bureaus, Al-Jazeera was building a serious global news network that would challenge the dominant discursive frames of North/South international news reporting.

As the United States presidential campaign of Donald Trump has amply demonstrated, on commercially based media, politicians and newsmakers in general claim more column inches and more airtime by using the language of belligerency, demonization, incitement, and fear. Such discourse attracts the curious and fascinates large audiences and is therefore profitable, amplifying its news value on corporate media. As CBS Chairman Les Moonves told a Technology, Media & Telecom Conference in San Francisco in February 2016, "It may not be good for America, but it's damn good for CBS." *Politico* noted the comment perfectly distilled what "media critics have long suspected was motivating the round-the-clock coverage of Trump's presidential bid" (Collins 2016).

By now this language is familiar to many across the globe; immigrants are rapists, terrorists, or murderers who should be feared and kept out the United States and on the other side of a great wall. Evelin Gerda Lindner and Linda Hartling dedicate their chapter, "Dignity in Times of Crises, Communicating the Need for Global Social Climate Change", to those who work at the forefront of global emergencies, and the global victims who experience and witness what they identify as a key psychosocial strategy of demonization—the aggressive discourse of humiliation. They explore the many ways groups, sub-groups and individuals are humiliated, and draw out the negative consequences that intensify crises and conflict. But what would the language of compassion and humanitarian policy sound like? What are the modes of communication, the psychosocial appeals, the terms, and language that would offer the possibilities of empathy and understanding? Lindner and Hartling offer specific ways to begin to dismantle the dynamics of humiliation, and replace it with a key expression fundamental to community and inclusion, that quality of human dignity.

On the other side of the communication divide are the dark terms of hate that are rehearsed over and over, and often repeated across media channels. In Chapter 5 titled, "When Media is Used to Incite Violence: The United Nations, Genocide and Atrocity Crimes", Adama Dieng and Simona Cruciani articulate how hate speech is defined, and draw out its possible consequences. Dieng makes the distinction between hate speech and incitement. Incitement is a very dangerous form of hate speech that can trigger violence and, in some instances, atrocity crimes and even genocide. He makes a distinction between a person standing on a street corner who may say vile, racist things, but such invective will not have the same impact as the words spoken by a national leader who calls for violence against a particular group at a time when political tensions are high. The International Covenant on Civil and Political Rights (ICCPR) states that, "Any advocacy of national, racial or religious hatred that constitutes incitement to discrimination, hostility or violence shall be prohibited by law."[1] Hate speech and its uses to incite hostility and violence is escalating in many parts of the world, increasingly spread over social media. Dieng and Cruciani discuss the many initiatives within the United Nations system aimed at countering hate speech and incitement, underscoring how seriously the organization takes this form of expression.

Against this backdrop, we might reconsider the hate speech of Donald Trump who began his presidential campaign by comparing Mexicans to rapists and criminals, and along the way he denigrated women and maligned and degraded Muslims and claimed allowing immigrants to enter the country would result in increased terrorism. In addition, Trump openly threatened violence against Black Lives Matter activists, and promised to subsidize supporters who commit violence against protesters. It may not be surprising then, that almost from the beginning his supporters "have been punching, kicking, choking, and harassing people at his events and in his name." By March of 2016, Kira Lerner (2016) noted, "As Trump's hateful rhetoric has increased, so have violent, often racist or xenophobic attacks against people at his campaign events."

On November 3, 2016, a Trump Pence campaign sign was plunged into the ground outside an early voting location on a college campus in Plano, Texas. The sign was blocking a "vote here" marker, and when a poll volunteer tried to remove the sign, he failed to see the shiny blades glued along the sign's bottom edge. His hand was sliced up.

The same day a fire was deliberately set at a historically black church in Mississippi— the spray-painted words "Vote Trump" were left behind. It is being investigated as a hate crime. The Center for American Progress Action Fund has chronicled Trump's Hate Speech throughout the 2016 campaign, and beginning in September 2015, the organization America's Voice tracked the times and places where Donald Trump, his supporters, or his staff harassed or attacked Latinos and immigrants (Lerner 2016). In addition, in the aftermath of Trump's election, over 900 incidents that chided, humiliated, and threatened violence against African Americans, Latinos, immigrants, women, and Muslins were recorded within the first few weeks.

Clearly the Trump campaign has taken hate speech into a national arena, and many argue that his words have led to violence across the country. As the news media continue to present the candidate as a legitimate political actor, and now the president, in what scholar Jay Rosen terms the "bogus neutrality" of authoritarian societies (Rosenberg 2016), the United States comes ever closer to normalizing speech that incites violence and violates internationally recognized Human Rights Covenants.

Note

1. International Covenant on Civil and Political Rights, Art 20, United Nations Office of the High Commissioner for Human Rights, Article 20 of the ICCPR, available at: www.ohchr.org/en/professionalinterest/pages/ccpr.aspx

References

Collins, E. (2016) "Les Moonves: 'Trump's Run is Damn Good for CBS,'" *Politico*, February 29, available at: www.politico.com/blogs/on-media/2016/02/les-moonves-trump-cbs-220001

Lerner, K. (2016) "How Trump Has Inspired Violence Across the Country, In One Map," Think Progress, March 17, available at: https://thinkprogress.org/how-trump-has-inspired-violence-across-the-country-in-one-map-6ab5e096a627#.1lre6uvul

Rosenberg, P. (2016) "Media Critic Jay Rosen on 2016 Campaign Coverage and the Rise of Trump: 'That's the Way Authoritarian Societies Work,'" *Salon.com*, November 6, available at: www.salon.com/2016/11/06/media-critic-jay-rosen-on-2016-campaign-coverage-and-the-rise-of-trump-thats-the-way-authoritarian-societies-work/?source=newsletter

1

MEDIA, POLITICS, COMPASSION, AND CITIZENSHIP IN THE POST-HUMANITARIAN DEBATE

Visual Storytelling and the Humanitarian Imaginary

Robin Andersen

As we outlined in the introduction to this volume, one of the main theoretical foundations for humanitarian action is articulated by Lilie Chouliaraki (2013), identified as the *humanitarian imagination*. The idea is built upon the concept of *cosmopolitan solidarity*, which has been best developed by Craig Calhoun (2010). These concepts coalesce to explain the ethics, motivations, and context for humanitarian action, understood as the public's response to the suffering of others—when confronted with the knowledge that people or groups, be they the same or different from us, find themselves in dire situations and in need of help, global publics are compelled to act to stop their suffering. The assumption of such a sensibility forms the basis of aid appeals. It also undergirds what has been called the CNN Effect, and later the Al-Jazeera Effect, because, of course, mobilizing such sentiments and the resulting public action, is dependent upon the mediations of humanitarian communication. How else would the public come to know about the suffering of those in need, or of the on-going campaigns to help them? We are dependent on media, the news photographs, the stories of suffering on television—both long and short—the latest word from the Internet and social media, accessed on our computers and hand-held devices, to bring the world to us. But the stories about the world are always, and can only be, media representations of the world and not the world itself. Unless we are the ones standing on the beach of a Greek island waiting for another boat of freezing refugees, or tracking the exploitation of children on a conflict-ridden island in the Philippines.

If not in the midst of helping or bearing witness, we must rely on those who see for us, who take the pictures, record the testimony, shoot the video, and tell the stories, either in print, on television, in an agency report, a Facebook page, or a YouTube video. But the process of mediation is always fraught; so many frames of reference from local to global can be applied to the news, some illuminating, others that only serve to obscure. Depictions represent or misrepresent the circumstances, explanations, and causes of disasters. They often contextualize those who suffer either as innocent or complicit, worthy or unworthy. As historical representations have also demonstrated, there are unintended consequences of the use of various media, the implicit assumptions they inherit from their embeddedness in social and economic relations—spectator and beneficiary, secure citizen of the global North and precarious victim in the global South. Media constructions often contain within them proscribed logics of compassion versus blame, familiar versus other, inevitability versus solutions. Ultimately media can influence and alter our understanding of events, our feelings toward the people affected, and our opinions about the official policies in response. In this way, such mediations can also either evoke compassion for the suffering of others and thereby reinforce the humanitarian imaginary, or they can fail to do so and the spectator/viewer is unmoved.

Many scholars have offered arguments about how and why media sometimes fail to address us in ways that evoke and confirm the humanitarian imagination. Many of those theories have developed over decades of assessment of the legacy of images of suffering in news and aid appeals. Some critics detail the long trajectory of loss of meaningful international news coverage and the failure to inform global publics in ways that nurture knowledge and citizenship. Other studies evaluate new media practices from the Internet to Social Media. Chouliaraki (2013) posits that the combination of media technology and strategic design of message appeals by competing aid agencies, have transformed our relationship to those in need of our help. In a commercial age when everything is defined as a *brand*, so too are humanitarian agencies. When we click on a donate button we often do so to affirm ourselves and establish an identity. Lost is our compassion for the suffering other—it is all about us, not them. We have become, in this way, *ironic spectators* to the suffering of others in a *post-humanitarian* age. Many scholars have also asserted that the visually driven imagery of those in need is so ubiquitous that it has led to *compassion fatigue* in the West with information overload and the perpetually flawed mediations of the suffering "other," and we have become overwhelmed and lost our ability to empathize.

This chapter explores the historical connections forged between human disasters, media representations, and humanitarian responses, as well as the theoretical conceptions used to assess those interconnections. Put another way, we can say it seeks to untangle the threads that tie images, stories, and narratives of suffering to the complex ways they pattern humanitarian action. The fabric of humanitarianism is woven from the photographs and videos, words and narratives of the long history of disasters, campaigns, and media strategies that currently make up what we now call the humanitarian community.

Of course, space prevents us from including all that is outlined above, but we will track key historical campaigns and mark important turning points in order to reveal the bonds and identify the challenges that tie, sometimes uncomfortably, media to our ability to engage in humanitarian action. Possibly more importantly, we will ask where we can go from here. Are there communication practices that result in effective action, and at the same time bolster our ability to empathize with others? Are there depictions and narratives that accurately represent the complexities of crisis that can lead to solutions based on humanitarian principles? Along the way we will address the ideas of a humanitarian imaginary, the benefits and drawbacks of humanitarian communication, the descriptive value of the idea of an ironic spectator, and the question of compassion fatigue in Western countries.

Early campaigns that forged the immutable bond between media and humanitarian disasters go back more than half a century. Those early images are a good place to start to tell the story of media and its unintended consequence for humanitarianism.

Biafra, Ethiopia and Sudan

Media and humanitarian action as we know it was forged in 1968 when a group of journalists flew to eastern Nigeria where Igbo separatist rebels had formed a new state they called Biafra. There two of the journalists, led by an Irish Father named Kevin Doheny of the Holy Ghost Order, were taken to a hospital where they saw severely malnourished children, victims of the Nigerian government's deliberate policy to starve the Biafrans through a land and sea blockade. UK reporter Alan Hart (2010) was filming for International Television Network ITN and the impact of the film, along with black and white images of starving children were widely published in the press and stunned the Western world. As one writer put it "within hours people worldwide were asking how they could donate money to stop the suffering" (Waters 2004). Frederick Forsyth (the fictional author) would later write:

> Quite suddenly we'd touched a nerve. Nobody in this country at that time had ever seen children look like that. The last time the Brits had seen anything like that must have been the Belsen pictures . . . Starving children were on the front page of every British newspaper, and from there to newspapers all over the world.
>
> (Harrison and Palmer 1986, 33)

Haunting news photographs depicted skeletal, swollen-eyed, mostly naked children struggling to survive, many about to die. Coverage led to an outpouring of charity, political activism, and, in France, the founding of the international, independent, medical humanitarian organization, Médecins Sans Frontières (MSF) or Doctors Without Borders. All this prevented many more from dying of starvation. The effects were monumental, as Franks puts it in this volume, "The shocking images of Biafran children starving became a cause célèbre for radical protest in western capitals. And for years to come the very word 'Biafran' was associated with these images of extreme starvation." But in retrospect, the images obscured as much as they revealed about the conditions depicted, and the complex politics in Nigeria at the time.

Over the decades since, the actual consequences of the relief effort in Biafra, and the nature and impact of the images that drove it, have been the subject of debate and analysis by writers, researchers, academics, media strategists, and documentary filmmakers seeking to understand the circumstances, and the interactions set up by visual representations and the public response to them. Many have provided pieces of this narrative explaining how the charity output also extended the Biafran war for 18 more months, ultimately causing tens of thousands more deaths. The relief efforts fortified the rebels, and brought in currency from landing fees that meant that the rebels could buy more guns (Barrow and Jenkins 2001). Though the Nigerian government actions starved a civilian population, rebel leaders were also willing to sacrifice civilians to press on with the conflict. A documentary film shows rebel leaders explaining their glee from the public response to what they considered a successful "propaganda" effort.[1] The plane that took the journalists to eastern Nigeria was actually part of the PR effort by a little-known agency based in Geneva that the rebels hired.

By 1984 another set of images from Africa would hold the West in its grip, and again confirm the power of the visual language of suffering, this time combined with dramatic prose, to evoke public concern. Ethiopians were experiencing mass starvation and world opinion galvanized around Michael Buerk's vivid stories that aired on the BBC. On October 23, 1984 the midday report opened this way:

> Dawn, and as the sun breaks through the piercing chill of night on the plains outside Korem, it lights up a biblical famine, now, in the 20th century. This place, say workers here, is the closest thing to hell on earth.

The historic broadcast of this "biblical" famine resulted in worldwide interest and donations. The footage was transmitted by 425 television stations worldwide, including major US news channels, some that retain Buerk's original British voice-over (Jackson 2015). "Coverage of the famine in UK tabloid newspapers went from 50 column inches in the first three weeks of October to nearly 1,200 column inches in the last 10 days of the month" (Nguyen 2013). It inspired pop star Bob Geldof to organize the Live Aid concert, and thus to the next step in the process of media, and now popular culture, intimately tied to humanitarian appeals fronted by performers and celebrity spokespersons. This in turn led to the unprecedented growth of foreign relief organizations, all of which would change the face of humanitarian organizing and fundraising.

But like the images and broadcasts of Biafra, they oversimplified the crisis and converted a famine with a long genesis and deep political roots into a natural disaster. The famine in Ethiopia was far from that. Starvation had become a weapon of war for the dictator Mengistu Haile Mariam in the battle against insurgents in the north. As in many conflicts, fighting caused problems with food supply. Just as in Nigeria, foreign currency brought in by aid agencies helped the conflict continue. In addition, both government and rebel forces diverted the vehicles used to distribute relief supplies (Nguyen 2013). Ultimately, the media-driven aid influx strengthened a bad government, and according to Franks, "did more harm than good" (see Chapter 15).

Picturing Famine Victims

Ethiopia followed Biafra and the images and their power chronicled a set of visual conventions, especially for famine in Africa that has been frequently repeated over the years since. As Zelizer (2010) notes the "visual standard for all of the images of famine that followed" were "depicted by pictures suggesting vulnerability and cued by bodily frailty" (163). Mostly children, and generally anonymous, they stood staring or sitting with distended stomachs, their hollowed out features showing little emotion. Close up and frequently shot from above—diminished— they often stared up at the camera, their pitiful eyes dominating bony, despondent faces. Images from Ethiopia included starving mothers and children similarly, many about to die, waiting for food deliveries.

Since then, the nature of the imagery itself has also inspired writers, theorists, and critics, all of whom have offered astute and original insights into the visual language of suffering. Theoretical and analytical frameworks track the politics of photographs, the psychosocial impact of visuals, their performativity in the humanitarian cultural imaginary, the impact of their form and content on viewers, and their meanings within the larger context of media and narrative tropes. In journalism studies, scholars question the limits and verisimilitude of imagery, and the influence such photojournalism has on the press, from framing news reporting and practices to journalistic ethics. These discussions also include the "rights of photographic subjects, the duties of producers, and the extent and degree of harm or benefit these images generate" (Fehrenback and Rodogno 2015). Probably the harshest critique was penned by Susan Sontag (2004) who noted that the images carried a double meaning. "The ubiquity of those photographs, and those horrors, cannot help but nourish belief in the inevitability of tragedy in the benighted or backward—that is, poor—parts of the world." To Sontag, they were part of an age-old practice of "exhibiting exotic, that is colonized, human beings displayed like zoo animals in ethnological conditions" (2004, 71).

Kevin Carter and the Starving Sudanese Girl

Toward the end of the 1980s the use of imagery and narratives had become a concern to the humanitarian community. By 1989 a Commission for Images published a Code of Conduct in which NGOs were advised to be "attentive to messages that over-simplify or over-concentrate sensational aspects of life in the third world."[2] Four years after that report, photojournalist Kevin Carter took a picture of a starving Sudanese child that was published in the front section of the *New York Times* on March 26, 1993. The picture would further shake the received wisdom that a photograph "is worth a thousand words," and that an image contained within it the power to explain and move the public to act. In Carter's picture the tiny girl is collapsed upon herself face down on the dusty ground and a large vulture lurks on its hunches just behind her in the frame, waiting for her last movement. Carter waited for up to 20 minutes to see if the vulture would spread its wings to look even more threatening before he settled for the shot he took (Marinovitch and Silver 2000). Readers responded to the picture immediately, demanding answers to questions about the child and what had happened to her. Much has been written and said about the image including a documentary about the life of Kevin Carter. Zelizer (2010, 166–172) offers the best, most recent discussion of the image and the responses to it, and its movement through a series of uses and controversies, including its Pulitzer Prize win and ultimately, the suicide of Kevin Carter.

Over a period of time the photograph circulated widely in the press. *Time* magazine published the photograph with an appeal for donations to relief organizations. The image also appeared on a publicity poster for a human rights campaign for Amnesty International in 1994. With its circulation came increased public demand to know more about what happened to the starving child, and neither Carter nor the editors who published the picture gave credible or consistent answers; some claimed she had continued on and probably found her way to a feeding station, others said they hoped she had. It is widely believed she died shortly after the picture was taken. It is not surprising that in the wake of the failure to provide any information about the child, criticism and discussion turned to the ethics and role of photojournalism, and to Carter in particular, raising questions about his intentions and motivations for taking the shot: Why didn't he try to help the child, pick her up or find out who she was? Zelizer (2013, 168) quotes from the *St. Petersburg Times*: "Viewers continued to express outrage, calling his actions 'shameful,' 'inexplicable,' and 'inhuman' and complaining that he had 'cheapened' both the prize and the news organizations that printed the image: 'which is the true vulture?' asked one reader."

The critiques of Carter's photograph resonate today in discussions of the visual imagery of suffering and its consequences to public discussion and sensibilities. In a way we have never gotten over the image, or Carter's death, or the images from Biafra and Ethiopia, as we continue to evaluate their power or explain their failures. Zelizer (2010, 170) offers this observation "Questions of content—of whether the girl in fact had died—were accompanied and exacerbated by discussion of form—of what Carter did or did not do." In Zelizer's view, photographs are works of interpretation—thus they are *subjunctive* forms, or inferences, not *indicative*, or representations of facts. Though they have a powerful claim to the real because of their documentary form, or what Messaris (1997) calls indexicality, assigning meaning to them is done through the work of viewers. Images of people about to die are suggestive images of death, not facts of that death.³ Photographs capture public imagination and evoke emotions, offering a range of interpretive possibilities through inference. Zelizer assigns the blame for the failure of Carter's image to its depiction of the famine wracked body of the child, arguing, sometimes "cues of bodily frailty do not navigate the inferential tensions necessary for images of possible death to work" like other images of impending death (Zelizer 2010, 165). Thus, if we draw out Zelizer's argument, we can say that the suffering of the child's body emotionally blocked the public's ability to generalize to the larger issues of famine, or imagine a way to help stop the suffering. After all, the child was beyond help, outside of rescue, she was hopeless and her death was inevitable (Andersen 2006). Public imagination responded to that quality of the photograph with indignation.

Another consequence of visual depictions of starving bodies is their departure from a political understanding of the roots and uses of starvation, "as the outcome of historical processes of systematic inequality in the distribution of resources" (Chouliaraki 2013, 58). Though the photograph records an actual moment frozen in time (Sontag 1977) and is therefore irrefutable evidence of an event, the fact remains it cannot interpret those events, offer explanations, causes or motivations (Benjamin 1969, Berger 1980, Berger and Mohr, 1982). In addition, when images of starvation dominate the news they shape the story and mold the frame, contextualizing famine as a problem of individual survival or what Edkins calls the "medicalization of famine" (2000, 39). The solutions proposed by that narrative call for treating the symptoms of famine through food relief, something that certainly saves many lives. But they leave a legacy of reporting (and practices of aid agencies) that obscures or mystifies the causes—saving individuals "rather than restoring the means of livelihood in the community" (Edkins 2000, 39). Over time these frames have troubling consequences; they fail to address the root causes of disasters and lead to highly naïve publics.

In addition, embedded within such images are the social relations of inequality and what many have identified as the *colonial gaze*—or the unequal relationship set up by the visual— where all the power is assigned to the viewer. Comfortable spectators are invited by broadcasts and publications, to gaze voyeuristically at a distant *other*, they have the privilege to act and relive the suffering, yet those in need sit passively, pleading, pitiful and barely human. Not only are we positioned as complicit with the suffering of others, within these images is the "immorality of distance" that makes the West the "benefactor of a world that it manages to symbolically annihilate" (Chouliaraki 2013, 60). Others have called this dynamic between the view and viewed, the "iconography of anonymous victimhood" (Bleiker and Kay 2007, 144).⁴

By the mid 1990s many aid agencies abandoned the use of such negative imagery and changed their appeals through the use of positive imagery (Chouliaraki 2013) showing smiling children who looked straight into the camera and the eyes of the spectator/donor. In contrast to the colonial gaze of negative appeals, such positive images establish a different performative logic, replacing the power relationship of inequality with a *sympathetic equilibrium* between victim and spectator (Boltanski 1999, 39). These images seemed to strike a more positive balance with a reciprocal emotional dynamic between the distant sufferer and the spectator as benefactor. The smiling child of the positive appeal "provides subtle evidence of the sufferer's gratitude for the (imagined) alleviation of his/her suffering by a benefactor and the benefactor's respective empathy toward the grateful sufferer" Chouliaraki (2013, 61). Arguably such images hold the child within the community of the living, elevate her in relationship to the spectator, and imbue her with a reciprocal sense of agency, but the image poses no real challenge to most of the other logics embedded in the negative appeal. In the cultural imaginary of the positive depiction, the child remains outside the bounds of explanation and understanding, the only thing that could lead to solidarity able to recognize the injustice of the child's plight. The new logic of the positive image glosses over the fundamental asymmetry between the sufferer and the would-be donor, subsuming the difference under the logic of Western conceptions. While such images appear to empower the sufferer though "discourses of dignity and self-determination," positive appeals actually disempower those depicted "by appropriating their otherness in Western discourses of identity and agency" (Chouliaraki 2013, 63).

The 2014 updated Code of Conduct on Images and Messages addressed the *smiling child*, referring to the appeal as a "new stereotype" saying:

> It is a welcome development that many organizations recognize that they have a responsibility to try and move away from prevailing "negative" images and messages. However, the tendency to directly replace the image of the "poor unhappy person" with the "smiling happy child" does an equal disservice to the context of many situations.

In addition, because the urgency of need is less evident, positive appeals have been shown to be less effective in garnering financial support (Cohen 2001, 183–184).

Compassion Fatigue

Evaluating the nature and dynamics of the photograph seems to be an endless and thankless task; as soon as one critique is made and corrected in the visual record, another appears in the lens. As Stanley Cohen (2001, 169) has noted, at this point "we know nothing worthwhile about the cumulative effect of media imagery." In light of the somewhat devastating criticisms of the history and conventions of humanitarian photography (only a portion of which we outlined above), many writers express an overall sense of failure of imagery to live up to the emotional and cultural demands placed upon it. Today the literature is filled with a general suspicion about the capacity of images to move the public or convey the world. One of the most common claims is the troubling accusation, according to David Campbell, that photographs of suffering including atrocity, famine and war, have induced "compassion fatigue" in the public at large. Currently at the World Press Photo Foundation, Campbell (2012) is widely published on the topic and in "The Myth of Compassion Fatigue" he refutes the claim, while noting its persistence in the literature. Susie Linfield (2010, 42) describes the thesis as "a contemporary truism, indeed a contemporary cliché" so much so that "to dispute this idea is akin to repudiating evolution or joining the flat-earth society." As defined by Campbell (2012, 3) the concept often starts with "an assertion about our media saturated world . . . At its heart is the notion that, far from changing the world, photographs work repetitively, numbing our emotional capacity and thereby diminishing the possibility of an effective response to international crises." Quoting Rancière (2009, 103) Campbell (2012, 3) notes that the suspicion of the visual is generated in part by a simplistic and totalizing assertion about the power of the photograph, "the disappointed belief in a straight line from perception, affect on, comprehension and action."

The foundational text that proposed compassion fatigue was Susan Sontag's (1977, 21) seminal work *On Photography* when she famously asserted that, "in these last decades,

'concerned' photography has done at least as much to deaden conscience as to arouse it."
Her statement that "images anesthetize," has been widely circulated, and by the power of
her rhetorical force, the idea of photography's responsibility for compassion fatigue has been
sustained and elaborated upon (Sontag 1977, 20). Nowhere is this more evident than in the
book titled *Compassion Fatigue: How the Media Sell Disease, Famine, War and Death* by Susan
Moeller (1999), which is also regularly cited in the literature of photographic analysis. But
Campbell points out that Sontag's words were written between 1973 and 1977, and the
grounds for this argument seem even weaker when "we consider that no more than seven
years later the world was moved to the largest charitable event ever by both still and moving
pictures of mass famine in Ethiopia." In addition, though Sontag posited the phenomenon
in the 1970s, in her later book *Regarding the Pain of Others*, she seemed to retract those earlier
claims:

> As much as they create sympathy, I wrote [in *On Photography*], photographs shrivel
> sympathy. Is this true? I thought it was when I wrote it. I'm not so sure now. What
> is the evidence that photographs have a diminishing impact, that our culture of
> spectatorship neutralizes the moral force of photographs of atrocities?
>
> (Sontag 2004, 23)

Of the many contradictions Campbell (2012, 4) points to, is the fear that compassion fatigue
may strike, even when circumstances negate the efficacy of the idea.

> Whenever there is a crisis, the claim of compassion fatigue is never far behind.
> Consider the 2010 earthquake in Haiti that killed more than 200,000 people and
> devastated the country. Media coverage was swift, extensive and intense. The focus
> on victims trapped in rubble or suffering as a result was, as in Ron Haviv's photo-
> graph, up close and personal. The charitable response was vast and global. Yet
> alongside the coverage and the response were frequent iterations of the worry about
> compassion fatigue setting in.[5]

Even in the face of a surge in charitable compassion, the fact that compassion fatigue can be
mobilized as a concept "demonstrates how empty it is as a signifier" (Campbell 2012, 13).
In addition to pointing to the fallacies of argumentation, Campbell notes that there is no
credible empirical evidence to confirm the loss of pubic compassion in response to humanitarian disasters. In fact he lists evidence that charitable giving is alive and well.

> In Britain there are 166,000 charities that received donations totaling £10 billion in
> 2009. In the United States, there are more than 800,000 charitable organisations, and
> Americans gave them more than $300 billion in 2007. The British public's response
> to disasters like the 2010 Haiti earthquake (for which the Disasters Emergency
> Committee raised £106 million) shows that the willingness to act on empathy for
> the victims of natural disasters is still considerable even when they are distant. The
> DEC conducts consolidated appeals for the fourteen leading aid NGOs in the UK,
> and a look at their various appeals over the last few years shows that there is a constant
> willingness to donate, albeit at variable rates, from the 2009 Gaza appeal's £8.3 million
> to the massive £392 million given for the 2004 Tsunami appeal. There are clearly
> *differential* responses, but these do not add up to a generally *diminished* response.
>
> (Campbell 2012, 22)

In the end Campbell makes a significant contribution to the analysis of visual language by pointing out that the problem may be using compassion as a singular concept, and a dominant mode through which to interpret the public response to extreme events. Compassion operates at an "individualizing level" and therefore cannot be the basis for political mobilization:

> because it is limited to a vicarious experience of suffering usually between two individuals (the one suffering and the spectator of that suffering), and can thus only ever deal with the particular rather than the general. As such, framing the problem in terms of either the diminishment or promotion of compassion means we are incapable of generalizing the move from singular expression to collective action.
>
> (Campbell 2012, based on Johnson 2011, 621–643)

Chouliaraki (2013, 28) argues that, "Contemporary citizenship largely depends on this moral acknowledgement of unfortunate others who, in being shown to suffer, mobilize the West as a public—a collectivity with the will to act." But citizenship must also be understood as the requirement to participate in a democratic process, a process in which decisions made by common persons are based on information and knowledge. We seem to be stuck singularly, in a psychosocial dimension that is certainly an important part of the process of public action; but also crucial to citizenship is information, and at least some knowledge of the systemic causes of a crisis. Only then can we participate in meaningful solutions, or what Chouliaraki terms revolutionary solidarity.

If we return to Sontag, we find another passage that qualifies the psychosocial response by positing a need for political context.

> What determines the possibility of being affected morally by photographs is the existence of a relevant political consciousness. Without a politics, photographs of the slaughter-bench of history will most likely be experienced as simply unreal or as a demoralizing emotional blow.
>
> (1977, 19)

If we draw out this logic, images of suffering are an "emotional blow" if they do not include a political explanation, and so the public cannot fathom a solution, and therefore a way to participate in alleviating the suffering at a political level. What many aid agencies have done is to bypass the need for political understanding of the root causes of crisis and their long-term solutions. They offer instead a way for the public to act, not necessarily as informed citizens, but as humanitarians supporting relief efforts. If we return to Carter's picture of the starving little girl, in the initial publication the photograph was used as little more than gratuitous illustration. Without a narrative or political context, the public was offered no way to act. No caring humanitarian was on the scene to help the child. No pathways were presented for the public even to imagine a way to alleviate the suffering, unlike the images from Biafra where children were actually being cared for—as much as could be done for them—and in Korem, where food was also on the way. The response was an emotional blow that ignited public indignation. But where might the fault lie, with Kevin Carter—or the publishers? Carter could not move freely in the area. He was under heavily armed guards and could not follow up on what he had photographed.[6]

Conceptualizing the real power of the photograph includes the narrative context and its ability to provide information from the micro to macro levels. But we have known this for a very long time through the writings of Walter Benjamin (1969) to John Berger (1980) and many others. According to Benjamin (1969), in an age of technological reproduction the photograph cannot explain on its own. It only captures the surface or the appearance of an event—it can suggest no further or deeper meaning. It cannot narrate an essence or tell us how or why something happened.[7] Nowhere has this become more important than in the field of humanitarian communication.

The point here seems to be that many factors are in play in determining the public's response to disasters. With so many "differentials," it would seem that evaluating humanitarian communications on a case-by-case basis will teach us much about the sincerity and efficacy of images, narratives and appeals. If we rethink humanitarian communication in the present image-rich landscape of contemporary media, we can point to mediations that nurture and expand the idea of a humanitarian imagination and citizenship. We will also find some parameters for evaluating a set of best practices. With this in mind, we now take a look at two humanitarian media campaigns.

The first is a 2:21 minute film produced by Brave New Films titled, *Nowhere to go: Shutting Out Syrians*, which includes images, footage, text, and audio—actuality of conflict, voice-over, and song. In addition, it presents a graphic shadow play of a couple in their home:

> In monochromatic hues we see footage of bombing within a woman's silhouette, overlaid with text noting: There are over 4.8 million Syrian Refugees. A song of lament is mixed with conflict audio. The next image is an old, sepia toned newspaper with massive headlines "Irish Refugees Turned Away, 1840, slow cut to another, Jewish Refugees Turned away 1939, then another, Salvadoran Refugees Run From Violence, 1985. The last: Syrian Refugees 52% Are Children. Each front page also carries a picture. As the final newspaper expands in the frame, an image of a Syrian child turns to video footage. The little girl sings a song in Arabic, and the captions read: "I yearn for my nation which knows no safety. I'm yearning for freedom." Suddenly the commotion in the street turns to chaos as a bomb goes off and we lose sight of the child.
>
> Upbeat music plays and the outlines of a house rise from the bottom of the screen. A shadow play begins. Syria's population in 2010: 21 million. A mother, in black silhouette within a gray house, moves in the space and cradles her infant; a voice says, "We had a safe life." As her husband arrives home and kisses her we hear a child's voice: "We didn't need money or anything from anyone. We used to stay up late telling bedtime stories." A bomb goes off and the man and woman crouch in the space. In what sounds like testimonial, a woman's voice says, "When the shelling became heavier I would tell them it was fireworks . . ." More bombing and missiles flare along the sides of the house and shapes of gray buildings are superimposed over street footage: ". . . but I could not lie any longer. The demonstrations, the arrests, our house was raided." A man pointing a gun enters the house and the people huddle against a wall. "One day, all of a sudden, the bombing started in our neighborhood." Conflict intensifies and a man's voice says, "The shop that I owned and worked at was looted." The people, fearful, dart back and forth, the fire continues outside. "And was hit by a rocket after that." Bold headlines now state that: "Half the population has been forced to flee their homes." The outlines of other buildings fall from view to the bottom of the screen and footage of a city in flames becomes more pronounced. "We never thought this would happen in Syria. My house was destroyed." The house finally falls away and the man and woman crouch together without shelter. "Syrian refugees undergo the most scrutiny

of anybody entering the US, requiring approval from numerous departments with no guarantee of acceptance." "The US has agreed to take in 0.2% of the Syrian Refugees. Tell Congress to help refugees, not turn their back on those escaping war and persecution. Sign the Petition at AmnestyUSA.org/SupportRefugees."

In a little over 2 minutes the film is packed with innovation and visual strategies that work on many levels. Through audiovisual story telling, it creates empathy without sentimentalism, provides information and invites public participation for a legislative campaign, all of which serve to nurture the humanitarian imagination. The shadow play selects fragments of home life in a narrative that reaches across cultural and religious differences. American audiences can empathize through the positions and commonality of members of a family—they tell bedtime stories, when their home becomes unsafe they try to protect their children. The father owns a small business, like many people in the US, and before the shelling started they did not need assistance from anyone.

Chouliaraki (2013) asserts that in the West the humanitarian imagination was fostered in the theater, going back to the classical conception of Greek tragedy; dramatic action—seeing the misfortunes of men—leads the audience to pity. As theater reemerges in early modern Europe the staged action becomes a "catalyst for solidarity" because, through drama, we "momentarily place ourselves in the sufferer's condition," which enables "a fleeting transfer of emotion as if the suffering were our own" (29–30). Because of the "moralizing potential of sympathetic identification," the drama reinforces a conception of solidarity with others, and thus the humanitarian imagination. Audience identification with sympathetic characters has long been understood in all types of storytelling from novels to films, but a re-focus on theater is useful here, as a newly emerging aesthetic technique of the shadow play has taken hold in political performance. The innovative style of the silhouetted family allows us to empathize with their worsening situation, yet doesn't collapse the distance between us and them, which would serve to deny the conditions under which only they suffer, not us. The actuality footage of conflict and the voice-over testimonial style brings real people within our perception, and underscores the violence from which they need to flee. The on-screen text offers historical comparisons, actual information and a way to take action at a political level, all bolstering the practices of citizenship and participation. This film is a partnership between Brave New Films and Amnesty International, yet it does not represent a media strategy designed to promote a brand, or position the viewer as an ironic spectator. The viewer is invited to act out of concern, based on empathy and information, and participate in a needed legislative action directed at national policy, not immediate gratification.

The next example also represents a partnership, this time between a photojournalist, an actor, and a number of campaigns, including Human Rights Watch. This multifaceted campaign includes one of the most entrenched conflicts in the world, and a media technology company. It educates and addresses the foundational technology and economics of new media on a global scale.

Intel and Conflict Minerals in the DRC

On January 7, 2014 Intel announced that its new microprocessors were "conflict free," meaning that the minerals were now sourced from clean mines in the Democratic Republic of the Congo. This was a major step. It meant the company would no longer be directly financing part of the conflict in the DRC. Four years earlier the company was approached by The Enough Project, an organization carrying out a campaign to stop the use of conflict minerals in the region. The campaign also featured the celebrity actress Robin Wright. Collaboration and partnership were thus the hallmarks of Intel's journey to conflict-free microprocessors.

The images of photojournalist Marcus Bleasdale provided visual records of the consequences of the global market in minerals. After decades working in Africa, Bleasdale's earlier alliance with Human Rights Watch (HRW) culminated in an exhibition titled, The Curse of Gold which examined how the global market for gold helped sustain the war. His photos of Congo were shown in Geneva in an exhibition organized by HRW, which influenced the decision of a leading gold mining company Metalor Technologies, to stop doing business in the DRC. David Campbell (2012) tells the story:

> With each trip to the DRC, even when he wasn't directly commissioned by them, Marcus worked with both HRW and The Enough Project, benefiting from their research and occasional logistical support, sharing images, and providing talks and testimony for their campaigns.

Bleasdale was also commissioned by *National Geographic* (2013) to be part of "The Price of Precious" exhibition, a story that made clear "the minerals in our electronic devices have bankrolled unspeakable violence in the Congo."

Commenting on the role of photojournalism in this process Bleasdale noted "We cannot stop wars with pictures, but we can provide the tools for the dialogue, which eventually will stop wars." He also noted, "it's difficult for photographs to do this work on their own. You need an advocacy group to partner with who can knock on the doors of Congress and corporations. This advocacy work is as satisfying to me as taking a photograph."[8]

From the "Photograph" to Visual Storytelling

Today our visual landscape demands that we re-conceptualize the nature and function of the "photograph." The single photograph has dominated the analytical and theoretical imagination for too long. The short film and the collaborations with Bleasdale's images expand our definition of imagery to include "multimedia," a combination of images, sound and graphics, all that contributes to telling a story.[9] As David Campbell has argued, the proliferation of imaging devices such as smartphones, video-enabled DSLRs, GoPros, drones, Google Glass, Oculus Rift, and the way we view images on so many screens and in varied contexts, has produced a "new media economy" that must re-envision the photographic, whether personal or professional, still or moving, "lens-based or computational." Visual storytelling is best understood in this context, and now includes documentary or editorial photography, mobile imaging, photojournalism, video journalism, and satellite imagery. A photograph cannot be considered an isolated or discrete object, but is now part of "networks of materials, technologies, institutions, markets, social spaces, emotions, cultural histories and political contexts."[10] The photograph no longer stands on its own in today's media geography, if it ever did. Indeed, we speak of the black-and-white pictures taken of starving children as singular images from Africa, but Biafra was also shot in video, and Ethiopia was primarily presented on film, in different venues and powerful narrations.

Over the years as photojournalists have continued to document the pain of others, as news reports narrate their stories, and aid agencies present images of crises (including development organizations and their beneficiaries), discussions of the ethics and nature of images and narratives, and the emotions they evoke continue to fill the pages of books, journals, cultural critiques, and humanitarian reports. Of central concern to the humanitarian community has been the dual question of empathy and compassion and the force of those sentiments to fund relief efforts for the next crisis or donate to the next urgent campaign. Political understanding and action should also be part of this discussion, and it seems to be finding its way onto the discursive agendas. As the 2014 Code of Conduct advises, "Choose images and related messages based on values of respect, equality, *solidarity and justice* [emphasis added]." But they also acknowledge "it is a reality of our world today that many of the images of extreme poverty and humanitarian distress are negative and cannot be ignored" (Dochas 2014, 7–14).

The Art, Aesthetics and Power of a Single Image

The history of photography is filled with examples of images so powerful they remain unforgettable, and many have served as catalysts for news reporting and public action. Consider for example the photograph of Aylan Kurdi, the 3-year-old Syrian boy whose body washed ashore on a Turkish beach. In Western-style dress, we see little legs in shorts. His arm is tucked under his body, his head to the side as if asleep. Yet his body faces toward the sea and his face is in a wave. The image sparked public action and information about the boy, his family, and the details of the journey that ended on the beach. News organizations around the world published the image, many with corresponding editorials expressing outrage that developed nations were not doing enough to help refugees.[11] An online petition in the UK urging Prime Minister David Cameron to accept more asylum seekers surged to more than 300,000 signatures from 40,000 the day before. In addition, the image of the drowned toddler quickly went viral.[12]

When Aylan's picture was taken, thousands of refugees had already drowned in the Mediterranean, but together with the visual/technical media economy, this image sparked a much-needed global dialogue that had been delayed, and finally emerged in legacy and online media. Charities and human-rights organizations reported a surge in donations.[13] The power of the image can be found in the visual anomaly it captured, and the feelings it evoked in the public. Aylan looks like an average little boy who is sleeping and, like anyone's child, he should be. Instead he has been drowned. It is this association and the resulting confusion between sleep and death, other and familiar, that jars the public. It acts like a poem by creating an aesthetically inspired association that changes one's perspective on the world. Indeed, memes placing him in bed, and many other situations, were widely circulated, some becoming quite controversial. Photographs, like art, can allow us to see from a different view, one able to focus a new light on an ongoing crisis. But that is a different form of signification than explanation, analysis, or reasoned exposition. We must evaluate the power of visual images not only by their ability to make us feel and interpret events, or even explain them, but by their ability to engage a visual economy and move through a participatory multimedia environment that can serve as a catalyst for action. Indeed the effects of the image of Aylan continue to resonate in the media. On August 1, 2016 the radio program *Marketplace* reported that a community group was helping resettle Syrian refugees in New Haven, Connecticut. They were inspired by the photograph of Aylan Kurdi a year earlier.[14]

Conclusion

For too long the single photograph has carried the burden of analysis, and time and again has struggled with the weight of the demands and expectations placed upon it. Contemporary multimedia practices can augment the photograph, offer context, captions, graphic displays, performance, and forums for discussion, all of which offer explanation and get us closer to finding solution, combined with other art forms that can bridge the gap between mediation, perception, understanding, public concern, and political action.

For the most part, images cannot speak on their own, and certainly not to all the needs of historical documentation, or to a public that must rely on information to engage in the world's humanitarian crises. Such positions lead us to blame viewers for a loss of compassion, relief agencies and their staff who risk their lives trying to save lives, and the photographers and journalists who risk theirs every time they move among the dispossessed, the displaced, the exploited, and those under fire.[15] A better way is to focus our discussion on a multimedia visual economy, considering images within the larger context of media geography, public action and global economic and political justice. We may well have crossed over into a post-humanitarian age, but that has more to do with the justifications for war and conflict than our ability to empathize with those who suffer.

Notes

1. This clip can be seen on "Goodies and Baddies," Adam Curtis: The Medium and the Message. BBC blog, March 28, 2011, available at: www.bbc.co.uk/blogs/adamcurtis/2011/03/goodies_and_baddies.html
2. Dochas, The Code of Conduct of Images and Messages, available at: http://deeep.org/communication/code-of-conduct/
3. The most notable "as if" is that of victims jumping from the Twin Towers on 9/11. "Viewers were never shown their impact of death, just victims plummeting towards it. In other words, the image of near death, or the 'as if' is more about what the image represents—the symbol it becomes, rather than that person's actual death." For a discussion of this language see *The Nation*: www.thenation.com/article/an-illustrated-guide-to-the-dumbest-things-republicans-have-said-about-refugees/
4. Chouliaraki (2013, 61) goes on to identify them as *negative appeals*, that "are defined by a performativity of guilt and indignation which claims authenticity through a realist imagery of suffering as 'bare life' and moralizes Western publics through the logic of complicity, thereby risking compassion fatigue and apathy."
5. "Haiti: Compassion Fatigue: Relief groups worried people may start tuning out," *Fox 25 News*, Boston, January 21, 2010, available at: www.myfoxboston.com/dpp/news/haiti-compassion-fatigue1264168069093; Clark Hoyt, "Face to Face with Tragedy," *New York Times*, January 23, 2010, available at: www.nytimes.com/2010/01/24/opinion/24pubed.html
6. By all contemporary indications he seems to also have been suffering from PTSD caused by the violence he'd experienced and documented for years in South Africa.
7. Even when it tells us what something looks like, it is an illusory appearance. Because the photograph is always a reproduction (a mediation) it is not immediately accessible to perception and must remain at a metaphorical distance from the viewers. It can leave us separated from the subject; physically as well as psychologically.
8. David Campbell, "How Photojournalism Contributes to Change: Marcus Bleasdale's Work on Conflict Minerals," January 14, 2014, available at: www.david-campbell.org/2014/01/14/photojournalism-contributes-change-marcus-bleasdales-work-conflict-minerals/
9. David Campbell, "'Multimedia,' Photojournalism and Visual Storytelling," April 29, 2013, available at: www.david-campbell.org/2013/04/29/multimedia-photojournalism-and-visual-storytelling/
10. Ibid.
11. And because Canada had turned down the family's bid for asylum, Prime Minister Stephen Harper was forced to defend his government's track record on refugee issues.
12. www.wsj.com/articles/image-of-syrian-boy-washed-up-on-beach-hits-hard-1441282847
13. Barbie Zelizer "Haunting Image Spurs Action on Refugees" (September 8, 2015), available at: www.philly.com/philly/blogs/thinktank/Haunting-image-spurs-action-on-migrants.html
14. Tracy Samuelson, "Think You Can't Help a Group of Syrian Refugees? Look at these Folks." Marketplace.org August 1, 2016, available at: www.marketplace.org/2016/08/01/world/think-you-cant-help-syrians-look-these-folks
15. As Don McCullin (1992, 124) wrote in his autobiography "the whiplash of compassion and conscience never ceased to assail me in Biafra."

References

Andersen, R. (2006) *A Century of Media, A Century of War*, New York: Peter Lang.

Barrow, O., and Jenkins, M. (2001) *The Charitable Response: NGOs and Development in East and North East Africa*, Oxford: James Currey.

Benjamin, W. (1969) *Illuminations: Essays and Reflections*, Hannah Arendt (Ed.) and Harry Zohn (Trans.), New York: Schocken Books.

Berger, J. (1980) *About Looking*, New York: Pantheon Books.

Berger, J., and Mohr, J. (1982) *Another Way of Telling*, New York: Pantheon Books.

Bleiker, R., and Kay, A. (2007) "Representing HIV/AIDS in Africa: Pluralist Photography and Local Empowerment," *International Studies Quarterly*, 51: 139–163.

Boltanski, L. (1999) *Distant Suffering: Morality, Media and Politics*, Graham Burchell (trans), Cambridge, MA: Cambridge University Press.

Calhoun, C. (2010) "The Idea of Emergency: Humanitarian Action and Global (Dis)order," in D. Fassin, and M. Pandolfi (Eds.), *Contemporary States of Emergency*, New York: Zone Books, pp. 29–58.

Campbell, D. (2012) "The Myth of Compassion Fatigue," (February 29) available at: www.david-campbell.org/2012/02/29/the-myth-of-compassion-fatigue/

Chouliaraki, L. (2013) *The Ironic Spectator: Solidarity in the Age of Post-Humanitarianism*, Cambridge, UK: Polity.

Cohen, S. (2001) *States of Denial: Knowing About Atrocities and Suffering*, London: Oxford.

Dochas. (2004) "Code of Conduct on Images and Messages," available at: www.dochas.ie/images-and-messages

Edkins, J. (2000) *Whose Hunger?: Concepts of Famine, Practices of Aid*, Minneapolis, MN: University of Minnesota Press.

Fehrenback, H., and Rodogno, D. (Eds.). (2015) *Humanitarian Photography: A History*, Cambridge, UK: Cambridge University Press.

Harrison, P., and Palmer R. H. (1986) *News Out of Africa: Biafra to Band Aid*, London: Hilary Shipman.

Jackson, A. (2015) "October 23, 1984: BBC report on Ethiopian famine sparks global fundraising campaign," October 23, available at: http://home.bt.com/news/world-news/october-23–1984-bbc-report-on-ethiopian-famine-shakes-the-world-into-action-11364012387968#article_video

Johnson, J. (2011) "'The Arithmetic of Compassion': Rethinking the Politics of Photography," *British Journal of Political Science*, 41: 621–643.

Linfield, S. (2010) *The Cruel Radiance: Photography and Political Violence*, Chicago, IL: University of Chicago Press.

McCullin, D. (1992) *Unreasonable Behaviour: An Autobiography*, London: Vintage.

Marinovitch, G., and Silver, J. (2000) *The Bang-Bang Club*, London: William Heinemann.

Messaris, P. (1997) *Visual Persusasion*, Thousand Oaks, CA: Sage Publications.

Moeller, S. (1999) *Compassion Fatigue: How the Media Sell Disease, Famine, War and Death*, London: Routledge.

National Geographic. (2013) "Conflict Minerals," available at: http://ngm.nationalgeographic.com/2013/10/conflict-minerals/gettleman-text

Nguyen, K. (2013) "New Book Examines Legacy of Media Coverage of Ethiopia's 1984 Famine," *Reuter's Foundation News*, October 4, available at: http://news.trust.org//item/20131004142501–3dpbh/

Rancière, J. (2009) *The Emancipated Spectator*, trans. G. Elliot, London: Verso.

Sontag, S. (1977) *On Photography*, New York: Farrar, Straus & Giroux.

Sontag, S. (2004) *Regarding the Pain of Others*, New York: Picador.

Waters, K. (2004) "Influencing the Message: The Role of Catholic Missionaries in Media Coverage of the Nigerian Civil War," *The Catholic Historical Review*, 90 (4): 697–718.

Zelizer, B. (2010) *About to Die: How News Images Move the Public*, New York: Oxford University Press.

Zelizer, B. (2013) "On the Shelf Life of Democracy in Journalism Scholarship," *Journalism*, 14 (4): 459–473.

2

COMMUNICATING FOR IMPACT, THE VOICE OF THE VICTIMS

The Role of Media Design in Humanitarian and Human Rights Organizations

Tamara Alrifai

My Dinner with George

I was in Los Angeles, having a meal with a group of old friends from school, some of whom I had not seen for nearly 20 years. Of course, the first questions we asked, after enquiring about our respective private situations (whether we had found partners, whether we had had kids . . .), were about our professional achievements. I put on my most serious face and boasted that I had been working in the field of humanitarian aid and human rights for over 15 years. "Oh my god", said one of them, "so you have actually lived in places like Darfur or Baghdad?"

That question was an instantaneous reminder that, to many people who are not directly involved in development-type work, humanitarian and human rights issues are often geographically remote topics, topics associated with faraway places, cities whose names have now become associated with global-scale catastrophes. Yes, I have been to Darfur a few times, I replied, while realizing that to my friends in Beverly Hills, Sudan, and now Syria, have mostly become associated with movie stars who adopt exotic-looking children, or who visit disaster-stricken areas and look genuinely moved by the scale of the human suffering they encounter.

While I carefully started to prepare myself to answer questions about women and children and the disastrous effects of armed conflicts on education, my friend Laura, now married to a young and talented Arab-American actor, looked up from her plate. Her eyes shone with the excitement of someone who had a story to tell. "When my husband had dinner with George, he told him how much he felt for these causes," she said. "Hmmm George?" I asked. "Oh sorry, Clooney," she answered. "Isn't that the kind of work you do, you know, taking celebrities to refugee camps and bring along big journalists to show the world how people struggle to survive catastrophes? You said you worked in communications for humanitarian causes, right?" she enquired, genuinely engaged. But before I even started to answer, the conversation became all about George and of course his gorgeous wife. "Hey she also 'does' human rights", said my friend. "Did you ever meet her?"

This is when I knew I had lost my storyline for the evening. With my naïve belief that I could capture and engage an audience who worked in Hollywood in a discussion on "issues" such as how political repression and lack of rights could only yield unhappy frustrated youths, or how aid could easily be politicized and manipulated by parties in an armed conflict, I quickly realized that despite all my storytelling skills it was difficult to maintain a discussion on humanitarian issues if it did not involve telling the stories of real people, and giving dramatic descriptions of someone's everyday life as a refugee, but also as a human being.

For professionals in the fields of development, aid or human rights, the world and politics are centered on the principles they defend: the right to life, the right to political and civil freedoms, the right to access humanitarian aid unhindered. To us, no political conversation is complete without a review of how much a country has respected universal principles of human rights[1] and no peace negotiations are possible without an unconditional acceptance of the role of humanitarian organizations. We often assume that everyone we talk to about politics will have these references in mind, but are surprised every time we see so many different angles in a news story; from economic themes to geopolitical security. It is precisely the angle of rights and the voice of the victim that humanitarian and human rights organizations seek to amplify through their various communications channels: campaigns, formal statements, audio-visual production, opinions pieces placed in media outlets, or interviews on television and radio.

During that dinner in Los Angeles, of course the conversation touched on Middle East politics a few times, mostly to lament the scope and scale of the damage in the region, but there was little space for discussing the humanitarian consequences of regional politics. In spite of what seemed to be genuine concern for the victims, there was little attention to, and almost no words to explain or understand, what could be done to contain their suffering.

A Changing Media Landscape

With the quasi quantum-leaps that the media industry has taken these last 20 years, and since satellite television networks have closely followed military operations, starting with the invasion of Iraq in 2003, at times even embedding their correspondents with the troops, humanitarian organizations, particularly those working in conflict areas,[2] have had more opportunities to send out their message clearly and, in fact, live, through aid workers whom journalists meet on location, while distributing food or registering refugees. And while the media is often primarily interested in reporting on the political and military developments around a crisis—though historically the root causes of crises such as famine are rarely illuminated (Franks 2014)—there has been an increased space for what has commonly become known as "humanitarian coverage," or covering the human cost of a conflict or a natural disaster.

The plethora of media outlets, including the increased private ownerships of media companies, the ease of communication, and the penetration of mass media to new communities have provided more space to be filled and enabled divergent views to be covered as the media is no longer controlled by a few businesses and a few governments, though only six highly conglomerated corporations own the US media companies. Moreover, after the collapse of the Soviet Union, humanitarian crises are no longer only politicized as a global confrontation between superpowers or at least no longer presented as such, thus giving non-political sources, such as humanitarian organizations, the possibility to comment on developments from their non-political perspective. For example NPR (2016) aired a story about community resilience to crisis featuring the role of music. Over the last 20 years, commentators have ceased being political commentators only, and there has been increased space for what has commonly been described as "the other voices," voices of victims, of people on the street, of humanitarian and human rights specialists.[3]

As a result, humanitarian and human rights organizations alike have gained more media space, have been able to place spokespersons on prime time to describe the situation from a humanitarian or legal perspective, or request more funding and political support for their work. They have regularly contributed to public debates, injecting legal arguments into a discussion that, until the end of the twentieth century, had primarily been political.

It is therefore now common to see a representative of a humanitarian organization talking on TV either directly from the location of the organization's projects (commonly referred to as "the field"), or from a studio with an anchor, sometimes in the presence of other guests or as part of a panel. Most media outlets in fact now give priority to a guest speaker from a humanitarian or human rights organization when covering a situation of natural or man-made disaster, many detailing how aid is best delivered to affected areas (Bloch 2016). These kinds of stories bring the human dimension to the debate.

Why Communicate?

Large and small humanitarian organizations generally depend on a set of traditional donors (governments and foundations) to cover the cost of their operations. And just as in the world of private companies, organizations need to demonstrate that they are relevant and worth investing in, providing services that make a difference in the lives of people they say they help. Organizations are accountable towards their donors in carrying out their planned activities and in responding to the needs of people affected by emergencies.

Organizations that also seek to instigate change and promote a culture of human rights, in addition to responding to needs through aid, rely on the support of public opinion to gain acceptability in the countries and communities they work in. They thus count on public opinion to promote their messages, and hope that public pressure can at least create awareness of the issues they promote or respond to. For example, launching a public campaign on the adverse consequences of a practice such as Female Genital Mutilation (FGM), a difficult subject to approach in a number of Arab and African countries (Egypt, Somalia, or Burkina Faso for instance) will help an organization raise awareness about the issue, and go hand in hand with efforts to help convince a government to enact legislation banning such a practice. It takes pushing from both ends, on policymakers and on the public, to bring about real change: laws that promote good practices and ban harmful ones, and public awareness that shows the issue from a different angle for people to think about and question practices they have inherited without challenging, ultimately leads to a change in behavior. Organizations such as UNICEF, UNHCR, WFP, MSF, Human Rights Watch, and Amnesty International manage to bring about change and report on the impact of their work can attract funds, including individual donations, from donor countries, hence generating more resources for them to continue their work.

Organizations therefore have a double interest in communicating about their work and issues: they demonstrate to their donors that they are effectively working in their fields, thus spending the funds wisely, and they seek acceptability by the people they want to reach and work with.

To do this, they increasingly resort to marketing-style techniques, slowly ditching their classic style newsletters and institutional stiffly worded press releases, in favor of more modern-style techniques such as tweeting live updates from a disaster-struck location, or promoting the impact of their work on real people, who give testimonies on camera. Are we back to George then? They increasingly use local languages and hire people who can communicate directly with the various communities they serve. Organizations may differ in their communication styles or in their level of assertiveness, they may also differ in the amount of resources they allocate to communications generally, but they have certainly all stepped up their communications efforts in the last decade, especially as the number of organizations competing for funds has risen.

There are therefore several reasons for aid organizations, international and non-governmental, to engage in public communications. First is to publicly report on their work, on the difference they make in a field that has become crowded with organizations: what is the added value of an organization, what sets it aside, what area of work does it specialize in, and how many people benefit from its services in a given context and worldwide? Second, an organization engages in public communications to promote certain values, principles or formal positions, as a way of advocating for a kind of change that needs to happen in order to improve a situation. Third, an organization communicates in order to directly engage with the community it works in, whether to give information on the kind of services it provides, or to give guidance to the people it serves on how and where to get help, or to get information from them that would make the organization able to understand local communities and adapt its work to expectations. Last, an organization communicates because today, comment is free and the space is open, and organizations that choose to work in silence only do so when they have concluded that discretion serves their interests and their objectives better, such as for example mediation efforts between parties in a conflict.

Branding vs. Advocacy

There are drawbacks in this increasingly crowded field of aid organizations. Shrinking resources and competition for funding among humanitarian organizations result from of a mix of donor fatigue and media fatigue, as well as from the recession and financial crisis of the last few years. In addition, the multiplication of smaller aid groups with lower running costs can come across as a more affordable and efficient alternative to big expensive aid machines. Organizations therefore look for creative and compelling ways to counter media fatigue, or the general state of cynicism that the media falls into after covering the outbreak of a crisis. A typical chief editor of a big media outlet will inevitably ask "What is the new angle of this story, why should we run yet another piece on refugees?"

Most international humanitarian organizations, including UN agencies and various components of the Red Cross and Red Crescent family have understood that communications, and their ability to position themselves in the public mind and space as relevant, play a crucial role in attracting and maintaining funds, by old and new donors, and access in crisis countries. Contrary to non-governmental organizations (including international NGOs operating in crisis areas), international and inter-governmental organizations tread a fine line in their relations to host governments, to which they are accredited, sometimes even enjoying diplomatic-like privileges). These organizations prefer a communication style that is engaging rather than confrontational, even when addressing issues at the core of their mandate, such as the need to put an end to child marriage or the need to empower women.

Just as in the marketplace, some organizations have a stronger brand than others, in the sense that they are generally more recognized in their field and recognizable by the general public. They are often too more visible, more present at public events. A few years ago, the Red Cross emblem was considered the emblem that was most associated, in people's minds, with aid and medical services generally, for example. Within the UN family, an organization such as UNICEF is generally more recognizable and vaguely associated with a product (here: children), than an organization such as UNFPA, which few people know is the agency in charge of closely monitoring and helping governments develop their population policies, including substantive support to governments in the fields of family planning and reproductive health. Organizations with a stronger brand can place their line or quote in the media more easily than smaller, less recognizable organizations. Their employees can negotiate better with host governments and work more easily in host communities, just on the strength of their brand and what it means to people. In that sense, success breeds success.

Aside from the marketing approach to branding an organization, humanitarian organizations, especially those whose mandate is enshrined in international law or those that extract their legitimacy from international human rights laws and standards, often have a double role to play: they deliver assistance to those in need, and advocate for a change in the behavior and policies of governments, warring parties or society, that would bring about more respect for people, in line with international rights standards. The International Committee of the Red Cross (ICRC), for instance, the world's leading international organization working in situations of armed conflicts, extracts its legitimacy from the Geneva Conventions of 1949, which stipulate that in times of international armed conflicts, the parties to the conflict are to give access to the ICRC to help, assist and protect those in need.[4] But the Geneva Conventions also give the ICRC the role of working with governments on drafting national legislations in line with the government's international commitments, since adhering to an international convention (on the protection of children or the ban on the use of certain arms for example) is meaningless without a national law that gives a national framework on how to address the issues (what happens if an individual or an entity disregards this law, or what monitoring and penalizing mechanisms exist, at the state level, to ensure respect, etc.) Likewise, agencies of the United Nations that base their work on universal legal documents, such as the Convention on the Rights of the Child,[5] or the 1951 Refugee Convention,[6] continuously refer to principles stipulated in them when advocating with governments in favor of victims or people.

These organizations are generally referred to as "rights-based," in the sense that they extract their legitimacy and that of their mandate from the broader framework of human rights and humanitarian and refugee laws and principles. It also means they have a role to play in spreading awareness about these rights and in advocating for their respect by governments and societies.

Humanitarian vs. Human Rights Organizations

When describing the rationale behind its communications style, the ICRC usually lists the following factors: security, raising awareness, giving visibility to victims and their plight, exposing the human cost of a conflict, and showing the humanitarian consequences in an attempt to garner support (including funds) for the humanitarian response that the ICRC can offer.[7]

Being able to spread news about relief work may contribute to an organization's safety, as some relief workers have explained over the years. Being able to demonstrate, particularly to parties to a conflict, that an organization is providing aid to those in need regardless of the side they are on may contribute to granting safe passage for convoys. Being recognized by those who hold territory, and being granted safe passage is something that big relief organizations rely on when designing their operations. In that sense, communication is an intrinsic part of any operation, and not an accessory that organizations add at the end of their planning.

Human rights organizations, for their part, see a large portion of their work centered on documenting human rights abuses and exposing them to the public, in an attempt to create public pressure that can eventually lead to change. They consider these efforts to be part of their public advocacy, and a way of shocking public opinion and shaping the discourse on rights.

International human rights organizations, or organizations more focused on exposing abuses after credibly documenting and authenticating them, such as Human Rights Watch (HRW) or Amnesty International, are generally considered bolder in their public messaging and less diplomatic in exposing perpetrators of abuses. In return, these organizations generally face access problems to countries they criticize, particularly countries where freedom of expression is generally limited. So, while international relief organizations such as the ICRC or UN agencies have formal presence in all capitals of countries they operate in, HRW and Amnesty International frequently undertake shorter and less formal missions into these countries, and are less frequently able to maintain a regular presence in a country they scrutinize for abuses. For such human rights organizations, continuous presence in a country is an advantage but not vital to their operations as it is for a humanitarian organization that delivers aid and services, and therefore needs to be physically present in a country in order to work effectively. Even without being permanently present in countries whose human rights landscapes these organizations analyze, they still manage to reach findings that become a reference for credible investigative journalists and legal practitioners, and sometimes become the basis for testimonies at the International Criminal Court.

In both cases though, these organizations seek visibility for branding, fundraising and advocacy purposes. In both cases, they can demonstrate that they are relevant to public opinion, that their findings and positions resonate in the public sphere, and can explain to their donors that they help shape public opinions and elevate the discourse on humanitarian and human rights principles through their communication.

Aid agencies directly involved in relief work or human rights defenders actively working in an emergency situation partly owe their strong brands to their frequent and lively com-munications, with the regular appearance of their representatives on big media platforms, where they give direct testimonies about what they witness and do. They also all rely on the regular production of digital material and modern tools such as interactive maps of their locations or infographic drawings, and promote these via various channels, including social media. Aid groups have learned that the use of Twitter can be an effective tool during a disaster (Burns and Burgess 2014). With nearly 6 million followers on Twitter, UNICEF accounts for the largest twitter community,[8] while UNHCR has 2.11 million followers,[9] and 1.39 million are following the World Food Programme.[10] Human Rights Watch talks to nearly 3.25 million followers via Twitter,[11] and Amnesty International to 899,000.[12]

Spokesperson for the Victims: Celebrities for a Cause

Some organizations use celebrities, whether from the movie or music industry, or from the literary and journalistic world, as spokespeople or as ambassadors for humanitarian causes, putting their reputation and outreach at the service of a cause (children, refugees, action to prevent hunger . . .) In a similar fashion, a few years ago, a group of famous musicians had organized to raise funds and awareness for the victims in Haiti, following the devastating earthquake at the end of 2009.

That Angelina Jolie appears in communications material by the United Nations High Commission for the Refugees (UNHCR), or that Susan Sarandon is seen helping refugees out of the water on Lesbos island in Greece at the height of discussions inside the European Union on how to face the migration crisis can both garner much social media activity and draw attention to the general plight of refugees. Celebrities, especially those who are genuinely passionate about and known for helping people, can definitely bring attention to an issue, and sometimes even raise funds to help cover an aid organization's financial commitments.

Celebrities can also benefit by attaching their name to such causes and maybe more than the victims in whose names these concerts are organized. Governments will continue to act in what they believe to be the economic and political interests of their countries. What is wrong then if the assumed interest of actors and governments end up helping the victims in Haiti? Maybe nothing is wrong. That people of international stature lend their name to specific causes and speak on behalf of people affected by a specific situation that can change is often a win–win, for the celebrity and for the cause.

Heads of credible organizations sometimes become celebrities in their own fields, speaking with authority and making headlines on the issues their organizations defend. When the head of UNICEF pleads for the protection of children, or when the head of HRW calls an act a severe human rights violation, these statements ensure a debate among journalists, practitioners, and sometimes governments in a way that helps shed light on the issues. In a way, heads of international organizations directly contribute to the debate on rights and relief because their positions make them de facto ambassadors for the people whose rights they seek to protect.

Conclusion

With the details about George's private life in the foreground, I sat back and thought about our cause, humanitarianism, and about our efforts to attract the world's attention to the poor, the oppressed and the destitute. I remembered days on end of activity by human rights and humanitarian organizations in the corridors of the United Nations Security Council in New York, pressing permanent and non-permanent members of the world's most power-ful political forum to include the issues of rights in the draft resolutions that they were about to table for discussion and then voting. In that sense, communicating on behalf of a humanitarian or human rights organization mostly meant communicating on behalf of a victim: a victim of a natural or man-made disaster or a victim of political oppression and persecution. It also meant prompting, through public communication, public opinion to exert pressure for change, thus counting on the public's emotional reaction to a drastic story, and its ability to influence, through pressure, a decision by politicians to engage in war or refrain from war or from help.

Does communication alone save lives? Certainly not, and it would be naïve to think that a public campaign alone will stop a war. But effective communication, with the ability to mobilize public opinion and create pressure on politicians will help release additional funds from government treasuries for aid groups, and might help influence political action, if only in a way that best serves these governments or at least does not undermine their interests. When the interests of governments intersect with those of a victim, then we can see a link between communications and saving lives. In that sense, smart communications might mean looking for opportunities where real change is possible if the right influencers are engaged both as a target and as a vehicle for messages, whether these are the media, the public or movie stars.

Notes

1. For a succinct outline, see "Human Rights Principles," the UNFPA, United Nations Population Fund, available at: www.google.com/?gws_rd=ssl#hl=en&q=universal+principles+of+human+rights

2. Though, for example in the early days of the invasion of Iraq there was almost no coverage of the humanitarian consequences of the war reported by embedded journalists—When Andersen (2006) asked a journalist if they would cover civilian casualties, the reporter responded by saying, "We are telling the US military's story."

3. There are of course exceptions. Here we might include the lack of adequate coverage of the humanitarian consequences of the involvement of US and Saudi Arabia in the devastating conflict in Yemen and the suffering of the people there.

4. International Committee of the Red Cross, "Geneva Conventions and Commentaries," available at: www.icrc.org/en/war-and-law/treaties-customary-law/geneva-conventions

5. United Nations Human Rights Office of the High Commissioner. "Convention on the Rights of the Child," available at: www.ohchr.org/EN/ProfessionalInterest/Pages/CRC.aspx

6. United Nations High Commission on Refugees. "The 1951 Refugee Convention," available at: www.unhcr.org/en-us/1951-refugee-convention.html

7. International Committee of the Red Cross, "Mission and Mandate," available at: www.icrc.org/en/who-we-are/mandate

8. The Twitter handle for the United Nations International Children's Emergency Fund is @UNICEF and the organization has 5.91 million followers as of February 28, 2017, available at: https://twitter.com/UNICEF

9. Most UN agencies and big NGOs have several accounts, with one main account usually in English and other regional accounts in different languages depending on where they are managed. The United Nations High Commissioner for Refugees twitter handle is @Refugees and it has 2.11 million followers as of February 28, 2017, available at: https://twitter.com/Refugees?ref_src=twsrc%5Egoogle%7Ctwcamp%5Eserp%7Ctwgr%5Eautho

10. The Twitter handle for the World Food Program is @WFP and the organization has 1.39 million followers as of February 28, 2017, available at: https://twitter.com/WFP

11. The Twitter handle for Human Rights Watch is @hrw and the organization has 3.25 million followers as of February 28, 2017, available at: https://twitter.com/hrw

12. The Twitter handle for Amnesty International is @amnesty has 899,000 followers as of February 28, 2017, available at: https://twitter.com/amnesty

References

Andersen, R. (2006) *A Century of Media, A Century of War*, New York: Peter Lang.

Bloch, H. (2016) "When Disaster Strikes, He Creates a 'Crisis Map' that Helps Save Lives." NPR, October 2, available at: www.npr.org/sections/parallels/2016/10/02/495795717/when-disaster-strikes-he-creates-a-crisis-map-that-helps-save-lives

Burns, A., and Burgess, J. (2014) "Crisis Communication in Natural Disasters: The Queensland Floods and Christchurch Earthquakes," in K. Weller, A. Burns, J. Burgess, M. Mahrt, and C. Puschmann (Eds.), *Twitter and Society*, New York: Peter Lang.

Franks, S. (2014) *Reporting Disasters: Famine, Aid, Politics and the Media*. London: Hurst.

NPR (2016) "A Story of Crisis and Resilience, Told Through Music," November 13, available at: www.npr.org/2016/11/13/501722840/a-story-of-crisis-and-resilience-told-through-music

3

THE AL-JAZEERA EFFECT

News Media Coverage of Global Humanitarian Emergencies

Yehia Ghanem

Since the late 1980s and until 1996, when Al-Jazeera was born, I always felt that Egypt's *Al-Ahram*, the oldest and the most prestigious newspaper in the Middle East and Africa, was the only voice in the wilderness crying out against humanitarian catastrophes, be they man-made conflicts or natural disasters. Indeed, we were in the middle of all wars, from the first Chechen one to the Serbo-Croatian and Bosnian wars, and the war in Afghanistan between the Taliban and Northern Alliance. Even though I was a war correspondent from the late 1980s until 1993, I hardly knew the pivotal role media could play in directing and redirecting humanitarian relief to disaster stricken areas. I realized the media's importance only after I received a note from the Supreme Committee of Humanitarian Relief in Egypt informing me that I was to be decorated as "Man of The Year" in recognition of my efforts to raise public awareness to the horrors and agonies the Bosnians were suffering. At that time, satellite television channels were newborns in the West and totally unknown in the Middle East. I received the award at the pinnacle of *Al-Ahram*'s success: we had a daily circulation of 1.3 million including the international edition, 1.7 million for the weekly Friday edition, and readership was up fivefold. *Al-Ahram* was at the height of its influence, setting the agenda for local television and to a certain extent for many TV stations in the Arab world. In the second half of the 1990s my war coverage was syndicated to at least 20 leading newspapers across the Arab world, which multiplied the paper's impact. It is worth mentioning that *Al-Ahram* was one of the few Arab media outlets at the time that covered wars in the Middle East.

Al-Ahram's prominence in conflict coverage remained almost unchallenged until Al-Jazeera was born in 1996. After that I started seeing colleagues from the channel in the same conflict zones that I covered. During those years, I saw that war reporters from Al-Jazeera would be essential to the programming, and that the channel would focus on covering conflicts more than other news topics. However, Al-Jazeera's coverage of both man-made and natural disasters came to distinction later on, at the beginning of the new millennium. Below, I outline the reasons for this shift, and follow the development of Al-Jazeera from a single channel to a giant network, which accounts for the evolution of its conflict coverage.

Phase I: 1996–2001 "The Opinion and the Other Opinion"

For at least half a century until 1996, the Arab world in particular and the Middle East in general had a media style that could only be characterized as monotonous speech controlled by dictatorial regimes that used media to consolidate their powers. Even in the 1990s when they had to allow private media, tyrannical regimes controlled them by controlling their crony businessmen who owned the media outlets. The main goal of Al-Jazeera from day one was to break the monopolies maintained for so long by dictatorships in the Middle East. The way the new channel did that was by introducing a vanguard logo that heralded a new era in the region, not only in media but also and more importantly, in political life. The logo was "Introducing the Opinion and the Other Opinion." In a region where one and only one opinion was voiced, that of the regimes, the open debate began to transform the previously controlled and heavily censored Arab media. This new political discourse shook up many dictatorial regimes and pushed them to effect some positive changes. During the years 1996–2001, the channel provided a platform for a multiplicity of differing voices in the Middle East, and in return earned the growing trust and credibility of the peoples in the region. As a consequence, Al-Jazeera and Qatar also became targets of animosity from many Arab leaders.

In his book, *Al Jazeera English: Global News in a Changing World*, Seib Philips argues that AJE, born in 2006, was first among its sibling networks to bring voice to the "voiceless" through its unique focus on the developing world in good times and bad. In contrast, I argue that this trend started on the first day that Al Jazeera's Arabic channel broadcast in 1996.

Phase II: 2001–2007 "The World vs. Us"; Time to Cover Wars

In 1999, I was assigned to cover the brutal war in the Democratic Republic of Congo (DRC). I quickly found that contrary to conventional wisdom this war was not an internal one, but could only be understood in the context of the regional conflict where all Great Lakes area countries, namely, Rwanda, Burundi, Uganda, and Tanzania, were involved directly by having combat troops inside the DRC. At that time, Al-Jazeera was still in Phase I, focusing on expanding freedom of expression in the Middle East. Of course, the DRC conflict appeared on Al-Jazeera screens but mostly through the work of news agencies. It was not until after the 9/11 attacks that Al-Jazeera leapt onto the international stage with extensive and intense field reporting, offering a unique perspective on the global war in Afghanistan. Its coverage was distinct because it offered on-the-ground reports from war zones and it was very close to the humanitarian side of conflict news. This was Al-Jazeera's moment. The network was no longer only important as a regional game-changer, its presence as an international broadcaster took off. The Afghanistan war coverage was unique for many reasons, one of which was the ability of Al-Jazeera's six crews to gain access to the most dangerous and important sectors on the frontlines of the conflict. These places were out of reach for other international Western networks. Also, unlike all competing networks covering the Afghanistan war, Al-Jazeera had almost exclusive access to many of the most influential sources involved in the conflict. Al-Jazeera's logo came to be seen on the screens of all international networks, as it became the exclusive source of news. Most experienced media professionals understand that such a major development does not happen overnight. It was clear that the management had been crouching for such a leap for years by properly staffing and training their teams, waiting to capitalize on the right event. Al Jazeera's unique coverage was applied to wars that followed the war in Afghanistan, especially the invasion of Iraq in 2003, the war against Lebanon in 2006, and later the war in Gaza.

Coverage of those wars represents the apex of Phase II, and the shift in focus to "Us, the Arabs & Muslims versus the World." During this time, major changes in the structure and organization of Al-Jazeera were in play, shifting the core of the channel work from a newsroom-based focus to a field-based operation. This was likely one of the reasons the channel management named Wadah Khanfar, a field reporter who headed the Baghdad bureau in September 2003, as the new Managing Director of the channel. He later went on to become Director General of the network that was comprised of more than ten channels. Khanfar was far better suited to lead such a powerful network during this new phase.

Coming from a field operation background, the management team with Khanfar at the helm realized that a new type of journalism would need to reflect the peripheries of power and focus on the humanitarian dimensions rather than serve as stenographers to the centers of powers. In other words, the channel became aware of the necessity of being *humanitarian centered* rather than *power centered*. In order to better grasp the new paradigm that Al-Jazeera chose in Phase II, we have to remind ourselves of the fact that most media firms are funded either by States or by corporations, and that is why they have always revolved editorially around these centers of power. They are more seriously influenced and driven by States' policies or by profit, both of which translate into power and are not necessarily in the best interests of the public (Klaehn 2008).

Explaining how Al-Jazeera managed to wiggle itself out of the mold of simply reflecting state power, Wadah Khanfar admitted in an interview for this article that Al-Jazeera is indeed funded by Qatar, and saying that Qatar is certainly not a charity:

> "However, and for the sake of accomplishing that vision of 'human centered paradigm', we decided to establish a separation between the State's interests and the network's interests, something that necessitated very powerful field operations," Khanfar said. "We believed that magnifying field operations and minimizing the role of news agencies is the way journalists can best interact with people on the ground, achieving authenticity and by doing so, building and enhancing credibility."

Seib (2012) describes Al-Jazeera English as a contradiction in terms: of an Arab government-financed channel, yet a pioneer of borderless journalism with a reputation for covering Arab revolutions. Translating that vision into reality led to the vast expansion of the network from 12 overseas bureaus in 2003 to 34 in less than two years, and to 80 by 2011. Soon after the network had more than 83 bureaus covering over 105 countries, and cemented a reputation for setting tough standards for its bureau chiefs. Among these standards was the policy that bureau chiefs had to be part of the societies they reported on, so better to reflect their cultures and social fabric. In addition, it was time to move from a "News Conference" style of journalism to one characterized as the "Impacts and Outcomes of News Conferences" on public lifestyle. It means the impacts that power centers have on people's lives. The difference in journalism is between power-centered and humanitarian-centered reporting, and it is what distinguished Al-Jazeera, along with other things, from most of the other networks.

Arriving at the core of the subject matter for this article—how Al-Jazeera covered global humanitarian emergencies—we can say confidently that such coverage was the focus from the very start. During Phase I, humanitarian crisis can be defined as the situation in which the distressed peoples of the Middle East had been deprived of freedom of expression for so long. Al-Jazeera relieved their distress by providing them with a platform to make their voices heard.

The Origins of Al-Jazeera English

Before Al-Jazeera International (English) was launched in 2006, a special committee was established to oversee a six-month debate among journalists with the goal of developing a mission statement for the network. That statement reads in part: "We are based in the Arab world but with a global perspective, seeking the truth by giving a platform to opinion and counter opinion." Because the network's stated vision is always to provide a global perspective to news from around the world—while based in the Arab world—scholars have investigated the extent to which AJE could address "the ongoing discourse of the 'clash of civilizations' in favor of a new discourse of 'dialogue between civilizations.'" In her important study published in 2007, *The Role of New Arab Satellite Channels in Fostering Intercultural Dialogue: Can Al-Jazeera English Bridge the Gap?*, Sahar Khamis asserts that AJE could reconcile the cultural chasm separating "civilizations." The following year Mohamed El Nawawy and Shawn Powers published *Mediating Conflicts: Al-Jazeera English and the Possibility of a Conciliatory Media*, and found AJE does serve as a conciliatory media source by moderating viewers' attitudes towards other cultures.

Expanding Coverage to the Global South

The first step that always needs to be taken to enhance global cultural understanding is a simple one—expanding news and information about people and their societies. From the start of Al-Jazeera English, the network sought to present a fuller picture of the global and alter the lens through which the world had been viewed. As Wadah Khanfar explained with their coverage of Africa:

> For instance, Africa has always been pushed aside by world networks; they have always included the continent on their agenda, stereotyped in four major stories: Famines, HIV/AIDS, conflicts and slavery. While not ignoring these important issues, we walked the extra mile by introducing the socio-political and economic realities of Africa to show, among other things, how the continent became what it is, and that the north had historical and present responsibilities to address these issues.

Al-Jazeera's coverage could always be distinguished from its network competitors like CNN, NBC, CBS, and Fox because it was the one and only network that represented the South, not only geographically but more importantly culturally, socially, and politically. International networks headquartered in the North represent a northern perspective quite distinct from the global South. For decades, the North had been the dominant voice in international news. Northern-based media corporations view the South from perspectives based on their own values. By doing so, most international broadcasts filter the world's data through a Northern lens. Nowhere was this more evident than in the coverage of the Ebola epidemic. As one media critic put it, behind the "fear-mongering and scare tactics" lie:

> very palpable undertones of colonialist attitudes of racism, xenophobia and cultural elitism. Identifying it as a consequence of the North/South divide, an academic term

that "roughly delineates the economic disparities between the countries of the Northern and Southern hemispheres." To put this another way, the developed, industrialized North assumes a relatively normalized stance that the underdeveloped, global South is both a misunderstood, backward place to be kept at a safe distance and a latent threat due to its political instability, poverty and foreignness.[1]

Consequently, the South has always been a topic that revolves around a Northern agenda, and seen as secondary, and therefore understanding its problems has been shallow, superficial and stereotyped. As a result, and being based in the South, Al-Jazeera, though not ignoring the North, has set its own news agenda to reflect realities in the South. Wadah Khanfar explained Al-Jazeera's attempt to change the perspective: "We believed that if we became powerful in telling our narrative, the North would listen to us."

Al-Jazeera and Humanitarian Crises

In Phase II, the effect of Al-Jazeera's news coverage of global humanitarian emergencies became more evident as it expanded and extended its coverage of war and concentrated on the human face and ugly consequences of wars. Since the turn of the twenty-first century, it was obvious that a decision was made that Al-Jazeera would be on the ground wherever there are humanitarian crises: whether man-made or natural disasters. At a time when US news networks were closing down overseas news offices (McChesney and Pickard 2011), Al-Jazeera was expanding its news operations. In order to cover such events effectively the network opened many overseas bureaus, especially in countries where disasters were likely to occur. For instance, at that time there was not much happening in Somalia, but shortly after an office was established a fierce famine hit East Africa and the Horn of Africa, and later on moved to West Africa. The world followed the tragedy on Al-Jazeera, which succeeded in breaking the silence, slammed by international media that failed to cover the story.

Partnering with Humanitarian Organizations

Al-Jazeera also set an important precedent by partnering with international humanitarian relief organizations that approached the network to maximize public awareness about the magnitude and severity of catastrophes. In return, the network had greater access to stricken areas. These partnerships worked full speed during the Indian Ocean Earthquake and Tsunami in 2004; coordination with humanitarian organizations enabled the network to dispatch and place crews in every stricken area, thereby allowing the network to provide more in-depth coverage of the tragedy affecting multiple countries.

In humanitarian crises, media tend to stay for a while and then move on quickly to other stories, although in many cases aftershocks of catastrophe are even more severe and dangerous than the initial event itself. The reason for such media behavior is the obsession with ratings, a point I will return to below. Unlike those flawed news practices, Al-Jazeera has made it a policy to remain even after most other international media leave. For example, in the case of the 2004 earthquake and Tsunami, followed by a relatively smaller Tsunami in 2006, it took the initiative of bringing teams of journalists from organizations across the Arab world to the stricken areas to follow up on the tragic results of the catastrophe for their own local media.

Apart from permanent bureaus providing coverage, in many cases, special assignments must be commissioned to areas where there are no offices. The decision-making process for those assignments in most networks is relatively lengthy and goes up the ladder to higher management. The process within Al-Jazeera, especially when there are humanitarian emergencies, is short, quick and effective. Both the planning and assignment sections are given a free hand in dispatching correspondents and crews to any humanitarian crises without the need for higher management approval. By doing so, the network has not missed covering a single humanitarian crisis from Haiti through sub-Saharan Africa, Latin America to Asia, up to the North Pole during that row over the melting of the polar ice-cap phenomenon, and also down to Antarctica (South Pole), wrapping up the whole globe with its crews on the ground par excellence. The mission has always been to connect Arabs, who have been ill served by media for so long, with the rest of the world and vice versa.

Ratings and Issues of Commercializing News Coverage

But are ratings, which have become a media obsession, totally ignored by the network? According to many Al-Jazeera officials, the relationship between the network and its audiences is uniquely dialectical. Ratings serve as a detector of the public pulse. However, in many cases the audiences come to Al-Jazeera because they trust its capability of choosing for them. It is a very long and sensitive process of building trust and credibility between the network and its audiences.

One former network director said in an interview for this article, "I have always been opposed to blindly running after the wish list of trending topics and following only those stories with the highest rating. Sometimes stories have to be pushed because they have meanings regardless of their ratings," the man explained.

> I remember being frequently asked during meetings of the planning department: how many Arabs would want to know about seals on the Southern shores of South Africa? My answer was: even if 5%; it remains to be an elite percentage within our Arab audience that deserves to be served by us; and by doing so we can expand these elite. Also, reaching for 5% of an influential audience who can effect positive societal change is not less important than obtaining the interest of 50% from those less capable of making such changes.

In Al-Jazeera, ratings are important but only to a certain extent for it is also part of commercializing media, which in many cases infringes on audience rights. The fact that Al-Jazeera shies away from commercializing news makes sense. Imagine if ratings showed viewers were uninterested in coverage of humanitarian emergencies, what would be the outcome in a profit driven network? Would that negatively impact such coverage? The realistic answer is: yes!

A better way to rate the network's coverage may be to look toward the public and the humanitarian community that the network serves. Perhaps the best institutions qualified to judge are humanitarian relief agencies. Many international humanitarian organizations frequently praise Al-Jazeera's news coverage for its role in helping to ease many crises by raising public awareness and mobilizing relief efforts. Al-Jazeera was decorated and re-awarded several times for such roles, especially when it comes to raising awareness of the tragic plight of refugees displaced in many parts of the world. In 2005, the United Nations High Commission for Refugees (UNHCR) recognized Al-Jazeera for its coverage of the tragedy of refugees produced by the wave of drought that hit West Africa during 2004–2005. Reporting began shortly before the drought hit, thanks to cooperation between the network and relief agencies. Such coverage played a key role in mobilizing international efforts to better deal with the tragedy. Aside from Al-Jazeera, there are no other media networks that have such unique and effective partnerships with humanitarian organizations.

Wings of the Newsroom

With tough standards set for its bureau chiefs and correspondents tasked with the forecasting of emergencies, Al-Jazeera, through its partnerships with specialized centers and agencies providing early warning of such crises, empowers itself to fly red flags through its news coverage. This growing sense of the importance of catastrophe-preventive assignments, which rarely exists within heavily commercialized media, was the main reason for the network to create two wings for its newsroom: Al-Jazeera Center for Studies, and Al-Jazeera Center for Human Rights. The latter, launched in 2008, was preceded by a conference organized in Doha by the network attended by most of the important human rights organizations and humanitarian relief agencies. The conference ended with the signing of memoranda of understanding between the newly established center for human rights and these organizations for future cooperation.

The idea for the Center for Studies was to provide background research using groups of experts and analysts who are not under the pressure of news gathering on a daily basis. Their job is to analyze and contextualize events for more in-depth coverage prior to passing this data and information on to the newsroom. The focus of the Center for Human Rights is to train journalists and to educate them on humanitarian law, to better enable newsrooms to tell the humanitarian side of the news. The two centers are actually two wings of the same network newsroom, and do not work independently. They actively contribute in setting editorial policy of the whole network, and in many cases, in formatting and framing news.

The Queen's Visit to Africa

A case in point: the Queen of the United Kingdom was going to Uganda to open the Commonwealth Heads of Government Meeting (CHOGM) in Kampala in 2007. Her agenda included a visit to an HIV/AIDS orphanage as part of her humanitarian work. All international networks focused on her visit and then the summit. In contrast Al-Jazeera, enabled by its Study Center and after discussions, made the decision that HIV/AIDS in Africa should be the network's focus because it is a disease that is a tragedy for the continent as it struggles against both HIV/AIDS and the profit-driven pharmaceutical companies trying to cash in on this catastrophe. Her Majesty the Queen's visit was just an entrance story to the main narrative, which was HIV/AIDS in Africa.

The two-pronged vision of the network is in-depth reporting and a humanitarian-centered orientation of the news. The Study Center enhances the first whereas the Center for Human Rights reinforces the second.

Phase III: 2007–2010, "Us vs. Us"

By the end of Israel's war against Lebanon in the summer of 2006, the Arab and Muslim world plunged into internal conflicts arising out of racial, sectarian and ideological issues. Being in the middle of that whirlwind, Al-Jazeera entered its third phase: "Arabs and Muslims vs. Arabs and Muslims." With such diverse newsroom staff within the network's channels:

Muslims, Sunnis, Shiites, Christians of all denominations, the real challenge was how to develop a strict code of reporting and conduct to assure the quality of reporting and not import those conflicts into the newsrooms.

Phase IV: 2010–Present, Arab Spring Revolutions and Beyond

Since its inception in 1996, Al-Jazeera was a virtual revolution in the Middle East and North Africa, and the Arabian Gulf, where media has been controlled and heavily censored by dictatorships or autocratic rulers. Its paradigm vision has always been the humanitarian side of the news. Since popular revolutions are humanitarian and humane acts against inhuman injustice, the network entered the next phase at full speed in terms of exclusive coverage from the Tunisian uprising and Tahrir Square in Egypt in the center, to Libya in the west, to Syria in the east and to Yemen in the southeast. Almost word-for-word, the world followed the Arab Spring Revolutions through Al-Jazeera.

With the apparent failure of all Arab Spring revolutions and the throw back of their countries to the era of dictatorships, injustice, and societal chaos at varying levels, the Arab and Muslim world has entered into an extremely complicated grey phase. It is now an era where visibility is blurred and clarity is scarce, especially with regard to many important issues of life and death, freedom, and economic survival. Long fixed paradigms are being shaken and some even shattered. Traditional alliances are falling and seemingly awkward new ones are on the way in. Who would have thought that Israel would side with Russia on many issues in the region and that Egypt, after the 2013 change of power, would pace up to join them, along with their Arab backers and financiers? Who would have expected to see the Gulf countries backing the counter-revolution in Egypt while supporting the revolution in Syria, then taking the extrajudicial steps (under the tenets of international law) to fight a counter-revolution war in Yemen? The trends nowadays in the Arab world are extremely unstable and definitely unpredictable. As a media organization, this is not a comfortable position to be in. This phase comes with many synchronized challenges, some of which include:

- Sailing in such rough, stormy and changing political weather patterns in the Middle East, how to keep your moral compass pointing in the right direction.
- Al-Jazeera Media Network broadcasts to 310 million unique homes every day. How will it accomplish the migration to a new and much more interactive media world without sacrificing its traditional type of media?
- How to attract the younger generation of below 40 by adopting newer technologies and structures without sacrificing its older audience, and keeping the depth, legacy and heritage that has been built over the years.
- How to marry two concepts without any disruption of either.
- Since its launch in 1996, Al-Jazeera has stayed true to its initial mission. Each new phase never negated its predecessor, and each told a humanitarian story. How can Al-Jazeera redefine itself while continuing the strong humane and humanitarian orientation that it always had?

As a professional war correspondent in this line of journalism for two decades, I hope and expect that Al-Jazeera will negotiate these headwaters successfully.

Note

1. Machado, Mario. 2014. "The Media Covering Ebola: Fear Tactics that Play on Racial, Economic Divides" (October 10, 2014) *The Huffington Post*, available at: www.huffingtonpost.com/mario-machado/ebola-media-coverage_b_5899790.html

References

El Nawawy, M., and Powers, S. (2008) *Mediating Conflicts: Al-Jazeera English and the Possibility of a Conciliatory Media*, Los Angeles, CA: Figueroa Press.

Khamis, S. (2007) "The Role of New Arab Satellite Channels in Fostering Intercultural Dialogue: Can Al-Jazeera English Bridge the Gap?" in P. Seib (Ed.), *New Media and the New Middle East*, New York: Palgrave Macmillan, pp. 39–51.

Klaehn, J. (2008) "The Propaganda Model," in R. Andersen and J. Gray (Eds.), *Battleground: The Media*, Westport, CT: Greenwood, pp. 388–394.

McChesney, R. W., and Pickard, V. (2011) (Eds.) *Will the Last Reporter Please Turn Out the Lights: The Collapse of Journalism and What Can Be Done to Fix It*, New York: The New Press.

Machado, M. 2014. "The Media Covering Ebola: Fear Tactics that Play on Racial, Economic Divides" (October 10, 2014) *The Huffington Post*, available at: www.huffingtonpost.com/mario-machado/ebola-media-coverage_b_5899790.html

Seib, P. (2012) *Al Jazeera English: Global News in a Changing World*, New York: Palgrave Macmillan.

4

DIGNITY IN
TIMES OF CRISES

Communicating the Need for Global Social Climate Change

Evelin Gerda Lindner and Linda M. Hartling

We are living in an age of cascading crises. Every day the media brings us news of devastating events that disrupt the lives of millions of individuals, families, communities, and nations around the world. For example, the 2015 United Nations High Commissioner for Refugees' annual report warns that global displacement has reached levels never seen before, estimating that "one in every 122 humans is now either a refugee, internally displaced, or seeking asylum," and this trend is growing (UNHCR 2015, para. 4). The UN expects that the number of forcibly displaced people will far exceed 60 million, with 20.2 million refugees fleeing violence and conflict (Nebehay 2015). Beyond conflict zones, the Internal Displacement Monitoring Centre reports that trends on displacement after disasters are equally troubling: "Latest historical models suggest that even after adjusting for population growth, the likelihood of being displaced by a disaster today is 60 per cent higher than it was four decades ago" (IDMC 2015b, 8).

Furthermore, there are mounting indications that "man-made factors" such as "rapid economic development, urbanisation and population growth in hazard prone areas" are increasing trends in disaster displacement (IDMC 2015a, para. 4). The growing displacement of millions of people throughout the world is one illustration of the cascading crises that could become suicidal for humankind.

All who live and work on the frontlines of these crises are witnesses and messengers bringing attention to countless forms of human suffering resulting from these events. While dodging ideological, political, and real bullets, their words and actions help us document and respond to unspeakable tragedies and disasters unfolding around the globe. In support of their efforts, this chapter offers a discussion of an acute twenty-first century social crisis that has been largely overlooked, even as it becomes a gathering storm. We could call this a *global social climate crisis*, a crisis triggered by a social dynamic that is running rampant in the world today.

In 2012, a 14-minute YouTube video unleashed an international firestorm of violent protests throughout the Middle East, Northern Africa, Asia, and Europe (Kirkpatrick 2011, 2012; Hudson 2012). The video presented shocking and degrading images of Islamic culture, fomenting outrage in more than 20 nations around the world (Kirkpatrick 2011). The wildfire reaction to this video illustrates the power of a dynamic that we suggest is not only stimulating a global social climate crisis, it is a dynamic that intensifies all other crises. This is *the humiliation dynamic* (Klein 1991).

This chapter explores the urgent need for *global social climate change* to address the consequences of humiliation, a social dynamic that contaminates efforts to effectively respond to existing and emerging crises. We will define and describe the operations of this dynamic and offer a discussion in support of media and human rights professionals, UN and government staff, academics, policymakers, and practitioners—all those who witness and experience the consequences of humiliation. Finally, we will examine ways to begin dismantling this dynamic using dignity as the key.

Humiliation in an Age of Historic Change

The world is going through a historic transformation that increases sensitivity to, and awareness of humiliating human behavior (Lindner 2006, 2009a, 2010b). Although this transition began centuries ago, the convergence of human rights ideals, the global information age, and 24/7 media have made humiliating social, political, and economic practices visible to all. Today people around the world are rising up against the powers that made them believe they were not deserving of dignity, rising up against individuals and systems that induce feelings of humiliation. Consequently, all who work to address crises need to sharpen their awareness of the specter and spectrum of humiliation that can accompany these events. Mindsets and practices of humiliation may be underwriting the hostile treatment of asylum seekers (Cobbe and Slatery 2015), disaster responses that ultimately fail (Freedland 2005), racially motivated police shootings (Leadership Conference on Civil Rights 2016), and countless terrorist attacks (Lindner 2009c).

Humiliation may be a fundamental *missing link* in the search for root causes of acute and chronic civil unrest, political instability, and violent conflict (Hartling et al. 2013). Kofi Annan, Nobel Peace Prize Laureate and former Secretary-General of the United Nations, observed: "All the cruel and brutal things, even genocide, starts with the humiliation of one individual" (Whack 2013). *The New York Times* columnist Thomas Friedman (2003) observed, "If I've learned one thing covering world affairs, it's this: The single most underappreciated force in international relations is humiliation" (para. 1). Based on more than three decades of research, we suggest that humiliation is "a nuclear bomb of emotions" (Lindner 2006, 32), perhaps the most toxic social dynamic of our age. It profoundly poisons social and global relationships, instilling indignation and fomenting deadly retaliation.

What is humiliation? It is complex. Recognition of this experience has evolved as human rights ideals have moved to the forefront of global awareness, especially over the last century. In 1948, *equal dignity* formally emerged as a global priority when the UN General Assembly adopted the *Universal Declaration of Human Rights*: "All human beings are born free and equal in dignity and rights. They are endowed with reason and conscience and should act towards one another in a spirit of brotherhood" (UN 2008, Article 1). This declaration brought global attention to the value of human dignity. *And*, concomitantly, it brought attention to *dignity violations*, i.e., the incalculable forms of humiliation. Within the context of human rights ideals, "humiliation" can be understood as:

the enforced lowering of any person or group by a process of subjugation that damages their dignity or sense of worth; "to be humiliated" is to be placed in a situation that is against one's interest (although, sadly, not always against one's will) in a demeaning and damaging way; and "to humiliate" is to transgress the rightful expectations of every human being and of all humanity that basic human rights will be respected.

(Lindner 2006, xiv)

From a broad perspective, humiliation can be examined as: (1) an internal experience (e.g., a feeling, an emotion), (2) an external event (e.g., a degrading interpersonal interaction, bullying, abuse, violent conflict, atrocity crimes, and genocide), or (3) as systemic social conditions (e.g., intractable poverty, discrimination, forced dislocation). Forms of humiliation are influenced by the cultural context in which they occur. Because of this, researchers who study humiliation must acknowledge that they are always working with *partial knowledge* (Minnich 1990). Sometimes they can only scratch the surface of the historical-interpersonal-social-political-economic-international context of humiliating events. Giving us a hint of the extent of this social iceberg, peace linguist Francisco Gomes de Matos (2012), founding member of The World Dignity University and cofounder of ABA Global Education, offers these words as examples of humiliation (Figure 4.1).

The most destructive consequence of humiliation is violence. An illustration of this may be found in the study of mass shootings, such as those that occurred in Norway (Mala and Goodman 2011) and in numerous locations in the United States—including the shooting of 26 children and adults at Sandy Hook Elementary School in Newtown, Connecticut (Barron 2012) and the community college shooting in Roseburg, Oregon (Muskal et al. 2015). Research is beginning to explore the complex link between humiliation and deadly violence.

What is Humiliation?

A Mnemonically Made Checklist

Francisco Gomes de Matos

- degradation
- dehumanization
- demoralization
- denigration
- depersonalization
- deprivation
- discrimination
- dislocation

- domination
- exploitation
- incrimination
- intimidation
- objectification
- subjugation
- terrorization
- vilification

Figure 4.1 What is Humiliation? A Mnemonically Made Checklist.

Jeff Elison and Susan Harter (2007) concluded that "adolescents who report high levels of aggressive anger in response to humiliation are more likely to have thoughts of killing others" (317). In another study, Julian Walker and Victoria Knauer (2011) concluded that "humiliation is a more common trigger for violence than other self-conscious emotions" (737).

However, humiliation does not always and necessarily lead to violence. In studies of Palestinians living in Gaza and the West Bank, Jeremy Ginges and Scott Atran (2008) found that humiliation may also suppress violent action, creating an "inertia effect" (281). Bernhard Leidner, Hammad Sheikh, and Jeremy Ginges (2012) observed that humiliation is accompanied by feelings of powerlessness. They suggest this leads victims to be less likely to engage in violence. In other words, humiliation can also induce powerlessness and inertia. This may be the depressogenic effect of humiliation described by Kenneth Kendler et al. (2003) in their study of over 7000 twins. Kendler identifies humiliation as the most powerful predictor of major depression, second to the loss of a loved one. Powerlessness and depression may be precursors to violence. Harter and her colleagues (2003) note the history and signs of depression in the school shooters. Although more research is needed, in some cases humiliation may inhibit violent action by inducing depression, while in other cases these feelings may erupt into violence in an instant or over time. Further research will help us understand what role humiliation plays in the incubation of active shooters (Harter et al. 2003; Torres and Bergner 2010).

Beyond the study of individual events, we must investigate what happens when humiliation affects global concerns, whether this is the stability of political systems and social institutions, the activities of militant organizations, or the evolution of entire nations (Fattah 2013). Evelin Lindner's global research examines the impact of humiliation on a score of urgent global issues, including the threat of international terrorism and conflict (2009b, 2010c), the intersection of gender and global security (2010b), the need for new economic models (2012a), education (2008), the impact of globalization (2007), and the need for sustainable disaster recovery (2010a). As a researcher, Lindner (2016) works in connection with a world community to provide a foothold also for other researchers investigating the pervasive and pernicious consequences of humiliation.

One of the fundamental reasons humiliation has been neglected in the literature until recent years may be because it is a *relational dynamic*, that is, it occurs in the context of interpersonal, social, institutional, and global relationships (Hartling and Luchetta 1999). The individualistic lens of Western psychology may have kept researchers from grasping the magnitude of this experience. When Donald C. Klein named this dynamic in 1991, he outlined the relational nature of humiliation as involving the interaction of three roles: (1) the humiliator, (2) the victim, and (3) the witness (Klein 1991). Probably the role that has received the least amount of study is the role of the witness. Those who work at the forefront of crises are often the firsthand witnesses of the humiliation dynamic in action.

Witnesses of Humiliation: Facing Dire Dilemmas

Media and human rights professionals, UN and government staff, academics, policymakers, practitioners, and others are the professional witnesses of the world. They put themselves in harm's way to document disasters, to respond to suffering, to expose injustice, to give voice to the vulnerable, and to uncover unimaginable atrocities. Yet, few of us may fully appreciate the magnitude of the danger these professionals are defying in today's world. To understand one must look back on human history. During the past millennia, the limits of communication and geography kept information about human interaction and activity compartmentalized.

Communication was confined to separate social, cultural, ideological, religious, or political spheres of existence (Lindner 2006). Between these spheres, fear of being attacked by surprise and subjugated or annihilated was a continuous concern. Political scientists call this the *security dilemma* (Herz 1951, 1957). The security dilemma is characterized by the arms race motivated by mutual fear. Within these conditions, a *dominator* strategy of survival evolved (Eisler 1993)—overpower others or be overpowered. To achieve security in this context, humans have developed more and more elaborate strategies of domination involving military might and weaponry. However, today we understand that the accumulation of sophisticated weaponry to enforce separate geopolitical spheres does not make communities or nations more secure. Indeed, these arms races bring about the insecurity they are designed to prevent, especially as the world becomes more interconnected and backlashes reach out globally. Moreover, might-makes-right dominator strategies frequently inflict, intensify, and entrench feelings of humiliation (Giacaman et al. 2007; Lacy 2011; Fontan 2012). The consequences of dominator strategies dramatically heighten the risk for those who work as witnesses to crises, e.g., journalists, humanitarians, and others. They get caught in the crossfire of today's alarming events (Harooni and Macaskill 2016).

Compounding the physical risks, those who act as witnesses to devastating disasters and violent crises are working in the context of a troubling transformation of news media. This transformation might be described as an information-based manifestation of a security dilemma. In competition for corporate profit, some say independent journalism is being displaced by *infotainment* (Manning 2015). Ted Koppel, former anchor and editor of the highly regarded *ABC* news program, *Nightline*, describes this development (Silverblatt 2007, 9):

> Now, every division of every network is expected to make a profit. And so we have entered the age of boutique journalism. The goal for the traditional broadcast networks now is to identify those segments of the audience considered most desirable by the advertising community and then cater to them.

What happens to our media when the most powerful "audience" becomes—covertly or overtly—a billionaire CEO, an intimidating political organization, or a ruthless dictator? The 2015 secretive sale of the *Las Vegas Review*, the largest newspaper in the state of Nevada, to billionaire casino magnate Sheldon Adelson is instructive (Folkenflick 2016). John L. Smith, a reporter for the paper, dared to cast doubt on the secretive and humiliating practices of this powerful gambling tycoon. As a result, he was accused of libel (i.e., humiliating the billionaire) and sued by Sheldon Adelson. The legal cost of defending himself ultimately drove Smith to file for bankruptcy, while his family was in the midst of a major medical crisis. This story illustrates why it is crucial for professionals to understand the dynamics of humiliation not only when they are in the position of witnessing crises and disasters, but also in the context of recent trends influencing the media. Ideally, the media plays a crucial role in exposing pervasive forms of humiliating behavior, events of violence, brutality, social injustice, atrocities, and so forth. Yet, powerful people can also use the media to spread a narrative that minimizes or obscures the truth of humiliation, especially if this serves their interests.

While being a professional witness in the world is growing more dangerous, witnesses working as journalists, humanitarians, policymakers, and scholars are humanity's eyes and ears. They are the feet-on-the-ground providing us with the vital information we need to address disasters and atrocities. Yet these witnesses must be wary. When they expose the dynamics of humiliation, they must be prepared for retaliation. These are the dangerous dilemmas facing all who act as witnesses in a world that is struggling with cascading crises.

Dismantling Dangerous Dilemmas: Dignity is the Key

Whatever we do, we cannot wait for our political leaders to address global social crises of humiliation. Everyone is called on to help dismantle this dynamic starting today, but how? International consultant and former Senior Secretary of the interagency UN Framework for Coordination on Preventive Action (FT) Gay Rosenblum-Kumar offers a clear direction in four words: "dignity is the key" (HumanDHS 2015). Whatever we do as professionals in the world, we must strive to protect, rebuild, and replenish the dignity of all people. In this way we strengthen the social fabric of humanity that allows us to prevent, address, and overcome all other crises.

This is the work of a global community known as the Human Dignity and Humiliation Studies network (Lindner et al. 2012). This group has joined together to support those who work to dignify the lives of all people, those who are striving to disarm all forms of humiliation. Cultivating dignity is both a method of inoculation and antidote to humiliation. If humanity is to survive, we must evolve beyond the toxic social climate generated by the security dilemma's motto: "Si vis pacem para bellum" ("If you want peace, prepare for war") (Lindner 2012a, 201). This logic has fueled the globalization of fear (including fear of humiliation). The security dilemma and the responses it elicits, including strategies of domination, are potentially suicidal for humankind (Reiss 2009), and while this was already true in the past, this truth is growing in intensity today. In a highly interconnected world, "Every war has two losers" (Stafford 2003, 8).

We can leave the mutually destructive practices of the dominator model behind and create space for a new *dignity model* of human engagement to emerge. This model would prioritize the development of mutually beneficial connection and cooperation, dialogue, and constructive change, across all fault lines. A dignity model is a model that can realize Mahatma Gandhi's message, "There is no path to peace. Peace is the path." It allows living the logic of *ubuntu*, described by Nelson Mandela (2007) as the "sense that we are human only through the humanity of other human beings" (para. 14). This new model can provide people with the opportunity to engage peacefully as equals in dignity, leading to what Lindner (2012b) would call, *the globalization of egalization* (short for "equality in dignity for all").

All of us, especially media and human rights professionals, UN and government staff, academics, policymakers and practitioners are called on to be the leaders we wish to see in the world today. If humanity wishes to survive and offer its children a dignified future, we must do what we can to create space for a dignity world to emerge. How can we begin?

Telling the Truth About Power

Uprooting the dominator model means telling the truth about power that perpetuates violations of dignity (a.k.a., humiliation). We can use our professional platforms to expose humiliating dominator practices that obstruct progress toward the globalization of egalization. Dominance is built on a foundation that involves the degrading restriction of another group, be it by race, class, gender, religion, class, sexual preference, cultural heritage, or other characteristics (Walker 1999; Walker and Miller 2001). It is not just the division by differences that is the source of the dominant group's power, it is that differences are "profoundly stratified"; subordinate and dominant groups are taught whom to regard as superior and whom as inferior, thus permanently denying the equal dignity of all people.

A deeply disturbing example of this miseducation can be found in Lindner's (2001) description of the events that led to the 1994 genocide of hundreds of thousands of Tutsis in Rwanda. When European colonizers arrived, they treated the Tutsis as the superior group and the Hutus as the inferior group. As Lindner states, "European colonists simplified and intensified the system of structured inequality within Rwandan society" (2001, 12). European colonists used their power to impose conditions that locked Hutus and Tutsis into decades of struggle that eventually led to the slaughter of thousands of victims.

The media played a powerful role in fomenting the atrocities in Rwanda, as described in a paper by Daniel Rothbart and Jessica Cooley (Rothbart and Cooley 2016, 82):

> In the prelude to the 1994 genocide, Hutu extremists launched an intense media campaign prior to the genocidal violence, spreading tales of Tutsi plans to conquer Rwanda and brutalize Hutus. After Hutu extremists established the Radio Télévision Libre des Mille Collines (RTLM) in 1993, they dominated the airwaves with horrific tales of Tutsis committing atrocities against the oppressed Hutus. Stoking the flames of aggression, the broadcasters reiterated the accusation that the Tutsi people planned to conquer the nation by infiltrating major institutions and claimed that Tutsis disguised their real intention of ultimate domination by lulling innocent Hutus into complacency.

Miseducation that is communicated through a media megaphone can easily spread lies that justify the denial of dignity and disseminate socially and psychologically disfiguring humiliation. Miseducation makes degrading practices seem necessary and eventually even normal. Thus, the dominant members of society gain tremendous power over the less powerful group in all realms, including economic, social, political, and cultural (Miller 2003).

Media and human rights professionals, UN and government staff, academics, policymakers, and practitioners are key leaders bringing attention to the humiliating operations of power that privilege one group over another. By refraining from a dominator's *dukes-up* approach, they can use the tools of inquiry and action that lead to dignifying dialogue. The Norwegian philosopher Arne Næss developed the notion of the "depth of intention," or the "depth of questioning" or "deepness of answers." Næss writes, "[O]ur depth of intention improves only slowly over years of study. There is an abyss of depth in everything fundamental" (Naess and Wetlesen 1978, 143). Greater depth means continuing to ask questions at the point at which others stop asking (Fox 1990). All of us can commit ourselves to telling the truth about power by asking questions. On the path to dignity, courageous and persistent inquiry is a powerful tool for telling the truth about power.

Dignify Stories of Good Conflict

Creating space for equal dignity also means learning to think differently about conflict. Unfortunately, violent conflict sells, even though it overwhelmingly involves violations of human dignity. Pictures of aggression and war fill newspapers, magazines, and news broadcasts: "If it bleeds, it leads" (NPR 2001, para. 10). The marketability of violence may be one of the reasons why people are confused about conflict. Violence, aggression, and war are presented in the media as synonymous with conflict. But the media's lens is narrowly focused. Images of conflict in the media are *conflict in the extreme*: deadly, destructive, and bloody conflict. Legendary psychiatrist, relational–cultural theorist, and social justice advocate, Jean Baker Miller (Miller 1976/1986, 1983), goes further. She explains that these images are, in reality, images of *failed conflict*, in other words, *bad conflict*.

Perhaps our limited conceptualization of conflict results from the history of the dominator model. Within that model, humanity came to believe that we have no option but to engage in combat (i.e., bad conflict) to address or suppress conflict (more bad conflict). Miller observed, "as soon as a group attains dominance it tends inevitably to produce a situation of conflict and that it also, simultaneously, seeks to suppress conflict" (1976/1986, 128). This perpetuates an endless loop of failed conflict and escalating spirals of deadly aggression, humiliation, and retaliation (again this is the security dilemma). Bad conflict perpetuates an endlessly contentious global social climate.

We need a wider lens for conceptualizing conflict. Conflict need not be confused with violence and aggression. Jean Baker Miller urged people to understand that conflict is not the problem; *it is the way people conduct conflict that is the problem* (1976/1986). She emphasized that conflict is a necessary and normal part of growth in all relationships. Rather than engaging in bad conflict, humanity can strengthen and expand the necessary relational skills to conduct what she calls "waging good conflict" (WGC), constructive conflict, conflict free of aggression and violence (132). This type of conflict begins by separating the energy of anger from the behavioral response of aggression. When aggression is set aside, the energy associated with anger can be focused on creating constructive change. Creating the conditions for WGC allows people to clarify their concerns in relationships and mobilize their energy to work for new possibilities. It results in deeper understanding, mutual growth, and, in the best scenario, healthier and more resilient relationships going forward.

Although Miller named this way of conducting conflict, she didn't invent it. WGC has been part of the history of human relational activity throughout the ages, as seen in effective parenting, teaching, and other human growth-fostering relationships. Skilled parents, teachers, and others apply sophisticated relational skills for WGC long before anger leads to aggression. Although the industrial age has undervalued and underappreciated relational skills (Fletcher 1999), in today's interconnected world these are the essential skills we need to disarm bad conflict and the dangerous dynamics of humiliation.

Media and human rights professionals, UN and government staff, academics, policymakers, and practitioners can help the world move in the direction of dignity and WGC by bringing conflicts to our attention early in the process, long before they become violent. They can spotlight stories of WGC with the same penetrating power used when reporting stories of violent crises. They can provide a counter-narrative to the deadly definition of conflict as violence, aggression, and war. The Center for Global Peace Journalism supports this effort in their first principle of peace journalism. It encourages journalists to be "proactive, examining the causes of conflict, and looking for ways to encourage dialogue before violence occurs" (Center for Global Peace Journalism 2016).

As frontline witnesses to bad conflict, humanitarians and those working in the media also need to be aware that some people may seek to capitalize on conflict by inciting indignation or framing events as humiliation. Recently, the Iranian Military Guard detained American sailors after their boats crossed into Iranian waters. Even though no one was killed and the conflict over releasing the sailors was quickly resolved, some sought to incite national indignation in America by describing this incident as a humiliation of the US Navy and the US President (Davis 2016). Provoking feelings of humiliation is an invidious way to perpetuate bad conflict. Evelin Lindner (2002, 128–129) calls this "humiliation entrepreneurship":

> the deliberate activation and manipulation of feelings of humiliation in others for the purpose of achieving personal, social, or political objectives. Humiliation entrepreneurship may be a very cost-effective method of undermining or eliminating

rivals or victims. For example, the "low-tech" mechanism of murder by machete was the basic technique used to perpetrate the large-scale genocide in Rwanda. The Hutu elite succeeded in inciting their population to buy their own weapons and take up arms against those they believed to be their would-be humiliators.

Fortunately, in the case of the detained US sailors, a counter-narrative reported that months of prior dialogue with Iranian leadership, leading to a successful nuclear weapons agreement and the lifting of sanctions in Iran, cultivated the conditions in which Secretary John Kerry was able to facilitate the quick and safe release of these sailors (Sanger et al. 2016). No guns were fired; no one was killed. When we develop relationships through dignified dialogue, far in advance of conflict, we are creating conditions for waging good conflict.

From Dualistic Debate to Dialogue

The metaphysical orientation that underpinned Western expansion over the past centuries is *dualism*. Dualism holds that ultimately there are two kinds of substance. René Descartes' dualistic view of a mind–body dichotomy is perhaps the most widely known expression of dualism. Even though contemporary academics recognize the limitations of this Western outlook, dualistic views still linger on in many spheres—not least expressions such as "the axis of evil" serve as evidence. Indeed, dualism offers the very metaphysical backdrop that pushes the world toward war. Dualism might be described as a kind of "master blind spot" in current Western approaches. In his book *The Psychology of War*, Lawrence LeShan (1992) dissects how creating and firing up Manichaean self/other and good/evil dualisms in people prepares them for violence and convinces them that wars are worth fighting.

Dualism can be thought of as an implicit theory, or core belief that frames people's interpretation of events. Dualistic thinking leads to simplistic categorizations and interpretations of events, such as categorizing people as "good or evil," "bad or good," "friends or enemies," and so forth. However, it is not just the overly simplistic categorization of human beings that makes dualistic thinking problematic. It is also the calcification of dualism that hinders our progress when it comes to finding ways to address aggression and conflict.

David Yeager (2013) and his colleagues conducted an interesting study that examined implicit theories of beliefs and *hostile attribution bias* or the tendency to interpret another person's behavior as hostile. He noted that over 100 studies have provided evidence that hostile attribution bias is a predictor of an individual's motivation to engage in reactive aggression. Building on the research of Carol Dweck (1975, 2008, 2014; Dweck and Heckhausen 1998; Dweck et al. 2004), Yeager et al. (2013) examined how holding a *fixed mindset* versus holding a *growth mindset* influenced interpretations of other people's hostile intent. A fixed mindset, a belief system also described as *entity theory*, is characterized by the core belief that human character, traits, and intellectual abilities are relatively fixed and unchanging (Dweck 2012). A growth mindset, a belief system also known as *incremental theory*, manifests the core belief that human character, traits, intellectual abilities are malleable, that is, that people have the potential to change.

In a meta-analytic study of eight independent samples that included 1,128 students, Yeager et al. (2013) found that a fixed mindset predicted hostile intent even when controlling for past experiences of victimization, and predicted hostile attributions equally for males and females and for students from communities with higher and lower levels of violence. In a following study, Yeager found that experimentally changing implicit theories to a more incremental growth mindset substantially reduced attributions of hostile intent in both urban and suburban schools. In a final study, Yeager found that a short-term intervention (two class sessions) could result in more benign intent attributions over an eight-month school year.

On the global level, earlier research exploring Jewish Israeli attitudes toward Palestinians, Eran Halperin (2011), a postdoctoral fellow working with Dweck and others, examined how holding fixed beliefs about the traits of certain groups (such as, they are evil and will always be evil) may perpetuate hatred and conflict. Halperin found that those who subscribed to a fixed mindset not only held more negative attitudes toward the other group, these attitudes predicted less support for peace-related compromises. However, he also found that merely *reading* articles about groups being malleable—without naming a particular group—led to more favorable attitudes about the opposing group. These favorable attitudes predicted a substantially greater willingness to make major compromises for peace and a greater willingness to interact with opposing groups (Dweck 2012).

Although more research needs to be done, one of the most problematic aspects of Western dualism is that it induces a fixed mindset, an entity theory of human behavior, rather than a growth mindset that recognizes humanity's potential to change. By virtue of being educated in Western dualism, humanitarians, journalists, and others working in the field may need to ask themselves whether they have been unconsciously conditioned to think in a fixed mindset. If so, what would happen if they consciously cultivated a growth mindset in their work?

The Human Dignity and Humiliation Studies (HumanDHS) network provides one example of such an effort (Lindner et al. 2012). Dedicating its work to advancing human dignity and healing cycles of humiliation in the world, HumanDHS is organized around the development of mutually beneficial, growth-fostering relationships. Rather than forming a traditional institutional hierarchy common to nonprofit organizations, HumanDHS has been shaping a relational ecology that resonates with a growth mindset, with the incremental theory of human behavior. What does this look like in practice? The HumanDHS network emphasizes dignifying dialogue, moving away from the dualist-debate model of engagement that frequently characterizes professional groups and meetings. Debates are about taking a fixed position and defending that position. Sociologist-economist and community organizer S. M. (Mike) Miller (2012), a member of the HumanDHS Global Advisory Board, describes the difference between the fixity of debate compared to the more fluid, incremental growth experience of dialogue:

> A dialogue differs from the debate stance that too frequently occurs in discussions. In a dialogue, we learn from and with each other rather than keeping to a fixed position. There are no winners or losers as in the debate exchange. Rather, at the end of a dialogue we are all enriched. We learn from each other and are stimulated or prodded to move beyond our outlooks and formulas.

We have to overcome our miss-training, and likely experience, to participate in joyful, enlightening, creative, helpful dialogue rather than indulging in debate and issuing (usually negative) verdicts on the other participants. The aim is to build together rather than to block one another. We change others by changing ourselves in the course of dialogue.

Rather than winning debates, the HumanDHS community emphasizes skills for engaging in dignifying dialogue. This does not mean the group shies away from differences or contentious topics. It means that members of this community work to engage their differences and disputes with unshakeable mutual dignity. A variety of relational skills are required to facilitate dignifying dialogue. They include practicing appreciative enquiry, listening to each other's voice, building on each other's ideas, waging good conflict, and recognizing that every person's idea deserves a fair hearing. The HumanDHS community reduces the relational roadblocks that inevitably accompany dualistic debate by practicing dignifying dialogue that thrives in the context of a growth mindset.

A joint project initiated by the United Nations Educational, Scientific, and Cultural Organization (UNESCO) and the Tunisian Ministry of the Interior illustrates a related promising approach to cultivating relational change through mutually dignifying dialogue (Clavaud and Mendel 2015; UNESCO 2016). This project brings together security forces and journalists to begin building constructive relationships that support individual freedom of expression while maintaining safety and security in the community. The training helps both security officers and journalists to engage in dialogue about their roles and responsibilities and offers them specific ways to address challenging problems that arise in the midst of public protests:

> Balancing legitimate demands for access to public information with the equally legitimate but sometimes conflicting need to maintain law and order in society is a challenge for any democratic society. In general, promoting respect for freedom of expression does not lead to disorder and instability, but creates opportunities for constructive dialogue both between different sections of society and between citizens and public authorities. The right of citizens to receive and impart information and ideas is a fundamental right, and experience has shown that promoting respect for this right strengthens social dialogue and helps consolidate democratic institutions.
>
> (Clavaud and Mendel 2015, 6)

These examples illustrate the potential for dignifying dialogue to move relationships in new directions, creating new possibilities and practices that will provide for the health and well-being of all involved. Yet, much more needs to be done.

Communicating the Need for Global Social Climate Change

In this age of cascading crises, media and human rights professionals, UN and government staff, academics, policymakers, practitioners, and other professionals are in a powerful position to witness and carry out the work that needs to done. They can tell the truth about the dynamics of power that inflict indignation and humiliation that foment and intensify our twenty-first century disasters. They can help everybody widen their lens on conflict, making the benefits of waging good conflict visible and thus more viable. They can play a pivotal role cultivating constructive change in human engagement by personifying the practice of dignifying dialogue. In every aspect of their work, they can be the leaders who help humanity jointly attenuate the security dilemma that drives the dominator model, creating space for a dignity model of the world to emerge.

More than ever before, humanity needs *global social climate change in the direction of equal dignity*. This may be our best hope for cultivating a relational ecosystem of mutual cooperation that serves humanity as a whole. Furthermore, dignity is the global-relational antidote to the viral crisis of humiliation that intensifies all other crises. We can't wait for political figures to lead us toward dignity. Media and human rights professionals, UN and government staff, academics, policymakers, practitioners, and others can speak up for dignity in every step of their efforts. They can communicate the urgent need to create an evergreen global social climate of equal dignity, a climate that generates the growth-fostering conditions that dignifies lives, relationships, and the planet.

References

Barron, J. (2012) "Nation Reels after Gunman Massacres 20 Children at School in Connecticut," *The New York Times*, available at: www.nytimes.com/2012/12/15/nyregion/shooting-reported-at-connecticut-elementary-school.html

Center for Global Peace Journalism (2016) *Peace Journalism: An Introduction*, Parkville, MO: Center for Global Peace Journalism.

Clavaud, P. D., and Mendel, T. (2015) *Freedom of Expression and Public Order: Training Manual*, [Project Office in Tunis] Paris, France: United Nations Educational, Scientific and Cultural Organization.

Cobbe, E., and Slatery, D. (2015) "Syrians Fleeing to Europe Get 'Treated Worse Than Dogs,'" *The New York Daily News*, available at: www.nydailynews.com/news/world/syrians-fleeing-europe-treated-worse-dogs-article-1.2350552

Davis, S. (2016) "Iran's Humiliation of Barack Obama Is Now Complete," *The Federalist*, available at: http://thefederalist.com/2016/01/13/irans-humiliation-of-barack-obama-is-now-complete/

Dweck, C. S. (1975) "The Role of Expectations and Attributions in the Alleviation of Learned Helplessnes," *Journal of Personality and Social Psychology*, 31: 674–685.

Dweck, C. S. (2008) *Mindset: The New Psychology of Success*, New York: Random House.

Dweck, C. S. (2012) "Mindsets and Human Nature: Promoting Change in the Middle East, the Schoolyard, the Racial Divide, and Willpower," *American Psychologist*, 67 (8): 614–622.

Dweck, C. S. (2014) "Motivating Students to Learn," Oregon Health Sciences University 2014 Brain Awareness Teacher Workshop, Portland, OR, March 8, 2014.

Dweck, C. S., and Heckhausen, J. (1998) *Motivation and Self-Regulation across the Life Span*, New York: Cambridge University Press.

Dweck, C. S., Mangels, J. A., Good, C., Dai, D. Y., and Sternberg, R. J. (2004) "Motivational Effects on Attention, Cognition, and Performance," in *Motivation, Emotion, and Cognition: Integrative Perspectives on Intellectual Functioning and Development*, Mahwah, NJ: Lawrence Erlbaum, pp. 41–56.

Eisler, R. (1993) *The Chalice and the Blade: Our History, Our Future*, London: Pandora.

Elison, J., and Harter, S. (2007) "Humiliation: Causes, Correlates, and Consequences," in J. L. Tracy, R. W. Robins, and J. P. Tangney (Eds.), *The Self-Conscious Emotions: Theory and Research*, New York: Guilford Press, pp. 310–329.

Fattah, K. (2013) "The Terrorist Mind," *Open Canada*, available at: www.opencanada.org/features/the-terrorist-mind/

Fletcher, J. (1999) *Disappearing Acts: Gender, Power, and Relational Practice at Work*, Cambridge, MA: MIT Press.

Folkenflick, D. (2016) "The Vegas Columnist and the Newspaper Owner Who Once Sued Him for Libel," *National Public Broadcasting*, available at: www.npr.org/2016/01/14/463070783/casino-magnate-and-new-newspaper-owner-has-history-of-suing-reporters

Fontan, V. (2012) *Decolonizing Peace*, Lake Oswego, OR: Dignity Press.

Fox, W. (1990) *Toward a Transpersonal Ecology: Developing New Foundations for Environmentalism*, Boston, MA: Shambhala.

Freedland, J. (2005) "Receding Floodwaters Expose the Dark Side of America—but Will Anything Change?" *The Guardian*, available at: www.theguardian.com/world/2005/sep/05/hurricanekatrina.usa5

Friedman, T. L. (2003) "The Humiliation Factor," *The New York Times*, available at: www.nytimes.com/2003/11/09/opinion/the-humiliation-factor.html

Giacaman, R., Abu-Rmeileh, N. M. E., Husseini, A., Sasb, H., and Boyce, W. (2007) "Humiliation: The Invisible Trauma of War for Palestinian Youth," *Public Health*, 121 (8): 563–571.

Ginges, J., and Atran, S. (2008) "Humiliation and the Inertia Effect: Implications for Understanding Violence and Compromise in Intractable Intergroup Conflicts," *Journal of Cognition and Culture*, 8: 281–294.

Gomes de Matos, F. (2012) "What Is Humiliation? A Mnemonically Made Checklist," Revised January 28, 2016.

Halperin, E., Russell, A. G., Trzesniewski, K. H., Gross, J. J., and Dweck, C. S. (2011) "Promoting the Middle East Peace Process by Changing Beliefs About Group Malleability," *Science*, 333 (23): 1767–1769.

Harooni, M., and Macaskill, A. (2016) "Suicide Bomb in Afghan Capital Targets Journalists, Kills Seven People," available at: www.reuters.com/article/us-afghanistan-blast-kabul-idUSKCN0UY1HU

Harter, S., Low, S. M., and Whitesell, N. R. (2003) "What Have We Learned from Columbine: The Impact of the Self-System on Suicidal Violent Ideation among Adolescents," *Journal of School Violence*, 2 (3): 3–26.

Hartling, L. M., and Luchetta, T. (1999) "Humiliation: Assessing the Impact of Derision, Degradation, and Debasement," *Journal of Primary Prevention*, 19 (5): 259–278.

Hartling, L. M., Lindner, E. G., Spalthoff, U. J., and Britton, M. F. (2013) "Humiliation: A Nuclear Bomb of Emotions?" *Psicología Política,* 46: 55–76.

Herz, J. H. (1951) *Political Realism and Political Idealism: A Study in Theories and Realities*, Chicago, IL: Chicago University Press.

Herz, J. H. (1957) "Rise and Demise of the Territorial State," *World Politics*, 9: 473–493.

Hudson, J. (2012) "A Map of Muslim Protests around the World," available at: www.theatlanticwire.com/global/2012/09/map-muslim-protests-around-world/56865/

HumanDHS (2015) "2015 Workshop on Transforming Humiliation and Violent Conflict: 'Honoring Alfred Nobel's Message'," 26th Annual Human Dignity and Humiliation Studies Conference, Columbia University, New York, December 3–4, 2015.

IDMC (2015a) "19.3 Million Displaced by Disasters but 'Mother Nature Not to Blame' Says New Report," January 5, available at: www.internal-displacement.org/assets/library/Media/201507-globalEstimates-2015/20150706-GE-2015Press-release-FINAL-v1.pdf

IDMC (2015b) *Global Estimates 2015: People Displaced by Disasters*, Geneva, Switzerland: Internal Displacement Monitoring Centre.

Kendler, K. S., Hettema, J. M., Butera, F., Gardner, C. O., and Prescott, C. A. (2003) "Life Event Dimensions of Loss, Humiliation, Entrapment, and Danger in the Prediction of Onsets of Major Depression and Generalized Anxiety," *Archives of General Psychiatry*, 60 (8): 789–796.

Kirkpatrick, D. D. (2011) "Anger over Film Fuels Anti-American Attacks in Libya and Egypt," *The New York Times*, available at: www.nytimes.com/2012/09/12/world/middleeast/anger-over-film-fuels-anti-american-attacks-in-libya-and-egypt.html?pagewanted=all

Kirkpatrick, D. D. (2012) "Cultural Clash Fuels Muslims Angry at Online Video," *The New York Times*, available at: www.nytimes.com/2012/09/17/world/middleeast/muslims-rage-over-film-fueled-by-culture-divide.html?_r=0

Klein, D. C. (1991) "The Humiliation Dynamic: An Overview," *Journal of Primary Prevention*, 12 (2): 93–121.

Lacy, D. (2011) "The Role of Humiliation in the Palestinian/Israeli Conflict in Gaza," *Psychology & Society*, 4 (1): 76–92.

Leadership Conference on Civil Rights (2016) "Race and the Police," in *Justice on Trial: Racial Disparities in the American Criminal Justice System*, Washington, DC: The Leadership Conference on Civil and Human Rights, available at: www.civilrights.org/publications/justice-on-trial/race.html

Leidner, B., Sheikh, H., and Ginges, J. (2012) "Affective Dimensions of Intergroup Humiliation," *Public Library of Science One*, 7 (9): e43675.

LeShan, L. (1992) *The Psychology of War: Comprehending Its Mystique and Its Madness*, Chicago: Noble Press.

Lindner, E. G. (2001) "Humiliation and the Human Condition: Mapping a Minefield," *Human Rights Review*, 2 (2): 46–63.

Lindner, E. G. (2002) "Healing the Cycles of Humiliation: How to Attend to the Emotional Aspects of 'Unsolvable' Conflicts and the Use of 'Humiliation Entrepreneurship,'" *Peace and Conflict: Journal of Peace Psychology*, 8 (2): 125–138.

Lindner, E. G. (2006) *Making Enemies: Humiliation and International Conflict, Contemporary Psychology*, Westport, CT: Praeger Security International.

Lindner, E. G. (2007) "In Times of Globalization and Human Rights: Does Humiliation Become the Most Disruptive Force?" *Journal of Human Dignity and Humiliation Studies*, 1 (1), available at: www.humilliationstudies.upeace.org/

Lindner, E. G. (2008) "The Educational Environment as a Place for Humiliating Indoctrination or Dignifying Empowerment," *Experiments in Education*, 36, *Humiliation in the academic setting: A Special Symposium Issue*, 3 (March): 51–60.

Lindner, E. G. (2009a) *Emotion and Conflict: How Human Rights Can Dignify Emotion and Help Us Wage Good Conflict*, Westport, CT, London: Praeger.

Lindner, E. G. (2009b) "Humiliation and Global Terrorism: How to Overcome It Nonviolently," in R. Summy (Ed.), *Nonviolent Alternatives for Social Change*, Oxford: Nonviolent Alternatives for Social Change, pp. 227–248.

Lindner, E. G. (2009c) "Why There Can Be No Conflict Resolution as Long as People Are Being Humiliated," *International Review of Education*, 55 (May 2–3): 157–181.

Lindner, E. G. (2010a) "Disasters as a Chance to Implement Novel Solutions That Highlight Attention to Human Dignity," in A. Awotona (Ed.), *Rebuilding Sustainable Communities for Children and Their Families after Disasters: A Global Survey*, Newcastle upon Tyne, UK: Cambridge Scholars Publishing, pp. 335–358.

Lindner, E. G. (2010b) *Gender, Humiliation, and Global Security: Dignifying Relationships from Love, Sex, and Parenthood to World Affairs*, Contemporary Psychology, Santa Barbara, CA: Praeger.

Lindner, E. G. (2010c) "Traumatized by Humiliation in Times of Globalization: Transforming Humiliation into Constructive Meaning," in A. Kalayjian and D. Eugene (Eds.), *Mass Trauma and Emotional Healing around the World*, Santa Barbara, CA: Praeger/ABC-CLIO, pp. 361–382.

Lindner, E. G. (2012a) *A Dignity Economy: Creating an Economy That Serves Human Dignity and Preserves Our Planet*, Lake Oswego, OR: Dignity Press.

Lindner, E. G. (2012b) "Fostering Global Citizenship," in P. T. Coleman and M. Deutsch (Eds.), *Psychological Components of Sustainable Peace*, New York: Springer Science + Business Media, pp. 283–298.

Lindner, E. G. (2016) "Evelin Lindner's Global Life World and Scientific Inquiry," 2016, available at: www.humiliationstudies.org/whoweare/evelin/09.php

Lindner, E. G., Hartling, L. M., and Spalthoff, U. J. (2012) "Human Dignity and Humiliation Studies: A Global Network Advancing Dignity through Dialogue," in T. Besley and M. A. Peters (Eds.), *Interculturalism, Education, and Dialogue*, New York: P. Lang, pp. 386–396.

Mala, E., and Goodman, J. D. (2011) "At Least 80 Dead in Norway Shooting," *The New York Times*, available at: www.nytimes.com/2011/07/23/world/europe/23oslo.html?pagewanted=all

Mandela, N. (2007) "Nelson Mandela's Speech at the Launch of the Elders," available at: http://theelders.org/article/nelson-mandelas-speech-launch-elders

Manning, P. (2015) "Chequebook Journalism: Blurring the Line between News and Infotainment," *The Guardian*, January 20, available at: www.theguardian.com/commentisfree/2015/jan/20/chequebook-journalism-blurring-the-line-between-news-and-infotainment

Miller, J. B. (1976/1986) *Toward a New Psychology of Women*, 2nd ed., Boston, MA: Beacon Press.

Miller, J. B. (1983) "The Necessity of Conflict," *Women and Therapy*, 2 (2): 3–9.

Miller, J. B. (2003) *Telling the Truth About Power*, in Work in Progress, No. 100, Wellesley, MA: Stone Center Working Paper Series.

Miller, S. M. (2012) *Dignifying Dialogue: How to Dialogue and Why*, Boston, MA: Center for Rebuilding Sustainable Communities after Disasters, University of Massachusetts, available at: http://youtu.be/COnuz9mubnY

Minnich, E. K. (1990) *Transforming Knowledge*, Philadelphia, PA: Temple University Press.

Muskal, M., Winton, R., and Gerber, M. (2015) "Death in a Classroom: Oregon Shooter Targeted His English Class," *The Los Angeles Times*, available at: www.latimes.com/nation/la-na-oregon-shooting-20151002-story.html

Naess, A., and Wetlesen, J. (1978) "Through Spinoza to Mahayana Buddhism or through Mahayana Buddhism to Spinoza?" in *Spinoza's Philosophy of Man: Proceedings of the Scandinavian Spinoza Symposium 1977*. Oslo: University of Oslo Press.

Nebehay, S. (2015) "World's Refugees and Displaced Exceed Record 60 Million," available at: www.reuters.com/article/us-un-refugees-idUSKBN0U10CV20151218

NPR (2001) "The Ratings Game," *Local News Online*, available at: www.pbs.org/wnet/insidelocalnews/ratings.html

Reiss, H. (2009) *Every War Has Two Losers: A Poet's Meditation on Peace*. Zinc Films.

Rothbart, D., and Cooley, J. (2016) "Hutus Aiding Tutsis during the Rwandan Genocide: Motives, Meanings and Morals," *Genocide Studies and Prevention: An International Journal*, 10 (2): 76–97. DOI: http://dx.doi.org/10.5038/1911-9933.10.2.1398

Sanger, D. E., Schmitt, E., and Cooper, H. (2016) "Iran's Swift Release of U.S. Sailors Hailed as a Sign of Warmer Relations," *The New York Times*, available at: www.nytimes.com/2016/01/14/world/middleeast/iran-navy-crew-release.html

Silverblatt, A. (2007) *Genre Studies in Mass Media: A Handbook*, Armonk, NY: M.E. Sharpe.

Stafford, K. (Ed.) (2003) *Every War Has Two Losers: William Stafford on Peace and War*, Minneapolis, MN: Milkweed Editions.

Torres, W. J., and Bergner, R. M. (2010) "Humiliation: Its Nature and Consequences," *Journal of the American Academy of Psychiatry and the Law*, 38 (2): 195–204.

UN (2008) "The Universal Declaration of Human Rights," *United Nations Website Services Section*, last modified October 13, 2008, available at: www.un.org/Overview/rights.html.

UNESCO (2016) *Training Security Forces on Freedom of Expression and the Safety of Journalists*, available at: https://youtu.be/_2u85rAwAzM

UNHCR (2015) *Worldwide Displacement Hits All-Time High as War and Persecution Increase*, Geneva, Switerland: United Nations High Commissioner for Refugees.

Walker, J., and Knauer, V. (2011) "Humiliation, Self-Esteem, and Violence," *Journal of Forensic Psychiatry and Psychology*, 22 (5): 724–741.

Walker, M. (1999) *Race, Self, and Society: Relational Challenges in a Culture of Disconnection*, in Work in Progress, No. 85, Wellesley, MA: Stone Center Working Paper Series.

Walker, M., and Miller, J. B. (2001) *Racial Images and Relational Possibilities*, in *Talking Paper*, No. 2, Wellesley, MA: Stone Center Working Paper Series.

Whack, R. C. (2013) *Guest Biography: Kofi Annan [Webpage and Audio Download]*, in *Maya Angelou's Black History Month Special 2013, Telling Our Stories*, Public Radio International: RCW Media Productions.

Yeager, D. S., Miu, A. S., Powers, J., and Dweck, C. S. (2013) "Implicit Theories of Personality and Attributions of Hostile Intent: A Meta-Analysis, an Experiment, and a Longitudinal Intervention," *Child Development,* 84 (5): 1651–1667.

5

WHEN MEDIA IS USED TO INCITE VIOLENCE

The United Nations, Genocide, and Atrocity Crimes

Adama Dieng and Simona Cruciani

Hate Speech and Incitement to Discrimination, Hostility, or Violence

Recent years have been difficult for those on the front line of the struggle to protect populations from atrocities crimes, the term commonly used to refer to the crimes of genocide, war crimes, and crimes against humanity. Humanity is confronted daily with the unimaginable horrors faced by civilians in many parts of the world, including in Burundi, the Central African Republic, Iraq, Myanmar, South Sudan, Syria, Ukraine, and Yemen, and jolted by reminders that the fragile peace in countries such as the Democratic Republic of the Congo is often punctuated by violence against civilians, including sexual and gender-based violence.

Regrettably, hate speech and incitement to discrimination, hostility, and violence have become the common denominator of atrocities committed worldwide. Most, if not all have been preceded and accompanied by these phenomena. In many other situations, where tensions between communities are growing, hate speech and incitement contribute to sowing the seeds of suspicious, mistrust, and intolerance. Increased inflammatory rhetoric, propaganda campaigns, or hate speech targeting communities or individuals, based on their identity, contribute to enabling or preparing atrocity crimes, and are hence indicators that those crimes are likely to be committed.[1] Of note, atrocity crimes and, in particular, genocide and crimes against humanity, are processes that take time to plan, coordinate and implement. They cannot be explained as isolated or spontaneous events that perpetrators commit without some level of preparation. Paying attention to the presence of hate speech and incitement in societies divided along identity lines and in situations where tensions are high can help detect an increased risk of atrocity crimes and contribute to early warning and prevention efforts.

While there is no legal definition of "hate speech," and the characterization of what is "hateful" is controversial, hate speech is normally defined as any kind of communication in speech, writing, or behavior, that denigrates a person or a group on the basis of who they are, in other words based on their religion, ethnicity, nationality, race, or other identity factor. Hate speech may suggest that the person or group—it is usually groups—is inferior and that they should be excluded or discriminated against on this basis including, for example, by limiting their access to education, employment, or political positions. While all incitement to discrimination, hostility, or violence is hate speech, not all hate speech constitutes incitement. A person standing on a street corner can say vile, offensive and racist things but the impact will be very different to that of a national leader who is calling for violence against a particular group at a time when tensions are already high. The International Covenant on Civil and Political Rights (ICCPR) defines incitement as "any advocacy to national, racial or religious hatred"[2] and links it to the potential it has to fuel or escalate violent acts. Incitement is therefore a very dangerous form of hate speech as it can trigger violence and, in some instances, atrocity crimes. For this reason, incitement is forbidden under international law, while hate speech is not.

There have been several initiatives aimed at identifying the factors that make speech so "dangerous" that it can trigger violence. Among these, scholar Susan Benesch developed guidelines for monitoring speech and evaluating its "dangerousness"[3] that call for an assessment of: (i) the speaker, (ii) the audience, (iii) the speech itself and how it could be interpreted, (iv) the socio-economic context, and (v) the means of transmission, taking into consideration the circumstances in which the message or the speech take place, the influence of the speaker over his/her audience, and the will and capacity of the audience to commit violence. Of note, also, is the policy brief of the non-governmental organization Article 19, which considers six factors—the severity, content, extent, imminence, likelihood, and context of the speech—to distinguish between hate speech and incitement and, based on this, identify messages that need to be criminalized.[4]

Criminalization of hate speech that constitutes incitement to discrimination, hostility, or violence should be exceptional and is controversial. While some countries oppose it in the name of absolute freedom of expression and opinion, others support some restrictions of freedom of expression and opinion in the interest of preventing incitement to discrimination, hostility or violence. It must be stressed, however, that any limits to freedom of expression and opinion used by States to suppress fundamental rights and freedoms are unacceptable. Blasphemy laws, for example, should be repealed, as they infringe on freedom of expression and opinion and freedom of religion and belief and can be misused to clamp down on political opponents.

Past and Present Cases of Incitement to Discrimination, Hostility, or Violence

History is full of cases where hate speech and incitement have paved the way to atrocity crimes, including genocide. In most cases, the media have been used to disseminate and multiply hateful and discriminatory messages to achieve violence more rapidly and massively.

Hate speech and incitement to violence were used extensively in Nazi Germany in the years leading up to the Holocaust to turn the population against the Jews, Roma, and Sinti, homosexuals, and others. From 1923 to the end of World War II, *Der Stürmer*, the weekly Nazi newspaper, was a significant part of Nazi propaganda and was vehemently racist and anti-Semitic, running caricatures of Jews and accusations of blood libel. As early as 1933, *Der Stürmer* included articles calling for the extermination of the Jews.

Before and during the Rwandan genocide of 1994, hate speech—including the use of cartoons and popular music—was used to deepen divisions between Hutu and Tutsi communities.

Kangura, a Rwandan tabloid, heavily contributed to shaping public opinion in Rwanda against the Tutsi population, disseminating anti-Tutsi propaganda well before 1994 and accusing the Tutsi of being the cause of the civil war between the government of President Juvénal Habyarimana and the Rwandan Patriotic Front. The radio also played a major role in the Rwandan genocide. When President Habyarimana's plane was shot down on April 6, 1994, *Radio Télévision Libre des Mille Collines* called for the extermination of "cockroaches," referring to the Tutsis, broadcasting which people to kill and where to find them.

During the ethnic cleansing campaign led by the Serbs against the Muslim population of Bosnia Herzegovina in the 1992–1995 Bosnian war that culminated with the Srebrenica genocide in July 1995, Serbian-controlled media sources such as Radio Television Belgrade ruled the airwaves, victimizing the Serbs and demonizing Bosnians. False reports that NATO troops were shooting and gassing Serbs were pervasive on television and radio. These messages built on preconceived ethnic hatred and led to increasing acceptance and support for the genocide of Muslim men and boys.

Regrettably, despite the global pledge of "never again" after the horrors of Rwanda and Bosnia, traditional and new media, including newspapers, radio and television broadcasters, the internet, and mobile phones, continue to be used on a daily basis to spread messages that stigmatize, marginalize, and denigrate the "other," and in certain instances incite to commit violence against groups of people based on their national, racial, religious, social, and political, identity. In recent years, hate speech has been used to incite to hatred, hostility and violence both in conflict and peace situations, including in Côte d'Ivoire, Iraq, Kenya, Kirgizstan, Libya, Myanmar, South Sudan, Syria, the United States, Yemen, and a number of European countries, including the United Kingdom, Germany, Italy, Austria, and Hungary.

During the violence that erupted in Kenya after the 2007 presidential elections, the Kenyan media stimulated and exacerbated the violence with ethnically charged hate speech, pitting Kenya's citizens against one another in the worst eruption of violence since the country gained independence in 1963. By the time the violence had subsided, over one thousand Kenyans had lost their lives, and a further six hundred thousand had been displaced; the blame placed on the (vernacular) media as radio KASS FM is epitomized by the current trial of Kalenjin-language broadcaster Joshua Arap Sang at the International Criminal Court (ICC), which began on September 10, 2013 and is ongoing. Sang's trial represents the first time a journalist has been tried at the ICC, making it an important precedent for determining the legal relationship between hate speech and violence.[5]

In Côte d'Ivoire, for years online and offline media have spread hateful messages that contributed to increasing the identity divide between the North and the South of the country. Hate speech was prevalent throughout the first Ivorian Civil War (2002–2007), as well as during the period of political transition that paved the way to Presidential elections held at the end of 2010. It is also widely acknowledged that vitriolic hate speech contributed to the escalation of violence that followed the 2010 Presidential polls and that resulted in over 1,000 civilian deaths as well as in the ICC indictment of ex-President Laurent Gbabgo, his wife Simone Gbagbo, and the leader of his youth movement, Charles Ble Goude, on charges of crimes against humanity and incitement to discrimination, hostility, or violence. Of note, due to high levels of hate speech and incitement in the country, particularly in political discourse, the mandate of the United Nations Peacekeeping Mission in Côte d'Ivoire has, since its establishment in 2006, been tasked to monitor "any public incidents of incitement to hatred, intolerance and violence", with the purpose of bringing to the attention of the Council "all individuals identified as instigators of political violence."[6]

In Libya, during the 2011 anti-government demonstrations that resulted in the fall of Muammar Gaddafi's regime, President Gaddafi appeared on State television several times, denigrating peaceful protesters and calling them "rats and mercenaries." His son, Saif Gaddafi, went further, warning that the protesters would be crushed in a bloodbath if the Government's offer of reforms was rejected. It is widely acknowledged that Gaddafi's speeches were a decisive factor in the approval of the Security Council of Resolution 1973, which authorized the international community to establish a no-fly zone over Libya and to use all means necessary short of foreign occupation to protect civilians.[7]

In Kyrgyzstan, during the 2010 ethnic riots between ethnic Kyrgyz and Uzbeks in southern Kyrgyzstan that followed the overthrowing of President Kurmanbek Bakiyev, many of the Kyrgyz-language newspapers—particularly *Forum*, *Alibi*, and *Kyrgyz Tuusu*—began publishing nationally biased articles that openly divided the society into "us-Kyrgyz" and "them-Uzbeks." At the same time, increasing online expression of interethnic polarization appeared in social media. Nationalistic and provocative messages also appeared in online forums and Twitter—with ethnic Kyrgyz accusing ethnic Uzbeks of wrongdoings and setting fire to Bakiyev's family house, and ethnic Uzbeks accusing ethnic Kyrgyz of hatred towards Uzbeks and of attacking private property. In the riots, some 420 people were killed while 80,000 were displaced.

In South Sudan, in April 2014 during fierce fights in Bentiu between the majority Dinka Government and Nuer rebels affiliated to former Vice President Riek Machar and that resulted in the targeting of the civilian population along ethnic lines, hate speech calling for certain groups to leave Bentiu and urging the men of one community to commit vengeful sexual violence against the women from another community was broadcast over local radio. More than 200 civilians were killed in the fighting in Bentiu in what was called the worst massacre in the South Sudan conflict. As the Security Council condemned the attacks against civilians, stressing that they might constitute war crimes,[8] the United Nations Peacekeeping Mission in South Sudan compared the hate speech and incitement broadcast by radio stations to what was heard in Rwanda 20 years before.

In the Middle East, hate and incitement speech have been particularly prevalent during recent years. For instance, hate speech along religious and sectarian lines has been present in Syria since the very beginning of the civil war. Graffiti calling for Alawites to leave Syria and for Jews to go back to Israel were seen in 2011 on the walls of Syrian cities. Moreover, since 2011, several religious leaders have issued *fatwas* calling for jihad against the Syrian regime and its Shi'a allies and have denigrated the beliefs of parties to the conflict and their allies, further fueling sectarian tensions.

The so-called Islamic State of Syria and the Levant (ISIL) spreads hatred, incites violence, and recruits new members through a very sophisticated use of social media, including Facebook, Twitter, YouTube, Instagram, Ask.fm, Tumblr, WhatsApp, Kik, SureSpot, and Vibe. It is important to note that not all its propaganda includes violent imagery intended to incite. Hate speech is often surrounded in messages that offer a sense of belonging, which contain within them a strong invitation to conform, such as, in the case of the so-called ISIL, videos that present the group as an exciting and heroic alternative to life in the West. This media presents the so-called ISIL as the powerful creators of a new state, to which all Muslims (male and female) have a duty to travel. When the so-called ISIL's official media groups release material online the group encourages supporters on social media to share the material—this is what gives the so-called ISIL its large reach, particularly among young people.[9] Moreover, in the territories it occupied in Iraq, Libya, and Syria, the so-called ISIL publishes its own magazine, *Dabiq*, aimed at attracting recruits from the West, as well as spreading misinformation about Western society and other religions and beliefs and inciting discrimination, hostility, or violence—including sexual violence—against those it terms "infidels." In Yemen, since the conflict erupted in 2014, the Yemeni branches of the so-called ISIL and Al Qaeda in the Arabian Peninsula (AQAP) have made extensive use of sectarian language to fuel divides and incite their followers to commit jihad against "infidels."

In Asia, hate speech and incitement to discrimination, hostility, or violence have been particularly virulent in Myanmar. In October 2012, violent attacks led by Buddhist mobs against Muslim Rohingyas in Rakhine State were fanned by a campaign of poisonous anti-Muslim and anti-Rohingya rhetoric, in which political and religious leaders were also implicated.[10] The attacks destroyed numerous Rohingya communities and displaced some 125,000 people. The lack of accountability for the 2012 violence has likely contributed to the outpouring of anti-Muslim hate speech that has since been prevalent not only in Rakhine state but in all of Myanmar. The Buddhist "969" movement, composed of extremist Buddhist monks, has been among the most visible instigators of violence against Rohyngas and Muslims and has been disseminating anti-Muslim propaganda—including stickers and posters —country-wide. In relation to this, pro-Buddhist online and offline media have spread "969"'s racist and discriminatory propaganda, contributing to creating a general climate of suspicion, mistrust and paranoia, deepening the divide between Buddhists and Muslims in the country. Of note are the speeches made by the leader of the "969" Movement, U Wirathu, who has been openly advocating the "cleansing" of Muslims from Myanmar.

The United Nations and the Prevention of Incitement to Hatred, Hostility, and Violence

Due to the proliferation of vitriolic rhetoric both in countries at peace and in conflict, the United Nations has increased initiatives aimed at reducing the negative effects of hate speech and preventing incitement to discrimination, hostility or violence. In 2013, the High Commissioner for Human Rights launched the Rabat Plan of Action on the prohibition of advocacy of national, racial or religious hatred that constitutes incitement to discrimination, hostility or violence.[11] The Plan of Action was the result of a series of workshops organized by the High Commissioner of Human Rights in all regions of the world and included recommendations, mostly to Member States, on ways to prevent incitement to discrimination, hostility or violence. While the Rabat Plan of Action recommended the adoption of comprehensive national anti-discrimination legislation with preventive and punitive action to effectively combat incitement to discrimination, hostility or violence, it also recognized the limits of this legislation, and called States, media, and the broader society to tackle the root causes of intolerance through policy measures, including in the areas of intercultural dialogue, education for pluralism and diversity, the empowerment of minorities and indigenous people. In this context, the Rabat Plan of Action also urged the media, as well as community and religious leaders, to be both more ethically aware and socially responsible.

The same year, building on the Rabat Plan of Action and in order to better tackle the issue of incitement to violence that could lead to atrocity crimes, the Office of the Special Adviser on the Prevention of Genocide and the Responsibility to Protect (the "Office"), with the support of the Special Rapporteur on freedom of opinion and expression, the Special Rapporteur on freedom of religion and belief, and the Special Rapporteur on contemporary forms of racism, racial discrimination, xenophobia, and related intolerance, as well as other experts, developed a policy paper entitled "Preventing Incitement to Atrocity Crimes: Policy Options for Action"[12] with recommendations for Member States, civil society organizations, the media and the international community on ways to prevent and curb incitement to atrocity crimes.

The Policy Options paper recognizes the important role played by journalists and media corporations in preventing incitement that could lead to atrocity crimes and in depriving such speech of its power. In particular, the paper recommended that the media enhance ethical standards and establish credible structures for internal self-regulation to promote the principles of truth telling, impartiality, and independent reporting. It also stressed the importance of journalists being trained in research and investigative techniques, as well as in counter and alternative speech. Finally, the paper called for ethical standards that apply to traditional journalism to be extended to the Internet, "which despite having unlocked extraordinary communication opportunities has also provided an unprecedented infrastructure for the dissemination of racial and ethnic hatred, as well as hate speech and incitement to violence."[13]

In the context of its recommendations for civil society, the Policy Options paper recognized that religious leaders "have a special role to play"[14] due to their position of leadership and their capacity to influence the behaviour of their followers. In other words, the paper spelled out clearly the link between religious discourse, ethical and responsible online and offline communication, and the prevention of incitement to violence.

Given that many past and present violent conflicts have had a religious or ideological driver, and given the alarming spike in religiously motivated hate speech and incitement, both online and offline, not only in conflict but also in peaceful situations, the Office has made the prevention of incitement to violence a priority and has focused particular attention on the role that religious leaders can play both in inciting violence and in countering incitement and preventing violence, including through the media. In some of the most serious cases of recent or ongoing violence, such as in Central African Republic, Iraq, Myanmar, Syria, and Yemen, religion has played a significant role and hate speech and incitement to violence have been prevalent. In addition, racist and discriminatory messages disseminated along religious lines, including by religious leaders, have become prevalent also in societies considered to be peaceful and democratic, in particular as a consequence of the increase in migration and refugee flows from conflict areas in the Middle East to Europe and North America.

Of note, the necessity of engaging religious leaders and actors, as well as the media to prevent atrocity crimes and their incitement has also been stressed by former Special Rapporteur on the freedom of religion and belief, Heiner Bielefeld, in his 2015 report to the Human Rights Council on Preventing Violence Committed in the Name of Religion. The report calls on religious communities and their leaders to challenge authenticity claims of religious extremists and foster religious tolerance and freedom. It also urges the media to promote a culture of public discourse that is able to counter hostile rumours and fearful narratives in order to prevent them from escalating into fully fledged conspiracy projections and, eventually, violence.[15]

In light of this situation, at the beginning of 2015 the Office launched an initiative, working with religious leaders to develop context-relevant strategies for the prevention of incitement to violence that could lead to atrocity crimes. The first forum with religious leaders took place in April 2015 in Fez, Morocco, and brought together religious leaders from different faiths and religions from around the world, with the support of the King Abdullah Dialogue Centre for Intercultural and Interreligious Dialogue and the Kingdom of Morocco. The Forum resulted in a draft Plan of Action[16] for religious leaders to prevent incitement to violence and the Fez Declaration, a declaration of principles. Four of the eight elements of the draft Plan of Action highlight the link between the media and the prevention of atrocities. The draft Plan calls for:

- monitoring and public reporting of incitement that could lead to atrocity crimes;
- developing, speaking out and circulating "alternative" messages or counter-speech;
- engaging in dialogue with the speakers and the potential audience;
- engaging in dialogue on "grievances," both directly and through the media.

These elements focus, in particular, on increasing the ability of religious leaders to monitor, identify and respond to hate speech and incitement in the media; prevent and counter hate speech; as well as engage with radicalized or at-risk youth both online and offline. In this context, it must be stressed that enhancing religious leaders' ability to engage online, through the social media, could contribute significantly to preventing and countering hate speech, incitement, and radicalization, given the prevalence of these phenomena online.

At the time of writing, the draft Fez Plan of Action is being reviewed and strengthened through a series of five regional meetings with religious leaders, which will also serve to develop strategies for implementing the Plan of Action in each region, once it has been finalized. Recommendations from each of the regional meetings will be used to finalize the draft Fez Plan of Action, which will be launched in late 2016. The first two regional meetings brought together religious leaders from the European, and the Middle Eastern and North African regions, respectively. Religious leaders at both meetings stressed the importance of training on the use of social media, the same media that are being used by the so-called ISIL and others to recruit followers.

Within the United Nations system, other entities are also working to curb hate speech and prevent incitement to discrimination, hostility or violence, including in the media. The Hate Speech initiative of the United Nations Alliance of Civilizations (UNAOC) puts emphasis on engaging media and journalists, particularly those who are well positioned to report, comment on, and investigate xenophobia, hate speech, violent extremism, and prejudice. With this initiative, the UNAOC aims at exploring the root causes of hate speech, its link to violent extremisms, and the treatment of migrants, as well as the different measures that have been taken globally to combat hate speech and their limitations. The initiative includes regional conferences and a media campaign.[17]

At the same time, the United Nations Educational, Scientific and Cultural Organisation (UNESCO) is focussing on expanding knowledge on how to prevent online hate speech. Its latest publication on Countering Online Hate Speech provides a global overview of the dynamics characterizing hate speech online and some of the measures that have been adopted to counteract and mitigate it. Is also highlights good practices that have emerged at the local and global levels. While the study offers a comprehensive analysis of the international, regional and national normative frameworks developed to address hate speech online, and their repercussions for freedom of expression, it also places particular emphasis on social and non-regulatory mechanisms that can help to counter the production, dissemination and impact of hateful messages online.[18]

Due the spike in violence by terrorist and violent extremist groups in recent years, curbing hate speech, in particular online, is also a priority in the fight against terrorism, as highlighted in the Global Counter Terrorism Strategy.[19] In this relation, the Secretary-General's Plan of Action to Prevent Violent extremism,[20] published in December 2015, reaffirms the relevance of combating incitement to hatred, hostility and violence with the purpose of preventing violent extremism. The Plan calls for a comprehensive approach to fighting incitement and violent extremism, involving all relevant actors, such as national human rights institutions, civil society, political parties and the media. The Plan also highlights the paramount role played by religious leaders in fostering intra- and inter-faith tolerance and understanding, as well as in voicing their rejection of violent doctrines by emphasizing the peaceful and humanitarian values inherent in their religious doctrines.

Conclusion

The proliferation of hate speech and incitement to discrimination, hostility, and violence in many parts of the world, increasingly spread through the social media, increases the risk of violence and atrocity crimes and represents a challenge for the maintenance of international peace and security. The multiplication of initiatives in the United Nations system aimed at preventing and countering hate speech and incitement is an indication of how seriously the organization takes these phenomena. But not only the United Nations must act, for if we are going to reduce the risk of atrocity crimes posed by the dissemination of hate speech and incitement through the media, all actors must play a role—including States, civil society, religious leaders, and, most importantly, those working in the media.

Notes

1. Framework of Analysis for Atrocity Crimes, United Nations Office on Genocide Prevention and the Responsibility to Protect, available at: www.un.org/en/preventgenocide/adviser/pdf/framework%20of%20 analysis%20for%20atrocity%20crimes_en.pdf
2. "Any advocacy of national, racial or religious hatred that constitutes incitement to discrimination, hostility or violence shall be prohibited by law," International Covenant on Civil and Political Rights, Art 20, United Nations Office of the High Commissioner for Human Rights, Article 20 of the ICCPR, available at: www.ohchr.org/en/professionalinterest/pages/ccpr.aspx
3. The Dangerous Speech Project, available at: http://dangerousspeech.org/guidelines/
4. www.article19.org/data/files/medialibrary/3572/12–12–01-PO-incitement-WEB.pdf
5. From Incitement to Self-censorship: the media in the Kenyan elections of 2007 and 2013, available at: http://freespeechdebate.com/en/discuss/124451/
6. S/RES/2226 (2015)
7. S/RES/1973(2011)
8. SC/11363(2014)
9. How Social Media Is Used to Encourage Travel to Syria and Iraq. Briefing Note to Schools, available at: www.gov.uk/government/uploads/system/uploads/attachment_data/file/440450/How_social_media_is_used_ to_encourage_travel_to_Syria_and_Iraq.pdf
10. All You Can Do Is Pray, 22 April 2013, available at: www.hrw.org/report/2013/04/22/all-you-can-do-pray/ crimes-against-humanity-and-ethnic-cleansing-rohingya-muslims
11. Rabat Plan of Action on the prohibition of advocacy of national, racial or religious hatred that constitutes incitement to discrimination, hostility or violence, available at: www.ohchr.org/Documents/Issues/Opinion/ SeminarRabat/Rabat_draft_outcome.pdf
12. Preventing Incitement to Atrocity Crimes: Policy Options for Action, available at: www.un.org/en/prevent genocide/adviser/pdf/Prevention%20of%20incitement.Policy%20options.Nov2013.pdf
13. Ibid.
14. Ibid.
15. Report of the Special Rapporteur on freedom of religion or belief, Heiner Bielefeldt, A/HRC/28/66, December 29, 2015, available at: www.ohchr.org/EN/Issues/FreedomReligion/Pages/Annual.aspx
16. Fez Plan of Action, available at: www.un.org/en/preventgenocide/adviser/pdf/Fez%20Plan%20of%20Action.pdf
17. Tracking Hatred: an international dialogue on hate speech in the media, available at: www.unaoc.org/what-we-do/projects/hate-speech/
18. Countering Online Speech, 2015, available at: http://unesdoc.unesco.org/images/0023/002332/233231e.pdf
19. A/RES/60/288(2006)
20. A/70/674(2015)

Part 2

DOCUMENTARY, NEWS, HUMAN TRAFFICKERS, AND THE RESCUE NARRATIVES OF GLOBAL MIGRATIONS

Humanitarianism and Human Rights
in an Age of Crisis

INTRODUCTION
TO PART 2

Standing on the shore of the Greek island of Lesbos, Dr. Alexander van Tulleken reaches out to a migrant who has just managed to cross the Mediterranean Sea in what looks to be a very unstable craft. This landing is only the first stop on a journey that will take thousands of refugees overland through Europe, crossing rough terrain, trekking through snow, and standing in long lines at border checkpoints. In "*Frontline Doctors: Winter Migrant Crisis*," Alexander and his brother Christoffer follow the migrants, document their struggles and the conditions of their health, record their illnesses, and most importantly try to understand their situation and aspirations, all the while offering what assistance they can. A production of BBC1, the documentary reached large audiences in the UK, and stands as a unique example of a media representation of the migrant crisis, offering a point of view from humanitarian doctors in the field willing to do what they can to improve the plight of refugees. In doing so, this non-fiction document, and the behind-the-scenes story of its making, conveys empathy and compassion, concern and outrage, and nurtures the humanitarian imagination of its viewers.

We are in the midst of what the United Nations has called the largest refugee crisis since World War II. For migrants crossing the Mediterranean, summer is the "season of death" as milder weather and a somewhat calmer sea results in more craft setting off, many of which are unseaworthy and full to the brim with human cargo attempting the voyage to Sicily, Malta or Greece. Illustrating how devastating the human cost of crossing the Mediterranean can be, the month of April 2015 was one of the most deadly. On April 15 a boat sank off the Libyan coast and about 400 migrants drowned with 150 rescued by the Italian Coast Guard. On April 16, 41 migrants drowned and four survived to make it to Sicily. In another incident 12 passengers perished after being thrown overboard. On April 19 a vessel capsized off the coast of Libya carrying about 900 refugees; an estimated 350 were Eritreans and 200 were Senegalese. Other passengers were from Syria, Somalia, Sierra Leon, Mali, Gambia, Ethiopia and the Ivory Coast. Despite the efforts of 18 rescue ships only 28 survived. Then on April 24, the Italian Coastguard saved 80 migrants who had set out from Libya. Soon after, over the weekend ending on May 3, Italian Coastguard patrol vessels rescued almost 6,000 refugees and migrants from Africa on a dangerously over-filled craft, after ten had drowned. By late spring 2015, an estimated 1,750 persons had perished, 30 times more than the previous year. A year later the situation had not changed dramatically and hundreds more drowned, yet the refugees and migrants would rather risk death than remain in their war-torn homelands.

Many of these humanitarian disasters are recorded on video camera and broadcast to global publics. For example, on May 25, 2016 the Italian Coastguard released dramatic footage to the world's media of an overloaded fishing boat keeling sideways. Over 400 African migrants were rescued and five bodies recovered. The European Union for its part pledged to design policies to redress the appalling death toll. However, as the number of migrants reaching Europe escalated, the situation was quickly defined as a crisis, and "security" policies were designed primarily to keep refugees and migrants from ever reaching the shores of Europe.

In Italy news coverage of migrants focused on the Italian Coast Guard's interception of small crafts loaded with people. In "A Humanitarian Battlefield: Redefining Border Control as Saving Victims," Pierluigi Musarò observes that through the course of patrolling the seas, reporting on the Italian Navy's efforts to intersect migrant vessels became a contested media terrain. Musarò examines the ways in which the narrative and visual strategies employed by the Italian Navy during operation Mare Nostrum transformed the threatening spectacle of the "migrant invasion" into the compassionate spectacle of the "humanitarian battlefield." Focusing on how the militarization of migration and border controls has been explicitly bound with notions of humanitarianism, the chapter explores how the current focus on both the securitarian and humanitarian sides of the phenomenon supports a more complex logic of threat and benevolence. He concludes by assessing this unusual development as a double-sided phenomenon where humanitarian governance of migration fuses the often conflicting concerns of care and control.

In Chapter 8, Elke Grittmann examines news coverage of the Syrian refugees in German media, and finds a trajectory of news frames over time. "From Pity to Control: Regulated Humanitarianism in German Media Coverage of Refugees and Asylum," Grittmann looks at how coverage of Syrian refugees evolved from humanitarian concerns to a focus on regulatory control and management. Since the onset of Syria's uprising in March 2011, it is estimated that a total of 4.8 million Syrians have fled ongoing violence in their country, and more than one million have sought asylum in Europe and Germany (UNHCR 2015). Syrian refugees constitute the largest number of refugees worldwide. The article shows that although frames of solidarity with refugees are strongly present, coverage is dominated now by control, regulation, and migration-management frames.

From a global media perspective, by the end of 2015, 65.3 million men, women, children and the elderly, were either refugees, asylum seekers or internally displaced persons (IDPs)—an increase of five million in a single year and the highest level ever recorded. From a forced migration perspective the UNHCR notes that this figure represents one in every 113 people on the planet, displaced in 2015 from their homes and that 12.4 million persons were newly displaced by conflict or persecution. Across the globe, 24 people per minute were forced to flee their homes. Half of all refugees are children under 18 years old. Despite the global media attention on "Europe's migrant crisis" the overwhelming number of refugees and migrants are not in Europe. Indeed, the UNHCR confirms that 86 percent of the world's refugees are being sheltered in low- and middle-income countries. Turkey is the host-country with the most refugees worldwide with 2.5 million people, trailed by Pakistan and Lebanon, with Libya not far behind. In "Regional Impact of Human Trafficking and Forced Migration: Looking for Solutions in Libya," Purnaka L. de Silva examines the regional impact of human trafficking and forced migrations. Silva draws on extensive fieldwork that documents the trafficking routes across sub-Saharan Africa focusing on the pivotal role of Libya, which is seen as a gateway or conduit to Europe. Rather than searching for solutions from European or Western perspectives, this chapter offers a rare perspective with recommendations voiced by Libyan nationals and researchers.

Amid the migration crisis in May 2016, the first World Humanitarian Summit was convened in Istanbul bringing together aid organizations from across the globe. As Pamela DeLargy observes, while the fine points of humanitarian accountability were discussed and the European governments and civil society pledged their commitment to the Core

Humanitarian Standard, Sudanese refugees were fending for themselves in a squalid camp in Calais without even basic sanitation and Syrian refugees were arriving exhausted on the shores of Lesbos but finding no shelter from the sun and no first aid unless they happened to be met by a kind local resident or a self-funded volunteer. In "The Drowning of SPHERE in the Mediterranean: What Has Happened to Humanitarian Standards in Fortress Europe?" DeLargy notes that despite the successes in some countries that generously took in and cared for thousands of asylum seekers and continue to provide for so many, the care for those stranded at borders or in limbo does not meet even the minimum of humanitarian standards that are provided in camps in Jordan or Sudan or Thailand. Less wealthy countries that host an even greater proportion of the world's refugees are watching Europe and are surprised to see that the conditions of those in the Greek camps or on the border of Macedonia are so poor, given the financial resources in European countries. Arguing that Europe is the birthplace of modern humanitarianism, the very place where the well-known humanitarian principles of impartiality, neutrality, and response based on need were developed and refined, DeLargy notes that it is both surprising and tragic that the continent seems to have left much of that commitment behind when it comes to caring for refugees and migrants recently arriving in Europe. DeLargy concludes that the labeling (of what might have been handled in a calm and organized fashion) as a "crisis" turned out to be prescient; it has truly turned into a crisis— a political crisis, above all. The mishandling of the in-migration has led to profound political instability within and conflict among European states. Xenophobia has become a feature in the national politics of almost every EU member state. The very survival of the European Union is at stake. And that political crisis is in full swing in the United States as well.

Nowhere has xenophobia, racism, and misogyny challenged humanitarian principles and core values more than in the United States with the election of Donald Trump. From the beginning of his campaign Donald Trump humiliated people of color, denigrated immigrants, labeled Muslims terrorists, and ignited white supremacists across the country. As President, Trump is beginning to set in place the mechanisms by which his campaign promises to build a wall along the US Mexican border, and to deport immigrants. Drawing out the consequences of Trump's immigration policies, Human Rights writer Stephen Hopsgood (2016) warned: "if the plan is really to deport millions of undocumented workers, then internment camps, dawn raids by thousands of armed government officials, deaths and killings in custody, border firefights and lacerating misery are almost inevitable."

As the country and the world brace themselves for the consequences of this new anti-immigrant, white nationalism, Americans across the country have gone into the streets to protest the election, its rhetoric, and the fact that Hillary Clinton won the popular vote by almost two million. The next four years will prove to be a defining chapter in the continuation of progress toward the development of global human rights discourse and humanitarianism in general.

References

Hopsgood, S. (2016) "Fascism Rising," *Alternet*, November 12, available at: www.alternet.org/election-2016/fascism-rising?akid=14872.19806.Ww1JCM&rd=1&src=newsletter1067068&t=4

UNHCR. (2015) "UNHCR: Total number of Syrian refugees exceeds four million for first time," available at: www.unhcr.org/en-us/news/press/2015/7/559d67d46/unhcr-total-number-syrian-refugees-exceeds-four-million-first-time.html

6

FRONTLINE DOCTORS

Winter Migrant Crisis
BBC1 (2016)

Alexander van Tulleken

Chris and Xand van Tulleken—doctors, part-time aid workers and twin brothers—want to see for themselves what conditions are like for migrants fleeing through Europe at the height of winter. They travel to Lesbos in Greece, through the Balkans and on to Berlin and Calais to understand what's being done on a medical and humanitarian level in response to the refugee crisis.

Spending time with medics, charities and volunteers in camps and clinics, at border crossings and transit points, they find out what the situation is like on the ground and, wherever possible, lend a hand in the biggest migration crisis of our times.[1]

Editor's Note

The refugees that have fled to Europe in this global crisis have been faced with a terrible choice. Stay and risk death in the midst of conflict, or leave and risk death in the Mediterranean and all the hazards and trauma of a continuing trek over land. Hundreds of thousands have chosen to flee, and what the BBC brings to viewers as they follow Chris and Xand van Tulleken, is the harrowing journey migrants experience once they leave Turkey. We don't see them jump into a small boat and onto a very stormy sea—we see them come ashore on the Greek island of Lesbos. Standing on a beach with a group of locals, Xand is well covered against the cold, still people scramble into the water grabbing children, women and men out of boats. Non-professional humanitarians greet and help them, directing them to safety as Xand helps treat a small boy and a young man for hyperthermia. As soon as the beach clears two more full boats are about to wash ashore under a grey sky.

This is the first port of call on a much longer journey that takes them 200 miles through the middle of Europe. A map shows the migration route that some 2,000 people a day follow as they travel northwest through Macedonia. *Frontline Doctors* was filmed in January, and as they press on, the cold, snow-covered landscapes cast a deep chill into the bones. Traveling mostly in families, across borders, through checkpoints, they wait in long lines to be "processed." In one of the most disheartening scenes, all must walk through the cold and snow, some limping, to be registered and recorded before they can get a hot drink and find warmth. "There are some minibuses, but not enough even for the old and ill. 'This is unbelievable,'" as Chris told *The Guardian*. "'We'll help—but not too much.' It's the response in microcosm. 'We'll be a bit nice, but not very, very nice'" (Mangan 2016).

The scene changes significantly in Germany where things are better. The Tempelhof airport has been transformed into temporary refugee housing. Under the huge roof, it's bright, white, and clean, with showers, toilets, hot meals, and living quarters—rows of cubicles configured in straight lines. We meet a man called Katobi, who was a surgeon in Syria, and says with a grin. "We are lucky!" But he will be moving on to Norway if he can get a chance.

At the cold center of the film is the "The Jungle," the refugee camp in Calais, which was bulldozed by French authorities shortly after the film was completed. It is here and at another camp in Dunkirk that the brothers find the worst conditions. They, and we, are also confronted with what must be described as the existential contradictions of the current humanitarian crisis, a crisis that is revealed in multiple layers of humanitarian detail, yet one that we come to understand is simply about people in need. As we press on with the doctors we too come to understand that the only way to resolve this crisis is through geologic shifts in global attitudes and circumstances. In the following piece, Dr. Alexander van Tulleken (Xand in the film) illuminates the complexities of the migrants' medical needs, and contemplates how those needs are sometimes overshadowed by their circumstances. Writing from the perspective of an experienced humanitarian doctor, he tries to answer the question, "What should we do?" In doing so, he also outlines why a global reckoning is the only way to end the crisis.

Robin Andersen

Contradictions and Complicity in the European Refugee Crisis

Alexander Van Tulleken

I spent 14 days in January 2016 filming a documentary about the medical aspects of the European migration crisis for the BBC. The premise was straightforward: to learn more about the health problems affecting migrants on different stages of their journeys. I have worked as a physician in humanitarian crises and for the last five years I have taught and written about humanitarian responses in my job as the Helen Hamlyn Senior Fellow at the Institute of International Humanitarian Affairs (IIHA) at Fordham University. I didn't think I was naive about the contradictions and complexities of humanitarian crises but those two weeks of filming presented me with the most appalling, astounding and complex set of circumstances I have ever seen.

I was co-presenting the documentary with my twin brother, Christoffer. We followed some of the migrants' possible journeys from their arrival on the shores of Lesbos in Greece, to Athens, to the Macedonian border and, for some, into Serbia and then Germany. We finished our journey in the camps in France at Calais and Dunkirk. Migrants are not a monolith: their origins, aims and ambitions vary so widely as to make the label almost meaningless and as a result, there is no common route they take through Europe. We chose these particular locations for filming because they are all places where people are forced to pause at a border and where, therefore, various organizations are attempting to meet humanitarian needs. We hoped we might be able to meet people as they paused and investigate their health problems and the organizations working to assist them.

Each of these locations revealed extreme need and vulnerability: trench foot, hypothermia, and exhaustion in Greece; frost-bite in Macedonia and Serbia; psychological trauma and depression in Germany; the extreme public health threats of the camps in France. And each site provoked the question: "What should be done?"

Health Conditions in "The Jungle"

In order to answer this question, let me describe the public health conditions I found in the Jungle Camp in Calais. I arrived at dusk (it is possible to simply drive off the main road and into the camp) and there was a dense pall of black smoke hanging over the crude, uninsulated wood-frame shelters that housed around 6,000 people at the time of filming. It was well below freezing and the black smoke was from fires that were burning a combination of plastic and wood—whatever fuel people could find—to keep themselves warm and to cook. The health hazards of burning plastic and air pollution are well documented: they are responsible for increased rates of respiratory tract infections, and other respiratory illnesses, which significantly increase mortality in vulnerable populations such as children and the elderly.

To this respiratory hazard was added, very shortly after I arrived, CS gas (tear gas), fired into the camp by the French police. CS gas is interesting as a public health problem. Despite its widespread use in the US, there has never been a legal action against the police in the United States where anyone has successfully proved damage on health grounds from the gas. The medical literature is rather vague on its potential long-term harms because it is very rarely used for routine, day-to-day law enforcement. But studies do suggest that exposure to CS gas can cause heart and liver damage, severe respiratory damage, and increased rates of miscarriage (Hu et al. 1989). It was clear to me after being CS-gassed once that this is an extreme hazard for the elderly, people with pre-existing respiratory problems, pregnant women, and children. I asked about why the gas was being fired and was told (by NGO workers, camp residents and volunteers) that it was done simply to torture the camp's residents. This was borne out by my experience: beyond simply being present in a group of people around a fire trying to keep warm, we had done nothing particularly to provoke the police. The ground around the periphery of the Jungle is completely littered with thousands of spent CS gas shells.

By the end of four days filming in the Jungle, the crew and I had hacking, productive coughs and our clothes and skin reeked of smoke. I spent an evening observing a clinic run by a camp resident, Shakir, a Pakistani nurse, who diagnosed us with "Jungle Lung." His most common request from people seeking his care was for cough syrup: I saw over 50 people in one evening visit his trailer (used as a mobile medical clinic) simply for this remedy. I've never put cough syrup very high on my list of essential drugs but for his patients it performed three roles: helped them, and the people crowded around them, to sleep; it suppressed their coughs so they had a better chance of silently hiding on a truck to get to the UK (the destination of choice for everyone in the camp); and perhaps most importantly, it provided a caring interaction more of the kind your mum might give than a medical professional. He ended every consultation with a wink, a blown kiss and—when English was the language of the consultation—a murmured "I love you." It was high-camp and hilarious. It got a grin from everyone.

The smoke and CS gas—and the respiratory and psychological problems they caused for the majority of residents—were the most immediately apparent health threats on arrival in the Jungle. But these problems paled in comparison to other public health hazards.

Over the four days I spent in the camp there was no running water available anywhere before 1pm (including the MSF/MDM clinic) because the pipes froze overnight. It is almost impossible to overstate the seriousness of this. It means that diarrheal illness can spread extremely rapidly. It means that people are unable to wash themselves or their clothes, a consequence that leads to a proliferation of skin infections and rashes as well as an epidemic of scabies (a kind of body louse) that seemed to be all but unstoppable in the Jungle. Being without water all morning makes staying hydrated extremely difficult. Even on warmer days, when the water points would be working constantly, there were far too few of them, and they were all located so far from the latrines that I—and I have a degree in Public Health—could hardly be bothered to wash my hands.

The latrines themselves were appalling. The provision of adequate toilet facilities is the most basic part of humanitarian public health and widely available guidelines describe the minimum standards: segregated by sex, no more than 20 people per latrine, they must be well maintained and hygienic, and so on (The SPHERE Project 2011). The latrines in the Jungle were unlit, so sparsely distributed, and frequently so disgusting, that, especially at night, many camp residents preferred to relieve themselves in the sand by their tents.

These water and sanitation problems were exacerbated by vast quantities of garbage. At any location in the camp it was possible to find discarded rotting food in large quantities. This led to rat problems, which presented further ways of transmitting infections as well as novel health hazards.

As people with weakened or vulnerable immune systems coped with smoke and gas inhalation, filthy latrines, lack of water, open garbage pits, and rats, the Jungle compounded these problems with overcrowding. A typical shelter of around seven by seven feet would hold five people sleeping next to one another. The children sandwiched into these sleeping arrangements had rarely had their vaccinations of early childhood as they had come from Syria, Iraq, Afghanistan, and other places where vaccinations rates are far below optimal.[2] The camp had six cases of measles during the time I was there—a statistic that should be terrifying to everyone: young children are extremely vulnerable to infectious disease and this disease can be fatal. And yet no mass-vaccination campaign had yet been undertaken. As well as the lack of vaccinations, the camp's residents' immune systems were weakened in other ways: the constant cold and damp, lack of sleep (due to cough, itch, over-crowding and fear), and anxiety and depression provoked by the appalling conditions. I visited many families whose shelter floors were thick with mold from the constant damp.

The nature of these threats to health is that they all add up: poor water and sanitation combines with over-crowding and weak immune systems to create a perfect storm of infectious health hazards. And there are further problems beyond the risk of infectious disease: the vast psychological trauma of a prolonged stay in this environment; the physical risks of the attempts to get onto trucks and cross the border to the UK; and the lack of physical security for women and other vulnerable populations due to lack of lighting in most of the camp.

The only sector of humanitarian need that was fairly adequately provided for was food and nutrition: many of the migrants can afford to eat at the many restaurants in the camps and the food distribution seemed to cover everyone that needed it. There has been no formal survey of nutrition status but this was my impression.

Answering the Question "What Should be Done"

So, the medical needs in Calais were straightforward to understand, and in theory, to fix: the health, overcrowding, and housing conditions we found at the Jungle are all problems that have been addressed in any manual on camp management. It is possible to find solutions to every single one of these problems with technology that exists, is widely understood and used on a regular basis by NGOs and humanitarian agencies. The simple answer to "What should be done?" is to improve every aspect that we identified by on-the-ground observations and assessment of these camps. Why then, in northern Europe, in one of the richest countries in the world, do these conditions continue to exist if the solutions are so simple?

The answer to this question could be found, at least in part, in the French Government's attempt to address the conditions in the Jungle at a cost of approximately $20 million. On the eastern edge of the camp there is an area that has improved on every one of the severe needs I have described: shipping containers in orderly rows have been converted to accommodation with insulation, electric lighting, and beds. There are well lit, numerous, secure latrines and the containers are on a well-drained gravel bed, free of trash or sources of disease. The compound is expanding but at the time of filming could accommodate over a thousand people with an area that was secured by a wire fence. To apply for accommodation here (priority is given to the more vulnerable) all you need to give is a name (any name, you need not present identification) and a hand-print which would electronically open the gate so that you could come and go at any time. I interviewed the manager of the site who insisted that the hand-print information would not, and indeed could not, be distributed to any immigration authorities.

Humanitarian Practices and the Aspirations of Migrants

But when I toured this facility it was almost empty, despite being surrounded by the appalling conditions I have described. I asked many residents why they didn't move into these far more comfortable accommodations and I always got the same five answers. First, people feared that their hand-prints would be handed to the authorities. Second, they feared that the open-access system would change so that they would be trapped in a prison. Third, people said that they need to be able to leave the camp for increasingly long periods to attempt to climb onto trucks and they knew that if they were absent for more than 48 hours they would lose their places and end up with nowhere to sleep. Finally, people mentioned that in the shipping containers they were not able to cook their own food, one of the last remaining rituals of family and social life.

These are compelling reasons and they represent the limits of humanitarian thinking. As long as the answer to "What should be done?" is framed in terms of public health needs and humanitarian norms and accounting (latrines per person?), rather than in terms of the ambitions and aims of the crisis-affected people, it will fail to address the real, lived experience of the crisis. But these two considerations are to some extent mutually exclusive. The French state's attempt to address needs necessarily severely constrained people, but how could it do otherwise? Public health is their foremost consideration (as it is a foremost consideration of all modern, western states) and this is a discipline and a set of practices that fundamentally seeks to govern a population and shape their behavior to optimize health. In order to make a population healthy it is essential to "measure" them: to know their demographics, to understand them in terms of epidemiology and biostatistics. But this is precisely what many of the people in the Jungle do not want: the vast majority of them seek to leave to the UK by means they know are illegal and they are unwilling to be registered and counted and constrained. And so the choice they are forced to make is to live outside the fence and risk their health in order to have what they believe is a chance at a better life in the UK. There is a possibility for formal, organized humanitarianism to make a significant impact and Médecins Sans Frontières and Médecins du Monde are cooperating on health, water, and sanitation provisions and many other projects that mitigate against the worst effects of the environment in the Jungle. But it is hard to conceive of solutions that would truly address the public health and humanitarian practices, which would not involve some severe constraints on the lives of the residents of the Jungle. This is a collection of problems that can really only be legitimately addressed by the state, and the state has few shared interests with the migrants.

The camp in Calais was the starkest example of the choices that many refugees face between immediate physical security and comfort, and their long-term aspirations and the freedoms they feel they need to construct a new life. For many of the people migrating in this crisis the choice is simply between one kind of danger and another: risking drowning in the Aegean to avoid the risk of death at the hands of Isis or Assad. In trying to make a film about health we were forced to confront the fact that, for many people, immediate health is a secondary priority to freedom and opportunity.

The Unresolved Contradictions of a Global Crisis

The sense I had at every stage of the journey was futility, as the question of "What should we do?" began to feel increasingly irrelevant. That question suggests a western "we" that does not really exist in the divided world that is modern Europe, and it implies that there might be a "solution" to a problem that is understood and experienced differently by almost everyone involved. Witnessed up-close, this massive movement of people felt less like a crisis and more like a reckoning: a demand from the citizens of many countries that the North service the longstanding debts of empire and post-empire wars. The roads around Calais that lead to the ferries and the Channel Tunnel are almost entirely enclosed with brilliant white high barbed-wire fences and there are vast numbers of armed and armored policemen patrolling for miles around the ports. It looked like every dystopian-future movie I've ever seen. But these efforts look absurd when considered in the light of the thousands of people arriving every day in Greece. I had a sense of the unsustainability of the vast North–South inequality that exists and the irrepressible human desire to redress that balance that exists in so many minds around the world. There seem to me to be two ways to react to this manifestation of people's desire for opportunity and freedom. First, it is possible to react in fear, and build barriers along borders. There are many policy proposals that detail the ways in which migrants can be excluded and returned that seem feasible. But the sense I had was that these plans are unlikely to stop the million migrants that Europe is expecting in 2016. The second way of reacting is to treat this movement as inevitable and to lean towards more open borders. The global order that the North relies upon is creating a pressure and a demand to move that is irresistible: open borders might compel us to address this crisis in a way that recognizes these contradictions and searing global inequalities.

Notes

1. This is how the BBC describes the documentary *Frontline Doctors*: www.bbc.co.uk/programmes/b073jh6b
2. http://data.worldbank.org/indicator/SH.IMM.MEAS

References

Hu, H., Cook-Deegan, R., and Shukri, A. (1989) "The Use of Chemical Weapons: Conducting an Investigation Using Survey Epidemiology," *JAMA*, 262 (5): 640–643.

Mangan, L. (2016) "*Frontline Doctors: Winter Migrant Crisis* review—paints a picture as bleak and unforgiving as the weather," *The Guardian*, March 8, available at: www.theguardian.com/tv-and-radio/2016/mar/08/frontline-doctors winter-migrant-crisis-review

Sphere Project. (2011) *Sphere Handbook: Humanitarian Charter and Minimum Standards in Disaster Response*, available at: www.refworld.org/docid/4ed8ae592.html

7

A HUMANITARIAN BATTLEFIELD

Redefining Border Control as Saving Victims

Pierluigi Musarò

The Ambivalent Narrative of Migration Crisis

With more than a million migrants and asylum seekers[1] reaching Europe, 2015 has become known as the year of Europe's "migration crisis." Nevertheless, the so-called "migration crisis" is neither new nor exceptional, especially when viewed through an historical lens. Indeed, since the early 1990s it has been high on the European agenda and a main cause of concern for European citizens, particularly those alarmed by the "invasion" of "illegal migrants" crossing borders, as well as those preoccupied with the humanitarian duty of rescuing the lives of the "victims" escaping war or poverty. The 1990s are marked as the period when the European Union began tightening and militarizing its borders, justifying its massive investments in border controls through the narratives of national security (combating human smuggling and potential terrorists) (Mezzadra and Nielson 2013; Vaughan-Williams 2015), and humanitarianism (rescuing lives and protecting asylum seekers' human rights) (Albahari 2015; Tazzioli 2015). As such, it becomes clear how the current focus on both the securitarian and the humanitarian sides of the phenomenon supports a more complex logic of risk and benevolence, of threat and vulnerability, allowing for a security–humanitarian response (Musarò 2013; Andersson 2014).

While this European crisis, which migration agencies define in terms of "mixed migration flows,"[2] is by no means a recent and man-made phenomenon, it constitutes a policy domain that frequently stirs strong emotions and controversies (Moore et al. 2012). It is a policy area where economic, political, humanitarian, cultural, and legal points of view often clash with particular force. The complexity of these migration flows is challenging current frameworks, and Europe is struggling to develop a comprehensive architecture that balances efforts to assist persons in need with efforts to secure its borders (de Haas 2007).

Presenting the Mediterranean Sea as the setting of a perpetual emergency, the representation strategies and discursive practices enacted by military authorities, politicians, and media have been representing migrants crossing borders as a significant problem to be managed in terms of a wider social, cultural, and political "crisis." Far outstripping any real crisis is the public anxiety about migration and asylum-seeking in Europe, which in part has grown due to the media coverage of the phenomenon as well as the rhetoric of politicians, who describe Europe as being besieged by people fleeing conflict or seeking a better life (Pastore et al. 2006; Musarò and Parmiggiani 2014).

Although 2011's political uprisings in Tunisia and Libya, resulting in an increased number of people attempting to cross the Mediterranean, were reframed as a "migration crisis" requiring emergency measures and the redefinition of the EU's priorities, the co-existence of the humanitarian narratives of saving lives and the spectacle of increasingly militarized and securitized borders has been particularly highlighted since the launch of Mare Nostrum. The military–humanitarian operation—targeted at both rescuing migrants and arresting smugglers, while stopping the illegal entry of unauthorized migrants—was established by the Italian government after two big shipwrecks off Lampedusa on October 3 and 11, 2013, which resulted in the deaths of over 600 migrants. It was launched on the wave of the compassionate reaction of citizens watching hundreds of coffins on their television screens. Although Mare Nostrum signified a strengthening of two other permanent missions coordinated and financed by Frontex and Italy operated in the Mediterranean during this period (Hermes controlled the border along the Italian coastline, while Aeneas controlled migrant flows), it constituted a transformative moment in the communication strategies of Italy, because it contributed to reshaping the relationship between the military and the humanitarian aspects of the operation.

The performance of crisis through spectacular interventions, such as Mare Nostrum, Frontex's Joint Operation Triton, EUNAVFOR/Operation Sophia, or the absence thereof such as in the case of people arriving on the Aegean islands of Greece, is part of the European migration management. In the meantime, attention to performances of crisis may well obfuscate the less visible work being invested in constructing the Mediterranean as a "migration crisis" space. As Calhoun (2010) argues, crisis demands an immediate response often thought to be outside of politics. It asks that the situation categorized as a crisis be managed in some way.[3] However, this crisis management is focused only on restoring the status quo, not on changing it. Meanwhile, questions regarding what this status quo looks like remain unaddressed (Jeandesboz and Pallister-Wilkins 2014).

Focusing on the relation between the migration narratives and the production of a military–humanitarian response, this article aims to answer the following questions: Which representational regimes did the media employ to describe the military–humanitarian mission in the Mediterranean? How have rescue and border control operations been explained? How does this visual representation rearticulate the relationship between military and humanitarian mechanisms of migration governmentality? Which conceptions of humanity does this military–humanitarian imaginary come to legitimize?

Drawing upon the role of the media in war and humanitarian crisis management, the article aims to analyze how representation strategies and discursive practices enacted by the Italian Navy transform the threatening spectacle of the "migrant invasion" (De Genova 2013) into the compassionate spectacle of the "humanitarian battlefield." It concludes with remarks on the double-sided nature of humanitarian governance of migration concerned with care and control.

The Mediterranean Sea as a Humanitarian Battlefield

"We need more than a humanitarian response . . . We need political leadership and action," said Filippo Grandi, the United Nations High Commissioner for Refugees (UNHCR), on March 8, 2016. Referring to the fact that "Europe is now seeing record numbers of refugees, and migrants, arriving on its shores," Grandi stressed that "this emergency does not have to be crisis, it can be managed." Grandi, who was speaking to the European Parliament in Strasbourg, did not mention to what extent, in recent years, the militarization of migration and border controls has been explicitly bound with notions of humanitarianism. Nevertheless, I guess he is aware that the current migration crisis is considered a crisis because Europe's borders have become sites of suffering and death with the production of a humanitarian response as a result. By seeing the deaths in the Mediterranean only in terms of crisis contributes to obscuring the structural role of European border policies and everyday practices in these deaths (Basaran 2015). As such, the consolidation of Europe's external borders, as a consequence of the implementation of Schengen and the restrictive visa regime, has a direct consequence on people's ability to seek safe and legal routes into the European Union.

Unfortunately, Grandi's concern is not new. The problematic relationship between humanitarianism and politics was clearly stressed by James Orbinski, Médecins Sans Frontières (MSF), 17 years ago, while delivering his Nobel Lecture: "Humanitarianism is not a tool to end war or to create peace. It is a citizen's response to political failure. It is an immediate, short term act that cannot erase the long term necessity of political responsibility."[4] The novelty is that Orbinsky was criticizing those interventions called "military–humanitarian," while Grandi is referring to ongoing migration management, too often framed as a humanitarian emergency.

Following Grandi's concern, on June 27, 2016 a coalition of more than 100 NGOs strongly condemned new EU policies to contain migration. Criticizing the EU's refugee deal with Turkey, the NGOs expressed

> their grave concern about the direction the EU is taking by making deterrence and return the main objective of the Union's relationship with third countries. More broadly, this new Partnership Framework risks cementing a shift towards a foreign policy that serves one single objective, to curb migration, at the expense of European credibility and leverage in defense of fundamental values and human rights.[5]

Furthermore, it is worth noting that on June 17, 2016 MSF announced that it will no longer accept funds from the EU and Member States, as a sign of protest against the closure of European borders to migrants and asylum seekers. Rejecting "the instrumentalization of humanitarian aid for the sake of border control,"[6] MSF depicts the Mediterranean as a "warzone," denouncing "a mass grave created by European policies."[7]

This association between European management of migration and war is not new. If in recent years some critical NGOs and researchers have spoken of a "war"[8] that is transforming the Mediterranean Sea into a "battlefield" (Rosière 2012; Reid-Henry 2013; Balibar 2015), on September 26, 2014 the president of Italy's lower house of parliament, Laura Boldrini, stated that the number of migrants drowning in the Mediterranean amounts to "a war."[9] Even though Bigo (2014, 212) has shown in his research that "most of the military personnel participating in border control, including those patrolling the seas, firmly reject this idea of a 'war' or a front line to defend against enemies," I think we might move the analysis of the "migration crisis" beyond the military's practical regime of justification. Being aware that the terminology of a "war on migrants" risks reducing the complexity of border control through a simplistic narrative of geopolitics and conflicts of civilizations, as Bigo states, I propose to consider several factors within the broader framework of this "war." On one side, we must include the strengthening of militarization of Europe's borders, the decision to involve NATO by deploying three warships in the Aegean Sea to target people-smuggling operations,[10] the focus on deportations, and the tragic death toll. On the other, we need to consider the way the Italian army adapts its practices to the new visual, moving, "live" technology, the focus on the suffering of innocent people as a major factor in the decision to intervene, the linked discourses and practices of humanitarianism, and the media coverage stressing the micro-level individual experience rather than macro-issues of the collective social good. All these elements are typical of the current "humanitarian" (Ignatieff 2001), "mediatized" (Cottle 2006) or "postmodern" (Hammond 2007) wars.

The coexistence of the humanitarian narratives of saving lives and the spectacle of increasingly militarized and securitized borders has been particularly highlighted since Mare Nostrum's inception. As we can read on the Italian Navy's website, Mare Nostrum was established "to tackle the dramatic increase of migratory flows during the second half of the year and consequent tragic shipwrecks off the island of Lampedusa." At the same time, "the naval and air units deployed by Mare Nostrum were necessary to improve maritime security, patrol sea lanes and combat illegal activities, especially human trafficking."[11] As such, the operation was led by military personnel and means, with the participation of voluntary healthcare operators. The Italian Navy, on the one hand, deployed amphibious vessels, frigates, helicopters, a Coastal radar network, and submarines to gather evidence of the criminal activities. On the other, they were supported by several humanitarian actors: the Fondazione Rava, the emergency services Corps of the Order of Malta, the Italian Red Cross Military Corps and Nurses, and Save the Children.

Speaking the language of combatting human smuggling and potential terrorists, while rescuing lives and protecting migrants' human rights, Mare Nostrum performs the spectacle of the "humanitarian battlefield." The concept of "humanitarian battlefield" can be better understood if we investigate the communication performances of Mare Nostrum within what Chouliaraki (2013, 318) defines as a "war imaginary":

> a structured configuration of representational practices, which produces specific performances of the battlefield at specific moments in time, with a view not only to informing and persuading us, as per the instrumental aspect of propaganda, but also to cultivating longer-term dispositions towards the visions of humanity that each war comes to defend.

Assuming, with Chouliaraki (2012), that the imaginary works performatively through a morality of virtue, that is "it draws upon familiar practices of aesthetic performance so as to engage spectators with images and stories about our world and, thereby, to socialize us into those ways of feeling and acting that are legitimate and desirable in a specific culture" (p. 44), we see how these images contribute to influencing public perception, while shaping the social imaginary through moral discourses of care and responsibility.

One Spectacle for Different Publics

The spectacle of the "humanitarian battlefield" is one spectacle, but different publics understand it differently. Like the different light refractions of the same kaleidoscope, the national spectacle of surveillance, policing, and border control is also the cosmopolitan spectacle of rescue and salvation. Mare Nostrum speaks different languages to different political constituencies: to migrants and to citizens, to smugglers and to transnational activists, to right-wing government coalition members, and to NGOs. A quick look at the visual politics of Mare Nostrum makes clear what types of political and epistemological implications this "spectacle" has. Consider, for example, that since the start of the operation, Italian soldiers on ships began producing photographs and videos about the operations on the high seas that were immediately distributed by mainstream media. As such, press releases, images, videos, and films produced by the Italian Navy during the 12 months of the operation (October 2013–October 2014) might not be considered only as material or digital artifacts. Rather, they are institutional nodes in the European public sphere and subjects whose visibility impacts public discourses, collective ways of thinking, and the decision-making processes around the "migration crisis."

The extent to which these images invite us to legitimize the operation (which costs €9 million per month), becomes clear if we adopt a "visual framing" approach that takes into account how the images of rescue operations are symbolically organized, the representational genres that they utilize to convey distant suffering, and the sorts of ideological and aesthetic positioning of actors involved in this process. The Italian Navy's choice of some keywords, key phrases, and images (as well as the omission of other elements that could suggest a different perspective or trigger a different sentiment) reinforces a particular representation of reality and a specific emotion towards it.

Let me point out that Mare Nostrum (our sea) was the Roman name for the Mediterranean Sea, picked up by Mussolini to frame fascist propaganda about the "Italian lake." As the same (ambivalent) name indicates, the possessive "our" imagines the Mediterranean as a European space of care and control, while it ambiguously refers to both Italy and Europe.

In order to understand how the Italian Navy represent "us" (European citizens) and "them" (migrants) as "imagined meta-communities" and construct borders at imaginary levels, I propose to examine the performative dimension of the selected publicity images available on the Italian Navy's website.[12] Most photographs trigger sympathy for the soldiers and pity for the migrants. There are plenty of images that portray the soldiers' activities with the aim of drawing us into a community of witnesses. Emphasizing practices and discourses of care, aid, and assistance, soldiers covered this operation as a programme of humanitarian, national benevolence that institutes an "imagined community" (Anderson 1991) between spectators and soldiers from the same country: a community in which the spectator is positioned as the possible savior, while the rescued bodies are the "other." Through such images it becomes clear that border control is being redefined within a moral imagination that puts emphasis on human vulnerability. The soldiers' activities are depicted like recurring imagery of aid delivery, with rescued, grateful migrants receiving food parcels and water. Women with tiny, innocent babies are the most commonly represented subjects.

Thank You Italya: The Video of the Operation

To what extent the legitimacy of the military–humanitarian operation Mare Nostrum depends on how it is described and explained through media becomes evident through the analysis of the official video of the operation.[13] As you can see, while in the first part of the video we are invited to witness the dramatic "emergency," feeling the pressure to be concerned or upset in response to the horrifying images; in the second part, the high-adrenaline spectacle pivots on the soldiers challenging the waves to resolve the catastrophe. We are invited to read the military-security dispositive of Mare Nostrum through the moral voice of the Pope— a religious authority who is here reframed through a secular humanitarian narrative, continuing the sacred salvational narratives of rescue. An intense apocalyptic musical score immediately erupts after the Pope's words. Images of soldiers rescuing people in the high waves alternate with those of medical care interventions as the rescued reach the technologically highly equipped vessel. The visual focus is on soldiers distributing food to starving children and exhausted women. In the last shot we are faced with the smiling eyes of two grateful rescued children, with a signboard on which they have written: "Thank you Italya."

The unique perspective of soldiers constructs a celebratory positive portrayal that dominates above all else. The credibility of the "heroes" is never questioned, nor is the legitimacy of their operation. At the same time, the victimization of refugees transforms them into objects of pity. It is properly in the name of this mechanism of representation, which establishes a generalized concern for the suffering "other," that the Italian Navy justifies and legitimizes the military–humanitarian mission. The moralization of the spectator takes place through a mechanism of aestheticization of suffering that is detached from any historical or geopolitical context.

Adopting the narratives of the "emergency imaginary" (Calhoun 2010), the selection of images in the short video depicts the Mediterranean as a place where the "state of exception" takes place and migrants are reduced to "bare life" (Agamben 2005): excluded from the sphere of human values, civic rights, and moral obligations. As such, this paternalistic spectacle constructs a hierarchy of pity that reframes the military logic as an affair of humanitarian concern.

Rather than promoting solidarity in the name of human dignity, the military–humanitarian narrative certifies the complex ontology of inequality that gives specific hierarchical value and meaning to human life, while providing support to neoliberal global governance in establishing an asymmetric (in terms of both agency and dignity) *moral geography of the world* (Musarò, 2013).

Catia's Choice

This re-articulation of the military as the humanitarian is even more evident in the docu-drama co-produced by the Italian Navy and broadcast at prime time in October 2014 by the Italian national television network (RAI): *Catia's Choice: 80 miles south of Lampedusa.*[14] Catia Pellegrino is the (female) lead character of this 92-minute docudrama, chronicling the rescue of refugees crossing borders during the last two months of the Mare Nostrum operation. Alternating images of the brave rescue operations with personal stories of the crew, the video focuses on the positive influence of Catia's strength and empathetic nature in serving others, while maintaining vigilance, keeping the seas safe on her watch. Catia is the candle that helps conquer some of the darkness of our world, lighting a path of hope to those in need. Next to security scenes depicting the fight against violent and brutal smugglers, we watch scenes in which a crewmember begins crying as he recalls the dead bodies he retrieved from the churning waters.

Through the hyper-emotionalization and psychologization of the marines, these images project a moral agency of emotional fragility that humanizes and "feminizes" the armed forces within the realm of those needing "protection" (Masters 2005, 114). Emphasizing the value of personal narratives, the marines appear closer to social workers than soldiers: *social workers with guns.* This attitude is in line with what Chouliaraki (2014) has defined "the empathetic soldiering self," which is infused by the spirit of benevolence and can be associated with the soldiers' effort to cultivate a military subjectivity that sees the "other" as the self and is committed to protecting her/him as one of "our own"—"thereby, paradoxically perhaps, effecting a new 'civilianization' of the military" (p. 615).

As in the video previously mentioned, the images of this docudrama exclusively highlight the effectiveness of the marines' efforts, rather than present the causes behind the operation. The issue of irregular migration flows is here construed as a journey without destination, as a tragic game of fate. As protagonists of a crisis that comes from nowhere, migrants are depicted at the same time as subjects who are forced to put themselves in danger—departing on unsafe boats—and as subjects at risk (of death and trafficking) who need to be saved. The story is about an aid operation, and the suffering party is only ever a recipient of aid, never an agent of his or her own destiny. Furthermore, it not only denies migrants' agency to decide to move, but also translates the very notion of "human" into "life to be rescued," and transposes the human rights discourse into securing migrants' lives at sea.

In summary, while reaffirming our cosmopolitan solidarity through the language of benevolence and compassion of "our soldiers," the spectacle of the "humanitarian battlefield" contributes to feed what Mbembe (2003) calls "necropolitics"—the symbolic practice of inserting death within existing hierarchies of human life, thereby perpetuating projects of territorial sovereignty and global power.

The World Outside the Compassionate Frame

Let me conclude with a recent example that unequivocally demonstrates the integration of the humanitarian discourse of assistance and protection within the on-going language of migration governance. On October 15, 2015, during his visit to the Italian Parliament, the UN Secretary-General, Ban Ki-moon, paid homage "to the Italian soldiers who saved thousands of human lives in the Mediterranean," and thanked "the Italian population for the efforts made to welcome and assist migrants." Concluding the event, the Italian Prime Minister, Matteo Renzi, affirmed: "the Italy that welcomes you is the country of the Italian officers who became nurses to deliver babies in the ships on the Mediterranean. It is an Italy of which we are proud."[15]

Furthermore, on March 7, 2016 Renzi gave each EU leader at a migration summit a DVD copy of *Fuocoammare* ("Fire at Sea"), a documentary about the plight of refugees as they wash up on the shores of the Sicilian island of Lampedusa, which won the top prize at the 66th Berlin Film Festival.[16]

As I have shown, in recent years the bio-political imperative of managing lives is visually expressed in an aesthetic of trauma, where war (on migrants) is represented both as an intimate experience of sorrow and a public act of peacemaking. As in other instances of humanitarian government, this aestheticization of war suffering situates the concept of security on the backstage of Mare Nostrum's performances, while legitimizing the "spectacle of migrant illegality" (De Genova 2013) and nurturing a "compassionate repression" (Fassin 2012) that fails to bridge the gap between "us" and "them."

If we consider borders not as mirror-like reflections of the divisions existing in the physical –cultural landscape, but as symbolic and political barriers enacted and performed as "discursive or emotional landscapes of social power" (Paasi 1996, 63), it becomes evident how the institutional framing of the prolific communication produced by the Italian Navy during Mare Nostrum contributed to feed both imaginary and concrete makings of borders. Indeed, while before Mare Nostrum media's attention was predominantly on the "frontierization process" of Lampedusa, renamed "the border of Europe" (Cuttitta 2014), the mediated performances of the Italian army moved the fight against clandestine migration and its compassionate spectacularization into the open sea.

Furthermore, I want to shed light on the double-sided nature of humanitarian governance of migration. While Mare Nostrum, through rescue operations carried out on the high seas as well as in the territories of third countries, represented an instrument for the inclusion of migrants into the European space; at the same time, this humanitarian process of inclusion appears as an act of compassion towards victims deserving pity rather than solidarity. This double-sided nature of the humanitarian governance (inclusionary and exclusionary) not only fails to take account of specific political circumstances (Barnett and Weiss 2008), it also contributes to the media's failure in properly comprehending and reporting the "migration crisis." Indeed, if migration is reduced to a humanitarian question of saving lives and to a question of combating the smugglers, its technocratic management appears to be beyond politics. Thus, the Mediterranean appears more and more as a de-politicized border.

Let me conclude with a final point: I am not affirming that militaries deliberately manipulate communication by denying us "the truth." In the last months, I had the chance to interview several militaries who took part in the operations and I sensed how passionate they are about their jobs. As one of them said to me: "Consider the despair of these people, you see that and you see a human being in danger and anyone who has a little bit of empathy will aid people who are in distress."[17] And I agree with him. My point is a different one.

I argue that although the enhanced capacity of soldiers to directly testify what they are witnessing and relay information to journalists can do much to expose the "crisis," it can do little to explain it. In other words, despite the emotional framing that invites us to empathize with the heroes or the victims, we must be aware that solidarity can be found only if we understand global political, financial, and ethical interests in the world outside the frame. In stark opposition to this framing, we should keep in mind what has been happening in the last months. The collective march of refugees across the Balkans has rendered the agency of migrants themselves highly visible, exposing the crucial role they play in challenging existing governance structures. As it becomes clear, people on the move challenge the subject position of helpless victims, and reassert their agency, their social and political identities, their hopes and dreams, their capacity to choose their own destiny.

Notes

1. Although there is a crucial legal difference between "migrant" and "refugee," it is worth noting that in the media these terms are often used interchangeably, depending on the period and its public sentiment (e.g. according to Google Trends data, throughout 2015, searches for "refugee" remained slightly higher than "migrant," spiking in early September around the time the distressing photos of Aylan Kurdi were released), available at: www.newsweek.com/refugee-vs-migrants-whats-right-term-use-371222

2. www.iom.int/jahia/webdav/shared/shared/mainsite/microsites/IDM/workshops/return_migration_challenges_120208/mixed_migration_flows.pdf

3. Thus, considering that Europe's intake of 1 million refugees in 2015 amounts to only 0.2 percent of its total population of 500 million, crisis narratives are, in fact, a form of appropriation by policymakers—a means by experts and institutions to manage the land and resources they deem under crisis, while justifying their interventions.

4. www.nobelprize.org/nobel_prizes/peace/laureates/1999/msf-lecture.html

5. http://statewatch.org/news/2016/jun/eu-joint-ngo-letter-reject-migration-proposals-6-16.pdf

6. www.euronews.com/newswires/3208246-msf-rejects-all-eu-funding-in-protest-at-eu-turkey-migrant-deal/

7. www.msf.org/article/msf-calls-large-scale-search-and-rescue-operation-mediterranean

8. Of interest is the Frontexit campaign, whose claim is "Europe is at war against an imaginary enemy," available at: www.frontexit.org/en/

9. As 2014's death toll topped 2,500, Boldrini stated: "There is a war underway in the Mediterranean. We are talking about a war, because during the last Gaza conflict around 2,000 people died," available at: www.thelocal.it/20140926/migrant-boat-deaths-amount-to-war-boldrini

10. "The goal is to participate in international efforts to stem the illegal trafficking and illegal migration in the Aegean," NATO Secretary-General, Jens Stoltenberg, available at: http://nato.int/cps/en/natohq/news_127981.htm

11. www.marina.difesa.it/EN/operations/Pagine/MareNostrum.aspx

12. www.marina.difesa.it/_layouts/15/MMIV2-Layouts/pages/MMI.GalleriaFullscreen.aspx?PageId=1f721c47-dd5d-408d-82ad-226b3a03c23e&Guid=a3cdcf80-1680-4816-9ef3-b89ae03a5236; and also www.marina.difesa.it/conosciamoci/notizie/Pagine/20141024_annomarenostrum.aspx

13. www.youtube.com/watch?v=H7LWma67WAA

14. www.youtube.com/watch?v=0MJWdxuG0Qo

15. www.onuitalia.com/eng/2015/10/15/thanks-for-60-years-of-italy-un-partnership-said-ban-ki-moon-in-rome/

16. www.ansa.it/english/news/2016/03/07/renzi-gives-eu-leaders-copies-of-fire-at-sea_d34fa393-dc9c-4f67-af41-e8df7308558f.html

17. Interview with Rear Admiral Cristiano Aliperta, conducted in London in March 2016.

References

Agamben, G. (2005) *State of Exception*. Chicago, IL: University of Chicago Press.

Albahari, M. (2015) *Crimes of Peace: Mediterranean Migrations at the World's Deadliest Border*. Philadelphia, PA: PENN.

Anderson, B. (1991) *Imagined Communities*. London: Verso.

Andersson, R. (2014) *Illegality, Inc. Clandestine Migration and the Business of Bordering Europe*. Oakland, CA: University of California Press.

Balibar, E. (2015) "In War," *Open Democracy*, available at: www.opendemocracy.net/can-europe-make-it/etienne-balibar/in-war

Barnett, M. and Weiss, T. (2008) *Humanitarianism in Question: Politics, Power, Ethics*. Ithaca, NY: Cornell University Press.

Basaran, T. (2015) "The Saved and the Drowned: Governing Indifference in the Name of Security," *Security Dialogue*, 46 (3): 205–220.

Bigo, D. (2014) "The (In)securitization Practices of the Three Universes of EU Border Control: Military/Navy ? Border Guards/Police—Database Analysts," *Security Dialogue*, 45 (3): 209–225.

Calhoun, C. (2010) "The Idea of Emergency: Humanitarian Action and Global (Dis)order," in D. Fassin and M. Pandolfi, M. (Eds.), *Contemporary States of Emergency*, New York: Zone Books, pp. 29–58.

Chouliaraki, L. (2012) *The Ironic Spectator: Solidarity in the Age of Post-Humanitarianism*, Cambridge, UK: Polity.

Chouliaraki, L. (2013) "The Humanity of War: Iconic Photojournalism of the Battlefield, 1914–2012," *Visual Communication*, 12 (3): 315–340.

Chouliaraki, L. (2014) "From War Memoirs to Milblogs: Language Change in the Witnessing of War, 1914–2014," *Discourse & Society*, 25(5): 600–618.

Cottle, S. (2006) *Mediatized Conflict*, Maidenhead: Open University Press.

Cuttitta, P. (2014) "Borderizing the Island: Setting and Narratives of the Lampedusa Border Play," *Acme. An International E-Journal for Critical Geographies*, 13 (2): 196–219.

De Genova, N. (2013) "Spectacles of Migrant 'Illegality': The Scene of Exclusion, the Obscene of Inclusion," *Ethnic and Racial Studies*, 36(7): 1180–1198.

de Haas, H. (2007) *The Myth of Invasion. Irregular Migration from West Africa to the Maghreb and the European Union*, Oxford: IMI research report.

Fassin, D. (2012) *Humanitarian Reason: A Moral History of the Present*, Berkeley, Los Angeles, CA, London: University of California Press.

Hammond, P. (2007) *Media, War and Postmodernity*, London and New York: Routledge.

Ignatieff, M. (2001) *Virtual War: Kosovo and Beyond*, New York: Picador.

Jeandesboz, J. and Pallister-Wilkins, P. (2014) "Crisis, Enforcement and Control at the EU Borders," in A. Lindley (Ed.), *Crisis and Migration: Critical Perspectives*. London: Routledge, pp. 115–135.

Masters, C. (2005) "Bodies of Technology: Cyborg Soldiers and Militarized Masculinities," *International Feminist Journal of Politics*, 7 (1): 112–132.

Mbembe, A. (2003) "Necropolitics," *Public Culture*, 15 (1): 11–40.

Mezzadra, S. and Neilson, B. (2013) *Border as Method or The Multiplication of Labor*, Durham, NC: Duke University Press.

Moore, K. Gross, B. and Threadgold, T. R. (Eds.) (2012) *Migrations and the Media. Global Crises and the Media*, New York: Peter Lang.

Musarò, P. (2013) "'Africans' vs. 'Europeans': Humanitarian Narratives and the Moral Geography of the World," *Sociologia della Comunicazione*, 45: 37–59.

Musarò, P. and Parmiggiani, P. (2014) *Media e migrazioni: etica, estetica e politica della narrazione umanitaria*, Milano: FrancoAngeli.

Paasi, A. (1996) *Territories, Boundaries and Consciousness*, Chichester: Wiley.

Pastore, F., Monzini, P. and Sciortino, G. (2006) "Schengen's Soft Underbelly? Irregular Migration and Human Smuggling across Land and Sea Borders to Italy," *International Migration*, 44: 95–119.

Reid-Henry, S. M. (2013) "An Incorporating Geopolitics: Frontex and the Geopolitical Rationalities of the European Border," *Geopolitics*, 18 (1): 198–204.

Rosière, S. (2012) "Vers des guerres migratoires structurelles?" *Bulletin de l'Association de géographes français*, 89 (1): 74–93.

Tazzioli, M. (2015) *Spaces for Governmentality, Autonomous Migration and the Arab Uprisings*, London: Rowman & Littlefield International.

Vaughan-Williams, N. (2015) *Europe's Border Crisis: Biopolitical Security and Beyond*. New York, NY: Oxford University Press.

8

FROM PITY TO CONTROL

Regulated Humanitarianism in German Media Coverage of Refugees and Asylum

Elke Grittmann

Introduction

In 2011, an unexpected wave of protest movements against authoritarian regimes in North Africa and the Middle East caused a profound reverberation in Western public discourse. Framed in the Western imagination as revolutions in the tradition of European struggles for democratic societies, the uprisings were labeled enthusiastically as the "Arab Spring," which began in Tunisia in 2010 and subsequently spread to other countries, e.g. to Egypt and Syria. The Syrian uprising quickly turned into a full-scale war. In 2014, António Guterres, the United Nations High Commissioner for Refugees (UNHCR), described the humanitarian consequences of the crisis in Syria as "the biggest humanitarian emergency of our era, yet the world is failing to meet the needs of refugees and the countries hosting them" (Edwards 2014).

Since the outbreak of the Syrian civil war, it is estimated that 4.8 million people have fled to neighboring countries such as Lebanon, Turkey, Jordan, and Iraq, approximately 1.1 million have sought asylum in Europe, and almost 400,000 have made their way to Germany (UNHCR 2016). Thus, the humanitarian crisis has become a pressing issue not only on a transnational, but also on the national and local level in Germany. As an important international organization and "frame sponsor" (Horsti 2013; cf. Gamson and Modiglianis 1989), the UNHCR has promoted a humanitarian perspective to engage public and political action in other countries. The humanitarian perspective is not only promoted by humanitarian organizations; the suffering of distant others has also been prominently reported in the international media (Höijer 2004; Chouliaraki 2006, 2008; Joye 2010) because of the increased importance of emerging transnational digital media networks and the amplified interconnectivity of transnational communication. News media privilege humanitarian crisis and feature suffering, so that their stories may engage Western emotions and promote identification with others (Chouliaraki 2008). In her study of television representations of distant suffering,

Chouliaraki (2006, 2008) has raised the crucial question of how pity, compassion, and empathy are evoked by Western media coverage. Her study elucidates how different representations and aesthetic strategies enable ethical positions and inspire action and solidarity.

The present study seeks to broaden the theoretical perspective on humanitarian communication by positing the idea that the "suffering of distant others" remains distant for Western audiences, and that, for these audiences, distant sufferers remain "strangers we will never meet" (Chouliaraki 2013, 3). But in a cosmopolitan, globalized world where the movement of people, ideas, and goods is fast-paced, this hypothesis remains questionable.

While German media covered the humanitarian situation of the "distant suffering" of Syrian refugees in the countries bordering Syria, they simultaneously reported the refugees' flight to Europe and their situation in European countries and in Germany. The transformation of Syrian refugees from "distant others" into "neighbors" raises larger issues than simply those of distance and proximity. When the distant others became neighbors, media coverage shifted significantly; the terms "refugees," "migrants," and "asylum seekers"[1] began to be used interchangeably, and the people to whom the terms referred were portrayed as a social problem, as objects without a voice or history (e.g., Butterwegge 1996; Pickerings, 2001; Horsti 2008).

It should be noted that it is not a coincidence that research on media and humanitarian communication is generally treated as a separate topic from coverage of migration, refugees, and asylum. However, in this article I propose to draw attention to the processes of "cosmopolitization" (Beck 2012), involving global power relations, social inequalities, ongoing deterritorialization, and increasing interdependency, by analyzing the transnational, national, and local dimensions of migration, flight, and asylum reflected in German media coverage. These processes are relevant even as a humanitarian "welcome culture" (in German: *Willkommenskultur*) was emerging in German society in 2014. Networks were founded in many cities and communities to help newly arrived refugees, and Chancellor Merkel called for support, asserting "We can do it" (German: "*Wir schaffen das*"). Humanitarian support worked perfectly within state policy. Therefore, the main research question is: How did the media cover and frame the situation of Syrian refugees in the neighboring countries of Syria, on the way to Europe, and on their arrival in Germany? And how did the humanitarian perspective change from a transnational to a local one?

For this purpose, the present article proposes a qualitative discourse analysis, using the sociology of knowledge approach to discourse (SKAD) (Keller 2011, 2012) with the aim of examining the "discursive construction of symbolic orders" and their power effects (Keller 2011, 48). This approach is useful as a way to enable the analysis of the different frames and knowledge dimensions reproduced in the discourse, such as problems, values, social actors' positionings, solutions, and causes in relation to each other. Furthermore, the approach uses Lilie Chouliaraki's concepts of solidarity of salvation and of revolution to elucidate the kind of humanitarian imaginary that is constructed by media. Chouliaraki's system of analysis offers a critical perspective on the moral and political framing of the conditions and consequences of forced migration.

This chapter consists of the following sections: First, I will discuss how refugees and migrants were represented in German media in the 1990s, taking into consideration the special socio-historical background. It was an important period in public discourse for migration and asylum in Germany. The next section will theorize the framing of refugee conditions in the light of Chouliaraki's concepts of humanitarian solidarity and political solidarity. In the same section, I will also propose theoretical and methodological considerations of SKAD, focusing on the relevant aspects for the analysis. The article will discuss the use of the concepts of humanitarian communication in understanding the representation of refugees in the national contexts of host countries. Though journalism has been challenged for more than a decade by the decline in print circulation and ad revenues resulting from the rise of digital media and globalization, in many societies news coverage remains dominant in the production of public knowledge. This empirical research examines the coverage of Syrian refugees in two German media outlets in 2014, namely, *Landeszeitung Lüneburg* (LZ), a small regional newspaper that focuses on local events and topics, and *Zeit Online* (ZO), the website of the quality newspaper *Die Zeit*, which focuses on national and transnational events and topics. I am particularly interested in the shift in coverage from a distant perspective, from discourses about refugees in neighboring countries around Syria and their flight to Europe, to a local perspective, when "distant others" became neighbors. Thus, local, national, and transnational perspectives are represented in the data. The third section will present the results of the discourse analysis. Finally, the implications of the findings for humanitarian communication will be discussed.

Representations of Refugees in Media Since the 1990s

In 2015 prominent Western media dedicated long commentaries and background stories to a political initiative by German chancellor Angela Merkel (e.g., Akrap 2015; Eddy 2015), as she proposed that Germany take in thousands of Syrian refugees who were stranded in Hungary. Merkel suspended refugee regulations and flung open the doors of Germany to the refugees, consequently receiving heavy criticism from fellow party members and other politicians. Pictures of Munich inhabitants warmly welcoming refugees at the train station were widespread and gave rise to the term "welcome culture." Even though this political act by Merkel seemed an extraordinary political case, the so called "Willkommenskultur" had emerged in German civic society almost two years before. In many cities and communities, very broad and densely connected networks were founded by Germans to assist refugees by teaching them the language and providing food, shelter, clothing, and administrative services. As a result of the impact of this welcoming culture, the "Association for the German Language" (German: *Gesellschaft für Deutsche Sprache* 2014) announced "Willkommenskultur" as "Word of the Year" for 2014. According to the Association, "Willkommenskultur" means the willingness to open doors for people in need seeking asylum (ibid.). It should be mentioned that this unprecedented humanitarian support was surprising in comparison to the 1990s, when hundreds of thousands of refugees sought asylum in Germany, but were met with a climate of hostility in the form of racism spurred on by right-wing extremism. In pogrom-like attacks in Hoyerswerda (September 1991) and Rostock-Lichtenhagen (August 1992) and arson attacks on the homes of Turkish immigrants in Mölln (November 1992) and Solingen (1993), many were killed or severely injured. Although anti-racism and anti-right-wing protests took place after the attacks, politicians decided to change the asylum law to the disadvantage of the asylum seekers. They restricted the right of asylum by amending Article 16 of the Constitution, which guarantees asylum (cf. Monforte 2014). Different studies (e.g., Brosius and Esser 1995; Butterwegge 1996; Jäger and Link 1993) show that the media played an ambiguous role in the coverage of refugees and asylum in those years. Refugees were referred to as "social parasites" and "trouble makers" and dehumanized with terms like "floods" and "masses" (Butterwegge 1996, 20–28). These metaphors became pictorialized by photos and collages. For example *Der Spiegel*, a leading German newsmagazine, published a manipulated cover photo in April 1992 that shows a huge mass of migrants or refugees struggling to enter a small gate to get asylum in Germany (*Spiegel* 1992). According to Brosius and Esser (1995, 215), the media coverage incited certain groups to use violence as what they considered a necessary and legitimate tool for dealing with the refugee situation at the time. Since the 1990s, studies on media representations of migrants have demonstrated that they have been increasingly depicted in a negative light (cf. Müller 2005; Bonfadelli 2007), and since 9/11 the religion of Islam has come to represent the other (refugee/migrant) in what scholars refer to as the securitization of migration. A majority of studies focus on migrants, asylum seekers, and refugees, as the terms are used more or less as synonyms, with "migrant" used in many cases as an umbrella term. Thus, the representation of refugees has rarely been the singular focus of study. In one study on asylum in Germany, researchers found that media primarily framed asylum seekers in a negative way (Hömberg and Schlemmer 1995).

Although my focus is Germany, other studies on media coverage illustrate the frames of victimization (e.g., Horsti 2013), of invasion and infection (e.g., Falk 2010), disasters (e.g., KhosraviNik et al. 2012), and threats (e.g., Pickering 2001), often combined with the criminalization of undocumented migration through border control discourses (e.g., Burroughs 2015). The "illegal migrant" is represented as the other, one who does not belong to the nation.

However, in 2014 public discourses seemed to have taken a different direction in Germany —at least for a short period (I will come back to the current discourse in the conclusion). So, as media play a crucial role in public discourse, the question here is how they framed the topic of Syrian refugees.

The Framing of Forced Migration in a Post-Humanitarian Age

The theoretical framework of this article makes reference to Chouliaraki's arguments on distant suffering, humanitarian communication, and the media in a post-humanitarian age, addressing the question of political and ethical perspectives on humanitarian crisis with a focus on the engagement of distant (Western) spectators. Furthermore, it is based on a Foucauldian approach and sociology of knowledge-grounded discourse analysis (Keller 2011). I will first outline Chouliaraki's concept and its application to the research question; I will then integrate the concept into the theoretical framework of SKAD.

The increased interconnectedness and distribution of mediated knowledge of humanitarian crises and disasters by media and the Internet raises the fundamental question of the changing relationship between spectators and sufferers. Inspired by Luc Boltanski's seminal work on "distant suffering" (1999) and the politics of pity and Roger Silverstone's theoretical reflections on the ethical, cosmopolitan obligations of journalism in a time of transnational "mediapolis" (Silverstone 2006), a new discussion of the moral and cosmopolitan responsibilities of news media has emerged within the last decade and has focused on how coverage enables or constrains moral engagement by their audiences towards distant other (e.g., Höijer 2004; Chouliaraki 2008; Robertson 2010; Pantti et al. 2012; Orgad and Seu 2014; Joye 2015). In reference to Boltanski, Chouliaraki provides a comprehensive theoretical and analytical framework on how transnational media (she examined satellite news) produce a "sense of moral agency" under specific conditions and aesthetic strategies (Chouliaraki 2008, 329). In her seminal work *The Ironic Spectator*, Chouliaraki (2013) integrates news media as one important site in the broader context of humanitarian communication. She argues that media, and in particular news, "fully participates in the humanitarian imaginary," as media provide "one of the most important stages for human vulnerability to appear in the West" (Chouliaraki 2013, 138). According to Chouliaraki, humanitarian communication in Western societies has moved into a "post-humanitarian age," characterized by a change in humanitarian communication that has transformed the Western audience into an "ironic spectator" that is at once skeptical towards truth claims and willing to engage morally (Chouliaraki 2013, 2). For the purposes of this article, I will in particular draw attention to her differentiation of Western humanitarianism towards the suffering of distant others between solidarity of salvation and a solidarity of revolution. Chouliaraki (2013, 24) argues that both variations are reflected in humanitarianism.

Solidarity of salvation can be described as apolitical, based on the "principles of neutrality, impartiality and independence" (Chouliaraki 2013, 11). It requires a moral response that seeks to help and support. In contrast, solidarity of revolution refers to political humanitarianism, which is dedicated to redistribution and social justice. This distinction provides a fruitful approach to the study of the news media's coverage of humanitarian crisis from both an ethical and an analytical perspective. But the concept should be extended. Chouliaraki positions the relation of spectator and sufferer in the field of global power, along the axis of "the West" and "the global South." Though this division is grounded in the historical and political context, the geographical dimension is still important in the image of "distant suffering." However, under conditions of what Ulrich Beck (2012) has defined as "cosmopolitization," which leads to new encounters of interconnectivities and interdependencies of "us" and "others" both between societies and, primarily, within societies, humanitarianism is not only a question of "distant others," but—as the current movements of forced migrations prove impressively— of "global others in our midst" (Beck 2011). A solidarity of salvation or revolution could also be enabled within societies—and media play a crucial role in this process, as they disseminate knowledge.

It is this both ambiguous and powerful ability of news media to produce particular frames— verbally and visually—and "truth" about reality that leads to the question of how this knowledge is constructed in news discourse. Reiner Keller's (2011) sociology of knowledge approach to discourse offers further theoretical and methodological considerations from a constructivist point of view to assess coverage on Syrian refugees. Drawing both on Foucault and on Berger and Luckmann's theory of knowledge, Keller (2011, 48) stresses the social construction of reality and directs attention towards the "*discursive construction* of symbolic orders." A key assumption of this theory is that the discourses are regulated and structured (ibid.) and that the social is constituted and realized by discourse. The sociology of knowledge approach to discourse is thus interested in the symbolic orders of knowledge produced by sign usage.

According to Keller (2011, 43), the purpose of the research endeavor is to analyze hetere- geneous processes of the production, circulation, and transformation of knowledge. This approach is not only concerned with the contents of discourse and knowledge configuration, but also with the conditions of discourse production and power effects (ibid., 57). However, the purpose is to explore mainly the knowledge configurations composed of interpretive schemes or frames, classifications, phenomenal structures, and narrative structures.

This study will primarily focus on the phenomenal structures of knowledge in news coverage and the interpretive schemes/frames, which can be analyzed on the basis of the phenomenal structure. The strength of this approach is the systematic exploration of phe- nomenal structures constituted of different dimensions related to each other: the definition of a "problem," for example, is ascribed to particular responsibilities, refers to particular causes, and is linked to specific solutions and values (there are obvious similarities to Entman's framing approach). With this qualitative approach, the relations between these dimensions are explored and the subjects' positioning (self-other) are analyzed. First, the research material has been coded according to the phenomenal structure scheme of SKAD (Keller 2011, 59), and the main schemes and frames have been analyzed. The second step focuses on the humanitarianism constructed in the coverage of Syrian refugees.

The study analyzes the coverage in two news sources, the *Zeit Online* (ZO) and the *Landeszeitung Lüneburg* (LZ) in 2014.[2] A period of two specific discursive events has been chosen, namely the emergence of the Islamic State terror group in northern Syria and the decision of the German government to accept a further 10,000 so-called "*Kontingentflüchtlinge*" (fixed number of refugees with a special status) in summer 2014. As a consequence of these developments, the topic of the Syrian war gained greater prominence in German media. This came at the time when "welcome culture" became popular. Hence, the study examines the coverage of Syrian refugees in the two German newspapers (print and online) in the months of May, August, and September 2014. Therefore, the results must be interpreted in this context.

The *Lüneburger Zeitung* is a regional newspaper with a circulation of approximately 31,000 (print and e-paper) in 2014, published in Lüneburg, a city in northern Germany. Though newspapers in general are facing a decrease in readership, regional newspapers are still important sources for regional information. The County of Lüneburg (about 178,000 inhabitants) has also accepted many refugees (about 4,400 in 2016, Landkreis Lüneburg 2016). The broad networks of local and civil society have welcomed the refugees with "welcome culture." Thus, the topic of refugees as well as their support by many organizations and networks sparked great interest in the local news. The *Zeit Online* is the online version of the national weekly newspaper *Die Zeit*, one of the leading quality papers in Germany, and provides daily news, mainly from a national and transnational perspective.

To state things up front, the discourse was quite different from what I expected. The data consisted of 170 articles only mentioning or mainly focusing on the condition and situation of Syrian refugees; 51 articles with a main focus were analyzed. In May, the sample of the coverage of Syrian refugees was rather weak. Only 11 articles were collected (six articles LZ, five articles ZO). After the development of ISIS in North Iraq and Syria 2014, the humanitarian crisis gained more prominence in coverage in August, thus the coverage published in August and a further month, September, has also been analyzed (21 articles LZ, 19 articles ZO). The *Landeszeitung Lüneburg* (27 articles) had a strong focus on local developments and events such as local support for refugees, or administrative and bureaucratic measures (11 articles), six articles covered issues of Syrian refugees on a national level, e.g. political discussions. Their journeys while fleeing from the Syrian borders and the situation at the borders of the European Union were prominent in ten articles; 11 of 24 articles from *Zeit Online* focused mainly on the situation at the borders of the neighboring countries of Syria and seven articles focused on the national level. Four articles reported about the events at the EU-Border and two covered transnational issues, e.g. the meeting of foreign ministers. We identified the following five frames in news coverage:

1. The Humanitarian Perspective: Fate, Claims, and Needs of Refugees

Some reports seem to fully participate in the "humanitarian imaginary" as defined by Chouliaraki. The history and situation of the refugees is told from their perspective. They become visible as subjects and have—though selected by journalists—voices to tell their individual life stories, their situations, but also their problems and needs. An example is the report on a so-called "reception center" in Germany (ZO 2014, June 8), where refugees are compelled to stay after their arrival. The article focuses on the repression of Christian refugees by Islamic refugees in the center, while the conditions of asylum application processes remain untouched. A second example is the report on the precarious situation of refugees in Egypt (ZO 2014, April 30) that focuses on the lack of support and empathy by the administration. In this case, the humanitarian perspective can be observed on an individual and structural level that, according to Horsti (2013, 80), is necessary to evoke both compassion and the desire for political change.

2. Humanitarianism of Salvation: Hospitality and Support

A second humanitarian frame can be distinguished as a shift in perspective from refugees as subjects to the transnational organizations and ordinary Germans supporting the refugees. The values of humanitarianism are mainly defined by Western organizations. The article "Masses fleeing terror" (LZ 2014, August 30) describes the disastrous situation of Syrian refugees fleeing their country. The article covers the problems *faced by* refugees and their physical and emotional exhaustion and traumatization and is accompanied by a harrowing photo of a group of Syrian women and children. The display of women and children is meant to elicit emotions from the audience, showing their hopelessness as they sit with all their worldly belongings in a field that resembles a desert. The women and children refugees remain anonymous in the report; their individual lives and suffering are not visible. The refugees appear more or less as an anonymous mass without a voice, their only voice coming from major international agencies such as the International Organisation of Migration and the UNHCR, represented by their goodwill ambassador, Hollywood actress Angelina Jolie. The celebritization of humanitarian solidarity, as discussed by Chouliaraki (2013), has become part of news coverage.

While international organizations such as the UNHCR are the main actors on the transnational level, defining the situation as a humanitarian crisis requiring a humanitarian solution, humanitarian support by Germans for the Syrian refugees is highlighted by local media coverage. For example, the *Landeszeitung Lüneburg* reported about a school that donated skateboards and scooters as a welcome gesture to young refugees who had enrolled at their school (2014, August 1). The key focus (in the sense of problem definition) lies in the support and help by Germans. In consequence, they are the main actors, who take care and are responsible. This is supported by a photograph showing Syrian children with their new skateboards and scooters in front of the class. They are smiling gratefully. The media highlights the compassion and support of Germans by portraying them as selfless givers, donating gifts and providing free language lessons to the refugees. As on the transnational level, refugees are not given a voice to speak and have no interpretive power. They are represented as victims or grateful and passive recipients of charity.

3. Refugees as an Administrative Problem in Need of Regulation

Based on an analysis of the phenomenal structures of the articles, many of them construct Syrian refugees as a problem contributing to a burden, a crisis beyond control, in both Germany and the rest of Europe. Coverage on the mass "influx" focuses continuously on the numbers of Syrians fleeing their country. These articles are mainly presented as objective, neutral, and fact-based, relying on statistics, numbers, figures, and comparisons. Expressions such as "more and more refugees" (LZ 2014, August 25, September 5) or "the number of refugees continues to grow" (LZ 2014, May 21), in both the headlines and reports highlight a looming sense of danger, a catastrophe that, if not controlled, will get out of hand.

An article in *Zeit Online* (2014, August 15) illustrates this clearly, with the headline "highest number of asylum applications." This article, which deals with statistics and quantitative data, begins by stating the staggering number of 20,000 asylum applications in Germany and goes on to state that it is the highest number of applicants in more than 20 years. With sentences such as "almost three times more applications," "the second largest number of applications are from . . .," "thirteen-fold increase in new applications," followed by data googlegoogleon the monthly increase ("75% more," "40% more," "62% more"), the article seems to be objective and neutral, but with its repetition of increase the sense of danger is reinforced.

The article defines the situation as a problem for the German bureaucracy handling asylum applications—"the Syrian civil war leads to more asylum applications in Germany"—and ends with the number of open asylum applications to be processed. As in many other articles, refugees are passively mentioned, while government or state actors are actively mentioned and described as responsible. For example, the article published in *Zeit Online* with the headline "more than 100,000 Syrian Kurds fled to Turkey" (ZO 2014, September 22) focused on the Turkish government and the Kurdish party PKK; the refugees were simply a problem to be dealt with: "Turkey feels overburdened by so many people." Furthermore, the country is faced with a "worst-case scenario." Similarly, "Athens is preparing for the worst" (LZ 2014, September 5). This frame is also displayed visually, in the iconography of bilateral talks of politicians discussing measures and ways of mitigating the refugee dilemma (ZO 2014, May 29). However, it should be noted that similar terms are used in reporting the refugee crisis in Germany at the local and national level. It is framed as a dilemma that, if not properly handled by political powers and bureaucracy, could potentially escalate. Military metaphors are also widespread, e.g., "communities have to be prepared and armed." By highlighting the great increase in various numbers and data, the media present Syrian refugees as an anonymous mass. The subject position on the national and local level is depicted as an "us against them" situation; this is also the case in reporting about other host countries. Although phrases and metaphors of invasion, of "refugee floods," "rush," and "masses" are used, it should be emphasized that these reports do focus on "objective" and "neutral" data. The same metaphor of big numbers can be observed in KhosraviNik's (2009) study on the coverage of refugees, asylum seekers, and immigrants in the British press. He concluded that the use of metaphors such as "flood" is not automatically negative in that context, for example, when the numbers are tied to the claim for humanitarian support (ibid., 487). However, I argue that the problem-focused definition of increasing numbers is a constitutive part of a frame that relates to particular responsibilities and therefore legitimizes the application of seemingly depoliticized migration management measures seen as necessary.

4. Refugees as Objects of Control and Surveillance

Borders are important liminal spaces, where the movement of refugees is negotiated as a question of legality or illegality, of security, surveillance, and control, thus evoking "the integrity of the nation-state" (Pickering 2001). The control and surveillance of refugees is represented as a necessary practice in some articles. The *Landeszeitung Lüneburg* reported that the police "picked up a group of refugees" on a train (LZ 2014, May 5). The article did not provide further detail on why they were arrested. Their mobility is indirectly criminalized. The control frame is displayed fully in the context of the refugees' journey from the Mediterreanean Sea by boat and in the description of the role of the Greek and Italian authorities in rescuing and relocating them in refugee centers (ZO 2014, May 31).

The *Zeit Online* (2014, May 31) reported that "within a few hours the Italian Navy rescued about 3,000 refugees," arguing that the operations by the Italian Navy "Mare Nostrum" caused the increased "flows." The argument is that rescue operations are an incentive for refugees to risk their lives on the Mediterranean Sea. Furthermore, media disseminates the strong suspicion that terrorists might be masquerading as refugees—hence the need for stricter and tighter border controls (ZO 2014, September 28). But asylum and border politics are also very much a subject of political discussion and claims, of the humanitarianism of revolution.

5. Humanitarianism of Revolution: Political Protest against Dublin III

The situation of the refugees is rarely discussed with regard to rights, citizenship, and social justice. In these accounts mainly politicians from different parties and NGOs give their opinions. They define the political debate against refugee policy, e.g. against Dublin III demanding change in the asylum laws and migration policy (LZ 2014, May 17; ZO 2014, April 9). In the sample these positions were only marginal.

Conclusion: Regulated Humanitarianism in a Posthumanitarian Age

After the racist attacks and pogroms against refugees and migrants at the beginning of the 1990s, a number of studies in the media and migration fields concerned the role of journalism in reinforcing the concept of the "other" and in creating hostile stereotypes, attitudes, and thoughts towards refugees and migrants by (re-)producing what Stuart Hall has called "implicit" racism (Hall 1989, 155) in media coverage. Scholars such as Christoph Butterwegge (1996, 216) have recommended that the media avoid heavily loaded terms such as the "full boat," which elicit a fear of the other, a looming danger. In 2014, more than 20 years later, coverage in German media seems to have changed. The *Landeszeitung Lüneburg* and The *Zeit Online* avoid using negative expressions when reporting on refugees; sometimes, in the political and bureaucratic context, they are called "asylum seekers." Furthermore, a humanitarianism of salvation as well as a "politics of revolution" were observable in favourable coverage of the Syrian refugees. The "humanitarian imaginary" unfolded on the local, national, and transnational level. KhosraviNik et al. (2012) also observed frames of humanitarianism and justice in the British press. According to them, these are at best a form of "victimization," not a positive presentation. This victimization can also be observed in the German media reports analyzed in this article. Refugees were rarely portrayed as subjects or individuals in a humanitarian context; they usually remain objects, passive receivers of help and support, anonymous masses, without a voice, while organizations or support networks are dominant in the discourse. Refugees remain "others" that must be regulated.

However, phrases and terms such as "flood" and "flow of refugees," of invasion and masses, have been used countless times in journalistic narratives. Though both papers studied focused on the humanitarian crisis, the moment Syrian refugees crossed a border and sought security, the humanitarian crisis turned into a "refugee crisis" of the hosting countries, characterized by military and technocratic vocabularies that evoke the imagery of an invasion. In media coverage, both the local and national newspaper constructed *refugees as a social problem* for the neighboring countries of Syria, for Europe, and for Germany, rather than focusing on *problems experienced by the refugees*. By defining refugee movements from Syria as a challenge to social order, nation states and their executive and administrative institutions were presented in public discourse as the main actors that had to solve and handle the "refugee crisis." The "problem" definition unfolded in multiple numbers, data, figures, and comparisons, which led automatically to debates on possible solutions on the political, but mainly on a bureaucratic, level. This perspective on migration management was especially relevant on the transnational, national, and local level. However, the apparently neutral and necessary requirements of bureaucratic procedures are, as Zetter (2007) has pointed out, part of larger state interests, of regulation, restriction, and control. Control is not restricted to border control; it includes the prerogative to regulate anything that seems to be getting out of control. The "refugee crisis" has mainly been defined as a crisis of inadequate political handling, administrative measures, and bureaucratic procedures. It was only a small step to a public discourse of "there are too many refugees" and of "how can access be restricted?" and from there to racist protests against refugees by the right-wing, populist political movement Patriotic Europeans Against the Islamisation of the West, Pegida, which started in winter 2014/15.

As the study shows, coverage of a humanitarian crisis can't be reduced solely to the discussion of humanitarian issues from an ethical perspective. On the contrary, the humanitarian imaginary that highlights those who give support and help or political justice plays only a small role in the larger public discourse. When we talk about a post-humanitarian age, we have to broaden our understanding. As to the humanitarianism of revolution, a political perspective was almost absent in coverage. Instead, there was an increase in use of quantitative data and statistics that evoke "objectivity" and define a "problem." Emphasis is put on the apolitical, bureaucratic, and administrative management and control of refugees and forced migration, without empathy, leaving the ideological level of political decisions and the power of the states untouched. The consequences are a dehumanization of refugees and a depolitization on the transnational, national, and local level.

Notes

1. I follow Zetter (2007, 11) in his statement that "anyone has a right to claim refugee status." The Geneva Convention, 1951, provides a particular definition. According to the Convention, refugee status is ascribed to people who are forced to flee their country in fear of persecution. Although, at first glance, it seems appropriate to use the term "refugees" in the case of Syrians fleeing their country in fear of the war, I would like to stress that it is a problematic term. The causes of flight are more complex and multifaceted. The use of the terms "refugees," "migrants," and "asylum seekers" terms refer to concepts that do not describe but rather construct and create social categories and identities (cf. Zetter 2007). The production of different categories of migrants, refugees, and asylum seekers legitimizes not only regulation and restriction of migration by restrictive control but produces at the same time "others," seen in contrast to a national identity (cf. Zetter 2007).
2. This article is the first part of a larger project on discourse about refugees in German media coverage since 2014. I started the project in the research project course "Humanitarian Communication and Media" in winter 2014/15. I would like to thank all students for their engagement in the research project, namely: Lydia Brandes, Madlen Golla, Franziska Krüger, Romy Manon Langkop, Jana Martens, Marie Schmidt, Martha Stiehler, Sophia Wolf, and Antonia von Lamezan.

References

Akrap, D. (2015) "Germany's Response to the Refugee Crisis is Admirable. But I Fear it Cannot Last," available at: www.theguardian.com/commentisfree/2015/sep/06/germany-refugee-crisis-syrian

Beck, U. (2011) "Cosmopolitanism as Imagined Communities of Global Risk," *American Behavioral Scientist*, 55 (10): 1346–1361.

Beck, U. (2012) "Redefining the Sociological Project: The Cosmopolitan Challenge," *Sociology*, 46 (7): 7–12.

Boltanski, Luc. (1999) *Distant Suffering: Morality, Media and Politics*, Cambridge, UK: Cambridge University Press.

Bonfadelli, Heinz. (2007) "Die Darstellung ethnischer Minderheiten in den Massenmedien," in Bonfadelli, H. and Moser, H. (Eds.), *Medien und Migration. Europa als multikultureller Raum?*. Wiesbaden: VS Verlag für Sozialwissenschaften (GWV), pp. 95–116.

Brosius, H-B., and Esser, F. (1995) *Eskalation durch Berichterstattung? Massenmedien und fremdenfeindliche Gewalt*, Wiesbaden: VS Verlag für Sozialwissenschaften.

Burroughs, E. (2015) "Discursive Representations of 'illegal Immigration' in the Irish Newsprint Media: The Domination and Multiple Facets of the 'Control' Argumentation," *Discourse and Society*, 26 (2): 165–183.

Butterwegge, C. (1996) "Mass Media, Immigrants, and Racism in Germany. A Contribution to an Ongoing Debate," *Communications*, 21 (2): 203–220.

Chouliaraki, L. (2006) *The Spectatorship of Suffering*. London: Sage.

Chouliaraki, L. (2008) "The Symbolic Power of Transnational Media: Managing the Visibility of Suffering," *Global Media and Communication*, 4 (3): 329–351.

Chouliaraki, L. (2013) *The Ironic Spectator: Solidarity in the Age of Post-Humanitarianism*, Cambridge, UK: Polity.

Eddy, M. (2015) "As Germany Welcomes Migrants, Some Wonder How to Make Acceptance Last," available at: www.nytimes.com/2015/09/06/world/europe/germany-welcomes-migrants-and-refugees.html

Edwards, A. (2014) "Needs Soar as Number of Syrian Refugees Tops 3 Million." UNHCR, August 29, available at: www.unhcr.org/news/latest/2014/8/53ff76c99/needs-soar-number-syrian-refugees-tops-3-million.html

Falk, F. (2010) "Invasion, Infection, Invsibility. An Iconology of Illegalized Immigration," in C. Bischoff, F. Falk and S. Kafehsy (Eds.), *Images of Illegalized Immigration: Towards a Critical Iconology of Politics*, Bielefeld: Transcript, pp. 83–100.

Gamson, W. A., and Modigliani, A. (1989) "Media Discourse and Public Opinion on Nuclear Power: A Constructionist Approach," *American Journal of Sociology*, 95 (1): 1–37.

Gesellschaft für Deutsche Sprache. (2014) "Die Wörter des Jahres 2014." [Words of the Year 2014] available at: http://gfds.de/wort-des-jahres-2014/

Hall, S. (1989). "Die Konstruktion von 'Rasse' in den Medien", in Stuart Hall (ed.) *Ausgewählte Schriften*, Hamburg/Berlin: Argument, pp. 150–171.

Höijer, B. (2004) "The Discourse of Global Compassion: The Audience and Media Reporting of Human Suffering," *Media, Culture and Society*, 26 (4): 513–531.

Hömberg, W., and Schlemmer, S. (1995) "Fremde als Objekt. Asylberichterstattung in deutschen Tageszeitungen," *Media Perspektiven*, 1 (95): 11–20.

Horsti, K. (2008) "Europeanisation of Public Debate: Swedish and Finnish News on African Migration to Spain," *Javnost—The Public*, 15 (4): 41–54.

Horsti, K. (2013) "De-Ethnicized Victims: Mediated Advocacy for Asylum Seekers," *Journalism: Theory, Practice, and Criticism*, 14 (1): 78.

Jäger, S., and Link, J. (Eds.) (1993) *Die vierte Gewalt: Rassismus und die Medien*, Duisburg: DISS.

Joye, S. (2010) "News Discourses on Distant Suffering: A Critical Discourse Analysis of the 2003 SARS Outbreak," *Discourse and Society*, 21 (5): 586–601.

Joye, S. (2015) "Domesticating Distant Suffering: How Can News Media Discursively Invite the Audience to Care?" *The International Communication Gazette*, 77 (7): 682.

Keller, R. (2011) "The Sociology of Knowledge Approach to Discourse (SKAD)," *Human Studies*, 34 (1): 43–65.

Keller, R. (2012) "Entering Discourses: A New Agenda for Qualitative Research and Sociology of Knowledge," *Qualitative Sociology Review*, 8 (2): 46–75.

KhosraviNik, M. (2009) "The representation of refugees, asylum seekers and immigrants in British newspapers during the Balkan conflict (1999) and the British general election (2005)," *Discourse and Society*, 20 (4): 477–498.

KhosraviNik, M., Krzyżanowski, M., and Wodak, R. (2012) "Dynamics of Representation in Discourse: Immigrants in the British Press," in M. Messer, R. Schroeder, and R. Wodak (Eds.), *Migrations: Interdisciplinary Perspectives*, Vienna: Springer Vienna, pp. 283–295.

Landkreis Lüneburg. (2016) "Flüchtlinge im Landkreis Lüneburg," available at: www.landkreis-lueneburg.de/Home-Landkreis-Lueneburg/Bildung-Soziales-und-Gesundheit-Landkreis/Fluechtlinge-willkommen/Allgemeine_Informatonen.aspx

Monforte, P. (2014) *Europeanizing Contention: The Protest Against "Fortress Europe" in France and Germany*, New York and Oxford: Berghahn Books.

Müller, D. (2005) "Die Darstellung ethnischer Minderheiten in deutschen Massenmedien," in R. Geißler and H. Pöttker (Eds.), *Massenmedien und die Integration ethnischer Minderheiten in Deutschland. Problemaufriss—Forschungsstand—Bibliographie*, Bielefeld: Transcript, pp. 83–126.

Orgad, S. and Seu, I. B. (2014) "The Mediation of Humanitarianism: Toward a Research Framework," *Communication, Culture and Critique*, 7 (1): 6–36.

Pantti, M., Wahl-Jorgensen, K., and Cottle, S. (2012) *Disasters and the Media*, London and New York: Peter Lang.

Pickering, S. (2001) "Common Sense and Original Deviancy: News Dicourses on Asylum Seekers in Australia," *Journal of Refugee Studies*, 14 (2): 161–186.

Robertson, A. (2010) *Mediated Cosmopolitanism. The World of Television News*, Cambridge, UK: Polity.

Silverstone, R. (2006) *Media and Morality. On the Rise of the Mediapolis*, Cambridge, UK: Polity.

Spiegel. (1992) Cover: "Asyl. Die Politiker versagen." 15/1992.

UNHCR. (2016) "Syria Regional Refugee Response. Regional Overview," available at: http://data.unhcr.org/syrianrefugees/regional.php

Zetter, R. (2007) "More Labels, Fewer Refugees: Remaking the Refugee Label in an Era of Globalization," *Journal of Refugee Studies*, 20 (2): 172–192.

9

REGIONAL IMPACT OF HUMAN TRAFFICKING AND FORCED MIGRATION

Looking for Solutions in Libya[1]

Purnaka L. de Silva

Background to an Unprecedented Humanitarian Crisis

Not since World War Two have there been such vast magnitudes of human beings, desperately seeking to escape the push factors of persecution, conflict, war, famine, environmental degradation, and economic malaise brought about through conflict, corruption, and bad governance. The majority of refugees and migrants come from sub-Saharan Africa, the Horn of Africa, the Middle East and North Africa (MENA), and South Asia. The United Nations High Commissioner for Refugees *Global Trends: Forced Displacement in 2015* report, estimates that by the end of 2015, 65.3 million men, women, children and the elderly, were either: refugees, asylum seekers, or internally displaced persons (IDPs)—an increase of five million in a single year and the highest level ever recorded. From a forced migration perspective, the UNHCR notes that this figure represents one in every 113 people on the planet, displaced in 2015 from their homes and that 12.4 million persons were newly displaced by conflict or persecution, and 24 people per minute were forced to flee. Half of all refugees are children under 18 years of age.[2]

UNHCR Chief Filippo Grandi sees a worrying "climate of xenophobia" in Europe that has led to incessant media coverage by a near-hysterical press, greater support for anti-immigrant far-right groups, and controversial anti-immigration policies, all of which fly in the face of democratic principles and human rights norms enshrined in international law. Grandi noted in a current press interview that European leaders needed to do more to coordinate policies and to combat negative stereotypes about refugees. He said: "Those who do the opposite, who stir up public opinion against refugees and migrants, have a responsibility in creating a climate of xenophobia that is very worrying in today's Europe." He noted that it was unfortunate that some decisions taken by the European Union (EU) to handle this unprecedented crisis "were not implemented," calling it "a missed opportunity."[3] The same can be said for sections of the media industry, and the tabloid press in particular, which in this context could best serve democratic humanitarianism by reporting the harrowing conditions faced by migrants but often promote fear-mongering instead.

Despite the focus, hype, and global media attention on "Europe's migrant crisis," the overwhelming number of refugees and migrants are not in Europe. UNHCR confirms that 86 percent of the world's refugees are being sheltered in low and middle-income countries that are significantly less well-off economically. Turkey is the host-country with the most refugees worldwide with 2.5 million people, trailed by Pakistan and Lebanon with Libya not far behind.[4] This fact somehow tends to be ignored or underreported by the majority of the global media industry, where news coverage appears to be more focused on special interest stories that cater to American and European geostrategic and transnational security. In this way, the belligerencies of other global and regional powers involved in exacerbating the migration crisis with actions that violate international humanitarian law (Brownlie 2002) and the laws of war (Best 1997) remain outside of the news agendas. Since 2014, overseas military adventures are no longer the singular province of the big powers. Smaller, wealthy regional players such as the Kingdom of Saudi Arabia (KSA) and United Arab Emirates (UAE) are now also involved. Military analyst Matthew Hedges identifies KSA as a regional linchpin that engages in a number of military campaigns, including in Libya, with support from UAE. He notes that:

> As a result of their growing military prowess and purchases, Arab states [KSA, UAE] have started exerting their will successfully upon the international community . . . Weapon transfers to Lebanon, Egypt and Libya have seen the UAE and Saudi Arabia play a leading role in regional politics, assisting the rise of friendly regimes [Egypt] whilst also opposing those acting contrary to their interests [Libya].[5]

On August 27, 2014 the UN Security Council (UNSC) unanimously approved a resolution on Libya calling an immediate ceasefire and sanctions on parties stoking the conflict. This resolution was a day after the Pentagon stated that it believed Egypt and UAE were engaged in secret aerial bombardment of Libya.[6] It is further alleged that Emirati Special Forces with support from Egypt played an active role in fueling internal rivalries and factional fighting in Libya. According to leaked Emirati emails, UAE was shipping weapons in the summer of 2015 to protagonists in the Libyan imbroglio in contravention of an international arms embargo.[7] Destabilizing Libya is particularly problematic given its role as a pivotal "transit-hub" for human trafficking as a Mediterranean "gateway" on the doorstep of Europe.

At the same time, it appears that French Special Forces[8] seem to be working at cross-purposes in support of the non-UN sanctioned "rogue" General Khalifa Haftar from the Gaddafi era allied to UAE, Egypt, and KSA. Using Chad as a springboard, France is also purportedly fueling unrest between Tebu and Tuareg tribesmen in southeastern Libya.[9] Clandestine French activities in Libya certainly do not further the cause of supporting humanitarian action to stabilize the country or combat human trafficking/forced migration. Rather the opposite is true, where instability fosters insecurity, risk, and criminality on all sides. Given all the military adventurism and external meddling it is not a surprise that Libyans are in their current predicament and a "transit-hub" for human trafficking.

One of the unintended consequences of this instability in Libya is the fate of the unseen, unheard "silent" majority of men, women, children, and the elderly who are caught up in increasingly violent bloodletting. They make up the ranks of desperate and vulnerable refugees and migrants. One refugee from Libya that I interviewed said "we are just numbers nobody really cares whether we live or die . . . the Europeans do not want us, the Libyans do not want us [those] who want us are the smugglers they take our money and much, much, more." Another said "and ISIS kill us because we are Christian and black."[10]

Regional Instability and the "Dark Economy"

Regional instability in the MENA and sub-Saharan Africa, as a result of years of political misrule, corruption, armed conflicts and civil war, human rights abuses, environmental degradation, lack of sustainable development and livelihoods has created a perfect storm. Amnesty International reports that the refugees and migrants that flee these conditions face unspeakable atrocities and hardships in their flight to seek safety and security in democratic countries in Western Europe. Tens of thousands have died with many cases simply unrecorded. The Italian Ministry of Interior noted that 170,000 migrants arrived in Italy by sea in 2014 and the International Organization for Migration (IOM) estimates more than 3,200 people lost their lives during the sea crossing. The IOM estimates more than 1,011,700 migrants traveled by sea, and almost 35,000 by land in 2015, while other agencies put that number much higher, and these numbers have kept rising in 2016. According to IOM spokesman Joel Millman, more than 257,000 refugees and migrants arrived in Europe by sea as of mid-summer 2016, and for the third straight year at least 3,000 died on this route. In 2016, of the 4,027 refugees and migrants who died worldwide, 75 percent perished in the Mediterranean. These figures represent a 35 percent increase on the global total for the first seven months of 2015.[11]

Movement of such vast numbers of peoples under life-threatening conditions has also created a "dark economy" where men, women, and children are treated as commodities in a multibillion-dollar human trafficking industry. Somewhat akin to the era of the slave trade of earlier centuries, profits are derived from the transportation, housing, processing, placement, forced labor, and/or repatriation of humans. Significant sums of money change hands at each stage of the trek made by every man, woman, and child—even when deportation takes place. This "dark economy" in human trafficking is organized as a criminal enterprise and is paid for by the most vulnerable—i.e. the millions of migrants and refugees.

According to EUROPOL-INTERPOL, travel by 90 percent of the migrants to the EU is predominantly facilitated by members of a criminal network. Key migratory routes that are identified as main corridors for human trafficking, are fluid and influenced by external factors such as border controls. The facilitators behind migrant smuggling are organized in loosely connected networks in a multinational business, negatively affecting transnational security, with suspects originating from more than 100 countries. The structure of migrant smuggling networks includes leaders who loosely coordinate activities along a specific route, organizers who manage activities locally through personal contacts, as well as opportunistic low-level facilitators. Human trafficking suspects tend to have previous connections with other types of crime. And refugees and migrants who travel to the EU are vulnerable to labor or sexual exploitation as they are forced to repay their debts to human traffickers. EUROPOL-INTERPOL note that while a systematic link between migrant smuggling and terrorism is not proven (thus far), there is an increased risk that foreign terrorist fighters may use migratory flows, as well as the decades-old trading routes of looted antiquities,[12] to (re)enter the EU (EUROPOL-INTERPOL May 2016).

It is no secret that organised criminal groups, including the Sicilian mafia,[13] make large amounts of money from people smuggling and trafficking. These profits actually exceed the contributions made by Western governments to address irregular migration. Cathryn Costello from Oxford University's Refugee Studies Centre has estimated[14] that smugglers' revenues in Turkey alone last year were as much as 800 million euros, while a joint report[15] published in May by Interpol and Europol estimated that migrant and refugee smuggling networks earned between $5 billion and $6 billion in 2015. For comparison, the entire EU Asylum, Migration and Integration Fund is 3.137 billion euros for seven years.[16]

The multi-billion dollar "dark economy" is driven by inhuman greed that involves not only human traffickers and organized criminals but also military units in transit countries from the sub-Saharan region (e.g. Mali, Burkina Faso, Niger, Chad) and MENA (e.g. Algeria, Tunisia, Libya, Egypt) that charge "tolls" for providing "safe passage" and "watering rights." It is alleged that among this mix are some corrupt UN Peacekeepers and French troops stationed in the region.[17] We should not be surprised at the insidious power of corruption where diplomats, bureaucrats, civil servants, and all types of shady "entrepreneurs" are allegedly involved making money from selling flimsy rubber rafts and lifejackets to the provision of all manner of services to the migrants who are exploited at every turn. France suspended its Honorary Consul Françoise Olcay in the Turkish port of Bodrum after France 2 TV secretly filmed a shop owner selling dinghies and life jackets to migrants seeking to reach Greek islands. Admitting to taking part in the trade, she accused local Turkish authorities of also being involved.[18] Turkish police impounded over 1,000 fake life jackets filled with non-buoyant material in the port of Izmir, from a four-employee workshop, two of who were young Syrian girls.[19] Such testimonies of the "dark economy" are not uncommon.

The so-called "European migration" crisis has caused heightened scare-mongering and significant political rifts within the EU with some fearful member states party to the border-free area created by the Schengen Agreement of 1985 putting up border fences and re-imposing frontier controls. The xenophobic backlash against migrants also helped fuel the "Leave" campaign in the United Kingdom (UK) that advocated Brexit[20] from the EU. The building of physical barriers along the external borders of the EU impedes the freedom of movement of millions of refugees and migrants leaving them trapped in limbo, making them more vulnerable to the predations of human traffickers operating on the margins of Europe, often with disastrous consequences.

The European bloc reached an agreement with Turkey in an attempt to limit the mass movement of people to the EU, a deal that has been heavily criticized by human rights groups as contravening international law on the treatment of refugees and the tenets of democracy.[21] In Turkey most Syrian refugees come under the Turkish government's temporary protection scheme and do not count as asylum claimants. So-called "solutions" at the macro-level involving bilateral "deals" such as that between the EU and Turkey to return refugees and migrants,[22] and at the micro-level such as individual transactions between refugees/migrants and human traffickers, are not solutions at all. They only serve to prolong the agony and suffering not to mention the continued success of the "dark economy."

The Dark Side of the Media, Populism, and Injustice

It is fair to say that millions of refugees and migrants have suffered injustices of all forms of unjust treatment that go unrecorded, including: prejudice, racism, xenophobia, sexual violence, torture, as well as extortion, beatings, starvation, and forced labor. Equally grievous, they are treated as "slaves" who are not worthy of human dignity particularly en route along the smuggling routes of sub-Saharan Africa and North Africa; and the Balkans and Eastern Europe for those using land routes via Turkey. Many pull and push factors have led to this unprecedented phenomenon, facilitated and serviced by human traffickers. It is a bloody gauntlet that must be run daily by millions of desperately vulnerable human beings seeking to escape their circumstances traversing hazardous land routes and the clutches of criminal traffickers before they can brave the deadly seas in flimsy craft to reach their "promised land" on the shores of Sicily or Greece. The preferred "dream destinations" for most refugees and migrants are richer northern European countries such as Germany and Sweden. This is reflected in the UNHCR's figures for new asylum applications in 2015, which shows that Germany was the largest single recipient of refugees followed by the United States and Sweden.[23]

It is tragic therefore that among many injustices meted out to refugees and migrants is having to face the brunt of xenophobia, racism and hatred of peoples because they are perceived to be a threat on the basis of their creed, language, or color of their skin. At best they are classified carte blanche as "economic migrants' or at worst they are equated with "terrorists" in Europe and America. Unspeakable acts of terrorism and murder carried out across Europe, and even America, by small fanatical units of Islamist militants and "lone wolves" affiliated with Daesh further compound hostility towards refugees and migrants, reinforces stereotypes and their marginalization. It also makes the Europe/North America-centric mass media and tabloid press increasingly unsympathetic to their plight, or in the case of Fox news, the assertion that migrants and terrorists are equivalent. Manufactured, exaggerated untruths and hostile rhetoric is broadcast on multimedia platforms by populist/right-wing anti-immigrant politicians in Europe such as Frauke Petry in Germany, Victor Oban in Hungary, Marine Le Pen in France, Marian Kotleba in Slovakia,[24] and Donald Trump in America. All of these actors have stimulated acts of hatred ranging from verbal abuse, threats, and physical attacks to changing mainstream political discourse where it is now "acceptable" to spout racist and offensive slurs. Intolerance and bigotry are indicators of bigger societal problems than human trafficking with potential for atrocity crimes to take place.

Needed Efforts

US President Franklin Delano Roosevelt noted when confronting the crisis of his generation during the Great Depression (also applicable when facing down Nazism and Fascism, often repeated by many world leaders, the latest being US Presidential nominee Hillary Clinton at the 2016 Democratic Convention): "So, first of all, let me assert my firm belief that *the only thing we have to fear is fear itself*—nameless, unreasoning, unjustified terror which paralyzes needed efforts to convert retreat into advance."[25]

Some of many questions that need to be examined in order to determine what constitutes "needed efforts" are: What should concerned multilateral and non-governmental actors do in practical terms? How can the multi-billion dollar criminal industry driving and feeding off this humanitarian catastrophe be combated? How can forced migration, racism, sexual violence, slavery, and xenophobia be effectively countered? What are the forced and voluntary factors that pull and push thousands of human beings to undertake precarious and life-threatening journeys across vast expanses of inhospitable deserts, harsh terrain, and deadly seas with little more than what belongings they can carry? Why is there a deficit of generosity and human kindness in the face of this unprecedented mass movement of peoples?

What is clear from the outset is that there are no "quick fixes" to what is arguably one of biggest humanitarian catastrophes of our generation. Shortsighted policies adopted by European and American legislators who are fearful of or influenced by populist/right-wing anti-immigrant leaders so often repeated in the press do not solve anything. For example, placing naval assets in the Mediterranean Sea offers only a false sense that "something is being done." Combating the scourge of human trafficking and forced migration necessitates a comprehensive understanding of the mechanics of how and why migrants and refugees embark upon their journeys. What is required is a complete re-evaluation and re-exploration of multilateral, regional and local policies and actions. It is the responsibility of concerned UN member states, UN agencies and civil society actors—including, quite importantly, religious and faith-related organizations—to address these issues. This unprecedented humanitarian crisis is in need of courageous leadership such as Pope Francis and Chancellor Angela Merkel, who stand up to the bigotry and ignorance of extremists and promote values of humanity, compassion and the greater good. In 2015, Chancellor Merkel refused to "shut the door" on genuine asylum seekers and welcomed more than a million refugees. Also in 2015, Pope Francis pleaded for every European Catholic parish/faith-based community to show solidarity and human kindness, and "take in one family of refugees," saying he would start with the Vatican.[26]

Changing the Media Discourse

Media debate so often revolves around questions of policy and security that the human-interest story is given short shrift, with the rare exceptions of National Public Radio (NPR) and PBS/Frontline in the US, and a few other outlets. It is often overlooked in current media debates that refugees and migrants are not only people in search of human security, and thus in need of protection and basic shelter, but are also individuals with diverse potential, skills, education, and capacity to contribute. They long for a peaceful future that is free of violence, and want to build their lives in new settings and make their own living. In addition to their inalienable human rights, each migrant and refugee the majority of whom are young people are a source of valuable social and human capital. They have the potential to benefit societies, especially those with largely aging populations, creating opportunities for industry, economic growth, and professional innovation to rich spiritual, religious, and cultural diversity.

In general, humanitarian themes are missing in media coverage, as they are incompatible with frames that imply or emphasize anti-immigrant fears. Changing the media discourse must entail fact-checks and counter-narratives to the multimedia messaging and rhetoric of anti-immigrant politicians who spread fear and misperceptions of vulnerable refugees and migrants. Such themes should include the articulation of international human rights laws and responsibilities by UN agencies, host country governments in Europe, as well as humanitarian organizations from the non-governmental/faith-based sector—to protect these people seeking sanctuary and new beginnings. Such legal obligations, political responsibility, and moral leadership should apply equally to the ruling elites in other host countries such as Turkey, Libya, Lebanon, Pakistan, and Afghanistan. It also applies to governance, law and order issues in sub-Saharan and MENA source and transit countries: Senegal, Nigeria, Ghana, Mali, Burkina Faso, Niger, Chad, Central African Republic, Sudan, Eritrea, Somalia, and Sudan, as well as Syria and Iraq.

Trouble with Global "News Makers" and Military "Adventurists"

A problematic aspect of media reporting on Libya came to the fore in 2014 with the outbreak of intra-Libyan factional hostilities. The exodus of American and European diplomats and Western journalists resulted in limited "eyes on the ground" with the exception of stringers and freelancers. News reports were sourced externally and became increasingly reliant on diplomatic and military intelligence "sources," which became regular fare as "the facts". Less-than-accurate briefings of the ground situation were rebroadcasted multiple times passed off as accurate news reports to global publics unaware of what was going on. Perception unfortunately makes up for reality in the 24/7 information age. A good case in point involves the rebranding of strongly pro-Western Libyan revolutionaries as anti-Western "Islamist" militants in 2014 by analysts sitting thousands or hundreds of miles away at their desks in America and Europe. Some of them had in fact invited very senior retired American and British general staff officers, British politicians, and top international legal experts to assist in attempts to build viable governance and national security/border protection structures.[27] Irrespective of all that, Libya has been labeled a "failed state" in the global media. Something that the UN-supported "Unity government" is addressing with new attempts to reintegrate and rehabilitate armed factions, and reconstruct the country and its very lucrative oil and gas industry. Unfortunately, "black gold" and mineral wealth are often a curse that invariably attract external meddling.

Global media networks play their part to spread disinformation and misinformation to suit the geostrategic and transnational security interests of hegemonic Western powers. For example, Western media reported that the so-called "Islamic State" (Daesh) had infiltrated the former Gaddafi stronghold Sirte in 2011–2014, and that these terrorists could possibly "take over" Libya, a country located just across from Western Europe. Pentagon officials claimed in 2016 that Daesh had around 6,500 fighters. Reports from sources inside Libya always maintained that at most there were only a couple of thousand.[28] The Pentagon's judgment was called into question when a brigade of Libyan fighters allied to the UN-approved "unity government," primarily from Misratah, overran Daesh positions in a rapid three-week offensive. These fighters and their operations room commanders are some of the very same pro-Western Libyan revolutionaries who had been wrongly accused months earlier.

Understanding Libya to Find Solutions

Given that some of the main land and sea routes to Europe traverse this vast and lawless country, the regional impacts of human trafficking, forced migration, and transnational security are examined through the prism of Libya. Such an approach sheds light on ways to address questions on transcontinental migration to Europe and the "dark economy" of human trafficking. Turkey is the other major transit-hub; however, mass migration by land routes has been impeded by internal instability and physical barriers at the external borders of the EU. This makes Libya a more "acceptable" if longer transit country, especially during favorable weather conditions for sea crossings from spring to autumn. Solutions to the problem of human trafficking must therefore be looked for in Libya. It is imperative that policymakers, legislators, international civil servants, media personnel and humanitarian actors understand Libya in its current state. They must avoid any varnish or wishful thinking or preconceived notions of official spokespersons, media professionals and analysts (many of who have not set foot in Libya).

Libya is simply massive by all counts and made up of an area of 1,759,540 square kilometers (679,362 square miles). Its total land boundary length is 4,383 kilometers (2,723 miles) that is shared with: Algeria 982 kilometers (610 miles), Chad 1,055 kilometers (686 miles), Egypt 1,1150 kilometers (715 miles), Niger 354 kilometers (220 miles), Sudan 383 kilometers (238 miles), and Tunisia 459 kilometers (285 miles). The Libyan coastline is 1,770 kilometers (1,100 miles) with a coastal plain that is frequently marshy. However, there are more than 1,600 kilometers (1,000 miles) of beaches with easy access to 22 kilometers (12 nautical miles) of territorial sea limits in the southern Mediterranean Sea.[29] These geographical attributes and the inability to effectively police such vast swathes of land and sea, make Libya an ideal haven and "transit-hub" for human traffickers. Only 520 kilometers or 280.77 nautical miles separates Libya from Sicily, which is the closest point in the EU. Invariably, human traffickers abandon their human cargoes in flimsy craft quite soon after the vessels leave Libyan waters.

First of all, post-2011 Libya is an unwilling host to refugees and migrants. The country perceives itself as being as much a victim of the negative consequences of mass migration as many European countries. Libyan officials, whatever power faction they support, speak from a common national legal position. They refer to "illegal immigration" (a term that is not accepted to be politically correct by international humanitarian organizations such as UNHCR, IOM) that involves the "clandestine movement of foreign citizens into their country" that does not fulfill the legitimate conditions or authorization to stay.[30] Libya is distinguishing between three types of "illegal immigration", namely, refugees/migrants who stay in Libya over the long term; pass through Libya to EU countries; and enter Libyan territory to cross into non-EU countries. Libyan officials summarize reasons for the phenomenon of "illegal immigration" as the lack of sustainable development, economic opportunities, civil war, corruption, poverty and unemployment in states that are a *source* of "illegal immigration"; the acceptance of illegal immigrants as "residents" by European countries and the provision of work opportunities or housing, healthcare, living benefits, and in some cases livelihoods; and the geographical location of Libya and its long Mediterranean coastline close to Sicily and its oil economy. Rampant corruption and the presence of organized criminal networks and armed gangs in source and transit countries bordering Libya (and EU) fuel human trafficking, which feeds off the multibillion-dollar human trafficking "industry" that boosts the growth of this phenomenon exponentially.

The Libyans also strongly point out the failures of EU and American Overseas Development Assistance (ODA) programs, and foreign policy, over many decades in sub-Saharan Africa and MENA countries; arguing that in fact American foreign policy since 9/11 and the years of President George W. Bush in particular destabilized countries such as Iraq and Afghanistan, adding to refugee and migrant flows; and that matters came to a head under President Barack Obama where Syria was allowed to implode and Libya made ungovernable after the initial "NATO-led intervention" to topple the dictator Gaddafi. They claim that American diplomats "did nothing" while UAE and Egypt with backing from the Saudis were allowed to contravene internal law and the laws of war, play favorites and meddle in Libya, triggering a violent power struggle since 2014. Libyans also blame this nexus of external forces for corrupting top diplomat Bernadino Leon, UN-Special Representative of the Secretary-General for Libya to play a "not-so-honest role" in the country's affairs. It is reported in leaked Emirati emails that SRSG Leon supported the UAE's position of favoring selected protagonists during peace talks that he chaired; turned a blind eye to alleged UAE sponsored gun running in contravention of the UNSC arms embargo; and that the UAE rewarded Leon with a high-paying job to ostensibly "train their diplomats," which he was offered

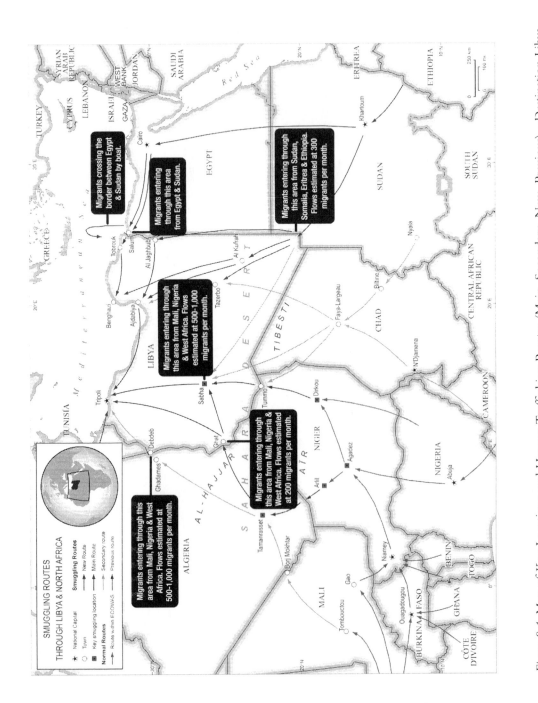

Figure 9.1 Map of Key Locations and Human Trafficking Routes (Main, Secondary, New, Previous)—Destination Libya.

Source: © ISSD Malta (Map by Guillaume Le Sourd based on ISSD Malta map/data).

when he was a "supposedly impartial" high UN official.[31] The five permanent members of the UNSC and the administration of Secretary-General Ban Ki-moon have kept quiet the "Bernadino Leon Scandal". Hand-in-hand with such disregard for international law and probity stands the global media industry, which has not presented accurate knowledge-based information about the country to global politics at the time of writing. The destabilizing of Libya has led to rampant corruption and porous borders that human traffickers have exploited to funnel their human cargoes to Europe. All of the above have contributed to the lack of development, economic opportunities, corruption, poverty and unemployment, low standards of living, and lack of basic services in countries that are a source of "illegal immigration," as well as armed conflicts, civil wars, political turmoil, instability, and "coercive" or "forced migration."

Libyans divide the most important source countries of "illegal immigration" into two groups, namely: *MENA and sub-Saharan Africa* (i.e. Egypt, Tunisia, Morocco, Sudan, Algeria, Somalia, Ghana, Mali, Ethiopia, Chad, Sierra Leone, Eritrea, Democratic Republic of Congo, Niger, Nigeria, Senegal, Cameroon, Mauritania, Ivory Coast, Djibouti, Zambia, Guinea, and Burkina Faso); and *West Asia and South Asia* (i.e. Iraq, Syria, Palestine, Lebanon, Jordan, Afghanistan, Pakistan, Bangladesh, India). Usually refugees and migrants from these countries obtain access to Libya through legitimate means and later travel to Europe illegally. However, there is also record of the entry of "illegal immigrants" from these countries, as well as cases of the use of fraudulent visas.

Libyan Realities of "Illegal Immigration"

The daily rate of migration of up to one thousand people and yearly approaching half a million or more represents a serious transnational security threat, especially if they centralize in the south of Libya, which is unstable. National estimates in April 2016 puts the figure at almost double the number, which indicates an increased inflow possibly because the Turkish and Balkan routes to the EU have been restricted somewhat. Human traffickers ferrying refugees and migrants are quite ingenious, and are already seeking alternate routes through Libya especially during a calmer Mediterranean from spring to autumn. Apart from these developments there is risk of very significant increases in rates of "illegal immigration" to Libya (more than expected yearly rates) for a number of reasons. For example, there is a possibility of sudden and dramatic collapse of governance and economic structures in neighboring countries to the south of Libya. Not to mention the emergence of starvation, famine, malnutrition, and disease caused by drought affecting arable land and decimating livestock, lack of potable water, desertification, climate change, and political and economic crises. Also, locusts and other pests and diseases destroying crops can impact negatively on the economies of these countries. Other factors include rebel groups, armed groups and warring factions causing conflicts, civil wars, extra-judicial killings, crimes against humanity, and even genocide, as well as increasing crime rates in neighboring countries especially to the south. Last but not least the encroachment of large numbers of Chadian Tebu tribes into southwestern Libya is dwarfing indigenous Libyan Tebu tribes and fueling conflict with Libyan Tuareg in this region.

Human Trafficking Routes

In looking for solutions to the problems of human trafficking and forced migration we have to go farther afield to countries where refugees and migrants originate and to transit countries

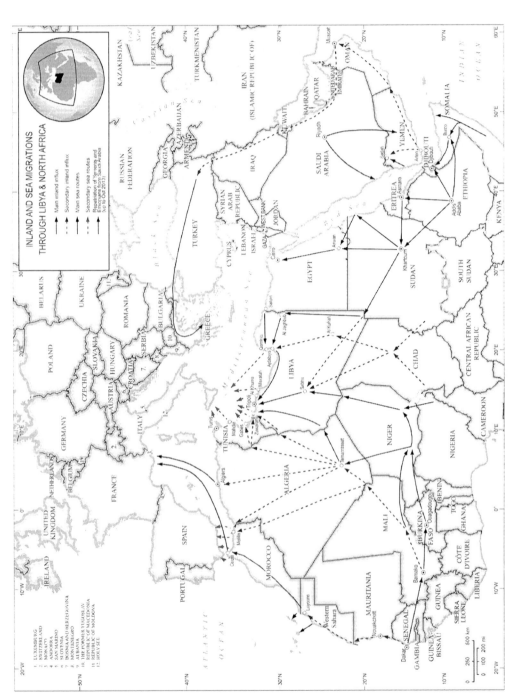

Figure 9.2 Regional Human Trafficking Routes—Destination Europe.

Source: © ISSD Malta (Map by Guillaume Le Sourd based on ISSD Malta map/data).[32]

bordering Libya. The best way to comprehend the scale of the phenomenon is to check out regional human trafficking routes in the map in Figure 9.2.

Negative Effects of "Illegal Immigration"

The increasing and exceptional numbers of refugees and migrants moving to EU countries has resulted in a number of negative effects. In particular, the rise to power of extreme right-wing "fascist" or "neo-Nazi" political parties using the pretext of an anti-immigration agenda to increase popularity. Such unforeseen "blow back" can have a long-term negative effect on global geopolitical stability and security. In Libya, the increasing rate of "illegal immigration" has had a significant adverse effect on the country's economic outlook, along with the inability to cope with providing basic needs to such huge numbers of often quite desperate people at a time of national instability and upheaval. The presence of large numbers of "illegal immigrants" indirectly affects the general budget and services provided by the Libyan state on account of population congestion and increased demand for rationed goods and supplies; and the inflow of huge numbers of illegal immigrants may result in an increased rate of inflation, unemployment and more crime in Libya. This situation is contributing to the spread of organized crime and growing human trafficking networks of all kinds— i.e. leading to breakdown in law and order (e.g. kidnapping, ransom, extortion, robberies, murder, rape, and general societal malaise). A recent Amnesty International Report is entitled: *'Libya is Full of Cruelty': Stories of Abduction, Sexual Violence and Abuse from Migrants and Refugees* (2015).

The falsification of documents to show "Libyan nationality" has enabled some "illegal immigrants" to infiltrate security and military institutions, which represents a serious threat to national security given that such people are not vetted or screened. There have been numerous instances of infiltration by wanted terrorists from Daesh, criminals and convicts posing as "refugees," which has even led to the breakout of violent anti-social elements from Libyan prisons. The infiltration of persons from neighboring countries who work in favor of the deposed Libyan dictatorship has led to further chaos, fear, and instability in the country. From a health standpoint there have been increased outbreaks of communicable diseases and problems caused by congested settlement in unsafe, unsanitary, and at times, appalling conditions.

There has also been an adverse effect on the social fabric of Libya with a growing illicit trade in drug trafficking, counterfeit currency and goods (including narcotics, spirits, and wines), spread of prostitution, alcoholism/drug abuse, and even contributing to black magic, sorcery, and superstition. Evangelical Christian proselytization has led to cases of unrest, as in the events of March 2013 in Benghazi, where a Coptic church and the Egyptian consulate were attacked, which worsened relations between the two countries. There have also been isolated reports of activity by certain Shiite advocates to spread Shia doctrine with the risks of this leading to sedition between members of the Libyan community. While there may be no direct correlation of some of these events to the mass movement of refugees and migrants, rumors abound, and in a world where perception is reality, local social media reinforces such prejudices against refugees and migrants.

Visual Effect

The photos in Figure 9.3 and 9.4—taken by ISSD Malta associated field researchers—provide a sense of perspective and illustrate the levels of organization required by human traffickers

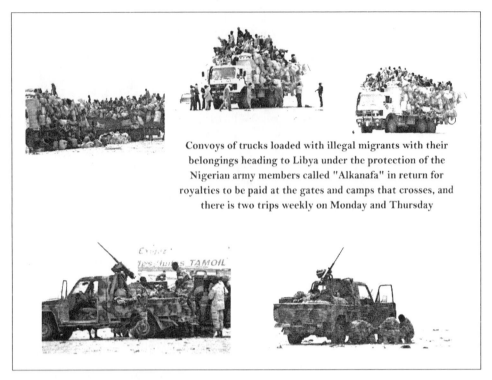

Convoys of trucks loaded with illegal migrants with their belongings heading to Libya under the protection of the Nigerian army members called "Alkanafa" in return for royalties to be paid at the gates and camps that crosses, and there is two trips weekly on Monday and Thursday

Figure 9.3 Correction: Niger (not Nigerian) army members called "Alkanafa."

Source: © ISSD Malta.

to traverse the inhospitable desert terrain. Southern Libya lies in the Sahara; eastern Libya, western Egypt, and Sudan are in the Libyan Desert. The ability to navigate trackless deserts and water are essential to the operation of human traffickers. The three largest oases in Libya's desert region are Al-Kufrah, Ghāt and Ghadāmis. In the southwestern Fezzan desert there are *ergs* or immense sand dunes hundreds of feet tall that cover 20 percent of the area. Here, *sabkhas* or depressions in the desert floor contain underground water aquifers that feed random oases. The Fezzan is largely on an even plane, with the exception of the southern Chadian border, where the craggy Tibesti Massif mountain chain sits. Encompassing a vast expanse of 9,065,000 square kilometers (3,500,000 square miles) the Sahara Desert covers the entire breadth of North Africa—i.e. from the Atlantic coast in the west to the Red Sea in the east; and the Mediterranean Sea and Atlas Mountains in the north to the southern Sahel area and the Sudan.[33]

Looking for Solutions in Libya

Libya seeks to address the issue of mass migration of refugees and migrants within the framework of multilateral cooperation and in accordance with international law. In order to do so, they seek support from leading nations, such as Germany and America, as well as UN agencies specializing in international human rights law. The objective is to design and implement a strategic action plan in order to "close the open door" to human trafficking by criminal networks and stop terrorist infiltrators using Libya as a launching platform. Bilateral

Figure 9.4 Convoy of Toyota Pickup Trucks Loaded with Human Cargo from Sub-Saharan Africa Ready for the Long Journey to Libya.

Source: © ISSD Malta.

and multilateral cooperation is envisaged in terms of goodwill and principles of human rights enshrined in international law with authority over all parties including refugees/migrants, source and transit countries bordering Libya, the Libyan State, EU countries, the UK, and the United States. Libya does not want to follow Turkey and hark back to the dark days of Gaddafi where mass migration was used as "political blackmail," and resulted in dubious financial practices where European governments paid the dictator to keep migrants away from the shores of northern Mediterranean countries.

Addressing the Phenomenon of "Illegal Migration"

There is general consensus that tackling the mass movement of refugees and migrants is well beyond the scope of a single country and certainly Libya. In fact, it engulfs the whole Mediterranean basin, MENA region, sub-Saharan Africa, and Europe. Libya must therefore cooperate with trusted bilateral and multilateral partners to develop a clear policy and strategic action plan. Such an objective can only be achieved through concerted efforts locally (i.e. between institutions and ministries concerned with the Libyan nation state), regionally (i.e. involving source, transit, and border countries to Libya), and internationally with relevant trusted bilateral partners such as Germany, the UK and US, and multilateral organizations. It must be noted here that the UN has not won the "hearts and minds" of the Libyan peoples by expressly ignoring citizens' sovereign rights to elect their own government.

What applies for a small country such as Libya is also applicable to powerful countries such as America or Germany. No state irrespective of size, geopolitical power, and economy strength can address these issues alone and combat the multibillion-dollar criminal enterprises

115

of illegal immigration and forced migration. There has to be cooperation, coordination, exchanges of information, collective use of media networks, and general goodwill between affected countries, as well as greater cohesion at the regional and international level. For this to happen however, *trust and respect* must be fostered and strengthened. Therefore French-sponsored conflict inside Libya harms these collective efforts, and sows distrust and disharmony.

The complexity of this situation requires media narratives able to extend the discussion of migration policies well beyond the standard parameters, which mostly focus on European or US responses. Combating human trafficking, forced migration and terrorist infiltration requires a carefully designed strategic and tactical action plan that covers many dimensions, including: security, intelligence, law and human rights, sustainable development, economics, social policy, and politics. Such an action plan perspective would aim to secure land borders and the seacoast of the Mediterranean basin. All participating border security (e.g. FRONTEX the European Agency for the Management of Operational Cooperation at the External Borders of EU member states),[34] intelligence, police, and military agencies need good communication and coordination with each other—which has not been the case thus far. Furthermore, the impact of the Brexit has yet to be calculated. EU countries and their American allies must accept the criticism that their overemphasis on a "counter-terrorism" strategy is a narrow focus that will not succeed; unless and until *adequate attention is paid in practice* in well-funded efforts to resolve short-term and long-term pull and push factors noted above in source, transit, and border countries to Libya, and other similar human trafficking "hubs" (e.g. Turkey, Greece, and the Balkans). Policies of affected countries and those of multinational inter-governmental entities such as the EU, African Union, the Arab League, NATO, INTERPOL, EUROPOL; and multilateral organizations such as those in the UN system must be redesigned without delay. They must reconcile *immediate needs* to "interdict" the flow of desperate refugees, migrants, and terrorists from traveling to Europe (something of a logistical impossibility) with *long-term holistic measures* aimed at stabilizing source, transit, and border countries, and hubs such as Libya. It must involve collective political will on the part of these entities to provide professional assistance and allocate adequate resources to improve governance, national/transnational security and economic performance/productivity.

Strengthening Laws in Libya to Combat Human Trafficking and Improve Transnational Security

In order to deter human traffickers and organized crime, strict new laws and regulations must be designed to prosecute persons engaged in such illegal activities. These laws must be capable of targeting their support networks and collaborators in source and transit countries, and focus on corruption and graft. Situation-specific, real-time requirements necessitate swift amendments to previous laws to be enforced, as opposed to taking multiple years. In particular, specific laws relating to nationality, naturalization, freedom of movement, work, property ownership, and residence need to be amended to curtail activities of criminal networks. Laws and penalties must be enhanced for visa fraud and all actions related to the unlawful transportation of refugees, migrants, and illicit workers. Current immigration laws and regulations should be modified to lawfully arrange for labor importation. And suitable work environments need to be created for qualified individuals that bring benefit to the national economy as practiced currently in Germany.

Libyan legal experts would like to see the amendment of Law No.6 of 1987 on the "regulation of entry and residence of foreigners in Libya" so as to make it comparable to laws in other countries; and to increase punitive sentences for criminal acts associated with human trafficking by any means. As with all laws, there are still those who are tempted to circumvent Libyan justice and security, and national and international laws, across the Mediterranean basin region and Europe. "Illegal immigration" has become a heavy burden for Libyan security because of the widening of the southern border and the porous nature of the desert region. To support these efforts Libya must apply a system that codifies the terms of entry and residence; determines legal measures to combat human trafficking and terrorist infiltration; and impose strict sanctions against criminal gangs and networks that operate human trafficking "enterprises" to deceive vulnerable people, many of whom dream of "safety and security", or "economic paradise" beyond the conflict ravaged, environmentally degraded and impoverished borders of their own countries.

There are a number of legal and transnational security procedures that Libya can adopt, such as developing a legislative system to criminalize human trafficking and "illegal immigration," and make the punishment of gangsters more punitive and stringent in order to deter and scale back their operations. Monitoring of agencies and travel companies involved in the ingress and egress (including deportations) of "illegal immigrants" must be tightened and intensified. At the same time victims of "illegal immigration" need to be dealt with in a manner that takes into consideration the fact that besides being victims of circumstances, they have suffered physically, psychologically, and morally—for example abduction, sexual violence, slavery, and other abuse of refugees and migrants (Amnesty International 2015). This is certainly not the case now. Likewise, there must be greater collaboration on national and transnational security matters between responsible Libyan authorities such as the Ministry of Interior, border guards, coast guards, and other institutions mandated to combat human trafficking.

At the international level there is urgent need for increased cooperation and coordination that includes violations of national Libyan laws, rights, duties, and interests. Libya needs to effectively implement international conventions on countering transnational organized crime with special focus on human trafficking and terrorist infiltration, which would have an extremely favorable impact on the transnational security of the Mediterranean basin region. Such acts would be complemented through intensified investigations in corridors used by human traffickers and police actions to arrest individuals active in arranging, gathering and trafficking refugees and migrants, particularly in seaports, fishing villages and beach areas. Libyan police action must involve regular communication, coordination with the International Police (INTERPOL) and the European Police (EUROPOL) on transnational law enforcement and other legal procedures to prosecute "overseas persons"—such as those in Gulf Cooperation Council (GCC) countries, the Balkans, Eastern Europe, Turkey, and Sicily—currently involved in human trafficking and terrorist infiltration.

Effectively countering human trafficking and forced migration requires genuine cooperation and coordination between the "exporting" (source), "transit," and "receiving countries" such as Libya, Turkey, and Lebanon as well as in Europe. Such transnational security cooperation must take place within a well-funded framework where there is exchange of necessary information, human intelligence (e.g. face recognition), and data comparison in real time to apprehend organized criminal gangs and networks involved in human trafficking and terrorist infiltration. Concerted education and awareness-raising campaigns must be conducted in the "launching areas" of human traffickers in Libya, especially in Zuwarah, Alzawia, Tripoli, Tajura, Qarapoly, Khoums, Zliten, Misratah, Tobruk, and Benghazi. The information and thoughts contained in this chapter are derived from detailed research conducted inside Libya, across sub-Saharan Africa, covering West Africa, Central Africa, and the Horn of Africa) and in MENA countries on combating human trafficking, forced migration, and terrorist infiltration. The research is ongoing and continuously being updated.

From a wider, transnational security perspective, it is imperative for peace and stability to reign in Libya so that policy recommendations, such as those contained herein, can be successfully implemented to bolster national and regional efforts. Libya is a comparatively wealthy country with a relatively small population of around 6,259,000 people. Provided there is "enough of the pie to go around" from the benefits of a rejuvenated oil and gas industry, maintaining peace and stability should therefore not be that much of a problem. Of course, as noted above, "external meddling" in Libyan affairs and military adventures must be brought to a complete halt. Libya has tremendous potential and could have an immense positive impact on the region in combating human trafficking and forced migration, as well as countering terrorism and safeguarding transnational security; a positive narrative of which the media industry, humanitarian agencies, international law enforcement, and global publics should be made cognizant and act upon for the greater good.

Notes

1. Early version presented at "Managing Migration: Solutions Beyond the Nation-State" Conference in Siracusa, Sicily, April 18–19, 2016 organized by the Institute of Global Affairs of the London School of Economics and Political Science.
2. UNHCR report "Global forced displacement hits record high," available at: www.unhcr.org/en-us/news/latest/2016/6/5763b65a4/global-forced-displacement-hits-record-high.html
3. UNHCR Chief Filippo Grandi's interview, available at: http://unhcr.org.ir/en/news/11421/UN-refugee-chief-warns-of-worrying-'climate-of-xenophobia'-in-Europe
4. BBC news report "Refugees at highest ever level, reaching 65m, says UN," available at: www.bbc.com/news/world-36573082
5. *Defense News* report by Awad Mustafa "Saudi, UAE Influence Grows With Purchases," available at: www.defensenews.com/story/defense/policy-budget/budget/2015/03/22/saudi-uae-influence-grows-with-purchases/25013385/
6. CNN news report by Laura Smith-Spark, Jomana Karadsheh and Schams Elwazer "U.N. Security Council passes Libya resolution amid concern over secret airstrikes," available at: www.cnn.com/2014/08/27/world/africa/libya-unrest/index.html
7. *The New York Times* news report by David D. Kirkpatrick "Leaked Emirati Emails Could Threaten Peace Talks in Libya," available at: www.nytimes.com/2015/11/13/world/middleeast/leaked-emirati-emails-could-threaten-peace-talks-in-libya.html?ref=topics&_r=1
8. *The Guardian* news report by Chris Stephen "Three French special forces soldiers die in Libya," available at: www.theguardian.com/world/2016/jul/20/three-french-special-forces-soldiers-die-in-libya-helicopter-crash
9. Jacques Foccart "ran Africa affairs" from his offices in Paris and the French "army dictated politics in its former colonies and reaped economic rewards" *The New York Times* diplomatic memo by Steven Erlanger "French Colonial Past Casts Long Shadow Over Policy in Africa," available at: www.nytimes.com/2011/04/18/world/africa/18francafrique.html?_r=0
10. Excerpt of personal interviews in Malta, April 2016. Just two of the testimonies of many, gathered over years of fieldwork (ongoing since 2011) by an "army" of volunteer field researchers associated with the Institute of Strategic Studies and Democracy, Malta, a small think-tank of which I am Director. Their commitment and sacrifices are duly acknowledged.
11. Reuters news report "Bodies found off coast of Libya as migrant toll climbs: IOM," available at: www.reuters.com/article/us-europe-migrants-idUSKCN10D0TQ
12. BBC *Magazine* news report by Simon Cox "The men who smuggle the loot that funds IS," available at: www.bbc.com/news/magazine-31485439; The *Washington Post* news report by Loveday Morris "Islamic State isn't just destroying ancient artifacts—it's selling them," available at: www.washingtonpost.com/world/middle_east/islamic-state-isnt-just-destroying-ancient-artifacts--its-selling-them/2015/06/08/ca5ea964-08a2-11e5-951e-8e15090d64ae_story.html
13. *Time* news report by Lorenzo Tondo "How the Mafia Make Millions Out of the Plight of Migrants," available at: http://time.com/4134503/mafia-millions-migrants/
14. *Forced Migration Review* (January 2016) *Destination: Europe*, Issue 51, Oxford University's Refugee Studies Centre, available at: https://issuu.com/fmreview/docs/fmr51_destination-europe

15. EUROPOL news report "EUROPOL AND INTERPOL ISSUE COMPREHENSIVE REVIEW OF MIGRANT SMUGGLING NETWORKS," available at: www.europol.europa.eu/content/europol-and-interpol-issue-comprehensive-review-migrant-smuggling-networks

16. Quoted from *IRIN* (The inside story on emergencies) Opinion on Migration by Melissa Phillips "IS involvement in people smuggling is a red herring," available at: www.irinnews.org/opinion/2016/08/05/involvement-people-smuggling-red-herring?utm_source=IRIN+-+the+inside+story+on+emergencies&utm_campaign=f026637acb-RSS_EMAIL_CAMPAIGN_ENGLISH_MIGRATION&utm_medium=email&utm_term=0_d842d98289-f026637acb-75432781

17. ISSD Malta field report, excerpts presented to senior members of *Deutscher Bundestag*, British House of Lords, NATO, EU/European External Action Service and UN.

18. BBC news report "French honorary consul sold boats to migrants in Turkey," available at: www.bbc.com/news/world-europe-34229332

19. BBC news report "Migrant crisis: Turkey police seize fake life jackets," available at: www.bbc.com/news/world-europe-35241813

20. *The World Post* featured an excellent analysis by Craig Calhoun "Brexit Is a Mutiny Against the Cosmopolitan Elite," available at: www.huffingtonpost.com/craig-calhoun/brexit-mutiny-elites_b_10690654.html

21. *The New York Times* news report by James Kanter on "European Union Reaches Deal With Turkey to Return New Asylum Seekers," available at: www.nytimes.com/2016/03/19/world/europe/european-union-turkey-refugees-migrants.html?_r=0

22. *The Guardian* news report by Jennifer Rankin "EU–Turkey deal to return refugees from Greece comes into force," available at: www.theguardian.com/world/2016/mar/18/refugees-will-be-sent-back-across-aegean-in-eu-turkey-deal

23. UNHCR report *Global Trends: Forced Displacement in 2015*, available at: www.unhcr.org/576408cd7

24 BBC news report by Rob Cameron "Marian Kotleba and the rise of Slovakia's extreme right," available at: www.bbc.com/news/world-europe-35739551

25. President Franklin Delano Roosevelt's first inaugural address, March 4, 1933, available at: www.infoplease.com/t/hist/inaugural/37.html

26. CBC news report on Pope Francis' appeal, available at: www.cbc.ca/news/world/refugees-pope-appeal-1.3217455

27. I was privy to three of these high-level meetings in October-November 2011 and 2012.

28. ISSD Malta field research reports.

29. Geography and topography of Libya, North Africa, available at: www.nationsencyclopedia.com/geography/Indonesia-to-Mongolia/Libya.html

30. ISSD Malta field research interviews.

31. *The New York Times* news report by David D. Kirkpatrick "Leaked Emirati Emails Could Threaten Peace Talks in Libya," available at: www.nytimes.com/2015/11/13/world/middleeast/leaked-emirati-emails-could-threaten-peace-talks-in-libya.html?ref=topics&_r=1

32. I am indebted to Guillaume Le Sourd, UN Geographic Information Systems Officer in New York, who evaluated the original map created in Arabic by my ISSD Malta colleagues.

33. Geography and topography of Libya, North Africa, available at: www.nationsencyclopedia.com/geography/Indonesia-to-Mongolia/Libya.html

34. FRONTEX border security operations, available at: http://frontex.europa.eu

References

Amnesty International (2015) *"Libya is Full of Cruelty": Stories of Abduction, Sexual Violence and Abuse from Migrants and Refugees*, London: Amnesty International.

Best, G. (1997) *War and Law Since 1945* (Revised ed.), Oxford: Clarendon Press.

Brownlie, I. (Ed.) (2002) *Basic Documents in International Law* (5th ed.), Oxford: Oxford University Press.

EUROPOL-INTERPOL (May 2016) *Migrant Smuggling Networks: Joint Europol-INTERPOL Report*, The Hague: EUROPOL-INTERPOL.

United Nations High Commissioner for Refugees (2015) *Global Trends: Forced Displacement in 2015*, Geneva: UNHCR.

United Nations Security Council. (2017) *Final Report of the Panel of Experts on Libya* established pursuant to Resolution 1973 (2011) (S/2017/466), New York: United Nations, available at: http://reliefweb.int/sites/reliefweb.int/files/resources/N1711623.pdf

10

THE DROWNING OF SPHERE IN THE MEDITERRANEAN

What Has Happened to Humanitarian Standards in Fortress Europe?

Pamela DeLargy

Europe and Modern Humanitarianism

Europe is the birthplace of modern humanitarianism, the very place where the well-known humanitarian principles of impartiality, neutrality, and response based on need were developed in the mid 1800s by Henri Dunant who founded the International Red Cross movement. These principles have guided global disaster and conflict response for more than a century (albeit sometimes more in theory than in practice) and have served as foundations for the development of European Union and bilateral humanitarian policies (ALNAP 2015). In the past few decades, European governments and civil society have also been strong proponents of establishing measures of accountability in global humanitarian assistance programs. They have played leading roles in the development of standards for humanitarian response, beginning with the standards set out in the SPHERE Handbook, first published in 2000 and updated regularly thereafter. The SPHERE Handbook sets out minimum standards for care in key life-saving sectors such as water supply, sanitation, and hygiene promotion; food security and nutrition; shelter, settlement, and non-food items; and health action (SPHERE 2011, 2015). European governments and NGOs have also played leading roles in the development of the consensus-based Core Humanitarian Standard on Quality and Accountability which, based on input from thousands of humanitarian workers and long consultations, sets out commitments that organizations can use to improve the quality and effectiveness of the assistance they provide. The Core Humanitarian Standard focuses very much on the rights of those affected by conflict and disasters and emphasizes "the right to life with dignity, and the right to protection and security as set forth in international law, including within the International Bill of Human Rights" (Groups URD et al. 2014).

European states and agencies have been particularly insistent on the importance of protection of vulnerable people in humanitarian settings and have been the strongest supporters of programs to prevent gender-based violence, to protect children from exploitation and to ensure that the needs of the elderly and the disabled are met. Given this history of European leadership in the global humanitarian community, it is both surprising and tragic that the continent seems to have left much of that commitment behind when it comes to caring for refugees and migrants recently arriving on the continent. Indeed, a cynic might ask whether those standards, which Europe has championed, are only applicable in faraway places but not on European territory.

As the fine points of humanitarian accountability were discussed in Istanbul during the World Humanitarian Summit in May 2016 and as European governments and civil society pledged their commitment to the Core Humanitarian Standard, Sudanese refugees were fending for themselves in a squalid camp in Calais without even basic sanitation, and Syrian refugees were arriving exhausted on the shores of Lesbos but finding no shelter from the sun and no first aid unless they happened to be met by a kind local resident or a self-funded volunteer. While the latest innovations in humanitarian communication were explored at the WHS, Eritreans and Somalis, abandoned by their smugglers on sinking boats in the Mediterranean were trying desperately to call for help. While the professional humanitarian community discussed ways to empower refugees and displaced people, some European governments were erecting fences and mobilizing border guards, leaving families stranded in muddy fields with no food or shelter. While European leaders advocated for gender considerations, women and girls who had experienced the most egregious sexual violence and exploitation in Libya were arriving in Italy; they were lucky to be rescued in the sea (many have perished) but will likely never receive any care for their trauma. And despite the lip service paid to protection of children, there are thousands of unaccompanied child refugees who have arrived and "disappeared" in Europe in the past 18 months. They are Egyptian and Syrian, Eritrean and Iraqi, Somali and Nigerian. Some as young as ten have made their way all the way from Afghanistan only to be living hand-to-mouth on the streets of Paris or in "the Jungle" camp in Calais (ODI 2016).

Eighteen months after the advent of the "migrant crisis" in Europe, thousands of people are stranded in squalid conditions after some European countries closed borders and while EU member states argue over whose responsibility the refugees are. Despite the successes in some countries that generously took in and care for thousands of asylum seekers and are providing so many with a chance for a better future, the care for those stranded at borders or in limbo without asylum and without means to go anywhere else does not meet even the minimum of humanitarian standards that are provided in camps in Jordan or Sudan or Thailand. Less wealthy countries in other regions who host an even greater proportion of the world's refugees are watching Europe carefully. They are surprised to see that the conditions of those in the Greek camps or on the border of Macedonia are so poor, given the easy availability of logistical, technical and financial resources in European countries. They ask why they are expected to respect humanitarian standards and refugee law when wealthy Europe has chosen not to. Indeed, after the European Union made a deal with Turkey to return refugees now in Greece, Kenya proceeded with plans to close Dadaab camp, the largest refugee camp in the world, and send the Somalis home, using the same arguments the European Union did. Which leads one to ask: Will Europe, the birthplace of modern humanitarianism, also sounds its death knell?

This essay seeks to provide some context for understanding the specific challenges to humanitarianism in Europe today as well as the implications for the global humanitarian enterprise. First, we must understand how the arrival of so many refugees into Europe fits into the global humanitarian discussions. Europe's "migration crisis" was only briefly seen through a humanitarian lens. Mostly, Europeans have seen the arrival of refugees through the lenses of regional and global politics, border security, and global terrorism, asylum rights, and social welfare policies. Humanitarianism fell very low on the list. But the labelling (of what might have been handled in a calm and organized fashion) as a "crisis" turned out to be prescient; it has truly turned into a crisis—a political crisis, above all. The mishandling of the in-migration has led to profound political instability within and conflict among European states. Xenophobia has become a feature in the national politics of almost every EU member state. The impact of the migration on European politics remains to be seen. The very survival of the European Union is at stake. Endless hours have been spent discussing one unrealistic migrant "burden-sharing" plan after another, and yet there is no coherent policy. If the Brexit vote in the UK is any indication, the impact may be dramatic.

Migration politics have dominated the European media for many months. Academics have weighed in on costs and benefits of migration and best practices in social integration. Policymakers have debated every aspect of asylum policies and procedures, and activists have organized around refugee and migrant rights. But there has not been commensurate attention to the actual situation of the refugees and migrants themselves. Hundreds of thousands of people have been on the move, many risking their lives on dangerous sea journeys or travelling on foot for thousands of miles. They are tired and scared and are arriving where they may not speak the language or understand the situation. Some are wounded or ill. Some have been severely traumatized by war or by hellish experiences en route, including the loss of family members or friends during the journey. They all took the greatest of risks simply to be safe and have a future but on arrival in Europe many were not afforded even the most basic humanitarian support and, worse, were often greeted with hostility or violence.

If such large refugee movements occurred in Africa, the Middle East, or Asia and were met with such a chaotic response, including neglect of basic needs and rights of refugees, global criticism would be quick and loud—and almost certainly led by Europe. Yet Europe's failure has shown the world's richest continent unable or unwilling to cope with just over a million refugees. The question is: why? For all the political hysteria over migrants, there has been remarkably little analysis or evaluation of its humanitarian aspects. The humanitarian community must have honest analysis of the challenges and the responses (or non-responses) in Europe, not only for the sake of those needing support in the region but also for the sake of the whole humanitarian enterprise. The migration dynamics and the responses in Europe have been peculiar, to be sure, but there are many lessons to be learned.

Humanitarian Challenges in Europe

The numbers were big, and sudden, but not entirely unpredictable; they were part of a larger set of population movements.

There had been a steady movement of refugees and migrants into Europe across the Mediterranean and from the East for decades, but from summer 2015 the rapid increase of people (mainly Syrians) taking the Balkan route was dramatic. Over a million people sought refuge in just a few months. Yet those who had been watching the larger (global) humanitarian situation carefully were not surprised. The flight to Europe is clearly connected to humanitarian failures in other places. The reason Syrians decided to leave are not difficult to deduce. The UN appeals for humanitarian funding for Syrian refugees in Jordan and Lebanon had not brought in nearly enough funds to maintain basic services for those who were in camps or supplementary assistance for those living outside of camps. Child education programs had to be cut back and there was even a nutritional emergency when the World Food Programme had to cut rations. Combined with restrictions on employment and the depletion of all savings, this led, inevitably, to the decision of many Syrian families to move on to places where they could have a more secure future. Given these goals and its geographic proximity, Europe was a natural destination. The movement had started much earlier and only escalated in 2015. For Eritreans in Sudan or Ethiopia, the motivations were similar—young (often urban) people who felt stranded and completely dependent on rural refugee camps with no options for education or employment decided to take their chances on the dangerous journey across the desert and the sea simply to have the possibility of a future. Thousands have died and they are well aware of that. But they see the risk as better than dying the "slow death" of dependence and idleness in desolate camps (Delargy 2016).

There were also other global dynamics at work. A few years ago, Australia adopted a draconian policy of interception of "boat refugees" to prevent any arrivals on Australian shores. The Australian government pays for those who are intercepted, to be sent to Nauru or Papua New Guinea where they remain in detention in desolate conditions. Abuses have been widely publicized and Australian policies condemned by most human rights groups. These policies also cut off a traditional migration route for Afghanis, which precipitated a Westward shift among Afghani asylum seekers; many joined Syrians on the Balkan route. The horrific destruction caused by the war in Yemen also pushed long-settled Somali refugees back across the Red Sea to become part of the flow of people from the Horn of Africa onward to Libya and Italy. Thus, the arrival of so many refugees on European shores reflects not only the understandable human desire for greater long-term security in a stable region, but also the inability of the humanitarian system to meet basic needs in other places.

Changing Demographics and the Demonizing of Refugees

Changing demographics, routes and destinations made it hard to plan for appropriate humanitarian response; demographics have also been used to demonize refugees.

Migration dynamics depend on a very wide variety of factors, both "push" and "pull." For most of those arriving in Europe, the original push factors have been clear—war, terrorism, climate change, oppression, or the mere search for survival. For many, the secondary migration decision (onward migration from the first place of safety) has depended on a more complex set of factors, including the presence of family or friends in destination countries, information (and misinformation) on conditions, routes, and asylum possibilities.

The demography of the recent migration flows to Europe has changed across time, along with the routes taken, depending on the opening and closing of borders, perceptions of migrants and refugees about safety or destinations, and on the smuggling businesses. Not knowing who was moving where and not predicting the migration dynamics impeded humanitarian response planning all across Europe. How could one know what food or shelter needs would be or what health conditions people would arrive in? Data and information systems to track arrivals had to be developed—but given the lack of precedents, it was also not clear whose job this should be.

The demographic composition of arrivals also shifted constantly. For a number of years until 2014, the central Mediterranean route (from Libya to Malta or Italy) had been most active, especially since the collapse of the Libyan government's ability to regulate its own borders. Most people arriving were young men from the Horn of Africa or West Africa who had survived the dangerous desert crossing with intention to try their chances in getting to Europe or just to get work in Libya, long a labor destination. In 2014, this began to change; more women and children also took the Libyan route, including ever-larger numbers of unaccompanied children. In 2015, the opening up of Germany to Syrian asylum seekers also led to a significant increase in families crossing to Greece from Turkey and taking the Balkan route. These shifts in demographic composition and routes have seriously affected the ability to plan for humanitarian response. In 2014 there was not much discussion of protection issues. But the dramatic increase in numbers of unaccompanied children, thousands of whom have "disappeared" across Europe and may be at high risk of exploitation and abuse, as well as the growing recognition of the levels of sexual violence experienced by many women and girls travelling the Libyan route, have brought protection needs to the foreground.

The demography of the arrivals has also been politicized and played into the xenophobia in many countries. Some of the European media and many populist politicians, noting the high proportion of young men in the early arrivals, questioned whether a legitimate refugee population would have so few women and children. The young men arriving were often accused of deserting their families, of not being willing to fight for their country, or even of being part of a planned religious invasion. The involvement of young males from immigrant families in terror attacks in France, Belgium, and Germany increased the suspicion and fear of young male refugees. When the demographics changed to include more children and families, there was slightly more sympathy—yet even then, the more xenophobic media looked for reasons to blame the refugees—with criticism of mothers crossing the sea to Greece for endangering the lives of their children or accusations that refugees were only seeking welfare benefits, not to work or go to school. In some countries in Europe, there has been outright refusal to recognize the asylum needs of Muslim refugees even though this is a direct violation of EU migration policies and the 1951 Refugee Convention.

Limited Experience to Manage Transient Populations

Humanitarian actors had limited experience with programming for transient populations.

In many emergencies, people fleeing conflict or disaster seek safety and arrive in a place (a camp or a shelter) where they stay until they can return home (though of course, they may stay for years); such settlement means that basic services (health, education, sanitation, etc.) can be established in a relatively stable setting. Humanitarian organizations have global experience with the delivery of such camp-based services. But a distinctive feature of the European refugee arrivals is that people have not remained where they first arrived. Most had other destinations in mind —places where they could join relatives or friends or where they thought they would find jobs—so they kept moving. When Germany opened its doors to asylum seekers in 2015, thousands of people moved through the Balkans with the intention to get to the German borders. For some, the urgency to keep moving—before a border closed or before they were registered (and thus, according to EU rules, forced to claim asylum in the country they were in)—became the greatest priority. A family on the Macedonian border today might not be there tomorrow; following up on their health needs was often impossible. On the Balkan route, it was only when people made temporary stops that their needs could be properly assessed. But the humanitarian responders, whether experienced organizations or spontaneous volunteers, had little experience designing responses for transient populations (Walker 2016).

Politicization of Refugee and Migrant Arrivals

Across Europe, the politicization of the refugee and migrant arrivals determined willingness to provide humanitarian support. The purposeful withholding of humanitarian assistance is part of an effort to deter arrivals.

The international humanitarian system that has developed over past decades was largely designed to deal with conflict and natural disaster displacement in other, poorer regions. It was blindsided by the sudden arrival of hundreds of thousands of refugees into Europe. Humanitarians used to working in other regions assumed that wealthy European states, replete with logistic and technical expertise, would assume responsibility for providing assistance to those arriving who needed care. But many European governments failed to organize any humanitarian response. Why? Reasons ranged from lack of preparedness to inexperience to simple hostility to the refugees (sometimes on religious or cultural grounds). Not only were many governments unwilling to organize and support humanitarian assistance for people arriving, their actions such as erratically closing and opening borders and having security forces deal with arrivals exacerbated the crisis by purposely making movement as difficult as possible. Thousands (including young children and the disabled) were forced to move long distances by foot (when it would have been relatively simple to provide transport). Some governments punished refugees with detention, left them on borders with exposure to the elements, separated families, or even condoned physical violence by security forces or local anti-migration groups. In short, state response to the population movements sometimes actually created a humanitarian crisis rather than managing the movements in an orderly fashion, with respect for human rights and humanitarian standards.

A consistent and overriding theme over the past two years in the European policy discussions and the media has been what will deter refugees and migrants from attempting the crossing into Europe. The desire to stop the arrivals has been the guiding principle of a series of EU negotiations and agreements with transit countries (e.g. Turkey, Morocco, Sudan), of a number of development assistance (and sometimes security support) programs in countries of origin (e.g. Eritrea, Ethiopia), and greater assistance to improve basic services in the countries with large numbers of (potentially onward moving) refugees such as Jordan and Lebanon. But the idea of deterrence has also been a major factor in determining humanitarian response inside Europe.

This notion of deterrence has been used as a justification for distinctly anti-humanitarian policies, including restricting or cutting back on maritime search and rescue missions in the Mediterranean (the British Home Secretary famously suggested that not rescuing people in danger at sea could solve the problem by deterring others from attempting the crossing). The situation of refugees and migrants in the camps outside of Calais is a prime example of the confusion of humanitarian response with migration politics. Calais has a long history as a transit site for migrants and refugees seeking to get to the UK from the European mainland. In an effort to keep refugees out of the town, the local government opened up an old recreational facility and the land around it, where thousands have now settled. Local volunteer groups were the only ones providing assistance until the government, under pressure and with EU funds, contracted a charity to provide food and minimal health care to a limited number of settlers in the area, but basic sanitation and hygiene services were not provided in the settlement until humanitarian groups took the local government to court (Dhesi et al. 2015) As the settlement grew, with help from volunteers from all over Europe (see Calaidipedia), the local authorities have responded with security forces and tear gas, bulldozing of dwellings and a refugee constructed church and mosques, and restrictions on volunteer support, while at the same time attempting to either repatriate refugees and migrants or get them to apply for asylum in France so that they are then "in the system." The UK (the desired destination of the Calais refugees) sees the congregation as a security issue, only, and has provided huge financial resources for security infrastructure in France. But almost all refugees who have successfully made it to the UK (smuggled under trucks or even walking the Eurotunnel) have been granted asylum—indicating that they are legitimately refugees and it has been well documented that many of the unaccompanied children in Calais have family in the UK and thus some claim to asylum there. Yet the refusal to provide basic humanitarian support to refugees and even to destroy shelters already built or to restrict volunteer support in such camps has been claimed as a humanitarian policy since it might "prevent more people from risking their lives on dangerous seas crossings." This policy shows a serious lack of understanding about migration decisions, but nevertheless persists. And it is a major reason for the poor humanitarian responses in many parts of Europe.

Failure of States to Respond

Even as the state failed to respond (or made things worse), the traditional non-governmental humanitarian actors had limited experience in the European context, no presence in the affected areas, or were hesitant to get involved.

International humanitarian organizations faced their own challenges when confronting the refugee situation in Europe—most of them had no operational agreements with European governments and no presence in refugee-affected areas. They also had no budget lines for work in Europe; their donors funded their work in other parts of the world and these funds could not (and should not) be diverted for activities in Europe. Many agencies also feared getting involved. They depended financially on European government donors and did not want to risk their funding by getting involved in controversial support for refugees and migrants in Europe. (Certainly, an agency that is dependent on UK government funding, would not want to be seen as helping out in Calais, given the official UK position about refugees there. It took some courage on the part of MDM and MSF to get involved there.) Among the traditional humanitarian organizations, there were long debates about mandates but also hesitance to spend any available core funds in wealthy Europe since the funds were desperately needed for people in emergencies in Africa or Asia. What this meant for refugees arriving in Europe is that the international humanitarian system—so often led by European NGOs and funded by European states and the EU—faltered when it had to be mobilized on European territory. Agencies, which had long experience negotiating humanitarian access in places such as Myanmar or Sudan seemed to have no idea how to negotiate with the local authorities in France or Greece. And the local authorities, no matter how sympathetic, were trapped in the regional politics of deterrence and the local politics of populist xenophobia. This, and the lack of a coherent (and accepted) European plan for relocation of qualified refugees as well as the lack of promised financial and human resources support from the EU, has resulted in the dreadful situation of thousands of men, women and children in substandard camps in Greece.

Humanitarian Support from the Bottom up

When states and the traditional humanitarian agencies failed to respond to needs, it fell to individuals and small groups to mobilise humanitarian support. A huge proportion of assistance in Europe has been provided by volunteers.

While the large agencies delayed and debated mandates, thousands of individuals across Europe and hundreds of small community groups began to provide help to those arriving by sea or land. Fishermen in Greece and Italy rescued people from the sea and local communities mobilized to receive and feed those arriving. Young people and retired people across Europe volunteered their services. Indeed, one of the most distinctive and impressive aspects of the European humanitarian response has been its dependence on largely untrained volunteers. A large part of the humanitarian assistance that states and humanitarian agencies would be responsible for on other continents has been carried out by local citizens.

The scale of volunteerism has been remarkable and diverse. Volunteers are conducting sea rescues (MOAS is surely the first private family-run maritime search and rescue ship and the Spanish lifeguard groups working on Greek shores have saved hundreds of lives), are setting up laundries (the Dirty Girls of Lesbos), collecting and distributing clothes, cooking meals, establishing schools and libraries (Jungle Books in Calais), building shelters, developing language and asylum application apps (Techfugees), assisting with family reunification and asylum applications, providing first aid and medical support, and even conducting censuses. In Calais, British and French volunteers organized themselves into health, sanitation, shelter, and protection groups—nearly replicating the "cluster" system utilized in almost all UN emergency response elsewhere. And a volunteer team from Birmingham University pro-vided the hygiene and sanitation assessment in Calais that was used in the court case that forced the local authorities to improve water and sanitation. It is also volunteers who have raised awareness of the problems and vulnerabilities of the thousands of unaccompanied youth; British volunteers and activists continue to press Parliament to accept those with family ties in the UK.

The role of volunteerism in the European migration response deserves serious study (Borton 2016). Many of those who worked first in Calais or in Italy with earlier arrivals later also volunteered in Greece when Syrians began to cross from Turkey. They helped local communities provide basic care for refugees long before any of the big humanitarian agencies began to respond. The humanitarian impulse is clearly vibrant in Europe—but it is more reflected in individual commitment than in state responses or even in the responses of the traditional international humanitarian community.

Although this individual humanitarian spirit is inspiring, dependence on volunteers also presents some challenges for effective humanitarian action. Most of the volunteers assisting new arrivals in Europe have not been trained in humanitarian response, are not familiar with humanitarian standards and principles, and some have inadvertently caused problems for the people they sought to help. The need for training of volunteers has been apparent since the beginning of the refugee arrivals. A well-known humanitarian training agency, RedR, recognized this early on and developed short courses for volunteers focused on both under-standing of humanitarian standards but also on planning and coordination skills. Ironically, due to lack of donor support (including those donors who were supposedly so insistent on humanitarian accountability), RedR had to mobilize initial resources for the training through crowdfunding.

This raises another unusual aspect of the humanitarian response in Europe; the use of crowdfunding has been widespread, not only for actual material support for refugees and migrants but for the travel costs and support of volunteers, as well. Any eventual calculation of the humanitarian response costs in Europe surely will be challenged to estimate the monetary value of the time and opportunity costs of volunteers and also the value of donations. It is also important to point out the support provided by refugees themselves to other refugees, as well.

Role of Social Media

The role of social media has been distinctive—both within the refugee movements themselves and in the European civil society response to refugee arrivals.

The "migration crisis" has been the major focus of political discussion at the regional and national levels in Europe and has taken up a huge amount of media airtime and ink space. Thousands of lines have been written debating the distinction between refugees and migrants, arguing about asylum policies and benefits, and presenting both sympathetic and accusatory human-interest stories. Photojournalism has been remarkable and media analysts have found rich ground to till. But there has been less analysis of the role of social media, which has played a major role in the humanitarian setting in Europe. While much has been made of the prevalence of smart phones in the refugee population, it has mostly been a questioning of whether "real refugees" would have access to such expensive items (this shows the general European perception of global refugees as poor and maybe even illiterate—which deserves a deeper discussion of humanitarian stereotypes) or a suspicion that the refugees' ability to communicate might be a threat to security, at worst, or at least provides a way for them to get information to strategize their "illegal" movements. But, in fact, the ability to communicate and to gather information via social media and use of mobile technology is a new and important factor in humanitarian situations. Refugees have certainly used this technology to gather information on routes and destinations, to stay in contact with families back home, to follow political and policy developments likely to influence their future prospects, and also, of course, to contact smugglers. They also use online translation applications, first aid instructions, and share videos of dangerous crossings with those who plan to follow. The refugees arriving in Europe today are as connected to news and friends as anyone else in Europe is; in this they differ greatly from earlier groups of refugees who left home with little hope of knowing what was happening with their families left behind, sometimes for years. Because of the wealth of information and communication available to today's refugees, their decisions can be based on much more accurate information. WhatsApp and Facebook can help a young Sudanese refugee in Paris find and connect with other people from his village who also made it to France. This can surely be helpful for his/her own adjustment. Those humanitarian responders dealing with the mental health or trauma treatment for refugees are only just starting to study how valuable the use of this technology can be.

Social media has not only been important for refugees themselves but has also played a major role in the organization of volunteerism in Europe. A search of Facebook will show hundreds of sites for volunteers who are sharing information on their activities. There are sites for particular camps, for the activities in the origin towns of volunteers, for a wide variety of sectors or professions, and even support groups for volunteers. For places such as Calais or Idomeni there are dozens of sites focusing on different issues or linked with different activist groups. As mentioned earlier, significant resources have been mobilized for volunteers and activities through crowdfunding sites. This is a relatively new phenomenon within humanitarian work and calls out for more investigation of all its possibilities to make humanitarian response more effective.

What are the Implications of the European Response for Global Humanitarian Commitments?

As described above, Europe has faced a number of challenges for provision of what, in other places, would be the expected humanitarian package of services. Some of the challenges could have been met with better preparedness, predictable funding, and improved use of technical and logistic resources available. And it is these types of technical and operational issues that made up the bulk of the discussion at the World Humanitarian Summit and on which some consensus could be gathered. Solutions to other, more politically fraught issues such as humanitarian access made less headway in the Istanbul meeting. But lack of access, so often mentioned by the humanitarian community in regard to reaching vulnerable populations in places such as Syria or South Kordofan or Myanmar, has actually been a major issue in Europe, as well. When refugees are detained by the state and are not provided with basic support but humanitarian groups are also not allowed to reach them or provide services (such as in some camps in Greece today), it is a serious humanitarian access issue. And when vulnerable people who organize their own shelter and support are faced with the demolition of their meager settlements and volunteers are not allowed to enter the area to assist them (such as in Calais), it is also an access issue. The politics may be different in Europe and in Sudan but the lack of access of vulnerable people to humanitarian support is due to political decisions, not to technical or operational problems. What determines humanitarian space in Europe today is lack of political will on the part of European governments to define the refugee arrivals as a humanitarian issue combined with the inability of the European Union to maintain consensus on humane migration and refugee policies.

It is important to remember that it is the current migration and asylum policies of European member states that have created the humanitarian emergency (which effective and humane management might have averted.) The mere fact that a refugee, desperate to reach a place of safety where he or she might have a future, must physically reach European territory in order to request asylum leads to all the dangerous sea crossings. In fact, the greater the European investment in security and border control, the more dangerous the trip becomes and the more lives are lost (Anderson 2015). Over 4000 people are known to have died so far in 2016 trying to reach Europe—and the number is surely greater than that since many are never found or known about. *Establishment of safe, regular, and orderly methods for seeking asylum would save lives, money, and avert political crises.* Acceptance of greater numbers of refugees under the UNHCR third country resettlement program could be part of such a strategy.

Sadly, many of the recent policies adopted across Europe to respond to the refugee arrivals completely undermine or even violate basic humanitarian principles. In 2015, the EU established a refugee relocation policy whereby 160,000 refugees would be relocated from the border-states to other countries. The program has failed, both due to refusals by some states to participate and due to poor planning. But also, it was restricted to only Syrian, Iraqi, and Eritrean refugees even though many Afghanis, Somalis, and others also have legitimate claims to asylum. The recent EU–Turkey agreement allows passage only for Syrians who register in Greece, not others who arrive, so they are separated and provided less support. This violates basic humanitarian principles. There is no neutrality or impartiality when some people rescued at sea or arriving across a border are provided assistance, based on religion or on nationality, when others are not. There is also no independence when humanitarian organizations are afraid to respond to needs for fear of their home government policies or because they worry about losing a traditional donor because that donor has labeled legitimate refugees as "illegal migrants." One fears for global humanitarian action when European governments, so adamant about human rights and humanitarian standards in other regions, conveniently look the other way when basic health, nutrition, or sanitation standards are not met in camps in Europe. Or worse, when spontaneous settlements are razed to the ground, purposely to disperse refugees and migrants as a deterrent to those who might follow. The concern expressed by hundreds of human rights and humanitarian organizations about the new EU migration "management agreements" with transit and origin countries (many of whom have serious human rights records) reflects another worry: Will Europe, already having abandoned commitment to humanitarian standards at home, also abandon human rights agreements and refugee law in an effort to stop the influx of refugees? What example does this set for other refugee-receiving countries that have even fewer resources to care for refugees or for whom the presence of refugees is politically controversial? The plan announced by Kenya for the closing of Dadaab camp and the expulsion of Somali refugees may only be a first response in a world where intolerance and xenophobia seem to be growing. Without setting a better example, how can Europe respond?

References

ALNAP. (2015) "International Humanitarian Law and Core Humanitarian Principles: humanity, neutrality, impartiality and independence," available at: www.alnap.org/resource/21824

Anderson, R. (2015) "The Illegality Industry: Note on Europe's Dangerous Border Experiment," *Oxford Border Criminologies Blog*, September.

Borton, J. (2016) "The Humanitarian Impulse: Alive and well among the citizens of Europe," *Humanitarian Exchange Magazine*, September.

Calaidipedia. Available at: www.calaidipedia.co.uk (a website established to serve the grassroots efforts at refugee assistance in Calais).

DeLargy, P. (2016) "Deadly Journeys and Disappointing Arrivals: The Role of Africa in Europe's Migration Crisis," *Africa at LSE Blog* January.

Dhesi, S., Isakjee, A., and Davies, T. (2015) "Environmental Health Assessment of the New Migrant Camp in Calais—October 2015," London: Economic and Social Research Council.

Groups URD, HAP International, People in Aid and the Sphere Project. (2014) *Core Humanitarian Standard on Quality and Accountability*, available at: www.corehumanitarianstandard.org

Overseas Development Institute. (2016) *Humanitarian Exchange Magazine*, Special Issue on Refugees and Vulnerable Migrants in Europe, September, London: Humanitarian Practice Network.

SPHERE Project. (2011) *The Sphere Handbook (Humanitarian Charter and Minimum Standards in Humanitarian Response)* (3rd ed.), Rugby, UK: Practical Action Publishing.

SPHERE Project. (2015) *The Core Humanitarian Standard and the Sphere Core Standards: Analysis and Comparison—Interim Guidance*, March 2015 (version 2), available at: www.spherehandbook.org/~sh_resources/resources/Sphere_Core_Standards_and_CHS.pdf

Walker, G. (2016) "Local, Dynamic, Flexible: Healthcare Provision in the Refugee Response," *Humanitarian Exchange Magazine*, September.

Part 3

GLOBAL HUMANITARIAN INFORMATION POLICY

Financing, Early Warning, and
Crisis Response

INTRODUCTION
TO PART 3

The collection of essays in Part 3 are original analyses and documentation by civil servants, professionals, scientists, and policy experts from Germany, Norway, and the United Nations who are responsible for designing policy and working in collaboration with national and international agencies on critical subject matter in the field of humanitarian action and international development planning. Information and communication have become essential in the planning process for dealing with complex emergencies, financing, and development within and between nations and regions. This examination of global humanitarian information policy helps provide a deeper understanding of the critical work involved in addressing some of the many challenges they face.

In Chapter 11, titled, "Forecast-based Financing, Early Warning and Early Action: A Cutting Edge Strategy for the International Humanitarian Community" the German team, which includes Alexandra Rüth, Laura Fontaine, Erin Coughlan de Perez, Konstanze Kampfer, Kevin Wyjad, Mathieu Destrooper, Irene Amuron, Richard Choularton, Meinrad Bürer, and Rebecca Miller, is a collaborative interdisciplinary, multi-stakeholder effort. Their work details an innovative forecast-based financing mechanism to deal with climate-related disasters. An Action Plan for Humanitarian Adaptation to Climate Change has been initiated by the German Federal Foreign Office. It represents a scientifically based funding system that enables practitioners and donors to react faster to natural extreme events. It also takes into consideration support for local communities, offering assistance and helping them adapt to increasing hazards by building up coping capacities. The German Red Cross coordinates the Action Plan with support from the Red Cross Red Crescent Climate Centre. Partners of the forecast-based financing approach include the World Food Programme and the International Federation of Red Cross and Red Crescent Societies. The essay highlights a number of in-country specific pilot studies carried out by the respective National Red Cross or Red Crescent Societies or other partners, where forecast-based financing is implemented to gather practical expertise required to successfully utilize the approach in a broader context. The achievements and challenges will in turn benefit experts and planners tasked with developing the general approach in an interdisciplinary multi-stakeholder dialogue platform, consisting of scientists, governmental representatives, humanitarian aid workers, and other institutional actors.

In Chapter 12, Anne Skjelmerud and Ivar Evensmo, both senior advisers at the Norwegian Agency for Development Cooperation, present a tour d'horizon of Norway's pioneering engagement to change the asymmetrical North–South news flow, a legacy of the colonial area, in order to improve the global flow of information. Their essay titled "Policy for Media and Communication in Humanitarian Action and Long-term Development Cooperation: Some Norwegian Experiences and Perspectives" is drawn from decades of field experience and professional analysis that involves media policy and humanitarian action. Norway discovered and explored a practical partnership approach to local media support for development, peace building, democracy, and human rights in the Balkans in the 1990s. They argue that a trusted relationship must be based on sound principles of collaboration, otherwise it may be vulnerable to opportunistic behavior from both sides.

The essay analyses how media development has emerged as a field of knowledge and practice. Norad's *Human Rights Approach* emphasizes people's rights to participation, non-discrimination, and accountability in life-saving operations. It covers development programs, advocacy and educational endeavors, while taking democratic engagement seriously. The essay gives examples of how media and communication can act as informational platforms for peace building, development and social change. However, this requires close collaboration between providers of peace and security, humanitarian and long-term development support. When done right, support to media and communication can have strong, long-term impact. They point out that today Norway is one of the ten largest international supporters of independent media and other activities promoting Freedom of Expression, which in turn has a tremendous impact on media coverage of the field of humanitarian action.

In Chapter 13, Ulrich Nitschke and Heike Wülfing discuss "The Correlation of Humanitarian Aid, North–South Development Cooperation, and the Media" from a German perspective, juxtaposing their identification of fact from fiction. Their findings are based on their professional experiences involving program management and media engagement during the 2004 Tsunami, humanitarian crisis situations in the occupied territories of Palestine, and the devastating floods in Myanmar. In this chapter the authors address the issue of what role the media may play in prevention of crisis and disasters, and the long-term consultative approaches in development assistance. The role of the media in any disaster is significant in raising public awareness that may result in funding and donations. Moreover, examining social media, the prevailing argument is that access to media sources is more and more democratized, where information is quickly disseminated and consequently turned into collective action. The authors argue that this assertion of the "democratization of the media" is primarily an illusion where more often than not media is dominated by power and money. While challenging some established thinking and structures in international cooperation, the authors try to negotiate the obstacles to collaboration in order to help bridge the gap for the benefit of so many people affected by natural and human-caused disasters. This chapter provides some guidance as to how the involvement of community and religious actors can serve as bridge-makers.

And in Chapter 14, Henia Dakkak argues from a pragmatic standpoint that more than 125 million people across the world are in need of humanitarian assistance. She notes that investment in global emergency preparedness by national governments, regional and multilateral organizations can save lives and contribute to resilience and recovery. Dakkak articulates the need to explore new information technologies and partnerships especially with communities, to give people a voice in emergency response. Technology and communications have given more people the means to express their needs, and offer their assistance more quickly. Yet, too often international assistance still works in traditional ways, focused on the delivery of individual projects rather than bringing together expertise to deliver better outcomes. It is important for national, regional, and international communities to refocus and place people at the center of these crises, moving beyond short-term, supply-driven response efforts toward demand-driven outcomes that reduce need and vulnerability. There is an urgent need for the international aid system, including the multilateral system of United Nations, non-governmental organizations, and donors to commit to working within a new paradigm marked by fundamental shifts that reinforce instead of replacing national and local systems, and that anticipate crises in order to prepare for them. In addition, planners must transcend the humanitarian–development divide by working towards collective outcomes based on comparative advantage and multi-year time-frames.

11

FORECAST-BASED FINANCING, EARLY WARNING, AND EARLY ACTION

A Cutting-Edge Strategy for the International Humanitarian Community

Alexandra Rüth, Laura Fontaine,
Erin Coughlan de Perez, Konstanze Kampfer,
Kevin Wyjad, Mathieu Destrooper,
Irene Amuron, Richard Choularton,
Meinrad Bürer, and Rebecca Miller

Part A: Background Information

Introduction: Why the German Government Is Advocating an Anticipatory Humanitarian System

Despite undisputable scientific evidence that climate related risks are on the rise with an increase in the number, frequency, and intensity of disasters, the amount of disaster-related humanitarian finance is stagnating. Due to increasing extreme weather events such as drought, floods, and cyclones, Germany's Federal Foreign Office stated in its governmental report on humanitarian assistance 2010–2013 (Federal Foreign Office 2014) that a paradigm shift in humanitarian assistance towards an anticipatory system is *sine qua non* needed to use funds in a more efficient way. All the important humanitarian donors and organizations state regularly the increased demand for humanitarian assistance—question marks are often the only answer provided in discussions on future needs and how to address those needs. The bitter reality is that funds for humanitarian engagement will most probably not increase. But the demand is getting higher and higher. As an outcome of the 34th Forum on Global Questions (June 17, 2014) the German Government decided to announce the Action Plan of the Federal Foreign Office for Humanitarian Adaptation to Climate Change and focus, with the help of different actors, on the creation of an anticipatory humanitarian system using a new approach called Forecast-based Financing (FBF). This new concept of humanitarian assistance utilizes the window between a forecast and the potential disaster manifesting. Many climate-related hazards can be predicted; but even today humanitarians do not always get the information about when and where extreme-weather events such as storms, floods, and droughts are expected. And even if humanitarians have this information, funding is mostly not available and they do not have plans how to use this information. Waiting for the disaster to happen also means accepting human suffering and spending enormous amounts of money, whereas often a fraction of this amount invested beforehand would have had a much stronger impact.

Thus FBF represents an opportunity to use resources in the most efficient way, by investing in early preparedness actions based on scientific forecasts. The early preparedness actions are predefined in Standard Operating Procedures (SOPs) including costs and the corresponding triggers for extreme weather events.

The Action Plan of the Federal Foreign Office for Humanitarian Adaptation to Climate Change, coordinated by German Red Cross, embraces different levels of actors: the humanitarian community, scientists, local actors, and policymakers. The main partners are the National Red Cross/Red Crescent Societies in the respective pilot countries, the International Federation of Red Cross/Red Crescent Societies (IFRC), the Red Cross/Red Crescent Climate Centre (RCCC), World Food Programme (WFP), United Nations Office for the Coordination of Humanitarian Affairs (UNOCHA), Welthungerhilfe, and the Nansen Initiative. In a multi-stakeholder event taking place twice a year in Geneva, the Dialogue Platform, additional partners such as Oxford University and University of Reading, as well as other scientists and humanitarian actors, meet to exchange results and lessons learned and to work on the FBF methodology. The main pillar of the Action Plan is the development and testing of FBF in high-risk pilot countries, under the guidance of German Red Cross (GRC) and WFP. Exchange between the different actors (i.e. scientists, humanitarian actors, policymakers and government representatives) is guaranteed by the Dialogue Platform in Geneva. The final result of the Action Plan is to develop a short-term funding mechanism, such as a Preparedness Fund, providing the financial resources for medium- to short-term preparedness actions based on forecasts, while closing the funding gap between long-term development and emergency response.

The following contributions to this paper reveal: (a) the different views and contexts of the pilot countries on FBF; and (b) the challenges inherent in an innovative process with regard to generalizing the experiences and developing one methodology. The article also analyzes the informational role media will play at the national and international level within the FBF framework.

The Challenge at the Policy Level

The challenge at the policy level is to convince decision makers and donors that preparedness is better than post-treatment and that FBF is a worthwhile investment. Specifically, from the donor constituency, a paradigm shift needs to take place in the way humanitarian funding is allocated. It should be evident that there is more value in saving lives and preventing loss and suffering than in responding after a disaster strikes. However, funds tend to be disbursed mostly in post-disaster settings. Such a process is often dependent on local, national, and global media coverage of disaster, which can have a detrimental effect on relief efforts. A fundamental culture change is required for donors and actors to act during the window between a forecast and a disaster. Not only does the approach require coordinated efforts by a range of stakeholders, including scientists, humanitarian and development actors, governments, donors, and communities, it also requires a clear understanding and acceptance that sometimes early action will be taken "in vain" when expected disasters do not eventuate.

Policy Recommendations

Humanitarian and development practitioners agree that the funding gap must be closed and a comprehensive strategy to support the development and operationalization of FBF systems at the national and international level is needed. The following policy recommendations are based on emerging experience with the small-scale forecast-based finance pilots conducted at the moment, and on discussions with policymakers, practitioners, and thought leaders already engaged in FBF concept development and operations.

Having pre-disaster financing arrangements (e.g. a "Preparedness Fund") earmarked and readily available at shorter timescales is essential for the sustainability and ability to scale up the success of this system. SOPs need to be elaborated, nationally and internationally. This will require donor collaboration and meaningful engagement with diverse stakeholders, including government, civil society, and the local private sector. Early experience underscores the importance of establishing clear and strong institutional arrangements, including multi-agency working groups, that involve beneficiaries for collective elaboration of standard operating procedures. Once developed, FBF systems need to be evaluated and revised on an ongoing basis.

Probabilities, Forecasts, Thresholds, and Actions: We Need Science to Make Decisions

Humanitarians are the first external responders after a disaster strikes. However, as climate-related risks are rising worldwide, just waiting for disasters to happen is not an option. Many humanitarian actions could be implemented in the window between a forecast and a disaster; for instance by storing drinking water for the elderly before a heatwave. Such forecasts are increasingly available; humanitarians can receive real-time information about when and where extreme-weather events such as storms, floods, and droughts are expected. In fact, forecasting systems have improved rapidly over the last 50 years, with for instance storm track errors for tropical cyclones going down significantly in the two decades alone (NOAA 2015, par. 5).

Such forecasts allow humanitarians to know the probability of an extreme event before the actual event happens. From a forecasting point of view, this often relies on a state-of-the-art technique called ensemble prediction systems (Cloke and Pappenberger 2009). Ensemble techniques take account of the uncertainties associated with modeling a nonlinear and complex chaotic system. The system runs multiple iterations of what could happen in the coming days and months to produce an ensemble prediction of future weather. At a simple level, the percentage of ensemble members that exceed a threshold (such as a temperature of 40 degrees Celsius) is assumed to give the probability of that particular event occurring.

Globally, hydrological models that include such ensembles are becoming more widely available. The Global Flood Awareness System (GloFAS) offers daily forecasts around the world indicating the probability of flooding in a specific river location (Alfieri et al. 2013).

The Key to a Forecast-based Financing System is Twofold

1. Define the "danger level," or the critical magnitude of the extreme event at which avoidable losses can happen. For example, a temperature of 40 degrees Celsius for three days causes avoidable hospitalizations and deaths in a particular location.
2. Identify what forecast probability of that "danger level" should trigger action. For example, hospitals might decide it is worthwhile to assign extra staff for the coming week if there is a 30 percent chance of reaching the danger level (three days of temperatures above 40 degrees).

Forecast-based Financing (FBF) proposes an automatic system that defines in advance what action will be taken based on which forecast trigger. Then, when the forecast trigger is reached, the system automatically funds preparedness actions before the potential disaster strikes. Such a system can minimize suffering through early notification systems, use humanitarian funds more efficiently, and contribute to long-term development.

To do this, an implementing humanitarian agency works with government officials, communities at risk, and forecasters themselves to agree on selected actions that are worth carrying out at specific trigger probabilities. Then each action is allocated a budget to be activated when a forecast is received.

The system is finalized in a set of SOPs that specify the danger level, forecast probability trigger, the action that will be taken, and how it will be communicated. In each SOP, the amount of funding is predefined, and can be released automatically based on a forecast. Roles and responsibilities are clearly defined, assigning who will do what when the forecast is reached.

However, no forecast is perfect. Sometimes, the triggered action will not be followed by the extreme event—the "danger level" is not reached. For example, the hospital could be overstaffed for a week if the temperatures do not rise enough to cause extra morbidity. This is acknowledged and taken into account when the triggers are defined; the actors agree that it is worth the risk of sometimes acting "in vain" because over time, the negative consequences of not taking early action are greater and the actions taken for acting "in vain" are still relevant.

The system will be designed so that "high regret" actions such as evacuation will only be done at high probability triggers, and actions that have "low regrets," such as extra staffing, can be done at lower probabilities. Broadly speaking, forecasts showing a greater likelihood of disaster will be matched with more expensive actions. Some actions, such as hygiene campaigns before a flood, will have lasting effects that are beneficial to the community even if the extreme event does not materialize. Ultimately, because SOPs are standardized, disaster managers will not face any blame if the disaster does not materialize.

Part B: The Practical Implications of an Anticipatory Humanitarian System

Disaster preparedness is an integral component of sustainable development. This was again emphasized during the Third UN Conference on Disaster Risk Reduction 2015 in Sendai, Japan:

> During the World Conference, States also reiterated their commitment to address disaster risk reduction and the building of resilience to disasters with a renewed sense

of urgency within the context of sustainable development and poverty eradication, and to integrate, as appropriate, both disaster risk reduction and the building of resilience into policies, plans, programmes and budgets at all levels and to consider both within relevant frameworks.

(UNISDR 2015, 9)

Yet in many countries, disaster preparedness plays only a minor role at the moment. Classic disaster management activities predominate. Also it is not always easy to differentiate between reactive disaster measures and disaster preparedness. Both react to a predetermined warning level, to reduce the negative impacts of natural extreme events.

The National Societies in the selected pilot countries and the GRC, in collaboration with the RCCC and with funding from the Federal Foreign Office of Germany, are piloting this innovative approach to disaster risk reduction. By using forecast-based thresholds to automatically release money that pays for pre-planned short-term emergency preparedness actions, the critical window of time before a disaster is used to an advantage. Emergency preparedness involves critical information sent to agencies, communities, and local actors in the days or even weeks before a disaster, and is an important complement to traditional disaster risk reduction efforts focusing on longer term infrastructure and capacity development.

Mozambique: The Role of Governmental Institutions in the FBF Approach

"Each country bears the primary responsibility for protecting its people, infrastructure, and other national assets from the impact of natural disasters" (United Nations 1994, principle 10). To adapt the FBF approach to specific countries, the core task will be to integrate the mechanism into existing governmental disaster management structures. Linking FBF with existing early warning systems and strengthening local actors in disaster preparedness measures is a precondition. This is most sustainable when using national coordination structures organized by the government and with the involvement of the local population, such as volunteers of the national Red Cross Red Crescent Movement.

Roles and Responsibilities

The human factor is crucial in supporting effective action from forecasting systems. Following this principle, local institutions in Mozambique, e.g. the National Institute for Disaster Management (INGC) and the Mozambique Red Cross Society (CVM), play a major role in the design and implementation of FBF actions. Prioritization of FBF disaster preparedness measures can only be done in collaboration with those key actors. Looking ahead, working groups will need to be created to elaborate the planning, implementation, and finalization phases of the SOPs for disaster preparedness. A particular challenge within the collaboration is to come to an agreement on the threshold that will trigger the planning process of a specific preparedness measure. However, this is a complex issue in Mozambique, as in many other countries in development, since the existing governmental technologies and know-how for early warning are limited to such an extent that often the warning concerning an extreme event is only sent out to the communities once the impacts of floods or tropical cyclones are already visible. Although it is commonly understood that the reduction of disaster risks before an extreme event strikes reduces human suffering and economic damage significantly, the Humanitarian Country Team (HCT) is at present mainly restricted to emergency response.

The FBF mechanism offers a solution for this current impasse, because it presupposes that the measures are funded and executed in response to specific predictions that can be communicated and acted upon in advance of the extreme event. Therefore, humanitarian actors can already become active in the field of disaster preparedness. This is the difference between improved disaster preparedness using the FBF approach and classical disaster preparedness. Until recently, disaster preparedness interventions in Mozambique were not linked to specific warning levels and humanitarian actors often had their hands tied because of the absence of governmental requests for action (Artur 2011, 59).

Determining the risk of a disaster based on a forecast is consequently the first major challenge of the FBF mechanism, as it requires participatory approaches at all levels. First, thresholds are scientifically elaborated with the RCCC, the National Institute for Meteorology (INAM), and the National Water Directory (DNRH). Then, in a second step, the selected thresholds need to be agreed upon with the implementing actors, and a plan for early warning communication needs to be established. That is why a close collaboration with governmental decision makers and civil society actors is decisive in determining the risk. Media organizations and their technological capacity at community and national levels must also be engaged and developed.

Organization

FBF preparedness operations exhibit a cycle of planning, implementation, finalization and evaluation of a preparedness measure, with and without extreme event occurrence. This is important because forecasts for floods and cyclones are always subject to uncertainty and the residual risk that the extreme incident fails to materialize is always there. For both alternatives, an impact-assessment is necessary for the revision of SOPs and documentation of lessons learned. Crucial in the case of implemented preparedness action without extreme event occurrence is risk communication at the local level. Considering that in Mozambique a significant part of the population is still illiterate and most of local communities have no or only a few years of school education, the rural population usually does not understand the weather forecasts emitted by the National Institute for Meteorology. An example for such a forecast is "Within the next 24 hours moderate to strong rainfall is expected, with 30–50 mm above normal in Zambezia Province." Thus, weather-related data used for early warning has to be translated into more user-friendly information and better disseminated to communities at risk. The information has to include behavioral instructions to reduce risks and to prepare the community for an effective coping mechanism (Kunz-Plapp 2007). For Mozambique, this means the warnings and measures to be implemented must be translated to the local language and additionally the local communities have to be educated about existing and future risks and associated uncertainties. It is very important that the people at risk, whom we are aiming to persuade toward effective actions before an extreme event occurs, are convinced of the benefit of those actions and of course take the decision to act. If for instance the traditional leader of a community is not convinced of a preparedness measure, it will become a challenge to persuade the rest of the community to react. Here the local DRR committees and the Mozambican Red Cross volunteers play a crucial role. They are trained to carry out disaster risk reduction measures and are intermediaries between the government, humanitarian actors, and civil society. A central point for humanitarian aid projects is therefore to partner with local communities for open lines of communication and mutual learning, combining traditional knowledge with awareness raising and training of volunteers that represent the local communities and are responsible for communicating risks and options for action in specific hazard prone villages. Another important role is played by the mass media. For example, local radio stations are essential for the dissemination of warning information in local language. Naturally this form of dissemination of risk information and call for action assumes that the intended target group owns radios (Bollin 2008, 253–267).

The pilot project in Mozambique is in the process of identifying options for FBF disaster preparedness actions and evaluating their quality based on criteria and practical experiences. Alternative strategies will also be considered, in case of non-occurrence of a forecasted extreme event. The standardized procedures developed for the FBF mechanism will be detailed and exercised in two pilot districts. Whether these options for action can be replicated in other districts will depend highly on the participation and advocacy of the governmental National Institute for Disaster Management (INGC). In order to institutionalize the mechanism in existing structures, it will be necessary in a second phase to integrate the designed measures for disaster preparedness and the available budget of the donor with the local contingency plans and to anchor the specific measures by making them multi-sectorial.

Bangladesh: Forecast Based Financing and Longer-term Resilience Building

FBF will enable the Bangladesh Red Crescent Society (BDRCS) to act in the days before a flood or cyclone to communicate early warnings and reduce community losses and ready itself to provide relief immediately after an event. This section briefly discusses the relationship between FBF and longer-term resilience building approaches to disaster risk reduction.

Linking Forecast-based Financing and Resilience Activities

Many traditional resilience efforts concentrate on developing infrastructure and capabilities over periods of months and years usually targeted through some form of baseline risk assessment. For example, flood protection systems are built in areas that are flood prone in general, rather than in response to a threat posed by a specific flood event. On the other hand, FBF focuses on short-term actions that can be done within days of notification in response to the threat posed by a specific forecasted hazard event. FBF is also directly tied to emergency response in ways that resilience building is not, in that forecast-based actions often either move response actions up to before an event, or are directly tied to facilitating a better post-event response. Thus, resilience building and FBF are both in essence risk reduction efforts, but have different underlying conceptions of risk and very different time-frames of action.

These differences make resilience building and FBF complementary. To maximize the benefits of complementarity, it is useful to maintain distinctions between the two spheres of activity. As a general rule, FBF in Bangladesh will concentrate on actions that either could not be done as part of traditional resilience programming, or, even if they could be done as part of traditional resilience, show clear benefits to implementation immediately before a hazard event. In other words, FBF actions will be actions that are more effective or efficient when implemented after a forecast before a disaster. This rule is being applied so that evidence generated from the Bangladesh pilot will show a clearly advantageous niche for the FBF approach, and to insulate the pilot from criticism that it is simply repackaging existing actions in a complicated way.

This means that FBF in Bangladesh is deliberately avoiding three main areas of traditional resilience building: infrastructure development, distribution of durable goods, and basic trainings. Developing infrastructure (e.g. embankments or cyclone shelters) requires longer timeframes than forecasts make possible, and should be targeted through baseline risk assessments to efficiently use resources. Most durable goods can be easily distributed without a forecast, and because these goods last for many years they are not appropriate for regular distribution via SOPs that will be activated frequently. Likewise, basic training can be done at any time, although refreshers prior to hazard events could well be beneficial and will be considered. Current FBF Bangladesh plans focus on providing cash grants to offset evacuation costs and assist participants to act to reduce their potential asset losses, distribution of water purification tablets to promote consumption of safe water, and internal community preparedness actions concentrating on waterproofing food and assets as well as coordinating the mobilization of volunteers to assist the most vulnerable community members and secure public assets such as school materials.

Taking a broader view, because FBF is linked directly to specific potential emergencies, it is by definition a last line of defense in terms of risk reduction. Ideally, resilience building would reduce the incidence of events that would require FBF activities to being relatively rare events. In flood-affected areas of Northern Bangladesh this would mean improving embankments and elevating houses/infrastructure to, for example, the 50 year flood level, and then establishing an FBF system on top of this foundation of resilience to reduce residual risk posed by extraordinary events. Static resilience and event-focused emergency preparedness activities are both important parts of an effective risk management framework, and ideally they should be implemented together in a coordinated way. Laying the groundwork for this comprehensive risk management approach will be a critical focus of the FBF Bangladesh project in 2016 and 2017.

Peru: Preparing for El Niño

You could hear it everywhere in July 2015: The "Godzilla" among weather phenomena, El Niño, would be striking the pacific region around winter 2015/2016. Scientists all around the globe were predicting a particularly strong event, with the effect of an anxious local population and the humanitarian community talking about what to do and where to get the funds.

Signals such as the warming of sea surface temperatures have to be taken seriously, because with a "Kelvin"-wave this warm sea surface water can come near the coast, change the climatological pattern and bring above normal rainfall around the equator and drought elsewhere. In the North of Peru, more than 1.2 million persons were affected by a strong El Niño event in 1983 (both floods and droughts) and over 500,000 persons were affected in an El Niño of 1997 (mainly floods). However, even a moderate El Niño can cause serious flash flooding in areas that are not used to dealing with huge amounts of rain.

So, we know what is likely to happen and have reasonable probabilities. Why wait for the emergency declaration? The Peruvian and German Red Cross National Societies mobilized the Red Cross branches of Piura and Lambayeque in the North of Peru and together with the Civil Defence ministry and the local governments seven key action groups were identified to strengthen community preparedness and coping mechanisms before the disaster strikes: (1) train community disaster preparedness units and carry out awareness raising in the community; (2) refresh and strengthen the community early warning system; (3) prepare Red Cross and community volunteers for first aid actions; (4) provide safe drinking water; (5) carry out sanitation activities and fumigation against dengue fever; (6) strengthen and protect at least 300 vulnerable houses and (7) provide 100 temporary shelters in the community. We choose a comprehensive approach in the likely most affected areas of Northern Peru.

A Pilot within a Pilot

With FBF, the Red Cross is developing a new approach and El Niño pushed the Peru team to advance their schedule. With the support from scientists at the Red Cross Climate Centre and Universities of Oxford, Reading, and Columbia, seasonal, monthly, and weekly forecasts were connected with the activities identified in the field to develop a set of "thresholds for early action." Different activity groups were connected to a forecast with low, medium, and very strong impact for the population, equaling a very strong El Niño as in 1983 or 1997. These were the first set of SOPs for early action, granted as an independent, fully costed project proposal with individual funding for each threshold being met by forecasts. Starting in time, or even "before time," has advantages: through early warning communication strategies people in the districts could face less suffering, donors should face more efficient and cheaper projects, and the humanitarian community, more time to prepare properly with the communities, decision makers and the national system. Of course, these expectations will also be measured after El Niño passes by.

After the Trigger: FBF in Action

In November 2015, a first seasonal threshold was reached and triggered the SOPs on community awareness raising and early warning. In January 2016 the subseasonal (1 month) threshold was reached. So, the Red Cross started to take early action measures for first aid, safe drinking water, hygiene promotion, and protection of houses—hoping for the best while prepared for the worst.

A Shift in the Humanitarian Model: World Food Programme's FoodSECuRE Project

"The humanitarian system is increasingly stretched financially and operationally as more weather disasters require responses in more places and for longer periods. We need new approaches," said the World Food Programme's Executive Director Ertharin Cousin at COP-21 in Paris at the launching event of its new Food Security Climate Resilience Facility (FoodSECuRE).

FoodSECuRE is the first WFP institutional mechanism to use climate forecasts to trigger anticipatory action and funds at community level before climate shocks occur, allowing WFP to scale-up programming so that the people it serves enter forecasted crises more resilient and prepared.

In addition to the anticipatory FBF element, FoodSECuRE will trigger early response by complementing existing corporate emergency mechanisms in response to large-scale climate shocks. It is stepping up its collaboration with the African Union's Africa Risk Capacity (ARC) agency to work with governments to double the climate insurance coverage of the most vulnerable. FoodSECuRE will also support post-disaster resilience building by providing predictable multi-year funding for resilience interventions.

WFP's Food Security Climate Resilience Facility will shift the humanitarian model from a reactive system to one that looks ahead and communicates rapidly, implementing faster and saving more lives, time, and money.

Development of a Forecast and Trigger Prototype

To achieve this ambitious goal, the WFP engaged in a strategic partnership with the International Research Institute for Climate and Society (IRI) from the Columbia University to develop a robust and country-tailored forecast and trigger mechanism using long-term meteorological data combined with cutting-edge tools from climate science. In the initial phase, the prototype will look at forecasting slow-onset disasters such as droughts, which can be forecasted a couple of months ahead, and extending to rapid-onset disasters e.g. floods and tropical storms in a later phase.

The tool provides the user with a series of forecast-based triggers to choose from to simulate a climatic shock at a user-defined threshold level e.g. likelihood of shock occurrence and exceedance of a specific percentile for precipitation.

In combination with information on water requirement of key staple crop and food insecurity and vulnerability information, anticipatory resilience building activities will be triggered. Most recently, in the context of the 2015/16 El Niño, FoodSECuRE has been activated in Guatemala and Zimbabwe using seasonal climate forecasts to trigger funding for community-level resilience activities before the anticipated shock occurs.

Early Action in Zimbabwe Builds Drought Resilience

In the case of Zimbabwe, the chosen trigger parameter is precipitation (3-month forecast) with the threshold set as equal or below 20 percent of the long-term climate median (significant extreme event) and a probability level of >50 percent. WFP has identified the Mwenezi district in the southern belt of Zimbabwe to be most affected, facing substantial reduction of agricultural production during the 2015/16 season, in particular of rain-fed maize, the staple crop, highly sensitive to water stress during the early stages of its development (November– January).

To reduce the anticipated negative impacts, WFP together with FAO and the Ministry of Agriculture's extension service (AGRITEX) is field-testing the FoodSECuRE early action modality to bolster the resilience capacity of 550 affected small holder farmer households through promoting the cultivation of drought tolerant small grains (local sorghum and millet). This will be combined with the promotion of soil and water conservation techniques to help food-insecure households to improve food production and marketing opportunities— reducing the impact of the drought on their food access and limiting the need for them to employ distress coping mechanisms.

The Benefits Are Evident

An anticipatory response not only protects people's lives, it also builds resilience, and new WFP research shows it also saves money. A 2015 (ex-ante) cost–benefit analysis on FoodSECuRE in Sudan and Niger shows that using a forecast-based system would lower the cost of the humanitarian response by 50 percent. The FoodSECuRE approach also has a resilience and recovery pillar and if that is added into the equation, the cost drops further.

FoodSECuRE brings cutting-edge tools from climate science and finance together for action with governments and communities through potential linkages to national safety net programs and WFP's traditional food assistance tools, to ensure operations do more than simply support recovery from a particular disaster; and build resilience, food security, and nutrition in the face of growing climate risks. These innovations promise to transform the way we work now and in the future.

Uganda: Sustainability of the FBF Concept

The Uganda Red Cross Society (URCS), in partnership with GRC, is implementing an Integrated Climate Change Adaptation project in North Eastern Uganda. This project focuses on building resilience in communities affected by flooding and associated risks. The selected project areas are vulnerable to the effects of climate change; flooding and long dry spells in particular. The project has a component of the Disaster Preparedness Fund to support actions triggered by a flood forecast. This innovative approach is supported by RCCC with regard to technical issues and the weather forecasts are based on the Global Flood Awareness System (GloFAS).

The Action

On November 12, 2015, the GloFAS model issued a trigger for Kapelebyong Sub County, one of the project areas in Teso region. This trigger was shared with the Red Cross teams and verified with the Uganda National Meteorology Authority. As a result and based on its SOPs, URCS mobilized its volunteers, notified the beneficiaries, and distributed non-food items to 369 households (1,815 people) from two parishes of Amemia and Okoboi. Each household received two jerry cans, two bars of soap, five sacks for food storage, one hoe, and 30 water purification tablets (to last one month). Prior to the distribution, a meeting was held with the local government officials of Amuria district and the beneficiary communities to explain this unique course of action. The forecasted region in Uganda is indeed now facing the impacts of floods. Rescue operations and emergency appeals have been activated. The communities reached by Forecast-based Financing are not included in the current emergency appeal that is seeking aid for the rest of the region.

Challenges

In the execution of the FBF concept, there were challenges encountered. (1) This was a new concept in that action (distribution of non-food items) was triggered based on weather forecast, in anticipation of a flood. However, URCS usually provides nonfood items in the event of a disaster and because of this there were some delays in the activation of the distribution as time was spent instructing staff about the FBF concept. (2) By the time the trigger was activated, the communities were already experiencing water logging and some areas were flooded. (3) The non-food item kit lacked some priority items such as tarpaulins as communities were already experiencing water logging/flooding.

Recommendations

URCS, GRC, and RCCC need to continuously raise awareness on the new FBF concept, internally and externally. There is need to define flooding vis-à-vis the community understanding. The trigger indicated a possibility of flooding within one month while the community insisted they were already experiencing flooding. The SOPs should be a living document that is continuously updated based on the learning and realities in the field. There is also a need to review the thresholds for which an action is triggered. Some of the target areas reported flooding but the flood model did not pick up on it. The FBF concept is sustainable within a running project, as is the case with the URCS/GRC supported projects, where there are strong linkages with ongoing initiatives, for instance if FBF is embedded within an existing project.

Part C: Forecast-based Financing and the Media

While risk communication needs to be improved between scientists and actors, the communication with governmental actors and other stakeholders is even more vital, and public perception of FBF is instrumental to the success of establishing it internationally. Since the actual funding process is decoupled from the media and only indirectly influenced by it, FBF is different from "conventional" humanitarian aid appeals. It is innovative in the sense that the donor response is not linked to the intensity and length of the media coverage of an event, but to the extent of harm it could potentially cause, because the approach is anticipatory, not reactionary. An action is triggered through a forecast with the likelihood of an event, so when funding is pledged it is before anything has actually happened that could be reported. Of course, the increasing risk has to be communicated internally and also externally, but there are no death tolls to report to encourage donor generosity. Public preconceptions and the tone and scope of potential media coverage are not vital to the actual efforts, since they were arranged beforehand. This also makes fundraising more complicated; raising money beforehand is harder than after a disaster has been reported and can be seen and perceived emotionally. But by objectively judging the scale and magnitude of an event relief operations and resilience building measures are planned not by how grave a situation is perceived to be, but by how best to mitigate impact. Also, disasters could potentially be avoided altogether, if for instance an evacuation is successful prior to a flood. Of course, then it is important to communicate this success to verify the approach. That is where evidence of the success of FBF projects needs to be well documented and communicated.

National Context

At the national level, providing climate services is a central part of the FBF mechanism. This means the dissemination of climate information to the public or a specific user in general, but also the translation of this information so that governments and humanitarian actors can take decisions on a national level, as well as providing communities with specifics so they can understand the increasing risk and why they need to act. Usage of climate information when defining thresholds is a multidisciplinary process where one has to ensure that all stakeholders are on board. The practical example for the Peru El Niño project shows that the use of climate information is not easy, especially concerning a joint understanding between scientists, humanitarian practitioners, and regular civilians. Specifically, questions on how to ensure that communities understand certain risk levels, how to communicate impacts, and why certain actions were chosen, need to be addressed. Media coverage is important in this context, since it can facilitate the communication with populations affected by future or current natural hazards or improve the effectiveness of aid itself, by explaining why an organization such as the German Red Cross is starting to act in the area. This also entails dealing with coverage of operations of acting "in vain" and public perception of measures taken. Here, it is important to involve and integrate all stakeholders (state and non-state) in the whole process, to make FBF a part of existing national contingency plans and the broader national public dialogue. Another aspect is updating all partners regularly on developments, with the idea of having a national steering committee for future processes or even a preparedness fund in the respective country with its own management structure.

International Context

Essentially it is all about the human factor—promotion of the approach is needed nationally and internationally. But especially when communicating FBF on a grand scale, evidence and success stories are needed to advance the application of the concept. That is why interventions such as the pilot projects in Peru and Uganda have been well documented and analyzed. Good monitoring and evaluation processes are necessary to follow up on the results and lessons learned. Only if the pilot projects can deliver proof that FBF is using funds in a more efficient way compared to longer-term preparedness activities, will the mechanism have a chance to enhance the humanitarian system. The Dialogue Platform is the pivotal element in the FBF approach; it provides exchange between everyone interested at different levels, serves as a dissemination point of expertise and information while also being a networking event and the public face of the FBF framework. Real-time communication through a collaborative workspace ensures that crucial data and results reach everyone and a peer-review mechanism provides guidance to those in the field. A website provided by the IFRC presents materials, reports, and documents while the internal workspace allows practitioners to work jointly on documents and procedures. Using information to change perceptions and provoke changes in thinking is not new, but it can be useful in this context; as mentioned in the paragraph on challenges at policy level, advocacy work is needed for FBF. One success was the inclusion of FBF in the World Humanitarian Summit Synthesis Report, mentioning "innovative finance triggered by the forecast of extreme events" (WHS 2015, 127). FBF has been presented widely, including through side events at the 2015 Paris Climate Conference (COP-21), also with joint press releases by the IFRC, GRC and WFP, the 2015 World Humanitarian Summit, the 2015 UN World Conference on Disaster Risk Reduction in Sendai, Japan and at the next meeting of the Working Party on Humanitarian Aid and Food Aid (COHAFA) in Brussels in 2016.

Part D: The Future of Forecast-based Financing

Key tasks for the immediate future focus on advancing the FBF agenda at the international level, connecting the Foreign Office Action Plan with other policy agendas and developing a flexible financing mechanism that can be used to utilize funds applicable to the approach, such as the Disaster Relief Emergency Fund (DREF).

Linking FBF and the Disaster Relief Emergency Fund

The Disaster Relief Emergency Fund was set-up by the International Federation of Red Cross and Red Crescent Societies (IFRC) in 1985 to provide National Societies with an access to quick and unearmarked funding to facilitate rapid local response (IFRC 2011). DREF is currently one of IFRC's basic tools for disaster response, providing immediate financial support to start up emergency appeals, until donor contributions are received.

With the number of applications increasing, it became clear that it was not enough to provide funding after a disaster but that there was a need for funding to be made available before a disaster to enable National Societies to be better prepared. A new mechanism of DREF funding was implemented in 2004 when it was agreed to start providing grants for short-term, predictable or imminent crises—from civil unrest to possible hurricanes (IFRC 2015). At the moment DREF does not, however, support disaster preparedness, the pre-positioning of stocks, or capacity building unless a crisis is clear, imminent, and exceptional.

Recent examples of DREF application based on a weather forecast illustrate the success and improved application of humanitarian aid. In 2013 the Belarus Red Cross Society (BRCS) applied for a DREF grant to scale-up its disaster preparedness following the national meteorological agency forecast of a rapid increase in temperatures and risk of flooding caused by an unusually heavy snowfall and cold weather earlier that year. This allowed time to train volunteers who practiced search and rescue tactics, which included pre-positioning tents, blankets and uniforms, reducing the average time to bring assistance from six days to four hours (IFRC 2013). Another example of improved utilization of an extreme weather forecast allowed communities to avoid the disastrous consequences of the Buzi river flood in Mozambique in 2007. After receiving a DREF grant, the Mozambique Red Cross accomplished evacuation in the river basin even before the end of the year and provided safe drinking water, food, health, and livelihoods for the resettled people (IFRC 2008).

The experience gained within the DREF is of particular interest to FBF and the development of a mechanism aiming at delivering resources before the crisis strikes. Both approaches underlie operationalization and usage of climate information as a tool for a more efficient and effective humanitarian response by taking anticipatory measures. Scaling-up the use of FBF will likely require the establishment of a centralized fund similar to DREF to reduce transactions costs and improve effectiveness.

Future Challenges

To follow the vision of a paradigm shift in humanitarian action, the FBF movement needs endorsements of actors globally, who advocate the system at national, but also regional, levels. The ultimate goal is to reach vulnerable communities and enable them to adapt to climate change proactively, instead of reacting to ever-increasing crises. To achieve this, a real tested methodology has to be in place in GRC's and WFP's pilot countries—this is the objective for 2016 and 2017. The antagonism of a general versus a tailor-made (i.e. adapted to national setups) approach will be a challenge, good research on cost–benefit and impact is therefore needed. At the same time, an assessment of existing financing mechanisms for either disaster preparedness or response can give insights into how FBF could be included and in what way a special preparedness fund should be designed (criteria, mechanism, management etc.). Including some sort of a certification process for countries or organizations as a requirement to access FBF funds is especially important on national level, since structures have to be established and triggers need to be defined. Lastly, continuous public relations work is key to establish FBF and to disseminate the results. In addition, the Dialogue Platform will be made accessible to major public interest organizations that are invited to participate.

References

Alfieri, A., Lorenzo, B. P., Dutra, E., Krzeminski, B., Muraro, D., Thielen, J., and Pappenberger, F. (2013) "GloFAS —Global Ensemble Streamflow Forecasting And Flood Early Warning," *Hydrology and Earth System Sciences*, 17 (3): 1161–1175.

Artur, L. (2011) *Continuities in Crisis: Everyday Practices of Disaster Response and Climate Change Adaptation in Mozambique*, Thesis, Wageningen: Wageningen University.

Bollin, C. (2008) "Staatliche Verantwortung und Bürgerbeteiligung—Voraussetzungen für effektive Katastrophenvorsorge," in C. Felgentreff and T. Glade, (Eds.), *Naturrisiken und Sozialkatastrophen*, Heidelberg: Akademischer Verlag.

Cloke, H. L. and Pappenberger, F. (2009) "Ensemble Flood Forecasting: A Review," *Journal of Hydrology*, 375 (3–4): 613–626.

Federal Foreign Office. (2014) *Bericht der Bundesregierung über die deutsche humanitäre Hilfe im Ausland 2010–2013*, Berlin: Hausdruckerei.

International Federation of Red Cross and Red Crescent Societies. (2008) *Early Warning Early Action.*

International Federation of Red Cross and Red Crescent Societies. (2011) *Disaster Relief Emergency Fund (DREF): Procedures and Guidelines.*

International Federation of Red Cross and Red Crescent Societies. (2013) *Disaster Relief Emergency Fund (DREF) Belarus: Floods Preparedness.*

International Federation of Red Cross and Red Crescent Societies. (2015) *Disaster Relief Emergency Fund (DREF): 30 Years of Saving Lives.*

Kunz-Plapp, T. (2007) "Vorwarnung, Vohersage und Frühwarnung," in C. Felgentreff and T. Glade (Eds.), *Naturrisiken und Sozialkatastrophen*, Heidelberg: Spektrum Akademischer Verlag, pp. 213–223.

United Nations (1994) *Yokohama Strategy and Plan of Action for a Safer World: Guidelines for Natural Disaster Prevention, Preparedness and Mitigation*, Yokohama: World Conference on Natural Disaster Reduction, available at: www.ifrc.org/Docs/idrl/I248EN.pdf

United Nations Office for Disaster Risk Reduction (UNISDR). (2015) *Sendai Framework for Disaster Risk Reduction 2015–2030.*

United States Department of Commerce, National Oceanic and Atmospheric Administration, National Hurricane Center (NOAA). (2015) *National Hurricane Center Forecast Verification*, available at: www.nhc.noaa.gov/verification/verify5.shtml

World Humanitarian Summit (WHS) Secretariat. (2015) *Restoring Humanity: Synthesis of the Consultation Process for the World Humanitarian Summit*, New York: United Nations.

12

POLICY FOR MEDIA AND COMMUNICATION IN HUMANITARIAN ACTION AND LONG-TERM DEVELOPMENT COOPERATION

Some Norwegian Experiences and Perspectives

Anne Skjelmerud and Ivar Evensmo

Introduction

Humanitarian and political reporting have always been deeply intertwined. The phrases, images and arguments used to describe human sufferings depend on our worldview and our perceptions of "the other." The more culturally distant a relationship is, or the more political a crisis is seen, the less emphatic and more biased the descriptions tend to be. Notoriously famous are the reactions in the League of Nations to appeals by Fridtjof Nansen to help refugees left stateless in Eastern Europe after the Russian Revolution and later to help fund the relief efforts in famine-stricken Russia in 1921. His appeals to action mostly fell on deaf ears of diplomats and politicians who feared more the consequences of the Russian Revolution than they felt empathy with millions of suffering humans.

This was possible 100 years back. Since then modern media have changed the situation fundamentally. It is no longer possible to hide human suffering of such scale from a world audience. Today, the world's eyes are in principle present everywhere—even in local pockets of conflict and natural disasters—although not necessarily attracting adequate attention and response. Diplomats and political decision makers are informed and pressured by media and interest groups to take a stand and to act. But the level of public and political attention and humanitarian response are dependent on the images that the media bring back to the powerful nations and their populations about who the sufferers are, where they live and what type of conflicts they are parts of. The Biafra secessionist war in Nigeria 1967–71 that failed and left four million people dead of disease, hunger and malnutrition, and the freedom fight in South Sudan that led to independence in 2011, but also at the cost of millions of dead civilians, are classic examples of how communication and media campaigns were used mainly by outsiders for the dual purposes of humanitarian aid and lobbying for political goals. In contrast, in ex-Yugoslavia and Rwanda modern communication tools were also used by the warring fractions to manipulate and control the affected population themselves.

Media and communication, including communication from humanitarian organizations play important roles in gathering support in the global North for people in the South who suffer and are oppressed, and for humanitarian as well as long-term development assistance. Despite the obvious role of the media, Norway did not have a *media support policy* for its international development operations until 2005. Part of the explanation is that many government policy analysts placed media issues into a governance perspective. At a deeper conceptual level however, this has also to do with the historical traditions and thinking in Norway as a Western liberal country.

In Norway, the media sector has for very long been "The Fourth Estate" among its principal democratic institutions and enjoyed wide self-autonomy from state interference. There was no tradition of government policies regulating the sector. Print media had always been free, while public broadcasting was de-monopolized in the late 1980s. Strong associations and interaction among journalist unions, editors' guilds and media owners had produced common norms for good journalism (Vær Varsom- og Redaktør-plakaten) and self-regulatory mechanisms for abuse of media power.

Out of that tradition, media projects were supposed to enhance democracy by focusing mainly on technical equipment and capacity building of journalists and editors. There was little understanding of media sector development within the broader national social and political contexts. On the other hand, many were quite aware of the very asymmetrical international information flow from North to South and wanted to change this situation. Norway started to support organizations that facilitated news flow in the opposite direction, for instance to Inter Press Service (IPS). It also initiated an International Program for Development and Communication in UNESCO, the only UN organization with a mandate to work on information and communication. In the 30 years that have passed since the IPDC started, it has funded more than 1600 media projects across all continents and generated a huge knowledge base in media development.

Part I—Historical Overview

Discovering the Issues: The Balkans as an Eye-opener and Learning Arena

Norwegian perceptions of communication and media support in the 1970s and 1980s changed dramatically in the 1990s. Although local media played an important part in the atrocities in Rwanda in 1994, it was the wars in ex-Yugoslavia that became the real eye-opener. The Balkans are part of "us," are part of Europe, historically, politically, and culturally. And Europe had civilized ways to deal with conflicts, we all thought, after having been responsible for starting two world wars in the last century; the greater was the shock then to wake up to the horror of more wars on our own continent.

The external world could witness the hugely negative impact of information blockades between former republics that had previously enjoyed multiple information systems, and how all political fractions used very sophisticated propaganda machineries in what became known as "Prime Time Crime." However, it took time before the truth sunk in and Norwegians began to understand that local media, based on democratic values and high journalistic standards, are fundamental both for development as well as for conflict prevention and good governance.

A small but important antidote to the poisonous mainstream of nationalistic propaganda was the Alternative Information Mreza (or network) AIM. It was a *news agency* founded soon after ex-Yugoslavia collapsed and reliable information flows from other parts of the country stopped. It was a simple but creative attempt to break this news blockade by using the by then quite new email technology. Professional editors in each of the former republics collected 20 news articles every day, uploaded and sent them to a small editorial staff in Paris who bounced them back to editors in all the other former republics for free distribution to local media outlets. So, every day 20 articles in local language were sent from one's own republic and back came 100 articles from the five other republics. It was a mixture of humanitarian, political news, features, and other reporting. Financial support came from the Council of Europe and a program called "Confidence Building Measures." AIM became a model for Norwegians in how to work *with* local media and build their capacity to reach local audiences, instead of working *through* them instrumentally to channel news flow from outside. Trust and confidence in the local media partners were at the heart of the matter.

The AIM editorial board had members from all parts of former Yugoslavia plus core staff in Paris and met every quarter somewhere in Europe to discuss strategy and internal matters, but also to inform and lobby political decision makers about the situation on the ground in the Balkans and speak with one voice about the need for support to local independent media. With support from the Norwegian Government, civil society organizations already engaged in humanitarian work in the Balkans ventured into the field of local media support together with a handful of other Western human rights and media support organizations. Famous is the history of B92, which grew from a small radio station in Belgrade into a huge media house for newsprint, radio and TV under the nose of the Milosevic regime and became the leader of ANEM, a collaborating network of electronic media outlets (local radio and TV stations) throughout Serbia and Montenegro. B92 was also the kingpin of a professional media center that became a very important meeting point for local, national and international media professionals and media support organizations.

The learning curve from these experiences was steep. The complex and protracted conflicts in the Balkans fostered holistic thinking about communication and how to strengthen capacity of local media outlets. It broke down the old distinction between humanitarian and long-term communication for development. A decade later when an independent evaluation assessed the impact of this support to freedom of expression and free media in Serbia (as well as in Macedonia and three countries in Africa), it concluded that Norway had made a significant contribution to a peaceful regime change.[1]

Other learning points were that running a media program was not much different from other humanitarian and development work when it came to needs assessments, appraisals, program implementation, and monitoring. What was fundamentally important was to be present on the ground and to understand the local context, identify good partners, show confidence in them, and develop a shared analysis of the situation. On that basis, respect for their integrity as media professionals was valued, and their professional, managerial capacity and editorial priorities as media organizations strengthened in a way that did not undermine confidence from their local audiences.

Donor coordination was fundamental. It provided synergy and cost-effectiveness, prevented duplication, and allowed for a division of labour according to capacities. This coordination depended on common understanding of the situation, agreement on strategies, transparency, plus willingness and time to cooperate.

From Field Experience to Institutional Learning in Norway

In the rather fragmented reality of media support that existed around 1997, a group of Norwegian media activists with a broad background came together and decided to take a more systematic approach. They had all experienced a very dysfunctional support system and shared a common vision to replace this with an analytical framework and tools for programming, monitoring, and evaluation of different intentions and types of interventions.

It resulted in a "tool kit" for assessing, deciding, designing, implementing, and evaluating media projects that brought conceptual clarity and was easy to apply in practice.[2] Three major categories were identified according to their objectives: *Humanitarian reporting, conflict resolution*, and *institutional building*. In reality, these categories would often overlap. It was also the first time that Norwegians working with media support saw the fundamental distinction between working with media *for* development in order to boost a message or a particular campaign, and working with media *in* development to build permanent local communication capacity.

Humanitarian reporting projects focus on exposed populations' need for information during crises. The goal is to empower people to make qualified decisions under highly complex and conflicting circumstances. Timely access to relevant and qualified information is the main guiding principle for such activities. Humanitarian reporting revolves around "news that people can use." Activities encompass much more than strict reporting on any conflict situation. Communication around health standards, information about communicable diseases, mine awareness, and how to get in touch with the right agencies in often a very confusing web of organizations present in a conflict situation are also typical subjects for humanitarian reporting. AIM, mentioned above, is a good example of such a project, but it also included elements in the other two categories described below.

Conflict resolution media projects aim at preventing, reducing, or resolving conflicts. They represent an alternative to the confrontational media that characterize a conflict situation and therefore aggravate rather than ameliorate. Such projects often combine building expertise in media management with applying conflict resolution techniques. They usually require a substantial amount of resources, as they emphasize program production. The "portfolio" of such programming can vary from news reporting based on a conflict resolution rationale to production of documentaries, drama, and music shows. Messages are usually conveyed to the audiences through a combination of hard-fact documentaries, music entertainment, and soap operas in a manner that fits the overall peace-building rationale. The BBC-Media Action is a world leader of such productions in local languages screened throughout the developing world.[3]

Democracy or institution building media projects support the development of a certain kind of political system, i.e. democratic pluralistic systems concerned with human and minority rights. Such projects are typical for post-conflict situations. Support will often be an additional dimension to other forms of donor involvement, for instance through multilateral channels such as UNDP. Although institution-building projects often have positive effects on the quality of reporting, their primary focus is structural/regime change.[4] The Zimbabwe Media Program which has been operated by the International Media Support for more than a decade and builds on an annually updated conceptual framework between donors and information sharing and collaboration on activities, belongs to the latter category, but includes also elements of conflict prevention and humanitarian reporting for instance on communicable diseases.[5]

The New Millennium: From Optimism to a Gloomy media picture

At the turn of the millennium, the world seemed open for more democracy, more respect for human rights, and more media freedom. Assaults and attacks on journalists and human rights activists were moderate, if not on a straight down-going curve. There was also technological optimism related to digital development, in particular to the expansion of the Internet, more access to information for all people and more participation and engagement by citizen journalism and social media. Funding increased steadily to a growing number of Norwegian and international media partnerships.

In 2005, the Norwegian Ministry of Foreign Affairs (MFA) issued a policy for media support in development assistance, and there referred explicitly to the good governance agenda:

> Free and independent media are an essential part of a viable democracy. All societies need open channels to be able to engage in social debate and to examine the exertion of power and authority in an independent light . . . The right to information is necessary for good governance, and good governance is perhaps the single most important factor in promoting development and fighting poverty.[6]

In 2008 the Norwegian MFA launched an initiative targeting violations of the right to freedom of expression. It highlighted the links between media, democracy, and development, and committed itself to provide more direct support to media in conflict areas. As a result, support to free media moved high up on the governance agenda. It also became the rationale for the Norwegian Agency for Development Cooperation's (Norad) shift from supporting a traditional communication for development approach to a new vision of building permanent media capacity in developing countries.

Then the Arab Spring, Libya, and Syria challenged the picture. In addition came social media, blogging, the mobile revolution, and Internet of Things as well as surveillance capacity, cybercrime, hate speech, and terrorism, and vamped the optimism. Media itself became a prime target for terrorist attacks, both targeting individual journalists and media houses. Fear and self-censorship increased. Press freedom indexes showed a declining number of countries with free or partly free media. Media manipulation and propaganda became more professionally done both online and offline. And the Internet was unfortunately a very easy means to use for such malicious activities.

The competition between digital media and traditional professional news agencies and media outlets has also intensified. There is more commercialization and concentration of media power than before. In countries in a state of fragility the media picture is more fractured and fragmented, where political actors take control over media, acquire their own media tools and use the Internet to manipulate, spread propaganda and wage media wars. This gloomy picture of world media trends may lead to self-fulfilling negative prophecies if not counteracted with evidence-based information and positive interventions. Especially in turbulent times, it is important to stand up for the universal right to press freedom, to protect people who use their right to speak, and to strengthen free and equal access to information for all. The whistle blower Edward Snowden put it this way: "When you say I don't care about the right to privacy because I have nothing to hide that is no different from saying I don't care about freedom of speech because I have nothing to say."[7]

Part II—Policy and Practice in Norwegian Humanitarian and Development Communication

Norwegian media policy for humanitarian actions and development cooperation has a twofold task: first, to provide the affected people with information vital for their coping capacity, and give them access to means of communication that will amplify their voices, promote their interests, and protect their human rights; second, to ensure that people in other countries get a sober and truthful picture of the political and humanitarian situation where there are crises and conflicts.

To work with good local partners who are trusted by their audiences as well as by the donor is essential in order to understand local problems and implement relevant programs. Confidence as a strategic approach can open hearts and minds, but is also vulnerable to opportunistic behavior. Mistakes are unavoidable, but costs can be greatly reduced if the selection process is well prepared. Likewise, it is critical to show local media outlets respect with regard to their credibility and editorial independence, and to ensure that funding is not awarded on the basis of ideology or as political favors.

What Norway learned in terms of policy development from its media support in the pioneering 1990s and onwards can be summed up in ten "golden rules." These rules are quite similar to other guidelines for Norwegian development assistance, but here geared particularly towards media support.

1. Enhance donor coordination
2. Identify and work with good local partners
3. Be flexible in project planning and design
4. Protect the credibility of local media
5. Develop capacity, not dependency
6. Plan for long-term donor commitment
7. Have exit plans ready
8. Diversify funding instruments
9. Promote conducive legislative/regulatory frameworks
10. Build sustainable media support institutions.

The purpose of media support is to develop capacity—not dependency—and refrain from imposing ideas, manipulative or crippling bureaucratic demands. Like all other development engagements such support is generally effective only after many years of sustained engagement; it cannot be known in advance how much time will be needed to achieve results, or what obstacles might emerge. It is necessary to be flexible in project planning and design. Media environments and other conditions change over time. Priorities and methods are not uniform, and choices and decisions must remain open as social and political situations evolve.

Norway also learned that it is essential not to destroy the local media market. In general, donors should refrain from giving grants to individual media outlets, although there will always be exceptions where such assistance will be necessary for political reasons. If available, soft loans from banks and other investment institutions are generally better options to develop the media market. But donors can without problems support journalists' organizations, branch associations, media research, and NGOs to avoid contradictions inherent to choosing recipients for direct support.

Finally, it is important to have strong self-regulatory press institutions within a system of stable, fair, media-supportive environment of law, courts, and regulators. For transitional countries coming from a totalitarian past where the regime used to manipulate and have full control over public opinion, this can be a very complex and time-consuming processes. To rehabilitate corrupted state radio/TV channels and turn them into public broadcasters is also extremely challenging, where both political will from national authorities and technical expertise from abroad are necessary. It might be easier for donors to help with temporary training until government institutions again are capable of providing sustainable media education.

Norwegian Development Cooperation

Norwegian development cooperation is well adapted, aligned, and harmonized with the OECD/DAC system, while the Norwegian system for humanitarian assistance connects closely with UN norms, guidelines, and procedures. Civil Society Organizations (CSOs) have since the beginning been a vital element in both contexts.

What makes the Norwegian system rather unique is the Information Grant Support Scheme (see box). It has facilitated a strong CSO impact in policy development. There are countless examples of debates started by CSOs, later followed by media campaigns that raised the public interest, then engaging political parties and finally ending up as Norwegian official policy.

Norad's Information Grant Support Scheme

The support program for Norwegian CSOs was established in the early 1990s, and the allocation is in 2016 well above 90 million NOK. CSOs can apply for support that enables them to build up their own professional communication departments on North–South issues and collaboration. Information and educational material are published on all media platforms, including paper magazines with an estimated yearly circulation of more than 700,000 copies. The aim is to gain and maintain support for the organizations, but also to be an independent voice and stimulate well-informed debates about development issues. The growing political conflict about this scheme revolves around the difficulty of distinguishing between what is public information work and organizational branding and public fundraising strategy.

Norad's Communication Department

Norad's own communication department has in recent years been reduced to mainly having the responsibility for information on development results. Norad's own newspaper *Bistandsaktuelt*, established in 1998, is still owned and financed by Norad, but has since 2011 been an independently edited newspaper under the same ethical norms as for other professional publications. *Bistandsaktuelt* now publishes on a multimedia platform and has a sustained and continuous coverage of the whole development sector.

The national campaign to drop charges against southern governments to repay "bad loans," given to them to finance Norwegian export of surplus ship tonnage, and Ban the Landmine Campaign are two success stories among many. This Norwegian model has been surprisingly effective in raising awareness about developmental issues both at home and internationally. CSOs have also acted as brokers and bridges in peace negotiations with so-called Track 2 activities (supporting and complementing diplomatic Track 1 activities providing broader public support for negotiations).

The Ministry of Foreign Affairs (MFA) Communication Department

The Ministry has always had a rather small communication unit and budget, and can only to a limited degree engage in open, informed, and thorough debates on development issues. Public media campaigns are for the most part outsourced to private companies, while their communication staff mostly comment on day-to-day issues, make press releases on special events, and do technical backstopping for their politicians. As a consequence, CSOs and their stand on many policy issues are more known to the public than the state institutions that fund them.

A New Strategy for Freedom of Expression and Independent Media in 2016

To elevate Human Rights values and political priorities the government submitted a White Paper to the Parliament in late 2014. *Democracy, rule of law*, and *equal opportunities for all* are priorities both in its foreign and development politics. The White Paper spelt out in greater detail how these three dimensions shall be strengthened in all sectors as well as being issues of concern for all development programs.[8]

In January 2016 the Norwegian Ministry of Foreign Affairs launched a new strategy for freedom of expression and independent media. It has three priority areas or pillars: (i) support to independent media, (ii) protection of journalists, HR activists, bloggers, artists, and others using their universal right to express themselves without fear of harassment, intimidation, assault, prosecution, and conviction, and (iii) access to information.[9] More emphasis shall be on international normative work, national legislation, promotion of more openness from governments, and business sectors about financial transactions, hindering blocking, filtering, and other forms of controlling information flows and promoting access and digital literacy for vulnerable groups.

Within the first pillar of the strategy, focus is on better competence among journalists and other media workers; stronger legal protection for independent media and media-related institutions; and contributing to media pluralism. The second pillar shall enhance protection of those who use their right to freedom of speech, including on the Internet, and reduce impunity of perpetrators against media workers. The third pillar concerns access to information and will assist countries in putting in place legal provisions to secure access to information. This can increase financial accountability mechanisms, transparency in public affairs and private finance transactions, and facilitate Internet access for disadvantaged groups.

Communication for Humanitarian Purposes

Norwegian humanitarian policy combines a rights-based operational approach with normative work, directed both towards the multilateral level and at individual countries. This normative framework rests on international humanitarian law and human rights and the four fundamental principles of humanity, non-discrimination, independence, and neutrality. Better coordination between humanitarian and long-term development cooperation is a major challenge.

UN appeals and the flow of continuous humanitarian reporting from the news agency IRIN form the basis for assessments and planning of support. International Media Support, Internews and other INGOs complement the UN information flow, along with humanitarian appeals from Norwegian CSOs such as the Norwegian Refugee Council, Norwegian Red Cross, Norwegian Church Aid, Norwegian People's Aid, Save the Children Norway. Many of them are active members in an international learning network called Communicating with Disaster Affected Community Network (www.cdacnetwork.org), also supported by Norway. CDAC does advocacy and advanced learning around the topic on effective Communication with Communities (CwC). The Norwegian Refugee Council in Oslo carries out the secretariat function of the network.

Communication for Development Goals

Communication, education and information are means used to achieve stated goals and objectives in development projects. Often also labeled "Behavior change communication" they are rarely mentioned in media policy documents and mostly left to the development organizations themselves to develop. The aim is not mainly to provide information or debate, but to facilitate change in the way people live and act. There are several ways to apply this approach.

Most common is the project approach preferred by those with little or no competence in communication and media. Staff members can be highly skilled in technical areas such as health, education, environmental protection, and so on, but use different communication channels and methods that are rather unsystematic and arbitrary. Usually they lack baseline data against which to measure change. However, even with a more professional approach, targeting groups with special information that is *necessary* to facilitate changes, it is not easy to know whether it really also is a *sufficient* condition for behavior change.

The more sensitive and private the desired change is, the more complex it is to find the right ways to communicate. For instance, when the aim is to end female genital mutilation/cutting, use condoms during sex, or stop smoking, a radio program, newspaper article, or billboard will rarely do the trick. Then, communication and information work must be combined with other methods that together might change the dynamics in social groups, so that their social norms change.

Our experience is that communication, whether through popular films that people discuss, newspaper articles, or radio programs where listeners join in the debates, can have a great influence on social norms. Dialogues and experiences shared in the community are probably most important. Successful community dialogue processes such as the methodology used by Steps International (a South Africa CSO) to create awareness about HIV/AIDs and behavioral change, have been able to create a demand for more information within the social target group.[10] In such situations, other media providers can join in and contribute with more information. Organizations and projects supported by Norad often use such communication as one of their methods.

Unfortunately, communication as a means to achieve behavioral change is seldom evaluated. Therefore, our knowledge is quite limited when it comes to how development communication may interact with other social factors and interventions in order to create maximum impact. From our own experience though, we will argue that group dynamics is the most important factor influencing individual changes, and that communication of various forms can influence such dynamics.

Another angle is to use information and communication tools for development through a community empowerment approach. Poverty is overwhelmingly linked to marginalization. And marginalization is caused by a number of different factors based on race, ethnicity, religion, sexual behavior, disabilities, culturally sanctioned gender discrimination, generational subordination, or a combination of all these factors. In all efforts to combat poverty and marginalization it is crucial to enhance communication capacity of marginalized groups in order to strengthen their self-identity, build cultural group self-esteem and give them the necessary political skills to negotiate a fair share of collective resources.

Historically, communication for development ("comdevt") efforts concentrated on information and communication campaigns. The main reason was that governments considered social mobilization through media as quite sensitive and therefore something they wanted to control politically. However, gradually, the barriers against use of modern communications technology for community participation, social animation and similar empowerment strategies have disappeared. Since the late 1980s Norway has worked closely with organizations such as Panos Network (originally called Panos Institute), a network of independent non-governmental institutes that use communication to promote public debate, pluralism, and democracy.[11]

The purpose of a community empowerment approach is to bridge the gap between an outside campaign approach with building the infrastructure and communication capacity from within communities and thereby amplify the voices of the poor. This is done through support to capacity building in communication skills—mainly through support to community radio stations and/or radios in the communities to help them cover development issues and investigative reporting/governance issues. Other programs deal with health, environment and natural resources management, with gender, human rights, and vulnerable groups as cross-cutting issues, partnering also with state channels and private mainstream media outlets.

A third angle is advocacy for change at a global level. In 2010, Norway started linking communication and advocacy in order to help design the UN Secretary-General's Global Strategy for Women's and Children's Health, and the revised strategy for the Sustainable Development Goals in 2015. The initiative worked through the platform of the "Every Woman Every Child" initiative and the Partnership for Maternal, Newborn and Child Health with 700 partners. A common agenda and key advocacy messages were developed through consensus and ownership building across seven constituency groups involved in maternal and child health. This constituency group was very comprehensive and diverse, and included partner countries, donors, civil society, academic/training and research institutions, UN and funds, health care professional organizations, and the private sector. When press releases based on such a broad constituency were published, they received wide coverage and helped create a platform for commitment to action ranging from the highest level of government/decision makers to implementers and activists on the ground. Professional communication experts worked together with technical experts to use communication and mobilization strategically for the global health cause.[12]

Conclusion: Some Topics for Further Policy Explorations

The new information technology not only changes the relation between citizens and states globally. It also creates an entire new configuration between human rights defenders, journalists and other information workers, media and communication specialists. It challenges our fundamental security systems, socio-political and economic development, peace, prosperity, and privacy.

Soon, most of the global population will have access to smart phones and the internet. As the digital world expands rapidly, intelligible communication becomes available on a variety of software platforms for different purposes. The technology can give us unlimited and unrestricted communication in real time, but also poses great challenges when it comes to the political objective of the Sustainable Development Goals "to leave no one behind." According to the World Bank 2016 Report on Digital Dividends the digital divide is growing, resulting in greater social and economic inequality for all those without Internet access, whether caused by poverty, ignorance, or digital illiteracy.[13]

Other challenges are that unverified information, rumors, and even false information travel worldwide in seconds and contribute to global misconceptions, distrust, and conspiracy thinking. Preventing hate speech and the misuse of communication technology are other major challenges. Access to lifesaving information and the right and ability to two-way communication must be included in the logistics and emergency planning and facilitated as part of a humanitarian response.

When an acute humanitarian crisis enters into a more long-term situation, communication systems must be built along with protection, shelter, food, and other fundamental human needs. Lack of safety for journalists is another major challenge. It creates no-go areas where objective reporting becomes extremely difficult. Building verification mechanisms in collaboration with local reporters on the ground should therefore be another high-priority area. This is very difficult to do unless there are already well-established relationships and trust on the ground between local media actors and outside support organizations. Communication must also be in a language that people understand. This is an extra challenge when working with minorities; it means understanding the local cultural codex, which again implies working closely with local media organizations.

Going back to where we started with Fridtjof Nansen and his deep frustration about the lack of response from European governments to give humanitarian assistance to millions of starving and dying people in Russia: Instead of passivity, he used his position as a highly respected international explorer and scientist, moral authority as the first League of Nations High Commissioner for Refugees, and his personal communication skills to organize an international campaign for which he later received the Nobel Peace Prize in 1922. In his Nobel Lecture, he said:

> The difficulty did not lie in finding the food or transporting it to those who were starving. No, there was more than enough grain in the world at that time, and adequate distribution facilities were available. The problem lay in obtaining funds, an obstacle, which has always bedeviled such attempts to supply aid—not least so at this moment. . . . In my opinion, the only avenue to salvation lies in cooperation between all nations on a basis of honest endeavor. . . . Honest work cannot thrive, however, except where there are peace and confidence: Confidence in one's self, confidence in others and confidence in the future. Here we strike at the heart of the matter.[14]

Confidence is the core, according to him, and confidence can only be built by broad and inclusive communication, through many channels and platforms, and can make a lasting difference in the field of humanitarian action.

Notes

1. "Evaluation of Norwegian Development Cooperation to Promote Human Rights," p. 71, Scanteam, August 2011.
2. "Local Media Support," Fafo Report 320, 1999.
3. BBC Media Action: Transforming Lives Around the World. www.bbc.co.uk/mediaaction/
4. "Local Media Support," Fafo Report 320, 1999.
5. International Media Support, available at: www.mediasupport.org/
6. Norwegian Guidelines for Support to Free Media in Developing Countries, p. 1, 2005, available at: www.norad.no/aktuelt/nyheter/2005/nye-retningslinjer-for-stotte-til-frie-medier/
7. Alan Rusbridger, Janine Gibson and Ewen MacAskill, "Edward Snowden: NSA Reform in the US is only the Beginning." May 22, 2015, available at: www.theguardian.com/us-news/2015/may/22/edward-snowden-nsa-reform
8. Meld. St. 10 (2014–2015) Report to the Storting (White paper) Opportunities for All: Human Rights in Norway's Foreign Policy and Development Cooperation.
9. www.regjeringen.no/globalassets/departementene/ud/vedlegg/mr/strategi_ytringsfrihet.pdf
10. Steps, "Documentary Films for Social Change: AfriDocs," available at: www.steps.co.za/
11. The Panos Network, available at: http://panosnetwork.org/
12. Every Woman Every Child, available at: www.everywomaneverychild.org/
13. The World Bank. "World Development Report 2016: Digital Dividends," May 7, available at: www.worldbank.org/en/publication/wdr2016
14. Fridtjof Nansen, Nobel Lecture, 1922. "The Suffering People Europe," December 19, available at: www.nobelprize.org/nobel_prizes/peace/laureates/1922/nansen-lecture.html

13

THE CORRELATION OF HUMANITARIAN AID, NORTH–SOUTH DEVELOPMENT COOPERATION, AND THE MEDIA

Facts and Fiction

Ulrich Nitschke and Heike Wülfing

Humanitarian aid and development cooperation are usually separate areas of intervention and the approach is to be determined in times of crisis and especially after crisis. Major donor countries are still struggling with the associated challenges. And there are certainly several good reasons to do so. It is not only the very different origins of these two fields of action—there are some more arguments. The key issue in humanitarian aid is focusing on the needs of people in emergency situations: to save lives and reduce suffering. While development cooperation concentrates on complex mid-term and long-term projects such as education and state building, another different aspect focuses on the relation to the concerned government: Realizing sustainable interventions, development cooperation needs to interact with governments, whereas humanitarian assistance requires less coordination with government entities but is sometimes highly volatile, since governments come later into the affected areas than humanitarian aid structures.

Despite this heterogeneity there are better reasons to overcome the divide, especially if we look into real-life cases. This chapter will provide some decent experience-driven historic crises that have simultaneously been calling for immediate response as well as some long-term planning and strategic development cooperation. Structures and institutions of humanitarian aid as well as of development agencies proved to fail to cooperate in most of the historic examples described here. But why is this the case in so many incidents and crisis situations around the globe? How can we overcome the "gap" and what specifically is the role of media in this regard? How can different institutions of humanitarian assistance and development cooperation enhance their modes of cooperation and link up needs and people-driven development, especially in times when fragility and crisis are increasing around the globe?[1]

Our essay provides some preliminary experience but cannot provide scientific research or data-based evidence on how to overcome the gap. There are already several studies proving that the lack of resources and capacities in terms of financial, human, and technical aspects and a low level of knowledge and education have emerged as root causes for several drivers of disaster risk.[2] Individual actions alone will not be sufficient if governments do not make the necessary changes at the structural level. The community affected by the crisis is crucial as well[3] and obviously this is one main reason to overcome the gap between humanitarian action and development cooperation. This chapter provides some guidance as to how the involvement of community and religious actors can serve as bridge-makers.

Furthermore, we provide arguments particularly regarding the role of media, to provide more prevention and long-term consultative approaches in development assistance. The role of the media in any disaster is significant to motivate the social climate and consequently motivate funding and donations. Moreover, examining social media, the prevailing argument is that access to media sources are more and more democratized, where information is quickly disseminated and consequently turned into collective action.[4] We think that this assertion of the "democratization of the media" is an illusion where more often than not media is dominated by power and money.

In this discourse, while challenging some established thinking and structures in international development cooperation, we try to motivate the ideologists of both fields of action to reconsider their positions and help to bridge the gap for the betterment of so many people affected by natural as well as man-made disasters.

The Tsunami 2004

It is December 26, 2004, and the worst ever Tsunami hits coastal regions in both Sri Lanka and India, as well as Thailand and Banda Aceh. In the space of the two hours it took for the first and second waves to strike, a total of 227,898 people[5] in 14 countries lost their lives, millions lost their homes, sources of income and livelihood, their relatives, and hopes for a decent life.

The media response was quick and events were documented[6] surprisingly earlier than any official statement. Videos, photos, and posts were circling the first social media fora around the world. These pictures of the waves and the sound of the screams of people in shock may never be forgotten. Like many other tourists from all parts of the world, some German tourists were affected as well. This may have been the reason why thousands of German compatriots donated so much private funding to the humanitarian assistance and development of the devastated region. The plight of the affected people and countries prompted a worldwide humanitarian response. Nations all over the world provided over US$14 billion in aid for the affected regions.[7] This incident has been extremely well documented because of the prevalence of video cameras and due to the fact that the tsunami struck highly frequented touristic areas where many tourists have their cameras at the ready.

In Germany, there was enormous media coverage, most likely caused by the tourists who were involved in this catastrophe and by Chancellor Schröder's Christmas address establishing linking village-to-village, school-to-school. Without this national interest, the overwhelming donation of nearly 1 billion euros would probably not have been given. At the end of January

2005 the sum already reached 650,000 euros, more than ever before in German donation history. These private donations in a fragile situation caused fragile solidarity—but what does "fragile solidarity" mean, especially for development cooperation? People were touched by the fact that German compatriots were hit by the tsunami wave. If no Germans had been involved, would solidarity have been weakened or even non-existent? Before trying to answer this question we will examine our responding tsunami-work in Germany. The Service Agency Communities in One World only started to work a few days after the tsunami, supplying emergency aid to the devastated coastal areas while considering sustainable shore protection and implementing a development education campaign in Germany to provide private donors with developmental sensitive information.

In order to gain an inside view into the very concrete working level, consider that there were 1,377 offers of relief and partnerships from federal states, municipalities, districts, schools, non-governmental organizations, companies, and private individuals that wanted to get involved with the rebuilding and development of the Asian regions affected by the flood. Two years later, 64 percent of the offers had been matched or had received project recommendations. The remaining part of the donators could not be placed, either because they had retracted their offer to help or because they were commercial offers.[8] In total, the Service Agency was able to identify 152 projects having a total volume of about 30 million euros and placed these successfully. For this, 321 different donations were bundled, in part significantly, to meet the demand of the respective rebuilding projects. According to the wish of many German donors to get involved with rebuilding efforts for children, most of the projects established were children- and school-related projects; many also got involved with re-establishing medical care and with activities for rebuilding infrastructure.

Both of us were at the forefront of German civil service and media efforts, and had to explain the difference between disaster relief and development cooperation and point out the necessity of sustainable rebuilding projects created in a cooperative manner. After the first project financing had materialized, intensified counselling and project monitoring became significantly more important. During the course of the projects, new questions and also some difficulties came up from the acting parties. A large part of the counselling service was devoted to imponderables of the rebuilding process: halting projects, reports on expenditure of funds, lack of communication, increased project funding, or new legislation in the countries—the Service Agency offered counselling and itself partly gained new information each day.

Beginning in the second half of 2005, targeted decentralized counselling services were offered that aimed to point out the possibilities of developing long-term partnerships. Even though project-partnerships were successfully established, implemented and completed, the establishment of long-term partnerships was achieved only sporadically. This is a consequence of fragile solidarity fading away with time, lasting no longer than the media response is present.

Regarding the media management, the Service Agency created some realms for the purpose of public relations that have been respected. A networking website where basic information concerning their work, the current situation, information regarding the countries, project successes, and hints and procedures was constantly kept up to date. In particular, service information and printed documents for relief initiatives were created. Moreover, the Service Agency was an information center and contact for the media—queries from more than 150 participants were processed.

And what about the NGOs in Germany? They came together united to perform better and enhanced their immediate response on the ground and founded the network "Bündnis

Entwicklung Hilft," a union of seven relief organizations. The decision to create this network was made right after the tsunami. The organizations implemented their aid measures independently, but discused them together and raised funds together in the case of urgent need. Cooperation with other NGOs meant their voices were heard by politicians, which helped to save costs and share knowledge.[9]

One lesson learned from the tsunami was the turning point for countries to see that risk management and early warning are essential public health functions and crucial for protecting people's health and investments. But what about a catastrophe that gets nearly no public attention? Does cooperation still work efficiently? Another crucial insight emerging from the tsunami relief funds concerns political backing of leadership on all levels (in Germany in a Federal system) you need their support—from mayors (e.g. the Mayors Forum on disaster and risk management that included the city of Bonn) to *Ländergovernments* to national level—as well as involvement of NGOs, which is key to gaining some implementation and new partnerships on the local level.

The Floods in Myanmar in 2015

In July and August 2015 Myanmar suffered the worst landslides and flooding in recent decades after unusually heavy monsoon rains and exposure to Cyclone Komen that passed by the country's southern coast. This natural disaster also struck other states in this region, such as the often affected Pakistan and India, for this is the world's most disaster-prone region with 88 percent of all people affected worldwide by natural disasters living here and the average number of people annually affected by floods amounting to 84 million.[10]

We would rather focus on Myanmar for the consequences of the floods, where they were worse than in neighboring countries. OCHA reports that 17 million people live in the most affected areas and about 1.7 million were displaced from their homes and 15,239 houses were destroyed.[11] Over 1.4 million acres of farmland were inundated, with more than 841,000 acres destroyed. Only 123,000 acres had been re-planted when the floods happened, at a time with just two weeks of the planting season remaining. Consequently, Myanmar required enough food for 2.9 million people, not only during the time of the emergency but until the end of June 2016.[12] The World Food Program provided life-saving food to 455,000 people during this emergency in summer 2015 and continued to provide food assistance to flood victims until mid 2016.[13] While the water receded in most areas, many roads and bridges were destroyed in the worst affected states and regions. In order to overcome logistical challenges, such as assessments and assistance delivery, it was necessary to strengthen the resilience of disaster-affected communities. Logistical barriers made it difficult for the government and humanitarian organizations to respond to the most urgent needs of displaced people and other affected people in Chin State, and cold temperatures further exacerbated the situation for people living in tents and other temporary accommodation.[14]

Millions of people were affected in nearly all of Myanmar's states and regions. They lost their homes, livelihoods, crops, and food stocks. So, how did the public react? Were there private donations for the victims affected by the flood? As there are hardly any official figures about donations, it's nearly the same as the funding for the Asian countries, where the needs are far from being met: In March 2016 the funding made available for meaningful relief was 99.1 percent unmet.[15]

When looking for reasons for this very mediocre willingness to donate, one must consider the media reaction towards this incident. Of course, all international and national relief organizations called for action but there was barely—compared to other natural disasters—

any reaction from traditional media, such as newspapers, television and radio, or on social media. In Myanmar no tourists were involved in this disaster and therefore no videos and photos circulated and there was little reaction from social media. In addition, foreign, security, political, and resource-linked interests are almost non-existent regarding Myanmar. Therefore, the floods in Myanmar may be a clear counterexample to immediate reaction and support. This is what we therefore call a second effect of fragile solidarity in such contexts. Ironically, without media coverage and victims from Western countries there are hardly any large-scale private donations compared to what was donated during the time of the 2004 tsunami.

West Bank and Gaza Conflicts

Between 2010 and the end of 2014, Ulrich Nitschke was assigned to the occupied territories of Palestine. The main purpose of the German bilateral cooperation in the governance sector was and still is capacitating municipalities and local communities to develop better citizens' services and enhance local authorities in democratic decision-making as well as in sustainable city planning. Admittedly, in the latter we failed because it is almost impossible to plan effectively under such a devastating occupation. When 62 percent of West Bank territories are under strict military rule and every construction above 70 cm in height has to have permittion from Israel, there is no room for long-term or strategic planning. As bad as it is in the West Bank, it is even worse under the siege in Gaza.

Bearing the region's long and tragic history in mind and not going beyond the scope of this essay, we consider the most recent Gaza war that happened in 2014. On July 8, 2014 the Israeli Defense Force started their military operation, Protective Edge, after missile attacks by Hamas and other Palestinian militant groups on Israeli territory. This ended on August 26, with a return to the cease-fire conditions of 2012. During those 50 days of battle more than 500,000 Palestinians were displaced at the height of the hostilities and over 100,000 people are still displaced. Approximately 18,000 houses were destroyed or severely damaged and consequently about 108,000 Palestinians were made homeless. By March 2016 more than 16,000 families—or over 90,000 individuals—remained displaced as a result of the 2014 Gaza–Israel hostilities.[16] And casting a glance at the terrible figures regarding the numbers of dead and injured people, 2,205 Palestinians were killed, including at least 1,483 civilians, including 521 children and 283 women; 71 Israelis were killed, including 66 soldiers, a security coordinator and 4 civilians.[17]

The ceasefire in Gaza is very particular since the fighting still goes on regardless. The figures from one month alone, December 2015, demonstrate the extent of this tragedy: 37 Palestinians were killed, 2,154 Palestinian injured, 2 Israelis killed, 41 Israelis injured, 13 structures demolished in the West Bank, 61 People displaced in the West Bank.[18] The end of 2015 had recorded 136 Palestinian deaths and nearly 14,000 injuries in the West Bank and Israel in the context of attacks and clashes. The bulk of the casualties were recorded in the last quarter of the year, in a wave of violence characterized by almost daily stabbings and ramming attacks by non-affiliated Palestinians, and widespread protests and clashes.[19]

In the first few months of 2015 the status of rebuilding and repairing these homes was slow, but after the agreement between Israel and the State of Palestine in June 2015 on the import of restricted building materials, the reconstruction gradually increased. By the end of January 2016, around 15 percent of displaced families were able to return to their homes and the repair of an additional 2,000 homes is ongoing. Despite this progress, at the beginning of 2016, still around 95,000 people had no home. And there is a funding gap for about half of them.[20] Furthermore, the displacement goes on, because 11,000 demolition orders are out-standing in the so-called "Area C" affecting 13,000 structures.[21] It has become very evident that the Palestinians urgently require legal assistance and advocacy to prevent displacement, and confirm the rule of law in the occupied, military-ruled territories.

The living conditions in the occupied territories are not only characterized by the lack of shelter, the Palestinians also suffer from high unemployment, low household incomes, and high costs of living. The erosion of livelihoods has led to continued high levels of food insecurity in the occupied Palestinian territories, which equates to 27 percent of all households that are moderately to severely food insecure. Nearly half of the households in Gaza—47 percent—and 16 percent of households in the West Bank are food insecure. Across the occupied Palestinian territory there is even higher food insecurity for female-headed house-holds with 32 percent and refugee camps at 39 percent.[22] One other aspect concerns access to essential services including water, sanitation and health, healthcare, education, energy, and housing, which are severely restricted for Palestinians in the West Bank and Gaza. Only 40 percent of Gaza's 1.7 million population receive just 5 to 8 hours of water supply every three days; 1.4 million people, including refugees, face restricted access to basic healthcare and 593,000 children need humanitarian interventions to access education.

The enclave is believed to have the world's highest unemployment rate at 43.9 percent[23] and almost 80 percent of Gaza's population is currently aid dependent.[24] Israel's land, air, and sea blockades as well as the most recent war pushed this to a record high of 43 percent in 2014. Youth unemployment, meanwhile, stands at more than 60 percent.[25] It is no wonder that Palestinians are hardly developing short-term, mid-term, let alone long-term, perspectives under such conditions. And again, even if Palestine has not suffered natural disasters and is barely comparable with the tsunami or Myanmar, where is the solidarity of private donations?

In face of all of these terrible facts, how come the world is not willing to offer more financial support for the victims of this ongoing conflict? The above-mentioned funding gap forces the supposition that people are more willing to donate money to victims of natural disasters than to "complicated" humanitarian emergencies that tend to be politically and socially complex.[26] And what about the role of media in this tragic history? Is there a lack of media response because no German tourists were ever present in Gaza while houses were bombed and people killed?

In contrast, the Gaza conflict is an excellent case to explore how social media is used to attempt to sway international opinion.[27] Both Hamas and Israel inform the public about the conflict,[28] giving a view of statistics and personal stories that have a very different effect on the recipients. Both sides advocate their actions to international audiences and know how to use social media as a tool for conflict.[29]

Let us now return to the affected people who are in need of support and who are experiencing a humanitarian crisis as a result of war. Although this cannot be compared with natural hazards such as the 2004 tsunami or the floods in Myanmar, the impact and conse-quences for human beings are pretty much the same. But the public reactions—concerning media and donations—are rather different. So how can we overcome the picture-driven fragile solidarity? Can this be done without becoming cynical about loss of lives and without losing the momentum obtained by people who lead secure lives and are seriously touched by a crisis and want to help? Can media be the answer to this dilemma? Regarding the possibility of involving and motivating people through information, there is still the ambiguity of information that can resemble manipulation. We do believe that something else is missing here. Fragile solidarity is driven by direct concerns with the effects of media in crisis and for sure by political agendas. It is difficult to compare but important to raise these issues concerning the role of media and their accountability in situations of crisis and disaster caused by natural hazards or war situations. We suggest differentiation between the agendas and topics by looking into some actors that are often not perceived as actors in crisis situations, who rather just do the job out of humanitarian or religiously motivated compassion.

Faith-based Organizations

Let us now look at a "new" or better long-term player who is typically not immediately considered in our fields of interest: religious or faith-based organizations (FBOs). In case of crisis they reach the place before any other organization arrives, they operate efficiently like all other humanitarian aid workers and continue their efforts constantly even after others have already gone. In some societies, they provide more than 50 percent of the health and education sector.[30] In sub-Saharan Africa a considerable proportion of social services is provided by FBOs, for example in Kenya the figure is about 40 percent and in Uganda more than 50 percent.[31]

More than 80 percent of the global population affiliate with a religion.[32] In some countries of development cooperation that percentage is even higher. Taking this into account, any development policy that respects people as individuals must also respect their individual worldviews, which for most people are fundamentally shaped by their religion.[33] This major part of the population is also decisive for the achievement of Sustainable Development Goals.[34] And the importance of the world's religions is rising; forecasts suggest that the share of people who identify with a religion will rise to 90 percent.[35] Moreover, religion can drive and motivate people to become socially engaged and thus improve the prospects for successful development.[36]

Looking at the local religious players and their role in humanitarian response there is a major review of over 300 studies that examines the evidence for the contribution of faith groups to community resilience in the context of humanitarian emergencies.[37] One reason is the role of religious players in their society: They are often firmly rooted and stand for accountability—both advantages that no external organization will be able to fulfil. FBOs incorporate these unique characteristics by working on the local level and always including their local players and often long-term experience.

Regarding the multitude of successfully working projects managed by FBOs, whether these are performed in cooperation with other national or international organizations or by interfaith networks,[38] it is difficult to present only one of those. Here, one best practice is showing the effectiveness of a coordinated religious development strategy. The northern part of Burkina Faso lies within the Sahel region where water is a rare resource. Over 90 percent of the growing and predominantly Muslim population depends on agriculture for their livelihoods and is always struggling against the drought. In 1969 some local leaders in the provincial town of Dori in the far Northeast of the country had already formed an association to improve the living and working conditions. This is where Cissé Nassourou, Grand Imam of Dori, and his Catholic counterpart Paul Ouédraogo, Bishop of Fada N'Gourma, work. They are members of the Union Fraternelle des Croyants de Dori, which in the initial years focused on hydraulic structures and resource conservation. The initiative has now evolved into an integrated regional rural development project that serves some 400,000 people. Priority is given to water management in order to improve people's access to drinking water and water for producing crops. This involves building rainwater reservoirs and installing solar systems to operate pumps to water the surrounding fruit and vegetable plots. The general levels of nutrition have improved significantly through consumption of the newly cultivated vegetables. This involvement by the religious communities is vital because the state does not offer any comprehensive extension and support programs for rural areas. Above all, the cooperation between Muslims and Christians is a model of good practice in terms of interfaith dialogue.[39]

The importance of collaboration and coherence between faith communities is evidently shown in this project. Many institutions and organizations as well as the UN have stressed the importance of these types of cooperation.[40] It is time to explore this promising approach of cooperation with FBO, as their capabilities, networks, and structures are essential for building local and global capacity. FBOs can be one part of the solution for bridging the gap between humanitarian aid and sustainable development cooperation.

Intrinsic Aspects Promoting the Gap

Let us now move away from the concrete working level and return to structural concerns. What about the competencies and responsibilities of governmental departments and administration in our fields of interest? How do states bureaucratically handle humanitarian assistance and development cooperation? There are mainly two different systems of management: One example for the division of sectors and funding is the German framework whereby humanitarian aid lies within the responsibility of the Federal Foreign Office:

> The lead ministry for the German Government's humanitarian aid abroad is the Federal Foreign Office, which provides humanitarian assistance swiftly, flexibly and without unnecessary bureaucracy. According to the principle of subsidiarity, the German Federal Government provides humanitarian assistance where the government of a country hit by disaster is unable or unwilling to do so itself on a sufficient scale.[41]

However, development cooperation belongs to the responsibility of the Federal Ministry for Economic Cooperation and Development:

> The BMZ develops the guidelines and the fundamental concepts on which German development policy is based. It devises long-term strategies for cooperation with the various players concerned and defines the rules for implementing that cooperation. These are the foundations for developing shared projects with partner countries and international development organisations. All efforts are informed by the United Nations Millennium Development Goals (MDGs), which ambitiously aim to halve poverty in the world by 2015.[42]

More contemporaneous of course are the UN Sustainable Development Goals (SDGs) and Agenda 2030.

The same structural divide applies for the United States. The United States Agency for International Development (USAID) mission statement

> highlights two complementary and intrinsically linked goals: ending extreme poverty and promoting the development of resilient, democratic societies that are able to realize their potential. We fundamentally believe that ending extreme poverty requires enabling inclusive, sustainable growth; promoting free, peaceful, and self-reliant societies with effective, legitimate governments; building human capital and creating social safety nets that reach the poorest and most vulnerable.[43]

It is the leading US Government agency that is responsible for long-term development cooperation. Humanitarian aid is the responsibility of the State Department:

> The U.S. Government provides life-saving disaster relief, including food aid, and other humanitarian assistance to people affected by natural disasters and complex, human-made crises. Within hours of a disaster, the U.S. Government—through its foreign assistance—mobilizes goods, services, and relief workers to assist survivors with food, water and sanitation, shelter, and health care, and to strengthen local capacity to respond to the humanitarian needs. These programs will strive to uphold international standards for the provision of humanitarian assistance. Where appropriate, we will restore sustainable livelihoods to encourage self-reliance and minimize the need for long-term assistance. In doing so, U.S. humanitarian assistance begins the process of stabilization and recovery as early as possible.[44]

In both countries the missions seem to have the same overall goal: improving people's lives.

Another, more holistic approach reigns in Sweden, where both fields of action are united under one ministerial roof. According to the multilateral cooperation in the Scandinavian country

> Development cooperation is about helping to enable poor people to improve their living conditions. Swedish development aid is often channelled through international organisations such as the UN and the EU. Humanitarian assistance refers to Sweden's activities to save lives, alleviate suffering and maintain the human dignity of those affected by natural disasters, armed conflicts or other similar circumstances.[45]

It can hardly be a coincidence that Sweden clearly shows an increased efficiency concerning its activities in this policy field. Based on ODA data as percent of Gross National Income (GNI), the Swedish figure reaches 1.10 percent—whereas the USA shows 0.19 percent and Germany 0.41 percent. This data may even convince skeptical players to no longer promote the separation of humanitarian aid and development cooperation.

Conclusion

Both fields of action, humanitarian aid and development cooperation, have worked together efficiently—as seen in the tsunami case. But there are other disasters—naturally caused ones such as in Myanmar and man-made as in Gaza—where these fields have not seemed to work well together. Political reasons and lack of media interest may be the causes for less efficiency. But shouldn't this be one more reason to establish a bridging management to reinforce all possibilities and resources to improve conditions and implement mechanisms to enhance coordination for the betterment of the most affected people on the ground?

The fragmented landscape of programs, projects, and players of both fields of action has to be connected by the overall nexus of responsibility towards people in need of support. This is a good ground for a mutual fruitful cooperation between old and new partners. There is no doubt about the need for more effective partnerships, including in the area of finance, that will maximize our impact.[46] Their experience and engagement will help to create the nexus of a new and common approach to development activities. To achieve a more responsible management of rescue, prevention, and reconstruction, the "division of labour"[47] has to diminish, as is already being practiced in some countries. A liberalization and renewal of established notions and structures in international and national cooperation will lead to more efficient changes—a simple but mostly convincing argument.

One possible way to achieve more and sustainable enhancements could be the establishment of a linking management mechanism. Therefore, for innovative platforms to induce links, to coordinate activities and exchange between NGOs and governmental institutions, organizations and community actors are required—as these are essential for the long overdue creation of synergies.

Additionally, and as shown, the entire portfolio of media plays a crucial role in getting people involved and engaged in all types of development work. Consequently, the media is requested to illuminate the indispensable necessity of a new correlation between formerly and still divided fields of development cooperation and humanitarian assistance. The influence of social media websites is enormous and their usage is affecting people to react. Regarding the fact that 74 percent of the world's online population use social media,[48] this can also change the world outside of the Internet.[49] To utilize this key role of special programs for media, development and training for journalists have to be designed.

Dialogue is a key to partnership; it involves developing new alliances and cooperation, and trying to build bridges between different approaches and capacities—so let us start getting into dialogue about correlating humanitarian aid and development cooperation—it is time to pool resources and enhance efficiency. The newly established International Partnership on Religion and Sustainable Development/PaRD under the stewardship of GiZ can be a model for that.

Notes

1. See Bertelsmann Transformation Index 2016, available at: www.bti-project.org/en/home/
2. German Committee for Disaster Reduction (Ed.). (2012) *Detecting Disaster Root Causes—A Framework and an Analytic Tool for Practitioners*, Bonn: DKKV Publication Series 48.
3. German Federal Ministry for Economic Cooperation and Development. (2016) *Voices from Religions on Sustainable Development*, Bonn: BMZ.
4. Thomas Zeitzoff. (2014) *Gaza: Does Social Media Influence Conflict? Evidence from the 2012 Gaza Conflict* (Working Paper), available at: www.zeitzoff.com/uploads/2/2/4/1/22413724/zeitzoff_socialmedia_2ndgaza_v2.pdf
5. *U.S. Geological Survey (2004) Magnitude 9.1—Off the West Coast of Sumatra*, available at: www.fiu.edu/~longoria/gly3034-sp/gly3034sp/sumatra.pdf
6. Facebook was founded on February 4, 2004.
7. Sisira Jayasuriya and Peter McCawley. (2010) "The matter of money," in *Asian Tsunami: Aid and Reconstruction after a Disaster*, Cheltenham, UK and Northampton, MA: Edward Elgar.
8. Service Agency in One World. (2007) *Zwei Jahre Partnerschaftsinitiative* (Two Years of Partnership Initiative), Bonn.
9. www.entwicklung-hilft.de/wir-ueber-uns.html
10. https://docs.unocha.org/sites/dms/ROAP/Mainpage/images/ROAP_10years_A4_final.png
11. http://reliefweb.int/report/myanmar/ocha-flash-update-no-2-myanmar-floods-emergency-03-august-2015
12. www.wfp.org/stories/myanmar-five-months-after-floods
13. www.wfp.org/stories/five-months-after-floods-and-landslides-chin-state-and-sagaing-region-wfp-continue-its-sup
14. http://reliefweb.int/report/myanmar/revised-flood-response-plan-myanmar-august-december-2015
15. www.unocha.org/myanmar
16. http://gaza.ochaopt.org/2016/02/reconstruction-of-15-per-cent-of-homes-destroyed-or-severely-damaged-during-the-2014-hostilities/
17. www.ochaopt.org/content.aspx?id=1010361
18. www.ochaopt.org/documents/ocha_opt_the_humanitarian_monitor_2016_01_05_english_dec.pdf
19. http://reliefweb.int/report/occupied-palestinian-territory/gaza-situation-report-126–14-january-2016
20. http://gaza.ochaopt.org/2016/02/reconstruction-of-15-per-cent-of-homes-destroyed-or-severely-damaged-during-the-2014-hostilities/

21. www.ochaopt.org/documents/hno_hrp_dashboard_english_2016.pdf

22. www.ochaopt.org/documents/hno_december29_final.pdf

23. wwwds.worldbank.org/external/default/WDSP/IB/2015/05/27/090224b082eccb 31/5_0/Rendered/PDF/Economic0monit0oc0liaison0committee.pdf

24. www.unrwa.org/newsroom/emergency-reports/gaza-situation-report-94

25. www.worldbank.org/en/news/press-release/2015/05/21/gaza-economy-on-the-verge-of-collapse

26. Jake Wheeler. (2013) *How Does Media Coverage Impact Disasters?* Center for Disaster Philanthropy, available at: http://disasterphilanthropy.org/disaster-lifecycle-2/media-coverage/how-does-media-coverage-impact-disasters/

27. Zeitzoff. (2014) *Gaza: Does Social Media Influence Conflict?*

28. Ruben Durante and Ekaterina Zhuravskaya. (2015) *Attack When the World Is Not Watching? U.S. News and the Israeli-Palestinian Conflict*, available at: https://papers.ssrn.com/sol3/papers.cfm?abstract_id=2566741SSRN-id2566741.pdf

29. Zeitzoff. (2014) *Gaza: Does Social Media Influence Conflict?*

30. Joint Learning Initiative on Faith and Local Communities. (2015) *Proceedings of the Religion and Sustainable Development Building Partnerships to End Extreme Poverty Conference*, Washington, DC, available at: http://jliflc.com/recources/rsd-conference-proceedings/

31. UNFPA. (2008) *Culture Matters: Lessons from a Legacy of Engaging Faith-based Organisations*, New York: UNFPA, available at: www.unfpa.org/sites/default/files/pub-pdf/Cultur_Matter_II.pdf

32. Pew Foundation. (2015) *The Future of World Religions: Population Growth Projections, 2010–2050*, Washington, DC: Pew Foundation, available at: www.pewforum.org/2015/04/02/religious-projections-2010–2050/

33. German Federal Ministry for Economic Cooperation and Development. (2016) *Voices from Religions on Sustainable Development*, Bonn: BMZ.

34. Joint Learning Initiative on Faith and Local Communities. (2015) *Proceedings of the Religion and Sustainable Development Building Partnerships to End Extreme Poverty Conference*, Washington, DC, available at: http://jliflc.com/recources/rsd-conference-proceedings/

35. Pew Foundation. (2015) *The Future of World Religions*.

36. Deutsche Gesellschaft für Internationale Entwicklung. (2016) *More than Anything: The Contribution of Religious Communities and Human Rights Organisations to Sustainable Development*, Bonn: GiZ.

37. http://jliflc.com/resources/local-faith-communities-and-the-promotion-of-resilience-in-humanitarian-situations-a-scoping-study/

38. Joint Learning Initiative on Faith and Local Communities. (2015) *Proceedings of the Religion and Sustainable Development Building Partnerships to End Extreme Poverty Conference*.

39. Deutsche Gesellschaft für Internationale Entwicklung. (2016) *More than Anything*.

40. Joint Learning Initiative on Faith and Local Communities. (2015) *Proceedings of the Religion and Sustainable Development Building Partnerships to End Extreme Poverty Conference*.

41. www.auswaertiges-amt.de/EN/Aussenpolitik/HumanitaereHilfe/WieHelfenWir_node.html

42. www.bmz.de/en/ministry/mandate/index.html

43. www.usaid.gov/who-we-are/mission-vision-values

44. www.state.gov/s/d/rm/rls/dosstrat/2007/html/82955.htm

45. www.government.se/government-policy/multilateral-cooperation/

46. *Poverty Conference*, Washington, DC, available at: http://jliflc.com/recources/rsd-conference-proceedings/

47. Bruno Riccio, Maria Benadusi and Chiara Brambilla. (2011) *Disasters, Development and Humanitarian Aid: New Challenges for Anthropology*, CERCO: Scuola di dottorato in antropologia ed epistemonlogia della complessità, Università degli Studi die Bergamo.

48. www.pewinternet.org/fact-sheets/social-networking-fact-sheet/

49. Taylor Kennedy. (2015) *The Influence of Social Media*, Senior Honors Thesis Paper 440, available at: http://commons.emich.edu/honors/440

References

Deutsche Gesellschaft für Internationale Entwicklung. (2016) *More than Anything: The Contribution of Religious Communities and Human Rights Organisations to Sustainable Development*, Bonn: GiZ.

German Committee for Disaster Reduction (Ed.). (2012) *Detecting Disaster Root Causes: A Framework and an Analytic Tool for Practitioners*, Bonn: DKKV Publication Series 48.

German Federal Ministry for Economic Cooperation and Development. (2016) *Voices from Religions on Sustainable Development*, Bonn: BMZ.

Jayasuriya, S. and McCawley, P. (2010) *"The matter of money" in the Asian Tsunami: Aid and Reconstruction after a Disaster*, Cheltenham, UK and Northampton, MA: Edward Elgar.

Pew Foundation. (2015) *The Future of World Religions: Population Growth Projections, 2010–2050*, Washington, DC: Pew Foundation, available at: www.pewforum.org/2015/04/02/religious-projections-2010–2050/

Service Agency in One World. (2007) *Zwei Jahre Partnerschaftsinitiative* (Two Years of Partnership Initiative), Bonn.

UNFPA. (2008) *Culture Matters: Lessons from a Legacy of Engaging Faith-based Organisations*, New York: UNFPA, available at: www.unfpa.org/sites/default/files/pub-pdf/Cultur_Matter_II.pdf

Zeitzoff, T. (2014) *Gaza: Does Social Media Influence Conflict? Evidence from the 2012 Gaza Conflict* (Working Paper), available at: www.zeitzoff.com/uploads/2/2/4/1/22413724/zeitzoff_socialmedia_2ndgaza_v2.pdf

14

GLOBAL EMERGENCY PREPAREDNESS AND MULTILATERAL ACTION IN AN INFORMATION AGE

Henia Dakkak

The global response to the January 2010 7.0 magnitude earthquake in Haiti showed how connected individuals are becoming increasingly central to humanitarian emergency response and recovery. Haitians trapped under rubble used text messaging to send pleas for help. Concerned citizens worldwide engaged in a variety of ways, from sending in donations via SMS, to using shared networks to translate and map requests for assistance. After a large-scale disaster, there is always a massive effort to collect and analyze large volumes of data and distill from the chaos the critical information needed to target humanitarian aid most efficiently. But the response to the 2010 earthquake in Haiti was different.

For the first time, members of the community affected by the disaster issued pleas for help using social media and widely available mobile technologies. Around the world, thousands of ordinary citizens mobilized to aggregate, translate, and plot these pleas on maps, and to organize technical efforts to support the disaster response. In one case, hundreds of geospatial information systems experts used fresh satellite imagery to rebuild missing maps of Haiti and plot a picture of the changed reality on the ground. The work—done through "OpenStreetMap"—became an essential element of the response, providing much of the street-level mapping data that was used for logistics and camp management.

Natural and human-made disasters have swept through various parts of the world and received much attention over the past decade. Meanwhile, many parts of the world suffer from a lack of basic necessities, including shelter, water, food, education, access to basic health care and safety, which have been identified among "humanity's top 10 problems over the next 50 years" (Smalley 2003). After the 2004 Indian Ocean Tsunami, humanitarian logistics and information gained additional traction among humanitarian agencies and among governments.

The responses to human suffering typically come from government, multilateral organizations, such as United Nations funds and programs, nongovernment organizations (NGOs) and the private sector with resources in the form of materiel, personnel, utilities, and transport capacity. Time is always a top priority with the key challenge being to properly prioritize the delivery of critical goods and services using available transport. Often, however, transport capacity is constrained not only by the number of ships, fixed wing and rotary aircraft, and trucks, but also by its requisite infrastructure that more often than not has been destroyed.

Christopher and Tatham (2011) note that there is a marked difference between commercial and humanitarian logistics. They offer an understanding of issues associated with humanitarian logistics: where coordinating the operations of a large number of unrelated organizations is challenging, given that they often operate with different missions and objectives; humanitarian relief poses requirements for types of materiel and services that vary from disaster to disaster; the human resources available often are volunteers with little or no training; the scopes of individual disasters are different; the operating environments are seldom the same; and the respective politics may require compromise when working in different countries and situations.

The key point raised by Christopher and Tatham (Ibid.), is the need for increased professionalism and training, specifically with regard to the capabilities of the people employed, the assets controlled, the information managed, and the metrics required. Clearly, there are some world-scale organizations such as United Nations World Food Program (WFP), the Red Cross/Red Crescent, the Fritz Institute, Médecins Sans Frontières (MSF), and others that have put into place professional logistics for their organizations.

They go on to point out that military logistics have been deployed and utilized in a number of disasters, such as in Indonesia, Kosovo, Pakistan, and the United States, and that there are similarities—and indeed there are more similarities than differences—between military operations and their humanitarian action counterpart. It is important to note, however, that although not every military organization has the requisite doctrine, training, and culture to effectively carry out humanitarian relief operations, many do and in recent decades have been so deployed in places to support humanitarian operations. Military and humanitarian logistics operations alike require a command system to coordinate large-scale operations, transportation capabilities, and security for the distribution system. Both also require an inherent flexibility to deal with a range of situations, both from the scale and nature of incident standpoints. There is, however, another common thread, which is the tangling of the commercial supply chains with the humanitarian and military equivalents. It is the commercial supply chains that link inventories of critical supplies with the means of delivery to the affected areas and many times may fill the end-to-end supply chain management, as witnessed in Walmart's capabilities in the aftermath of Hurricane Katrina. Walmart is touted among UN disaster specialists as a good example of a private enterprise responding more effectively than FEMA, especially their ability to have a command center and mobilize resources fairly quickly with good inventory management. Their local knowledge and logistics capacity enabled Walmart to bring aid quickly. The failures of FEMA and other US government agencies during Hurricane Katrina have been widely reported and I will not discuss this aspect here. What is quite interesting is that less focus has been given to meaningful private sector humanitarian action during Katrina and its after effects. Walmart and other privately owned businesses weighed in effectively by all accounts. This does not mean that international and governmental humanitarian actors can simply copy such private sector endeavors.

Effective logistics operations are a critical component of addressing these needs. The challenges in humanitarian logistics are great and include, among others, limited availability of resources and infrastructure to address needs, high uncertainty and urgency characterizing response efforts, and the presence of multiple stakeholders who often act with different objectives. Therefore, it is important to develop humanitarian logistics that takes into consideration the following:

Demand analysis
Develop a basic framework to model the demand based on historical data, past experiences, and most-likely scenarios. Start with a disaster design: type, magnitude, location characteristics, and other defining attributes.

Inventory planning and control
Adequate inventory levels are critical given the high uncertainty of delivery lead times for relief supplies. Inventory prepositioning is a suitable strategy to face uncertainty, especially when local supply might be very limited. Inventory management systems are useful to keep track of valuable information about quantity and quality of the inventory on hand.

Regional coordination and synergies
Process standardization helps facilitate regional cooperation, but effort should also be placed on decentralized models of smaller coalitions among neighboring cities or countries with similar characteristics. Economies of scope in established emergency response systems support joint operations; and partnerships with multi-location and international corporations bring flexibility, robustness and agility to the supply chain.

In-kind donations management
Consolidate donations so they can be classified and then redistributed, or reassign them to local organizations (e.g. faith-based organizations such as churches, registered charities, the Salvation Army, etc.) who are equipped to deal with these donations. These organizations can either identify those items that can be used or sell some items to raise funds for relief efforts. Always enforce planning, communication and collaboration for in-kind donations processes. For example, a practice known as "donations in contract" can enable more robust supply chain processes. Donations are only physically transferred when they are requested by the receiving organization according to the terms of the contract.

Collaboration among organizations
Governments and multilateral organizations should play a leadership role in determining what critical resources the region needs and achieving coordination among the NGOs and all related organizations. Alliances should be sought between for-profit and non-profit organizations and between non-profit organizations, but these partnerships should be built before a disaster occurs as part of preparedness. Other strategies to facilitate collaboration include information sharing and organization specialization, which may reduce competition among organizations.

Understanding regional political, economic and socio-economic conditions
Awareness of the local conditions is crucial for the success of the humanitarian operations. Arrange cultural awareness training programs to create opportunities for a given organization to meet with others that have previously worked in the region. It is essential to involve the community in the preparedness processes and to understand their coping mechanisms before imposing other preparedness measures.

Utilizing local capacity and capabilities
Find out what capacity is already in place. Using local capacities and assets (e.g. local volunteers, mules, carts, etc.) offers the added benefit of giving community residents dignity and opportunities to participate in the response and recovery operations.

Constant communication

Information from and communication with the people in the field, right where the disaster took place is of critical importance. Information and communication emergency systems should be built in advance. The use of mobile phones, when possible, has obvious advantages; moreover, telecommunications companies may see an agile disaster response as a marketing opportunity. Satellite phones might be purchased in advance in case terrestrial cellular service becomes unavailable. Various technologies such as GIS (Geographic Information System) and GPS (Global Positioning System) are available as part of robust current information systems.

Socio-economic impact assessment

Potential negative socio-economic impact of humanitarian operations is undeniable, but it could be reduced. Past experiences and information sharing could be helpful. First, consider what is or is not likely to be needed in the affected region. Second, offer aid that is sustainable by the local communities (e.g. provide the parts needed to fix a donated water pump). Finally, keep tradeoffs between the short-term effectiveness of the response and the long-term impacts in good balance.

Humanitarian operations evaluation

Humanitarian operations form a continuous improvement cycle that requires measurement. After a disaster, all learned lessons should be discussed and documented. Tracking the results of the humanitarian operations is particularly important; avoid strategies such as "truck and dump" that fail to document whether the supplies reach those in need.

Humanitarian organizations should be measured not only in terms of efficiency and effectiveness but also with regard to outreach and public perception. Information technology, education and research are important enablers of successful implementation of disaster relief or developmental aid programs. IT allows collecting, storing, analyzing, and disseminating all the data gathered before and after a disaster hits or as long-term aid operations progress. To make adequate use of IT, identify the questions one wants to answer, the information that is needed, how the data will be collected and codified, and by whom, and how the information will be administrated.

For humanitarian logistics to be recognized as a profession, adequate education is needed. Training and informing the entire community is crucial, and all stakeholder organizations should take responsibility for raising public awareness. Finally, universities have the ability to act as neutral parties and create a broad network that goes beyond borders among researchers and educators to develop new ways to improve humanitarian operations. Academicians should also be exposed to and understand the real aspects of humanitarian problems to make sure they are working to solve problems that are important in practice. Operations research and management science (OR/MS) methodologies and tools have already been developed extensively to benefit for-profit supply chains, and they should be adapted to the particular requirements of humanitarian supply chains. Researchers need to focus efforts on innovative solutions to develop radical, instead of incremental, approaches to address these pressing challenges.

Most crises are imposing great stress on the response capacity and resources of local authorities and front-line offices of national governments as well as on those of central authorities. Crises can rapidly assume an international dimension. This includes when they occur along or across national borders or in international waters. Natural disasters, such as a hurricane or earthquake or tsunami, can often have an effect on several countries at the same time, calling for cooperative responses among the affected countries, including structured regional arrangements.

The wider international community can become involved in a number of contexts. International intergovernmental organizations have specialized expertise that can be made available to national governments and many have logistical capabilities that can be deployed rapidly. This is also true of international non-governmental organizations, notably those that are focused on providing emergency responses and humanitarian assistance. Foreign governments have interest in their nationals who are in a country when an emergency occurs.

While crises and emergencies put systems of national governance and public management under tremendous stress, this is particularly true of developing countries, which as a rule are significantly less well placed to prepare for crisis contingencies or to respond when they occur. For such reasons, the international community is more likely to become involved in responding to crises in developing countries, placing enormous challenges of coordination and consultation on national governments that for both structural and circumstantial reasons are not well placed to cope either with the crisis or the international response, however well intentioned. Recovery efforts can also involve measures to rebuild or strengthen national governance capacity generally as well as in the area of contingency planning and crisis response specifically.

The Emergence of Public Sector Crisis and Contingency Management Institutions

Management of crises and emergencies has received increasingly systematic attention in recent years as a public administration and public management concern, leading to the emergence of crisis and emergency management as a distinct field; this requires major elements of multi-lateral action that involve coordination among national and international crisis management capacity and response, with a particular focus on their governance, public administration, and communication dimensions. As a result, the international community typically plays a signifi-cant part in supporting national crisis responses in developing countries, and at times it is called upon to take the place of national governments, notably in some failed state situations. Bilateral aid donor organizations are also involved in providing humanitarian assistance and emergency relief as well as supporting longer-term reconstruction efforts.

Most of the national crisis and contingency management cycle is organized around: Preparedness, Prevention and Mitigation (eliminating or reducing risks); Response and Recovery; and Evaluation and Learning, thus providing a basis for planning and preparedness for the future as well as for measures to reduce future disaster risks. Each stage calls for high-level government decision making, engaging the institutions and processes of governance. However, a central focus is preparedness, as many of the most crucial decisions are taken in the advance deployment of resources and the creation of processes—and a supporting culture—that are activated when a crisis occurs. These advance decisions can have a major influence on the effectiveness of decision-making under stress when a crisis occurs and can make the difference between crisis and disaster. A national crisis and emergency management capacity must be integrated within the national system of governance and public administration while being in a position, when called upon, to move effectively into action—with varying degrees of autonomy, according to the circumstances.

Coordinating foreign and domestic aid agencies—major disasters in all countries gen-erate responses from non-governmental, governmental, and intergovernmental aid agencies.

This creates coordination challenges that are significant but that can also be anticipated in national contingency planning—pointing to the desirability of involving potential international partners in the planning process. In crises that have attracted significant international attention this can impose severe strains on national governance and public management capabilities, and there is a high risk of international agencies—and in the case of institutionally weak or failed states, the international community as a whole—circumventing national institutions, with potentially serious longer term implications.

Effective Partnerships and Complementarity

The importance of strategic private sector engagement beyond the provision of material support is a great example of the role of business and the private sector. The deployment of private sector focal points for the responses to typhoon Haiyan and the Ebola outbreak facilitated consultations and meaningful support from the private sector in supporting multilateral agencies such as the UN.

Private businesses and civil society organizations, as well as individual residents, are usually among those affected by crises and should be aware of contingency plans that might affect them. They can also play a central role in responding to crises, with respect to both their own situations and the community at large such as in mobilizing and organizing volunteer responders and in obtaining financial and other contributions from private individuals and organizations in communities to supplement public resources.

Crisis management is not a new field. With the onset of wars in modern history, engaging civilian populations as well as military combatants, European governments in particular developed civil defense mechanisms during World War I and especially World War II, much of it to protect civilians from aerial bombing. This was expanded during the Cold War, as governments addressed the probable effects of airborne nuclear attack—which the bombings of Hiroshima and Nagasaki at the end of World War II had demonstrated would be widespread and indiscriminate—on their civilian population and infrastructure and on the operations of government itself.

Most developed countries established dedicated emergency preparedness organizations during this period and prepared contingency plans that involved all levels of government and civil society. An example of the enduring legacies of the Cold War period was the Internet, which at least in part grew out of planning for restoration of the US telephone system after a nuclear attack (Rowland 2006). From the beginning, emergency preparedness was also concerned with non-military hazards, and many societies have experience of dealing with natural and public health hazards and disasters that dates to ancient times. In practice most of the crises that actually required emergency responses, especially in developed countries, involved major accidents or natural disasters. The emphasis shifted even more in that direction with the end of the Cold War in the late 1980s and the reduced apprehension of nuclear conflict. The approach to crisis management became more systematic in the wake of a series of well-publicized industrial accidents and natural events. Another development has been globalization of transportation and communications, which has accelerated the movement of people, with associated hazards such as easier spread of infectious diseases, but has also raised awareness of disasters in previously isolated parts of the world.

The creation of the United Nations and its system of specialized organizations and agencies—which includes the World Bank and the International Monetary Fund (IMF)—represents the core of today's multilateral arrangements. The multilateral system as it appears today represents an assortment of intergovernmental structures and institutions, comprising the UN and its system, financial institutions, including the Bretton Woods institutions, World Bank and IMF, regional organizations, and a host of other international organizations. While some multilateral organizations are not universal in terms of membership, they may nevertheless be global in terms of their interests, outreach, and ramifications of action, especially in relation to humanitarian assistance, human security, human rights and economic and social development.

Emergence of some global hazards has increased both the pressure on the international community to become involved in crisis responses and its ability to do so. Global warming and associated climate change are also producing a new category of mega problems and may be linked to an increase in severe weather disasters in some regions and severe drought in others. In addition, in the past decade there has been a renewed concern with security-related crises, in particularly those involving terrorist attacks: i.e., the use of violent means by non-state actors in pursuit of political goals, generally directed at civilian targets.

Therefore, the international community has assumed a major role in crisis response. A number of international organizations, notably agencies in the United Nations system and international non-governmental organizations, were established to deal with the refugee and related crises that existed in the aftermath of World War II. Although the International Committee of the Red Cross (ICRC), was created earlier, these organizations have continued to grow in number, range of functions, expertise, and logistical capability, and such international organizations have taken on an important role in most major disaster situations. The UN has created an Office for Disaster Risk Reduction (UNISDR), which coordinates the ten-year *Hyogo Framework for Action*, ending in 2015 with the creation of the Sendai platform, which provides a common international framework for national disaster response efforts, including the development of global and regional platforms for disaster risk reduction and fostering of resilience in the face of disasters. International linkages are particularly important for developing countries, where national public management capacity is weaker in general and more vulnerable to the effects of a crisis.

The possible responses to crises can be as complex and diverse as the crises themselves. This is an emerging field of public management and one that by its nature does not lend itself to a single public management model. Crises are not programmed or expected and they are not ordinarily included in the government planning cycle; however, categories and probabilities of possible crisis situations can be anticipated, even if their precise timing, location, or magnitude cannot. Contingency planning, informed by risk analysis, risk management, and learning from past crises, is thus a central feature of crisis management.

Crises can seriously affect public facilities and services, but generally their greatest impact is on non-governmental social and economic institutions and on individual citizens and communities. Crises are no respecters of social or economic status or of other divisions in a society. In that sense, they are a basic test of citizenship and of a government's concern for its citizens. Non-governmental and civil society groups are frequently victims of disasters but they also have a major role in responding to them. A central feature of all crisis response, therefore, is communication, consultation, and coordination with groups outside government and with the public at large.

Informing and Supporting the Public

One of the most vital functions of any emergency response is keeping the public fully informed. This requires ensuring that there are adequate communications channels as well as informed and authoritative spokespersons. A central goal of emergency response efforts is to enable members of the public to become as autonomous as possible as quickly as possible, and effective communication is an essential part of this effort. The communication needs to be two-way, ensuring that the circumstances and needs of individuals, families, and the community in general are known to decision-making public authorities, and their perspectives and advice are drawn upon as fully as possible.

When Hurricane Katrina devastated the US Gulf Coast in 2005, Facebook was still new. There was no Twitter for news updates, and the iPhone was not widespread. By the time Hurricane Sandy slammed the eastern seaboard, social media had become an integral part of disaster response, filling the void in areas where cell phone service was lost while millions of Americans looked to resources including Twitter and Facebook to keep informed, locate loved ones, notify authorities, and express support. Gone are the days of one-way communication where only official sources provide bulletins on disaster news.

Communicating with, and providing information to people affected by crisis is increasingly being recognized as vital in humanitarian response. Communicating with communities is a growing field that helps to meet the information and communication needs of people affected by crisis. Modern communications and social networking technologies mean that an emergency in any part of the world instantly becomes a global event within seconds and minutes. Managing media interest becomes a major challenge for crisis managers but it also represents an opportunity to mobilize international attention and support from governments, NGOs and the global public. Individuals and communities with personal and family ties with an affected country who live elsewhere are interested in determining the status of people and areas that they know and also in providing assistance. A different dimension occurs when the crisis is near or straddles international borders or when it creates transnational environmental risks, the most open-ended case being hazards to the atmospheric environment or international waters.

Powered by cloud, crowd, and SMS-based technologies, individuals can now engage in disaster response at an unprecedented level. Traditional relief organizations, volunteers, and affected communities alike can, when working together, provide, aggregate, and analyze information that speeds, targets, and improves humanitarian relief. This trend toward communications driven by and centered on people is challenging and changing the nature of humanitarian aid in emergencies. Some researchers have now started publishing data on the use of social media in disasters, and lawmakers and security experts have begun to assess how emergency management can best adapt. The convergence of social networks and mobile phones has thrown the old classic response playbook out of the window.

With the rise and uptake of new information and communication technologies (ICTs), such as social media and mobile phones, the role of regular citizens in disaster management becomes more visible and influential as they are active not only in being informed about a disaster but also being involved in information sharing that is needed at pre-disaster and aftermath stages. This calls for multilateral and humanitarian organizations' attention in utilizing these technologies and the growing power of collective intelligence in formulating their disaster programs. Nonetheless, knowledge is still limited as to whether and how increasingly prevalent online information behaviors transfer to different aspects of disaster management (e.g. disaster preparedness, mitigation).

Since the rise of the Internet in the early 1990s, the world's networked population has grown from the low millions to the low billions. Over the same period, social media have become a fact of life for civil society worldwide, involving many actors—regular citizens, activists, nongovernmental organizations, telecommunications firms, software providers, and governments. The leading social networks are usually available in multiple languages and enable users to connect with friends or people across geographical, political, or economic borders. Approximately 2 billion Internet users are using social networks and these figures are expected to grow as mobile device usage and mobile social networks increasingly gain traction.

There are more than 320 million active Twitter users per month and one billion unique visits monthly to sites with embedded tweets and other social media such as Facebook that now has more than 1.44 billion monthly active users. Of those, 1.25 billion are mobile users, with 936 million daily active users and 798 million mobile daily active users which means about 65 percent of Facebook's members use the service daily, and 64 percent of its mobile members use it daily on mobile.

In the wake of the global information age and with the recognition that communication is a vital component of humanitarian response, in 2009, as a transformative strategy, the CDAC network was founded by a group of UN, INGO and media development organizations to facilitate collective work on making communicating with communities an integral part of emergency response. Today the CDAC network brings together over 30 member agencies from humanitarian and media development organizations, UN agencies, the Red Cross, faith-based groups, translators, technology providers, and those with expertise in mass marketing-type surveys. This extended network comes with connections to the private sector, civil society groups, communities, and national governments. The vision of the network is of a world in which people affected by crisis are agents of their own response and recovery, and the network seeks to catalyze communities' ability to connect, access information, and have a voice.

CDAC Network Members are committed to supporting and implementing the coordinated provision of information and communication with disaster survivors in all humanitarian responses. Members focus on how partnerships, particularly with media development organizations, telecoms companies, and technology providers, can deliver effective and appropriate outcomes. The Network delivers through four pillars: research and learning, capacity strengthening, convening and advocacy. Convening is one of the Network's most critical roles: it is unique in its capacity to bring together humanitarian and media development organizations and, increasingly, specialist technology and other service providers. The Network helps founding members step out of silos and collaborate to identify opportunities for partnership, bring about innovative and effective field practice, and increase mutual understanding of the challenges they face. The Network and its Members advocate for the development of communicating with communities as a predictable, consistent, and properly funded aspect of preparedness, response, and recovery.

In the context of humanitarian action, communication with communities (sometimes abbreviated to CwC) refers to activities where the exchange of information is used to save lives, mitigate risk, enable greater accountability, and shape the response, as well as support the communication needs of people caught up in conflicts, natural disasters, and other crises.

Without the power to communicate, disaster survivors cannot access information. Without information, neither can they access assistance or make the best decisions to ensure their and their families' survival. Nor can they reconnect with their wider family and community networks, ask questions or get answers about the situation they find themselves in, or express their needs and concerns. In circumstances when communities cannot be reached physically, information such as home treatments for disease is literally lifesaving.

Communicating with affected communities also benefits disaster responders. It leads to better relationships between humanitarians and survivors, resulting ultimately in a more effective, more equitable, higher quality, and more transparent humanitarian response. But while communicating with, and providing information to, people affected by crisis are two of the most important elements of humanitarian response, they continue to be difficult to implement in practice. Those working on communicating with communities are seeking to change this. On the ground, they help disaster survivors to access the information they need and to communicate with the people assisting them as well as with each other. Examples of communicating with disaster-affected communities projects include information needs assessments, humanitarian radio broadcasting, hotlines, newsletters, SMS surveying, and the development of independent feedback systems for disaster survivors.

At the global level, those working on communicating with communities advocate for systematic change and for the importance of communicating with communities to be reflected in everything from standard operating procedures, coordination and humanitarian architecture to staffing, project design, and funding. Communicating with communities is an approach and a philosophy that needs to be applied at every stage of the disaster cycle, from preparedness to long-term response.

The use of Social Media (SM) during a disaster has significantly advanced in recent years and is acknowledged for its role in supporting humanitarian response efforts, particularly in enhancing situational awareness. However, its use for disaster preparedness and disaster risk reduction (DRR) is significantly less developed. Disasters such as the 2015 Nepal earthquake generated vast amounts of SM data—digital volunteers mapped and verified over 5000 images and 7000 tweets (Meier 2016). Within the humanitarian sector, an increasing number of organizations are taking the time and effort to engage with SM for disaster response, even going so far as employing Social Media Analysis Tools (SMAT) in order to derive greater efficiency from their SM activities. Yet this use of SM and SMAT within DRR and disaster preparedness is less developed.

In the domain of disaster management, SM are used for gathering information from other humanitarian organizations and emergency-related government agencies. Organizations also use SM for sharing information about early warning prior to disaster and posting situational updates during disaster. The target audiences for the disaster communication include the general public and other humanitarian organizations within and outside the country. Nonetheless, despite the opportunities and advantages, lack of manpower dedicated to SM posts/management stood out as the biggest obstacle encountered by humanitarian organizations in adopting social media for their work on disaster preparedness.

As SM is increasingly a part of everyday life in many countries for both humanitarian actors and the general public, it is critical to bring the two together and use SM for DRR and preparedness work. Managing and analyzing engagement and the amounts of SM data this produces can be facilitated by the use of SMAT.

SMAT can provide insights into SM data that can aid humanitarian actors' work in disaster management. However, the ways in which SMAT are used for disaster response can differ from those for DRR and preparedness. This implies that different SMAT could be used for different purposes. Currently SMAT are more widely used for purposes related to disaster response than preparedness and risk-reduction activities.

The reach of preparedness communications can be increased by identifying and targeting influential users. Certain SMAT can show influential users in relation to a particular hashtag, which can give an impression of the relevant users to engage with. For example, SMAT can be used to identify the number of SM users having conversations or sharing information about a campaign. Preparedness messages can be scheduled in advance to be posted in a particular period or date. For example, preparedness-related information can be planned to be sent out in the period leading up to seasonal hazards or posted on a relevant date such as the anniversary of a well-known earthquake, reminding people that preparation can save lives.

Using SMAT to perform keyword searches and monitor conversations can provide information regarding potential risks that SM users are discussing. Certain SMAT can subsequently send out alerts to the organization that has set up the keyword searches, warning organizations of such impending risks for early interventions. For example, if there is a sudden increase in a hashtag set up to monitor floods in country or an area, it would be valuable to receive a notification of such an increase. Managing the risk of humanitarian challenges and taking action before they become large-scale crises must be a priority for all actors. A risk-based approach is needed to save more lives today and avoid crises tomorrow, while reducing costs, especially in protracted crises.

References

Christopher, M. and Tatham, P. (Eds.) (2011) *Humanitarian Logistics: Meeting the Challenge of Preparing for and Responding to Disasters*, London: Kogan Page.

Meier, P. (2016) *DIGITAL HUMANITARIANS: How Big Data is Changing the Face of Humanitarian Response*, Boca Raton, FL: CRC Press.

Rowland, W. (2006) *Spirit of the Web: The Age of Information from Telegraph to Internet*, Markham, ON: Thomas Allen Publishers.

Smalley, R. (2003) "Top Ten Problems of Humanity for the Next 50 Years," in *Energy and Nanotechnology: Strategy for the Future Conference*, Houston, TX: Rice University.

Part 4

FAMINE, VIOLENCE, AND COMPASSION

The Politics of News, Perception, Aid, and Security

INTRODUCTION
TO PART 4

These essays offer a variety of perspectives on news coverage of humanitarian issues, dating from the early reporting of starvation and famine, to the global conflicts of contemporary times. They evaluate the consequences of image-driven story lines that often shock viewers, and detail the ways in which news is shaped and positioned through framing devices that often dictate themes and outcomes.

In "Reporting Humanitarian Narratives: Are We Missing Out on the Politics?" Suzanne Franks discusses how the visually dominated storytelling of famines in Africa distorted the causes of famine and therefore obscured the most effective solutions. As journalists struggled to document the depths of human suffering, humanitarian communication in these early stages raised compassion, concern, and actions of all sorts, but also helped to extend the conflicts and misled global publics by offering simple explanations for complex circumstances. In addition, it left in its wake a legacy, and a visual convention of stereotypic imagery, of *The Starving African*; anonymous, vulnerable, powerless, and forever waiting for food from the West.

Writer Heather Bourbeau finds that in a crisis, media professionals and humanitarian aid providers negotiate a delicate balance between thorough and consistent coverage, and coverage that sensationalizes a crisis and leads to hysteria, misery, and fatigue. In "Front Pages and Frontlines: How the News Cycle Impacted Humanitarian Assistance in Liberia and the Democratic Republic of Congo," Bourbeau compares the media coverage of the Ebola crisis in Liberia to reporting on the Second Congo War in the DRC. She finds that when the topic is a contagious disease outbreak, media themes can swing the international community into action, but can also create unnecessary fear in countries far from the affected areas. By contrast, ongoing conflicts such as the war in the DRC often become background noise relegated to the back pages of major newspapers, if covered at all by the international press. She concludes that without continued media interest and informed coverage the international community's response becomes dulled or muted and atrocities can be overlooked despite a continuous need for assistance and diplomatic efforts.

No war in the Middle East has been more drawn out, contentious, and disturbing than the Israeli–Palestinian conflict. Emma Heywood's study of humanitarian news titled "Compassion as a News Value: Comparing French and UK Humanitarian Coverage of the War in Gaza 2014," examines the theme of compassion as it is applied as a news value in reporting of that conflict. She compares the stories produced by French news media outlets to those that emanate from the United Kingdom, and finds differences in the ways compassion is presented and discussed. She notes the various responses from viewers in both countries, finding that national foreign policy can be understood by prime viewers' responses to the themes of conflict, compassion, and victimhood.

The "war on terror" has become a news-framing device for press coverage across the globe. The frame emphasizes as a primary value, border security. It dictates a belligerent response to lone-wolf and organized terrorist attacks that leaves out international legal avenues for redress, cuts off themes that could point to diplomatic or negotiated resolutions to conflict, and in general obscures a pathway to peace and reconciliation. As media analysts seek to understand the global consequences of this framing device, we find that, particularly when it is applied to local conflicts and violence, it obscures much and illuminates little. In the following two chapters, the authors find the war on terror frame in operation, and seek to illuminate its consequences.

In another international comparison of media coverage, Maria Konow Lund and Eva-Karin Olsson understand the ways in which historical news framing affect both local and global reporting. In "News Frames and Global Terrorism Coverage in the UK and Norway: Context and Consequences for Humanitarian Issues," the authors compare the coverage of the July 5, 2005 terrorism attack in London to the July 22, 2011 Norwegian attacks. The chapter focuses in particular on the impact of historical analogies for creating meaning and framing news. In both cases, local frames of reference and meaning addressed citizens' emotional and communal needs, such as solace, a sense of historical legacy, and identity concerns. However, the global frame of reference differed. In the British case, historical analogies were foremost means of connecting that terror event to the broader "war on terror frame," which facilitated the identification of motives and policy responses. In the Norwegian case, no such analogies existed. They find that for journalistic accounts to create meaning and comfort to global audiences, stronger efforts should be made to communicate humanitarian values by using inclusive, comprehensible, and relevant global analogies.

At the height of the Central American refugee crisis in 2014 in the United States, 68,000 unaccompanied minors arrived at the border fleeing the horrific gang violence in El Salvador, Guatemala, and Honduras. In the past two years that number has dropped by half, and the refugees' stories have receded from the headlines. However, the ongoing humanitarian catastrophe continues. These numbers have not declined because of a decrease in violence in Central America, or because people have stopped fleeing the violence. They are instead the consequence of Obama Administration policies that outsourced border security further south—to Mexico. Just as the Europeans secured their borders by outsourcing the problem to Turkey, the US provided millions of dollars in equipment and training to Mexico to halt the flow of immigrants along its southern border with Guatemala and Belize. As Woodhouse (2016) notes, "Apprehensions in Mexico have gone up by 71 percent without an accompanying expansion of screenings for legitimate asylum claims." This travesty is now covered on alternative media, such as *The Intercept*, which draws out the consequences of US policies:

> As a result, many refugees are being summarily deported back to the countries they fled—countries in which they have been personally targeted for murder, rape, and gang conscription—before ever having a chance to present their claims for asylum before an American immigration judge. In the meantime, they're warehoused in prisons and treated by American immigration courts as if they were the violent gangsters they risked their lives to escape.
>
> (Woodhouse 2016)

In "The Central American Refugee Crisis, Securitization, and the Media," Adrian Bergmann examines the news narratives and the causes for the flow of refugees from Central

America and Mexico. For years, state and non-state actors such as local and transnational organized crime, gangs, death squads, police, and the military, have been locked in a dynamic of armed confrontation that is fueling the crisis of forced displacement within and across borders. Using El Salvador as a case study Bergmann shows how an entrenched, militarized approach to gangs has shaped the transnational relationship with the United States, and how the media politics of security have turned into a major obstacle to peace by peaceful means in the region. Bergmann finds that the predominant response to the flow of refugees may be exacerbating the logic of war that is driving hundreds of thousands from their homes.

Reference

Woodhouse, L. A. (2016) "Running for Their Lives: Fleeing Gangs, Central American Refugees Fight Deportation from the U.S.," *The Intercept* (May 18, 2016), available at: https://theintercept.com/2016/05/18/fleeing-gangs-central-american-refugees-fight-deportation-from-the-u-s/

15

REPORTING HUMANITARIAN NARRATIVES

Are We Missing Out on the Politics?

Suzanne Franks

Introduction

Western audiences have become accustomed to the way the media report crises in the developing world. The framing of the coverage frequently focuses upon the *humanitarian* dimension of the crisis, often to the exclusion of other aspects. This chapter will discuss how the nature of this coverage has evolved and the extent to which the trope of humanitarian reporting is closely connected with how many NGOs seek to interpret and portray faraway suffering. It will also highlight the notable contrast with the manner in which crises in developed nations are interpreted; where there is a more rounded and nuanced understanding of the origins and effects of the problem. The chapter will further investigate how the focus of attention upon the humanitarian dimension in the reporting can mean that there is diminished evidence of a political understanding of the nature of such crises in faraway places.

There is a well-understood argument that faraway crises are constructed by media coverage, because without the media, in most cases there would be no awareness or knowledge of such events (Benthall 2010). Indeed, many serious crises are hidden from view and the wider world is barely aware they exist (Humanitarian Practice Network 2002; Hawkins 2008; Sen 2011). Yet even when there is reporting, the nature of the coverage is not necessarily sufficiently well informed to give audiences an adequate picture. According to Ian Smillie, what we experience is "random, fickle and incomplete" because reporting and understanding faraway places and in particular "news about the developing world is authorless, anchorless and impossible to understand or follow" (Smillie 1995, 133).

All too often the reporting of humanitarian crises in the developing world and particularly in Africa follows a familiar narrative. Its emphasis is upon distant suffering of helpless civilians who are usually awaiting some kind of salvation from external forces. This has been well examined, originally by (Boltanski 1999) in *Distant Suffering* and more recently by Chouliaraki in *The Spectatorship of Suffering* (Chouliaraki 2006). It is apparent that the tone and focus of this coverage of humanitarian crises from the developing world is very often disconnected from wider explanations and understanding.

Unlike the coverage of crises in more developed regions, the suffering is often highlighted in exclusion from and not linked to causes, explanations, and even possible solutions. Invariably this simplification and intense focus upon suffering—usually in the form of shocking visual images—leaves out so much else. In particular, there is no emphasis upon political causes underlying the problem or political processes as a means to solve the issues (Calhoun 2016). Or at best these are dealt with in a superficial and stereotypical manner, or sometimes misconceived and inaccurately described. The pattern of this kind of reporting cannot be viewed in isolation as only a failing of the media. Sometimes it is in the particular interests of the political players, both the donors and those in the country where the crisis is situated to minimize the role of politics. This framing is also part of a narrative conveyed by NGOs involved in fundraising for humanitarian crises who may wish to downplay contradictory and complicated factors at the expense of a simplified story of suffering that requires urgent outside assistance.

Origins of Humanitarian Reporting

The birth of what has become known as "humanitarian reporting" in the modern era began with the international coverage of the Biafran war in the 1960s. The consequence of the fighting between the Igbo secessionists and the Nigerian state was widespread starvation and suffering among the civilian Igbo population. During the course of that conflict a new form of crisis reporting was born and this eventually became the dominant influence on the way that western media came to interpret disasters in the developing world for the decades that followed. Shocking visual images of civilian suffering, including starving children, became headline news on mainstream international television output and very unusually even in the tabloid press. It was a confluence of several factors that led to this new form of coverage; developments in technology that made the mass media use of such images a daily possibility, a developing awareness among NGOs of the potency of such images, a highly media-literate group of advisers who surrounded the rebel forces and journalists who were interested in a new way of reporting that gained them extraordinary visibility (Harrison and Palmer 1986).

Colonel Ojukwo, leader of the rebel Biafrans, had used the services of a Geneva based PR agency Markpress to promote his cause. He also attracted some high-profile and media literate supporters, such as Frederick Forsyth (the future thriller writer), who disappeared from his post as a BBC reporter covering the war in order to become a cheerleader for the Biafran cause. A number of key aid agency workers—in particular those working for the Irish-based Catholic relief mission—became passionate advocates for the suffering Biafran civilians (Harrison and Palmer 1986). And other relief workers such as Bernard Kouchner (the future French foreign minister) were so moved by the suffering that they founded the relief agency Médicins sans Frontières in response to their desire to offer solidarity with the Biafran cause. The shocking images of Biafran children starving became a cause célèbre for radical protest in Western capitals. And for years to come the very word "Biafran" was associated with these images of extreme starvation.

This support for the Igbo cause mediated through the use of shocking images of hunger and suffering translated into a huge flow of aid and assistance provided by independent NGOs prepared to challenge the Nigerian blockade. There were dramatic night time flights into Biafra conveying food and medical aid (and, it eventually transpired, arms and ammunition were also being smuggled aboard). More cynically the rebel regime charged "landing fees" and an unrealistic exchange rate that became its prime source of foreign currency and was in turn used for purchasing arms (Barrow and Jenkins 2001). This "back story" to the Biafran crisis only emerged much later and became a complicated twist to the dominant narrative conveyed by the terrible images. Yet it was an important and political context because it eventually emerged that the use of the pictures of hungry children had unintentionally enabled the rebels, whose cause was ultimately a hopeless one, to continue fighting for months if not years longer than they would otherwise have been able, inevitably leading to far more suffering and death. In this way the aid, which was raised internationally and donated to Biafra as a result of the propaganda effort, could be viewed as having done "more harm than good." The overriding imperative was to end the suffering of starving civilians whose plight was plastered across popular media—print and television—rather than a more nuanced discourse able to understand the complicated political situation, and the complex assessments needed to resolve the crisis. One of the journalists who had covered the story, Colin Legum, later commented that "Your head was telling you one thing but your heart was telling you something very different" (BBC 1995).

Famine in Ethiopia

Some years after Biafra there was another worldwide transmission of a report of African suffering when the 1984 story of the Ethiopian famine broke on BBC Television (Harrison and Palmer 1986). The reporter Michael Buerk (and the Visnews cameraman Mo Amin) travelled to Tigray in northern Ethiopia and broadcast a news report containing harrowing pictures of widespread starvation which was then transmitted on over 400 stations worldwide and won countless awards. Buerk memorably used the phrase "biblical famine" to describe the grim scenes he witnessed there (Buerk 2004). Once again this was a complicated and unpleasant story of competing military and political actors who were largely indifferent to civilian suffering (Rieff 2002; Buerk 2004). But this uncomfortable dimension to the suffering was largely absent from the ensuing media coverage. Despite the work of Amartya Sen and others on the significant social and political origins of famine, this barely resonated in the way the story was portrayed, as it reverberated around the world including mainstream tabloid outlets (Sen 1981; de Waal 1997). Instead the international attention, on a scale that was without precedent with its accompanying powerful images, focused upon what was apparently a "natural disaster." A singular narrative depicted an unfortunate population starving due to lack of annual rains. The accompanying celebrity involvement and in particular the birth of "compassion through rock music" under the aegis of Band Aid and Live Aid reinforced this simple and uncomplicated coverage (Harrison and Palmer 1986).

Ethiopia in 1984/5 thereby assumed the narrative of a story of "pure humanitarian suffering" that required straightforward humanitarian assistance. It was even characterized as "a golden age of humanitarianism," which referred to the apparent nature of the suffering and the worldwide compassionate response (Robinson 2002). This became the dominant frame both at the time and in popular memory, largely through the collective experience of Live Aid and the associated fundraising. Yet there is clear evidence that even as the famine unfolded there was a wider political dimension that was being conveniently sidelined, both internally in the causes of the famine and externally in the international response.

The original report of the famine that became such a momentous news sensation was treated as a *sudden event*, yet self-evidently famine is a long and slow process. This sense of a breaking news story is what propelled the issue into the international headlines. However, it is clear that Western governments had been aware of the famine for many months, so it is rather strange that the day after the BBC report there was an emergency statement to the UK Parliament reacting to the revelations in the news and promising emergency relief. For the diplomats, Foreign Office officials and Ministers this was not breaking news. Yet they reacted as if the images were a shocking revelation of an unknown and humanitarian crisis, a natural disaster. The internal group within the UK government set up to monitor the public response was called the "Ethiopian Drought Group" (Franks 2013). Yet in fact the causes of the famine were well beyond lack of rains, but the title ignored the social and political origins of the crisis.

Paradoxically it could be argued that at the time it was specifically because there *were* wider political reasons that the international response was largely limited to dealing with what was framed as a non-political humanitarian crisis. The dominant cold war ideology still infused much of Western foreign policy. As Ethiopia was firmly within the Soviet sphere, this meant that long-term engagement in development was out of the question for Western countries. They were prepared to send emergency aid, but even in doing this they were determined to use evidence of the donations as a means of criticizing the "other" side. Both the US President Reagan and in the UK Prime Minister Margaret Thatcher made much of the contrast between the generosity of the Western nations providing humanitarian relief, compared with the Eastern bloc that were only interested in supplying arms (Franks 2013). Western aid was given a high media profile. For example, there was a determined priority encouraging Royal Air Force air drops of food which made for great television pictures, even though aid workers criticized this for being an expensive and inefficient way of providing relief. The overriding message was that this was a natural disaster and the aid kindly supplied by generous Western donors would feed the suffering and solve the problem.

It is a further paradox that the same attitude toward the crisis was apparent from within the Ethiopian regime, despite their very different ideological alignment. The problem was only ever described as a drought (Article 19, 1990). For obvious reasons, there was no willingness to acknowledge the political background to the famine in Tigray and Eritrea. The war against the secessionists despite being on a huge scale was conducted largely in secret from both the national and international media. For example, one of the medical aid workers described how during that period she once stumbled across a ward full of wounded Ethiopian soldiers who were usually kept out of sight of foreigners (Bertschinger 2005). Similarly, the deliberate policies against the civilians in those areas were not being acknowledged and this included the brutal villagization or resettlement policy that caused many thousands of deaths (Brauman 1988). In fact some assessments claim that it was as deadly as the famine itself (Clay 1989). So, there was a convenient labeling of the crisis as solely attributable to lack of rainfall, rather than the vanishing entitlements of a vulnerable population attributable to political and military decisions (Giorgis 1989). Crucially, this again played into the convenient and simple narrative of humanitarian suffering devoid of political causes that could therefore be relieved by the transfer of aid.

The preference of the Ethiopian regime—as in many other similar crises from Myanmar to Somalia—was that they distrusted international NGOs and therefore wanted where possible, to keep the delivery of aid within their own ambit. This was not just for straightforward political reasons of control but also because aid could then sometimes be diverted elsewhere—something that Polman (2011) argues inevitably takes place to a greater or lesser extent, against a background of conflict. It was particularly significant in this crisis because the Ethiopian government was seeking to use the aid for its forced resettlement program of moving the population away from the northern areas affected by the famine (Clay and Holcomb 1986). This became highly controversial and when Médecins Sans Frontières

(MSF) spoke out publicly against this policy and the way that international aid was being used to support it, the doctors were subsequently expelled from the country (Brauman 1988). Other agencies including the UN were accused of being complicit by not preventing this use of aid to fulfill such a policy. In some cases the Ethiopian government insisted on making the supply of food to hungry children contingent upon their parents' agreement to being resettled.

MSF argued that NGOs and the UN needed to engage with the political realities of relief rather than allowing the Ethiopian government to manipulate them. But by trying to keep the agenda to a simple one of looking after the needy and not enquiring further or avoiding confrontation, many of the agencies and of course the government of Mengistu were limiting the problem to a pure humanitarian crisis, with potentially devastating consequences for the population of the affected areas. The Article 19 report *Starving in Silence* highlighted this dilemma and concluded that "it is essential that the coverage is politically informed. Over-hyped naively 'humanitarian' reporting can be as bad as no reporting at all." The report went on to say "the Band Aid factor distracts attention from the need to address the political causes underlying the famines in Ethiopia" (Article 19 1990, 97).

Rwanda and its Consequences

A further and very prominent example of how a story of humanitarian suffering became disconnected from a wider political context occurred in the aftermath of the Rwandan genocide, when millions of refugees fled across the border to Eastern Congo in 1994. There was a well-reported crisis in the camps dealing with this huge influx of refugees, which was linked to a major aid appeal to Western nations. Hundreds of NGOs descended upon the area to minister to those who had arrived in the camps. Yet it was only some time later that it emerged that many of those receiving succor were in fact from the Interahamwe, the Hutu genocidaires and their families who had left Rwanda when they feared that they might be sought out by the invading RPF armies. David Rieff makes the following comparison "It is as if two hundred thousand SS soldiers had taken their families out of Nazi Europe as it fell to the Allies, to somewhere they could hope to be sheltered from retribution, by sympathetic NGOs" (Rieff 2002, 53).

The fault for this misinterpretation and misunderstanding of the refugee crisis in and around Goma in 1994 lay both with the NGOs and with the media (Terry 2002). The aid agencies that arrived in unprecedented numbers were caught up with the immediate challenge of caring for a huge volume of refugees. There was plenty of competitive posturing in this as it was also a valuable fundraising opportunity because of the focus of attention (Dowden 2004). Yet they failed to ask the right questions of who was being helped. Meanwhile the media too were failing to understand and to probe into what was going on. It is well known that journalists neglected the Rwandan genocide, partly because it coincided with a major story in South Africa—the inauguration of Nelson Mandela as President—so in the aftermath of the genocide few journalists had sufficient understanding of what was really happening. George Alagiah of the BBC for example admits that for a week he (along with many others) failed to comprehend and properly report the story of the refugee crisis (Alagiah 2001, 120).

With this wholesale misinterpretation of major stories of crises, we are left to question whether delving into the complexities of such events matters less when the crises occur in Africa. *If we compare coverage of Africa to coverage of commensurate crises in Europe, we find that media reporting differs greatly.* The reporting of difficult confrontations in other parts of the world such as the long drawn out Northern Irish crisis or the fighting in the Balkans in the

1990s were subject to different standards of reporting (Myers 1996). The humanitarian suffering in the Balkans in the 1990s was never encapsulated solely as a story of hopeless victims engaged in an inexplicable suffering. There was a repeated explanation of the background to the suffering images, well-understood causes for the fighting between the groups involved, and ultimately an explicable political process. At no point was this simply an impossible story of "warring tribes." On the other hand, the shorthand and frequently lazy formulation of "ethnic conflict" is used all too often in African crises (Allen and Seaton 1999) from Darfur to Rwanda to Kenya. The contrast between the explanation of the Bosnian and Rwandan crises makes clear how the reporting differs and how this in turn gives a very different frame (Myers 1996).

"Pure Humanitarianism"

The problem with these cases is that media's acceptance and promotion of simplistic narratives of humanitarian crisis, devoid of complexities and context, has historically led to unintended consequences. As Andersen (2006) has argued in the case of the Civil War in El Salvador, lack of political context when reporting conflict has historically led to the trope of hopelessness in news coverage. When media mystify the causes of conflict and viewers are offered no understanding and therefore no pathways for action, human suffering becomes as hopeless as it is inevitable. Hopelessness without political context has been characterized by the filmmaker Adam Curtis as the phenomenon of "O Dearism" (Curtis 2009). He describes this "pure" decontextualized version of humanitarian events, where the focus is on faraway victims and inexplicable suffering, as a disconnected exclamation of "O Dear," an attitude of helplessness and inability to deal with the problem. His film makes a plea to reinsert the political understanding necessary to engage with so many apparently "humanitarian" crises. Curtis links the end of the Cold War the origins of O Dearism because of the disappearance of an overarching framework of ideology, but in fact the disconnected framing of humanitarian suffering had begun well before this point and was evident already in the coverage of the crisis in Biafra.

So, who is at fault for the omission of politics and for the problem of the "pure humanitarian" interpretations? There are at least three substantial and interconnected sets of causes we can identify. First, news reporting allows the political dimension to be left out. In particular, the reliance upon images and the unwillingness to explain the complexities and confront the stereotypes have far reaching consequences.

Second, there is the complex role of the NGOs, many of which are now global multimillion dollar brands. As a consequence, what are now relatively powerful institutions may seek a consciously apolitical position in many of these situations, which is particularly significant given their increasingly direct use of media to report events in the field (Cooper 2011). As Nieman (2009) argues, many NGOs are seeking to preserve a role for themselves and their own brand using effective public relations, and media are influenced by these strategies. The uncomfortable reality may therefore not be acknowledged that on occasion it could be better not to intervene or even to withdraw because humanitarian aid might not be achieving its goals (Howard 2010). In addition, these complications make it increasingly difficult to determine when and whether relief agencies and international NGOs are the best actors to take on the burden of humanitarian relief. In some cases, shouldering a burden that may be better shouldered locally may absolve those intent on fighting of responsibility (Holmes 2013). This is a version of what is sometimes referred to as "fungibility" where support from aid agencies allows recipient governments to shift resources around and pursue other agendas, even those that extend conflict. Indeed, Linda Polman (2010, 2011) in her critiques of the aid world cites many examples where humanitarian intervention led to worsening outcomes.

This links to the third set of causes for the absence of politics, which derives from the intentions of those who are participants. There are many reasons why certain actors involved in a crisis, both directly as protagonists or indirectly for example as donor nations, would favor a limited interpretation of humanitarian crisis, preferring wherever possible that disasters remain "natural." At a global level, many in the international community might wish to preserve the status quo. In many cases where aid is required, the recipients, even in "normal times," are living very close to the edge of extreme poverty and potential hunger. Addressing the overall causes for such huge disparities would itself be viewed as destabilizing and a challenge to the hegemony that governs the international distribution of power (Chouliaraki 2012). Not engaging with the complex inequities and balances of global power is a result of avoiding a discussion of deep structural economic inequalities that characterize the global North and South. Meanwhile participants on the ground, in particular competing violent groups, may have their own agendas. Linda Polman's argument is that many want aid as a tool for their own ends and to exploit as a potential powerful commodity, rather than a resource for helping needy civilians (Polman 2011). In other crises, protagonists above all favor a lack of interference, insisting that the international community should just provide the aid and keep themselves at arm's length. Such is the case that has played out for some years in Somalia for example with the resistance by groups such as Al Shabab to NGO relief work (Holmes 2013, 403).

John Holmes was the UN under-secretary general for humanitarian affairs and in this capacity between 2007 and 2010 dealt with a range of devastating crises ranging from Darfur to Haiti (Holmes 2013). In the account of this period, *The Politics of Humanity*, Holmes became convinced of the overwhelming need to understand the nuance and complexity of the political dimensions of these problems, arguing that "media coverage is not interested in nuance and the experts are not listened to because what they say is not black and white enough to conform to our prejudices." It is apparent from so many of the crises he describes, such as the Democratic Republic of Congo or the Sri Lankan Tamils, that instead of simple dichotomies between good and evil, or black and white, only multiple juxtaposed shades of grey actually exist. And the civil war in Syria has provided a further example of this with multiple warring groups where outsiders find it almost impossible to decipher and understand who is worthy of support.

Situations like this do not provide a ready narrative either for media or the public because they are too complex and indecipherable. As a consequence, once again the focus becomes the overwhelming scale of humanitarian suffering, a frame disconnected from the complicated political causation. In this way even a crisis such as the Haitian earthquake in 2010, which by all appearances is purely a "natural" disaster, also has a profound political dimension. The ongoing chaos of relief efforts in Haiti and the failure after years to satisfactorily rebuild despite the huge scale of aid and involvement of thousands of NGOs, indicates the profound political background to such a crisis (Katz 2014).

Understanding Africa

This history of media coverage of Africa has left its mark on the global perception of the continent, and that in turn has deeply affected the ways in which humanitarian crises have been understood, narrated, and responded to. The absence of a political understanding of the often messy political realities in continuing African crises has led to a particular dilemma. For some years there has been a debate about the persistent negative reporting of Africa (Hawk 1992; Wainaina 2005; Bunce et al. 2016). The term "Afro-Pessimism" conveys the lack of positive news in the way that Africa is depicted in the international news media, with the continual emphasis upon unpleasant suffering rather than the more balanced news frames that are used in reporting other areas of the world. This has led on to a determined effort to try and highlight "good news stories" in the reporting of Africa (Gault 2007) to try and counter Afro-Pessimism. But the origins of this negative framing in the coverage can also be traced back to the same absence of political understanding (Pawson 2007). Since those original powerful images used in the Biafran crisis, a key characteristic of reporting from Africa was a disconnected story without a context of politics and the ability to politically solve anything. As a result, the reporting became a parade of misery, a succession of wars, famines, and disasters—punctuated by the occasional celebrity story of someone famous coming to "help."

If the frame of the story is terrible suffering, conveyed by such images with little means to engage with how the crisis could be understood and potentially solved, then there is inevitably a degree of hopelessness, which has thus been characterized as "Afro-Pessimism." In many ways this is a direct legacy of the power of images to override a complex and difficult to interpret narrative. The saying goes that "a picture is worth a thousand words" but equally so there are many cases where a picture can obscure and distort the words that a journalist might be seeking to convey (Luyendijk 2010). And in the new media and social media environment there are even more ways in which pictures can be misleading (Cooper 2011; Cottle and Cooper 2015).

David Clark has written in particular about the production of the contemporary famine image (Clark 2004) and the immense (global) resonance that surrounds these pictures as a recent phenomenon. But as we have seen, it was the Ethiopian famine (and the Biafran conflict beforehand) that established the trope of the images of distant suffering. In addition, such imaging corresponded to the significant rise in NGOs, which were experiencing a powerful impact from these new forms of global communication.

> 1984/5 was a crucial moment in the trajectory of NGOs. It brought their work prominence and assured them greater prestige and a much larger income than they had experienced previously. These benefits were achieved by virtue of a hyper-inflation in images of Africa.
>
> (Lidichi 1993, 107)

Such image tropes are shocking and powerful, but they also result in a paradox. If their simplistic "pure humanitarian frame," which reduces the trope to the simple suffering victims, obscures an awkward and complicated message of political realities, where for example multiple unpleasant protagonists vie for control, and in turn are offered aid, that may in turn result in worse harm.

Rethinking African Images

The images surrounding the coverage of the Ethiopian famine were able to yield such extraordinary reactions that it prompted some thinking by a group of aid agencies about the potency and power of such pictures. In particular it led to soul searching about the ways that Africa was being depicted through a kind of biblical suffering this visual style portrays (van der Gaag and Nash 1987). This deliberation led eventually to agreements and codes of conduct by NGOs on the use of images, starting with Article 10 of the Red Cross Code in 1992. Yet many years later it is still apparent that many of the images used regularly by some (but not all) NGOs in their marketing and fund raising are far from being "responsible." The agenda of many NGOs is to highlight suffering and achieve donations and this "commodification of suffering" remains the most effective way to achieve those goals, even if it reduces the message to an oversimplified and distorted one (Aid Thoughts 2009).

The way that NGOs portray themselves and relate to crises has received some attention in the recent literature (Kalcsics 2011). At the most basic level they want simplicity, a message that will enhance and not impede fund raising. A humanitarian crisis, caused by a complex emergency where multiple unpleasant warring factions are in a protracted conflict, is not a good message to distill to the charity-giving public (Smillie and Minear 2004). The ongoing conflict in the Congo, which since the mid 1990s has seen more loss of life than any other war since 1945, is a prime example of all these difficulties. Referred to as "Africa's hidden world war" (Benn 2004), it has remained relatively unreported, and therefore notoriously difficult from a fundraising perspective. There have been specific aspects of the conflict, in particular the repeated incidents of mass rape, that have managed to highlight sporadic attention, but those stories have been rather disconnected from the broader political context and the inevitable negotiating process that would be the only way to curtail this situation for good (Holmes 2013). There are plenty of stories and fundraising for rape crisis centers and medical assistance but as Holmes argues there is insufficient wider political will to engage with the underlying causes of the suffering.

Urs Boegli a former head of the ICRC media services made the observation:

> Far too many disasters with political causes and for which there can only be political solutions are today labelled "humanitarian crises" . . . After all, rape is rape . . . no one would describe it as a "gynaecological disaster." Yet conflicts, which are referred to as "humanitarian disasters," are often much more than that. This steers the international response in the wrong direction, towards purely humanitarian action in cases where political action is required.
>
> (Boegli 1998)

Boegli and many others are seeking to find ways to explain and interpret that do not present a distinct "pure humanitarian" story set apart from other analysis and concerns. In this way, we should look for a unified narrative that reflects the far more nuanced way that we report from within our own societies, rather than using the frame of a *humanitarian* narrative, which is about the hopeless, inevitable suffering of a distant "other," reporting devoid of political nuance, explanation, and public understanding.

The message that many aid professionals have unthinkingly used and that media have promoted is that "A starving child knows no politics." The assumption is that it should be a straightforward matter of providing help for such a (blameless) victim and that there is somehow a neutral zone where that is achievable, without having to engage with complex surrounding political realities. In this scenario, the role of the relief worker is simple: cut through the middle, provide the aid and, unquestioningly, save lives. Yet in the context of many complex emergencies this now appears to be naïve, simplistic, and ultimately counter-productive. As Alex de Waal has argued "A hungry child is created by politics" (de Waal 1997). To end the cycle of on-going humanitarian crisis, it is imperative that relief agencies, recipients, governments, and the media all acknowledge and engage the complex political and social realities that increasingly define the context of disaster. Only then will donors, agencies, governments, and publics be able to understand disasters and respond in ways befitting a global humanitarian community.

References

Aid Thoughts (2009) Available at: http://aidthoughts.org/?p=69.

Alagiah, G. (2001) *A Passage to Africa*, London: Little Brown.

Allen, T., and Seaton, A. J. (1999) *The Media of Conflict*, London: Zed Books.

Andersen, R. (2006) *A Century of Media, A Century of War*, New York: Peter Lang

Article 19. (1990) *Starving in Silence*. Available at: www.article19.org/resources.php/resource/3/en/starving-in-silence

Barrow, O., and Jenkins, M. (2001) *The Charitable Response. NGOs and development in East and North East Africa*, Oxford: James Currey.

BBC. (1995) *Nigerian War Against Biafra 1967–1970*, available at: www.youtube.com/watch?v=J3ReFoFp0Gs

Benn, H. (2004) BBC-World Service Trust/DFID conference "*The Media and Development; Communication and the Millennium Development Goals*," November 24, available at: http://webarchive.nationalarchives.gov.uk/+/www.dfid.gov.uk/news/files/speeches/bennmedia24nov04.asp

Benthall, J. (2010) *Disasters, Relief and the Media*, London: Sean Kingston.

Bertschinger, C. (2005) *Moving Mountains*, London: Doubleday.

Boegli, U. (1998) "A Few Thoughts on the Relationship Between Humanitarian Agencies and the Media," *Dispatches from Disaster Zones*, available at: www.icrc.org/Web/Eng/siteeng/html/57JPJG

Boltanski, L. (1999) *Distant Suffering*, Cambridge: Cambridge University Press.

Brauman, R. (1988) "Refugee Camps, Population Transfers and NGOs," in J. Moore (Ed.), *Hard Choices: Moral Dilemmas in Humanitarian Intervention*, Lanham, MD: Rowman & Littlefield, pp. 177–193.

Buerk, M. (2004) *The Road Taken*, London: Hutchinson.

Bunce, M., Franks, S. and Paterson, C. (Eds.) (2016) *Africa's Media Image in the Twenty First Century: From "Heart of Darkness" to "Africa Rising"*, London: Routledge.

Calhoun, C. (2016) "Keynote speech: *Everyday Humanitarianism. Ethics, Affects and Practices at London School of Economics*," April 14.

Chouliaraki, L. (2006) *The Spectatorship of Suffering*, London: Sage.

Chouliaraki, L. (2012) *The Ironic Spectator: Solidarity in an age of post-humanitarianism*, London: Polity.

Clark, D. (2004) "The Production of a Contemporary Famine Image," *Journal of International Development*, 16: 693–704.

Clay, J. (1989) "Ethiopian Famine and the Relief Agencies," in B. Nicols, and A. G. Loescher, (Eds.), *The Moral National: Humanitarianism and US Foreign Policy Today*, Notre Dame, IN: University of Notre Dame Press, pp. 232–277.

Clay, J., and Holcomb, B. (1986) *Politics and the Ethiopian Famine*, Cambridge, MA: Cultural Survival.

Cooper, G. (2011) *From their own Correspondent. New Media and the Changes in Disaster Coverage. Lessons to be Learnt*, Oxford: Reuters Institute for the Study of Journalism.

Cottle, S., and Cooper, G. (2015) *Humanitarianism, Communications and Change*, New York: Peter Lang.

Curtis, A. (2009) *O Dearism*, available at: http://archive.org/details/AdamCurtis-OhDearism

de Waal, A. (1997) *Famine Crimes: Politics and the Disaster Relief Industry in Africa*, Oxford: James Currey, and Bloomington, IN: Indiana University Press.

Dowden, R. (2004) "War Reporting in Africa," Private seminar at St Anthony's College, Oxford, November 4.

Franks, S. (2013) *Reporting Disaster: Famine, Aid, Politics and the Media*, London: Hurst.

Gault, C. H. (2007) *New News out of Africa*, London: Yale University Press.

Giorgis, D. W. (1989) *Red Tears War, Famine and Revolution in Ethiopia*, Trenton, NJ: Red Sea Press.

Harrison, P., and Palmer, R. (1986) *News out of Africa: From Biafra to Band Aid*, London: Hilary Shipman.

Hawk, B. G. (1992) *Africa's Media Image*, New York: Prager.

Hawkins, V. (2008) *Stealth Conflicts: How the World's Worst Violence Is Ignored*, Aldershot, UK: Ashgate.

Holmes, J. (2013) *The Politics of Humanity: The Reality of Relief Aid*, London: Head of Zeus.

Howard, R. (2010) *No Good Deed Goes Unpunished: Complications of U.S. Humanitarian Aid*. London, Webster University: ProQuest Dissertations Publishing.

Humanitarian Practice Network. (2002, March) *Silent Emergencies: Humanitarian Exchange*, 20.

Kalcsics, M. (2011) *A Reporting disaster? The Interdependence of Media and Aid Agencies in a Competitive Compassion Market*, Oxford: Reuters Insitute Fellowship Paper.

Katz, J. (2014) *The Big Truck That Went By: How the World Came to Save Haiti and Left Behind a Disaster*, New York: Palgrave.

Lidichi, H. (1993) "All in the Choosing Eye: Charity, Representation and the Developing World." Open University: Unpublished PhD thesis.

Luyendijk, J. (2010) *Hello Everybody. One Journalist's Search for Truth in the Middle East*, London: Profile Books.

Morozov, E. (2005) *The Net Delusion: How Not to Liberate the World*, London: Penguin.

Myers, G. T. (1996) "The Inscription of Difference: News Coverage of the Conflicts in Rwanda and Bosnia," *Political Geography*, 15 (1): 21–46.

Nieman. (2009) Available at: www.niemanlab.org/ngo/.

Pawson, L. (2007) " Reporting Africa's Unknown Wars," in S. Maltby, and R. Keeble (Eds.), *Communicating War: Memory, Media and Military*, Bury St. Edmunds, UK: Arima, pp. 42–54.

Polman, L. (2010) *The Crisis Caravan: What's Wrong with Humanitarian Aid?* New York: Picador.

Polman, L. (2011) *War Games: The Story of Aid and War in Modern Times*, London: Viking.

Rieff, D. (2002) *A Bed for the Night. Humanitarianism in Crisis*, London: Vintage.

Robinson, P. (2002) *The CNN Effect: The Myth of News, Foreign Policy and Intervention*, London: Routledge.

Sen, A. (1981) *Poverty and Famines: An Essay on Entitlement*, Oxford: Oxford University Press.

Sen, A. (2011). *Marginal on the Map: Hidden Wars and HIdden Media. Conflict in India's Northeastern States, the Response of the State, How It Affects People and How It Is Reported in the Media. Media in Conflict and Peacebuilding*. Oxford Peace Conference.

Smillie, I. (1995) *The Alms Bazaar*, London: ITP.

Smillie, I., and Minear, L. (2004) *The Charity of Nations Humanitarian Action in a Calculating World*, Bloomfield, CT: Kumarian Press.

Sobhee, S. K., and Nath, S. (2010) "Is Donors' Concern about the Fungibility of Foreign Aid Justified?: A Panel Data Analysis," *The Journal of Developing Areas*, 43 (2): 299–311.

Terry, F. (2002) *Condemned to Repeat: The Paradox of Humanitarian Action*, Ithaca, NY: Cornell University Press.

van der Gaag, N., and Nash, C. (1987) *Images of Africa: The UK Report*, Oxfam.

Wainaina, B. (2005, Winter). How to Write about Africa. *Granta 92*, available at: https://granta.com/how-to-write-about-africa/

16

FRONT PAGES
AND FRONTLINES

How the News Cycle
Impacted Humanitarian Assistance
in Liberia and the Democratic
Republic of Congo

Heather Bourbeau

Introduction

In a crisis, media professionals and humanitarian aid providers must negotiate the delicate balance between thorough and consistent coverage, and a drumbeat that leads to hysteria, misery, and fatigue. This chapter examines the media coverage of two very different humanitarian crises. First, the Ebola crisis in Liberia was characterized by sensationalized themes and personalization. Such media themes can swing the international community into action but can also create unnecessary fear in countries far from the affected areas. Sensationalized and inaccurate media representations can also be detrimental to effective international responses. In contrast, after an initial dramatic crisis, coverage of the Second Congo War in the Democratic Republic of Congo (DRC) became background noise relegated to the back pages of major newspapers, if covered at all outside of the affected region. This chapter explores these two distinct situations to understand the need for consistent and continued media interest, and the effects such coverage can have on the international community's responses to conflict and emergencies. I also consider the role of the press in exposing atrocities that could otherwise be overlooked despite a continuous or increased need for assistance and diplomatic efforts.

Several factors distinguish the situation in Liberia during the Ebola outbreak (2014–2015) from that in the DRC during the Second Congo War (1998–2003). One occurred in West Africa and the other in East; one involved an epidemic and potential pandemic with thousands of cases across multiple continents, while the other was a more conventional war that involved several neighboring countries. The former lasted a little over a year, while the latter officially ended after nearly five years, though fighting continues in the eastern part of the country. The differences and important similarities in the media cycles and their impact on donor engagement are significant and instructive for media professionals and humanitarian actors.

Each situation had a distinct media life cycle of initial momentum with sustained coverage followed by a tapering off, and each was a part of a media environment wherein 24-hour international coverage influenced humanitarian and foreign policy responses—also known as "the CNN effect." This cycle of coverage amid constant news feeds, leads us to ask several questions: How do media outlets hold readers' or viewers' attention on a topic that has been covered repeatedly? How do consumers and producers of news avoid the loss of viewer interest that often comes with a prolonged crisis or 24-hour coverage? As a situation leaves the headlines, what are the deleterious humanitarian impacts of reduced news coverage, including drops in financial assistance and other aid?

There is no doubt that during the height of the Ebola outbreak, Liberia (and the neighboring countries of Guinea and Sierra Leone) received more consistent and broader coverage across many news sections than the DRC received during even the beginning of the Second Congo War. What marks both these crises is the severe drop in coverage after a rush of international attention. For the DRC, the drop-off came after the second year of the war in 1999–2000, and for the Ebola epidemic it came even before the last patient was cleared in Liberia. At the time of this writing, there are still four Ebola patients in Guinea, though the media coverage is nearly non-existent.[1] However, a recent study published in *The New England Journal of Medicine* that suggests Ebola's genetic material can persist in semen nine months after infection has gotten some media attention (Sprecher 2015).

At times the initial rush to cover a shocking crisis can lead to robust responses by the international community. Sometimes, however, the aid is not flexible enough or context-sensitive enough to be effective, as we will see with Liberia. In Liberia, the inevitable drop-off led to a reduction in outside scrutiny, funding streams, and other support. Private and individual donors have the most rapid and direct response to extensive and often alarmist media coverage, as they do not have to contend with parliaments, constituents, or large bureaucracies to give financial or other assistance (while multilateral and country donations usually take longer to organize, plan, and process).

The interconnections between media coverage and humanitarian response is further complicated by the varying influences of continuing coverage. As different factors sway an on-going media trajectory, outcomes can vary. For example, if media interest continues but no new angle or new significant development is reported, a resulting desensitization to continuing coverage will likely hamper humanitarian responses. On the other hand, as we will see in the DRC, sometimes extraordinary coverage after the main crisis has abated will result in meaningful responses.

Ebola Epidemic, Liberia

The first case of Ebola in Liberia was confirmed on March 31, 2014 (nearly four months after "Patient Zero" died in Guinea). The disease spread quickly through the country, particularly as cases were discovered in the densely populated capital of Monrovia. Much of Monrovia lacks sanitation and a citywide electrical grid, and most people still get their water from public pumps, all of which can accelerate the spread of disease.

In late June, Médecins Sans Frontières (MSF) called the epidemic "out of control." By the end of September, the WHO Ebola Response Team (2014) reported 5,800-plus cases and 2,800 deaths, noting the high fatality rate and stating that the "current epidemiologic outlook is bleak." On September 23, the US Centers for Disease Control and Prevention

(2014) suggested that Ebola cases could reach at least 550,000 to 1.4 million by January 2015. And a CNN poll (2015) that month found (unsurprisingly given the dire statements by the world's public health officials) that one quarter of Americans worried about getting Ebola.

As of October 15, 2015, there had been 28,466 reported confirmed, probable, and suspected cases, and 11,297 reported deaths in Guinea, Liberia, and Sierra Leone.[2] The United States had seen 11 patients and two deaths, the UK had three patients, and France had two patients with Ebola. However, these numbers belie the real threat of the Ebola epidemic. The outbreak was unprecedented and took public health officials off-guard in part because it had never been found in that part of Africa before. There had been less-than-effective infection control at the outset, and there were regional burial customs and insufficient health-care services that exacerbated the crisis. There would need to be a focused and thorough response. As Centers for Disease Control and Prevention Director Dr. Tom Frieden told Congress at a hearing in August 2014, "If you leave behind even a single burning ember, it's like a forest fire. It flares back up."[3]

The coverage was also unprecedented and often hyperbolic. In October 2014, Matt Drudge told his Twitter followers to "self-quarantine," and CNN's Ashleigh Banfield said that the terrorist group ISIS might "send a few of its suicide killers into Ebola-affected zones and then get them on some mass transit, somewhere where they would need to be to effect the most damage" (Beutler 2014). To be fair to her segment, one of her guests, Dr. Amar Safdar, an associate professor at New York University's Langone Medical Center, pointed out that unlike SARS, MERS, or the common flu, Ebola is not easily communicable.[4]

The fears of reporters and editors themselves were reflected in news reports. "During the Liberian civil war you knew if there was fighting in one neighborhood, and you would go somewhere else," notes *New York Times* reporter Norimitsu Onishi. "Ebola is invisible." This disease could not be seen or anticipated, and its unpredictable, yet "exponential" spread was unlike the more familiar conflict frames or combatant coverage of war reporting. Few professionals had experience treating or covering this disease. Before 2014, the biggest cases of Ebola were limited in their scope and usually restricted to rural areas. The largest outbreak had occurred in Zaire (now the DRC) in 1995, affecting 315 people and killing 254.[5] As the new epidemic spread rapidly, news organizations showed up starting in mid September 2014, but stayed only a short time as editors and producers were concerned about the safety of their reporters. Some journalists were pulled after only a few days covering the epidemic. "It was the fear of an unknown epidemic that people had never seen," says Onishi.

The CNN Effect

Much has been written about the 24-hour news cycle and the need to fill the airwaves. The amplification and repetition of 24-hour news, now coupled with the declining revenues, staff, and outlets of traditional media,[6] leads editors, producers and publishers to go for the stories that will garner the most viewers, listeners, and clicks. With new technology and social media, websites, Twitter, Facebook, and Instagram all distribute content at a relentless pace globally. Coverage in prominent news media is now augmented and can influence not only the public but also policymakers. It is sometimes referred to as "the CNN effect," which posits that continuous coverage of a particular story can influence foreign policy agenda setting and decision making (Livingston 1997).

Disease Contagion and the Personal Safety Frame

There are significant differences in the public responses to foreign conflict coverage and to that of global pandemics. Whether warranted or not, people believe that they may contract the disease in an epidemic and therefore have greater interest in stories about the disease. Global publics are also eager to hear about the latest, official emergency and abatement efforts. Contrastingly, few people believe they will be directly harmed by conflicts happening thousands of miles away, particularly if their national military is not involved. Viewers/readers have a more intense relationship with the coverage of international pandemics, one that can influence editors' decisions to run continuing stories with prominent placements.

Media and Donor Responses

The donor response to Ebola was significantly ramped up only after there were American and European patients. It can be argued that the United States, which was the largest donor to fight Ebola, gave too late and with less of an impact than that of local residents and community leaders inside Liberia, according to some public health officials. The US spent $1.4 billion on Ebola eradication in West Africa, sent military (which cost $360 million) and opened treatment centers. Yet the United States did not give the bulk of its aid until the second half of the year, after Ebola had already reached US shores. Therefore, by the time the US opened their first treatment center, the number of cases had already started to drop. Centers were left empty. Indeed, the health care system in Liberia still suffers from serious infrastructure issues that might lead to another large-scale infectious disease outbreak.

Second Congo War, the Democratic Republic of the Congo

The Second Congo War, lasting from August 1998 until July 2003, has been called "Africa's World War." It was the deadliest conflict since World War II, involving nine countries and several shifting rebel groups. It was preceded by an earlier conflict, referred to as the First Congo War from 1996–97 that involved neighboring countries Rwanda, Uganda, Angola, and to a lesser extent Burundi and the Angolan rebel group, UNITA. That initial fighting led to the overthrow of Mobutu Sese Seko by Laurent-Désiré Kabila.

The Second Congo War began as a rebel insurgency with Angola, Zimbabwe, and Namibia supporting Kabil;, and Rwanda, Uganda, and Burundi supporting the rebels. In January 2001, Kabila was assassinated by one of his bodyguards and succeeded by his son Joseph soon thereafter. The instability spread into Uganda and Rwanda. On April 19, 2004, Kabila referred the DRC to the International Criminal Court, which opened an investigation two months later. The duration and brutality of the conflict was devastating to the civilian life, characterized as it was by rape, sexual violence, and the use of child soldiers. From 1998 until 2003, millions of Congolese died, hundreds of thousands were raped and sexually assaulted (Harvard Humanitarian Initiative 2009). Despite ceasefire agreements, fighting continues in the eastern part of the country, particularly in the resource-rich North Kivu.

The United Nations Office of the High Commissioner for Human Rights released a report titled "DRC: Mapping Human Rights Violations 1993–2003" that documented 617 incidents of human rights abuses (339 during the Second Congo War)—the vast majority of which "may constitute crimes against humanity or war crimes, and often both at the same time" and where "the apparent systematic and widespread attacks described in this report reveal a number of inculpatory [incriminating] elements that, if proven before a competent court, could be characterized as crimes of genocide" (UNHCR 2010).

Unlike the extensive media coverage of the Ebola epidemic, the conflict-based humanitarian crisis in the DRC did not continuously occupy the headlines of major global news outlets. How could so many violations against human rights occur without an uproar? The answer is multifaceted and includes governmental media restrictions, a repressed and distrusted local press, remote and difficult locations, and misery fatigue on the part of editors and news consumers.

The press is severely restricted in the DRC. In 1996, a law was passed under Mobutu, the 1996 Press Law, that requires news outlets to support the government's war efforts. Offenses punishable by death for journalists include the betrayal of the state during wartime, insulting the army, and demoralizing the nation. Any reporters or editors charged with these crimes are tried by the Court of Military Order, whose rulings cannot be appealed (Committee to Protect Journalists 2001, 2003). During Kabila's first three years in power, the Committee to Protect Journalists recorded 130 press freedom violations, involving more than 200 journalists and 75 news outlets (Committee to Protect Journalists 2002).

Also factoring in coverage of events in the DRC was the general Congolese skepticism regarding the media, particularly of French and US news outlets, which were considered offshoots of the respective administrations. Because many Congolese believed that the US was backing Rwanda in the conflict, there was a belief that US coverage was inherently biased. To give further context to this view, in the DRC, many media outlets were and are funded by political parties or wealthy businessmen with an agenda. Most people cannot afford a newspaper but instead rely on radio. Many of the country's urban-based radio and television stations were also owned by political and business leaders with specific agendas (Infoasaid 2012). Moreover, the DRC is Africa's second-largest country, home to over 75 million people, with a total land area of 2,267,000 square kilometers.[7] The remote, dangerous, and extremely chaotic nature of the violence in the DRC reduced media access.[8] As *The Economist* wrote in 2002:

> Simply finding out what is happening in Congo is a challenge, as your correspondent discovered while accompanying militiamen on patrol by the shore of Lake Kivu last week, when he was forced to hide in a bush to avoid 200 hostile Rwandan soldiers passing by.
>
> (*The Economist* 2002)

A lack of media coverage was concerning to many covering the region. Michela Wrong, the former *Financial Times* reporter covering DRC during that time, claims that the end of the Cold War (when the then-Zaire was a close anti-Communist ally of the United States) worked to reduce the newsworthiness of the conflict in the eyes of Western media. In 2004, John F. Clark, Associate Professor of International Relations at Florida International University, argued that the Congo war was largely ignored, despite being "one of the most deadly, but also most interesting, conflicts of the post-Cold War world" (Soderlund et al. 2012).

The DRC was on Doctors Without Borders' (2007) annual list of the top ten most underreported humanitarian stories from 1999–2007 (MSF 2007; Soderlund et al. 2012). While the *New York Times* was more supportive of Africa coverage in general and the DRC specifically, Norimitsu Onishi was often alone in DRC covering the war, with help periodically from the Southern African bureau. In an interview for this article, Onishi noted, "When the Second Congo War broke out, interest was high and then the war dragged on for four or five more years. There was not sustained coverage. There were periodic bursts." Onishi notes that as the war persisted, it became more difficult to get stories onto the front page.

During the first year of the Second Congo War (August 1998–August 1999), *The Times* (of London) ran 71 stories about the war, *The Globe and Mail* ran 50, *The New York Times* 19, and *The Washington Post* 14. However, during the 2001 calendar year, *The Globe and Mail* ran an impressive 51 stories. However, *The Times* (of London) ran 31 stories, *The Washington Post* 22, and *The New York Times* only two. If we take out Zimbabwe (which was in the midst of its own elections and involved in the DRC conflict) in the search results, the numbers drop even further: *The Times* (of London) ran five stories, *The Globe and Mail* 28, *The Washington Post* 13, and *The New York Times* only a single story.[9] This drop in coverage came despite events that many would consider quite newsworthy under other circumstances: the UN Security Council approved a peacekeeping operation with over 5,500 observers and troops; Rwanda's government announced a phased withdrawal from the DRC; the diamond industry launched discussions in South Africa on how to stop the trade in conflict diamonds; fighting between former allies Uganda and Rwanda in Kisangani left 700 dead; and over 10,000 refugees were driven into northern Zambia.

While the scale of the war was unlike anything seen in Africa, it was nonetheless a very conventional conflict over territory and resources, and this ordinary horror made it less newsworthy. And unfortunately, the opposite of the CNN effect is the impact of near silence. It can be argued, in direct contrast to the CNN effect, that a lack of reporting often leads to lack of resources and placing an event or issue lower on a government's agenda.

A study by John S. Kim of Georgetown Public Policy Institute found that when an epidemic or war in a developing country is mentioned in a major US media source even once a year over a five-year period, the country in which the humanitarian crisis is happening receives almost 1 percent more in US aid per capita (Kim 2005). Douglas A. van Belle found that coverage by *The New York Times* had a "substantive" influence on the levels of aid that was greater than the recipient country's political or economic ties to the US. He noted a similar influence with *The Globe and Mail* coverage in Canada. With regard to French aid, *Le Monde* coverage was second only to the recipient country's adoption of the French language, and with UK aid, the coverage in *The Times* was second only to commonwealth membership (Rioux and Van Belle 2005; Van Belle 2010). In addition, in an interview for this chapter, Van Belle notes that reductions in news coverage impact the decisions of "aid bureaucrats who want to give money away," but need to justify the aid. Often there will be a burst of giving from countries when a crisis is making headlines, as the tax-paying public will accept the temporary increase in donations to respond to a critical need. "However, if coverage drops and they have secured desired funding, then it doesn't impact the distribution," says van Belle. And if the donor country aid officials (such as the US Agency for International Development or the UK's Department for International Development or DFID) want to secure additional funding, they will want a second peak in media coverage to secure those funding streams. Van Belle hypothesizes that the multilaterals, such as the United Nations humanitarian agencies, are even more sensitive to media coverage because they have to justify their donations to an even greater number of constituents. But when situations become chronic, such as the Second Congo War and continued violence in the DRC, it becomes more difficult to get the kind of media coverage that will help boost humanitarian support. In an interview for this chapter, Susannah Sirkin, Director of International Policy and Partnerships and Senior Advisor at Physicians for Human Rights said, "There is donor fatigue and paralysis. There is a numbing," and "People just shut down. The numbers are too big, they can't grasp it."

As Vava Tampa (2012), founder of Save the Congo, wrote in a CNN editorial:

> As an activist, I believe that the editors of news organizations such as CNN, Al Jazeera and the BBC must flood the airwaves with vivid images and news stories on the human sufferings in Congo. . . . Unless they tip that balance a little and force policy makers in Washington and internationally to pay more attention and act, the killing, raping and looting . . . could continue to unfold undetected by the camera lenses of Western media and excluded from Western political agenda.

Increasing the Coverage of an On-Going Long-Term Conflict

The International Rescue Committee Report

After the Second Congo War, while eastern DRC was still embroiled in conflict, at least one organization found a way to boost coverage of and political response to the situation. The International Rescue Committee published a report titled, "Mortality in the Democratic Republic of Congo: An ongoing crisis," that estimated 5.4 million people had died in the DRC since 1998. IRC conducted a series of mortality surveys that became the story rather than the millions of lives lost and damaged by the ongoing war. They noted that more than 10 percent of all deaths "were due to violence, with most attributed to easily preventable and treatable conditions such as malaria, diarrhea, pneumonia and malnutrition" (International Rescue Committee 2008).

While this report garnered a lot of press, some of it was focused on the methodology and not the war. Other researchers looked over IRC's research and came up with new methodologies that showed the death count was overestimated, but still horrific at anywhere from one to three million. In their assessment of IRC's report, the Human Security Report Project wrote, "Some critics believe that individual NGOs deliberately exaggerate death tolls in order to secure more funding, while others argue that lack of experience in survey design and implementation is the problem" (Human Security Report Project Part Two 2010, 126). And in terms of fundraising, these studies can be very effective. After IRC published their 2000 mortality survey (which helped inform the 2008 report), total humanitarian aid increased by over 500 percent, with US assistance increasing by a factor of over 25 (Brennan et al. 2006). According to the United Nations' Office for the Coordination of Humanitarian Affairs (OCHA) Financial Tracking Service, which tracks all humanitarian aid, donor funding to the DRC in 2000 was nearly $29 million, in 2002 was $177 million,[10] and in 2003 was $187 million.[11] (By contrast, the funding for the Ebola crisis (not separated by country) was $4.17 billion in 2014.[12])

This uptick in funding came not just because of the IRC report, but also because of the media coverage and political reaction to the report. While overall coverage of the DRC dropped in 2001, the report garnered some key placements in media outlets. *The Globe and Mail* and *The New York Times* each ran a story citing the then 2.5 million deaths IRC calculated. In early May 2001, there was testimony about the DRC on Capitol Hill before the International Operation and Human Rights subcommittee of the House International Relations Committee. In her opening remarks Rep. Ileana Ros-Lehtinen, Chair of the Subcommittee noted, "It is thus our hope that this hearing will help ensure that the 2.5 million reported dead by the International Rescue Committee's survey, and all the other innocent victims unaccounted for, do not go unnoticed" (United States Department of State 2001).[13] Two weeks later, on May 27, 2001, then-Secretary of State Colin Powell was asked about the report in a press conference with Ugandan President Yoweri Museveni.[14] *The Washington Post* ran an editorial on August 26, 2001 citing the IRC 2000 Mortality Survey, and ABC's *Nightline* devoted five programs to the war in September 2001, again using the IRC figures to frame the story. In fact, host Ted Koppel spent two weeks with IRC in eastern Congo for the series.

In a 2006 opinion piece about the toll of continued violence in the DRC in *The Washington Post*, Richard Brennan, director of IRC's Health Unit, and Anna Husarska, an IRC senior policy advisor, noted that because of the need for both instant and continuous news, more attention is paid to those who die violently than to those who die of disease. In IRC's mortality survey of DRC, only 2 percent of the deaths were attributable to the conflict directly. Yet the large overall figure would later grab headlines:

> When there is media coverage, aid increases. Large donors may be more inclined to press for a greater presence of international peacekeeping forces to protect civilians and humanitarian assistance teams. And the presence of peacekeepers makes it easier for the media to report.
>
> (Brennan and Husarska 2006)

Significantly, the Human Security Report Project (2011) notes that IRC's 2008 report effectively drew the world's attention to "the previously ignored plight of the Congolese and has helped successfully pressure the international community into providing more humanitarian assistance and increasing the number of peacekeeping forces. This has made a real difference to the lives of millions."

"Certainly without this kind of international attention and in donor nations, humanitarian response would be much weaker, but whether the human rights response would be weaker is harder to say," Sirkin says. There is a belief that attention to a crisis or issue is a means of preventing worse atrocities, but that is not always the case. There are many other factors that play into an international response, including the cooperation of the government where a crisis is happening and the political agendas of key international players, which are often at odds with each other (for example, the current US and Russian response to Syria or the impasse on arms embargo and financial restrictions on Zimbabwean leaders following post-election violence in 2008 as China and Russia objected to international involvement in what they considered a domestic issue.)

There is still an urgent need for the combination of media coverage and overwhelming international political will. The Ebola epidemic was apolitical by its nature and thus was able to garner a large and relatively immediate international response once it was considered a threat to more countries than the three in West Africa.

The IRC's report and the controversy and coverage surrounding it made people more aware and put more pressure on the international community. In large part due to international and industry pressure, there has been significant progress toward creating conflict-free minerals trade, and 70 percent of the tin, tantalum, and tungsten mines are free of armed groups, including the army (Enough Project 2015). But calm is unlikely to come in the next several months as President Kabila threatens changes to the country's constitution that would allow him to stay in power beyond the current mandated two-term limit. There have been protests that have been met with violence by the government security forces, which killed at least 38 demonstrators (Roth and Sawyer 2015).

Current Situation

Today the DRC is home to the largest and most expensive UN peacekeeping operation, MONUSCO (the United Nations Organization Stabilization Mission in the Democratic Republic of the Congo), with over 23,000 personnel and an approved budget of $1.33 billion.[15] Nonetheless, the eastern provinces are still unstable with dozens of armed groups actively competing for resources. And funding commitments for the DRC, according to OCHA, are $431 million, over 14 times the amount committed in 2000 during the height of the war.[16]

Meanwhile, Liberia has seen the opposite effect. The country is Ebola-free, but many medical facilities that were unable to handle treating infected patients closed during the outbreak and are now offering only reduced services that cannot accommodate the needs of patients with other highly contagious infectious diseases such as measles (MSF 2015). In order to create a more resilient public health system, the Liberian Ministry of Health announced a seven-year plan that will include the establishment of a national public health institute, emergency risk management, and improved overall safety and quality at public and private facilities. The plan is expected to cost $1.7 billion. (To give some context to this request, the 2015 federal annual budget for the Government of Liberia was $604 million, including $73 million for "health sector strengthening."[17]) Funding sources for the proposed health plan have not yet been confirmed (Sonpon 2015).

Conclusion

Despite some prominent news organizations covering the war in the DRC, it was not until the IRC mortality reports burst on the scene that humanitarian assistance in terms of dollars, programs, and protection increased significantly. There is still a great need for quality media coverage of the developments in the DRC, as well as humanitarian assistance and public–private efforts that curb the extraction and sale of resources by armed groups, particularly in the eastern part of the country. And despite the fast-paced coverage that increased fears and funding, the factors that exacerbated the quick spread of Ebola (poor sanitation infrastructure and inadequate public health system) are still present in Liberia. It will take many years for the public health system to become robust.

Media professionals and humanitarian aid providers must both negotiate a delicate balance between constant communication and a drumbeat that leads to hysteria, misery fatigue, or inaction during chronic crises. It is, therefore, important to examine different angles of a story and provide consistent and quality follow-up to the stories from the early days of an exceptional event or situation. Moreover, it is critical that when a large-scale crisis begins to drop off from the 24-hour news cycle and the front pages, reporters and editors see what research academics, public health officials, humanitarian aid organizations, and human rights organizations may have produced that examines an overlooked consequence or development, or puts a crisis in a new light.

Reporting on developments in a way that does not provoke panic, but does perhaps provoke action, will help ensure the crisis stays on the minds of not only the general public, but also donor countries and international policymakers. Informed, rather than reactionary, journalism can be a tool in preventing further atrocities and securing essential international assistance.

Notes

1. *Ebola Situation Report for 14 October 2015*, World Health Organization.
2. *Ebola Situation Report for 15 October 2015*, World Health Organization.
3. CBS News. 2014. "Scale of Ebola Crisis Unprecedented, CDC Director Says," August 7, available at: www. cbsnews.com/news/scale-of-ebola-crisis-unprecedented-cdc-director-says/
4. CNN, October 6, 2014.
5. *Ebola Virus Disease Fact Sheet Number 103*, World Health Organization, August 2015.
6. For example, the number of journalists in US newspapers in 1989 was 59,000 and in 2012 that number dropped to 36,000, according to the Brookings Institution, available at www.brookings.edu/research/essays/2014/bad-news#
7. *World Bank Data Sheet Democratic Republic of Congo*, 2015.
8. Liberia, while still off the beaten path with few flights into the capital of Monrovia, is still less remote than eastern Congo, or even Kinshasa. This means it is easier and less expensive for news organizations (that have decreasing budgets) to send reporters to cover events.
9. Lexis-Nexis search using the terms "Democratic Republic of Congo" and "war" for August 2, 1998–August 2, 1999 and January 1, 2001–January 1, 2002.
10. "*Congo, Democratic Republic of the in 2002—Related Emergencies*," Financial Tracking Service, the United Nations Office for the Coordination of Humanitarian Affairs.
11. "*Congo, Democratic Republic of the in 2003—Related Emergencies*," Financial Tracking Service, the United Nations Office for the Coordination of Humanitarian Affairs.
12. "*Ebola Virus Outbreak—West Africa—April 2014*," Financial Tracking Service, the United Nations Office for the Coordination of Humanitarian Affairs.
13. "*U.S. Congress Examines Humanitarian Crisis in Congo/Kinshasa*," US Department of State, May 2001.
14. FDCH Political Transcripts, "Colin L. Powell Holds Media Availability with President Museveni," May 27, 2001.
15. "*MONUSCO Facts and Figures*," United Nations Organization Stabilization Mission in the Democratic Republic of the Congo, 2016.
16. "Democratic Republic of the Congo 2015," Financial Tracking Service, the United Nations Office for the Coordination of Humanitarian Affairs.
17. Executive Mansion, "*President Sirleaf Presents FY 2015/2016 Draft National Budget of US$604.04 Million to the National Legislature on Monday, June 1, 2015*," May 31, 2015.

References

Beutler, B. (2014) "Republicans Want You to Be Terrified of Ebola—so You'll Vote for Them," *The New Republic*, October 16.

Brennan, R., and Husarska, A. (2006) "Inside Congo: An Unspeakable Toll," *The Washington Post*, July 16.

Centers for Disease Control and Prevention. (2014) "New Modeling Tool for Response to Ebola Virus Disease," September 23, available at: www.cdc.gov/media/releases/2014/s0923-ebola-model-factsheet.html

CNN. (2015) "CNN Poll: One in four Americans worry about Getting Ebola," September 16, available at: www. cnn.com/2014/09/16/politics/cnn-poll-ebola/

Committee to Protect Journalists. (2001) "Attacks on the Press in 2000—The Democratic Republic of the Congo," February.

Committee to Protect Journalists. (2002) "Attacks on the Press 2001: Democratic Republic of Congo," March 26.

Committee to Protect Journalists. (2003) "Attacks on the Press 2002: Democratic Republic of Congo," March.

Doctors Without Borders (Médecins Sans Frontières). (2007) "Top Ten Most Underreported Humanitarian Stories of 2007," available at: www.doctorswithoutborders.org/news-stories/special-report/top-ten-most-underreported-humanitarian-stories-2007

Doctors Without Borders (Médecins Sans Frontières). (2015) "Liberia: Rebooting Public Health Services," April 1.

The Economist. (2002) "A Report from Congo, Africa's Great War," July 4.

Enough Project. (2015) "Conflict Minerals: Progress and Challenges on Conflict Minerals: Facts on Dodd-Frank 1502 in Eastern Congo," October.

Harvard Humanitarian Initiative. (2009) Final Report for the Open Society Institute. "Characterizing Sexual Violence in the Democratic Republic of the Congo: Profiles of Violence, Community Responses, and Implications for the Protection of Women," August.

Human Security Report Project. (2010) "Human Security Report 2009/2010."

Infoasaid. (2012) "Democratic Republic of Congo Media and Telecoms Landscape Guide," December.

International Rescue Committee. (2008) "Mortality in the Democratic Republic of Congo: An ongoing crisis," January.

Kim, J. S. (2005) "Media Coverage and Foreign Assistance: The Effects of US Media Coverage on the Distribution of US Official Development Assistance (ODA) to Recipient Countries," Georgetown Public Policy Institute. May 2.

Livingston, S. (1997) "Clarifying the CNN Effect: An Examination of Media Effects According to Type of Military Intervention," John F. Kennedy School of Government's Joan Shorenstein Center on the Press, Politics and Public Policy at Harvard University.

Rioux, J-S., and Van Belle, D. A. (2005) "The Influence of *Le Monde* Coverage on French Foreign Aid Allocations," *International Studies Quarterly*, 49 (3): 481–502.

Roth, K. and Sawyer, I. (2015) "Joseph Kabila Forever: The Dangers of an Extended Presidency in the Democratic Republic of Congo," in *Foreign Policy* (July 28).

Soderlund, W., Briggs, E. D., Najem, T. P., and Roberts, B. C. (2012) *Africa's Deadliest Conflict: Media Coverage of the Humanitarian Disaster in the Congo and the United Nations Response, 1997–2008*, Waterloo, ONT: Wilfrid Laurier University Press, p. 46.

Sonpon III, L. M. (2015) "Liberia: U.S.$1.7 Billion to Build Resilient Health System," *Daily Observer* (Liberia), October 29.

Sprecher, A. (2015) "Handle Survivors with Care," *The New England Journal of Medicine* (October 14).

Tampa, V. (2012) "Why the World is Ignoring Congo War," CNN, November 27, available at: www.cnn.com/2012/11/27/opinion/congo-war-ignored-vava-tampa/ CNN

United States Department of State. (2001) "U.S. Congress Examines Humanitarian Crisis in Congo/Kinshasa," May.

United Nations Office of the High Commissioner on Human Rights. (2010) "DRC: Mapping Human Rights Violations: 1993–2003," August.

Van Belle, D. A. (2010) "Media Agenda? Setting and Donor Aid," in P. Norris (Ed.), *Public Sentinel: News Media & Governance Reform*, The World Bank.

WHO Ebola Response Team. (2014) "Ebola Virus Disease in West Africa: The First 9 Months of the Epidemic and Forward Projections," *The New England Journal of Medicine*, 371: 1481–1495.

17

COMPASSION AS A NEWS VALUE

Comparing French and UK Humanitarian Coverage of the War in Gaza 2014

Emma Heywood

Introduction

Compassion, or "a painful emotion occasioned by the awareness of another person's unde-served misfortune" (Nussbaum 2001, 31) is a contemporary news value increasingly used to raise public awareness of the civilian population as victims of conflict (Boltanski 1999; Tester 2001; Chouliaraki 2006; Silverstone 2007). As a news value, it not only raises the news-worthiness of a report but also gives it authenticity, and according to Bell's "journalism of attachment" where journalism "cares as well as knows; [and] is aware of its responsibilities" (1998, 16), raises the public's awareness of victims in conflict and injects a moral aspect into the coverage. Viewers are thus called upon to empathize with culturally different victims and deliberate not only the causes and effects of conflict but also who is considered responsible and what actions can be taken.

This new news value complements the more traditional list of factors devised by Galtung and Ruge (1965), which, in combination, are considered to increase the newsworthiness of broadcasts. Some of the more well-known factors, such as negativity value, are frequently encountered in foreign conflict reporting as the aggression and violence of war and fighting "sells". Similarly, the actions of global leaders and their nations (power elite and elite nation values) also dominate as solutions to the conflict become newsworthy once any potential interest in the fighting fades. Another important group increasingly receiving attention in media coverage of conflict is the victims, or the sufferers. Compassion in the way they are portrayed has the potential to elicit an emotional response to those suffering in distant places. The quality of compassion involves both the viewers' relationship with remote "others" and their recognition that these "others" are also part of a common humanity, regardless of where, or who, they are. But appealing to a single humankind has also been criticized for dehumanizing the "other" and reinforcing West/rest, resulting in humanitarian power relations (Silverstone 2007) and protecting geopolitical hierarchies between "effective and ineffective states" (Duffield 2007, 122).

Themes of compassion obligate viewers to engage with an ethics of care, or to imagine putting themselves in the position of the victim (Silverstone 2007). Yet, it has been argued that the sheer volume of broadcasts depicting human suffering desensitizes viewers, therefore blocking emotional responses and resulting in "compassion fatigue" (Moeller 1999; Tester 2001; Sontag 2003; Campbell 2012). Such saturation coverage of conflict and suffering must therefore be tempered to highlight events that are dramatic and that occur over short periods of time to heighten their newsworthiness (Carruthers 2000, 231).

Because cultural and geographical proximity is also important in determining levels of compassion (Moeller 1999), the media is key in determining not only what is shown to viewers but how it is portrayed and the extent of the graphic nature of the suffering.

Chouliaraki developed a typology of Western news discourse to facilitate analyses of victim portrayals. She determined three qualitative levels of suffering: *adventure* news depicts the subject from a distance and offers no cause for concern or action; *emergency* news produces pity with a corresponding demand or option for action to alleviate suffering; and in *ecstatic* news the victim is considered to be "one of us" allowing the viewer to identify with those suffering (2006, 94).

We will now apply these theoretical formulations of the news values of suffering and the corresponding viewers' responses to the humanitarian coverage of foreign conflict by two different news providers, BBC's *News at Ten* and *20 Heures* produced by France 2's broadcasting service. By investigating the various representations of victimhood in their coverage of the Gaza war in 2014, we seek to determine how the broadcasters perceive "victims" and whether or not they consider compassion as a news value that determines the newsworthiness of their output. The analysis applies these compassion typologies to the broadcasters' coverage of the war over time, tracing shifts from one category to another. This qualitative content analysis will help identify the proximity of the victims to the potential audience and the newsworthiness of the depictions of suffering in relation to other potentially more newsworthy aspects of events.

The Case Study and the Two Broadcasters

The chosen broadcasters (from France and the UK) are comparable as they are the flagship channels of their countries. The news programs in question are the main evening news broadcasts of these services. These are *News at Ten* from the nominally independent BBC, a British public service broadcaster; and *20 Heures*, also a public service broadcaster, from a media system with a long history of state intervention.

The case study is the 2014 war in Gaza, chosen because it is part of the Israeli–Palestinian conflict which represents a conflict of long duration and high visibility in the global media. Additionally, both reporting countries have similar connections to the broader Middle East region, both historically and domestically. They have the largest Jewish and Muslim populations in Europe, which associate them with Israel and the broader Middle East. In addition, both have suffered increases in anti-Semitism and Islamophobia since 9/11, incidents that escalate when there are flashpoints in the Middle East (Hecker 2012; Reader 2014).

The 2014 war occurred within the context of Israel's on-going occupation of the Palestinian territories and Hamas rocket fire into Israel. Israel's blockade of Gaza since 2007 had resulted in the degradation of human rights and a critical economic situation (HRC 2015). Simultaneously, there had been an increase in the construction of tunnels and rocket attacks from Gaza into Israel. According to the UN Human Rights Council (HRC) report, "the risk of a flare-up of the situation was evident" (2015, 17). On July 12, 2014, three Israeli teenagers were kidnapped and murdered in the West Bank, leading to extensive search and arrest operations by the Israelis. A 16-year old Palestinian was then burned alive in a revenge attack, resulting in a severe escalation of tensions. On July 8, 2014, the IDF started the operation it named "Protective Edge" to stop Hamas rocket attacks, and ground operations were launched to "locate and neutralize additional cross-border assault tunnels" (Israel Ministry of Foreign Affairs 2015). An unconditional ceasefire was announced on August 26, 2014 following 2251 Palestinian and 73 Israeli deaths respectively, and extensive destruction of Gaza's civil infrastructure. Though the HRC (2015) suggests that both sides may have commkiitted war crimes, numbers of dead indicate an imbalance in the humanitarian loss.

Using Galtung and Ruge's traditional news values (1965) and also Chouliaraki's typologies of humanitarian reporting, this study evaluates similarities and differences between the broadcasters' coverage of the war in 2014 to determine the ways they draw on the news value of compassion to raise the newsworthiness of reporting. It also considers whether compassion, as a news value, meets the moral challenges of humanitarian coverage by enabling a relationship to be created with the unfamiliar, other, or whether the victim remains distanced from the viewer (Silverstone 2004; 2007). The study will also determine whether hierarchies in victims emerge in the coverage that might demonstrate that compassion is culturally constructed and can vary between different groups, societies, and broadcasters (Höijer 2004). We consider two possible responses of viewers, defined by Boltanski (1999), to suffering portrayed by the media. The first of these relates to feelings of injustice regarding the suffering and the denunciation of those perceived as accountable; and the second relates to feelings of empathy and the appropriate care to be given and by whom. The analysis also applies Chouliaraki's definition of victim involvement ("*motion*—where the sufferer participates in concrete, purposeful activity, *gaze*—where the sufferer enters an active relationship with the camera and *condition*—the sufferer symbolizes a 'universal' human state of existence" (2006, 124)). The study focuses on different points of this 51-day long conflict. We first evaluate initial coverage when reports were short, factual, and with little attempt to humanize victims. The second stage considers the reach of the conflict and examines French coverage of pro-Palestinian demonstrations in July 2014, which included anti-Semitic violence in Paris. The French coverage of these protests demonstrates how compassion for victims in Gaza was quickly sidelined and then replaced by outrage and emotive coverage of victims of the Paris riots who are no longer the "other" but now "one of us." The third is the shelling of the Jabalia UNRWA School on July 30, 2014.

Compassion News Values in the Initial Reporting

The initial coverage following the IDF's launch of Operation Protective Edge on July 8, 2014 exemplifies Chouliaraki's *adventure* news discourse, in which the distant other is presented as no cause for concern or action. Both broadcasters provide seemingly balanced reportage in accordance with their objectivity guidelines (France Télévisions 2011; BBC 2015) and broadcast separate reports from Israel and Gaza highlighting two distinct groups of victims. Yet clear divisions emerge, replicating not only the asymmetry of the conflict but also, to some degree, the stances taken by the respective governments. The French government initially strongly supported Israel and criticized Hamas aggression (elysee.fr 2014). This sentiment was reproduced on *20 Heures*, questioning its independence as a public sector broadcaster, and the events were reported not only in detail from within Israel but also from an Israeli viewpoint. The correspondent interviews residents who are named, who talk directly to the camera and who are humanized and allowed to discuss their distress. *20 Heures'* principal emphasis is on the inconvenience caused to the Israelis by the ongoing Hamas rocket fire from Gaza which is attacking the civilized "us" represented by those in Tel Aviv. "We can't live like this. These are our main summer holidays. It's not fair," complains one resident and, "we need to stop this once and for all," encouraging viewers to empathize with the Israeli residents and making little attempt to reduce the emotional distance between the viewer and Gazan "others."

This distance is accentuated by the contrasting techniques *20 Heures* uses when covering events in Gaza. The latter is represented as physically remote, its people are dehumanized and the mounting death toll is minimized. The voiceover refers to the Palestinians in terms of numbers rather than as individual human beings ("twenty-two have allegedly died in Gaza this Wednesday," "the Israelis have hit 550 Hamas targets in Gaza" and "seventy-five deaths"). On the first three days' coverage, *20 Heures* provides no context to this operation and everything is reported in a singular space time. We, as the viewer, are shown a series of images of explosions in Gaza towns, of culturally different victims aimlessly picking over the remnants of their houses, women mourning, and families grieving over the dead body of a child. These reports offer no engagement with any of these sufferers and we remain onlookers. In contrast are the portrayals of the Israelis, who are shown in their domestic and social environments, while the Palestinians are reported from afar. Through the camera perspective and angle, viewers are positioned alongside Israelis who watch bombs explode on Gaza from hilltops in Sderot, some recording the bombings on their smartphones.

The events in Gaza are narrated in terms of who, where, and how with no suggestion of why, or of any solutions to this situation or its origin. *20 Heures* shows a map of the region on July 10 but it focuses on the West Bank, not the Gaza Strip where the conflict is being played out, and there is no useful geopolitical context to this map. There are background references to the 1993 Oslo agreement and to recent failed peace negotiations and the leaders involved on both occasions, but the omission of detail about the present conflict fails to inform the viewers and results in lack of viewer comprehension of the conflict. This, together with the exclusion of any attribution of causality for the suffering, hinders any meaningful engagement with the Gazan victims. The latter remain dehumanized and viewers are kept away from the living context of the victims. Thus, despite frequent references to the geographical proximity of Gaza to Israel (mainly to emphasize the closeness of the danger to Israel), the distance between the viewer and the victims in Gaza increases.

News at Ten's coverage resembles that of *20 Heures* as it provides little, if any, opportunity for viewers to engage with Palestinian victims. Yet, despite criticism of bias from both sides within the UK (Schlosberg 2014), its perspective is not so emphatically from the Israeli point of view, thus it detaches itself from the geopolitical interests of the UK government in spite of the fact that the Foreign Secretary had issued a clear statement supporting Israel's right to defend itself (gov.uk 2014). Noticeably absent from the coverage are interviews or direct communication with Gazan victims; instead, their situation is portrayed through a series of unconnected images linked together by the correspondent's fact-giving voiceover. The victims, as on *20 Heures*, are nameless, have no functions or roles, and are simply labelled "the Palestinians" or "the family", with no further details. Some reports included the deaths of "seven Palestinian civilians" and "one man who had a lucky escape" but there is no further elaboration. Compassion as a news value is sidelined and *News at Ten* prefers instead to draw on the negativity and sensationalistic value of explosions and bloodied victims being dragged from the rubble, and on representations of dehumanized masses of Palestinians at a funeral. Some context to the conflict is provided on July 9, when it is noted Hamas proposes a halt to the blockade and the release of political prisoners. On the other side, Israel wants rocket attacks from Gaza to stop. But this reporting is superficial and provides no additional or meaningful information on the broader conflict and the reporting is therefore devoid of historicity.

Although leaders are shown by both news providers, there are no suggestions of causality, agency or possible benefactors at this stage and the varying representations of the victims are framed in ways to suggest that nothing can be done to stop the conflict or alleviate the suffering, which seems to occupy a frame of inevitability and resignation. Both broadcasters portray the events as yet another flare-up in the long-running conflict not ultimately deserving greater attention. There is the prevailing sentiment that the newsworthiness of the conflict is minimal; "we've seen it all before—it's not the first time, it won't be the last" (*20 Heures* July 10).

French Demonstrations

This section shifts to the French domestic arena and, although it focuses exclusively on *20 Heures*, it provides a valuable discussion of *ecstatic* news discourse and shows how coverage of remote victims can quickly be displaced by domestic victims who are considered more newsworthy simply by being "one of us." In summer 2014, pro-Palestinian demonstrations were organized throughout France, as they were in many other countries. However, clashes between pro-Palestinian and Zionist demonstrators led to the marches in Paris being banned by the authorities and to subsequent questioning of republican values in France. Despite the ban, protests went ahead and targeted Jewish-owned businesses and a synagogue in the Parisian suburb of Sarcelles. Extensive coverage by *20 Heures* depicted not only, but predominantly, the Jewish community as now living in fear as victims. Now occupying the lead position in the running order, the coverage of the demonstrations was significant and, although it did not replace reportage of Gaza, it reduced the airtime available for it. In doing so, this phase of reporting revealed a hierarchy of victims. Suddenly, there was fear that, as President Hollande stated, the conflict was being "imported" into France. A different order of victims— the French Jewish community—emerged who were now "one of us"; they were not directly involved in the conflict but their suffering had been brought about by it, albeit indirectly. The increased cultural and geographical proximity of the events significantly increased the newsworthiness of the coverage. The distance that had existed between the remote Palestinian victims and (French) viewers had consequently lessened. Viewers became aware that the war in Gaza was affecting them in their safe zone of France and was being transformed into a very real and direct threat.

The protests, which caused new victims—the French Jewish community replacing the Palestinian victims—and new protagonists—the demonstrators—led to a discursive frame that questioned the fundamental democratic principles of the French republic: "you can't impose a ban [on demonstrating] like this, not in a country like France which is a democratic country . . . which stands for human rights" (July 19, 2014). The French victims, in contrast to the *adventure* news portrayal of the Gazan victims, are now thoroughly humanized. Individuals are allowed to speak directly to the camera and provide testimonial evidence of their suffering and the injustice of the attacks by the demonstrators given that "*we* are French, just like any other French citizen." Not only are the viewers and victims of the same nationality but so are those going to the aid of the victims. The victims are no longer the "other," they have a history and their integration into society represents core French values. Compassion as a news value for these new victims is augmented with the introduction of its counterpart, denunciation, not only by community leaders but also by heads of the state and religious leaders, whose elite news value is drawn upon in speeches and also through the visual narrative. The situation is so serious that the Prime Minister, Manual Valls, is shown condemning the attacks stating, "France will not allow provocative minds to feed . . . conflict between communities," (gouvernement.fr 2014) and *20 Heures*' coverage of the French victims now acts to unify the nation in the face of domestic political and ethnic fallout from the Gaza conflict. The newsworthiness of any compassion in the humanitarian coverage of the Gazan victims has now been supplanted by a fusion of news values in the coverage of the French protests and a clear message is relayed that the nation's values will not be shaken by hitherto distant events that now threaten domestic identity and politics.

July 30—Jabalia UNRWA School

This section examines the *emergency* news discourse exemplified by the broadcasters' coverage of the Israeli shelling of the Jabalia Elementary Girls School. This UNRWA designated emergency shelter accommodated 3,000 people when it was struck by Israeli artillery on July 30, 2014. The Israeli forces, which had been notified 28 times in 14 days that this was a UNRWA shelter, stated it had been the scene of armed clashes with Hamas militants. Between 17 and 18 people were killed including three children and at least 99 were injured (HRC 2015). The attack, for which no advance warning was given, received strong international condemnation.

A contrast emerges not just between coverage of the chosen events but also between the approaches of the two broadcast services. Approximately three weeks had passed since the IDF's launch of operation Protective Edge and no realistic end was in sight. Humanitarian ceasefires had collapsed and the asymmetry of the war was increasingly apparent from almost daily broadcasts of the rising death toll; 1336 Palestinians compared to 58 Israelis. The coverage reflected a growing sense of engagement with Gazan victims and, although they remained the "other," the remoteness that initially existed between them and the viewer lessened. In contrast with the initial understated *adventure* news discourse, reports now elicited pity from the viewer with phrases such as "this room was full of women and little children, all fast asleep when the explosion took place" (*20 Heures*); "the terror of conflict etched on to the face of a five-year-old girl" and "two little girls lying side by side bloodied and bruised" (*News at Ten*). The earlier minimal description offered became more complex narratives that display the characteristics of *emergency* news. Later reports exemplified Boltanski's mode of denunciation. *News at Ten*'s pivots from its previous depictions of personalized reporting (Heywood 2015) to more emotive narratives containing robust denunciation—or blame-filled compassion. Drawing also on the news value of elite leaders and nations, the coverage opens with clear condemnations of Israeli strikes from top UN officials, with Ban Ki-moon reflecting, in direct rather than reported speech, global outrage at the bombing he describes as "unjustifiable and [which] demands accountability and justice." Criticism from Obama is also mentioned, as is the fact that there is no "shortage of diplomatic outrage tonight." As images of the bomb site are shown there are instant judgement calls for accountability by the *News at Ten* correspondent stating that the "debate will begin immediately about who is responsible for this," implying that a limit had now been reached and the world could no longer ignore such atrocities.

News at Ten reveals the scale of the atrocity by flashing the death toll on the screen and by showing distressing images, for which a warning has been given, of grieving relatives, crowded hospital scenes and wounded victims, the majority of whom are children. A hierarchy of sufferers emerges with iconic images of children, women, and elderly men being frequently included in the narrative as they are considered suitable victims for inclusion. According to Moeller (1999) and Christie (1996), these groups are ideal victims and have greater news value than men. Footage of several injured little girls is shown, crying, bewildered and representing the "youngest and most vulnerable." On each occasion their gaze is directly at the camera, they are accompanied by family members, their stories are told and they are given the chance to articulate their pain. The viewer can engage with these humanized victims through their age and distress and the direct relationship built with them via the camera, and the correspondent's emotive pieces-to-camera and narratives of these "simply appalling scenes." Men, being lower down the victim hierarchy, are assessed through their actions, and they are shown toiling en masse and engaged in purposeful activity. On one hand, this has the effect of promoting their own agency but on the other highlights the world's abandonment of them, as they remain the other, obliged to look after themselves, despite being part of a common humanity.

News at Ten seems to provide an element of balance by broadcasting reports from Israel but these are framed in such a way as to provoke outrage from the viewer. One Israeli is shown refusing to apologize for the deaths of Palestinian children and another group of activists chants "no more children left" in Gaza. An IDF spokesman downplays the bombing, describing it as an "incident" that, when this is juxtaposed with images of death, injury, and destruction, serves only to increase indignation at the bombing. The asymmetry of the war is also foregrounded by a series of images of Israeli tanks and technology. In the knowledge that photographic images are considered accurate depictions of reality, and that audiences do not question their reality status (Silverstone 2007), it would seem hard for French viewers not to align themselves with those in Gaza. It is hard to deny the destruction and injury of children pictured in bombed-out refugee shelters.

In contrast with *News at Ten*'s heavily humanized coverage of this event, *20 Heures*' reports are less accusatory and the Gazan victims remain more emotionally distanced. An element of cultural interest is injected into the report during an interview with the French-speaking Commissioner General of the UNRWA when visiting Gaza. Indeed, his presence appears more newsworthy than that of the victims. There are some value judgements ("the UN is accusing [Israel] directly," "unheard of violence"; and Ban Ki-moon's words of condemnation are reported indirectly), yet a note of caution prevails, as advocated by the commissioner general, while waiting for the results of an enquiry.

There is little personalization value in *20 Heures*' coverage with few close-up images of the unpleasantness of human suffering. Instead, the focus is on wide-angle shots of Palestinians wandering over rubble or simply waiting in groups on various floors of the school. The correspondent reports from bombed-out classrooms and it is only through her that the viewer gains a personalized aspect; she reports on the situation—stating, for example, that this room had been full of women and children—rather than speaking directly to the sufferers themselves, which was the case on *News at Ten*. The coverage does not elicit sentiment for the victims nor is there discussion or call for humanitarian assistance despite reference to a call to the international community. The verbal commentary has a greater role than the images that, in many cases, are there to support the narrative rather than to provide an empathetic visual pathway to victims. Because the report is infused with statistics, the viewer can however comprehend both the scale of the bombings and also the importance of UN aid to the region.

20 Heures provides balance with reports from the Israeli point of view. Rather than questioning civilians about their opinions on the bombings, which could have had the effect of increasing levels of indignation as on *News at Ten*, *20 Heures* reports on Israeli accusations of Hamas using civilians as human shields and on tunnels being constructed into Israel, showing a Hamas video of these tunnels. In general, reporting of the school bombing and the dehumanized portrayal of victims is non-emotive, with few avenues available for viewer compassion. Nevertheless, as one report ends with graphic images of wounded Palestinian civilians, accompanied by "further unheard-of violence," a condemnatory tone is taken.

Both broadcast services attempt to address the moral aspects of the shelling and both sets of their coverage encourage viewers to relate, to different degrees, to the victim and consider them as part of common humanity. *News at Ten* provides personalized coverage that evokes pity for the victim and outrage at the Israeli actions. *20 Heures* is more reluctant to bridge any remoteness between viewers and victims with the former remaining onlookers. Reports are structured in ways that reinforce the us/them divide.

Conclusion

This chapter examined compassion as a news value in the humanitarian coverage of the 2014 war in Gaza by French and UK broadcasters to show the extent to which victims of foreign conflict can be portrayed with greater and lesser degrees of compassion. It is argued that such differences elicit diverse responses from their viewers. In addition, portrayals of leaders and governments also vary with significant consequences for the assigning of blame and responsibility. Findings demonstrate the different degrees to which broadcasters drew on compassion as a news value to increase the newsworthiness of their reports and retain the attention of their audience. The study demonstrates that compassion as a news value is highly contextual, and in some cases was found to be insufficient as a dominant news characteristic. Coverage displayed other dominant news values such as negativity, violence and graphic imagery of the dead and wounded, and the elite value of world leaders. It confirmed that a hierarchy of victims can be identified in coverage of humanitarian suffering. For example, coverage by *20 Heures* of related protests in Paris revealed that domestic victims may quickly displace remote others because of their cultural and geographical proximity. *News at Ten* provided a predominantly humanitarian coverage with direct interaction with victims while *20 Heures* preferred less emotive and more one-dimensional coverage supported throughout with analytical, factual information.

The findings not only provided insight into compassion as a news value but also shed light on it as an emotion among the warring parties, demonstrating the difficulty, if not impossibility, of displaying compassion for the enemy, regardless of their state of suffering. This was exemplified by the callousness of Israeli civilians when interviewed by *News at Ten* about the Palestinian deaths and injuries in Gaza. If, as Sontag stated, "pity is considered to be the emotion we owe only to those enduring *undeserved* misfortune" (2003, 59), the lack of feeling of these Israelis, which reflects not only the blame they attach to the Palestinians for the deaths in Gaza but also the potential threat they pose to Israelis, supports her suggestion that compassion must be justified.

The study does illustrate that, in certain instances, compassion as a contemporary news value has a place in humanitarian news reporting and that awareness of distant suffering can be raised through its inclusion in broadcasters' reports. Yet the emotional and physical gaps between the viewer and the on-screen victims remain. In fact, compassion reinforced the us/other divide as it only served to foreground differences and therefore exclude those who do not fit "our" cultural norms. The question therefore remains about the merit of broadcasting increasingly emotive reports on human suffering: Is the purpose of compassion as a news value only to raise the newsworthiness of a report or can it, as Chouliaraki suggests for *emergency* news, also trigger a demand or option for action among viewers to participate in alleviating suffering? On-screen denunciation of those responsible appears to increase in direct proportion to the on-screen levels of compassion and emotion yet achieves little. Compassion may be newsworthy, but might only occasionally provoke a reaction among viewers, especially given the ever-increasing desensitization of viewers. Without doubt, other conflicts that are more newsworthy for whatever reason will soon come along as replacements. Distant victims will remain remote and the power play between them and the viewer will continually be reproduced with compassion as a news value delivering predictably sensationalized news, marginalizing victims, and contributing to reports that do little more than act as passing acknowledgment of sufferers' plight.

References

BBC. (2015) *Editorial Guidelines: Section 4: Impartiality*, available at: www.bbc.co.uk/editorialguidelines/guidelines/impartiality/principles

Bell, M. (1998) "The Journalism of Attachment," in M. Kieran (Ed.), *Media Ethics*, London: Routledge, pp. 15–22.

Boltanski, L. (1999) *Distant Suffering: Politics, Morality and the Media*, Cambridge, UK: Cambridge University Press.

Campbell, D. (2012) *The Myth of Compassion Fatigue*, available at: www.david.campbell.org

Carruthers, S. L. (2000) *The Media at War: Communication and Conflict in the Twentieth Century*, Basingstoke, UK: Palgrave Macmillan.

Chouliaraki, L. (2006) *The Spectatorship of Suffering*, London: Sage.

Christie, N. (1996) "The Ideal Victim," in E. A. Fattah (Ed.), *From Crime Policy to Victim Policy*, London: Macmillan Press, pp. 17–30.

Duffield, M. (2007) *Development, Security and Unending War: Governing the World of Peoples*. Cambridge, UK: Polity. elysee.fr. (2014) "Entretien avec le Premier ministre israélien—14 July 2014," available at: www.elysee.fr/communiques-de-presse/article/entretien-avec-le-premier-ministre-israelien/

France Télévisions. (2011) *Charte des antennes de France Télévisions*, available at : www.francetelevisions.fr/actions/charte-des-antennes

Galtung, J., and Ruge, M. (1965) "The Structure of Foreign News: The Presentation of the Congo, Cuba and Cyprus Crises in Four Norwegian Newspapers," *Journal of International Peace Research*, 2 (1): 64–91.

gouvernement.fr. (2014) "Discours pour le 72e anniversaire de la rafle du Vél' d'Hiv—20 July 2014," available at: www.gouvernement.fr/partage/357-72e-anniversaire-de-la-rafle-du-vel-d-hiv-discours-du-premier-ministre

gov.uk. (2014) "Foreign Secretary Statement on Gaza—14 July 2015," available at: www.gov.uk/government/news/foreign-secretary-statement-on-gaza

Hecker, M. (2012) *Intifada française? De l'importation du conflit israélo-palestinien*, Paris: Ellipses.

Heywood, E. (2015) "Comparing Russian, French and UK Television News: Portrayals of the Casualties of War," *Russian Journal of Communication*, 7 (1): 40–52.

Höijer, B. (2004) "The Discourse of Global Compassion: The Audience and Media Reporting of Human Suffering," *Media, Culture and Society*, 26(4): 513–531.

HRC (Human Rights Council). (2015) "Report of the Detailed Findings of the Independent Commission of Inquiry Established Pursuant to Human Rights Council Resolution S-21/1," June 23, 2015.

Israel Ministry of Foreign Affairs. (2015) "2014 Gaza Conflict, Israel's Objectives and Phases of the 2014 Gaza Conflict—14 June 2015," available at: http://mfa.gov.il/MFA/ForeignPolicy/IsraelGaza2014/Pages/Objectives-and-Phases-of-the-2014-Gaza-Conflict.aspx

Moeller, S. D. (1999) *Compassion Fatigue: How the Media Sell Disease, Famine, War and Death*, New York: Routledge.

Nussbaum, M. C. (2001) *Upheavals of Thought: The Intelligence of Emotion*, Cambridge, UK: Cambridge University Press.

Reader, K. (Ed.). (2014) "France and the Middle East." Themed issue of *Modern and Contemporary France*, 22 (1).

Schlosberg, J. (2014) "Media Wars over Gaza: Why British Broadcasters Are Still Failing in Their Scrutiny of Israeli Officials—31 July 2014," available at: www.opendemocracy.net/ourkingdom/justin-schlosberg/media-wars-over-gaza-why-british-broadcasters-are-still-failing-in-thei

Silverstone, R. (2004) "Proper Distance: Towards an Ethics for Cyberspace," in G. Liestol, A. Morrison and T. Rasmussen (Eds.), *Innovations*, Cambridge, MA: MIT Press, pp. 469–491.

Silverstone, R. (2007) *Media and Morality*, Cambridge, UK: Polity.

Sontag, S. (2003) *Regarding the Pain of Others*, London: Penguin.

Tester, K. (2001) *Compassion, Morality and the Media*, Buckingham, UK: Open University Press.

18

NEWS FRAMES AND GLOBAL TERRORISM COVERAGE IN THE UK AND NORWAY

Context and Consequences for Humanitarian Issues

Maria Konow Lund and Eva-Karin Olsson

Introduction

News media is often accused of simplifying complex events in order to fit those events into a media logic that demands conflict, dramatization, and personification (Atlheide and Snow 1979). In this chapter we take a close look at how historical narratives are applied to complex terror events as ways to explain and interpret those events for national and international publics. History (and the analogies through which history is often re-told) is a powerful journalistic tool in connecting the past to the present (Edy 1999). Thanks to their narrative power, historical analogies regularly crop up in relation to emotionally powerful events such as crises, war and acts of terrorism. Here, history becomes a means not only of negotiating under-standings but of embedding and strengthening political messages in the analysis or aftermath of an event. Yet, little is known in regard to how historical analogies are applied in times of severe societal distress such as terror attacks.

To reveal the applications of historical analogies in times of terror, we have selected two internationally reported terror attacks that share some significant similarities, but that took place in two different national, historical, and cultural contexts: the July 7, 2015 London bombing and the July 22, 2011 Norway attacks. We are interested in understanding how analogies may appeal to national and global audiences alike, that is: How can history, and the way that it is narrated, contribute to creating meaning for contemporary terror attacks, and provide comfort at different levels to different audiences? The following research questions have guided our study: (1) How were the terror attacks in the UK and Norway reported on in a global context through historical analogies? (2) How were these attacks reported in a national context through historical analogies?

Terrorism, History, and Media

Historical Analogies

References to history and collective memory in the news media are crucial objects for this study since they play an important role in providing the public with understanding and emotional comfort in times of crisis and, in doing so, they guide society in reaffirming its core values and norms (Edy and Daradanova 2006). That is, history is an effective narrative tool for connecting the present to the past and allowing journalists and readers to make meaning from apparently senseless events (Kepplinger and Habermeier 1995). Moreover, history is important for the creation of not only logical arguments but also emotional responses and, as such, is closely related to "national identity"; no matter how intangible and shifting that particular notion is (Bell 2003; Ryan 2004). According to Winfield et al. (2002) *historical analogies* can be used to compare or align the present to the past. As such, they are specific and concrete references to historical events, as opposed to more generic and abstract understandings of history (Khong 1992, 26). Hoskins (2011) refers to historical key events as "nodal," a meeting juncture, due to the fact that they have "acquired a substantial and recognizable memorial status" (p. 270) in the discourse between the media and the public. From a journalistic perspective, *historical analogies* are significant because they are perceived as factual and objective, as opposed to editorials or news analyses, and as such they take on an evidential capacity in news reporting.

Framing Political Conflict

Scholars with an interest in political conflicts have demonstrated that the news media tend to make use of all-embracing narratives, or so-called global macro-frames; the Cold War frame, for example, "highlighted certain events as international problems, identified their sources, offered normative judgments, and recommended particular policy solutions" (Norris 1995, 358). In the wake of the terror attacks in the United States on September 11, 2001, scholars have traced the emergence of another such macro-frame as well, that is, the war-on-terror-frame (Norris 2003). Like its predecessors, this frame demonstrates a propensity for linking local conflicts to global ones; for instance, linking the case of 9/11 with the Al Qaeda movement. Governments, non-state actors, and the media apply this frame to justify and explain both political and military strategies, particularly in dealing with state opponents (Ryan 2004; Ruigrok and van Atteveldt 2007;). The ideological dimension of obscuring motives for and reasons behind conflicts (and their management) has generated much scholarly interest in comparing this macro-framing work within different national contexts. Even though terror reporting since 9/11 has been inspired by the "war on terror" frame, cross-national journalism studies have shown how terror coverage is redefined for various contexts and adapted to specific circumstances (Haes 2003; Reese 2007, 67; Papacharissi and de Fatima Oliveira 2008; Gerhards and Schäfer 2014). In general, the inclusion-versus-exclusion dimension of this frame tends to be pivotal where Muslim "others" are framed as "radical, oppressive, irrational," and, as such, as the antithesis of the orderly, rational, civilized West (Roy and Ross 2011, 3). Historically, there have been two alternative ways of framing terrorists—as disturbed lone wolves or as coordinated collectives acting within structures derived from political conflicts—where the latter dominates today's media coverage. Domestic terrorists have proven more likely to be portrayed as lone and mentally unstable individuals but also as persons with desirable human attributes such as intelligence. Typically, international terrorists are depicted as evil extremists who have strong ties to larger political-driven networks (Matusitz 2013).

In the empirical section we will take a closer look at how historical analogies create meaning in the two selected cases, by highlighting or subduing certain logical, emotional, identity-related, or political arguments.

Method and Material

Interestingly, it can be noted that both attacks were executed by individuals born in the country in question—British-born sons of Pakistani immigrants (except for one) in the first attack, acting in the name of Islam, and an ethnic Norwegian in the second attack, violently expressing a right-wing extremist message. Moreover, the countries differ in regard to their cultural and historical backgrounds. The UK has an imperial past, a tradition of engagement in world politics, and the absence of foreign military occupation. Norway, on the other hand, is a rather new nation state and has a long history of occupations and unions with the Nordic countries, including its recent experience of Nazi German occupation during World War II. The empirical material for this study was derived from two major media outlets in each selected country—*The Guardian* and the *Daily Telegraph* in the UK, and *Aftenposten* and *Verdens Gang* (*VG*) in Norway. We analyzed all of the material published in these newspapers within a ten-day period from each of the respective attacks. This time frame was chosen based on our interest in historical analogies as sense makers and sources of comfort, and both of these mechanisms are most likely to take place in the acute phase of crisis news reporting. Within this time frame, we qualitatively analyzed the material with the aim of identifying and contextualizing the historical analogies used to report these events.

Empirical Analysis

Global Level

London Bombings

In the empirical material, one of the key characteristics of the news coverage was the way in which it linked the London bombings to a series of similar events, typically starting with 9/11. Evoking references to these other events was a powerful way of showing that the London bombings were not isolated but rather part of a long and sprawling campaign. This campaign was depicted as one part of a larger all-encompassing Al Qaeda network operating on a global scale and threatening additional attacks. Along those lines, the *Daily Telegraph* quoted British Prime Minister Tony Blair as saying that he blamed

> Islamist extremist terrorists of the kind who over recent years have been responsible for so many innocent deaths, in Madrid, Bali, Saudi Arabia, Russia, Kenya, Tanzania, Pakistan, Yemen, Turkey, Egypt, Morocco, of course in New York on September 11, but in many other countries too.
>
> (*Daily Telegraph* July 12, 2005)

Consequently, it would be just a matter of time before the UK would join the list of countries struck by Al Qaeda attacks. This perspective is well illustrated by a quote published in the *Daily Telegraph*: "We knew they were coming, but didn't know when. Since 9/11—and even more starkly since the Madrid bombings in March 2004—Mr Blair has confronted this question every morning: Will this be the day?" (*Daily Telegraph* July 10, 2005a). Hence other articles argued that the "war on terror" frame had been misleading people into believing that there is a "real" war out there (*The Guardian* July 9, 2005b).

Besides geographical assimilation, the war on terror, and its references to previous events, also influenced how the concept of time was reported. In an attempt to counter the suggestion that the UK and the US military involvement in Iraq and Afghanistan might have compelled the terror attacks (*The Guardian* July 9, 2005a), the war on terror was narrated as a story having its origins prior to 9/11 and thereby shifting the "blame" away from the US and UK:

> There are those who will blame British involvement in Iraq for yesterday's attacks. That is to misread the nature of the struggle. Its modern manifestation goes back to the 1993 assault on the World Trade Centre in New York, the same which was destroyed eight years later. This was followed by bombings in Saudi Arabia in 1995 and 1996, . . . In 1998, the American embassies in Nairobi and Dar-es-Salaam were targeted; two years later, suicide bombers blew a 40 ft hole in the destroyer USS Cole, killing 17 sailors. So, well before September 11, 2001, Osama bin Laden and his likes had taken the battle to the enemy.
>
> (*Daily Telegraph* August 7, 2005)

The ability to link certain news events with certain time periods was advantageous for certain actors (those in the West) over others (those in Islamic radical movements) in terms of responsibility for a given attack.

In the next section, we will look at the historical analogies applied in the Oslo case.

Terror Attacks in Oslo

Before the identity of the perpetrator and motives were known, associations were directly made to previous Islamic-connected terror events, and journalists allude to how Al Qaeda had been directly and indirectly threatening to attack Norway (*Aftenposten Morning* July 23, 2011). According to one of the articles, "Now it has happened. Terror is here. This is our 9/11" (*VG* July 23, 2011). In fact, initially most of the coverage was very similar to the British coverage, including the incorporation of a chronological overview of previous global terror attacks performed by Islamic terrorist groups (*Aftenposten Morning* July 23, 2011). Also similar to the British coverage, this was a way of placing the event within the "war on terror" frame that allowed journalists to understand the event as an Islamic-terrorist-inspired attack on Norway (Ottosen and Bull 2012). These historical analogies were powerful tools in underpinning the journalistic gut-feeling of pointing to Muslim terrorism before the terrorist was identified as an ethnic Norwegian. After the first day when it became clear that the perpetrator was in fact a Norwegian with a middle-class background, the coverage radically changed.

Journalists continued to refer to other countries that had experienced terror attacks but they did so without relating the Norway attack to the "war on terror" frame. As a result, attempts to link the event to other geographical places lost all meaning in terms of politics and motives. One journalist at *Aftenposten* lamented the challenges involved in reporting on a terrorist who was "no stranger" but an integrated part of Norwegian society: "In spite of all unanswered questions, it is possible to affirm one thing: This terror is in some way part of the Norwegian society itself. It was not international but national" (*Aftenposten Morning* July 24, 2011). That is, the perpetrator was not one of "them," but actually one of "us." When the "war on terror" frame was no longer suitable, the question of motives was emphasized less and portrayed as too complicated to address or respond to, which was also mirrored by the lack of suitable analogies. When suitable analogies (such as references to the first attack on the World Trade Center in 1993 and the Oklahoma bombings in 1995) did exist, they seemed too random and mechanical to offer any insight into the *modus operandi* of the Norwegian attack (*Aftenposten* July 23, 2011).

The majority of journalists looked for explanations by trying to apply suitable historical analogies to, for example, school massacres in order to understand what motives drive individuals to such actions. One article stated that a terrorist is the "worst mass murderer of all times" (*Aftenposten* July 25, 2011). The article then continued by going through the most macabre massacres in recent history. By categorizing Breivik among globally well-known mass murders, the journalists, at the same time, placed the attack within a category of events that are almost impossible to explain and comprehend. Most of the articles expressed a need to understand the event, but also the awareness that it would be difficult to understand it without knowing the mental state of Breivik.

In sum, the Norwegian empirical material does not engage in any in-depth analyses of the attack by drawing upon historical analogies; rather, journalists make use of random references to previous attacks.

National Level

London Bombings

In the British press, the use of national analogies includes similar global events such as the IRA movement and World War II (in particular, the Blitz). While these analogies do not help to explain why the London bombings occurred, they provide emotional comfort by creating a sense of British belonging and an evocation of British identity: "This weekend, that glorious beast growls defiance more angrily than ever. Since the attacks, much has been made of the return of the 'Blitz spirit'" (*Daily Telegraph* July 10, 2005c).

The Blitz analogy functioned as a means of depicting the stoic British national character: "We all love it when the British people shrug their shoulders and move stoically on in the face of attack. It is a powerful national myth, and a true one" (*Daily Telegraph* July 9, 2005). If the "war on terror" frame focused on the global threat facing Britain, the more localized analogies emphasized resistance. In short, London had lived through it all, from Luftwaffe to the IRA, and there was no threat the city could not shrug off:

> There was no panic at Westminster, just anger and a determination to return to business as usual. How dare they spoil everything now? London has been through this before. The IRA bombed shoppers, city workers, Army horses, children and tourists. This city can't be stopped. . . . In a series of tableaux, London is seen burning in the Blitz, Spitfires chase German bombers and the Queen Mother goes for a walk-about in the East End. London didn't crack then and it won't now.
>
> (*Daily Telegraph* July 8, 2005b)

The bombings become an excuse to recall what is perceived to be Britain's glorious past. "But there are times when they [the British] know precisely what is needed. 'What kind of a people do they think we are?' asked Churchill in 1940. The Nazis found out soon enough; so will the bombers" (*Daily Telegraph* July 11, 2005).

Along with its capacity to provide emotional comfort and encourage resilience, the Blitz analogy also resonated with the "war on terror" frame—the more severe the threat, the more heroic, stoic, and determined the everyday Londoner would become. The "civilized" British way of responding to the attacks was to do the exact opposite of terrorism and uncivilized hatred (*The Guardian* July 8, 2005). Also akin to the "war-on-terror" frame, the World War II Blitz analogy (although localized) allowed journalists to position the bombings in the general context of an ongoing "war." However, others did not accept this frame and portrayed it as individuals being brainwashed by political extremists and as such "it had far more in common with the IRA mainland bombing campaign than the Blitz" (*Daily Telegraph* July 10, 2005b).

In reference to the IRA attacks, the following quote relates less to fighting back than to carrying on with one's daily life and embracing resilience:

> London is not given to panic, with memories of IRA bombs hard-wired into general consciousness. Its millions of denizens have a certain canny élan, accustomed to hard-headed calculations of the odds against being one of the unlucky few in the wrong place at the wrong time. Remember how we mocked Sylvester Stallone and other macho-muscled Hollywood stars who refused to fly to London for fear of bombs, unable to make that simple risk assessment.
>
> (*The Guardian* August 7, 2005)

Nationally, the press uncovered and celebrated a British identity expressed in a shared history of war, terror, and resilience. Yet the picture is not so straightforward. What about when the bombers are British? "If they pass the 'cricket test,' how do we stop the suicide bombers?" one headline read (*Daily Telegraph* July 17, 2005). History even offers multiple interpretations, relating the story of Britain as a successfully multicultural society with a large Muslim population but also allowing for this: "We have blindly allowed our country to be a haven for fanatics. The official line is that this is the work of a criminal minority, and should not be blamed on Islam or the wider Muslim community" (*Daily Telegraph* July 8, 2005a).

Terror Attacks in Oslo

As with the British case, the World War II historical analogy played an important role in the media coverage of the terror attacks in Oslo. The terror attacks were considered to be the most severe incident on Norwegian soil since World War II, as conveyed in the following statement: "Yesterday's attacks were the first hits directed toward civilian targets and the state authority in Norway since 9th of April 1940" (*VG* July 22–23, 2011). As a result of Norway's history, the Norwegian media's evocation of the war analogy was different than that in the British media. In the British case, the July 22 bombings and the Blitz are firmly equated within the "war on terror" frame portrayed as unexpected attacks by a foreign enemy. The Oslo incident, on the other hand, was significantly different since it lacked any explicit connection to a foreign enemy. Rather, World War II and the terror attacks in Oslo were linked in time since both were described as "unthinkable" and "inconceivable." In addition, the fact that Norway was an occupied country during World War II adds yet another dimension to the Norwegian war analogies. While the British national character emerges from the legendary resistance to the Nazis, the Norwegian national character must contend with the fact that there were both sympathizers as well as resisters regarding the German occupation.

To resolve the dilemma presented by a homegrown, lone wolf terrorist, this person must be positioned as an enemy of democratic ideals. When asked what it would mean for the Norwegian society to respond to the terror attacks with a renewed commitment to democracy, former Norwegian Prime Minister Gro Harlem Brundtland said: "First of all it means that we should be steadfast to our basic values and beliefs, not be frightened by violence and threats but go ahead and create a wider, more inclusive democracy" (*Aftenposten* July 29, 2011). In this context, the World War II analogy can then activate memories of a time when the Norwegian people suffered but stood up for their ideals of democracy and freedom. In the confused aftermath of the July 22 Oslo attacks, media references to World War II and lyrical statements about how the "best" have died resonate clearly with the British Blitz analogy in their attempt to comfort through the solace of historical precedent. In an interview with the former Swedish editor-in-chief of the newspaper *Dagens Nyheter*, Arne Ruth summarized the complexity of how Norway processed the domestic attack and the fact that it was instigated by profoundly un-Norwegian values:

> The cruelty of this massacre is incredible—rarely has something touched me so deeply. The lack of emotions that can occur in a so-called normal person, with a fairly normal childhood, a person that once was an ordinary Norwegian in the normal sense, is incomprehensible . . . It [nationalism in Norway] has historical roots dating back to 1814, May 17th celebrations in 1905, and the resistance during the war [World War II]. This laid the foundation for the Norwegian sense of national unity and freedom . . . Breivik, in his cruel manner, misused this strong tradition of national independence. He turned this national unity upside down by believing that anyone who is not Norwegian [by birth] should not be accepted in Norwegian society.
>
> (*Aftenposten* July 30, 2011)

Obviously, the Norwegian journalists must struggle with contradictory emotions regarding the fact that Norwegian society both nested and groomed the person behind this horrific and backward-looking deed. In short, the national analogies in connection to the July 22 attack have strongly suggested that news coverage is subtly embedded with specific national values that are closely connected to the history of a country. Even though such analogies serve the purpose of providing understanding and comfort at the national level, they may also exclude global audiences.

Conclusion

In what follows, we will discuss the findings of our study and the implications for further research regarding the use of historical analogies in creating meaning during traumatic events such as terror acts. One of the most significant challenges the media faces during such moments is to provide a story that can help explain the apparently inexplicable and, in doing so, contribute to restoring a sense of normalcy. In times of shock and uncertainty there is a need to rejuvenate and remember heroic contributions, national values, and moral obligations (Kitch 2003). The analysis in the empirical section suggests that historical analogies allowed journalists to connect the terror attacks to earlier events as a way of providing understanding but also to encourage resistance and supply solace.

Despite the differences between the two cases, both terror attacks were carried out by perpetrators who were citizens in their respective countries. Yet, two different stories were told: one as a foreign-born, Islamist-inspired act and the other as a lunatic domestic lone wolf.

Starting with the British case, the "war on terror" frame relies upon the "us vs them" rhetoric, and its power derives from its ability to link local conflicts to global ones and thereby activates certain existing political and military strategies. In the British case, historical analogies provided a backdrop for understanding the London bombings in terms of the terrorists' motives and the political ramifications of the attacks. It linked the terror attacks to similar events across time and geography, so that key historical analogies become "nodes" in the chain of events, which are requisite for a viable "war on terror" frame. These nodes describe a common Islamic threat directed to the society at large, and this global frame supplies a contextual understanding for any given terror attack positioned within it. In the British case, historical analogies were powerful rhetorical devices in connecting the past with the present, making it more vivid, understandable and undisputable. At the same time, Bhatia (2005) points out that the strong reliance on the "war on terror" frame masked complexity as well as local and historical differences and as such this frame did not provide the audience with any deeper understanding of the British terror attacks; rather, it provided journalists with a standardized way of reporting terror.

Similar to the London case, the Norwegian journalists initially made references to previous Islamic-inspired acts of terror. However, historical references disappeared when the perpetrator and his motives became known. Rather, the perpetrator was depicted as a lone wolf, which made it much harder for the journalists to localize the event in question and it became portrayed as an isolated occurrence. The empirical material does not provide much insight into why it was portrayed in this manner but one suggestion is that political motivation did not fit well into the story that the Norwegian journalists wanted to tell. Another explanation might be that there was a lack of in-depth knowledge about similar cases of domestic terrorism.

This reminds us that history is an arbitrary act highlighting some historical facts while ignoring others and often told by focusing on certain narratives. Being unable to draw upon any influential analogies, the terror attacks in Oslo were left largely unexplained and, rather, depicted as extraordinary and incomprehensible in terms of political motives. These differences had crucial political implications. The foreign Islamist-inspired stories generated blame allocation and triggered the desire for repercussions. On the other hand, the domestic lone-wolf frame steered attention away from political motives and in turn, this made the issue of ramifications ambiguous.

In general, analogies at the global level focused on uniting and comforting or generating the idea of a common threat, and analogies at the national level functioned as a means of evoking feelings related to national identity and belonging. At the national level, for the newspapers in both countries the dominant analogy was World War II. The British fight against the Nazi regime and the Norwegian resistance to the Nazi occupation became historical examples of resilience both of which serviced to reclaim and recall specific national identities. In the British case, history reinforced the notion of the perpetrators as strangers, that is, as not being part of British society and its way of life. This was manifested both in the analogies made to previous events around the globe as well as in relation to the World War II analogy which reminded the British people of their "inherent" strength in together fighting a foreign enemy. The Norwegian case is more complex, where World War II evokes memories not only of resistance and heroism but also of betrayal and cowardliness, making the understanding of the event more multifaceted, and from a journalistic point of way, a more complicated story to tell. Yet interestingly, the entire Norwegian story is never explicitly told. Rather, the Norwegian journalists chose to highlight just one aspect of the World War II analogy, that is, the story of national identity and values. These selected analogies were used by journalists to tell the story of resistance, resilience, and courage. In general, it is less likely that such analogies will have the same effect on members of a global audience since they are not part of the same community and, as such, lack a common contextual foundation.

In sum, this study has demonstrated that historical analogies are powerful journalistic storytelling devices that play important roles for responsibility allocation, threat images, and societal healing processes, especially when societal sense-making is vital. In our opinion, the ability to choose and use history is a double-edged sword. That is, analogies can facilitate audiences' understanding by connecting the unknown to something familiar and understandable. As such, historical analogies can serve to bring order to chaos. At the same time, the use of analogies can limit other explanations and arguments and, as such, hamper crucial knowledge on context and background information that is essential in creating informed publics.

While embedding current events within a past historical frame, most analogies also contain within them an assumed interpretation, a given emotional response, and a predefined course of action. In an era of conflict and global instability, referring back to policies applied to conflicts of the past for comfort and direction may serve to perpetuate past failures instead of seeking out alternative explanations, solutions, and policies. Another observation is that analogies are often nationally contextualized. In this study we showed that national analogies were applied in order to create resilience and comfort. This is not surprising given the fact the worst trauma is felt at the national level; nevertheless, stronger efforts should be made to communicate such values by using inclusive, comprehensible, and relevant global analogies.

Further Reading

Freedman, D., and Thussu, D. K. (Eds.). (2012). *Media and Terrorism: Global Perspectives*, London: Sage.

Jackson, R. (2005). *Writing the War on Terrorism: Language, Politics and Counter-terrorism*, Manchester, UK: Manchester University Press.

Zelizer, B. (1992). *Covering the body: The Kennedy Assassination, the Media, and the Shaping of Collective Memory*, Chicago, IL: University of Chicago Press.

References

Aftenposten (July 23, 2011) "Resemblance to the Terror Attack in Oklahoma."

Aftenposten (July 25, 2011) "Worst Mass Murderer of all Times."

Aftenposten (July 29, 2011) "Everything Will Be Different."

Aftenposten (July 30, 2011) "Will the Terror Change Norway?"

Aftenposten Morning (July 23, 2011) "These People Have Threatened Norway with Terror."

Aftenposten Morning (July 24, 2011) "He Is Not a Stranger."

Altheide, D. L., and Snow, R. P. (1979) *Media Logic*, Beverly Hills, CA: Sage.

Bell, D. A. (2003) "Mythscapes: Memory, Mythology, and National Identity," *British Journal of Sociology*, 54 (1): 63–81.

Bhatia, M. V. (2005) "Fighting Words: Naming Terrorists, Bandits, Rebels and Other Violent Actors," *Third World Quarterly*, 26 (1): 5–25.

Daily Telegraph (July 8, 2005a) "Al-Qa'eda Link Hides Multitude of Suspects."

Daily Telegraph (July 8, 2005b) "Your Luck Has Turned—But We Won't Be Stopped."

Daily Telegraph (July 9, 2005) "Where Is the Gandhi of Islam?"

Daily Telegraph (July 10, 2005a) "Blair Proves Equal to the Long-dreaded Day."

Daily Telegraph (July 10, 2005b) "Here's a Challenge: Link the al-Qaeda Bombs to Poverty and Global Warming."

Daily Telegraph (July 10, 2005c) "This Glorious Beast Now Growls More Defiantly than Ever Before."

Daily Telegraph (July 11, 2005) "A Stirring Display of Courage and Restraint."

Daily Telegraph (July 12, 2005) "New Anti-terror Laws Could Be Brought Forward."

Daily Telegraph (July 17, 2005). "If they pass the 'cricket test,' how do we stop the suicide bombers?"

Daily Telegraph (August 7, 2005) "A Dark Day from Which We Will Emerge Stronger."

Edy, J. A. (1999) "Journalistic Uses of Collective Memory," *Journal of Communication*, 49 (2): 71–85.

Edy, J. A., and Daradanova, M. (2006). "Reporting through the Lens of the Past: From Challenger to Columbia," *Journalism*, 7 (2): 131–51.

The Guardian (July 8, 2005) "In the Face of Danger."

The Guardian (July 9, 2005a) "I Pray for the Victims, Here and in Iraq."

The Guardian (July 9, 2005b) "We Have to Keep on Dancing."

The Guardian (August 7, 2005) "Let the Olympics be a Memorial."

Gerhards, J., and Schäfer, M. S. (2014) "International Terrorism, Domestic Coverage? How Terrorist Attacks Are Presented in the News of CNN, Al Jazeera, the BBC, and ARD," *International Communication Gazette*, 76 (1): 3–26.

Haes, J. W. H. (2003) " September 11 in Germany and the United States: Reporting, Reception and Interpretation," in A. M. Noll (Ed.), *Crisis Communications: Public and Media Responses to 9/11*. Lanham, MD: Rowman & Littlefield, pp. 125–132.

Hoskins, A. (2011) "7/7 and Connective Memory: Interactional Trajectories of Remembering in Post-scarcity Culture," *Memory Studies*, 4 (3): 269–280.

Kepplinger, H. M., and Habermeier, J. (1995) "The Impact of Key Events on the Presentation of Reality," *European Journal of Communication*, 10: 371–390.

Khong, Y. F. (1992) *Analogies at War: Korea, Munich, Dien Bien Phu, and the Vietnam Decisions of 1965*. Princeton, NJ: Princeton University Press.

Kitch, C. (2003) "'Mourning in America': Ritual, Redemption, and Recovery in News Narrative after September 11," *Journalism Studies*, 4 (2): 213–224.

Matusitz, J. (2013) *Terrorism and Communication: A Critical Introduction*, Los Angeles, CA: Sage.

Norris, P. (1995) "The Restless Searchlight: Network News Framing of the Post–Cold War World," *Political Communication*, 12 (4): 357–370.

Norris, P. (Ed.) (2003) *Framing Terrorism: Understanding Terrorist Threats and Mass Media*. New York: Routledge.

Ottosen, R., and Bull, C. A. (2012) "22 July. Understanding-explaining Preventing," in S. Osterud (Ed.), *Abstrakt*, pp. 246–271.

Papacharissi, Z., and de Fatima Oliveira, M. (2008) "News Frames Terrorism: A Comparative Analysis of Frames Employed in Terrorism Coverage in U.S. and U.K. Newspapers," *International Journal of Press/Politics*, 13 (1): 52–74.

Reese, S. D. (2007) "The Framing Project: A Bridging Model for Media Research Revisited," *Journal of Communication*, 57 (1): 148–154.

Roy, S., and Ross, S. (2011) "The Circle of Terror: Strategic Localizations of Global Media Terror Meta-discourses in the U.S., India and Scotland," *Media, War and Conflict*, 4 (3): 1–15.

Ruigrok, N., and van Atteveldt, W. (2007) "Global Angling with a Local Angle: How U.S., British, and Dutch Newspapers Frame Global and Local Terrorist Attacks," *Harvard International Journal of Press/Politics*, 12 (1): 68–90.

Ryan, M. (2004) "Framing the War Against Terrorism: US Newspaper Editorials and Military Action in Afghanistan," *International Communication Gazette*, 66 (5): 363–82.

VG (July 22–23, 2011). "22.07.2011."

VG (July 23, 2011) "When Terror Arrived."

Winfield, B. H., Friedman, B., and Trisnadi, V. (2002) "History as the Metaphor through Which the Current World Is Viewed: British and American Newspapers' Uses of History Following the 11 September 2001 Terrorist Attacks," *Journalism Studies*, 3 (2): 289–300.

19

THE CENTRAL AMERICAN REFUGEE CRISIS, SECURITIZATION, AND THE MEDIA

Adrian Bergmann

Introduction

In July 2015, president Peter Maurer of the International Committee of the Red Cross spoke with *The Guardian* about how the changing scenarios of global conflict impinge on humanitarian action. He emphasized that, "while conflicts have expanded and deepened and transformed, actors have transformed and humanitarian assistance is transforming" (Jones 2015). Months later, he told the same newspaper that "we see a transformation of warfare from the big armies and battlefields in open spaces to a fragmentation of armed groups and smaller armies, which move into city centres, which increasingly become the theatre of warfare" (Chonghaile 2015). This is certainly true of Iraq and Syria, but also of far less prominent conflicts around the world.

Deep in the shadow of international terrorism and great power standoffs, El Salvador, Guatemala, and Honduras—known as the Northern Triangle of Central America—make up the most homicidal region in the world (United Nations Office on Drugs and Crime 2013). Twenty years after the last peace accord was signed, country-level homicide rates far surpass those of, say, Afghanistan and Iraq. Even so, Central America receives scant concern or coverage in the international press, academia, and policy circles, and the humanitarian aspects of the regional security crisis is only of late receiving significant attention.

In large measure, this increase in interest was catalyzed by events of 2014, notably the surge in the number of unaccompanied minors arriving in the United States from the Northern Triangle, and the kidnapping and presumed massacre of 43 students of the Ayotzinapa Rural Teachers' College in southern Mexico. In May 2015, Central America and Mexico made a forceful appearance in the annual report of the Internal Displacement Monitoring Centre (2015) and, in October, the United Nations High Commissioner for Refugees (2015, 49) warned of a "looming refugee crisis" in the region.

Violence in the region is being driven by an array of state and non-state armed actors, including local and transnational organized crime, gangs, death squads, police, and military,

231

locked for several years in a dynamic of armed confrontation. Humanitarian actors are struggling to come to terms with these contemporary scenarios of armed conflict, and to develop effective strategies for addressing them (Internal Displacement Monitoring Centre 2016). Here, I ask whether the predominant response to the humanitarian crisis may be reinforcing the dynamic of armed confrontation that is driving hundreds of thousands from their homes.

"An Urgent Humanitarian Situation"

While the Honduran state has acknowledged and taken some first steps to address the contemporary forced displacement of its citizens, El Salvador, Guatemala, and Mexico have been reluctant to do the same. In a particularly succinct conclusion, the Special Rapporteur on the Human Rights of Internally Displaced Persons reported to the United Nations Human Rights Council in April 2016 that, across Mexico and the Northern Triangle, "a lack of resources and attention means that most internally displaced persons are left to fend for themselves." In his assessment, "internally displaced persons are not provided with the protection and support to which they are entitled and immigration and asylum policies and practices fail to live up to international standards required for those fleeing violence or persecution" (United Nations Human Rights Council 2016, 19).

Further north, in June 2014, the startling number of unaccompanied minors arriving in the United States from the Northern Triangle prompted US president Barack Obama to denounce an "urgent humanitarian situation" (Zezima and O'Keefe 2014). Even so, it would only be a few weeks before he called for an "aggressive deterrence strategy" for border crossers (Nakamura 2014), the striking contradiction between humanitarian urgency and aggressive deterrence notwithstanding. Two initiatives are key to the response, and both seek to move deterrence and enforcement outside the United States and away from its borders.

First, in July 2014, the Mexican government launched the Southern Border Program, aimed at stopping migrants before they reach the United States. Since then, Mexico itself has been receiving a rapidly increasing number of asylum applications, while detaining more than 425,000 mostly Central American migrants between 2014 and July 2016—almost all of whom have been deported (Suárez et al. 2016, 3).

Second, in January 2015, US vice president Joseph R. Biden announced the Alliance for Prosperity, a billion dollar aid package for the Northern Triangle, later cut back by Congress to about 750 million. The primary condition for this massive injection of capital into the small Central American states is their active collaboration in the implementation of the aggressive deterrence strategy, while presumably overseeing "systemic change" at home. In an op-ed in *The New York Times*, Biden (2015) asserted that, "as we were reminded last summer when thousands of unaccompanied children showed up on our southwestern border, the security and prosperity of Central America are inextricably linked with our own."

In line with Biden's analysis, both programs and the broader aggressive deterrence strategy bundle together economic, security, humanitarian, and migration policy, and are in part based upon an assumption that a large number of those who migrate from the Northern Triangle do so in the pursuit of economic interests, rather than to flee violence and persecution. In a February 2016 report, Hiskey et al. (2016, 2) tested this assumption, and found strong evidence from surveys in El Salvador and Honduras that direct, personal experience with crime "emerges as a critical predictor of one's migration intentions," as "those individuals who have been victimized by crime are considerably more likely to consider migration as a viable option than their non-victim counterparts" (Hiskey et al. 2016, 6). The authors concluded that the deterrence campaign "successfully sent the message to residents of the primary sending countries in Central America that the United States will 'send you back'." "Yet," they found, "Central American men, women, and children continue to make the trip," for "no matter what the future might hold in terms of the dangers of migration, it is preferable to a present-day life of crime and violence" (Hiskey et al. 2016, 11).

Beyond the headlines of the past few years, the long-term, transnational relationship between the United States and its southern neighbors is key to understanding the response to the present humanitarian crisis, and goes a long way toward explaining why the response may be informed as much by inadequate thinking about security as the principles for humanitarian action. For 10, if not 20 years, gang policy has played an important role in shaping that relationship, as well as the political arenas in the Central American states themselves. El Salvador will serve here as a case study.

"How the Street Gangs Took Central America"

Before and throughout the postwar era, the two main areas of policy concern for Salvadorans have been the economy and security—at once the policy areas that create the most confrontation between political parties and within them. Yet, security policy, and especially gang policy, was not an important political battleground until the turn of the century.

Analyses of media discourses and public policies on crime, youth, and gangs show that the run-ups to the 1999 and 2004 presidential elections were central to the transformation of gangs from a social issue among many to a key security issue in El Salvador (Hume 2007; Wolf 2012). In the tightly fought 2004 vote, outgoing president Francisco Flores of the National Republican Alliance (ARENA) employed strategic messaging and put gang policy front and center, as he launched a massive campaign of repression directed at gangs, known as "mano dura." The policy included a wave of discretionary arrests, constriction of due process guarantees, and increased participation of the military in policing. Mano dura would become a cornerstone of ARENA candidate Antonio Saca's successful bid for the presidency, and similar policies and the rhetoric that were introduced in Guatemala and Honduras at around the same time.

Alisha Holland (2013) argues that rendering gangs as a grave and urgent threat to society served to overcome tensions within ARENA, and to consolidate a voter base by using security policy to drive a wedge between ARENA and the main opposition party, Farabundo Martí Front for National Liberation (FMLN), which protested the new policy. Ever since, gang policy has been the key campaign issue for any party.

When Sonja Wolf (2012, 52) reviewed 2,874 news items concerning gangs in El Salvador's two main newspapers between 2003 and 2006, she found that "the press played a key role in selling the supposed effectiveness of suppression, chiefly by turning Mano Dura into a spectacle and publishing indicators of policy success." Furthermore, she concluded that, "rather than disclosing and challenging the human rights violations and a priori convictions of supposed offenders, the media were complicit in their occurrence" (Wolf 2012, 53).

International media and scholars, along with US government and law enforcement officials, largely got behind this framing of gangs as a threat and an enemy, and violent repression as the right response to them. Prominent examples include *Foreign Affairs'* publication of Ana Arana's (2005) "How the Street Gangs Took Central America" and *National Geographic Channel's* broadcast of "World's Most Dangerous Gang" (Shaffer 2006), while the Federal Bureau of Investigations set up an anti-gang task force in San Salvador.

Meanwhile, at the US Army War College, a group of scholars set out to read the situation through the lens of urban counter-insurgency, with treats such as Max G. Manwaring's (2005, 33) observation that if gangs such as El Salvador's Barrio 18 and Mara Salvatrucha "look like ducks, walk like ducks, and act like ducks—they indeed are insurgent-type ducks." More recently, Douglas Farah (2016) saw fit to claim that the Mara Salvatrucha "is actively looking" to learn from groups such as al-Qaeda and the Islamic State of Iraq and the Levant, because police had found evidence of internet searches on these groups on one gang member's computer.

Over the years, the demonization of gang members and the dynamics of violent confrontation between gangs and state security forces became ever more entrenched, and the security crisis progressively deepened. Nonetheless, when ARENA lost the presidential elections to the FMLN in 2009, after 20 years of continuous rule, the new president, Mauricio Funes, would come to oversee several dramatic shifts in gang policy.

"Government Negotiates Reduction in Homicides with Gangs"

Under the headline "Government Negotiates Reduction in Homicides with Gangs," the Salvadoran online magazine *El Faro* broke the story on March 14, 2012:

> Last week, between Thursday and Saturday, around 30 gang members, leaders of the Mara Salvatrucha and Barrio 18, were moved from El Salvador's maximum-security prison to less secure jails. . . . The transfers were part of a pact between the gangs and the Salvadoran government.
>
> (Martínez et al. 2012)

The agreement had been reached a week earlier, and stipulated that the gangs ensure a stiff reduction in homicides—which they did. Between March 2012 and June 2014, the mean number of homicides in El Salvador declined from 354 to 218 per month, in sum sparing "about 5,501 lives" in that period (Katz and Amaya 2015, v).

At least two conditions were crucial to the effectiveness of the homicide reduction strategy, widely known as the "truce." On the one hand, over the preceding decade, the main gangs in El Salvador had achieved a high degree of internal cohesion and effective organization. Unlike in Guatemala and Honduras, this allowed a fairly small group of gang leaders to pull the rank and file along on a path of negotiations. On the other hand, while the government's public position on the truce was highly contradictory, its practical support was indispensable.

What developed over more than a year into a full-fledged, gang-led peace process, stands out as an important learning opportunity for nonviolent engagement with non-state armed actors (Whitfield 2013; Cruz and Durán-Martínez 2016). It was also a forceful demonstration that "key stakeholders have the capacity to renegotiate existing norms of violence and that at least some gangs have the capacity to exert substantial informal social control over their members that can result in reduced violence" (Katz and Amaya 2015, 39). Gradually, however, the Salvadoran process unraveled, and the reasons for that are just as important to understand and learn from.

While there was no clear-cut moment at which the truce was over, and the renewed increase in homicides was slow, it is clear that the underlying politics of peacemaking crumbled. The truce had defied both popular opinion and the long-standing, official line of non-engagement with gangs, but the unprecedented homicide reduction afforded gang leaders, mediators, and state sponsors with some time and room to maneuver. That time, however, would run out. As the 2014 elections drew closer, the window of opportunity was definitively closed, with all political parties—including the FMLN—swearing never to "negotiate with terrorists."

In an interview in late 2015, chief mediator Raúl Mijango looked back at the truce and lamented that "the political factor is the one that can make the most damage to any action that seeks to resolve the problem of violence. Why? Because the [political] parties, in a spectrum as polarized as the Salvadoran, always want to make political gains" (Valencia and Martínez 2015). That is to say that, although the truce made a dramatic break with established policy, it did not substantially alter the political and electoral dynamics that surround gangs.

Furthermore, in an incisive analysis of security policy during the 2009–2014 presidency, which puts the truce in context, Chris van der Borgh and Wim Savenije (2015, 174) remark that, "while some types of dialogue seem to be unavoidable, such a strategy is extremely unpopular among many relevant audiences and therefore difficult to communicate publicly." As such, the challenge extended well beyond changing party and electoral politics. Ultimately, the truce's sponsors failed to establish its legitimacy as a homicide reduction strategy in the eyes of large sections of the Salvadoran public, and were thus unable to garner the support necessary to sustain and strengthen any processes of broader, negotiated change.

"Although Some Say We Are at War, There Is No Other Way"

After years of targeting one another, Salvadoran gangs and state security forces have become immersed in an increasingly antagonistic relationship, infused by intense, mutual hatred. As both gang members and police officers have told me repeatedly, at this point, "too many have died" for either side to break the cycle of violence.

In 2015, more than 20 years after the end of the war, El Salvador was the world's most homicidal country, relative to its population. In a land of less than six and a half million people, August saw days with 40, 42, and 43 homicides.

The stage for a gut-wrenching year had been set during its first months, as the president, vice president, justice and security minister, and director-general of the police signaled to the security forces to clamp down on gangs with lethal force, while the inspector-general of the police assured that his office would not open disciplinary proceedings against officers who injure or kill in the line of duty (Ávalos and Cabrera 2015).

A year later, at the beginning of March 2016, president Salvador Sánchez Cerén told the press that "although some say we are at war, there is no other way" (Rauda Zablah 2016). Days later, vice president Óscar Ortiz followed suit, assuring that "now, no option is left to us but confrontation" (Calderón 2016a). The end of that month, though, would see a steep decline in the number of homicides, and presidential spokesman Eugenio Chicas attributed the reduction to a decision made by the gangs, who called for dialog with the government. Even so, Chicas maintained that "the only solution is head-on combat" (Calderón 2016b).

In El Salvador and beyond, violence seems to breed not only more violence, but also the inability to see any other way forward.

Over the past five years or so, Salvadorans have witnessed a rise in the numbers of homicides in general, multiple homicides, homicides of women, and homicides in rural areas, the brunt of which is most commonly attributed to gangs (Segovia 2016). Meanwhile, in parallel to these developments, the limits on state-sponsored violence are also expanding. A particularly stark expression of this has been the sharp increase in the number of armed "confrontations" between state security forces and gang members, including numerous cases of extrajudicial killings.

In off-the-record conversations over the course of the past decade, various high-ranking public officials in El Salvador have told me that the overall, repressive approach is unproductive or indeed counterproductive to security, and does not make sense in terms of long-term violence reduction. While some fail to see any other way, others lay out alternatives that they think should be employed, but stress that they're unable to because the alternatives aren't "politically viable."

Herein lies a profound paradox, which El Salvador, Guatemala, and Honduras share with much of Latin America and the Caribbean: Large-scale, multi-year surveys show that a majority of people believe that increasingly repressive policies are not working. Yet, a majority of people do support increased repression (Lagos and Dammert 2012, 46). In other words, it would seem that people support repression not because it works, but because it's *right*.

This resonates with the argument of veteran Latin Americanist Jenny Pearce (2010, 289):

> The Latin American state increasingly claims its legitimacy not from a monopoly of violence but from its lack of such a monopoly. It is this lack which provides the state with the social outcasts and sources of disorder (criminals, drug mafias, youth gangs) which it must respond to with new forms of order, violently imposed, to win its authority.

As David Keen (2012) might have it, waging wars may be more important than winning them.

"A Chilling Effect"

In Guatemala, new online outlets—including *Nómada* and *Plaza Pública*—are changing the dynamics of the media landscape, and played an important role in mobilizing for popular action and bringing down a corrupt government in 2015. In Honduras, Ismael Moreno Coto, a Jesuit priest at the head of a radio station and an action research center, was awarded the 2015 Rafto Prize, recognizing him as "fearless spokesperson who works tirelessly to investigate and communicate the reasons for the violence and abuse committed against vulnerable groups in society."

However, the vast majority of domestic reporting on violence centers on violence in public spaces, and especially homicides, with little effort made to tell actual stories of the affected people and communities. Newspaper headlines emphasize violence attributed to gangs, and coverage overwhelmingly relies on official sources (Vásquez Monzón and Marroquín 2014, 93).

A gross example of the latter concerns the death of eight young people—two of them minors—at a farm called San Blas, an hour's drive south of the capital. Most all media outlets reproduced the official version of events: In the early hours of March 26, 2015, eight gang members were plotting a massacre and started shooting when the police approached, eventually getting killed in a prolonged exchange of gunfire (Canizalez 2015). After months of investigation, *El Faro* was able to uncover the details of what turned out to be eight extrajudicial killings and a subsequent cover-up at the hands of the police (Valencia et al. 2015). In the weeks that followed, *El Faro* received several death threats, and some of its journalists sought temporary refuge outside of El Salvador (Rauda Zablah 2015).

Not only journalists are in a difficult position, though. In May 2016, mediator Mijango was arrested along with dozens of public servants who facilitated the truce, and is set to stand trial for his dealings with the "terrorists." Three months later, Salvadoran prosecutors conducted a major raid directed against the Mara Salvatrucha, and among those arrested was former gang member Dany Romero. He has been the director of a non-governmental organization for over a decade and, at the time of his arrest, was busy documenting well over a hundred cases of alleged extrajudicial killings (Mackey 2016).

The July raid was accompanied by a fierce media campaign, presumably coordinated by prosecutors. Press reports would have it that Romero's organization, Opera, is nothing more than a front that channels and launders money for the gang (Focus 2016). This is not actually mentioned in the prosecution's legal case, but no journalists bothered to check. Speaking with human rights activists in other organizations, many tell me that they perceive Romero's arrest as a way to shut down and discredit his work, as well as a signal to those who investigate extrajudicial killings in the country.

Indeed, in El Salvador, it has long been the case that many of the individuals and organizations that work directly with gang members try as best they can to fly well below the media's radar. Romero had always been one of them. Their conviction is firm that the very fragile processes they've been able to establish will immediately crumble under the media spotlight. With the existing antiterrorism legislation, the fear of prosecution is real, but so is the worry that programs will collapse or funding will be cut, not to mention the potential for public scandal and social stigma attached to gang intervention. With respect to humanitarian organizations' engagement with non-state armed actors elsewhere in the world, Michiel Hofman (2015, 333) aptly described this as a "chilling effect."

Conclusion

Without doubt, Central American refugees and internally displaced persons must be protected and provided safe and legal avenues to asylum, in accordance with international humanitarian law, so that persons fleeing violence and persecution are not forced to turn to human traffickers. All the while, lest we also understand and talk about both the driving forces of this humanitarian crisis differently, the suffering is bound to be exacerbated.

First, the way violence and "the violent" are talked about shape our understanding of them, and thus our responses to them. As Keen (2008, 168) has emphasized, "challenging media stereotypes is also part of challenging the way enemies are defined and demonized, and this means examining the discourse of the 'enemy' circulating within richer countries as well as within the poorer countries that bear the brunt of disasters."

Second, journalists, scholars, and activists alike stand before a momentous challenge as regards documenting and denouncing the systemic character of abuse carried out by state security forces, as well as the criminal justice and prison systems, and interrogating the expansion of the limits on state-sponsored violence.

In turn, international agencies and donors must carefully consider the extent to which their policies and programs may feed the logic of war and dynamics of violent confrontation between states agents and citizens. Of special urgency is to unpack humanitarian and security policy, most notably in relation to the US' aggressive deterrence strategy against migrants.

Finally, there is a long-term challenge of legitimizing strategies for peace by peaceful means. Here, the media in particular have a role to play in terms of generating space in the public sphere for talking about the alternatives to violence. As the Salvadoran gang truce taught us, a peace process is only viable if nonviolent engagement with armed actors is seen as a legitimate path to peace.

Further Reading

Thierry Balzacq, Ed., *Securitization Theory: How Security Problems Emerge and Dissolve* (Abingdon, UK and New York: Routledge, 2011), provides an updated framework for the analysis of securitization processes.

Elana Zilberg, *Space of Detention: The Making of a Transnational Gang Crisis between Los Angeles and San Salvador* (Durham, NC and London: Duke University Press, 2011), unpacks the security-migration nexus.

Ellen Moodie, *El Salvador in the Aftermath of Peace: Crime, Uncertainty, and the Transition to Democracy* (Philadelphia, PA: University of Pennsylvania Press, 2010), engages the changing meanings of violence and peace in postwar El Salvador.

References

Arana, A. (2005) "How the Street Gangs Took Central America," *Foreign Affairs*, 84 (3): 98–110.

Ávalos, J., and Cabrera, A. (2015) "Gobierno insta a los policías a disparar sin temor," *La Prensa Gráfica*, January 22, available at: www.laprensagrafica.com/2015/01/22/gobierno-insta-a-los-policias-a-disparar-sin-temor

Biden, J. R. Jr. (2015) "Joe Biden: A Plan for Central America," *The New York Times*, available at: www.nytimes.com/2015/01/30/opinion/joe-biden-a-plan-for-central-america.html?_r=0

Calderón, B. (2016a) "Ortiz advierte aumentarán confrontaciones y violencia en próximos meses." *La Prensa Gráfica*, March 17, available at: www.laprensagrafica.com/2016/03/17/ortiz-advierte-habra-aumento-de-confrontaciones-y-violencia-en-proximos-meses

Calderón, B. (2016b) "Ayer hubo cuatro asesinatos en El Salvador, GOES atribuye reducción a pandillas," *La Prensa Gráfica*, March 29, available at: www.laprensagrafica.com/2016/03/29/ayer-hubo-cuatro-asesinatos-en-el-salvador-goes-atribuye-reduccion-a-pandillas

Canizalez, L. (2015) "Los ocho pandilleros muertos planificaban masacre en repudio a marcha por la paz," *Diario1*, March 26, available at: http://diario1.com/nacionales/2015/03/los-ocho-pandilleros-muertos-planificaban-masacre-en-repudio-a-marcha-por-la-paz/

Chonghaile, C. N. (2015) "Urban Warfare Has Altered the Nature of Humanitarian Work, Says Red Cross Chief," *The Guardian*, November 13, available at: www.theguardian.com/global-development/2015/nov/13/urban-warfare-humanitarian-work-international-committee-red-cross-peter-maurer-cities-conflict

Cruz, J. M., and Durán-Martínez, A. (2016) "Hiding Violence to Deal with the State: Criminal Pacts in El Salvador and Medellin," *Journal of Peace Research*, 53 (2): 197–210.

Farah, D. (2016) "Central America's Gangs Are All Grown Up," *Foreign Policy*, January 19, available at: https://foreignpolicy.com/2016/01/19/central-americas-gangs-are-all-grown-up/

Focus. (2016) "Estas son las dos organizaciones 'benéficas' que servían de fachada a la Mara Salvatrucha," *El Diario de Hoy*, July 29, available at: www.elsalvador.com/articulo/nacional/estas-son-las-dos-organizaciones-beneficas-que-servian-fachada-mara-salvatrucha-120523

Hiskey, J. T., Córdova, A., Orcés, D., and Malone, M. F. (2016) "Understanding the Central American Refugee Crisis: Why They Are Fleeing and How U.S. Policies Are Failing to Deter Them," Washington, DC: American Immigration Council, available at: www.americanimmigrationcouncil.org/sites/default/files/research/understanding_the_central_american_refugee_crisis.pdf

Hofman, M. (2015) "Non-State Armed Groups and Aid Organizations," in R. M. Ginty and J. H. Peterson (Eds.), *The Routledge Companion to Humanitarian Action*, Abingdon and New York: Routledge, pp. 324–336.

Holland, A. C. (2013) "Right on Crime? Conservative Party Politics and Mano Dura Policies in El Salvador," *Latin American Research Review*, 48 (1): 44–67.

Hume, M. (2007) "*Mano Dura*: El Salvador Responds to Gangs." *Development in Practice*, 17 (6): 739–51.

Internal Displacement Monitoring Centre. (2015) *Global Overview 2015: People Internally Displaced by Conflict and Violence*, Geneva: Norwegian Refugee Council.

Internal Displacement Monitoring Centre. (2016) *New Humanitarian Frontiers: Addressing Criminal Violence in Mexico and Central America*, Geneva: Norwegian Refugee Council.

Jones, S. (2015) "Spread of Global Conflict Transforming Humanitarian Work, Says Red Cross Chief," *The Guardian*, July 8, available at: www.theguardian.com/global-development/2015/jul/08/conflict-humanitarian-assistance-red-cross-chief-peter-maurer

Katz, C. M., and Amaya, L. E. (2015) *The Gang Truce as a Form of Violence Intervention*, San Salvador: Fundación Nacional para el Desarrollo.

Keen, D. (2008) *Complex Emergencies*, Cambridge UK: Polity.

Keen, D. (2012) *Useful Enemies: When Waging Wars Is More Important than Winning Them*, New Haven, CT and London: Yale University Press.

Lagos, M., and Dammert, L. (2012) "La seguridad ciudadana: el problema principal de América Latina," Lima: Corporación Latinobarómetro, available at: www.latinobarometro.org/documentos/LATBD_La_seguridad_ciudadana.pdf

Mackey, D. M. (2016) "The U.S. Government Accused a Salvadoran Human Rights Activist of Gang Activity—Now He's in Jail," *The Intercept*, August 8, available at: https://theintercept.com/2016/08/08/the-u-s-government-accused-a-salvadorian-human-rights-activist-of-gang-activity-now-hes-in-jail/

Manwaring, M. G. (2005) *Street Gangs: The New Urban Insurgency*, Carlisle: Strategic Studies Institute, U.S. Army War College.

Martínez, Ó., Martínez, C., Arauz, S., and Lemus, E. (2012) "Government Negotiates Reduction in Homicides with Gangs," *El Faro*, March 14, available at: www.elfaro.net/es/201203/noticias/8061/

Nakamura, D. (2014) "Obama Calls for 'Aggressive Deterrence Strategy' for Border Crossers," *The Washington Post*, June 30, available at: www.washingtonpost.com/news/post-politics/wp/2014/06/30/obama-calls-for-aggressive-deterrence-strategy-for-border-crossers/

Pearce, J. (2010) "Perverse State Formation and Securitized Democracy in Latin America," *Democratization*, 17 (2): 286–306.

Rauda Zablah, N. (2015) "El Faro denuncia amenazas contra sus periodistas," *El Faro*, August 13, available at: www.elfaro.net/es/201508/noticias/17263/

Rauda Zablah, N. (2016) "Sánchez Cerén: 'Aunque algunos digan que estamos en una guerra, no queda otro camino,'" *El Faro*, March 7, available at: www.elfaro.net/es/201603/el_salvador/18180/

Segovia, A. (2016) *El Salvador: Nuevo patrón de violencia, afectación territorial y respuesta de las comunidades (2010–2015)*, San Salvador: Instituto Centroamericano de Investigaciones para el Desarrollo y el Cambio Social.

Shaffer, M. (2006) "World's Most Dangerous Gang," *National Geographic Explorer*, Washington, DC: National Geographic Channel.

Suárez, X., Knippen, J., and Meyer, M. (2016) *A Trail of Impunity: Thousands of Migrants in Transit Face Abuses amid Mexico's Crackdown*, Washington, DC: Washington Office on Latin America, Fundar, and Casa del Migrante, available at: www.wola.org/wp-content/uploads/2016/09/A-Trail-of-Impunity-2016.pdf

United Nations High Commissioner for Refugees. (2015) *Women on the Run: First-Hand Accounts of Refugees Fleeing El Salvador, Guatemala, Honduras, and Mexico*, Washington, DC: United Nations High Commissioner for Refugees, available at: www.unhcr.org/5630f24c6.pdf

United Nations Human Rights Council. (2016) "Report of the Special Rapporteur on the Human Rights of Internally Displaced Persons on His Mission to Honduras." A/HRC/32/35/Add.4, New York: United Nations.

United Nations Office on Drugs and Crime. (2013) *2013 Global Study on Homicide: Trends, Contexts, Data*, Vienna: United Nations Office on Drugs and Crime, available at: www.unodc.org/documents/gsh/pdfs/2014_GLOBAL_HOMICIDE_BOOK_web.pdf

Valencia, R., and Martínez, C. (2015) "Hoy toca que los sedientos de sangre, los de las pandillas y los del gobierno, se sacien," *El Faro*, October 12, available at: www.salanegra.elfaro.net/es/201510/entrevistas/17432/

Valencia, R., Martínez, Ó., and Caravantes, D. V. (2015) "La Policía masacró en la finca San Blas," *El Faro*, July 22, available at: www.salanegra.elfaro.net/es/201507/cronicas/17205/

van der Borgh, C., and Savenije, W. (2015) "De-Securitising and Re-Securitising Gang Policies: The Funes Government and Gangs in El Salvador," *Journal of Latin American Studies*, 47 (1): 149–176.

Vásquez Monzón, O., and Marroquín Parducci, A. (2014) "Entre gritos y silencios: La narrativa de la prensa salvadoreña sobre la tregua entre pandillas," *Nueva Sociedad*, 249: 86–96.

Whitfield, T. (2013) "Mediating Criminal Violence: Lessons from the Gang Truce in El Salvador," Oslo Forum Papers 1. Geneva: Centre for Humanitarian Dialogue.

Wolf, S. (2012) "Creating Folk Devils: Street Gang Representations in El Salvador's Print Media," *Journal of Human Security*, 8 (2): 36–63.

Zezima, K., and O'Keefe, E. (2014) "Obama Calls Surge of Children across U.S.–Mexican Border 'Urgent Humanitarian Situation,'" *The Washington Post*, February 6, available at: www.washingtonpost.com/politics/obama-calls-wave-of-children-across-us-mexican-border-urgent-humanitarian-situation/2014/06/02/4d29df5e-ea8f-11e3-93d2-edd4be1f5d9e_story.html

Part V

VOICES AT THE TABLE, ON THE INTERNET, AND OVER THE AIRWAVES

Expanding the Global Dialogue
on Science, Religion, Civil Society, and
Human Rights

INTRODUCTION
TO PART 5

A truly vibrant media environment able to serve the needs of democratic publics is inclusive. Its mandate is to provide public forums that give voice to a multiplicity of people and groups, their concerns, experiences, ideas, and knowledge, and to articulate the on-going discussions and debates that take place within and across communities around the globe. The international news organizations based in different countries cover the world for global publics and offer only a glimpse of this vast global community. Civil society groups, the United Nations, NGOs, aid and development organizations, faith-based organizations, research centers and universities, health providers, and researchers, all serve as rich sources of information and analysis covering global issues and humanitarian affairs. Yet often these rich resources lie outside of mainstream representations or remain balkanized within tiny enclaves of localized publics. All too often the focus of international news is defined by those in power and emanates primarily from government officials that speak of the geopolitical concerns and the nation state. People, their cultures and communities, their experiences and knowledge, their struggles and visions are too frequently left out of the frame of media discourses. This section offers a pathway into the global world not often depicted in mainstream media (or many times misrepresented) and the wealth of knowledge that can be found amidst these voices.

The World Humanitarian Summit held in 2016 brought the humanitarian community together in an unprecedented gathering held in Istanbul, Turkey. In "Now You See Me, Now You Don't: Faith-based NGOs and Humanitarian Work—A Story from the World Humanitarian Summit," Azza Karam describes the inclusive nature of the event, and details the many faith-based organizations and their leaders who came together to express a shared vision, and were unified in their commitment to do whatever they could to make the world safe, equitable and inclusive.

In "The Role of Media in Public Advocacy and Countering Violent Extremism," Nadia Sraieb-Koepp shares her experiences designing participatory media campaigns and visual strategies that helped facilitate the democratic transition in Tunisia in 2011. She offers her thoughts about the need for inclusive social media strategies designed to counter recruitment messages targeting youth by violent extremists.

In the second decade of the twenty-first century as global climate change continues unabated, recent data from the World Resources Institute show that ten countries produce around 70 percent of global greenhouse gas emissions, and the United States is second on the list after China. As the earth's climate system continues to destabilize, the United Nations braces for global displacements and other crises caused by a warming globe. An estimated 80 percent of the work of the United Nations will focus on migrations, mostly climate caused, in coming years. Yet in the United States during a bullishly long presidential campaign season, global warming was rarely on the news agenda, and candidates were infrequently asked about climate policy. More importantly, in the United States, the words of climate deniers have consistently been given equal weight to the voices of climate scientists, those who raise concerns about the burning of fossil fuels, or those who point to the connections between extreme weather and global warming. We now find ourselves in a dire situation. Just as global agreements begin to openly recognize the need for action to abate further warming, Donald J. Trump was elected to the White House and threatens to dismantle the Environmental Protection Agency and ignore the Paris Agreement on Climate. These developments amount in themselves to a serious indictment of the mainstream news media's failure to explain, debate, and in general produce knowledge-based journalism able to inform the American public about the science behind climate change. As news media have increased their reliance on corporate press releases for news content, and dismantled units that once reported on science, the public falls further away from understanding even basic scientific principles. Indeed, as the Pew Research Center found in October 2016, of registered voters who support Trump, only 17 percent believed that climate scientists understand that global warming is occurring; 15 percent believe that scientists understand the causes of climate change; and only 10 percent of those who supported Donald J. Trump believe that scientists understand the best ways to address the issue. Clinton voters were better informed on the topic, but with 51, 41 and 32 percent respectively, there is still much room for improvement (Kennedy 2016).

As people and communities across a warming world become more susceptible to increasingly virulent diseases, it is even more imperative that global media provide consistent and serious coverage of disease outbreaks that does not incite fear and confusion. Media must step up and explain the science behind disease outbreaks, and resist sensationalized reporting motivated by the padding of their bottom lines. In Pat Fast's study of the science behind two disease outbreaks titled, "Ebola and AIDS: Harnessing Science and Human Nature to Combat Two Modern Plagues," she explains the nature of the diseases, how they are transmitted, what dangers they pose to the public, and the best ways to treat them. When we compare the media coverage of the two illnesses to the science behind them, we find very few details, if any, were accurately reported about the diseases during the height of the outbreaks.

As many have frequently pointed out, children and the youth of today will inherit the planet we leave for them tomorrow. While pictures and stories about children and young people have been widely circulated in the global media on coverage of the current humanitarian crises, the actual voices, opinions, hopes and desires of children and youth are rarely presented. As Jordi Torrent has long known, youth are infrequently invited to actually participate in media creations, productions and programs in a meaningful way to tell their own stories or to engage in public dialogue. In "Plural+ Media Literacy, and Voices of the Young: Platforms for Including Youth-Produced Media in Humanitarian Dialogue," Torrent argues that it is the work of educators, media producers, United Nations organizations, and NGOs to include youth media in global dialogue. Outlining the need for media literacy education and support, Torrent documents the successes of global youth video festivals that feature expressive and essential youth-produced media.

People and communities around the globe gather in World People's Forums to share knowledge, experiences and visions of a future better able to address the needs of humanity and create a world based on sustainability, justice and peace. In "The Voice of the People in an Age of Environmental Crisis: Pope Francis, the Earth Community, Human Rights, and Independent Media," Robin Andersen and DeeDee Halleck open their discussion of the voices of global change with the Encyclical Letter of Pope Francis. In *Laudato si* the Pope made an urgent appeal for a new dialogue that could shape the future of our planet, and called for a conversation that includes everyone. The authors describe the global gatherings at People's Forums and analyze their importance for defining new directions and visions. They find that many of the ways that Pope Francis re-conceptualizes a new role for humanity on an ecologically sustainable planet parallel the discussions at the People's Summits. This chapter outlines an alternative vision for the globe and offers a glimpse of the vast global movements taking place around the world and the people who risk their lives documenting their struggles. These stories and visions offer a path to an alternative future not dominated by environmental chaos, humanitarian disasters and endless militarized conflict. But this narrative demands confronting the "root causes," in the words of Pope Francis, of global instability and environmental destruction, and it is a narrative told mostly in the margins, by the people themselves, infrequently heard over mainstream global media channels.

Reference

Kennedy, B. (2016) "Clinton, Trump Supporters Worlds Apart on Views of Climate Change and Its Scientists," Pew Research Center (October 10), available at: www.pewresearch.org/fact-tank/2016/10/10/clinton-trump-supporters-worlds-apart-on-views-of-climate-change-and-its-scientists/

20

NOW YOU SEE ME, NOW YOU DON'T

Faith-Based NGOs and Humanitarian Work—A Story from the World Humanitarian Summit

Azza Karam

A thing is not necessarily true because badly uttered, nor false because spoken magnificently.

(St. Augustine)

It took a long time for the 9,000 participants who had finally registered, after months of intense work and sleepless nights on behalf of the organizers of the first World Humanitarian Summit (WHS), to clear multiple layers of security around the perimeter of the Conference Center in Istanbul on May 23, 2016. The lines at the various security "checkpoints," which were politely and efficiently staffed, were long on the day of the opening, so much so that many attendees were late getting to the diverse sessions. The WHS was organized by the UN Office for the Coordination of Humanitarian Affairs (OCHA), and hosted by the Turkish authorities, which were taking no chances with security. Much was at stake for the host government. Not only had some NGOs declined to attend due to concerns about security, but many heads of state, whose attendance is a sign of "political blessing" for the venture, ultimately did not show up.

For the UN organizers, the credibility of the entire endeavor was also a concern, especially when one of the leading international humanitarian NGOs, Médecins Sans Frontières (MSF), or Doctors Without Borders, pulled out only weeks before the meeting began. MSF released a statement outlining its reasons for not attending, which detailed a number of issues I will address below. But in that statement, MSF actually mentions one of the strengths of the WHS—the inclusiveness and the diversity of actors "brought under the humanitarian tent."

The WHS has done an admirable job in opening up the humanitarian sector to a much wider group of actors, and leading an inclusive process . . . However, with regret, we have come to the decision to pull out of the summit. We no longer have any hope that the WHS will address the weaknesses in humanitarian action and emergency response, particularly in conflict areas or epidemic situations.

Instead, the WHS's focus would seem to be an incorporation of humanitarian assistance into a broader development and resilience agenda. Further, the summit neglects to reinforce the obligations of states to uphold and implement the humanitarian and refugee laws which they have signed up to. . . . Summit participants, whether states or UN agencies or non-governmental organisations, will be asked to declare new and ambitious "commitments". But putting states on the same level as non-governmental organisations and UN agencies, which have no such powers or obligations, the Summit will minimise the responsibility of states. *In addition, the non-binding nature of the commitments means that very few actors will sign up to any commitments they haven't previously committed to* [emphasis added].

The last sentence expresses a skepticism that MSF actually shares with many in the United Nations itself, with regard in particular to faith-based actors. But in fact, the large umbrella for humanitarian dialogue provided by the WHS resulted in an unprecedented number of commitments by governmental actors, non-governmental actors, and private sector entities. Faith-based actors *did* "sign up to commitments they haven't previously committed to" and they did so, across religions, regions, genders, and issues. Sadly, this unique moment of commitment barely registered in the media-informed collective consciousness of humanity. Because the moment was virtually ignored by global news reporters not drawn to the gravity of the story, or who had no words for its narration, it seems now already erased, as if it never happened and cannot matter. If remembered at all, this moment may even have been rendered redundant by the killings in the name of religion, which have already taken place since May, some of them in the very same city that hosted the WHS.[1]

This article will seek to narrate the story of this historic event where faith communities came together, *specifically with their faith identities and representative capacities,* and in an unprecedented manner, listened to one another, rubbed shoulders with other humanitarians, politicians, developmentalists, and committed to peaceful collaboration and to affirming their respect for both human rights as well as international humanitarian law. This is a story of a moment in time that is of significance not only because of its potential, but also because of the deafening media silence around it. It offers an important lesson about media and humanitarian work in an age when lack of coverage can translate into a moment lost and a possibility unrealized. The media failure was abetted, ironically, by the oversight of the very same organizers who made this moment possible in the first place.

The World Humanitarian Summit was the first ever global gathering on any and all matters humanitarian. It was explained as "necessary at a time when we are currently facing humanitarian needs on a massive scale . . . [because] we must continually seek better ways to meet the needs of millions of people affected by conflicts and disasters."[2] The Summit had three main goals: to reaffirm a global collective commitment to humanity and humanitarian principles; to initiate actions and commitments that enable countries and communities to prepare for and respond to crises and be more resilient to shocks; and to: "share best practices which help save lives around the world, placing affected people at the centre [sic] of humanitarian action and alleviating suffering."[3]

The Story that Is/Was Told

What the WHS Achieved

In some ways, the summit's structure was both its strength and its weakness. Unlike COP-21[4] and most big UN summits, the WHS was not an inter-governmental process in which governments try to agree on a specific text in advance. Rather, it sought a range of ideas from all actors involved in aid, including civil society organizations and the private sector. This meant it was unwieldy and unfocused. But it also meant that many voices that do not traditionally have power were heard. The fact that the summit took place in the chaotic and directionless way that it did was in itself a tacit recognition of a narrative that has become increasingly popular: the humanitarian sector is an "eco-system" rather than a top-down, command-and-control system. By bringing such a variety of actors to the table, the summit also helped put humanitarian issues higher on the agenda in the politics, business and society at large.[5]

The participants at the WHS included a dizzying array of heads of state and other government representatives, private sector representatives including those from international financial institutions, young people, people living with disabilities, all manner of humanitarian actors, media, academics, those impacted by humanitarian crises, and NGOs from all countries and regions of the world. In spite of the cynicism expressed by many around the WHS outcomes, even the frank dismissal as a "fiasco" that some detractors have articulated,[6] there were some important points made at the WHS that are worthy of note. Even if these may seem obvious to some, this global summit brought together major stakeholders from all walks of life to affirm the same realization. What follows is a selection of the achievements as seen through the diverse press releases, social media tweets, newspaper articles, and online blogs.

Education

One recognized achievement at the WHS that received wide coverage is the importance of education as a humanitarian priority. Arrived at after years of lobbying, the consensus that emerged and was celebrated at the launch of the Education Cannot Wait Fund was that education is just as important as food and shelter in a crisis, at a time when, on average, less than 2 percent of humanitarian aid goes towards education.[7]

Collaborative Initiatives

Arguably one of the most concrete outcomes of the summit was the so-called "Grand Bargain," in which 30 donors and aid agencies signed an agreement making humanitarian aid more efficient by harmonizing time-consuming donor proposals and reporting, reducing overhead costs, introducing collective needs assessments, and earmarking less funding to specific projects. Importantly, a shift towards greater use of cash transfers was generally endorsed. This was advocated for also by Islamic humanitarian NGOs facing restrictions in money transfers due to counter-terrorism legislation.[8] Here again, a faith-based NGO, World Vision, pledged that half of their programming would be in the form of cash by 2020.

Financing

Facing a funding gap very roughly estimated at US$15 billion in responding to crises, the summit emphasized the need for innovative approaches to financing. Several initiatives were announced, including a *humanitarian impact bond*, in which private investors make an initial investment into a humanitarian response programme and are reimbursed (with a profit) by traditional donors only if certain outputs are met; an autonomous, global Islamic endowment fund for humanitarian needs; and a private-sector-led *initiative* to increase risk financing in the most vulnerable countries (backed by a fund to help pay the premium). Hundreds of companies also signed up to a new initiative to better coordinate the private sector's involvement in humanitarian action.

Protracted Conflict as the "New" Pivot of Humanitarian Work

Most humanitarian work is tailored around natural disasters, while 80 percent of humanitarian response takes place against a backdrop of protracted conflict. The Syrian war and resulting refugee crisis have forced the realization that protracted conflict must be at the core of humanitarian work, a point crystallized at the WHS. The acknowledgement that the global humanitarian response needs to be re-jigged towards a system that is focused more on addressing protracted conflict in a more coherent and systemic way, is a critical "paradigmatic" shift for the business as usual of humanitarianism.

The Untold Story

For all the talk of putting people affected by crises "at the centre" of humanitarian action, the subject didn't feature much at the summit. It was left out of the secretary-general's report framing the summit's priorities, despite being a major theme in the preceding consultations.[9]

Actually, "putting people at the centre" is precisely what the faith-based organizations and religious leaders gathered at the WHS specifically spoke to in the historic *Charter of Faith-Based Humanitarian Work* that they agreed to as an Outcome Document of their Special Session on Religious Engagement, which took place on May 23 itself. As one of the many commitments made, the representatives of faith communities specifically noted "We *commit* to keeping affected persons at the center of all assistance planned and provided, maintaining robust beneficiary feedback mechanisms."[10]

Also of little interest and excluded from media narratives was the fact that summit participants included over 250 representatives from religious organizations and faith communities, representing all faiths known to humankind and from every continent. The large majority of these faith representatives came at their own expense out of a sense of deep commitment to and extensive experience in humanitarian work. There were senior-most religious leaders, including the Ecumenical Patriarch—the Orthodox Pope, a Filipino Cardinal and President of the largest Catholic humanitarian NGO, a Hindu Swami from India running a large Ashram in his State and managing a nation-wide campaign for clean water; Anglican Church heads from Africa and Asia, and distinguished political cum religious figures such as the Nigerian Sultan of Sokoto—to name but a few.

There were several heads of religious NGOs—from those who controlled budgets in the billion dollars to those who could boast only a few thousand dollars, from those who had headquarters in rich Western capitals to those whose bases were in remote areas, far away from cities and yet their followers easily numbered in the millions. They also varied in religion, country, gender, race, ethnicity, thematic expertise, scope of influence, political affiliation, proximity to political office, style of work, and means of engagement—among many other differences. But what they shared in common was a commitment to dedicate their lives to working in and across their communities and nations, to serve the needy during war and peace, natural disaster, hunger and malnutrition, through all manner of strife, as well as in times of relative peace and prosperity—always inspired primarily by their faith. These are the stories of people and commitment rarely heard amidst the more dramatic conflict narratives—especially those of non-state actors.

How the Story Unfolds: Logistical Preparation for the WHS Special Session on Religious Engagement

On January 4, 2016, the Convenors of the United Nations Inter-Agency Task Force on Engaging with Faith-Based Actors (IATF-FBO) were contacted by the WHS Secretariat, and requested to provide support to "faith-based engagement at the WHS."

The WHS Secretariat communicated their intention to convene a special event as part of the main WHS (to be distinguished from "side events"), on religion. The request was made of the IATF-FBO to deliver a "Special Session" on Religious Engagement at the Summit. The Session attendants would have to comply with UN criteria for religious engagement, and the Session was designed in such a way that it would enable the faith communities to showcase their humanitarian contributions. In this process, the IATF-FBO was also specifically asked to be on call to advise UNOCHA colleagues on "all matters related to religion in the broader WHS." With the above rationale forming a common terrain of agreement between the UN agency members of the IATF-FBO and the Advisory Group composed of representatives from all major religious organizations doing humanitarian work, the objectives of the Special Event on Religious Engagement eventually crystalized into ensuring that the WHS would be an opportunity to provide a space for religious organizations to discuss their activities as key stakeholders in global, national, and local humanitarian action and response efforts, peacebuilding, and long-term resilience. In doing so, the Special Session would also require a critical examination of the challenges and opportunities for increased humanitarian partnerships with FBOs and religious leaders in order to invest in the local capacities and social capital provided by religious actors in humanitarian contexts. Another objective of the Special Session would be to secure public commitment from religious leaders and lead humanitarian agencies on strategies and mechanisms to: enhance humanitarian effectiveness; reduce vulnerability and risk; effectively attend to the needs of people in conflict; continue innovative means of serving communities and nations; and secure efficient partnerships with governmental and other non-governmental humanitarian and development counterparts.

The UN IATF-FBOs set out to realize several activities in preparation, all expected within a four-week deadline. The first of these were to collate their own UN criteria for faith-based outreach, adapt these to the humanitarian context, and use these same criteria to provide a list of 250 humanitarian FBO partners for OCHA to consider inviting to the WHS. At the same time, given some important work had already taken place by a group of civil society organizations (many of which were faith based) in anticipation of hosting a two-day "Religious Summit" of humanitarian actors prior to the WHS, the UN IATF-FBO reached out to the same group to act as informal Advisors to the preparation for the Special Session.[11]

The UN's Faith-Based Selection Criteria and the Challenges of Convening the Faith Representatives

There are approximately ten criteria that capture the main elements of the respective UN offices' and agencies' own engagements and outreach with faith actors. The general criteria call for the representation, in any event, in a manner proportionate to religious percentage of the particular terrain being engaged. This includes attention to ensuring the inclusion of diversity *within* the largest faith traditions (e.g. Catholic and Protestant Christians) as well as ensuring that traditional and indigenous faiths are also represented. This has been a challenge for many in the UN for a number of reasons, one of which is the difficulty of identifying the non-Christian organizations. Christian groups tend to be easily identified and have a long-standing record of engagement (thanks to the missionary colonial legacies many of them have). As a result, several UN events still tend to be limited to ecumenical (Christian) organizations, many of them often repeatedly invited over and over again, such that one may almost speak of the "top five" FBO partners of the UN.[12]

Another criterion is to ensure that the FBOs and religious leaders also represent different regions of the world. This criterion can often be another challenge since the "top five" FBOs share headquarters representation in the same cities and regions of the world where the UN itself is headquartered, thus rendering it easier to focus on the northern-based—and often the largest and richest—FBOs. Legal registration of the FBO is also an important guidance used to select which faith-based entity to engage. This particular criterion is necessary to distinguish between religious entities that may be providing critical services to their communities, but are not legally acknowledged and thus tracked by the national governments. These actors should be beyond the purview of the UN's outreach.

A gender balance between the faith actors is another criterion the UN system aspires to. To date, the majority of the religious representatives at many UN-sponsored events tend to be male religious leaders—a fact that can significantly diminish the validity of the experiences, needs, and realities of religious communities being discussed.

For the WHS Special Session additional particular criteria were employed that included giving preference to organizations actually active in humanitarian contexts, followed by religious leaders with a record of engagement around/in humanitarian relief situations. Moreover, FBOs should not have standing objections from any UN country office regarding a criminal case, nor should they be on the UN's terrorist list(s). Lastly, another requirement ensured participation by academics and think tanks with a track record of research on the intersections of religion and humanitarian work.

Why the Story Deserves to Be Told: Understanding Religious Resourcing for Humanitarian Work

Faith-based development and humanitarian organizations are among the oldest service institutions and networks of support known to humankind. For centuries, temples, mosques, and churches have been places of worship and spaces of public service. Schools, hospices, orphanages, clinics, and major hospitals have been provided through, or run by, these religious institutions. Even in the supposedly rich and developed United States, *The Economist* estimated that

[A]nnual spending by the church and entities owned by the church was around $170 billion in 2010 (the church does not release such figures). We think 57% of this goes on health-care networks, followed by 28% on colleges, with parish and diocesan day-to-day operations accounting for just 6% and national charitable activities just 2.7%.[13]

While this data applies to only one religious institution in a developed country, it is not difficult to imagine how significant the numbers would be for religious institutions in a developing country where government-run social services already suffer from an inability to reach major urban populations—let alone rural and more-difficult-to-reach peripheries.

During humanitarian crises when central governments struggle to reach vulnerable populations in situations of danger and desperate need, the role of faith-based entities—not just religious institutions but also faith-based NGOs–becomes even more significant and pronounced. In short, faith-based entities are the first recourse of refuge and the "first responders" in most cases, and especially during humanitarian crises. Embedded in local communities when disasters hit, they are on the ground and remain long after international actors have withdrawn. Religious institutions and faith-based groups provide critical social services to their communities, ranging from health to education to sanitation—all of which contribute to serving basic needs and reducing the vulnerability of affected populations.

The fact that many religious leaders and religious institutions are also cultural gatekeepers in most communities around the world, also means that they can be the source of some of the most egregiously harmful practices taking place. Conversely, religious authorities are well placed to tackle negative practices, such as FGM, early marriage, and gender-based violence, including sexual violence during conflict. These realities, in addition to being rooted within strong spiritual traditions, strengthen their psycho-social service advantage wherein some of them also may serve a role in protection and healing of vulnerable groups, including abused women and children.

Recognition for the many roles played by FBOs is infrequently communicated within the broader humanitarian community itself, making it difficult to find its way into public discourse. While the significant roles of FBOs engaged in the provision of humanitarian assistance during disasters is increasingly acknowledged in academic literature,[14] those working in this field often argue that

> Much of this work remains poorly communicated and understood and has not been integrated into humanitarian coordinating mechanisms and technical policy forums, thereby undermining operational effectiveness. Concerns also remain related to the perceived non-neutrality of religiously inspired humanitarian action and associated risks of proselytization.[15]

In his address at the Vatican on February 22, UN OCHA Undersecretary-General O'Brien noted the "unique relationship that faith-based groups have built with communities, which makes them well-equipped to contribute to the shifts required to put vulnerable people at the centre of global decision-making."[16]

The Secretary-General's Report highlights five core responsibilities of humanitarian engagement which the WHS was to target:

- global leadership to prevent and end conflict;
- upholding the norms that safeguard humanity;
- leaving no one behind;
- changing people's lives—from delivering aid to ending need; and
- investing in humanity.

Each of these relates, in diverse ways, to the work of religious leaders and faith-based organizations, especially given they are the closest, and often part of, the local communities themselves. Investing in humanity is perhaps the most relevant, from the faith-based standpoint:

> Accepting and acting upon our shared responsibilities for humanity requires political, institutional and financial investment. As a shift is needed from funding to financing *that invests in local capacities*, is risk-informed, invests in fragile situations and *incentivizes collective outcomes*. We must also reduce the funding gap for humanitarian needs. [emphasis added][17]

As Stephen O'Brien pointed out, "Faith-based groups already mobilize resources on a massive scale in response to crises—now we must identify innovative ways to extend this to reducing vulnerability and shoring up resilience."

It is precisely these capacities to mobilize resources (human, financial, social, and even political) that require better appreciation and understanding—both among the faith-based communities themselves, and the wider developmental and humanitarian communities. Particularly in a time of diminishing Overseas Development Assistance (ODA) together with the rise in anticipated humanitarian disasters (due to diverse factors including climate change, compromised financial systems, and increasing intra and inter-state conflicts) it behooves the international community to be better informed about innovative means of mobilizing resources.

To that end, and with a view towards the World Humanitarian Summit in May, UNFPA, in its capacity as the Coordinator of the UN IATF-FBOs, hosted an informal policy roundtable on "Religious Resourcing for Humanitarian Work" on March 29, 2016. The invitees to this policy roundtable included UN development and humanitarian agencies, select Secretariat offices, the World Bank, bilateral donors/governments, and a coordinating entity (International Partnership of Religions for Development), as well as major FBOs who partner with the UN at the policymaking and practical delivery levels.

The idea was to come together to level the playing field of knowledge between different international faith-based actors. The topics discussed covered how to mobilize resources (human, financial, and social) especially in the absence of other funding streams, and how the different approaches could be instructive for the UN and NGO partners.

The means of funding for the various FBOs is highly varied and depends on the faith-based entity and its origins and mandate. Sources include individual giving, contributions from foundations and corporate donors (e.g. pharmaceuticals). Some donations are received through specific appeals, and others are derived from the governments themselves. Other sources include grants received from the UN when FBOs act as implementing partners (such as Catholic Relief Services and Islamic Relief). In some instances, campaigns are designed around specific issues, for example to support refugees or in response to a humanitarian crisis/disaster (such as those carried out by World Vision). Private fundraising is yet another means (this includes annual collections in almost all Catholic parishes (as is the case with Catholic Relief Services/CRS), as well as donations by private citizens (here the Buddhist Tzu Chi Foundation is another example), as well as contributions from member churches (the World Council of Churches (WCC) and the Episcopalians mentioned this form of resourcing). Last but by no means least, many FBOs mentioned special collections during crises as a means of raising resources.

For Muslim humanitarian NGOs, a distinct form of giving was elaborated that referenced the centrality of the Islamic tradition of endowments, to be used to support community development (schools, hospitals, etc.). Moreover, the wealth tax on Muslims (2.5 percent of savings) was also mentioned as a resource, with generations estimated at around USD600 billion annually. Islamic Relief Worldwide, as well as its US-based counterpart, benefit from these sources, which can be used for a variety of causes, including peace building/conflict resolution; combatting slavery—human trafficking; and general support to vulnerable communities. Legacy giving and bequests are also a source of support to FBOs. Islamic Relief as well as the American Jewish Committee (AJC) share this, with AJC noting that much of the organization's funds come from bequests that, in turn, go to organizations that meet specific needs.

The unique positioning of FBOs—given their enormous cache of private, untied resources, their volunteer staff human resources and familiarity and longevity in communities—make them not only important to humanitarian response but more likely rather indispensable, particularly in light of the dire funding prospects of international NGOs, multilateral and bilateral donors/implementer community. Juxtaposing the resources for crises raised through international appeals versus those that can be raised (from private funders) by FBOs is hugely telling and suggestive of the influence and criticality of FBOs to the overall humanitarian system.

Faith-based NGOs are not a monolith, and the diversity among them is generally positive. The gulf between the major international FBOs and more localized ones was also stressed as an important aspect in attempting to distinguish between the world of faith-related humanitarian service. Some discussion exists as to whether they may benefit from a coherent body or architecture through which they engage with and message the larger Humanitarian Assistance community. Currently, the "faith-based" humanitarian scene tends to be uncoordinated, and the general lack of coherence may render it easier to dismiss or overlook their efforts, or even take them for granted—given their proximity to national communities particularly in the face of a crisis when system coherence is very much needed.

The deep legacy and experience working within the SPHERE[18] define minimum standards (indeed, drafting them) for many decades. Within the UN cluster system, however, SPHERE still needs to be known/amplified for all around, leading up to and at the WHS, and after. The perception (or lack of knowledge) of FBOs as not working within SPHERE and international standards of impartiality etc. should be challenged and rectified.

Another distinguishing feature between the diverse FBOs engaged in humanitarian work related to the intentionality of referencing women's specific needs (or the lack thereof) with clarity as to the proven economic and social viability, as well as benefits to communities and nations of safeguarding gender equality, together with the need to ensure women's leadership and engagement. These sets of issues are also considered challenges of FBO engagement—in terms of being seen as like-minded players by the secular organizations.

Especially for smaller and locally rooted faith-based NGOs, there are capacity building and service delivery challenges that can constitute deficits, so there is a call for funding their capacity-building needs both by the larger FBOs, but also through the UN's own efforts in countries. In this regard, one of the questions that presaged the WHS discussions was how to make capacity building and local empowerment—particularly through cash transfers—a core principle and value of humanitarian engagement. Noteworthy in this regard was the example of one such FBO approach, the Buddhist Tzu Chi, which is based on local procurements and engaging only local businesses in humanitarian donations and delivery. Starting out as housewives in China donating 2 cents a day 20 years ago to a multi-million dollar international entity today, this FBO speaks to cost effective and locally owned means of empowering the very same recipients of humanitarian support.

The value of volunteer time and human resources, free labor, is a tremendous resource that FBOs are uniquely positioned to provide, and is not sufficiently acknowledged by global actors.

These relatively more organic, community-based sources of funding that diverse FBOs are able to avail themselves of are especially noteworthy given that so much has been written about the negative effects of other appeals that exclusively use persuasive communications and public relations strategies for funding. Narrative analysis points to the avoidance of articulating the root causes of crisis that might alienate donors (Lugo-Ocando 2015), and others point to the tendency for such "branded" appeals to alter the emotional response to giving by taking donors way from feeling concern for those who suffer (Chouliaraki 2013). Given the benefits of FBOs community-based sources of support, they should be taken very seriously indeed.

Strengths of Faith-based Organizations (FBOs) and Their Approaches

All prophets are calling us to save humanity . . . Saving humanity is partnership in action.
(Dr. Hany El-Banna—The Humanitarian Forum, Egypt)

Genuine international cooperation must engage local communities. Yet the UN fails to recognize and engage with faith-based institutions. Faith-based organizations . . . are in the communities before, during and after the crisis. Caritas is convinced that an essential responsibility of the Humanitarian system is to put people at the center and involve them in the response. But one size does not fit all.
(Cardinal Antonio Tagle—Caritas Internationalis, The Philippines)

Even when the bravest NGOs leave, the FBOs stay, because they are community.
(Mr. Antti Pentikäinen— Network of Religious and Traditional Leaders, Finland)

Partnering with local churches and religious institutions that are the first respondents and care-takers of communities during crisis, and can also be service deliverers in addition to the usual religious and spiritual services they deliver, is an asset to any humanitarian approach. Most FBOs are unique in that they have both a value-based religious approach *and* adhere to SPHERE. This combination of a commitment inspired and justified by the specific faith tradition, together with being steeped in the principles of humanitarian response, provides the FBOs with a distinctive characteristic relative to other humanitarian actors. This is not to argue that they are better or worse, but simply to affirm their specific value-added that can often appeal to many communities in general, and to those suffering humanitarian disasters in particular.

FBOs have some of the oldest and largest youth networks, a fact not always acknowledged by the UN. This positions the FBOs to be able to actively involve youth who are normally forgotten, left out, and isolated in humanitarian settings, and provide them with opportunities for involvement. These strengths are linked to yet another wherein FBOs are often closely tied to—if not generically part of—grassroots communities. The experience of the Salvation Army, among others, shows there is a deliberate focus by the larger FBOs on training local people to respond to needs. As the Salvation Army's Dean Pallant noted, "this encourages and enables local people to respond immediately to their local situation using local resources, [thus rendering] external funds and support as a second line of support." Local people are both mobilized and enabled to raise their own resources.

Moreover, the inclusion of especially vulnerable populations is a key approach of most FBOs in line with putting people at the center and addressing their needs. Knowing a community's needs is a *sine qua non* of effectiveness and relevance to community members. Examples of populations referenced as examples by the fathered FBOs, include the Druze community in danger of Shi'a proselytization as well as persecuted Muslims in places as far apart as Rakhine State, Myanmar, and in the Central African Republic.

Because all major international FBOs often have strong reputations for value-based services and some of the larger ones have a track record of delivery as well as results-based management, many governmental donors tend to send money when there is need. The ability to combine resources with other FBOs and civil society organizations and initiatives increases individual FBO capacities. Each of the large FBOs is often quick to acknowledge the value of partnering with other faith-based and secular agencies to focus on particular issues (e.g. statelessness), yet another feature that resonates with potential donors. While raising resources, FBOs are both mobilizing active and needed support *and* building political will for advocacy at political levels. Some FBOs argue that there is value in FBOs' flexibility in how to use funds, rendering more feasible the possibility that they can be channeled according to greatest need, and used to develop creative new approaches and to build long-term capacity of local partners. This feature, however, is not necessarily considered an advantage, if the FBO happens to be a Muslim one, as the next paragraphs note.

Muslim FBOs and Specific Challenges

The "Muslim" or "Islamic model" of resourcing humanitarian relief work is built on the belief in fulfilling duties to communities, both local and elsewhere and on the tradition that beneficiaries have a right to your wealth. As Mr. Sharif Ali of Islamic Relief noted: "it is not a question of charity, but rather an obligation." The structural barriers to operations faced by Muslim NGOs, shared by Ms. Omayma El Ella of the UK's Muslim Charities' Forum, are related to foreign terrorist financing restrictions. Neither governments nor the UN can afford to vilify and undercut local Muslim organizations, she warned, especially given that they are the only ones capable of delivering in high-volatility areas. According to Islamic Relief International's presentation, "75% of crises in the last 15 years took place in Muslim-majority contexts," which underlines the criticality of Muslim fundraising and local Muslim organizations in responding.

Specific challenges to Muslim humanitarian and development NGOs include the increased number of regulatory policies, legislations, and donor requirements that are directly affecting the capacity of Muslim charities to receive contributions. Lengthy due-diligence processes (of both givers and recipients) limit the ability of Muslim relief entities to work in specific areas or to work with "prescribed" groups. While donations are often anonymous (in line with the religious injunction that disparages claiming credit for giving of one's money), this effectively puts charities at risk of being associated with terrorist groups, and adversely affects their reputation. In addition, there are increasing tensions between donors (including banks) and charities, given that "all risks are now placed solely on the Charities' shoulders" (UNFPA 2016). While internal oversight mechanisms and controls are acknowledged as needed and adhered to by the Muslim FBOs who are part of the international humanitarian networks, it is nevertheless noted that there is a trade-off between actually reaching and serving those in need, and spending significant time and effort delivering on the control requirements.

Last but by no means least, continuing (Western) media antagonism to Muslim charities is consistently identified as a significant challenge.

More than 250 faith-based leaders and representatives of the world's largest humanitarian organizations, representing all major world faith traditions, gathered at the World Humanitarian Summit's Special Session on Religious Engagement on May 23, 2016. These included representatives from all regions of the world, both religious leaders as well as NGOs, actively engaged in humanitarian relief work in all corners of the globe. The speakers called upon the international community to recognize and affirm their significant and often unique holistic contributions to humanitarian work, to consider them as equal partners in humanitarian and development work, and to scale up efforts to support their important work in communities around the globe. In turn, these major faith-based humanitarian actors committed, *together*, in an unprecedented and historic fashion, to serving the most vulnerable in humanitarian settings; upholding and expanding the significant humanitarian response of faith-based organizations; overcoming the manipulative and abusive attempts to link religion with violence, terrorism, or exclusion of others; keeping affected persons at the center of all assistance planned and provided; maintaining robust beneficiary feedback mechanisms; ensuring that women and girls' rights are protected, their needs are met, and their ability to engage in decision making is enhanced; and continuing to play an active role in response coordination.

But their voices were silenced.

Conclusion: "See FBOs, Know FBOs, Work with FBOs"

Particularly at a time when religion is being branded—and seen, rightly or wrongly—as the "big bad wolf" behind violent extremism, and when "countering" or prevention of violent extremism is the buzzword of foreign policy and financial market stability, how can we afford not to engage with faith-based organizations with a track record in development and humanitarian services worldwide? The question is, therefore, not whether we should engage, but *how* can the UN—with the willful blindness of some of its offices on the one hand, and the instrumentalization of religious actors intended by others on the other—better engage with faith-based actors? What follows are some recommendations made by the FBOs themselves in the course of the journey of the WHS.

See FBOs: Focus on Communication

Given the specific instance of failed reporting and documentation of the faith-based presence and achievements at the WHS, the focus on communication was a key part of the recommendations. In this regard, working with FBOs to also actively target and (re)build the communication infrastructure in humanitarian contexts was noted by the World Association for Christian Communication (WACC) as a key ingredient in not only acknowledging and supporting FBO contributions to humanitarian relief, but also as a means of ensuring that communities themselves are better empowered to deal with humanitarian crisis situations. In this regard, concrete recommendations included engaging the FBOs in the development of community-level emergency communication plans. These plans, however, should be tailored for actors that involve local and community media, and should also entail listening, rather than mere dissemination of information. WACC's own experience underlines the need to focus on enabling community media to become communication hubs during emergencies.

Know FBOs: Widen/Deepen Knowledge

Encouraging greater literacy about the intersections of religion with developmental and humanitarian issues and engagement would open the door to greater recognition of the types of faith groups, faith-based "assets," and faith-inspired models of resource mobilization, partnership, and service delivery. Rather than reinvent the wheel, however, it is important to build on existing resource and knowledge bases while also collating some of these rich references and making them available to a range of international, regional and local humanitarian and development entities.

Compiling and segregating data sources on FBOs' own financing capabilities in situations of humanitarian need was seen as important for both faith-based as well as secular actors. This was necessary in order to better identify—zero in on—the specific contributions of faith-based actors. While some of this data is available, it has yet to be compiled—and its contents checked for veracity—especially regarding non-Western-based FBOs.

Work with FBOs: Streamline Approach

The FBOs strongly emphasized the need to shift from the current sector-based cluster system, to area-based flexible approaches for coordinating disaster response. Many FBO actors maintain that individual, family, and community needs do not fit in neat sectoral buckets, and since they seek to respond more holistically and not just sector by sector, some argue that their assessments, planning and implementation are better organized around specific locations, rather than sectors.

An oft-repeated plea made by many of the FBOs, locally based and international ones alike, was to make both the UN and government-pooled funds more streamlined, available, and accessible to FBOs. Faith groups, especially local ones, need to be able to access UN funding streams in emergencies so their work can be adequately, fairly, and quickly resourced. Yet FBOs, like other NGOs, have to be routed through the national government's own funding mechanisms. Given humanitarian contexts where the state infrastructure itself is weakened, the importance of the UN as a key interlocutor is significantly underlined. This begs the question of how to develop and implement a common, streamlined partnership framework across the multiple UN agencies so FBOs, especially local ones, can partner effectively and efficiently while maintaining their respective roles. The plethora of complex applications and reporting requirements of all the UN agencies (as well as other donors) is a barrier to entry for many FBOs, especially many smaller yet capable ones that meet critical human needs but lack this specific capacity.

Muslim FBOs in particular argued for the UN to consider them "as investment opportunities," which would further encourage greater cross-sectoral cooperation and facilitate multi-faith coordination without taking away from their specific value-added in some contexts—e.g. where being Muslim can position them favorably vis-à-vis certain communities and possibly governments, and even non-state actors as is the case in Syria and parts of Iraq.

Systematically Include and Engage FBOs[19]

This would entail engaging FBOs in pre-disaster cooperation/collaboration focusing on shared goals of peace, risk reduction, resilience, and growth for the development of relationships with faith communities; as well as integrating faith groups in the planning and pre-positioning of relief items and delineation of zones of distribution, thus complementing FBOs' asset of presence with government and UN assets of logistical support, all while seeking to provide FBOs with some means of operational freedom. This would also entail engaging FBOs in pre-disaster technical collaboration to build specific FBO capacities, address gaps, scale up models of professional practices/principles, as well as recognize their role in national risk reduction efforts and preparedness plans.

Moreover, a specific ask was made of the UN and other humanitarian actors to provide the opportunity for faith-based voices in the case referral chain and cluster response mechanisms and to invite and integrate faith groups into national dialogues and networks (pre-disaster and during responses), thus effectively ensuring that faith-based partners are part of the practice—and visibility—of documentation and reporting around humanitarian contexts.

How Can the UN Engage FBOs Better?

Last but by no means least, the gathered FBOs had some very concrete recommendations specifically for the UN actors to engage FBOs better, presented here, to conclude, in some of their own words, but respectful of the fact that some of these were shared under Chatham House Rules:

> The UN should continue to leverage its unique convening power, but not ask FBOs, Religious Leaders or community based religious actors to become "more like the UN" or other secular NGOs.
>
> (Senior-most leader of an Orthodox Church)

> The UN should continue to provide logistical coordination support in humanitarian contexts—but be more deliberate about identifying and including faith-based community actors and ensure the extension of due inclusiveness and civility afforded other humanitarian actors.
>
> (CEO of a Muslim NGO)

> The UN needs to demystify the UN system and its bureaucracy to faith-based partners at the global, regional and national levels, and with a view to doing so particularly in humanitarian contexts.
>
> (Senior Operations Office in a Hindu NGO)

> The UN needs to be explicit about its desire to invest in this crucial sector, and why it is doing so.
>
> (CEO of a Catholic NGO)

> The UN should consider embracing the selflessness valued in the FBO partners.
>
> (CEO of a Buddhist NGO)

> The UN needs to clarify and share patterns of optimal coordination between FBOs and governments, and what are the needs to realize those. This may help reduce anxiety by some FBOs as regards being coopted by government actors, or losing credibility with at-risk communities.
>
> (Senior Executive in Jewish NGO)

The clarity—and simplicity—of the above recommendations further underlines the need to ensure that when faith actors gather to join hands for peace, to save lives, and to save heritage, no media or secular institution should silence these voices, especially not at a time when so-called "counter-narratives" to terrorism are being much sought after. For the work—and words—of these humanitarian and developmental FBOs is already an existing faith-inspired counter-narrative.

Charter for Faith-Based Humanitarian Action

Provision of Aid to All Those Who Need It

Our religious teachings, although diverse, teach us the importance of compassion and of one common shared humanity, where each human being is important in him/herself. Human dignity and the welfare of all people are the main objectives of faith and religion, with the principal role to serve other people. Learning from faith-based organizations, which are known to provide selfless service to all in need, irrespective of their faith, ethnicity, gender, and geography, we (faith-based organizations and other humanitarian actors), *commit* to upholding the principles of compassion, humanity, and impartiality in our provision of humanitarian assistance and protection in alignment with fundamental humanitarian principles.

Contribution to Peace and Reconciliation

In a world where conflicts, violence, and natural disaster affect millions of people, faith-based entities share a critical responsibility and role in working for peace, both at local and national or international levels. We facilitate sustainable behavior and relationship changes based on faith and worldview, offering mediation and sacred space for dialogue between parties.

We *commit* to uphold and expand the significant humanitarian response of faith-based organizations and to overcome the manipulative and abusive attempts to link religion with violence, terrorism, or exclusion of others. By so doing, we aim to resolve conflicts and work to promote reconciliation.

We *call* upon religious communities to use their social capital to amplify humanitarian diplomacy and to promote compliance with International Humanitarian Law as this contributes to the maintenance and restoration of peace.

We call upon the United Nations, international organizations, regional and national authorities to acknowledge and support these roles, and to encourage them.

Proximity to Communities

Through local faith communities and grassroots NGOs, faith-based actors are uniquely placed to engage in humanitarian action: faith-based actors often enjoy close proximity to, or are part of the populations affected by wider crises, and have therefore developed special relationships of trust, as well as insights and access to community members compared to many other actors; we are often present before crises, and are first responders when disasters hit. We are key providers of assistance and protection during crises and their aftermath.

We *call* upon international organizations to recognize and affirm the significant, and often unique, contributions of religious communities and NGOs, and to consider them to be equal partners, opening up access to adequate funding to support our efforts.

We (faith-based and other humanitarian actors) *commit* to working together to better contextualize humanitarian response, leveraging our added value to reach people in need of assistance and protection, and using our influence to mobilize our local communities in support of these efforts.

Notes

1. As of the writing of this article, so-called "Islamic State" terrorists have killed innocents in Turkey, in Bangladesh and in Iraq.
2. http://whsturkey.org/the-summit/aboutwhs
3. Ibid.
4. The United Nations Framework Convention on Climate Change (UNFCCC) is an international environmental agreement on climate change. The 21st annual Conference of the Parties (COP) in Paris took place from November 30 to December 11, 2015. · This Climate Conference is more commonly known as COP-21.
5. www.irinnews.org/analysis/2016/05/26/world-humanitarian-summit-winners-and-losers
6. www.ipsnews.net/2016/05/humanitarian-summit-the-big-fiasco/
7. www.irinnews.org/analysis/2016/05/26/world-humanitarian-summit-winners-and-losers
8. Specific targets in this regard were limited to individual pledges among NGOs rather than by governments.
9. www.irinnews.org/analysis/2016/05/26/world-humanitarian-summit-winners-and-losers
10. See the *Charter for Faith-Based Humanitarian Action* in the conclusion of this paper.
11. The idea of a Religious Summit was eventually put on hold. Meanwhile, those who were planning for it, agreed to become the Advisory Group for the UN IATF-FBO. The Advisory Group themselves represented diverse religions, regions, and included at least one governmental counterpart. They provided support in the design, management, overall guidance, as well as political and media outreach for the Special Session.
12. The "top five" FBO partners now most often seen at UN and World Bank religious events include Caritas Internationalis, World Vision, the World Council of Churches, Lutheran World Relief, and Islamic Relief.
13. "The Catholic Church in America: Earthly Concerns", in *The Economist* blog, available at: www.economist.com/node/21560536
14. Riddell (2007), xv, 316; Ager et al. (2015).
15. Alistair Ager and Helen Stawski, unpublished Concept Note for a Summit of Religious Leaders, January 2016.
16. UN OCHA, 2016: Speech delivered at the Vatican by Stephen O'Brien, available at: https://docs.unocha.org/sites/dms/Documents/USG%20OBrien%20remarks%20at%20Vatican%2022%20Feb%202016.pdf
17. *One Humanity: Shared Responsibility: Report of the United Nations Secretary General for the World Humanitarian Summit.* New York: United Nations, 2016.
18. *The Sphere Handbook: Humanitarian Charter and Minimum Standards in Humanitarian Response*, available at: www.sphereproject.org/handbook/
19. These recommendations are derived from detailed ones made by World Vision representatives at the WHS preparatory meetings, and were endorsed by many other FBO representatives.

References

Ager, J., Fiddian-Qasmiyeh, E., and Ager, A. (2015) "Local Faith Communities and the Promotion of Resilience in Contexts of Humanitarian Crisis: A Scoping Study," *Journal of Refugee Studies*, 28 (2): 202–221.

Chouliaraki, L. (2013) *The Ironic Spectator: Solidarity in the Age of Post-Humanitarianism*, Cambridge, UK: Polity.

Lugo-Ocando, J. (2015) *Blaming the Victim: How Global Journalism Fails Those in Poverty*, London: Pluto Press.

Riddell, R. C. (2007) *Does Foreign Aid Really Work?* Oxford: Oxford, UK University Press.

UNFPA. (2016) *Highlights from Religious Resourcing for Humanitarian Work*, New York: United Nations, unpublished conference proceedings.

21

THE ROLE OF MEDIA IN PUBLIC ADVOCACY AND COUNTERING VIOLENT EXTREMISM

Nadia Sraieb-Koepp

How can we contribute to a world that is strengthened by our differences and not defined by them, a world in which violent extremism no longer has its place? I would like to touch upon new trends with huge potential to shape public opinion, educate, raise awareness, and counter violent extremism in the world. Beyond the scope of the "information mission" of media—whether we talk about traditional media such as radio, TV, and written press—or the new information technologies such as the Internet and social networks—there is a real potential for media to be used more efficiently by engaging in digital activism; and using other sorts of borderless technologies to propagate counter-narratives and positive messages and to promote fundamental rights, freedom, and democracy.

In the face of the rise of violent extremism, and especially Islamist extremism and terrorism, one can point to multiple sources for the spread of this phenomenon, including repressive secular governments in the Middle East, local injustices and divisions, the hijacking of the internet for terrorist propaganda, and American interventions in the Muslim world from the anti-Soviet war in Afghanistan to the invasion of Iraq. Nevertheless, there seems to be very little doubt anymore about the notion that Saudi Arabia bears a great deal of responsibility for the current wave of extremism and jihadist violence. The world today is a more divided, dangerous, and violent place because of the cumulative effect of five decades of oil-financed proselytizing of a rigid, conservative and fundamentalist strain of Islam known as Wahhabism. As William McCants (2016), a Brookings Institution scholar notes, "The Saudis promote a very toxic form of Islam that draws sharp lines between a small number of true believers and everyone else, Muslim and non-Muslim," thus providing ideological fodder for violent jihadists. But what are the keys to this successful rise of Wahhabism in the world, an ideology that has disrupted local Islamic traditions in dozens of countries and touched every nation with a Muslim population as the result of lavish spending on religious outreach for half a century, estimated in the tens of billions of dollars. Even though the support has come from the Saudi government, the royal family, Saudi charities, and Saudi-sponsored organizations including the World Muslim League, the World Assembly of Muslim Youth, and the International Islamic Relief Organization, the message has effectively been amplified by media and social media.

Being from Tunisia, I witnessed firsthand the power of media in changing people's beliefs, opinions and even behaviors. When the Tunisian government authorized satellite dishes in the late 1980s, little did it know about the tremendous impact the programs dedicated to the preaching of the Wahhabi ideology would have in the country. El Arabia and Al Jazeera were the main satellite TV channels people watched as they were in Arabic, a language every Tunisian understood. Though many of the programs these satellite channels aired contained quality informational content, others included highly conservative religious themes, and very quickly one could witness the shift from a traditional Islam, deeply rooted in Sufism, towards a more conservative Islam often with a political agenda. There was no counter-narrative to this form of preaching as the main theology institutions, such as the Zitouna, had been closed in Tunisia ever since the Bourguiba era, and there was no proper theology or civic education in the schools or elsewhere. Furthermore, imams and muftis very often had no formal training in theology. As a result, Tunisian people who never doubted their faith up until then, started to split along the lines of religious conservatism and traditional belief. The powerful media machinery of the Gulf States started the spread of an entirely different interpretation of Islam without any authority or media outlet capable of countering this endeavor. Unfortunately, Tunisia is not an isolated case in the Muslim world or even in the West. Media and the Internet may not have been the only tools used to propagate this ideology, but they certainly are among the most powerful ones.

As pointed out by Majid Nawaaz, in his TED talk on "a global culture to fight extremism," we are moving from the age of globalization, the era of citizenship—where people could be from multiracial, multiethnic backgrounds, but also be equal citizens in a state—into a new age, "the age of behavior." This Pakistani man, born and raised in England, who used to be an Al Qaeda recruiter before turning into a pro-democracy activist, defines the age of behavior as a period of transnational allegiances, where identity is defined more by ideas and narratives. According to him, the people who have truly capitalized on this age of behavior and transnational allegiances by using digital activism and other sorts of borderless technologies, those who have really been benefiting from this, have been extremists.

If we look at Islamists, if we look at the phenomenon of far-right fascists, one thing they have been very good at, one thing that they have actually been exceeding in, is communicating across borders, using technologies to organize themselves, to propagate their message, and to create truly global phenomena. What were previously localized parochialisms, individual or groupings of extremists who were isolated from one another, have become interconnected in a globalized way and have thus become, or are becoming, mainstream because the Internet and connection technologies are connecting them across the world.

Why is it that extremist organizations, whether of the far right or Islamist extremism, are succeeding in organizing in a globalized way, whereas those who aspire to a democratic culture are falling behind? For Nawaaz, there are several reasons including complacency—those in power do not feel the need to advocate for that culture. Another reason is political correctness, because going out to propagate one's view is associated with either neoconservatism or with Islamist extremism and hardly ever with democracy, human rights, or fundamental freedoms. The power of these borderless technologies has also been proven more recently, since the so-called Islamic State (also called Daesh) self-proclaimed itself in the summer of 2014. Nobody has been spared the graphic visuals of this militant group that have been relayed in mainstream media all over the world. We witnessed beheadings and other horrific images that were directly provided to media outlets by the very criminals who committed them. The expected results were immediate: fear and stigmatization of Islam even though the largest number of IS victims are Muslims. However, to a large extent, the real success of the communication strategy of

IS lies also in the successful recruitment of new members in the Middle East and in the western world. But it is by conveying highly positive images of an idealistic "Caliphate" (Islamic realm), mainly on the Internet and social media, that IS has proven to be very effective in mobilizing and convincing thousands of young men and women to join their cause.

At the University of Arizon's School of Journalism, Shahira Fahmy describes in her article "Illusions of the 'Caliphate': Understanding the Visual Communication of the Islamic State" how

> IS runs an intensive media operation, one that is akin to an entire militia of media professionals. According to a 2015 article in *The Washington Post* written by Miller and Mekhennet, the IS media division is led by skillful foreigners, most of which have production expertise based on their previous jobs in media and technology related companies. The senior media operatives are immediately engaged in the group's strategic decisions and are regarded as *emirs* (rulers/leaders) of similar rank to their military counterparts. These privileged men lead hundreds of media professionals and enjoy status, high salaries and good living arrangements. IS has set up a decentralized media apparatus, responsible for producing and disseminating a huge amount of material inside and outside of its *wilayat* (provinces).

Over time, the IS media experts have ramped up the group's propaganda: alongside the "instagrammification" of the group's visuals, they launched several print magazines in Arabic but also in different languages, such as *Dabiq* that is published in English, *Istok* in Russian, *Konstantiniyye* in Turkish, or *Dar al-salam* (the House of Peace) in French. Whether through pictures or magazines, Daesh tends to emphasize—more often than not—a peaceful, attractive, prominent, and competent Caliphate, according to Fahmy. It is undeniable that the group uses visuals very efficiently to frame its dominant narratives and to highlight its legitimacy and power to IS audiences.

In the face of such powerful media/propaganda apparatuses, it appears more urgent than ever to counter these narratives with the same "weapons" and on the same platforms. In order to succeed, what is missing is grassroots activism on the ground to trigger a genuine demand for democracy and to promote values such as human rights, religious freedom, freedom of expression, tolerance, mutual respect, and fundamental freedoms. We should not be ashamed or embarrassed to advocate for these values, starting in schools, universities, and mainstream media. In many parts of the world, this has never really been done up until now, and in other parts it has been taken for granted in recent times. Our youth should be entitled to have other alternatives than rigid regimes, dictatorships, or theocracies. Our women should be entitled to equal rights and be treated as equal citizens, and our planet should be allowed to survive. Religion and ethnicity should no longer be the instruments of division and conflict. Unfortunately, without a massive effort to educate and raise awareness about these issues everywhere in the world, it will be very difficult to succeed and it is about time we used the same tools as extremist groups have been successfully using over the past two decades.

As Nawaaz puts it, what the Muslim world needs "is a genuine transnational youth-led movement that works to actively advocate for the democratic culture—which is necessarily more than just elections." He has made a start for that in Pakistan with his movement called Khudi, which works on the ground to encourage youth to create a genuine conducive environment and demand for a democratic culture. His call has seemed to resonate lately in the Middle East and Africa (MEA). In that part of the world that is gripped by protests and upheavals, real news junkies, at home and abroad, know how to go straight to the source: citizen journalists and bloggers help make sense of the chaos and shape public opinion especially for the younger generations. Others opt for more open forms of activism while relying on social media to reach out to wide audiences. One common feature across the MEA region is a young, Internet savvy generation that has hijacked the public debate and can no longer be ignored by the entrenched power structures. It is their collective voice that helped the youth of the region to reclaim their place in the public sphere. Unfortunately, what is missing is a similar attitude in mainstream media in order to amplify these messages.

My personal experience definitely echoes this call. At the beginning of 2011, right after the Tunisian revolution, I launched *Engagement Citoyen*, a not-for-profit organization dedicated to facilitating the democratic transition process in Tunisia through communication and media campaigns as well as grassroots level advocacy initiatives in the period leading up to the first free elections in Tunisia that took place in October 2011. The first months we focused on raising awareness among women and youth about what was at stake in the upcoming first and free election, and why it was important for them to embrace their role as citizens, including by voting or running for office. Nevertheless, the closer we got to the election date, the more obvious it became that the country was confronted with the problem of a potential low voter turnout.

After 23 years of President Ben Ali's dictatorship, Tunisia now had over 1,600 candidates to choose from and an over-exposure to political advertising and messages. As a result, people were confused and many had completely lost interest in politics. A few days before the first free and fair elections in Tunisia, the polls predicted 55 percent at best would go and vote. In order to turn this apathy into action we needed to reawaken people's sense of political engagement with a strong and effective reminder. We had to create an "electroshock" to get people to the polls and exercise their new democratic rights, so we pointed out the real danger of abstention: the possible return of dictatorship. We did it in a provocative and visually engaging way. Four days before polling day, we put back a giant poster of ex-President Ben Ali in the suburb of La Goulette, the exact same one that had been torn apart in the first hours of the revolution. The poster inevitably provoked the people, leading them to direct action. They reacted as planned and decided to tear it down but when they did so they discovered another poster underneath saying "Beware, dictatorship can return. On October 23rd, go out and vote." The entire event was filmed and posted online. It immediately went viral generating tens of thousands of posts and reactions and 461 percent more visits on *Engagement Citoyen*'s website. In the evening it aired on all Tunisian Arabic TV channels' news programs. The next day, it spread worldwide generating millions of views, comments and likes and free media coverage everywhere, but most importantly, 88 percent of voters turned out on the day of the elections, far higher than the expected 55 percent. Ironically, it's a symbol of dictatorship that helped build a new democracy.

Later on, our social media campaign, *"The return of Dictator Ben Ali"* (https://youtube/um5QvW5XHwY) was recognized for its public advocacy impact, its creativity, and innovative character by the international press and media as well as in the advertising world. It won, among others, five Clio awards in New York, including the Gran Clio, three Lions d'Or in Cannes, as well as the TED "Ads worth spreading" and the OSOCIO award.

Just to name a few other examples of positive social media and Internet campaigns in the realm of public advocacy in Africa and the MENA region, one should recall Ory Okolloh, the Kenyan activist, lawyer, and blogger, who was formerly the Policy Manager for Africa with Google. In 2006 she co-founded the parliamentary watchdog site Mzalendo (Swahili: "Patriot"). When Kenya was engulfed in violence following a disputed presidential election in 2007, Okolloh helped create Ushahidi (Swahili: "Witness"), a website that collected and recorded eyewitness reports of violence using text messages and Google maps.

In Tunisia, Amira Yahyaoui, President and Founder of the organization Al Bawsala (the compass), became a public figure overnight. The work of this young human rights advocate really had an impact during the period right after the Tunisian revolution and up until now. Her public policy and accountability NGO monitored the work of the Tunisian Parliament, the Constitutional Assembly, and Tunisian city halls, and nowadays the work of the new ARP (Assembly of the Representatives of the People) using technology to make relevant information accessible to citizens but also to monitor the work and attendance of elected members of these assemblies. Al Bawsala also advocates for a better way of governing and citizen inclusion through lobbying and technical assistance to government officials. While still a teenager, Amira was banned from her homeland for her activism and fled to Paris where she was stateless for several years. Following her country's revolution in 2011, Amira returned to Tunisia for the transitional period that also coincided with the writing of the new Tunisian constitution.

Amira is the recipient of the Vital Voices global trailblazer award as "Women Transforming the Middle East and North Africa"; the Norwegian Linderbraeke Award for Human Rights; the French Fondation Chirac award on conflict prevention; she was ranked one of the most powerful Arab women, by the Arabian Business magazine; and one of the most influential African women, by Jeune Afrique, Global Shaper, World Economic Forum, and Yale World Fellow.

Another frontliner in the Tunisian revolution was Lina Ben Mhenni. Born in 1983, Lina became a prominent Internet activist, a pro-democracy activist and a blogger, who used to be tracked down and censored under the Ben Ali regime. Even before the Tunisian revolution, Lina was in the frontline in shedding some light on the tense situation in places such as Sidi Bouzid and Kasserine with her blog "A Tunisian Girl," writing about freedom of expression, human rights (women's and students' rights in particular), and social problems faced by Tunisians. In May 2010, Ben Mhenni and her cyberactivist friends organized a peaceful demonstration against the government's censorship of media via the Internet. When the uprisings then started in December 2010, Ben Mhenni's blog became one of the most important sources of information for both Tunisians as well as the international media. Ben Mhenni also used social networks such as Facebook and Twitter to defend freedom of expression, write about the reality of the human rights situation in Tunisia, and mobilize people to take to the streets and protest against Ben Ali and his government.

Following the revolution, Ben Mhenni continued to track the progress of human rights and press freedom in Tunisia. She even tried to boycott the Constituent Assembly elections, as she believed that the Islamist Al-Nahdha party, then the leading party in the polls, would buy votes and possibly only pretend to be moderate and modern. In 2011, Ben Mhenni published her book *Get Connected*. It received the "Best Blog" award by the Deutsche Welle's BOB Awards. She was nominated for the Nobel Peace Prize.

Another such young activist is Khalid Abdallah, the British Egyptian actor who became, in 2011, one of the founding members of the Mosireen Collective in Cairo that filmed the ongoing revolution and published videos that challenged the state media narratives. He provided training and equipment to his young partners and compiled an extensive library of footage. His experience and that of several other protesters is recorded in the documentary *The Square*, a film that won the Audience Award for best world cinema documentary at the Sundance film festival and was tipped for an Oscar.

And finally in Morocco, one should mention Hisham Almiraat, blogger and cyberactivist as well as co-founder of the media platform Mamfakinch, a collaborative website that advertised the February 20 movement in Morocco.

After these examples of meaningful digital activism, let us turn now to the "Entertainment–Education" process, which consists of purposely designing and implementing a media message to both entertain and educate. This is done to increase audience members' knowledge and understanding of educational, societal, political, and environmental issues, to lead to favorable attitudes and influence behavior and cultural norms. Whether it is through TV sitcoms, radio programs, or social network campaigns, there are real opportunities to shape public opinion, offer counter-narratives to inflammatory or divisive rhetoric but also to increase audience members' knowledge and understanding of the issues at stake.

These "media tools" can help to tackle very sensitive issues in a non-threatening way, when possible with humor, and allow the messages to reach millions of people all over the country, including those cannot read and other marginal segments of society. They should stimulate discussions in the communities and promote changes in attitude, public opinion, and behavior.

The story-telling approach for social issues has already been used in South America to fight domestic violence through educational telenovelas and radio programs, often written in collaboration with the local population. In other parts of the world it was used to promote prevention in the fight against HIV/Aids and other diseases. And even in the developed world, sitcoms have greatly impacted public opinion on topics such as gay marriage or race, including in the United States.

A strategic combination of the new information technologies with traditional media but also other media tools such as radio and TV "education–entertainment" sitcoms and programs could definitely be a key factor in shaping public opinion, raising awareness, and mobilizing targeted audiences around a wide range of causes and topics. Such a savvy combination allows the messages to reach much wider audiences, the "connected" and the "non-connected" ones.

The challenge for mainstream media, at the local and at the international level, whether it is traditional or social media, as well as for mainstream activists, is to pick up on the experience of digital activism and media activism as practiced by extremists in the past decades, and expand those tools through participatory culture able to convey counter-narratives and relevant arguments and information.

When it comes to the United Nations, and more specifically UN peacekeeping and humanitarian assistance it is striking to see that they only make the headlines when Blue Helmets are accused of "bringing cholera to Haiti"; when the UN is accused of "having known for months about the starving in Madaya, Syria"; when Saudi Arabia allegedly becomes the "President of the UN Human Rights Council," or when there are alleged rapes committed by UN peacekeepers. As stated in a recent article in the Foreign Policy Magazine from January 15, 2016: "The U.N.'s handling of the Madaya crisis has prompted outrage from Syrian medical and rescue workers, who accused the international body of kowtowing to Assad's regime." In an open letter published on January 13, 112 Syrian humanitarian workers from besieged areas accused the United Nations of "chasing permission you do not even need" from the Assad regime in light of two UN Security Council resolutions demanding that humanitarian assistance flow freely, which should have given aid officials all the authorization they needed. The failure to more aggressively address the plight of starving Syrians, the letter said, had transformed the United Nations from "a symbol of hope into a symbol of complicity."

Unfortunately, this kind of story is rarely balanced by positive reporting, which undermines all the good work peacekeepers and humanitarian personnel are doing day in day out, at the risk of losing their lives. It tarnishes the image, the credibility and the legitimacy of the organization and jeopardizes any future actions on the ground. Considering the gravity of these facts, the media is more than right to uncover and expose them, as long as it is done in a balanced way, which has not always been the case, as the example of the stories about the alleged Saudi presidency of the Human Rights Council proves, when in fact it was only presiding over a Human Rights Council panel. At the same time, the UN also has a responsibility for getting the right messages out in real time.

Nevertheless, with currently more than 169,000 Blue Helmets deployed in 36 UN missions in 30 countries, it should not come as a surprise that there will be a few deviant actors among them and that occasionally problems will arise. But what about all the other UN peacekeepers and humanitarian staff members, including those who lost their lives in the line of duty. Does the media not have a responsibility towards them as well, at the local and international levels? Should not the general public be better informed about how UN peacekeeping works, as explained in the chapter by Pierre-Olivier François while discusing his film about the Blue Helmets in this volume.

As stated in the recent exhaustive peacekeeping review initiated by the UN, one of the new objectives for peacekeepers is to be "closer to local populations." But how can they be closer when the number of targeted attacks by terrorist and non-state actors has more than doubled every year over the last three years. In order to develop a relationship of mutual trust and respect, people on both sides need to be informed and to have fluid channels of communication and this is precisely where local media could pave the way.

To conclude, let us emphasize that the tools to change the narratives, to educate and inform, to raise awareness, and to inspire exist and it is up to the media world, to activists and bloggers to use them efficiently as extremists have unfortunately done so successfully in the past decades. TV and radio channels, Google, and other social media outlets have to start playing a more meaningful role in public advocacy by amplifying positive messages and reoccupying the space used so far by these extremist groups for their propaganda.

I personally believe that we must work towards a world that is strengthened by our differences, and not defined by them. But in order to get there, values such as democracy, religious freedom, freedom of expression, human rights, and gender equality are crucial and need to be defended and advocated for in a much more powerful way.

In a world that is more and more interconnected, the Internet, social media, and mainstream media are powerful instruments to support fundamental freedoms and democracy. By sharing images, opinions, and facts, we can bridge cultural differences and create a more tolerant, open, and vibrant world.

References

Fahmy, S. (2016) "Illusions of the 'Caliphate': Understanding the Visual Communication of the Islamic State" in S. Staffell and Akil Akwan (Eds.) *Jihadism Transformed: Al-Qaeda and Islamic State's Global Battle of Ideas*, Oxford: Oxford University Press.

McCants, W. (2016) *The ISIS Apocalypse: The History, Strategy, and Doomsday Vision of the Islamic State*, New York: Picador.

Ben Mhenni, L. (2011) *Vernetzt euch!* [Get Connected!], Berlin: Ullstein.

Miller, G., and Mekhennet, S. (2015) "Inside the Surreal World of the Islamic State's Propaganda Machine, National Security," *The Washington Post*, available at: www.washingtonpost.com/world/national-security/inside-the-islamic-states-propagandamachine/2015/11/20/051e997a-8ce6–11e5-acff-673ae92ddd2b_story.html?postshare= 1691448242309174&tid=ss_tw

22

EBOLA AND AIDS

Harnessing Science and Human Nature to Combat Two Modern Plagues

Pat Fast

Editor's Note

In the 1980s when the AIDS epidemic struck in the United States, no one knew what caused it, and because the first people diagnosed with the disease were gay men, it was initially called "Gay Cancer," or the "Gay Plague."[1] On July 3, 1981, a *New York Times* headline read "Rare Cancer Seen in 41 Homosexuals." The association of gay men and the disease restricted the focus of reporting, and Cullen (2003) argues that AIDS became a "moral panic," in the Western media. In addition, Karpf (1990) observed that the "gay plague" metaphor depicted HIV/AIDS as a contagious disease, one that could be transmitted with a hand shake, and helped fuel fear and stigma among the public that homosexuality and homosexuals caused the disease. Anti gay sentiment effectively blocked information and understanding of the disease, and stalled the US government's public health response to AIDS resulting in untold suffering and death (White 2004). As *The Guardian* reported in 2015, amidst a recent flair-up of new sensationalized reports of HIV in the British Press, "Elton John is right that HIV will only be overcome 'by eradicating its most deadly symptom: stigma'" (Jones 2015).

Years later, Ebola coverage in the US media was also inaccurate, distorted and sensationalized. Television broadcasts designed graphics that screamed Ebola, and many news outlets ran bold headlines with dire predictions of potential global disease outbreaks. Sensationalized coverage on Fox Network was so extreme that it became the subject of ridicule on news satire. On the *Daily Show*, Jon Stewart (2015) mocked the contrived visuals, fearful alarmist headlines, and rudimentary graphics. The iconic microscope image of the virus itself so often repeated in the media became a meme that mocked the lack of substantive and informative coverage. Coverage was pervasive and repetitive, and raised fear among viewers that they could contract the virus. By January 2015, a CNN poll (2015) found that one quarter of Americans worried about getting Ebola. Researcher Janet Kwami found that US media coverage portrayed Africa in stereotypic terms, denigrated cultural rituals and blamed the people there for spreading the epidemic.[2] On August 29, 2014 *Newsweek* rekindled racist tropes of Africans with a cover story featuring a large portrait of a mountain guerrilla and a bold text claiming "A Back Door for Ebola: Smuggled Bushmeat could spark a US Epidemic."

In this highly informative chapter, Pat Fast presents the science behind these diseases, the actual health issues they raise, and the hope for discovering vaccines. By separating fact from fiction, the author allows the reader to compare the diseases to their media portrayals, and in doing so reveal the issues that need to be addressed to ensure accurate and informative reporting in the future.

Robin Andersen

Introduction

Epidemics, widespread and devastating spread of infectious disease, have existed throughout recorded history. The Bubonic Plague in the fourteenth century is thought to have killed at least half the European population, and influenza in 1917–18 killed many tens of millions, far more than direct WWI casualties. In modern times we have more and better tools to fight epidemics, but with a far larger and more interconnected population they have become more frequent and almost unlimited in size.

This article will discuss two modern plagues; Acquired Immunodeficiency Disease (AIDS), caused by Human Immunodeficiency Virus (HIV), and Ebola Virus Disease (EVD), caused by Ebolavirus (EBOV). Although these viruses are quite different, each has raised important issues with respect to popular understanding of disease, posing ethical dilemmas and challenging physicians, scientists, policymakers, and journalists to improve communication with those affected or at risk, in order to end these epidemics.

EVD and AIDS share some features—both started as mysterious, lethal diseases caused by viruses that frequently strike the young and healthy, without specific treatments. Both originated in Africa with viruses that jumped from animals to humans, and were identified about 35–40 years ago. In each case avoiding contact with infected people or their secretions is protective, though intimate contact is required to transmit HIV. There are, however, many important differences. Perhaps most important is that EVD moves fast; it strikes within days and about half the victims die. Those that do not, recover within a few weeks, though disability and occasionally low-level infection can linger. HIV infection is often silent for several years before it causes a lingering illness, and no one is cured. We now have highly effective treatments for HIV that keep HIV positive people healthy and reduce their chances of passing the infection to contacts. Some of these HIV drugs can even protect people from becoming infected. For EVD, there is no drug known to be effective for treatment or to prevent transmission. In 2014 HIV killed far more people, but EVD was viewed by the public as far more frightening.

HIV and AIDS

Nature of the Virus

HIV is a retrovirus (this article will use "HIV" to refer to HIV-1; a similar virus, HIV-2, which evolved independently, is much less widespread). Retroviruses use a unique method of reproducing that had initially been thought impossible. In our cells, the genes are made from deoxyribonucleic acid or DNA (the double helix), and information encoded by an "alphabet" of four chemical building blocks defines our nature. The information in DNA is translated to a similar code in ribonucleic acid (RNA), which in turn causes specific proteins to be assembled, making up the basic building blocks of cells and controlling the chemical reactions within them. The retroviruses work backwards—their genes are RNA, and once they invade a cell, they make DNA and insert it into the cell's own genetic material (a process called integration). Once integrated, the retrovirus genes cause RNA and protein to be made—which form the HIV virus. In the last 30 years, medicines have been created to block all these steps: virus entry into cells, creation of the DNA from the RNA viral genes, integration of DNA into the host genome, and formation of the new virus RNA. When used in combination these drugs can be highly effective for treatment, but they cannot eliminate HIV, which has hidden by integrating into many cells of the body.

HIV changes frequently; there is a small change in almost every virus particle made within an infected person's body (early in infection, billions of particles are produced). These changes allow the virus to "escape" from drug inhibition. They also make it a very elusive target for vaccines.

History

HIV has killed about 35 million people in 35 years. First described in 1981, the disease spread with increasing rapidity for over two decades, with a recent decline to "only" two million cases per year. Deaths, likewise, followed an increasing trajectory until the highly effective treatments, first developed in the mid 1990s, became widely available. As of the end of 2014, over 30 million people had died and about 37 million were living with HIV.[3]

When AIDS was first described, the cause was unknown. Something was destroying patients' immune systems, leaving them vulnerable to microorganisms that were usually harmless, and to some unusual cancers. An infection was suspected, but other possibilities were considered. Initially described in gay men in the US, similar symptoms were also found in the Caribbean, Africa, and Europe, in men, women, and infants. After several laboratories identified HIV as the cause of AIDS, diagnostic testing soon became a reality, and the harsh truth emerged about the enormous extent of the spread of this virus—it is a pandemic, an epidemic involving the entire world. HIV can cause illness shortly after infection, but this usually ends within weeks, and most people have no symptoms for several years. As a result, the virus spreads silently.

Prevention

Prevention of HIV infection is, in theory, straightforward: avoid intimate contact with the body fluids of people who are infected with HIV. This is hard to put into practice for many reasons, among which is that many HIV positive people do not know they are infected, and therefore do not take precautions to protect others. For example, in the United States, about 14 percent of all those infected with HIV are not aware of their status and the Centers for Disease Control and Prevention (CDC) estimates that these individuals may be responsible for about one third of the ~50,000 new infections annually (Hall et al. 2015). Frequent diagnostic testing, coupled with skilled counseling is one approach to reducing this pandemic, particularly when committed sexual partners are tested and informed together.[4]

Antiretroviral Drugs for Treatment and Prevention

With highly effective HIV therapy, death from AIDS is no longer inevitable, but lifelong treatment is needed. An enormous investment in AIDS treatment has gradually expanded drug availability.[5] Thanks in part to investment by richer countries, and in part to cheaper generic drugs made in middle income countries, many in the poorest countries can now receive this treatment. The situation is not stable: two million people are infected each year, their numbers are increasing, because HIV positive people live nearly as long as those without HIV infection if treated appropriately. New studies show that we should start treatment immediately after diagnosis, both to protect the health of the patient and to prevent him or her from transmitting it to others (Treatment as Prevention, TasP). To treat everyone infected with HIV now, our investment must roughly double. HIV negative people exposed to HIV can also be protected if they take the anti-retroviral drugs in advance (Pre-Exposure Prophylaxis, PrEP). Some governments are now recommending PrEP for people who have multiple exposures, or whose partner refuses treatment.[6] TasP and PrEP can only work in an environment with good education about HIV and easy access to diagnostic testing and to the drugs; the press/media can help decrease stigma and help HIV-infected people understand that they will benefit from early treatment.

Antibodies

Human antibodies (proteins that can attach to HIV) can neutralize HIV, that is block entry into human cells. A few HIV-positive humans make antibodies that are very strong and neutralize most of the many different HIV strains found worldwide. Some of these antibodies have been molecularly cloned and mass produced. Clinical studies are now just starting to find out whether the antibodies can prevent HIV infection, treat or even cure patients with HIV (Barouch and Deeks 2014).

Vaccines

Vaccines to prevent HIV infection have been elusive. Hundreds of vaccines have been designed and over 250 clinical trials have evaluated the best of these.[7] Although a vaccine was expected in the 1980s, the first evidence of protection by a vaccine was not available until 2009, and the vaccine (tested in Thailand) made history by providing some protection (Rerks-Narm et al. 2009), but it was not effective enough to be licensed. Several types of vaccine can protect animals against AIDS-like disease, caused by a similar virus. Vaccine development for HIV has been excruciatingly slow, hampered in part by scientific uncertainty, financial and bureaucratic obstacles, despite substantial government and private investment. The story of Ebola vaccine development, however, has cast new light on some bureaucratic and financial barriers to rapid vaccine development (see below).

Ebola Virus Disease (EVD)

Nature of the Virus

Ebolavirus has genetic material made of ribonucleic acid or RNA; it is in the Filovirus family (thread-like viruses). (There are five types of Ebolavirus, but in this article we will focus on Ebolavirus Zaire). An enzyme copies the virus's RNA genome, creating new viral genomes, and the RNA is translated to make EBOV proteins that assemble into new virus particles. EBOV can infect a number of different animals; apes and monkeys become ill like humans, but fruit bats in Africa are apparently carriers that suffer no harm. They and perhaps other animals form a "reservoir" from which the virus can emerge at any time.

History

EVD was described in the scientific literature in 1976. EBOV has a short incubation period, with symptoms appearing days to a few weeks after exposure; it kills more than half of those infected, and the others recover within weeks, though some effects may linger. The virus is found in secretions and on the skin, once symptoms begin and even after death, so it spreads to family or caregivers with relative ease.

EBOV caused about two dozen outbreaks between 1976 and 2013 in central and East Africa and in Gabon; about 400 people died in the largest outbreak. No outbreak had been identified in Guinea, Liberia, or Sierra Leone. In 2013, a new outbreak began in a remote region of the West African country of Guinea, near the borders of Sierra Leone and Liberia. The "public health" response to EVD, isolating patients and their contacts, providing protective equipment for health care workers, and burying bodies safely, had always limited outbreaks in the past, and appeared to be bringing the outbreak under control, leading to a deadly delay in recognizing how serious this outbreak was. Guinea and its neighbors were vulnerable; each had very limited health systems, due to low investment and the destructive civil wars in the region. EVD had not been seen previously in these countries, so the proper responses were not well understood. The isolated rural populations initially affected did not understand infectious diseases well. Borders were porous, and there was no good mechanism for a coordinated response. The people had little trust in their own governments, and less in foreigners. The outbreak smoldered, nearly died and recurred twice and then, spurred in large part by sick people traveling to the crowded capital cities, spread with frightening rapidity. A few doctors and organizations such as Doctors without Borders raised the alarm, but it was not until August 2015, about nine months after the outbreak was first identified, that the World Health Organization declared a Public Health Emergency of International Concern, and—belatedly—many international charities and government agencies swung into action.[8]

In September, the number of identified cases was doubling every two weeks, and it was predicted that, if the public health response did not reduce this rate, there would be over a million cases by January 2015. Fortunately, basic sanitation, isolation of sick patients, and safe burials did have an effect. By the end of the epidemic, in mid 2015, there had been over 11,000 identified deaths caused by EVD. But the greater toll, which may never be properly documented, was the extraordinary disruption of fragile and overstretched medical systems. Of the very small numbers of health workers in these countries, hundreds died. Ordinary illnesses remained untreated, either because travel and health care were disrupted, or because of fear—the population was afraid of a health system full of EVD patients, and health care workers feared to treat any patient with a fever, such as a pregnant woman who needed a caesarian delivery.

Prevention

Past outbreaks were controlled by basic "public health measures," such as providing protective clothing for health care workers, preventing contact between healthy people and the sick and dead, and isolating people who may have contracted the disease until it is known whether they are infected. These measures initially failed due to the extensive spread of EBOV, including to cities, the extreme lack of resources in the countries affected, and a failure of communication: given their history and worldview, it was very difficult for the affected communities to accept sanitation practices that contravened their social and religious practices.

Treatment

When people become sick with EVD, basic care such as providing fluids for rehydration, treating other conditions such as malaria and bacterial infections can save many lives. During the recent EBOV epidemic, dozens of potential virus-specific treatments were suggested; after these were evaluated at WHO by an international committee of experts (based on safety and effectiveness in animals), a few were tried. To date, no medicine has been proven effective against human disease.

Antibodies

People who have recovered from EVD have antibodies in their blood. During the epidemic, facilities were set up in West Africa to collect blood, treat it to make it safe, and use these antibodies for treatment. For logistic reasons, the studies started relatively late and data were limited. Like HIV, scientists have been able to molecularly clone and produce large quantities of very potent antibodies that neutralize EBOV. These show great promise in animal experiments, but because they were in very short supply during the EVD epidemic, they were not adequately tested, nor did they impact the epidemic significantly.

Vaccines

A number of potential vaccines against EBOV have been developed, and several can protect animals against the virus. During the recent epidemic, evidence was developed that one of them can protect humans. There is a lot to learn from the story of how testing of drugs and vaccines was managed during the EVD epidemic.

Vaccines for Prevention of EVD and AIDS

For both viruses, a major focus of scientific research has been to find a preventive vaccine. For AIDS, the search has gone on for nearly 30 years with very limited success. Several candidate vaccines work well to prevent infection of monkeys by a similar virus, called Simian Immunodeficiency Virus or SIV. Investment in AIDS vaccines has been enormous, with both academic and industry work largely subsidized by the US and European governments, and a significant investment from Canada, Japan, China, and India and from philanthropies, most notably the Bill & Melinda Gates Foundation. Testing so far has led to only one small success—a complex vaccination regimen tested in Thailand reduced the infection rate by 31 percent. Research continues, with exciting basic scientific discoveries and a new crop of candidates slowly approaching their definitive tests for protective efficacy.[9]

For EVD, investment in vaccine development by the Canadian and US governments meant that several candidate vaccines were in development when the disease struck in 2014. Two, in fact, had been extensively tested in animals and were ready in vials for human clinical trials. (Other vaccines had been tested, but were not as far along.) However, in part due to a limited sense of urgency, neither vaccine had gone through the necessary small clinical trials that are needed to prove they are safe and induce immune responses likely to be protective. Once the epidemic was officially recognized by WHO, an international effort was mounted to test these vaccines.

EBOV vaccine testing in clinical trials occurred with extraordinary speed, and lessons can be drawn from this both for HIV vaccine development and for other future epidemics.

Ethical Dilemmas

In 2014, as the world's experts met repeatedly in Geneva and near Washington DC to discuss testing of vaccines, antibodies, drugs, and diagnostic tests for EBOV, the discussions of what would be ethical played out publicly and fast. Among the questions were

1. Who should receive experimental treatments or vaccines, and when?
2. How should the trials be conducted? Given widespread discomfort with using placebos (harmless but useless substances indistinguishable from the active drug or vaccine), how could data from trials be interpreted?

To make sure that comparisons between treated and untreated people are valid, clinical trials use random assignment and usually compare the drug or vaccine to a placebo using a code (blinding) to keep staff and trial participants from knowing who gets the experimental medicine and who gets placebo. Most officials from the EVD-affected countries were not willing to accept placebos. How could one explain to a terrified and critically ill patient the idea that a coin toss would determine whether they would get an experimental medicine or a sugar pill or salt water injection? The alternative, randomization to experimental treatment versus basic treatment without giving a placebo, was not as widely discussed. Most trials of treatments proceeded in a relatively uncontrolled manner, and little useful information was gleaned. As of today, there is still no proven therapy for EVD (Cohen and Enserink 2016). The concept of randomization and blinding of clinical trials is one that is far from intuitive for most people, and a great challenge for journalists is to explain how these concepts lead to the most reliable and rapid decisions (Cox et al. 2014).

For vaccines, as pointed out by the US National Bioethics Commission, the issues are different. People receiving the vaccines are healthy, though there is a risk they will be infected, and they can give consent. The US Food and Drug Administration (FDA) took a strong stand that randomization and blinding were essential for interpretable results in vaccine trials. Still, many felt that all who would be at risk of exposure to EBV should get the vaccine; this was based on a belief that the vaccine would work, even though in reality there was a chance the vaccine would be useless or even harmful.

Vaccines are among the safest of medical interventions, and some wondered whether these untested vaccines could be immediately used in West Africa, in the hope that they would quell the growing epidemic. But tradition dictated that small safety tests should come first, and there was also concern that Africans would feel they were being used as "guinea pigs," a common accusation that has some basis in historical events. As a result, even though the death toll was doubling every two weeks, in the late summer of 2014 the decision was taken to start with small trials, enrolling people who were not at risk of infection. Plans were for rapid Phase 1 trials in the US, Europe, and in African countries that were not affected by EVD, then proceeding to larger trials in the affected countries to prove whether the vaccines were protective. A program such as this would normally require 5–10 years. How fast could it be done? The risk was great that two opportunities would be lost—first, to prove whether the vaccines worked or not, and second (assuming they would work) to help stop the spread of EVD.

Ebola Vaccine Trials

The Phase I trials started in September–November of 2014. The trials were supported by the Wellcome Trust and the Bill & Melinda Gates Foundation and by the US, Canadian, and

European governments. The process moved at (comparatively) lightning speed, with bureaucratic processes streamlined, funding and regulatory decisions made in a tenth the usual time, various ethical, scientific, and regulatory committees working in parallel instead of sequentially, and many sleepless nights. The answers, from the US, Canada, Switzerland, the UK, Germany, Kenya, Mali, and Gabon were all clear—the vaccines were safe enough for deployment in larger controlled trials, and they did evoke immune responses that would be expected to protect people.

In February of 2015 (an astoundingly fast progression), the first of the efficacy trials started in West Africa. Trials in the three affected countries were designed very differently. A coalition led by the US National Institutes of Health (specifically the National Institute of Allergy and Infectious Diseases) worked with the Liberian government, the US CDC, planned a trial in Sierra Leone. The Liberia and Sierra Leone trials were fairly conventional, requiring enrolment of over 20 thousand participants, a very time-consuming procedure. As the EVD epidemic was brought under control, the chance of completing the trials slipped away.

A coalition led by WHO (supported by the Wellcome Trust) and the Norwegian Government worked with the Guinea government on a trial called "Ebola ça suffit" (meaning "Ebola this is enough").[10] The WHO trial in Guinea was a very innovative and unconventional design, using the principle that eventually wiped out smallpox—"ring vaccination." Rather than vaccinating everyone in a region, the trial focused on the people at highest risk. When a case of EVD was discovered, a team raced to the village involved and asked everyone eligible if they would agree to participate in the trial. All willing participants received the vaccine. Half of the villages were randomly selected to be vaccinated immediately, and half to get the vaccine three weeks later. The number of cases in the delayed vaccination versus immediate vaccination groups was compared. This trial provided evidence that the vaccine is highly effective (Henao-Restrepo et al. 2015). Because of the unconventional design, short experimental period, and small size, the evidence is not considered final proof.

Social Context

Both EVD and AIDS evoke great fear, and people who are infected, or who are thought to be at risk, may be stigmatized (Gonsalves and Staley 2015). In the early days of the AIDS epidemic, women who were found to be HIV positive in Africa were sometimes blamed for bringing infection into the home and beaten or thrown out of their homes. The US AIDS epidemic was initially characterized as associated with gay men and minority populations. In New York and elsewhere, some hospitals or doctors refused treatment for AIDS patients and undertakers refused to accept bodies for burial. Children were prevented from attending some schools in the earlier days of the epidemic. Immigration bans were instituted by many countries.

During the AIDS epidemic, many public and private acts of heroism helped to turn the tide of discrimination. In the US, when sports stars such as Magic Johnson and Arthur Ashe, and Elizabeth Glaser, the wife of a popular actor, revealed that they were HIV positive, it helped to turn public opinion. Of course, this influence was due largely to the media and public attention they garnered. More influential over time, perhaps, was the repeated experience of realizing that friends or family members—"people like us"—were at risk or infected with HIV.

For EVD in West Africa, there was also fear, stigma, disbelief, and conflict with the government. In the isolated rural region initially involved, many people lacked a clear understanding of viruses and how they cause disease. Deep suspicion of governments, exacerbated both by ethnic divisions and by recent civil wars, led to reluctance to accept government warnings. A conflict arose, in particular, when the health authorities forbade traditional burial customs that involved washing and touching the bodies of the deceased. This was known to carry a very high risk of infection, but these rites were an integral part of traditional burial rites. Even when EVD reached the crowded capital cities, there was initial skepticism about the reality of EVD. People heard that EVD was not real, while official messages emphasized it was lethal, there was no treatment (in fact, basic care can be life-saving), and those suspected of infection should be taken to hospitals. Once at the hospital, patients were separated from families, even though traditionally African families stay with patients to provide food and care that often cannot be provided by under-resourced, crowded hospitals. So, the sense that revealing one's illness meant dying, alone, far from home, and possibly neglected, did not encourage compliance.

In West Africa, during the EVD outbreak of 2014–15, some travel restrictions were instituted and some communities suffered from being restricted to the extent that obtaining water and food was very difficult. Africans (in general) were subject to discrimination or heightened scrutiny in travel to many countries. Volunteers who went to Africa to care for EVD victims were sometimes quarantined when they returned home. These problems were due, in part, to fear generated by news stories about EVD that did not explain that risk for disease transmission begins when symptoms begin.

Community Interactions

The rural regions where the initial outbreak began are remote, and access to modern communications is limited. In addition, cultural beliefs are very different from those of Western medical professionals who design public health interventions and clinical trials. Illness is often believed to be due to a disruption of the natural order, which involves obtaining an expert diagnosis of a person's cultural or spiritual transgressions as a cause of illness and a need to separate death of village members from that of outsiders, including those who are literally away from the village and those who have strayed from the cultural norms. Burial rituals, which involve washing a body, are considered necessary for the spirit of the dead to be at peace (Fairhead 2016).

It is easy to understand how these beliefs clash with the routine procedures of case finding, contact tracing, transport of patients or even those suspected of incubating the infection to remote Ebola Treatment Units or hospitals, and prohibiting anyone from touching a dead body. Communities were "reticent" or even rebellious. Covert resistance involved hiding sickness and helping those who were ill to flee, which served to spread the epidemic to neighboring villages, across national borders, and to crowded capital cities. Some resistance was violent, and teams travelling to the countryside were at some risk of being killed.

To counter the lack of trust and resistance, the international anthropology community set up the Anthropology Response Platform, with specific projects for Guinea, Liberia, and Sierra Leone. Teams were set up to consult in person with community leaders, to build trust, and to find culturally acceptable approaches to public health measures, and to train villagers and traditional healers in how to minimize disease transmission.

Communication Challenges: Present and Future

Both EVD and AIDS epidemics have benefited from extraordinary public investments, particularly on the part of the United States, Canada, and European countries. Attitudes toward the disease are undoubtedly shaped by the press, reporting both on the danger to ordinary citizens in these countries that they might be directly affected and to their spirit of altruism and concern. A corollary is that novelty sometimes overrides other factors, leaving the public with an unreasonable degree of fear, followed by an unreasonable degree of complacency. In-depth reporting is needed to allow the public and policymakers to understand the true situation, that rapid action to contain new and old epidemics is the right thing—for both humanitarian and self-protective reasons.

A particularly difficult area is explaining the process of clinical trials. Even to very sophisticated medical professionals, the concept of involving an individual in an experimental clinical trial is difficult. Traditionally, those who carry out a trial and those who participate are not aware whether they are using an active drug or vaccine or an inactive but identical-appearing placebo. Explaining the need to use randomized and blinded trials is an important role for an educated and skilled journalist.

Conclusion

The epidemics of AIDS and EVD share many characteristics—highly lethal viruses that jumped from animals and then spread by contact between humans. These two modern plagues, which began to spread over three decades apart, have much in common. Medically, they differ, but the response to the initial identification of these epidemics had many common features. Fear, ignorance, and stigmatization of those suffering from the illness have played obvious roles in our failure to contain these viruses; their control (EVD) or mitigation (AIDS) owes much to changes in public understanding and community action, as well as to scientific advances. In each case, there was a heroic response by a relatively small cadre of medical personnel and lay persons.

For both diseases, the risk is not over (with 2 million new HIV infections per year, and a menacing reservoir of Ebola virus in animals). Continued education of the public and policy-makers is needed to support the moral, political, and financial commitment needed to conquer these diseases. Each has extraordinary lessons to teach us about the need to involve communities in every aspect of the fight, from containing spread through humane and well-accepted public health measures to designing and executing complex clinical trials. An informed and sophisticated ethical discussion is essential, taking into account both scientific and cultural realities. Communications must be viewed in the broadest context, methods include newspapers, radio and television, scientific journals, the internet, social media, popular culture, and face-to-face community discussions led by mediators who understand both worlds.

For most of us, the personal risk from EVD is vanishingly small. HIV, however, is all around us, taking a continuing personal and economic toll. And hovering on the horizon are new risks—Zika, Chikungunya, and Dengue viruses and, dwarfing all of these, lethal Avian Influenza viruses in wild birds and domestic fowl, should they evolve to spread from person to person. Many other potential epidemic or pandemic diseases lurk, and it will behoove us to examine these histories and draw lessons, celebrating successes and learning to respond better in the future. Delays are deadly, concerted action can pay off in control of disease and development of new diagnostics, medicines, and vaccines. We need to prepare now, to cooperate and break the paradigms of bureaucratic delay, to invest in medical advances before the crisis (Farrar and Piot 2015; Plotkin, Mahmoud, and Farrar 2015), to listen and communicate in whatever way is needed, to support affected populations and the heroes who work on the front lines. Most of this was accomplished for EBV in 2014–15, but now we need to finish the job—rebuild the medical systems in West African countries that were affected and get a licensed vaccine into our stockpiles. And for the plagues to come, we must be ready.

Notes

1. See for example, "Remembering the Early Days of Gay Cancer." NPR, May 8, 2006, available at: www.npr.org/templates/story/story.php?storyId=5391495
2. Paper presented by Janet Kwami, "From News Magazines to Twitter: African Stereotyping in Global Media Coverage of Ebola" (Ferman University) IAMCR Annual Conference, Montreal, July 2015.
3. UNAIDS website, available at: www.UNAIDS.org
4. CDC, "Couples Testing and Counselling Intervention and Training Curriculum," available at: www.cdc.gov/globalaids/resources/prevention/chct.html.
5. www.UNAIDS.org
6. www.avac.org
7. IAVI Clinical Trials Database, available at: www.iavi.org
8. www.who.int
9. IAVI Clinical Trials Database, available at: www.iavi.org
10. www.ClinicalTrials.gov

Further Reading and Resources

AIDS Vaccine Advocacy Coalition (AVAC), www.avac.org (Advocacy and information on HIV/AIDS prevention.)

Center for Disease Control and Prevention, http//cdc.gov (A valuable source of information on epidemics and protective measures.)

Clinical Trials Database, www.clinicaltrials.gov (A comprehensive registry of US based or funded clinical trials. Other useful databases are created by WHO and its member states and regions.)

CNN. (2015) "CNN Poll: One in four Americans worry about Getting Ebola," September 16, 2015, available at: www.cnn.com/2014/09/16/politics/cnn-poll-ebola/

Ebola Response Anthropology Platform. www.ebola-anthropology.net/ (A consolidated web site for various anthropologists' work on Ebola, describing community outreach and mobilization of the Diaspora.)

David France, director "How to Survive a Plague," 2012. FILM. (Shows the intense conflict surrounding the early AIDS epidemic and contribution of activists to development of treatments.)

International AIDS Vaccine Initiative (IAVI), www.iavi.org, including its Clinical Trials Database with comprehensive information on all HIV vaccine clinical trials to date.

Journal Websites

The Lancet Ebola Resource Centre, www.ebola.thelancet.com/

Science Ebola Collection, www.sciencemag.org/site/extra/ebola/

The New England Journal of Medicine: Ebola Outbreak, www.nejm.org/page/ebola-outbreak.

(These journals provide easy access to their articles on EVD through disease-specific portals.)

Shilts, R. 1987. "And the Band Played On: Politics, People, and the AIDS Epidemic", St. Martin's Press (A comprehensive description of the early days of the AIDS epidemic.)

United Nations AIDS, UNAIDS.org (Definitive source on the AIDS epidemic.)

World Health Organization, apps.who.int/ebola/ebola-situation-reports (Definitive source on the Ebola outbreak.)

References

Barouch, D., and Deeks, S. (2014) "Immunologic Strategies for HIV-1 Remission and Eradication," *Science*, 345 (6193): 169–174.

Cohen, J., and Enserink, M. (2016) "As Ebola Epidemic Draws to a Close, a Thin Scientific Harvest," *Science*, 351 (6268): 12–13.

CNN. (2015) "CNN Poll: One in four Americans worry about Getting Ebola," September 16, 2015, available at: www.cnn.com/2014/09/16/politics/cnn-poll-ebola/

Cox, E., Borio, L., and Temple, R. (2014) "Evaluating Ebola Therapies: The Case for RCTs," *The New England Journal of Medicine*, 371 (25): 2350–2351.

Cullen, T. (2003) "HIV/AIDS: 20 Years of Press Coverage," *Australian Studies in Journalism*, 12: 64–82.

Fairhead, J. (2016) "The Significance of Death, Funerals and the After-life in Ebola-hit Sierra Leone, Guinea and Liberia: Anthropological Insights into Infection and Social Resistance," Draft—October 2014 j.r.fairhead@sussex.ac.uk, available at: www.heart-resources.org/wp-content/uploads/2014/10/FairheadEbolaFunerals8Oct.pdf

Farrar, J., and Piot, P. (2014) "The Ebola Emergency: Immediate Action, Ongoing Strategy," *New England Journal of Medicine*, 371: 1545–1546.

Gonsalves, G., and Staley, P. (2014) "Panic, Paranoia, and Public Health: The AIDS Epidemic's Lessons for Ebola," *New England Journal of Medicine*, 371: 2348–2349.

Hall, H., An, Q., Tang, T., et al. (2015) "Prevalence of Diagnosed and Undiagnosed HIV Infection: United States, 2008–2012," *Morbidity and Mortality Weekly Report*, 64 (24): 657–662.

Henao-Restrepo, M. A., Longini, I., Eggar, M., and Dean, N., et al. (2015) "Efficacy and Effectiveness of an rVSV-vectored Vaccine Expressing Ebola Surface Glycoprotein: Interim Results from the Guinea Ring Vaccination Cluster-randomised Trial," *Lancet*, 386 (9996): 857–866.

Jones, O. (2015. "We Can't Go Back to the Deadly HIV Stigma of the 1908s," *The Guardian* (November 11, 2015), available at: www.theguardian.com/commentisfree/2015/nov/11/hiv-stigma-1980s

Karpf, A. (1990) *Doctoring the Media: The Reporting of Health and Medicine*, London: Routledge.

Plotkin, S. A., Mahmoud, A. A., and Farrar, J. (2015) "Establishing a Global Vaccine-Development Fund," *The New England Journal of Medicine*, 373 (4): 297–300.

Rerks-Ngarm, S., Pitisuttithum, P., Nitayaphan, S., Kaewkungwal, J. et al. (2009) "*Vaccination with ALVAC and AIDSVAX to prevent HIV-1 infection in Thailand*," The New England Journal of Medicine, 361 (23): 2209–2220.

Stewart, J. (2014) "Au Bon Panic," *The Daily Show* (October 14, 2014), available at: www.cc.com/video-clips/kgr74h/the-daily-show-with-jon-stewart-au-bon-panic

White, A. (2004) "Reagan's AIDS Legacy/Silence = Death", *SFGate* (June 8, 2004), available at: www.sfgate.com/opinion/openforum/article/Reagan-s-AIDS-Legacy-Silence-equals-death-2751030.php

23

PLURAL+ MEDIA LITERACY, AND VOICES OF THE YOUNG

Platforms for Including Youth-Produced Media in Humanitarian Dialogue

Jordi Torrent

In the current humanitarian crisis, pictures and stories about children and young people have been widely circulated in the global media arena. Such media coverage serves to illustrate the refugee crisis, to evoke compassion, to persuade global publics to donate, to aid organizations, to accept, and to care enough to effect governmental policy on migrants and immigration. What rarely appears in media are the actual voices of children and youth themselves, their ideas, desires, demands, hopes, and fears. In essence, they are rarely invited to actually participate in media creations, productions, and programs, in a meaningful way to tell their own stories or to engage in public dialogue.

Of course youth, as well as adults, are largely dependent on media organizations and humanitarian workers to tell their stories during crises, as well as during the often prolonged periods of displacement. But youthful voices are also usually excluded from the wider global dialogue that includes humanitarian affairs in public discourse in general. Yet they are disproportionately affected by the humanitarian crises that have come to define our world. So many aspects of current crises affect young people; particularly the issue that was debated at the first World Humanitarian Summit in Istanbul, Turkey in May 2016; that is "protracted crises" and the relationship between crisis, displacement, and refugees:

> Protracted crises are the new normal. Humanitarian appeals today last for seven years on average and 89 percent of humanitarian financing goes to crises lasting more than 3 years. The most shocking statistic is that the average length of displacement is now 17 years. *This is enough for a child to be born, schooled (or not tragically) and reach adulthood. Doing so with nothing but basic, short-term humanitarian assistance is an outrage to the idea that all children in the world deserve development opportunities.*[1] [Emphasis added]

Indeed, this phenomenon holds true in times when young people are not part of a humanitarian crisis. Yet the wider global dialogue that includes humanitarian issues carries on without their voices, even as they are disproportionately affected. This is ironic, as we constantly speak of youth,[2] of youth challenges, of youth shortcomings, of youth innovative trends, of youth violence, of youth crime, of youth fashion, etc. But we seldom facilitate venues and opportunities for youth to significantly express themselves in ways that their visions and voices are really heard and taken into consideration by the adults. In the absence of youthful voices, adults are making decisions about the world that young people themselves must live in. On a global level adults are in control of a discursive environment that defines the parameters of debate from local issues to foreign affairs. Yet in a short period of time, youth will be asked to manage a world they will inherit from adults.

While it is true that most young people in the industrialized world are in fact constantly communicating,[3] with their dozens of followers on YouTube, their hundreds of friends on Facebook, their fans on Instagram, or Snapchat, how often do adults see such communication or take into consideration the media messages that youth produce? Certainly, digital marketers are sniffing out social media platforms for the betterment of the micro-target-placement of their commercial products. But the great majority of youth media messages are not within the ken of the adult world. When adults do pay attention, it is usually because of the recurring media agenda decribing the latest youthful "moral panic," a common framework of press reporting on youth media issues. Driscoll and Gregg (2008) identify this phenomenon as "panic" over social networking sites that dominate current media coverage of the activities of "wired" youth."[4] In this environment the voices and media of young people are usually not taken into consideration by political analysts drafting policies, regulations, and social frameworks.

We only really hear about youth when the news media communicate to us about entertainment, moral panics, sports, crime, or crisis. At most, we see them screaming (do we hear them?) at mediatized political marches and demonstrations. We seldom, if ever, hear, stop, and listen to young people's opinions on social affairs of political relevance. If we take into consideration that about 20 percent of the current world population—about 2 billion individuals—is between 10 and 24 years of age, this lack of opportunities for youth to voice their opinions and visions by participating in public dialogue is indeed a shortcoming of our societies. Such exclusion could result, and in some places has, in violent forms of expression.

As a society there are many way to incorporate young people into public discourse, to encourage and pay attention to their ideas, desires, and visions. We need to set in place channels of authentic communication, to actively engage in outreach and help youth find their voices and produce media messages of political relevance. And we must do so not as a form of "cultural luxury" or "political afterthought," but as a way to peacefully provide opportunities for the advancement of a humanity that is seriously taking into account the United Nations Sustainable Development Goals (SDGs).[5]

Media Literacy

The question is no longer, if it ever was, "to what extent does the opportunity to produce media empower young people?" Of course youth-produced media empowers youth. But to truly empower youth on a global level, youth media productions must also empower the broader social frameworks of public debate. They must allow the voices of youth to be heard at all levels of social discourse and to participate in ongoing discussions and debates that affect the lives of the young. In addition, for young people to become more than simply passive receivers of adult messages we must foster the means to help them articulate their own philosophical foundations and social visions. This would require that they are able to communicate in a way that adults can truly hear their voices. Youth media truly empowers them and society when produced within the framework of Media Literacy. Media Literacy provides young communicators with an ethical context and a framework for critical thinking. When applied to young people producing their own media, it allows the young to elevate their messages to relevant communication, to messages that adults should pay attention to. It is media on target, even if the aim, at times, is "solely" artistic creativity.

Expanding the Liminal Space of Youth Media

Youth media and Media Literacy experts call our attention to the "liminal" peculiarity of youth-produced media.[6] Youth are producing media in this space situated between the "school" and "home." This liminal uniqueness of youth-produced media is in fact directly connected to the essence of youth itself: between childhood and adulthood. It is the uniqueness of that liminal moment in the development of our life and character that makes youth strong and fragile at the same time.

I would like to argue that youth-produced media should not be a "liminal" activity but, on the contrary, an activity right at the forefront of education. Media Literacy curriculums should be developed to offer courses at all primary and secondary school levels. This can be done through interdisciplinary collaborations between communication and the liberal arts; developing courses in media and history, social studies, language and art, etc. Just as we are teaching children to read and write and reflect on printed texts, we should also include instruction on how to decode the wide range of audiovisual messages that flood young media, exposing young people to thousands of commercial and social messages on a daily basis. Situating the media messages that infiltrate and are embedded in all aspects of youth's life within a critical and analytical framework is essential to any contemporary educational project. As we have said many times, the concept of "literacy" needs to be expanded and must include these other forms of literacy, in which individuals need to be fluent in order to be truly active members of contemporary societies. We do a disservice to the young when we fail to impart such skills. We leave them to be misled and influenced by commercial messages when we don't provide the analytical tools needed to discern differences between persuasive messages and information, between serious news reporting and biased discourse.

Youth-produced media should not be considered a liminal activity but an integral part of education itself and, in fact, developed as part of the normal experience of being aware in our mediatized societies. But, again, Media Literacy should be the platform, the knowledge, the ethical framework, that facilitates—and encourages—the production of youth media. As part of this practice, channels supporting the distribution and outreach of these youth-produced media messages should be put in place. In fact, all mainstream media platforms (TV and radio networks, corporate media Internet pages, etc.) should include as part of their programming and content youth-produced programs and messages.

These actions would certainly facilitate a process where youth feels included in the decision-making activities of their communities; or, at least, feel included in the information package that feeds the arguments of policymaking practices. Youth will then feel truly included in the societies they inhabit. Becoming actual participants in the process of building a new world, a world moving toward the full implementation of the United Nations Sustainable Development Goals.

PLURAL+

An example of these kinds of efforts currently being put into action is the PLURAL+ Youth Video Festival on Migration, Diversity and Social Inclusion. Developed by the United National Alliance of Civilizations (UNAOC) and the International Organization for Migration (IOM), PLURAL+ (along with the support of its partners), is a multi-media platform of distribution that organizes and facilitates global outreach for youth-produced media. We encourage young producers to use media to tell their stories and express their opinions on migration and other social inclusion topics.[7] We do this by reaching young people through our partners, and by announcing a call for video productions online, and we receive (scores) of short videos.

Youth-Produced Media Festivals

Empowering young people through the distribution of their media messages is a strong signal that points to the fact that we adults take seriously social inclusion by of all members of our communities, young and old alike.

PLURAL+ videos have been seen over a million times on different Internet platforms and are constantly being presented at conferences and festivals around the world, providing in this way a true opportunity for young people's voices to be present in the adult's conversations. We also create Discussion Guides that summarize the material. Through this process, PLURAL+ videos are being used as points of departure for in-depth conversation on social topics in formal and informal educational settings.[8]

There are also other organizations and NGOs engaged in encouraging youthful voices in public dialogue by enhancing media skills through training. These relevant initiatives support youth-produced media and provide opportunities for the outreach of youth voices in the media around the world. Just to mention a couple, among many: WADADA News for Kids[9] and UNICEF's OneMinutesJr.[10] But I would like to address something else; something that I think is of capital importance, something very much connected to the significance of Media Literacy as the ethical framework that I mentioned above.

Youth, Media, and Global Citizenship

We live in an era of conflict and instability brought about by worsening economic, social, and environmental conditions globally. In this historical moment much attention is given to "Preventing Violent Extremism" (PVE) initiatives. In light of these concerns, Media Literacy should be at the forefront of such initiatives. They provide a pointed opportunity to call attention to current, now global, education policy that focuses primarily on curriculum defined as STEM—science, technology, engineering and math. In our opinion, the singular priority given to science is a recipe for trouble. Insisting on STEM education and pushing aside the Humanities—art, sociology, history, literature—will only further develop mindsets formed on immobile views of the world. These trends in education are part of the global movement toward business priorities in education and the corporatization of our schools. The insistence on STEM education is justified by the assertion that STEM's skills are marketable values in the professional world of the "knowledge societies"; that youth well versed in STEM will find jobs and prosper in global competitive market economies. But the fact is that the percentage of STEM-educated youth joining terrorist groups is proportionally much larger than youth following Humanities (religious) education. "Immunizing the Mind," a research paper by Martin Rose published by the British Council in November of 2015, confirms this trend.[11] Danielle Allen, Professor at the Harvard Graduate School of Education, echoes these concerns in her May 2016 article "What is education for?" She argues that "civic education" should be taught as compensatory pedagogy to our societies insistence on STEM. Allen says "if the STEM fields gave us the mass in "mass democracy," the humanities and social sciences gave us the democracy."[12]

Within this framework Media Literacy is viewed as an essential component for the training and nurturing of global citizenship. Media Literacy taught within a humanities curriculum, in addition to nurturing the skills needed for youth-produced media, should be essential components of the core curriculum of primary and secondary schooling. We must remind our policymakers that the development of critical thinking skills and the advancement of civic education—key to the "pursuit of happiness" promised to all by our legal charters—are indeed part of the Media Literacy educational context.

Examples of Youth-Produced Media

The mission to support the mediatization of civic education through youth-produced media is a key element of the critical thinking skills developed through Media Literacy pedagogy, which is supported by PLURAL+. PLURAL+ videos often illustrate magnificently this enticing combination of technology, critical analysis, and civic education. Just to showcase a few:

Maina: The Little Bride

This video was produced by a teenager in India. It very subtlety criticizes, through the gaze of children, the story of young Maina, following her as she becomes a child bride. As her story unfolds, viewers see many details of the cruelties inherent in child marriage. As an underage mother, the weight of her responsibilities reaches far beyond her young age.[13]

Airstrip

"Airstrip" is a production by a First Nation teenager from Quebec, Canada. It poetically and poignantly presents the viewer with the emotional, cultural and environmental impact that the building of a military airstrip has on the Anishnabe people.[14]

Lost

"Lost" is a documentary production from 24-year old Mohammed Alfaraj in Saudi Arabia. The piece describes the effects that the *stateless status* given to individuals in that country has on the identity formation of children.[15]

These are just three recent examples of the kind of videos that PLURAL+ recognizes and supports through multi-platform global distribution. These videos are good examples of youth-produced media that promote ethical narratives and critical thinking about important and relevant social topics.

The last couple of years PLURAL+ has received many videos produced by teenage Syrian refugees living in camps in Jordan and Lebanon. They are the result of informal media education workshops run by NGOs such as Save the Children, Beirut DC, as well as UNICEF and other United Nations agencies. These are the young people who are displaced and have grown up in refugee camps once thought to be temporary housing. These videos offer extraordinary and intimate counter-narratives to the dominant media representation of refugees so prevalent in mainstream media. In this regard, internet fare is not much better or more comprehensive. The videos created by young refugees on the other hand, are able to bring the variety of complex issues relevant to youth into humanitarian discourse. Through visual storytelling youth-produced video articulates the hopes, dreams, and interior landscapes of young refugees, providing them with much-needed inner emotional release. In these videos young refugees talk to us directly, not through the mediation of foreign media professionals, but through the media messages that they themselves produce. Visual storytelling also connects young refugees with the world, and sparks dialogue about humanitarian issues with adults in global venues wherever they are shown. Supporting this kind of global outreach and providing distribution channels and networks to facilitate such media production and its discussion is the main purpose of PLURAL+.[16]

Notes

1. S. Cliffe (2016) "Why We Urgently Need More Collaboration to Solve Long-term Humanitarian Crises," *The Guardian*, May 24, 2016.
2. We understand "youth" as the age group recognized as such by the United Nations: individuals between 15 and 24 years of age, un.org/youthenvoy
3. Although 97 percent of humanity has access to cellphones, currently only 40 percent of humans have access to the Internet. And just about 30 percent have access to smartphones.
4. C. Driscoll, and M. Gregg (2008) "Broadcast Yourself: Moral Panic, Youth Culture and Internet Studies," in U. Rodrigues, and B. Smaill (Eds.), *Youth, Media and Culture in the Asia-Pacific Region*, Cambridge: Cambridge Scholars Press.
5. Regarding UN Sustainable Development Goals, please see: un.org/sustainabledevelopment/sustainable-development-goals
6. Please see S. Goodman and C. Cocca (2014) "Spaces of Action: Teaching Critical Literacy for Community Empowerment in the Age of Neoliberalism," Department of Politics, Economics, and Law, State University of New York; and R. Hobbs and D. Cooper Moore (2015) "Cinekyd: Exploring the Origins of Youth Media Production," *Journal of Media Literacy Education*, 6 (2): 23–34.
7. Please see: pluralplus.unaoc.org
8. Please see: pluralplus.unaoc.org/resources/plural-discussion-guides-multilingual
9. Please see: wadadanewsforkids.org
10. Please see: theoneminutesjr.org
11. Please see: britishcouncil.org/sites/default/files/immunising_the_mind_working_paper.pdf
12. Please see: bostonreview.net/forum/danielle-allen-what-education
13. See the video here: pluralplus.unaoc.org/2013-winners/maina-the-little-bride
14. See the video here: http://pluralplus.unaoc.org/2015-winners/airstrip/
15. See the video here: http://pluralplus.unaoc.org/2015-winners/lost/
16. Look for videos coming from Jordan and Lebanon here: http://pluralplus.unaoc.org/2015-winners/

24

THE VOICE OF THE PEOPLE IN AN AGE OF ENVIRONMENTAL CRISIS

Pope Francis, the Earth Community, Human Rights, and Independent Media

Robin Andersen and DeeDee Halleck

I urgently appeal, then, for a new dialogue about how we are shaping the future of our planet. We need a conversation which includes everyone, since the environmental challenge we are undergoing, and its human roots, concern and affect us all.
(Laudato si, Encyclical Letter, Pope Francis)

We know the best thing is to give voice to the voiceless, and in our area the women are voiceless . . . The listeners are so inspired by the programs. They realize that these are real issues that we are facing.
(Lydia Ajono, founder of a radio station in the town
of Bolgatanga, Ghana at the 2015 Indymedia
Convergence in Accra, Ghana)

The community where Lydia Ajono lives, in the Upper East region in Ghana (a 20-hour bus ride from the capital Accra), is suffering from illegal logging of mahogany trees within tribal lands. Cutting the trees has changed the moisture balance and the streams are drying up. Ajono's radio programming has been key to the community's response to the logging company and brought the issue to the forefront of debate by local political leaders. In his Encyclical Letter on ecology, Pope Francis refers openly to the plight of the poor in an age of environmental crisis offering a critique of industrial practices and their destruction of the natural world, and of humanity itself. He argues that preserving human cultures is as important as guarding against any further loss of biodiversity. Both Ajono and the Pope understand that an inclusive dialogue is needed if humanity is to reverse the on-going destruction of the planet and forestall further human suffering. Such solutions will require fundamental transformations in the way we live and the way we conceptualize our place within the natural world.

This chapter explores the role Indymedia has played in giving voice to those whose struggles, experiences, traditions, and ideas have been largely excluded from public discourse. Global mainstream media covers official meetings such as the G8 summit and the Copenhagen and Paris Climate talks where élites meet to determine future economic and environmental policies. At these meetings the people with alternative visions are on the margins, relegated to the outside spaces of the streets, and as such have become the victims of state violence. Media coverage of demonstrators focuses on themes of disruption and social chaos, but rarely if ever gives voice to the ideas, objections, reasons for resisting, or alternatives to the policies being discussed inside, "at the table." That is left to alternative media, which occasionally make an incursion into mainstream coverage, but certainly does not lead to full and uninhibited discourse in global media.

The people mostly excluded from such debates are those with little wealth and power; they are the ones on the frontlines of climate change, those who lose their land and livelihoods as first-world demands for commodities and financial gain lead to the exploitation of the last of the dwindling resources of a globe already heaving under pollution, drought, over extraction, and militarized response. These people are the bulk of humanity and also comprise the people in solidarity with them. They do not include corporate wealth, the extractive and financial industries, or their official representatives. They constitute the vast abstract numbers of those now living everywhere on earth, in the global south, as well as in the world's most developed countries, and they are a wealth of knowledge. Their struggles for human rights— for drinkable water, to defend their tribal lands—is a struggle extending all the way to new conceptions of our place in the natural world and the assertion that "Another World is Possible." They struggle for a future globe, one defined by peace and security, instead of ever-increasing humanitarian crises, with the knowledge that we must re-conceptualize "humanity" to ensure the survival of the planet. This knowledge is also imparted at global meetings, ones with titles such as the World Social Forum, or the World People's Summit on Climate Change and Rights of Nature, and they work in collaboration with Indymedia. Such ideas and experiences are also shared at Indymedia convergences, which support community members and help give voice to their experiences and traditional knowledge.

These are at least some of the voices that Pope Francis calls into the global dialogue. In addition, many of the ways in which the Pope re-conceptualizes a new role for humanity on an ecologically sustainable planet, parallel the discussions at the People's Summits. This paper can offer only a glimpse of the vast global movements taking place around the world and the people who risk their lives documenting their struggles. This is also a story of the development of the idea for "human security," and a new way to conceptualize an alternative future, one not dominated by environmental chaos, humanitarian disasters and endless militarized conflict. This narrative demands confronting the "root causes," in the words of Pope Francis, of global instability and environmental destruction, and it is a narrative told mostly in the margins, by the people themselves, infrequently heard over mainstream global media channels.

We will begin at the turn of the twenty-first century, with an illustration of the treatment, by police and media, of those who formed part of the movement calling for an end to corporate globalization, neoliberalism, and the economic polices that have led to the extremes of wealth and poverty that we see today. The first World Social Forum brought 20,000 people to Porto Alegre, Brazil in 2001 as a human-centered counter-narrative to the G8 Summit held in Genoa, Italy. The motto was "Another World is Possible."[1] We can say that the First World Social Forum was born out of the violence perpetrated by the Italian police against the demonstrators in the streets of Genoa protesting the G8 Summit, to which we will now turn.

The Police, the Media, and the Protesters

More than 100,000 people went to Genoa to object to global economic policies. The vast majority of them were peaceful. Police, about 20,000, were on hand, armed with tear gas, water cannons, and military hardware. *Italian authorities had prepared the city by ordering 200 body bags and as the BBC reported, designating a room as a temporary morgue at the local hospital.*[2] Part of the city was cordoned off in a so-called "ring of steel," or "red zone," with many railways and roads closed and air traffic shut down. US media routinely glossed over this militaristic response, invoking it as "proof of the threat posed by globalization activists." FAIR (2003, July 30, 2001) noted that:

> Even the killing of Carlo Giuliani—a protester who was shot in the head, run over and killed by police after he threw a fire extinguisher at a police vehicle—is recounted by U.S. media as a timely "lesson" for activists that, as *Time* magazine put it, "You reap what you sow."

Sensationalistic coverage of violence left no room for the substantive political concerns motivating the protests—they were all but ignored.

Two days into the protest, Italian police carried out a night raid on a school being used as a dormitory in Genoa for anti-globalization protesters. It was adjacent to the Indymedia center covering the events. At least 150 masked officers wearing unnumbered uniforms attacked the school the night of July 21, 2001. As John Hooper in *The Guardian* reported in 2010:

> Such was the ferocity of the beatings that followed that one commander said the school was left resembling a "Mexican slaughterhouse," its walls splattered with blood. Twenty-eight of the injured were taken to [the] hospital and three were put on the critical list.

As FAIR documents, the raid received largely indifferent coverage in the US at the time, but reports by Indymedia and the non-US press indicated that some 200 police officers brutally beat sleeping activists and more than a dozen of those arrested were seen being carried out on stretchers, some unconscious. Of the 93 people taken from the school in the night, 72 suffered injuries. All were eventually released without charge. NBC *Nightly News* (July 22, 2001) can be commended for its reporting that devoted more significant attention to the attack and repeated the organizers' claim that all the arrestees were non-violent and "the latest victims of police brutality."[3]

According to the police, the school was the headquarters of the demonstrators. They said they found Molotov cocktails there, and that one of the police officers had been attacked with a knife. But in January 2003, an Italian court ruling found that none of the victims had been involved in violence, the petrol bombs were planted, and the knife attack was faked. FAIR was unable to find a single mention of the courts finding in 2003 in any major US newspapers or magazines, national television news shows or wire service stories. FAIR took media to task for this lack of coverage:

> Considering how fond U.S. media are of dramatic stories about protester/police "clashes," they should be able to find the energy to carefully investigate such incidents. This is crucial journalistic work; the right to peaceful assembly is central to democracy. The public deserves to have access to follow-up investigations of what happened at Genoa's "violent" protests.

It wasn't until 2010 that some of the top Italian policemen were convicted in the brutal night raid that involved a nine-year cover-up. British citizen Mark Covell, who was beaten into a coma that night responded to the verdict, which overturned many of the conclusions reached by the judges at the original trial in 2008, this way, "The Italian judiciary has recognized the truth of what happened. Human rights have finally been respected here. Italians will now recognize their cops do not have immunity" (Hooper 2010).

The chief prosecutor of Genoa told judges that they could not overlook "the terrible injuries inflicted on defenseless people, the premeditation, the covered faces, the falsification of statements by the 93 anti-globalization protesters, the lies about their alleged resistance [to arrest]."[4]

At the time, Amnesty International (AI) characterized the arrests at the school as illegal, saying police at the summit showed "scant concern" for human rights. AI cited reports that detainees were:

> slapped, kicked, punched and spat on and subjected to verbal abuse, sometimes of an obscene sexual nature . . ., deprived of food, water and sleep for lengthy periods, made to line up with their faces against the wall and remain for hours spread-eagled, and beaten if they failed to maintain this position.

In addition, "some were apparently threatened with death and, in the case of female detainees, rape."[5] Detainees also reported being denied prompt access to lawyers and medical care.

Berlusconi's Mousetrap

The website of the Irish IMC, part of the Indymedia network, summarizes the G8 meeting this way:

> The Protests against the G8 in July 2001 in Genoa Italy were the biggest and most significant protests in Western Europe since the Poll Tax riots in the UK. Italian Prime Minister Sylvio Berlusconi, wanting to impress his new best mate George W. Bush, orchestrated a brutal Media/Police preemptive strike on the Anti-Capitalist Movements' biggest First World mobilization to date.
>
> (Carolan 2005)

This media center produced *Berlusconi's Mousetrap*, a film that begins with the build up to the protest and the transformation of Genoa city centre into a fortified military zone. Next, protestors are shown arriving from all over the world and taking part in a march in support of immigrant rights; "an event that was characterized by a joyful sense of possibility and solidarity" (Carolan 2005). But the next day the police moved against the demonstrators with unbridled force as they marched towards the perimeter of the red zone. With extraordinary footage, the film documents the police brutality in grueling detail. In one almost nightmarish sequence the film is slowed down, showing the police repeatedly pummel and kick people, sweating from exertion, while the voiceover narrates the testimony of an Irishman who was attacked by the police and then arrested, where he endured beatings and death threats and relates how delirious and jubilant cops beat, threatened and pissed upon other detainees while forcing some of them to sing fascist songs. Again and again we see the police gassing and attacking people without provocation.

Yet in the mainstream media Genoa became a kind of shorthand for "violent protesters" in mainstream media,[6] a deviant manifestation that justified police actions. (One can only marvel at the double standard when ten years after condoning police brutality against protesters in Genoa, a US military-led intervention was carried out to protect violent protesters under the guise of a "humanitarian war" in Libya. Of course, the media's role in offering two very different interpretations facilitated the carnage in both cases.)

Another World Is Possible: World Social Forums

In spite of such brutality and human rights violations, people continued to struggle against inequality and the unequal distribution of global wealth and power. Such topics continue to be the themes at workshops taking place at social forums around the world. By 2011, at the 10th World Social Forum held in Dakar, Senegal, the numbers of participants had expanded to 80,000. In Dakar, the focus was on water shortages, climate justice, land-grabbing, food crises, and the policy of the International Monetary Fund (IMF). In a changing world speakers and workshops addressed alternative solutions to poverty, understanding that the financial crisis showed that the market often causes more problems than it solves. The Indymedia website summarizes the WSF meetings this way, "For many people, the WSF has become a symbol of hope for a just world." These meetings celebrate civil rights and human rights, and offer an international exchange on new forms of politics—for example, the proposal for a planetary social citizenship. The international community must expand its definition of human rights, it was argued, to go beyond civil rights to the right to food and water. As Indymedia reports, WSF is a global people's "movement from below that can have a great effect when its themes are spread over the globe." And that is exactly what has happened.

Indymedia Africa

At the 2015 Indymedia Convergence in Accra, Ghana, a radio volunteer working at the same station as Lydia Ajono in the town of Bolgatanga, Akolga Samuel asserted that "Programs enlighten people to understand the terrain of policies and understand how to fight for their rights." Both Ajono and Samuel were active participants at the meeting in Ghana where the importance of radio to local struggles was emphasized.[7] This work is especially important given the environmental crisis in Africa and the burgeoning US military presence there, a point we will return to below.

There have been many Indymedia initiatives in Africa and the Convergence that took place in Ghana was the sixth, which brought together media activists from eight countries. Their meeting was timed to coincide with the annual AMARC Conference (Association Mondiale des Radiodiffuseurs Communautaires). Radio activists caravanned from several countries, and held skill-sharing workshops, building radios, training with computer software for radio and exchanging tips for organizing in their countries. Long-time AMARC members and media practitioners contributed their skills and breadth of knowledge to those who attended the Indymedia Africa meeting, just as the presence of Indymedia/Africa's activists expanded the diversity of AMARC's gathering.

In the continuing series of African Convergences, the previous meeting in 2014 held in Dakar, Senegal, was scheduled to coincide with the African Social Forum. Valentine Eben (Sphinx) from Cameroon is the coordinator behind all six of the African Indymedia convergences. Sphinx was interviewed on a Canadian station before leaving for Ghana:

> The effort is to build community owned and operated media capacity and infrastructure. In the last couple of years huge international donor organizations tried to literally appropriate the spaces that have been opened by organizers and this has been very counterproductive. In response we are trying to build community owned media, which in the case of Africa is mainly radio. In Africa one in four Africans have access to radio.[8]

But only one in 160 have access to the internet. One of the benefits of building radios in a community is that the computers that are part of the radio infrastructure can be made available to local citizens.

The Indymedia movement has been criticized for the prominence of male leadership. For the African Convergences, an effort was made to ensure that women would also be part of technical training and skill sharing. In the Dakar Convergence, the gender balance was enhanced by the skilled participation of women activists from the Niger Delta, the site of long struggle against oil extraction by Exxon-Mobile and Royal Dutch Schell that devastated tribal lands, chronicled in the film, *Delta Boys* (2012).[9] Their skills at organizing helped create a vital Indymedia presence in the Dakar Social Forum march.

The importance of community radio for popular mobilization was evident when the Kenyan government reacted with violence. One of the African radios affiliated with Indymedia is Equator FM at the University of Maseno in Kenya. On October 15, 2015, the university was the scene of violent police repression after state police shot live rounds into a campaign vehicle carrying candidates for student government positions. Two of the campaigners were killed and several others seriously wounded. In response, students barricaded highways and burned down the administration buildings. The entire university was shut down. The Maseno student radio has been a key information provider in the midst of these protests. Universities throughout Africa are important hubs for students to gain access to radio and the internet. In this environment, Indymedia has a key role to play in connecting activists and defending their right to communicate within the universities and with other student movements.

Work as an Indymedia journalist in Africa is not without danger. Much can be at stake when communities struggle to get their voices heard. They are frequently demonized as "terrorists," but they are often the victims of terror by state and non-state actors. There have been attacks on Indymedia journalists. Stephen Nyash, a participant at the Dakar Indymedia convergence, was a radio journalist at KOCH-FM, in the shack community of Korgocho, Kenya, the third largest slum in the world. A skilled organizer and talented media professional, he was the founder of Ghetto Films. Fellow Indymedia activist John Bwakali wrote an obituary for Nyash, who was murdered one year after the Dakar workshops. "From the moment that he knew about Kenya Indymedia, Nyash became not just an active participant but fellow leader of the movement . . . Upon return [from Dakar, Senegal], he immersed himself into the vision and work of Kenya Indymedia." After the Dakar workshops he had continued his work in developing the KOCH-FM radio. But his work in broadcasting news about corruption in the Korogocho slums and his organizing of Ghetto Films had made him a target for repressive forces.

For media activists in Latin America and Africa, as in many parts of Asia and the Middle East, the work of reporting the truth is dangerous. Nyash is recognized as the third Indymedia journalist to be killed for his work. On June 29, 2004, Lenin Najera of Indymedia Guayaquil, Ecuador was assassinated by agents of the Ecuadorian government, and on October 27, 2006, Brad Will was murdered by the Mexican paramilitary in Oaxaca.

History Lessons

Aside from the skills learned in technical and organizing workshops at the African convergences, there were other unusual aspects of these meetings. Both of the last two African Indymedia convergences ended in visits to learn of Africa's history of slavery. Dakar's meeting ended with an emotional tour of the slave dungeons at Goree Island, and the Accra group visited the port in Ghana, where tens of thousands of chained and garroted Africans were loaded onto commercial ships, headed to Charleston, Newport, Rio, Havana, Port Au Prince, and other ports for sale. There was also a tour of the W.E.B. DuBois library in Ghana. DuBois, pioneer scholar and influential historian of African American culture, emigrated to Ghana in 1960 and his grave and library/museum are in Accra. This sort of connection to history for young media activists from around the continent is also emblematic of the larger global peoples' movement that seeks to expand the knowledge base as they seek solutions to local as well as global issues.

The global Indymedia infrastructure, as we have seen, holds convergences often in tandem with other alternative media and social forums, and in this way is able to provide technical support and skill sharing to community groups, many of which would be silenced otherwise. Indymedia brings the experiences from areas with more resources and funding, to regions struggling for support often experiencing violations of human rights, corporate globalization, conflict, war, and colonialism. This type of support and sharing is a key function, and what makes the Indymedia movement part of the larger struggle happening all over the globe.

Ecology Meets the Economic Critique: The Politics of Eco-Philosophy

Scientists have recently identified the present era as the age of the Anthropocene,[10] a geologic term that identifies human activity and its impact as the defining influence on the earth and its systems. Though it has been decades, indeed centuries in the making, in the twenty-first century humanity is living on a globe ravaged by industrial production. As World Watch Institute (Assadourian 2010, 4) documents: "Between 1950 and 2005, metals production grew sixfold, oil consumption eightfold, and natural gas 14-fold. In total, 60 billion tons of resources are now extracted annually—about 50 percent more than thirty years ago." Currently humans are using about a third more of the Earth's capacity than is available. The Millennium Ecosystem Assessment Board (2005, 5) warned, "human activity is putting such a strain on the natural functions of Earth that the ability of the planet's ecosystems to sustain future generations can no longer be taken for granted." Most disturbing is the loss of the planet's ability to regulate climate.

Environmental disaster will be the root cause of humanitarian crises for future generations. Human populations will face social and economic disruption, forced migration from drought and rising sea levels, water scarcity, loss of biodiversity and food production, disease, and the collapse of ocean fisheries. In the global south, poor, rural communities are already experiencing such disruptions, accelerated by corporate globalization that results in land seizures, pollution, water scarcity, and over extraction of resources. These realities are ignored by mainstream media agendas. The Indymedia movement is tied to people's struggles, providing information, forums for discussions, community solutions, organized resistance and global awareness. With the scientific and biological consensus that future generations and human sustainability are at stake, global economic activities are now re-conceived outside of the once dominant political categories that have become increasingly meaningless. This global social movement has tied economic activity to environmental crisis, and led to new theoretical formulations that re-position human activity within an "Earth Community." To do so they draw on direct analogies to the biological processes of the natural world, and posit that humans must mirror the pattern of ecological interactions for the species to survive.

World People's Summit on Climate Change and Rights of Nature

Against the backdrop of the failure of the Copenhagen Climate Talks, South African legal scholar Cormac Cullinan was a plenary speaker at the World People's Summit on Climate Change held in Cochabamba, Bolivia April 2010. His presentation outlined the need for social transformation and featured the development of a butterfly as a metaphor to reconceive the way humanity must change. In eloquent prose he detailed the veracious appetite of the caterpillar, who "eats and eats." He then goes on:

> [But] if it continued eating it would grow enormous and it would die. Fortunately Mother Earth imposes limits, and the caterpillar eats and eats and grows fatter until one day it stops, goes to a quiet place and becomes still. Because there is no future for the caterpillar who eats and eats, and grows forever. The point must be reached when a transformation occurs if the caterpillar is to survive.[11]

As a legal scholar and the author of *Wild Law: A Manifesto for Earth Justice*, Cullinan goes on to say that the law works the same way—like the DNA of the caterpillar. The law is the DNA of the social world, "it restricts or allows for the transformation of a society." The Wild Law movement seeks to establish "the rights of Mother Earth in a way that will be taken up by legal systems throughout the world."[12] Earth Jurisprudence is another term for the practice that enjoins nation states to legally codify the rights of nature. Indeed, the legal code addresses fundamental human survival as well. As Cullinan (2010, 144) argues, "Humans are, of course, but one of many species that have co-evolved within a system they are wholly dependent on. In the long term humans cannot thrive in a degraded environment anymore than fish can survive in polluted water." Cullinan follows in the footsteps of many ecologists from Aldo Leopold to thinkers who propose a fundamental shift in the framework of global policy discourses, one that replaces a human-centric global policy with an "Earth community" where humans can no longer dominate, or replace, all other members of the community that sustains them. The attitude that Earth is simply a store of natural resources for humans to consume is no longer viable. It is safe to say that these ideas are never brought into political debates on economics and environment policy in mainstream policy discourses.

The World Social Forums: Montreal, Canada August 2016

The most recent World Social Forum (WSF) took place in Montreal, Canada in August 2016. Many African Indymedia activists scheduled to attend were not given visas by the Canadian government and they were not present. The keynote address that appears on the first page of the WSF website was delivered by Italian political analyst Riccardo Petrella titled "Education, Environment and Eco-Citizenship, The Art of Living Together." Petrella tied inequality to corporate globalization, ecocide, and the consumerist lifestyles promoted by media. Petrella estranged the common, hidden practices of daily life; the fact that genetically modified organisms have become ordinary, to the fateful economic transactions that happen every thousandth of a second. The largest corporations that span the globe now "create life," define the value of our inventions, our possessions, and our identities. "We have monetized life, but life does not have a price, and the human being should not levy a charge upon it." He called for a declaration to make poverty illegal, and for an end to war, saying we have to stop wars that allow us to produce weapons for economic reasons.[13] He called for a new way of thinking about humanity as one part of the larger community of Mother Earth.

In his words can be heard a new political eco-philosophy that has emerged through the confluence of a number of powerful social, economic, and environmental forces at play since the turn of the twenty-first century. These include the current global political economy that, through decreased regulation and international trade deals, has solidified corporate power and ensured the dominance of market forces worldwide. With hurricanes and super storms, drought and flooding, the gravity of the environmental crisis and its increasing global manifestations are at the forefront of these discussions as well. Added to these increasingly urgent environmental developments is the dominance of militarism, and its obvious failure as a solution to global disputes and conflict (including its spread into other sectors such as law enforcement). This triad has led to a break from traditional modes of thought, and led to expansive theoretical perspectives on sustainability, peace, and planetary survival. It is a uniquely ecological point of view, but places the love for humanity and humanitarian values at its center. For example, when Petrella spoke of the renewal of the cycle of life and of nature through its diversification, whether wildlife or flora, he included human cultures or "even the various cultures that are on different continents." Indeed, Pope Francis has made these same points.

Pope Francis and the Peoples' Movements, and Eco-Spirituality

Many parallels can be found in Pope Francis' Encyclical Letter and the writings that emerge from global meetings of activists that take place annually at world forums. If we compare the text of the People's Agreement from Bogata in 2010, published by the Portland Independent Media Center, part of the Indymedia network, we find many parallels to the writings in the Encyclical Letter.

Pope Francis

> I will point to the intimate relationship between the poor and the fragility of the planet, the conviction that everything in the world is connected.

People's Agreement

> Today's environmental crisis is "based on the oppression and destruction of human beings and nature . . . which today encompasses the entire globe."

Pope Francis

If we approach nature and the environment without this openness to awe and wonder, if we no longer speak the language of fraternity and beauty in our relationship with the world, our attitude will be that of masters, consumers, ruthless exploiters, unable to set limits on their immediate needs. By contrast, if we feel intimately united with all that exists, then sobriety and care will well up spontaneously.

People's Agreement

The People's Agreement bluntly shows that humanity today faces the final disjunctive: Either continue the devastating path of capitalism towards depredation and death, or start paving the way to a model of society that learns to live in harmony with nature and respects and cherishes life.[14]

Pope Francis

Even as the quality of available water is constantly diminishing, in some places there is a growing tendency, despite its scarcity, to privatize this resource, turning it into a commodity subject to the laws of the market. Yet *access to safe drinkable water is a basic and universal human right, since it is essential to human survival and, as such, is a condition for the exercise of other human rights.* Our world has a grave social debt towards the poor who lack access to drinking water, because *they are denied the right to a life consistent with their inalienable dignity.*

People's Agreement

The document states that capitalism is a mode of production and consumption which has the sole purpose of seeking unlimited profits, alienating humans from nature and converting everything into a commodity: water, land, the human genome, our ancestral cultures, biodiversity, justice, ethics, people's rights, death, and life itself.

Pope Francis

In the meantime, economic powers continue to justify the current global system where priority tends to be given to speculation and the pursuit of financial gain, which fail to take the context into account, let alone the effects on human dignity and the natural environment. Here we see how environmental deterioration and human and ethical degradation are closely linked . . . As a result, whatever is fragile, like the environment, is defenseless before the interests of a deified market, which become the only rule.

People's Agreement

[This] model of civilization based on the oppression and destruction of human beings and nature, which had been sharply accelerated by the industrial revolution and which today encompasses the entire globe. It states that this model of civilization—

capitalism—has ruthlessly imposed on us its logics of competition and its notion of "progress," which equals wellbeing with unlimited economic growth, no matter the consequences.

In case there is any doubt of the wisdom of these critiques—of the connections made between financial gain and its effects on human dignity and the natural world, the call for access to water as a human right, of humans and nature as defenseless before the interests of a deified market—or the need for a new vision of humanity on the planet, consider the case of the on-going humanitarian crisis happening to the largest indigenous population in Colombia.

The Wayuu People of Colombia

The Wayuu people of La Guajira, Colombia are experiencing an on-going humanitarian disaster. Over the past eight years, the Inter-American Commission of Human Rights (IACHR) has documented the deaths of 4,770 children as a result of thirst, malnutrition, and preventable disease, a staggering number in this community of 100,000. (The Wayuu claim that over 14,000 children have died.)

As FAIR points out, this crisis has been largely ignored by mainstream media, but in August 2016, the plight of the Wayuu was brought to the attention of readers of the *Huffington Post* when it published an article by Human Rights Lawyer Dan Kavalik, who visited the Wayuu for the Washington Office on Latin America (WOLA). In a piece titled, "Colombia's Largest Indigenous Group is Dying with Media Complicity," Kovalik (2016) reports that the biggest threat to the Wayuu children is lack of drinkable water. He writes:

> The water that The Wayuu once had has been stolen from them—both by climate change which they had no part in creating, and by the damming of The Rancheria River which once fed their communities but which is now being used for the private benefit of coal mining giant Cerrejon.

The Cerrejon Mine opened in 1983 as a joint venture between Colombia and Exxon, and has been displacing indigenous and Afro-Colombian communities ever since (Chomsky et al. 2007). After the dam was built in 2011 for the coal mining company, the Wayuu lost access to the Rancheria River. Kovalik reports "Cerrejon now uses 17 million liters of water a day, while residents of the region have an average of 0.7 liters a day to live on" (Kovalik 2016).

In addition, Kovalik found that the chief advocate who works for the IACHR on behalf of the Wayuu, Javier Rojas Uriana, has received death threats by right-wing paramilitaries trying to pressure him into halting his legal actions to protect the Wayuu. Such threats are common in the region and have been well documented by researchers working in the area. The Colombian mineworkers union reports that human rights violations are disproportionately highly concentrated in Colombia's profitable mining and energy zones, where large foreign corporations use military and paramilitary forces to secure their investments (Cuellar and Chomsky 2005). Colombia is the third-largest recipient of US military aid.

The Colombian authorities have done next to nothing to alleviate the suffering of the Wayuu children. Finally, on August 1, 2016, Colombia's Supreme Court ordered the government to ensure that the Wayuu have access to the basics of survival, including drinkable water.

This order followed the December 11, 2015 directive by the IACHR to the Colombian government to take immediate "precautionary measures" to ensure the lives and personal safety of Wayuu children (Kovalik 2016).

Kovalik concludes by pointing out the consequences of the lack of media coverage:

> Just as remarkable as the dire situation facing The Wayuu is the almost total lack of press coverage regarding their situation. Thus, while the press covers the shortages in Venezuela nearly every day, and in a quite histrionic fashion which ignores the complexities and subtleties of the situation there, there is almost a total blackout of the real famine confronting The Wayuu of Colombia just over the border. And, it is this media blackout, even in the face of major rulings by both the IACHR and Colombia's high court, which of course allows this famine to continue without pause.

Give Them "Gummy Bears," and They "Rely on Smuggling"

Janine Jackson of FAIR did find media mentions of the Wayuu, and draws attention to a story on CNN's website in December of 2015 that told how "Colombia's wild northeast is slowly making its way onto the tourist map. But patience and a fair dose of discomfort are required to enjoy this barren outpost" (Jackson 2016). Reference is made to the Wayuu when readers are warned they'll be pestered by them for money and candy, so they are told to bring "a bagful of gummy bears." One *New York Times* piece in September 2015 that covered Venezuela closing its border, also mentioned these indigenous people when the paper informed readers in the final paragraph that "many Wayuu have long relied on smuggling to earn a living" (Jackson 2016).

Thus are the lives of people and communities deemed expendable by the coalition of extractive industries, the military and corporate media, discussed in the corporate press. This makes alternative media, and especially Indymedia vital to the survival of the planet and its peoples.

Tactical Media

With the failure of most twenty-first century corporate media to narrate the lives of the poor, or tell the story of their struggle accurately, many practitioners of Indymedia define what they do as tactical media, a term that brings a different attitude to documentation, testimonial, and representation. It is media that narrates from a different point of view, through the eyes and words of the people affected by disasters and human rights violations. It bears witness to people's struggles, giving them voice through testimonial and documentation. Tactical media applies to first-world struggles as well, such as the G8 summit and the organized protests that took place at US political conventions throughout the 2000s. On the eve of the 2004 Republican National Convention, organizers sent an open letter to mainstream journalists urging them to ensure fair and accurate coverage of the demonstrators and their actions. It read in part, "We are concerned by the slant of some of the media coverage that has focused on potential violence or made unsubstantiated and sensationalist claims about the activists who will be demonstrating."

Along with the vast numbers of protesters in New York City, well over a thousand Indymedia journalists worked out of the Independent Media Center (IMC) there. Alternative

Radio's *Democracy Now* interviewed filmmaker Richard Rowley who talked about covering people's movements in New York and around the globe. When we film with people in the streets he explained:

> it is your responsibility [as much as possible] to assume the risks of the people who you are filming with. I go to Palestine and I go armed to the teeth with the weapons of privilege. I come with my skin and my passport, which makes me not impossible to kill, but a lot more difficult to kill. But it's our responsibility there to at least put our bodies and our cameras on the front lines with people.

Rowley is co-founder of Big Noise Films, and he spoke about filming *The Fourth World War*, a documentary about global protests in Argentina, Mexico, South Africa, Palestine, and Korea.

> This is a film that would have been impossible to make even five years ago. It was made possible through a global network of activists in movements, independent media people around the world that really has not existed before. When we arrive in a place like South Africa, the day we arrive, we're traveling around and filming with South Africa Indymedia, which is basically a wing of the anti-eviction campaign and the anti-privatization movement is connected with grassroots movements on the ground.

Tactical media is also a counter-reaction to dominant conflict frames and visual coverage that sees war through the eyes of weapons not people:

> we see the war abroad shot from the noses of bombs in Iraq. We hear it narrated by generals . . . we wanted to create the possibility for an identification with people on the other side of that massive military and media machine. So we put the cameras in the streets with people who are putting their bodies on the line every day.

Militarism and Africa: Failed Policies and Humanitarian Crises

Perhaps the most important work for Indymedia is on the African continent, currently suffering from drought caused by climate change, the extraction of "conflict minerals," and the legacy of colonialism. As both the United States and China increase their involvement in Africa, Indymedia Africa's role in giving voice to the voiceless there is a crucial arena in the struggle for justice and against the new form of colonialism—militarism.

The last decade has seen a huge expansion of US military bases and operations on the African continent, as AFRICOM became an independent command. AFRICOM boasts that it "neutralizes transnational threats" and "prevents and mitigates conflict," while training local allies and proxies "in order to promote regional security, stability, and prosperity."[15] Since AFRICOM was established, however, the very opposite has occurred. There has been an increase in the numbers of lethal terror attacks across the continent from Chad to Niger, and from Nigeria to Kenya. To give just one illustration, today 13,000 displaced people sit in appalling conditions in make-shift camps in Nigeria, forced to flee their homes to escape the brutality of Boka Haram attacks. The terrorist group was bolstered by an influx of weapons, a consequence of the "humanitarian war" that led to chaos in Libya and the weapons flow to terrorist groups in surrounding African and Middle Eastern countries.

As military analyst Nick Turse points out:

> data from the National Consortium for the Study of Terrorism and Responses to Terrorism at the University of Maryland shows that attacks in Africa have spiked over the last decade, roughly coinciding with AFRICOM's establishment. In 2007 just before it became an independent command, there were fewer than 400 such incidents annually in sub-Saharan Africa. Last year, the number reached nearly 2,000.

Even in the midst of such failed policies, generals are not brought to accountability, or for that matter even questioned by the civilian government meant to oversee them. Turse points out that US Senators in oversight committees don't ask obvious questions about why terror groups and attacks are proliferating as US operations, bases, manpower, extractive corporations and military engagement across the continent grow.

> In an era of too big to fail generals, an age in which top commanders from winless wars retire to take prominent posts at influential institutions and cash in with cushy jobs on corporate boards, AFRICOM chiefs have faced neither hard questions nor repercussions for the deteriorating situation.

Similar records of failures and heavy setbacks with no victories have been repeated for the last 15 years by Washington's war chiefs in Afghanistan and Iraq. Nor have these failures ever led to official calls for some sort of accountability.

Human Security

But there is growing realization that war and weaponry only destroy homelands and lead to further global instability. Some in the humanitarian and academic communities now look to peace building as a way of addressing human security as a concern distinct from national security. In the book *Freedom from Fear, Freedom from Want: An Introduction to Human Security*, Canadian scholars Hanlon and Christie (2016) have identified a new interdisciplinary approach that builds on the work of the 1994 "Human Development Report" by the United Nations Development Program (UNDP) that began to outline the concept. In an address a year later, Burmese opposition leader and human rights activist Aung San Suu Kyi quoted from the report saying that human security "is not a concern with weapons—it is a concern with human life and dignity." This field continues to develop practical and theoretical knowledge to further refine the idea that human security involves freedom from want and freedom from fear, and that those freedoms are essential to global security.

Conclusion

> *Those in power attempt to spread the idea in the entire population that their way of life is the only way. There is only one homogenous linear moment in which everything in the future is the same as the present and the past. You cannot hope for any kind of change; there are no ruptures in history. But there are ruptures, tremendous ruptures that shatter this dominant history.*
>
> (*The Fourth World War*, Big Noise Tactical Media:
> Jacquie Soohen and Richard Rowley)

As global populations face humanitarian crises caused by the conditions of poverty and inequality, violence from state and non-state actors, and environmental degradation, their stories are rarely the subject of media reports. Yet these voices are heard across the global, emanating through the practices of communities and people, documented through tactical media, articulated by visionaries, ecologists, academics, many humanitarians, and the spiritual leader of over 1.2 billion of the world's people. These are the voices that reveal the actual practices of corporate globalization from Latin America to Africa, and the consequences of market commoditization that consumes resources, steals the lives and livelihoods of indigenous communities, and destabilizes the planet's climate system. This unified voice has been excluded from the political arena, silenced by government and police violence, and mostly ignored by mainstream media. All of these voices, from the very local to the global, articulate the root causes of humanitarian disasters and offer visions of a different world. The combined total of their words and ideas amounts to far more than the voices heard in global mainstream media by an order of magnitude. These are the visions and this is the knowledge that must be brought by global publics into the discussion of world politics and policies.

Notes

1. Coined by Susan George of the Transnational Institute and Attac in France in 1996.
2. BBC, June 21, 2001.
3. A couple of weeks later, it emerged that some of the victims were American. The three nightly newscasts then showed somewhat more attention to the issue of police brutality, running reports that included footage of the blood splashed on the floors and walls of the school (ABC, August 8, 2001; CBS and NBC August 11, 2001). CBS distinguished itself poorly again by introducing its follow-up report with excuses: "However provoked the Italian police were during the rioting around last month's summit in Genoa, their behavior has become the subject of an embarrassing domestic inquiry in Italy."
4. Under Italian law, the prosecution as well as the defense can appeal (Hooper 2010).
5. *The Wire*, September 2001.
6. This frame only lost dominance after the attacks on Occupy protesters by New York City police and around the country. These attacks were not acceptable to the public and resulted in similar court cases.
7. Thanks to Norman Stockwell, resource consultant for Indymedia Africa, who wrote about the Bolgatanga radio in an issue of Cultural Survival, available at: www.culturalsurvival.org
8. From an interview with a Canadian youth radio that Sphinx posted on Indymedia Africa.
9. Brendan DeMelle, "*Delta Boys*: Powerful Documentary Chronicles Niger Delta Oil Struggles," (December 16, 2012), available at: www.huffingtonpost.com/brendan-demelle/delta-boys-documentary_b_1971133.html
10. Working Group on the Anthropocene, "What is the Anthropocene?" Subcommission on Quaternary Stratigraphy, available at: http://quaternary.stratigraphy.org/workinggroups/anthropocene/
11. http://therightsofnature.org/cormac-cullinan-on-wild-law/
12. Ibid.
13. Grand Conference: Education, Environment and Eco-Citizenship, The Art of Living Together (August 12, 2016), available at: https://fsm2016.org/en/grande-conference-ecocitoyennete-et-education-a-lenvironnement-lart-de-vivre-ensemble/
14. http://portland.indymedia.org/en/2011/03/407439.shtml
15. Nick Turse, "The US Military Pivots to Africa and that Continent Goes Down the Drain," TomDispatch.com (August 2, 2016), available at: www.tomdispatch.com/post/176171/tomgram%3A_nick_turse,_the_u.s._military_pivots_to_africa_and_that_continent_goes_down_the_drain/

References

Assadourian, E. (2010) "The Rise and Fall of Consumer Cultures," *State of the World 2010 Transforming Cultures: From Consumerism to Sustainability*, New York: W.W. Norton.
Carolan, J. (2005) "If Seattle was 'Star Wars,' Then This Is 'The Empire Strikes Back,'" Independent Media Center. June 12, 2005, available at: http://archive.indymedia.org.nz/article/69701/if-seattle-was-star-wars-then-empire-str.html

Chomsky, A., Leech, G., and Striffler, S. (2007) *The People Behind Colombia Coal*, New York: Casa Editorial Pisando Callos.

Cuellar, F. R., and Chomsky, A. (2005) *The Profits of Extermination: Big Mining in Colombia*, Boston, MA: Common Courage Press.

Cullinan, C. (2010) "Colonization to Participation" in 2010 State of the World, *Transforming Cultures: From Consumerism to Sustainability*, New York and London: W.W. Norton.

FAIR. (2003) "Media Missing New Evidence on Genoa Violence," January 10, 2003, available at: http://fair.org/take-action/action-alerts/media-missing-new-evidence-about-genoa-violence/

Hanlon, R., and Christie, K. (2016) *Freedom from Fear, Freedom from Want: An Introduction to Human Security*, Toronto: University of Toronto Press.

Hooper, J. (2010) "Top Italian Policemen Get up to 5 Years for Violent Attack on G8 Protesters," *The Guardian*, May 19, 2010, available at: www.theguardian.com/world/2010/may/19/g8-italian-police-sentenced

Jackson, J. (2016). "Humanitarian Nightmare for Colombia's Wayuu Fails to Awaken Corporate Media," FAIR August 15, 1016, available at: http://fair.org/home/humanitarian-nightmare-for-colombias-wayuu-fails-to-awaken-corporate-media/

Kovalik, D. (2016). "Colombia's Largest Indigenous Group Is Dying with Media Complicity," *The Huffington Post*. August 2, 2016, available at: www.huffingtonpost.com/entry/colombias-largest-indigenous-group-is-dying-with-media_us_57a102c1e4b07066ba1fdc64

Millennium Ecosystem Assessment Board. (2005) *Living Beyond Our Means: Natural Assets and Human Well-Being*, Nairobi: UNEP, available at: www.millenniumassessment.org/documents/document.429.aspx.pdf

Part 6

COMMUNICATION, HUMANITARIANISM, AND CRISIS

Case Studies from the Global Community

INTRODUCTION
TO PART 6

The collection of essays in Part 6 is comprised of case studies covering a number of geographical areas including the Horn of Africa, the Philippines, the Arab Gulf, Northern Iraq and Syria, and Latin America. They cover a range of topics dealing with the complexities of global famine outbreaks, the interplay between media and aid, disaster management, and the role for organized labor unions. They discuss UNICEF's communication and media strategies for child protection applied in conflict zones, and detail the root causes of ethnic and cultural genocide affecting minorities. Finally, the discussion turns to the complexities of environmental degradation, poverty, and corruption, which must be addressed together to find solutions.

In Chapter 25 Aregawi Berhe the former military commander of the Tigrayan People's Liberation Front (TPLF) writes passionately in the "Horn of Africa: The Politics of Famine, Media Activism, and Donor Aid" about his experiences in Tigray and Ethiopia, and the Horn of Africa, addressing the recurrence of famine as a humanitarian disaster. He argues that political, ethnic, and cultural fault lines, together with drought and conflict make famine an ever-present danger that lies in wait even in the twenty-first century. This is particularly disheartening, given the advancement of science and technology, particularly in food production and processing, that has reached astounding heights. By famine, he is referring not to a brief deprivation of food or a casual hunger, but prolonged mass starvation, which takes the lives of millions of people in an agonizing manner—something that he has personally witnessed during the famines of 1973, 1974, 1983, 1984, 1985 in Ethiopia. He states that he has been in the middle of mass starvation and the politics of famine since the late 1950s, a time span of almost 60 years. He argues that some would rightfully characterize this phenomenon nowadays as "genocide by starvation."

Berhe notes that a number of factors such as climate change, civil war or insurgency, internal political or economic crises, uncalled-for external involvement, and other interacting factors may play a role in the causation of the recurring famine in the Horn of Africa. Arguing that some factors may have more weight than others, he identifies the decisive actors in the causation of this persistent problem. Understanding this dynamic is absolutely necessary for a lasting solution. He begins by asking questions such as: Why is this scourge occurring thick and fast in this corner of the world when human beings elsewhere have developed the capacity to produce plenty or even surpluses of food and know no famine? Where exactly does the principal cause of the recurring famine in the Horn lie? Is famine really the fault of nature or human-made? If the latter, who is responsible for the frequently arising devastation of human beings and their habitat? What is the way out of such a painful brunt? What role can the media play? Based on a number of studies conducted so far, and also from personal observation, this author addresses these crucial and related questions and identifies the root causes of the famine that still haunts the Horn of Africa. In doing so he clears a path for possible remedies.

In Chapter 26 Kim Scipes notes in "Disaster Management in the Philippines: Media, Unions, and Humanitarian Action" that, as the planet continues to heat up, all expectations are that there will be more and more "natural" disasters in the world and the people most at risk are those in the island nations. These are often small, atoll island nations—such as the Maldives Islands, the Marshall Islands, and Tuvalu—but this also extends to larger island nations, such as Indonesia and the Philippines. Also at risk are low-lying mainland areas, such as the Ganges Delta in Bangladesh. He notes that most of the emphasis to date has been on government and non-governmental organizations' (NGO) responses to disasters, and that their people are among first responders, and are also the focus of media attention when covering responses to such disasters. However, once the TV cameras leave, the remaining recovery work is often desultory, taking years for an affected area to fully recover. This has been the experience of the Philippines in addressing the problems of Typhoon Haiyan, which hit the country in November 2013. Studies of natural disasters tend to ignore the social impact of such events. This study foregrounds this, and argues that progressive trade unions and their allies should be involved in responses to natural disasters. Discussing the KMU Labor Center of the Philippines, this study argues that the KMU has qualities that would help overcome the impact of natural disasters on affected communities. Further, Scipes suggests that active involvement with media can lead to better news coverage of natural disasters through providing media access to affected communities, while utilizing organizational strengths to help communities mitigate and recover from the impact of such disasters. He concludes, that organized labor groups are an important and overlooked resource that might bridge the gap between natural disaster victims and government/NGO responders during and after national disasters.

In Chapter 27 Fadwa Ahmed Obaid, who is a Saudi media professional, discusses her experiences and insights in "Humanitarian Response and Media in the Arab Gulf Countries." Two major media revolutions transformed the humanitarian response to disasters facing the Arab Gulf States, namely the 1991 launch of Pan-Arab satellite TV channels, and the 2010 advent of social media. Drawing on her own professional experience, she argues that both media revolutions have had positive effects on humanitarian response in GCC countries and the Arab region. She explores the impact of mainstream Pan-Arab satellite TV channels in successful fundraising through telethons and 24/7 news reporting, resulting in an increasing awareness of humanitarian needs. A new public understanding of accountability in the distribution of mobilized resources has also emerged. Obaid has detailed the use of social media and the connections forged between volunteers, donors, and the victims of conflict and disaster. Both facets of the media revolution have the potential to become more relevant and effective in raising awareness of humanitarian crises, delivering relief, and helping the victims recover. Technological empowerment and skills-based media training will facilitate media accessibility and use, and are the ways forward in creating sustained, effective, and timely humanitarian response in the Arab region, and beyond.

In Chapter 28 Purnaka L. de Silva discusses future prospects for minorities in "Quo Vadis? Ethnic and Cultural Genocide: Chaldean and Assyrian Christians and Yazidis in Northern Iraq and Syria." He provides a careful examination of the antecedents to the ethnic and cultural genocide that have been inflicted upon Chaldean and Assyrian Christians and Yazidis among others in Northern Iraq and Syria. He argues that it represents an ongoing saga of human misery and crimes against humanity. The depopulation of ancient civilizations and willful destruction of diverse cultural and religious identities begs the question Quo Vadis? There are many fissures in the makeup of governmental and local authority in Northern Iraq and Syria, which have enabled extremists to gain a foothold. Ongoing debates to determine the fate of millions trapped are yet to be concluded. Nevertheless, it is necessary to examine the role of ideology and the use of media that have resulted in a humanitarian catastrophe— where indeed—as noted by Voltaire in a different time and context, "If we believe in absurdities we shall commit atrocities."

In Chapter 29 Priti Vaishnav delves into "Child Protection and UNICEF's Communication and Media Strategy: A Conflict-related Study from Mindanao, the Philippines." She bases her analysis on five years of fieldwork in the conflict zones of Mindanao, the Philippines, where child protection is of critical importance. She works with the Nonviolent Peaceforce, which specializes in Unarmed Civilian Protection in close cooperation with the United Nations and UNICEF to report and respond to Child Protection issues in Mindanao and the surrounding islands. In the field, she sought to implement the humanitarian principles of neutrality and impartiality among the parties to the various conflicts. She established an active presence, and gained access to remote conflict-affected areas. Such work seeks to document and ultimately protect children, civilians and internally displaced persons (IDPs) who are suffering as a result of the armed conflicts. This chapter offers a close examination of UNICEF's communication and media strategies, as well as behind-the-scenes advocacy and in-person contact under difficult physical conditions and terrain.

Finally, Rudelmar Bueno de Faria's chapter, entitled "Environmental Degradation, Poverty and Corruption: Media, Power, Humanitarian Action, and Sustainable Development Goals (SDGs) in Latin America," is based on decades of hands-on experience at the grassroots level in a number of Latin American countries—most recently assisting to finalize the peace treaty between the FARC and the government of Colombia. Bueno de Faria provides a rich discussion that examines three areas that influence the well-being and prosperity of the lives of millions of Latin Americans. Top of the list is environmental degradation, which has local and regional consequences as well as global ecological impacts because the Amazon region serves as "the lungs of the earth." He offers a complex analysis that includes the effects of poverty and government corruption on development imperatives, which he argues, are interrelated issues. He looks at the role the media play in articulating and framing these challenges to development and prosperity, and highlights areas that require greater cooperation from civil society, governments, and multilateral bodies alike. He finds humanitarian goals and principles for redressing some of the many negative realities faced by Latin Americans across the region.

25

HORN OF AFRICA

The Politics of Famine, Media Activism, and Donor Aid

Aregawi Berhe

Overview

Ethiopia, which is bordered by Eritrea to the north and northeast, Djibouti to the northeast, Sudan to the north and northwest, South Sudan to the west, Kenya to the south, and Somalia to the east and southeast is a geostrategic country in the Horn of Africa region. This ancient country, landlocked since 1991, is fractured along many political, ethnic, and cultural fault lines and the recurrence of famine in the aftermath of drought and conflict is an ever-present danger. It lies in wait even in the twenty-first century when the advancement of science and technology, particularly in food production and processing, has reached astounding heights (in many instances beyond the comprehension of the ordinary citizen). By famine, we are talking not of a brief deprivation of food or a casual hunger, but prolonged mass starvation, which takes the lives of millions of people in an agonizing manner—something that I have personally witnessed during the famines of 1973, 1974, 1983, 1984, 1985 in Ethiopia and shall never forget as long as I live. I have been in the middle of mass starvation and the politics of famine not only one or two years but since the late 1950s for almost 60 years. The recurrence of this scourge, commonly known as famine or, as some would rightfully characterize it nowadays, "genocide by starvation" or famicide (Howe 2007, 345) and its consequences, is then the focus of our investigation.

A number of factors such as climatic change, civil war or insurgency, internal political or economic crises, uncalled-for external involvement, and other interacting factors may play a role in the causation of recurring famine in the Horn. Although some of the factors may have more weight than the others, identifying the decisive actors in the causation of this persistent problem is absolutely necessary if we are looking for a lasting solution. We may therefore begin by asking some pertinent questions such as: Why is this scourge occurring thick and fast in this corner of the world when human beings elsewhere have developed the capacity to produce plenty or even a surplus of food and know no famine? Where exactly does the principal cause of the recurring famine in the Horn lie? Is famine really the fault of nature or human-made? If the latter, who is responsible for the frequently arising devastation of human beings and their habitat? What is the way out of such a painful brunt? Based on a number of studies conducted so far, and also from my personal observation as well, this essay addresses these crucial and related questions by way of identifying the root causes of famine that still haunts the Horn and clearing the ground for possible remedies.

Comprehending Famine

Famine, as "mass starvation leading to death," has been well known since Biblical times around 3,450 years ago (*The Holy Bible*, Genesis 45: 6–11) and people of different persuasions have been grappling to fully understand and control it. Yet it looks as if there is no conclusive understanding of the centuries old term, famine, which is still with us. Why? Perhaps it has to do with the complex nature of its evolution, as it is partly political, economic, social, and environmental. And it occurs also because there is a lack of will among influential actors who have the power to root out famine.

Despite the abundance of literature on famine and never-ending controversies concerning representations of famine, we may cautiously proclaim that the days of characterizing famine as an act of punishment of people by God, or simply nature's provision, are almost past. Indeed, these contentions were simplistic and inadequate excuses to avoid accountability on the part of those who allowed famine to befall. Nonetheless, the discourse on famine has continued unabated among humanitarians, media professionals, forecasters, legislators, academics, and so on, with no conclusive discernment or a path to solve this ageless scourge.

As the factors contributing to the emergence of famine appear to be many, the emphasis given to the different factors varies depending on the outlook of the concerned scholars on the matter—an outlook, which in turn is influenced by the decisive actors that will be identified below. In other words, human activities in general, fluctuation of weather, governance, vulnerability of communities (poverty coupled with lack of education), natural calamities, over-population, wars, and conflicts, are some of the factors that are commonly implicated as culprits, while the magnitude that these variables contribute to the occurrence of famine is gauged at different levels by different scholars. To most scholars, what seems to be evolving as a common theme is that famine is "human-made." Jenny Edkins' analysis of the problem, that famine is "a socio-economic process which causes the accelerated destitution of the most vulnerable and marginal groups in society" (2000, 20) and the suggestion of substituting the term "famine" with "mass starvation" to elicit effective response and account-ability, looks practical for the purpose this paper is set to accomplish.

Natural phenomena such as drought or extreme weather may or may not cause mass starvation and death. That depends on the capacity and readiness of the people affected to withstand the incidental event. The capacity and readiness of a people in turn depends on how far they are organized over a period of time and what type of leadership or governance they possess. People who are organized under an accountable democratic government, although they may encounter drought or extreme weather at any time, will not slide into a famine situation, for they are entitled to develop through time the capacity and coping mechanisms to withstand the calamities that they may encounter. On the other hand, people under a repressive and unaccountable government are stripped of their entitlements—natural or legal—and are neither allowed to freely organize themselves and forge a policy of their making nor develop the capacity to avert such calamities. In this manner, unorganized and oppressed communities are compelled to remain vulnerable and at the mercy of natural afflictions that are often harsh.

Famine occurs in a situation where there is a vulnerable way of life overseen by inept governments. This is why famine is attributed as human-made infliction and has no direct or rather intrinsic correlation with drought or other natural calamities. People can be starved to death or encounter famine because of self-centered policies and decisions made by cruel or inept authorities. As climate change depends on a number of natural factors including large-scale activities of humans, it follows then, lack of rain, i.e., drought, could occur at any time or any place because of one of the factors affecting the balance of nature. Many drought-prone countries, led by accountable governments, do not experience famine. Only where there is failure of authorities to arm their communities with the necessary capacity to withstand the impact of natural disasters does famine evolve. This happens because irresponsible governments neglect the factors that give rise to famine while investing the lion's share of their time and energy on power consolidation and fighting their political opponents, real or potential. Therefore, famine is caused not by scarcity or failure of rain, change of weather, over-population etc., but by the failure of authorities to enable their communities to withstand natural calamities. Their international benefactors who reinforce the prevalence of such inept and corrupt authorities in power are also in like manner responsible for the occurrence of famine.

Famine in the Horn

Historically, the Horn of Africa situated along the Red Sea and across the Arabian Peninsula was the conjoining region for trade and diplomatic relations between the West and the East. Its geostrategic importance grew centuries ago when the Nile River was the main highway of communication in the region before the Red Sea took over. The Red Sea that connects the Mediterranean and the Indian Ocean through the narrow passage of Babel-Mandeb is situated in the Horn. Through this passage passes the bulk of the trade merchandise between China, Japan and the rest of Asia and the West. One third of the world's oil and natural gas passes through this passage of the Horn of Africa every day. The Horn's geostrategic importance, however, had its own downside. Its significance came with an unavoidable cost that made it prone to conflicts. The inference is that who controls the Horn controls the greatest commercial passage in the name of national interest.

Through centuries of foreign invasions and expansions, the region was exposed to all sorts of war calamities. The Arabs, the Turks, the British, the French, and the Italians have made several repeated attempts to control the region causing the inhabitants of the Horn to engage in protracted defensive wars and consequently face the havoc that accompanies war. The impact of the wars on the environment was ruinous and on the population incendiary, causing mass displacement, destruction of farms and animals, scarcity of food, and soaring prices, and hence famine. The social and economic life of communities was uprooted to the core and stable political vitality was a long way off.

The external factors that have thrown the entire region into disorder had also upset the internal cohesion and continuity of each country of the Horn of Africa. An old state such as Ethiopia, situated at the center of the Horn, for instance, was ruled by warlords who partitioned the country into 28 fiercely competing regions for at least a century, from 1755 to 1855 (Henze 2004, 119). It was a century of wars and pillage amounting to self-destruction that led to a chain of famines. The predicament in other parts of the Horn was by-and-large similar and the entire region has been ravaged by proxy wars, the repercussions of which were dreadful. Even today, the trend of indulging in proxy wars seems not to go away. In general, this circumstance has led to the formation of dependent states in the Horn whose governments are not accountable to their people, but to external powers that finance them, supply them with arms and diplomatic leverage to stay in power. Obviously, external forces have their own regional as well as global agendas that entice them to intervene in the region in the first place. Hence, famine or other calamities that threaten the lives of the ordinary people are not of prime concern to the national government and the external powers that uphold them.

Why Famine Recurs and Who Is Responsible

All countries of the Horn have been enduring, more or less, similar pitiable famine for decades. Famine in Sudan, for instance, killed 70,000 Sudanese in 1998 (O'Grádá 2009, 24), while in Somalia between 2010 and 2011 more than 260,000 were dead as a result of famine (UN News Center, May 2, 2013). As many analysts have argued, contemporary famine in the Horn, as well as in other parts of Africa, is a system of wider and long-term economic and political difficulties: economic decline, political fragmentation and growing food insecurity (Duffield 1992; Woodward 1996, 2003). Twenty-four years after Mark Duffield made this critical observation, the Horn of Africa finds itself still in growing food insecurity and political instability as a result of extant poor systems of governance where accountability is non-existent. In a more explicit stance but without identifying the real actors in the famine saga, Devereux (2007, 23) delineates:

> In the past, the cause of and response to famine were localized; now they are globalized. All contemporary famines are fundamentally political, in the sense that political decisions contribute either to creating famine conditions or to failure to intervene to prevent famine.

Now let us delve into the perpetuity of famine in the Horn to identify the local and global players. However, since it is beyond the scope of this paper to cover the entire history of famine in the Horn countries, the focus shall be on the most populous country, contemporary Ethiopia, which by and large represents the other Horn nations as far as famine is concerned.

In 1973–1974, during the reign of Emperor Haile Selassie, the worst famine in memory took the lives of over 300,000 Ethiopians (Ofcansky and Berry 1991). As a result, the Emperor, together with the feudal system he represented, was overthrown and replaced by a military junta called Derg. "The decisive event was perhaps the big famine in the north of the country, which drew a very belated and callous response from the government and which revealed its inadequacy to care for its own people" (Abbink 1995, 65). Again, under the Derg's military government of Colonel Mengistu Haile Mariam, one of the deadliest disasters in the twentieth century occurred in 1984–1985, when a famine took the lives of over one million Ethiopians (Gibson 2012, 268). The world was alarmed after the distressing scene of the famine appeared on TV screens, thanks to the concerned journalists of the international media.

Although both governments were overthrown primarily as a result of the rebellion triggered by the devastation of the famines that were allowed to occur under their watch, similar depressing stories continued to reign throughout Ethiopia under the incumbent government as well. After the Derg was toppled in 1991, the leader of the EPRDF, Meles Zenawi, seized power and promised to deal with famine once and for all, "making it a history." For the following 21 years, until his death in 2012, he had repeated the same pledge without any apparent result. Despite the rhetoric of Meles and his allies, and their publications of a double-digit growth economy, Ethiopia in 2016–2017 finds itself in need of massive emergency relief aid. The UN-WFP writes, "According to the 2016 Humanitarian Requirements Document, 10.2 million people in Ethiopia need emergency food assistance."[1]

Table 25.1 aims to show the number of Ethiopian people who were in need of emergency relief aid and the frequency of such a predicament since the advent of the twenty-first century to this day. The data was collected from reports of the United Nations Food and Agriculture Organization (FAO) and World Food Program (WFP), as indicated chronologically.

Table 25.1 Relief Index 2000–2016

Year	Starving People (Millions)	Source
2000	2.3	WFP
2000–2003	12.6	WFP
2004	7	FAO/WFP
2006	7.2	FAO
2008	10	FAO/WFP
2009–2010	5	FAO/WFP
2011–2012	13	WFP
2013–2014	5	WFP
2015	10	WFP
2016	10.2	FAO/WFP

Source: FAO and WFP.

As one can observe from Table 25.1, millions of Ethiopians were and are still in need of emergency aid almost every year. The need for such emergency aid is prompted by widespread starvation that could kill en masse. For unqualified reasons, various academics use different wordings such as chronic hunger, extreme malnutrition, severe food shortage, etc., to describe the mass starvation that leads to numerous deaths. The point of concern in the present discussion, however, is not the selection of language but whether the stated different characterizations end up in famine that takes the lives of numerous people or leaves them on the verge of death. Isn't this what matters most if we believe in the right to food and to life? Why are these painful deaths of fellow human beings repeating themselves every year in this part of the world?

If there is one thing the Horn is most known for at least since the early 1970s, no doubt it is famine. Conflict may come next to famine as a contemporary stigma of the region, but when the numbers of victims in each case are statistically gauged, those of famine are excruciatingly high. The number of people who were killed by famine in Ethiopia in 1984–1985 was over one million, and in Somalia in 2010–2011 it was 260,000, according to the UN reports of 1985 and 2011 respectively. Conflict-induced deaths, on the other hand, are much fewer, the rare case being the Ethiopian–Eritrean war of 1998, which took almost 70,000 lives from both sides (Reuters, 2007). Yet, while the latter triggered massive international uproar, condemnation of and sanctions against the government authorities that set the war in motion, those governments that allowed deadly famines to evolve, causing hundreds of thousands or in some cases millions of deaths, got by without even the slightest condemnation.

The causes of drought—failure or inadequacy of rain—are befittingly associated with nature although large-scale human activities obviously impact on the environment and could lead to aridity and desertification. The expansion of the Sahara Desert southwards is a case in point. Famine, on the other hand, which is among other factors related with drought, is entirely human made. Unlike drought, which may or may not occur seasonally, famine is a cumulative effect of prolonged failure to create a sustainable basis of life and could engulf vulnerable societies even when drought is not a matter of contention. Many drought-prone countries or countries known for their arid climate do not experience famine simply because they design long-term ways and means to generate agricultural produce that keeps their population well fed and does not allow the negative impact of drought to lead to famine. Durable irrigation systems or sustained water conservation schemes could effectively reduce the impact of drought, thereby not allowing famine to occur. Such undertakings are manageable by a government worthy of its responsibilities. Bad governments, on the other hand, neglect their responsibilities and by not implementing the right policies at the right time expose their people to a position of vulnerability. Strictly speaking, drought that could have been overcome with responsible planning, such as investment in water and soil conservation or irrigation schemes, when left to take its course can lead to famine. Thus, the famine in the Horn is not simply down to the weather or conflict driven—it occurs because correct measures to curb it have not been set in place.

If we compare the severity of drought in Ethiopia and Egypt, a neighbor of the Horn, one may sum up Egypt as being in perpetual drought although we do not hear of famine affecting its people. Ethiopia, on the other hand, with average rainfall and contributing as much as 80 percent of the water to the River Nile flow that continuously feeds northern Sudan and Egypt, suffers from drought-driven famine. "The incredible irony is" says Ghelawdewos Araia (2002, 1):

> while Ethiopia encounters drought and famine almost every decade (now perhaps every half a decade) despite the blessings of hundreds of major rivers and thousands of streams, Egypt with an ecology that does not witness rainfall and the country depending on the Nile waters of Ethiopia, is a major exporter of food crops, especially beans.

This looks paradoxical, yet the explanation lies in the system of governance that presides over the people affected. The authorities that run the state that controls and manages the human and material resources of the country are at the center of the infliction. "Therefore, the eradication of famine and poverty requires a radical transformation of the exercise of state power" Tseggai Mebrahtu (2002, 6).

Famine and the Tigray People's Liberation Front (TPLF)

Despite drought, we have demonstrated that famine is preventable if and only if the mechanisms to prevent it—water conservation and irrigation schemes among others—are set in place. This resolve, of course, requires a system of governance that gives primacy to the welfare of the people by confronting drought before it leads to famine. In the countries of the Horn where the bulk of the population depends on rain-fed agriculture, conserving rainwater would have sufficed to grow enough crops to feed the entire population, thereby averting the possibility of famine from striking. Setting in place systems of irrigation that could undercut the impact of drought would also help produce the necessary yield to block the possibility of famine arising. This is amenable to a government that takes accountability, food security, and water management seriously. In Ethiopia, as evinced earlier, the failure to prevent famine and tackle it once it ensued was arguably the main cause that brought the downfall of the governments of Emperor Haile Selassie and Colonel Mengistu Haile Mariam in 1974 and 1991 respectively. Much has been written about the role these two regimes played in creating and covering up the famines that took the lives of millions of Ethiopians, hence there is no need to go into detail about the "famine crimes" perpetrated by these two governments.

In this section, however, I shall dwell on the role played by the "liberation" fronts as epitomized by the TPLF—a relevant segment to the general account but often brushed aside or construed in a rather unethical way. The engagement of the "liberation" fronts in general and that of the TPLF in particular in the famine discourse was barely touched upon. I would therefore like to incorporate the TPLF's share in the famine riddle as it happened, for I believe it contributes to a complete picture of the recurring tragedy, with the objective of arriving at a lasting solution.

More than most regions of Ethiopia, the northern part including Tigray (the home base of the TPLF) was devastated by a series of wars and unforgiving famines for generations. It was the dismal situation of the people that gave rise to the formation of the TPLF which vowed to resolve the generations-old problems, famine being at the top of the list. The people of Tigray plainly trusted the front and gave everything including their sons and daughters to the struggle, hoping the TPLF would end their misery and bring about peace and prosperity. Soon, the time came when the TPLF was to be tested.

Following severe droughts in most parts of the region, experience had made it clear that famine would occur if nothing was done in advance to avert it. Not heeding such bitter experiences and as the 1984–1985 famine was fast looming, the TPLF was preoccupied with preparations for celebrating its tenth anniversary and the formation of a new party, the Marxist Leninist League of Tigray (MLLT) within the front. Suggestions to postpone the ceremonial hustle and pay due attention to the impending famine by members of the Front were flatly rejected by the politburo of which I was a member and privy to all inner debates and discussions (for details see Berhe, 2009, 177). What transpired was folly.

At a time when the greater part of Tigray was facing the worst famine in memory, the responses of both the government and the front were much the same and unnerving. The intended response of the Mengistu government was to resettle the affected people in southern Ethiopia, far away from the TPLF-held territory. By so doing, the regime surmised it would deny the support the TPLF used to garner from the people. Dubious as it was, the plan could only work partially as the vast majority of the affected people were far beyond the reach of the government; it was the TPLF that controlled the greater part of Tigray and its people.

The TPLF's actual response, on the other hand, was to move the affected people to Sudan where international publicity was readily available and food aid could be generated. Therefore, according to the plans of the TPLF, thousands had to make a trek of hundreds of kilometers under the scorching sun of the Ethiopian and Sudanese lowlands. There was no adequate preparation, nor capable people to handle the mass exodus, which "included the evacuation of over 200,000 people to Sudan" (de Waal 1997, 129). Many perished on the way for lack of basic support of food, medicine and guidance. Seyoum Mesfin, then head of the TPLF foreign bureau, reported to the TPLF congress held at the time that 13,000 people were buried in the sand on the way to the Sudan.

At this moment, TPLF leaders and cadres stationed abroad were rushing from Sudan to Worii, one of the base areas of the TPLF, in Tigray where a founding congress of the new ultra-left party, the Marxist Leninist League of Tigray, was to be held from July 12–15, 1985. Seyoum Mesfin led the overseas-based TPLF contingent and had brought US$100 million with him. The money was part of the emergency relief fund collected from donors on behalf of the famine victims and was handed over to the organization's office of the Central Committee (CC) at Worii. Because the Mengistu regime made it extremely difficult to get food aid into the rebel-held territories of the north, another channel of collecting money by the front was the scheme called "internal purchase," when donors come with their cash to the "liberated" zone of the TPLF, ostensibly to buy grain as food for the starving population. What actually happened was veteran TPLF cadres posed as merchants to receive the aid money to buy grain, which in fact was pre-arranged stocks of the Front. A controversial story entitled "Ethiopia famine aid 'spent on weapons'" was compiled by the BBC World Service Africa editor.[2] At the end of July 1985, the Central Committee of the TPLF/MLLT met to determine, among other things, the budget of the Front and the then established party, MLLT. The allocation of the money in hand went as follows: 50 percent to MLLT, 45 percent to TPLF and 5 percent to famine victims. There was no considerable opposition to the financial outlays, except for one powerless voice that pleaded to raise the amount for famine victims in whose cause the fund was collected.

The appropriation of the fund and its subsequent allocation was a pattern that has been going on under the pretext of financing various organizational relief and developmental projects. This pattern of diverting relief aid for political and military purposes continued until the TPLF ousted the military regime in May 1991. In a rather carefully worded statement but asserting that the front used the aid money for its war projects, Alex de Waal (1997, 130) who wrote extensively about the TPLF asserts, "The front used its aid far better: it mobilized people in a war against tyranny, while Mengistu used relief to reinforce oppression." Although there was no evidence to support the idea that the TPLF is less tyrannical than Mengistu, de Waal's assertion reflects only that the TPLF used the aid for war. De Waal (1997, 129) does not stop there but continues, "In mid-1984, the TPLF made its *strategic priority* the struggle against famine. . . . The TPLF was not a conventional army diverting relief grain, rather it was a political front mobilizing a classic 'people's war.'" Finally, he declares, "The TPLF ultimately *won its war against Famine*" (de Waal 1997, 130, emphasis added. The reality on the ground, however, was diametrically opposed to these assertions. One could simply refer to the annual (2016 included) reports of the FAO or WFP as partly cited above. Nineteen years after de Waal wrote those words, famine and the TPLF are still prevailing in Ethiopia. De Waal theorizes about famine crimes but does not say a word about those who could also be considered famine opportunists such as Meles and Sibhat Nega, head of the economic department of the TPLF and its Chairman for some time.

Here we must ask whether aid agencies were primarily preventing famine from recurring or promoting regional or global objectives there by allowing famine to persist rather than fade away.

Funding Agencies and the Front

Conversant with the humanitarian activities of neighboring fronts in Eritrea and Sudan, the TPLF felt the need to establish a humanitarian wing right from the beginning of its struggle against the much stronger army of the military government in Ethiopia. In 1976, the TPLF formed its own humanitarian branch called the Relief Society of Tigray (REST) and Abadi Zemo, a veteran cadre, was posted as its director. REST was entrusted with the task of designing relief and/or developmental projects and raising money from voluntary funding agencies. The projects designed ranged from water and soil conservation to building terraces and from "internal purchase" of grain for food to farm equipment and oxen. On paper, all the designs pass as excellent projects that could transform the lives of impoverished communities in Tigray. Given the well-crafted project proposals, there was no problem of procuring large amounts of resources both in cash and in kind from the humanitarian aid agencies.

On the ground, however, the version was totally different; either the projects did not exist or there were only symbolic projects that helped keep the continuation of the fund flow. One vivid example was the Shiwata project of water and soil conservation, which began in a few plots of arid land in the vicinity of a village called Shiwata, in the district of Abergele, Tembien. As it started, it showed promising results of voluminous harvest, and funding agencies showed their determination to continue their support after looking into the pictorial reports of the initial outcome of the pilot project. Sadly enough, the project could not stretch from its pilot standing to cover the small village let alone expand to other arid districts. The TPLF had aborted the promising project by diverting the funds to its war efforts. The self-serving leaders of the Front eclipsed a project that could have been developed to a level that sustained the livelihoods of millions of farmers and their families. Thirty-five years later, after the induction of the Shiwata project, drought driven famine is still tearing down the district and its environs.

Shiwata is just one case among numerous projects through which funds were generated to finance the costly war project of the TPLF. The Front by then had an army of about 35,000 regular fighters and double that number of militias. It had to feed and equip its big army to fight the government forces, which were financed and armed by the former Soviet Union. Though the Front claimed to have the support of the people, there was no way to translate the claimed support materially. Famine stricken people in no position to support themselves justifiably could not support the costly war project of the Front.

The flow of relief and development aid that started at least since the Ethiopian famine of 1958, which took 100,000 lives while leaving nine million people destitute (Mariam 1986; Zewde 2003), is still going on; 58 years later 10.2 million people are starving to death and in need of emergency relief aid worth US$1.4 billion.[3] The famine situation in Somalia and South Sudan is for the most part the same, with 1.3 million people in Somalia (Reliefweb 2016) and 2.8 million in South Sudan (UN WFP 2016) on the verge of death. The flow of the enormous amount of aid for almost six decades has not changed the situation of famine in the Horn of Africa. The famine and the same ill-suited actions to tackle it are still with us.

It is imperative to scrutinize the engagement of the powerful governments in this huge business of relief and developmental aid in relation to the footing of the TPLF. This may also throw light on the overall aid business to African countries that has been running for more than five decades now but without apparent success. This very question into the role played by powerful governments such as the US is a crucial matter that is blocking a thorough understanding of famine and its ultimate solution.

To run its protracted war against the heavily armed military government of the Derg, the TPLF needed huge funds that could not be procurable from the impoverished people. The bulk of the fund, which the TPLF utilized for its military ventures, came mainly from European public donations and government grants through voluntary agencies commonly known as NGOs in the form of relief aid. NGOs obviously are obliged to operate within the legal bounds and approval of their respective governments. The NGO–government linkage thence entails a political chemistry to which both sides adhere, particularly in relation to who should be supported and why. This complex and undeclared component of the relationship reflects the often-reiterated rationale that "there is no aid without strings." To illustrate this point, in her 1987 article "Ethiopia and the Politics of Famine Relief," Gayle Smith, then a journalist and currently the Administrator of USAID, quoted former US Secretary of Agriculture John Block, who said: "In the coming years, food aid will prove to be the most powerful weapon of the US" (Smith 1987, 35). She goes on to note that:

> In early 1985, Vice-President George Bush flew to the Sudanese capital accompanied by aid Administrator Peter MacPherson and officials of the American-based Christian Broadcasting Network and Americares Foundation, both key players in the 'private aid' network supporting the contra rebels in Nicaragua. . . . All signs indicated that the EPLF and/or the TPLF might be tapped to serve as Reagan's contras in the Horn of Africa.

In her conclusion, Smith frames a striking case in point:

> As long as famine prevails, the US will be able to maintain some leverage over all parties to the conflict. Far from being simply a crisis requiring a humanitarian response, the African famine which began in 1982 bears grave political consequences for the Horn and for the entire continent.
>
> (Smith 1987, 37)

Indeed, famine has been an instrument of political objective and will remain so as long as the politics of the big powers does not change.

Let us look into the actual thinking of the leading US policy formulators. US Senator Hubert Humphrey in 1957 said:

> I have heard . . . that people may become dependent on us for food. To me that is good news—because before people can do anything they have got to eat. And if you are looking for a way to get people to lean on you and be dependent on you, in terms of their co-operation with you, it seems to me that food dependence would be terrific.
>
> (Hayter 1983, 86)

If food dependency is considered a terrific matter by powerful authorities, they all have their reasons to sustain poverty in its "ugliest" form, famine. This malignant notion continued to reverberate with other leaders of the US administration. President Nixon for one puts it nakedly: "Let us remember that the main purpose of aid is not to help other nations but to help ourselves" (Hayter 1983, 83–84). Seemingly contradictory, President Reagan was widely quoted in the media to have said, "A hungry child knows no politics" (Natsios 1997, cited in Howe 2007, 356). But for the Reagan Administration, the famine that struck in 1984 provided the opportunity to intervene more directly in Ethiopia's role in the Horn of Africa. "Between 1977 and 1983, US policy towards Ethiopia was shaped in reaction to the presence of the Soviet Union" (Smith 1987, 35). It set in motion "an Inter-Agency Task Force on the Africa Famine comprising representatives of the Department of Defense, the CIA, the Joint Chiefs of Staff, AID and the Department of Agriculture." Headed by General (ret.) Julius Bectin, the Task Force would play a critical role in determining who was fed and who starved in Africa's Horn. Smith concludes, "It now appears that the decrease in food assistance to Ethiopia and the failure to provide relief until the famine had reached catastrophic proportions was primarily a means of positioning the US," to exert more regional influence (1987, 36)."[4]

The goal of extending aid often seems to be to energize agreeable partners such as the TPLF in the global or regional confrontation against real or potential adversaries and not to curb the impact of famine.

Evidently, the aid flow had started at least since the late 1950s, but more was forthcoming from 1974 after the BBC journalist Jonathan Dimbleby in a TV documentary revealed to the world the horrifying famine in northern Ethiopia. The aid might have saved some lives, but certainly did not end famine. Ten years later famine struck again, as reported by Michael Buerk and Mohamed Amin of the BBC in 1984, despite the continuous flow of relief and developmental aid in between. Aid and famine continued to exist side-by-side although the former was intended to stamp out the latter. By maintaining this unholy balance between aid and famine, the TPLF toppled the military regime and seized power in Ethiopia under an umbrella organization known as Ethiopian People's Revolutionary Democratic Front (EPRDF) in 1991. Yet 28 years later, the nature of the aid and the recurrence of the famine have not changed. As we speak, over 10.2 million Ethiopians are in need of emergency relief aid according to the 2016 reports of UN-WFP/FAO, Oxfam, Menschen für Menschen (MfM), USAID, Relief Web, etc. The rebel-turned-government of the TPLF/EPRDF, moreover, continued the aid business as usual, but this time officially with the donor governments while famine lingers routinely.[5]

The emergency relief aid that has been flowing for the past 50 plus years may have saved some lives at every famine event and triggered the overthrow of repressive governments, but miserably failed in arresting famine itself. While the situation of the age-old famine persists, the relationship of the front-turned-government, the donor governments, and the aid agencies remains intact and the famine business goes on as it used to be. When the objective of the Front falls within the bounds of the strategic objective of the powerful government, reminiscent of the Cold War alignment or nowadays of anti-terrorism alliance, evidently the donor governments strive for ways and means to bolster the position of their partner in the interest of the global or regional strategy. This situation leaves the vulnerability of the people as it is and the imminence of famine alive.

Famine and the Role of Media

In the above deliberation we have seen how and to what end Western powerful states have been intervening in the famine-prone region of the Horn of Africa. They have been working with inept regimes in Africa whose policies have been paving the way for the recurrence of famine for decades. In this perplexing process, the international media has been active in playing both positive and negative roles. Without losing sight of the role the media have played in mitigating the impact of famine by alerting and mobilizing people to help the already victimized people, it is compelling to explore the role of the media in these issues.

Media bring the tragedy of famine to the attention of the international audience, partly to initiate donors and streamline their donation to save lives. This task of motivating and mobilizing remotely situated publics, NGOs, and donor governments to raise relief aid is not an easy one and is complementary to a genuine humanitarian endeavor. By the same action, the media exposes the responsible authorities that overlooked the outburst of such calamity. No doubt this is a worthwhile humane contribution and the media has to be commended for this role.

Yet every time famine strikes, the media rush to the scene of the tragedy once the famine has already inflicted a visible proportion of damage. Then the media covers the story for a brief period, usually until the horrifying scene subsides. The next time one hears from the media is when and if a similar famine strikes again. The same old coverage followed by the same fundraising effort repeats itself without looking deeper into the real causes and lasting solutions to the famine. In this case, the media to this day have failed to underscore the fact that relief aid is only an emergency or temporary solution and cannot prevent famine from happening again, but from the outset, they give the impression that they are there to mediate a solution once and for all. The immediate step of providing first aid, understandably, captures massive popularity in the face of a starving mass. In this manner, relief aid bears the marks of a legitimate solution, disguising the root causes and the permanent solution of famine. However, the big question is why is famine recurring year after year and decade after decade? What are the root causes of famine and how should famine be tackled once and for all? These are questions the media fail to answer. Johan Helland (2000, 1) rightly points out:

As famine evolves, resources are mobilized, mostly through the attention of the international media and eventually successful famine relief effort, (by and large) are

317

organized. If such efforts were exerted to identify and tackle the root causes of famine which is the more important approach of solving the problem of famine all together, people would not have to suffer in a recurring famine.

This does not mean however, that there were no attempts by daring journalists and other writers to dig into the intricacies surrounding the famine predicament, including reports of how relief aid was diverted by the TPLF to feed its army and buy weapons. The evidence of the misuse of the relief aid was procured from veteran TPLF members who were part of the decision-making process and execution of diverting the relief fund. In the midst of the crisis, a CIA report stated that aid was "almost certainly being diverted for military purposes."[6] Also, in *Mail Online* March 17, 2010, Richard Dowden notes:

> Bob Houdek, a former US ambassador to Addis Ababa, revealed that former rebels now in government had admitted to him that some of the food aid was 'monetarised'—i.e. sold for money to buy weapons.

Indeed, a 105-page investigative report published by Human Rights Watch (2010) documented the ways in which the EPRDF regimes continued to manipulate relief aid for political power. It states, "The Ethiopian government is using development aid to suppress political dissent by conditioning access to essential government programs on support for the ruling party." If famine is to be prevented effectively such that it may not ravage fellow human beings and undermine our common humanity again and again, the role of the media has to be exposing the root causes of famine that spark permanent remedies. In this age, when human beings have already developed the capacity to harvest valuable assets from outer space and below the surface of the earth, it could not have been that complex to prevent famine. The media ought to question and unmask the root causes of the failure to end famine. In a stark comparative observation, Bahru Zewde (2003, 7), notes: "Surprisingly enough, the extent and severity of famine has tended to be directly proportional to the sophistication of our development strategies and the redoubling of our efforts to combat famine." Being at a vantage point, the media is tasked to place accountability where it belongs. Once the root causes of famine are well established, all efforts could be directed towards tackling the dilemma and concerned actors would be in positions to take the necessary steps. For one, local governments, international agencies and NGOs could focus on long-range ethical investments rather than perpetuating inadequate emergency aid that has taken us nowhere.

Conclusion

When people starve en masse to death, it is famine, i.e. genocide by starvation instead of by bullets. This devastating phenomenon is still a reality in the Horn of Africa. Even in this year 2017, millions of people are trapped in famine. As always, emergency relief aid has been the response to the recurring calamity. Although such emergency response may have saved the lives of some lucky ones, the long-term dismal impact on the population affected and the shadow it casts over the root causes of the disaster is immense. This process obstructs the realization of essential remedies and allows famine to surface again and again.

Given adequate knowledge—among others, the "famine early warning systems" run by governments, the UN, and NGOs and the advanced capacity to produce the necessities for life and harness the vagaries of nature developed by many nations and international bodies—the fact that all attempts to curb famine have failed so far tells us that either the root causes of the scourge were not bluntly addressed or were knowingly ignored. Evidently, where the preponderant concern of national governments and international forces is not the well-being of their people but power through which they could impose their will by restraining their adversaries, ordinary people are exposed to multiple challenges in this permanently changing world. There are no chances of famine emerging when such challenges are confronted by a government that is ethically principled and accountable. It is therefore the failure of the authorities at the helm of state power that have the ability to mobilize and command the human and material resources of a nation and advance preparedness in the event of calamities that are at the center of the problem. When such authorities secure the backing of international forces for reasons other than the well-being of the people, the chance of famine re-emerging is self-evident, as one can observe in the Horn of Africa at present.

The real cause of famine lies in the irresponsible practices of political forces at national and international levels (Thurow and Kilman 2010). As long as these forces pursue the same old path of tackling famine that has brought the entire Horn to where it is now, things will only get worse with conflicts, displacement of people, desertification, and other looming disasters. Paul Streeten has observed, "'It is not political will that we should be studying'— or worry about—'but how to create the political base . . . to demand of our leaders an increased commitment to fight hunger across the world'" (Streeten 1984 cited in Devereux et al., 2008, 138). Our goal should be creating the political base to empower leaders who literally feel the pain of starving people and stand on their behalf. Evidently, famine and all related quandaries are preventable, but require the conviction of accountable, governing bodies together with the scrutiny of bold media and the endeavor of critical visionaries who are an integral part of an organized civil society.

Notes

1. A joint Government and Humanitarian Partners' Document, the *2016 Ethiopia Humanitarian Requirements Document* can be accessed online: www.humanitarianresponse.info/en/system/files/documents/files/ethiopia_hrd_2016.pdf

2. The BBC news report "Ethiopia Famine Aid 'Spent on Weapons'" by Martin Plaut, the Africa editor of the BBC World Service, can be accessed online: http://news.bbc.co.uk/2/hi/8535189.stm

   After a complaint from the Band Aid Trust about this report, the BBC concluded that there was no evidence that Band Aid funds were diverted to rebels to buy guns, a point that the journalist made in the report. The BBC concluded that such allegations "should not have been broadcast." www.bbc.co.uk/complaints/comp-reports/ecu/ecu_bandaidmoneydonatedethiopia

3. The official press release by the Permanent Mission of Ethiopia to the United Nations Office at Geneva and Other International Organizations in Switzerland can be accessed online: www.ethiopianmission.ch/2016/04/06/drought-in-ethiopia-humanitarian-partners-call-for-more-action/

4. The BBC news report "Ethiopia Famine Aid 'Spent on Weapons.'"

5. www.wfp.org/countries/Ethiopia, 2016; www.usaid.gov/ethiopia/food-assistance; http://reliefweb.int/report/ethiopia/humanitarian-action-children-2016-ethiopia

6. The CIA report can be accessed online: www.cia.gov/library/readingroom/document/cia-rdp86t00589r000200160004-5

References

Abbink, J. (1995) "FOCAAL," *Journal of Global and Historical Anthropology*, 25, 57–97.

Araia, G. (2002) *Uprooting the Root Causes of Famine in Ethiopia*, available at: www.tisjd.net/FAMINE.htm

Berhe, A. (2009) *A Political History of the Tigray People's Liberation Front (1975–1991): Revolt, Ideology and Mobilization in Ethiopia*, Los Angeles, CA: Tsehai, available at: http://countrystudies.us/ethiopia/46.htm

Devereux, S. (2007) *The New Famines: Why Famine Persists in an Era of Globalization*, London and New York: Routledge.

Devereux, S., Vaitla, B., and Hauenstein Swan, S. (2008) *Seasons of Hunger: Fighting Cycles of Quiet Starvation Among the World's Rural Poor* (A Hunger Watch Publication), London: Pluto Press.

De Waal, A. (1997) Famine Crimes: Politics and the Disaster Relief Industry in Africa, Oxford, UK: James Currey; and Bloomington IN: Indiana University Press.

Dowden, R. (2010) "'Get Real Bob - Buying Guns Might Have Been Better Than Buying Food': After Geldorf's Angry Outburst, an Africa Specialist Hits Back," available at: www.dailymail.co.uk/debate/article-1257735/Get-real-Bob--buying-guns-better-buying-food.html

Duffield, M. (1992) *War and Famine in Africa* (Oxfam Working Papers Series—Book 5), Oxford: Oxfam Professional.

Edkins, J. (2000) *Whose Hunger? Concepts of Famine, Practice of Aid*, Minneapolis, MN: University of Minnesota Press.

Gibson, M. (2012) *The Feeding of Nations: Re-defining Food Security for the 21st Century*, London and New York: CRC Press.

Hayter, T. (1987) *The Creation of World Poverty: An Alternative View to the Brandt Report*, London: Pluto Press.

Helland, J. (2000) *Pastoralists in the Horn of Africa: The Continued Threat of Famine*, Bergen: Chr. Michelsen Institute, available at: http://bora.cmi.no/dspace/bitstream/10202/245/1/WP2000.15%20Johan-07202007_9.pdf

Henze, P. B. (2004) *Layers of Time: A History of Ethiopia* (3rd ed.), New York: Palgrave Macmillan.

Howe, P. (2007) "Priority Regimes and Famine," in S. Devereux (Ed.), *The New Famines: Why Famines Persist in an Era of Globalization* (Routledge Studies in Development Economics), London and New York: Routledge, p. x.

Human Rights Watch. (2010) "Ethiopia: Donor Aid Supports Repression," October 19, available at: https://www.hrw.org/news/2010/10/19/ethiopia-donor-aid-supports-repression

Mariam, M. W. (1986) *Rural Vulnerability to Famine in Ethiopia: 1958–77*, Rugby, UK: Practical Action Publishing.

Mebrahtu, T. (2002) *Famine: The Price that Ethiopia Pays as a Result of Neglect of the Rule of Law by Its Rulers*, available at: www.ethiopiafirst.com/news2002/Nov/Neglect_of_the_Rule_of_law.html

Natsios, A. (1997) "Feed North Korea: Don't Play Politics with Hunger," *The Washington Post*, February 7.

Ó Gráda, C. (2009) *Famine: A Short History*, Princeton, NJ: Princeton University Press.

Ofcansky, T. P., and Berry, L. (Eds.) (1991) *Ethiopia: A Country Study*. Washington: GPO for the Library of Congress, available at: http://countrystudies.us/

Reliefweb. (2016) "Somalia Call for Aid—Drought and El Niño" available at http://reliefweb.int/report/somalia/somalia-call-aid-drought-and-el-ni-o-march-2016

Reuters. (2007), available at: www.reuters.com. January.

Smith, G. (1987) "Ethiopia and the Politics of Famine Relief," *MERIP*, March, 145, pp. 31–37.

Streeten, P. (1984) *Basic Needs: Some Unsettled Questions*, Cape Town: University of Cape Town.

The Holy Bible—Containing the Old and New Testaments, ESV edition 2011. Wheaton, IL: Good News.

Thurow, R., and Kilman, S. (2010) *Enough: Why the World's Poorest Starve in an Age of Plenty*, New York: Public Affairs, a member of the Perseus Books Group.

UN News Center. (2013). "Somalia famine killed nearly 260,000 people, half of them children", available at: www.un.org/apps/news/story.asp?NewsID=44811#.V9Zal63_PcQ

UN WFP. (2016) available at: www.wfp.org/countries/south-sudan

Woodward, P. (1996) *The Horn of Africa: Politics and International Relations*, London and New York: I.B. Tauris.

Woodward, P. (2003) *The Horn of Africa: Politics and International Relations* (International Library of African Studies), London: I.B. Tauris.

Zewde, B. (2003) "What Did We Dream? What Did We Achieve? And Where Are We Heading?" *Economic Focus Bulletin of the Ethiopian Association*, 5 (3): 1–18, available at: www.eeaecon.org/sites/default/files/publications/Economic%20Focus%20_Vol.%205%20No.3%20_%20Bahru%20Zewde_what%20did%20we%20dream%20What%20did%20we%20achieve%20and%20where%20are%20we%20heading_0.pdf

26

DISASTER MANAGEMENT IN THE PHILIPPINES

Media, Unions, and Humanitarian Action

Kim Scipes

As the planet continues to heat up, all expectations are that there will be more and more "natural" disasters in the world. Perhaps the people most at risk are those in the island nations. These are often small, atoll island nations—such as the Maldives Islands, the Marshall Islands, and Tuvalu—but this also extends to larger island nations, such as Indonesia and the Philippines, and will extend to low-lying mainland areas, such as the Ganges Delta in Bangladesh.

Most of the emphasis to date has been on government and NGO (non-governmental organizations) responses to disasters. Their people are often among first responders, and certainly that is who the media focus their attention upon when covering responses to such disasters. However, once the TV cameras pack up and leave the area, the remaining recovery work is often desultory, taking years for an affected area to fully recover. This has been the experience of the Philippines in addressing the problems of Typhoon Haiyan, which hit the country in November 2013.

Typhoon Haiyan was a "super typhoon" that struck the country in its midsection, the Visayas, with particular impact on the islands of Leyte and western Samar. Tacloban City, on the island of Leyte, experienced winds of approximately 195 mph. According to Weather Underground's Jeff Masters, "Haiyan is the strongest storm to ever make landfall" (Fischetti 2013). The resulting death count throughout the country was over 3,600 people, and the property damage was extensive and intensive. According to the UN office for the Coordination of Humanitarian Affairs, over 4.3 million people were affected across the country (Hodal 2013). Government officials estimated that storm damage would "probably shave 0.3–0.8 percentage points from the expected GDP rate of 7.3 percent this year" (Landigin 2013), suggesting major economic damage from the storm. One of the most impressive things about the aftermath was the global response. Many countries sent aid, resources, and money to aid the affected country (see extensive list of resources, "Typhoon Haiyan," *Wikipedia* 2014). This was heartening.

However, like many developing countries, the Philippines have limited governmental resources, especially financial but perhaps more importantly, in trained disaster responders. Reuters reported, "The government [in the local region that was hit] has been overwhelmed by the force of the typhoon" (Reuters 2013). And the international media also criticized the government for its lack of prompt response to the ravages of the typhoon (Pangco Panares 2013).

The Social Impact: A Shattered Cup

One of the primary impacts of natural disasters—especially after the immediate loss of life, destruction of property and loss of resources—is the impact on the social order or society. In contrast to British Prime Minister Margaret Thatcher's absurd claim that "there is no such thing as society" (see Tice 2010), it is the extensive social ties between individuals that allow social orders to develop and exist, especially in local areas. A natural disaster of any size can have an impact on a community and, obviously, the greater the disaster, the greater the impact. And, these kinds of impacts are similar to a military attack, or a major economic producer closing down factories and other productive operations in a local area (for the latter, see Moore 1989). For the affected area, the social impact can be suggested by throwing a cup down on a concrete floor: the cup (representing local society) shatters.

The social impact of natural disasters can be extensive and can linger over a long period of time. Michael Lindell and Carla Prater (2003) note that social impacts are multiple, and can include psychological, sociodemographic, socio-economic, and sociopolitical impacts. In other words, the social impacts go beyond just the threat to life, limb, and economic sustainability, and these impacts tend to intensify in places where social resources are limited. In turn, these factors generally are not understood, much less addressed.

Another source of conflict is the contrast between a personalistic culture in many victim communities, which is based upon bonds of affection, and the universalistic culture of the alien relief bureaucracy, which values rationality and efficiency over personal loyalty even when engaged in humanitarian activity. This conflict typically manifests itself in differences in emphasis regarding a task (material/economic) versus social–emotional (interpersonal relationships/emotional well-being) orientation toward recovery activities (Lindell and Prater 2003, 180).

However, and interestingly, these researchers also note, "In many cases, recovery is facilitated when outside recovery organizations hire local 'boundary spanners' to provide a link between the two disparate cultures" (Ibid.). The researchers note, "Perhaps the most significant sociodemographic impact of a disaster in a stricken community is destruction of households' dwellings." And after discussing four stages of housing recovery, they point out that:

> Particularly significant are the problems faced by lower income households, which tend to be headed disproportionately by females and racial/ethnic minorities. Such households are more likely to experience destruction of these homes because of pre-impact locational vulnerability. This is especially true in developing countries.
>
> (Lindell and Prater 2003, 179)

It is argued here that an important and overlooked resource that might bridge the gap between natural disaster victims and government/NGO responders is the country's labor movement.

Labor Movement

Now, before moving forward, it must be quickly added that we have to apply considerable nuance to what we mean by "labor movement": labor, like any other social force, is not monolithic; it is particularly heterogeneous, has multiple approaches and visions, and is chock full of contradictions. This author is not saying all labor organizations meet these goals of being life enhancing, pro-people and willing to fight for a better world.

To delve further into this idea, however, we must be able to disaggregate labor. A key way to do this is by "labor center"—these are conglomerations of affiliated labor unions, their unifying labor organizations, and their central organizations—as there are often multiple and competing labor centers in a country, so it is insufficient (and often inaccurate) to tie them together in a unified labor "movement." Labor centers have been identified according to their approach to unionism, and three different types of unionism—economic, political, and social movement unionism—have been identified (Scipes 1992a, 1992b, 2014b). Further, variations within both economic and political unionism—identified as "forms" of the different "types" of trade unionism—have been delineated (see Pillay 2013; Scipes 2014b).

Accordingly, these can be reconceptualized as "business" unions and "progressive" unions, featuring a narrow or broad approach to trade unionism. Within each of these categories, they can be further delineated between "more democratic" and "less democratic," but that is beyond the scope of this essay.

Business unions take a narrow approach to trade unionism, and generally only care about wages, benefits, and working conditions they can win for their members at work, ignoring their affects on other people, whether positive or negative.

Progressive unions take a broad approach to trade unionism. They generally try to improve their members' lives in the workplace, but also tackle issues that affect their members outside of work. These efforts vary by who determines organizational developments, the relationship to the industrial relations system of the country, and by the relationship to the social order of their particular country (Scipes, 2014b).

Three categories of trade unionism can be subsumed under the progressive label. These include "social justice unions"—a form of the economic type of trade unionism, and examples from the United States include the United Packinghouse Workers of America of the 1930s–1960s, which confronted racism inside the packinghouses, in their union, and their communities (see Scipes 2003), as well as a number of contemporary unions such as the International Longshore and Warehouse Union (ILWU), the United Electrical Workers (UE), and perhaps a few others today. There are also political types of unions that have been created to advance the interests of particular nationalist, socialist, social democratic, or communist parties in their struggles to advance their self-defined interests (see Pillay 2013; Scipes 1992a, b). These types of unions generally place the interests of their initiating organization over the direct interests of the union members, although not always, and when they address interests of their members, they generally take a broader approach. And finally, there are labor organizations that have developed that recognize not only the oppression of the workplace, but also how conditions in the workplaces are integrally linked to both the national situation and the global political–economic networks in which their country is enmeshed. Thus, they recognize that they have to confront issues at these other levels as well as in the workplace if they hope to improve the lives of these members and their families. Unionism of this more encompassing kind is called "social movement unionism" (Scipes, 2014b).

For another level of nuance, there are labor organizations that have been established by dictatorships—an example is the Trade Union Congress of the Philippines (TUCP), which was created by the Marcos Dictatorship—and they can act in ways that *oppose* progressive, pro-people labor centers and organizations. As detailed in an earlier book, *KMU: Building Genuine Trade Unionism in the Philippines, 1980–1994*, a TUCP-affiliated union—ALU (Associated Labor Unions)—collaborated with corporate management, the military, reactionary municipal officials and an identified death squad (no exaggeration) to try to defeat an affiliate of the progressive, pro-people *Kilusang Mayo Uno* Labor Center in a certification election at Atlas Mines in that country during the late 1980s. Fortunately, the KMU affiliate prevailed despite all of this—winning 5,025 votes in the government-sponsored election to ALU's 292 (Scipes 1996: see especially pp. 116–125; for a more succinct account, see Scipes 2010, 48–56).

The point—which hopefully by now is obvious—is that not all unions are progressive, pro-people, and willing to use their power to fight for changes that will benefit all. In fact, most are not willing to do anything more than to support their members, and their members alone and separate from the rest of their society. Thus, we must recognize the multiplicity of experiences that are encompassed by the term "labor movement."

However, at the same time, we must recognize that there are progressive unions that seek to address issues for their members not only in the workplace, but in the larger society as well. While how much further they will go varies; nonetheless, for these unions, their willingness to transcend traditional, narrow business unionism is considerable. And it is these unions, grouped herein under the term "progressive unionism," that I suggest can articulate progressive, life-enhancing values and pro-people interests, and can develop the power to force both the state and corporations to either back-off and give space to pro-people's organizations and their social programs, and/or limit the oppression of the majority of the population. Thus, it is suggested the larger social importance of these progressive unions extends considerably beyond traditional trade unionism and the workplace.

Labor in the Philippines

As noted above, not all Filipino labor organizations are progressive, life-enhancing, or even fight for anything beyond what the leaders perceive as necessary to give to their members to maintain their organizational affiliation. The TUCP has been mentioned previously.

However, there is another labor center the endeavors of which are much more interesting and relevant to this essay: the *Kilusang Mayo Uno* (KMU) or May First Movement. I argue that there is a lot to learn from the KMU in general (Scipes 2014a), but that there are things that can be learned from thinking about the KMU regarding responding to natural disasters.

The key thing needed to understand about the KMU—which has existed since May 1, 1980—is that it is a democratic and member-run Filipino labor organization based on building power and effecting social change for working people. It is a collective response to oppression in their factories, plantations, and department stores. It recognizes, however, that to change conditions in the workplace, both the national situation and the global political–economic networks in which the country is enmeshed must be changed. It understands that these changes cannot be made by workers alone, but that they must coalesce with other disempowered sectors of society, including peasants, women, students, the urban poor, the youth, etc., to make the changes necessary for the good of the entire social order (see Scipes 1996, 1999). This broader vision of trade unionism is known as "social movement unionism," a term that has gotten terribly confused but that has recently been disentangled (see Scipes, 2014b).

The KMU builds upon this broader vision. They have developed an education program that has included every member, not just leaders or shop stewards or other worker representatives. They have built an impressive organizational structure, combining both vertical and horizontal relationships, that has enabled them to survive vicious repression over the past 36 years. They consciously ally with other sectoral organizations—such as peasants, women, and so forth—to expand their power far beyond individual workplaces. And they recognize the need to build global labor solidarity, having developed an elaborate six-point program (see Scipes 2000), including the creation of a unique "International Solidarity Affair" (ISA) that has invited workers and labor leaders from around the world to come to the Philippines to experience the reality of Filipino workers, and this has been carried out around every May Day since 1984 (see Scipes 2015, for a report of the 2015 ISA; see Scipes 2014a for a discussion of what can be learned from the KMU).

The argument here is that the KMU and its sectoral allies provide an experienced, in-place nation-wide organization that is based on collectivity and is consolidated around the idea of improving the lives of the broad masses of Filipinos, most of whom live vulnerable lives inside a vastly unequal social order. In other words, the argument is that there is no comparable organization in the country that can provide better services to towns, villages, and dispersed communities in cases of natural emergencies; and it is comprised of people very similar in position and place to those most likely to be displaced and otherwise impacted. This organization does not have to be created in response to a natural disaster, but it is already in-place and established, with clear lines of communication coordinating workers' efforts nation-wide. And it is recognized across the country as being a pro-people organization.

Ideally, the government of the Philippines would recognize these attributes of the KMU, and work with them to help respond better to natural disasters: this seems a "no brainer." Yet the governments of that country—in common with those of many others—lack the vision required to act accordingly. It is either that, or they are more concerned with maintaining control by the elites over their country than taking care of disaster victims.

It is being suggested, therefore, that the KMU recognize its potential central role to natural disaster relief in the country, make this a nation-wide educational campaign for its members, and establish a conscious program to build support in the media to pressure the national, regional, and local governments to provide the resources to the KMU so it can actualize its potential regarding natural disaster relief. This governmental support could include providing money, equipment, and legitimacy for the KMU's efforts, including money to pay wages (established under collective bargaining agreements) for replacement workers should KMU members be needed outside of their own communities in response to natural disasters.

Media

Media in a developing country has an outsized impact on the people of that country simply because it can serve as a unifying force for the population; and this seems especially important in a good-sized archipelagic country such as the Philippines.

However, despite the "myth" that the media provides a fair representation across the social order as a whole—a myth promoted most by the media itself—it really does not, especially in "normal" times. In reality, there is no set definition of what is "news," which means that individuals placed in high-level positions inside the media corporations make choices and actually determine what is news; news is a social construction. Accordingly, what is defined as news is based on what is expected to garner the most public attention, according to the portion of the "public" that outlet has targeted, while not offending advertisers, who are the most important audience to any mainstream media dependent on making a profit for corporate survival/expansion.

In general, this means that the media will present news focused on the activities and statements of government officials, corporate leaders, and members of the socio-economic–political elites in general (see Herman and Chomsky 1988; Croteau and Hoynes 2014). The affairs and concerns of working people, much less their organizations, generally do not get included in the large majority of media activities.

However, there is generally one exception to this reality: in the face of natural disasters, the media will generally transcend its narrow "business as usual" approach to life and will report—at least for a few days—public service warnings in advance, and immediate responses thereafter. This coverage will often bring the situation and sufferings of the general public to national attention in ways different from any other time.

To provide this coverage, however, requires reporters and TV camera crews to go into these affected areas, see the devastation first hand, and report on the sufferings and turmoil in affected people's lives. Experiences like these can literally be life changing for the media folks.

The interesting question, then, is how do they do their job—and well? The simple, and traditional, way is to go to governmental officials or NGO staff and get their viewpoints. That will meet minimum requirements for their reporting. Does that meet the needs of the people who have been affected by the natural disaster? Mostly likely it does not.

The key to understanding what is going on in depth—and thus being able to help people— is to get access to them. Generally speaking, it is not enough for a reporter to walk up to someone and ask, "Do you want to talk?" or "Do you have something you want to say?"

The problem is that most people—and this would seem even more likely during periods of social disruption—do not generally trust others they do not know. "Why are you asking me questions?" or "What are you going to do with the information that I might give to you?" would seem to be questions reporters get immediately asked.

Accordingly, to get good information, one must have someone who knows the community well enough to gain access. It is not enough simply to walk into a barangay; one must have a "guide," a contact person known beforehand and who can verify to residents that this person is respectful of them and their situation, one who will treat them and their suffering with respect, and who is really trying to understand their plight, and who will report accurately on what they have learned; someone who is really trying to understand and share that understanding with many beyond the disaster area.

That seems to provide direction both for reporters and for KMU unions. For reporters, this means recognizing the important role that progressive unions and their community allies play in any community, and especially within a disaster zone. Their social bonds within the community are usually strong enough to withstand the largest disasters, so going through unions and their allies gives reporters access to see how people are responding to the disaster as active protagonists, and not merely as individual victims. Getting this viewpoint will provide more accurate coverage, and will support the affected community by focusing on their strengths rather than their weaknesses. It will also result in better, more accurate news reporting, while getting perspectives those government officials and outside NGO staff members cannot provide.

For the KMU and its allies, this analysis suggests that they reach out to reporters who have seen the damage first hand, and work with them to build support for an on-going campaign to get the government to recognize the importance of established labor and social organizations being included and actually providing resources to them to help in responding to natural disasters.

Taking this approach—reaching out and building support with news reporters and their editors before natural disasters develop—also requires that the KMU take an active approach toward the media; it cannot simply sit on its hands and hope that the media will approach the KMU (see Downing 2001). KMU national headquarters in Quezon City clearly is ahead of the game, and has built support among the media; but that is not enough. It is important that KMU organizations in the various regions do so as well. This means that it needs to train people in the regional and local organizations to understand and work with the media, and seek opportunities to do so. Relationships need to be created and enhanced.

Media work needs to be consciously developed in the local unions and in members' communities. One of the things discovered in my 2015 trip to the Philippines is that even in the most remote rural communities, people had access to cell phones, computers, and i-Pads. These provide multiple ways to record and document developments in local communities, and means to transmit them, and this needs to be utilized to people's advantage. They need to be taught how to develop their own reporting of events, and especially natural disasters (see Ryan 1991). This way, with responsive reporters, they could provide visual accounts of affects on communities that were chosen by community members, and not outsiders.

Conclusion

In this essay, a different way to approach reporting on natural disasters has been suggested. It requires news reporters and their editors to recognize that there are progressive unions and allied organizations that exist, and because of their rootedness in their various communities across the country, that they can help provide more honest and accurate accounts of natural disasters than can be gained from government officials and outside NGO staff-members. It has been argued that gaining access through these local organizations can provide approaches to news reporting that actually help the affected community heal, by portraying survivors as active protagonists to overcoming the death and destruction instead of helpless victims.

Concurrently, this essay also argued that progressive labor centers such as the KMU and its affiliated organizations need to recognize that they can further contribute to the well-being of people affected by such disasters, and should work to develop the organizational capacity to do so, while reaching out beforehand to sympathetic news reporters and building strong relationships. Focusing on the media from this perspective suggests how progressive unions, their allies, and their partners in the media can enhance people's ability to survive and transcend the social disruption caused by natural disasters.

References

Croteau, D., and Hoynes, W. (2014) *Media/Society: Industry, Images and Audiences* (5th ed.), Thousand Oaks, CA: Sage.

Downing, J. D. H. (2001) *Radical Media: Rebellious Communication and Social Movements*, Thousand Oaks, CA: Sage.

Fischetti, M. (2013) "Was Typhoon Haiyan a Record Storm?" *Scientific American*, November 12, available at: http://blogs.scientificamerican.com/observations/was-typhoon-haiyan-a-record-storm/

Herman, E. S., and Chomsky, N. (1988) *Manufacturing Consent: The Political Economy of the Mass Media*, New York: Pantheon Books.

Hodal, K. (2013) "Typhoon Haiyan: Desperate Survivors and Destruction in Flattened City," *The Guardian*, November 11, available at: www.theguardian.com/world/2013/nov/10/typhoon-haiyan-dead-aidLandigin, R. (2013) "Typhoon Haiyan: Philippines Reflects on Traumatic Week," *Financial Times*, November 15, available at: www.ft.com/intl/cms/s/0/ed124ba2-4dfd-11e3-8fa5-00144feabdc0.html#slide0

Lindell, M. K., and Prater, C. S. (2003) "Assessing Community Impacts of Natural Disasters," *Natural Hazards Review*, 4 (4): 176–185, available at: www.nifv.nl/upload/179148_668_1168611941109-lindell-2003.pdf (Must be put in browser.)

Moore, M. (1989) *Roger and Me*. A film available from Amazon.com.

Pangco Panares, J. (2013) "Govt Slow Response Hit," *Manila Standard Today*, November 14, available at: http://manilastandardtoday.com/news/headlines/133454/govt-slow-response-hit.html

Pillay, D. (2013) "Between Social Movement and Political Unionism: COSATU and Democratic Politics in South Africa," *Rethinking Development and Inequality*, 2, Special Issue: 10–27.

Reuters. (2013) "Typhoon Haiyan: Desperate Philippine Survivors Turn to Looting." *Chicago Tribune*, November 13, available at: www.chicagotribune.com/news/chi-philippines-typhoon-haiyan-20131113-story.html

Ryan, C. (1991) *Prime Time Activism: Media Strategies for Grassroots Organizing*, Boston, MA: South End.

Scipes, K. (1992a) "Social Movement Unionism and the Kilusang Mayo Uno," *Kasarinlan* (Third World Studies Center, University of the Philippines), 7 (2– 3) (4th Qtr. 1991–1st Qtr. 1992): 121–162, available at: http://journals.upd.edu.ph/index.php/kasarinlan/article/view/1393/pdf_38

Scipes, K. (1992b) "Understanding the New Labor Movements in the 'Third World': The Emergence of Social Movement Unionism," *Critical Sociology*, 19 (2): 81–101, available in English at: http://labournet.de/diskussion/gewerkschaft/smu/The_New_Unions_Crit_Soc.htm

Scipes, K. (1996) *KMU: Building Genuine Trade Unionism in the Philippines, 1980–1994*, Quezon City, Philippines: New Day Publishers.

Scipes, K. (1999) "Global Economic Crisis, Neoliberal Solutions, and the Philippines," *Monthly Review*, 51 (7): 1–14, available at: http://monthlyreview.org/1999/12/01/global-economic-crisis-neoliberal-solutions-and-the-philippines

Scipes, K. (2000) "Communicating Labor Internationalism: The KMU's 'International Solidarity Affair.'" January, available at: www.antenna.nl/~waterman/scipes.html

Scipes, K. (2003) "Trade Union Development and Racial Oppression in Chicago's Steel and Meatpacking Industries, 1933–1955," unpublished PhD Dissertation, Department of Sociology, University of Illinois at Chicago.

Scipes, K. (2010) *AFL-CIO's Secret War against Developing Country Workers: Solidarity or Sabotage?* Lanham, MD: Lexington Books. (Paperback edition published in 2011).

Scipes, K. (2014a) "Building Global Labor Solidarity Today: Learning from the KMU of the Philippines," *Class, Race and Corporate Power*, 2 (2), Article 2, available at: http://digitalcommons.fiu.edu/classracecorporatepower/vol2/iss2/2

Scipes, K. (2014b) "Social Movement Unionism or Social Justice Unionism? Disentangling Theoretical Confusion within the Global Labor Movement," *Class, Race and Corporate Power*, 2 (3), Article 9, available at: http://digitalcommons.fiu.edu/classracecorporatepower/vol2/iss3/9

Scipes, K. (2015) "Celebrating May Day—KMU Style," *Countercurrents.org*, October 8, available at: www.countercurrents.org/scipes081015.htm

Tice, A. (2010) "'No Such Thing as Society': a Book Review by Alistair Tice," *The Socialist*, November 25–December 1: 10, available at: www.m.socialistparty.org.uk/pdf/issue/648/10.pdf

Wikipedia. (2014) "Typhoon Haiyan," available at: https://en.wikipedia.org/wiki/Typhoon_Haiyan

27

HUMANITARIAN RESPONSE AND MEDIA IN THE ARAB GULF COUNTRIES

Fadwa Ahmed Obaid

Introduction

The Arab Gulf Countries (referred to here as the Gulf Cooperation Council countries or GCC countries) and countries of the Arab region in general have seen inter-state wars, conflicts, armed struggle, civil wars, and popular uprisings especially since the early years of the twentieth century. The most agonizing and painful conflict of all is the tragedy of the Palestinian people and their suffering either under Israeli occupation, or within the context of refugee camps in various Arab countries or as a part of a worldwide diaspora. Furthermore, there were political uprisings during the 1950s and 1960s and changes in regimes in various countries through a number of coups d'état that have left their impact on the quality of life of the people of the Arab region: the 1956 tripartite war of France, the UK, and Israel against Egypt, the Six Day War of 1967, the civil war in Lebanon from 1975 to 1990, including the Israeli invasion of Lebanon in 1982, the Iraq–Iran war of the 1980s, the Iraqi invasion of Kuwait in 1990, the USA invasion of Iraq known as the Gulf War of 2003. And now the region faces other forms of internal conflict, worsened by the involvement of regional and European powers, with the disintegration of the nation state in Iraq, Yemen, and Libya and the potentially complete disintegration of the nation state in Syria. And to top it all, there are various forms of terrorism from Al Qaeda to ISIS (Daesh) to the other smaller splinter groups, all claiming they are killing Muslims in the region or others outside the region in the name of Islam, or as some argue, taking revenge on the historical occupations and imperialism.

The tragic reality of the Arab countries pours its darkness on the whole region and certainly on the GCC countries and their people, who are not immune to violence and terrorism. Violence in any of its manifestations, especially wars, destroys countries and their infrastructures. But most importantly, it destroys the people themselves, not only physically, but also psychologically, mentally, and spiritually. War takes away people's sense of dignity, security, and safety, destroys their self-respect, and steals their sense of belonging and their power to manage their own lives and control their own destiny. War and violence in all their forms destroy the very spirit of the people, which is much harder to rebuild than the country's physical infrastructure. All this has increased the need for humanitarian efforts in the Arab world, most of which come from the GCC countries. The human cost of these "human-made" disasters is devastating, as is the damage to infrastructure, health, education, and sustainable economic and social development. Only one acute case of natural disaster occurred in Saudi Arabia and it will be included among the examples in this chapter. Within this tragic context, many institutions in all three sectors, governmental, private, and civil society, have contributed to humanitarian relief through funding and providing other daily survival commodities.

Media play an increasingly important role in the humanitarian challenges that the region must confront; they cover the crises, inform the people, and report on relief efforts. This chapter details the development of media technology, and transformations that have resulted in new forms of programming and increased public awareness and responses to humanitarian emergencies in an age of conflict in the Arabian Gulf.

Satellite TV News Channels

A media revolution took place from the early 1990s in the countries of the GCC region and Arab region; namely, the launch of Pan-Arab satellite TV news channels and the multi-channel satellite TV networks (Sakr 2001; Gunter and Dickinson 2013). These channels changed the media response to humanitarian disasters, those that were close to home or in other parts of the world. Social media has also played a major role in communicating the people's response to crises. These regional developments were part of a global seismic shift in the media landscape: how they are produced, who controls them, how far they reach, how they are consumed, how they set agendas, and how citizens increasingly became central players, no longer on the margins of media narratives and discourses. Expanded media discourse brought a new dimension of public engagement to world politics and its impact on the Arab region— its conflicts and contradictions— and especially to humanitarian issues. I will detail these media transformations and their public dynamic, taking into consideration the limited available references and research material that document such practices, supplemented by my own experience as a TV broadcast executive, program editor, producer, and media specialist who worked with various TV and media institutions in the GCC region.

One important aspect of this global shift is the role of media in general and social media in particular in the process of promoting, in practical terms, the right of people to access information—to know as much as possible and to act upon it. It is about the democratization of information and its free movement in the communities, in other words, the accessibility to a wide range of information from various sources freely. While this was not obvious in the early phases of satellite TV and social media, it has become very visible in the events of the twenty-first century known as "The Arab Spring." Though this article does not cover this subject (except briefly in the case of Syria which is an ongoing humanitarian disaster engulfing the region and beyond in Europe), it is important to highlight it here because one can see the seeds of "wanting to know and see everything and act upon it" as responses to the desperate humanitarian needs brought about by wars, armed conflicts, and natural disasters.

A Historical Overview

When the Saudi owned Pan-Arab satellite TV news channel MBC (Middle East Broadcasting Center) was launched in London in September 1991 as the first free-to-air private satellite channel, with 24/7 news, current affairs programs, and entertainment programs, a new era of TV broadcasting in the GCC and Arab region was born (Sakr 2001; Gunter and Dickinson 2013). In 1998, a series of Pan-Arab 24-hour satellite TV channels were launched by Abu Dhabi TV, Dubai TV, and Kuwait TV. Al Jazeera satellite TV News Channel was launched in 1996 and was considered the "CNN of the Arab region." Together they reach over 150 million Arabic speaking viewers and have had far-reaching consequences on the political, cultural, and social landscape. Equally significant was their coverage of political events and conflicts such as the Al-Aqsa Palestinian Intifada (known as the Second Intifada) from September 2000 to February 2005. The invasion of Kuwait was followed by the US launching of Operation Desert Shield, also known as the First Gulf War (from August 2, 1990 to February 28, 1991). Then the US invasion of Iraq, also known as the Second Gulf War (from March 20 to May 1, 2003), the 2006 Lebanon War with Israel (from July 12 to August 14, 2006), the Second Sudanese Civil War (1983–2005), as well as other conflicts and environmental disasters ensued regionally and globally. Images were broadcasted 24/7 to homes in the GCC countries and Arab region as these conflicts unfolded and audiences saw the human cost of these wars.

MBC, Abu Dhabi TV, and Al Jazeera Satellite News channels were competing for leadership positions and audience share across the region and internationally to all Arabic-speaking communities. They offered high journalistic standards, professionalism, and immediacy and up-to-date coverage and analysis. MBC TV News, Abu Dhabi TV News, and Al Jazeera TV News channels modeled themselves on CNN News, after it became a global and a regional phenomenon during the First Gulf War. CNN's 24/7 coverage included the battle front lines, from journalists and reporters with the US/International/Arab military coalition armies. The Pan-Arab satellite news channels were launched soon after and followed the same journalistic and broadcast practices as CNN. The numbers of satellite dish owners per household grew in GCC countries and the Arab region, and public venues such as cafés and social clubs featured televisions set to news channels. The voracious appetite for news, facts and updates grew to include less censored, more informed judgments, balanced political analysis, and open debate (Sakr 2001; Gunter and Dickinson 2013).

"The CNN Effect" became a phenomenon worthy of study and analysis because of its powerful impact in framing the news and narrative of events of conflicts, wars, and humanitarian disasters. CNN influenced how governments, policymakers, international organizations, relief agencies, and citizens formed understandings of these events and thus affected their response (Robinson 2002). Equally MBC, Abu Dhabi TV, and Al Jazeera Satellite TV, News Channels had a similar impact regionally. They offered an alternative to CNN in terms of local perspectives, reporting in the Arabic language on regional and world events, thus increasing their share of audiences. Because of this impact, this article will review the "Al Jazeera effect" and the effect of the other Pan-Arab satellite channels on coverage and response to humanitarian disasters (Seib 2008).

Social media heralded, globally and regionally, a new age of citizen journalism, witness accounts, and second-by-second sharing of the human cost of disasters, natural and man-made. Saudi Arabia and the other GCC countries are at the highest end of use of social media globally, especially Twitter (Gunter et al. 2016). It also marked a turning point in terms of raising awareness, advocacy, call to action, and mobilization at local community and regional levels. These far-reaching media developments in the GCC countries had a significant effect on humanitarian response.

FADWA AHMED OBAID

Pan-Arab Satellite TV Broadcasting and Humanitarian Response in the GCC Countries

New media developments include innovative programming, such as the live 24-hour telethons sponsored by the Pan-Arab satellite TV channels. The main objectives of such programs were fund-raising and awareness-raising. Through dramatic imagery, these telethons highlighted the destruction resulting from the various conflicts and wars, magnifying the human suffering of the civilian victims, loss of life, and the destruction of homes and other infrastructure. TV broadcasters dedicated all technical, journalistic, and creative resources to cover these major regional conflicts though a series of actions: ensuring that local bureaus and journalists were reporting on the ground, providing special reports about the conflicts and the human costs. Images were beamed live via satellite broadcasting and Outside Broadcasting (OB) units. Technical advances meant that smaller broadcasting OB units, satellite phones, and satellite communication devices that could be carried anywhere by reporters including to the front lines of conflicts provided live coverage from remote areas.

TV Satellite broadcasting using a variety of formats from news, current affairs, and 24-hour telethons, highlighted relief efforts undertaken by local, regional, and international organizations, non-governmental organizations (NGOs), and community volunteers. They made visible the activism and volunteerism of citizens, especially Arab women and youth, but they also showed the gaps and weaknesses in the official responses to these events. They became the critical eyes through which the communities assessed the efficacy of relief efforts.

In addition, fundraising TV broadcasts invited prominent guests in the studio such as politicians, writers, academics, artists, musicians, actors, public opinion writers, and those with public standing and influence that represented the different political spectra. This facilitated a broader discussion of the background of these conflicts and wars and brought to life stories of their human cost. They motivated individuals, communities, and relief organizations to take action and to be part of the humanitarian response underway, with the specific objective of alleviating the suffering of the innocent victims. Media fund-raising events and TV telethons (including at times radio and print) provided volunteer teams devoted to answering calls from the public and accepting donations live on air. As money was donated, a tally of the amounts raised would be shared on screen. Millions of Saudi Arabian Riyals (SAR), Kuwaiti Dinars (KWD), and UAE Dhirams (AED) were raised to fund humanitarian response activities by various organizations. To highlight the humanitarian efforts, NGOs, relief organizations, and community volunteers were interviewed and their work was highlighted. The public became directly involved and had a stake in the relief response—they wanted to know where the funds were going and how assistance was delivered.

The screens projected real-time 24/7 images of victims as well as the destruction and loss of lives, homes, schools, hospitals, and other institutions and infrastructures. Images and reports were beamed to every home in the Arab region so that the events and the response became part of every home and entered into the consciousness of viewers. This real-time broadcasting created a "we are all in it together" experience, incentivizing the citizens of the GCC countries to donate, volunteer, and play a role in alleviating the suffering of those affected; in particular, supporting Palestinians and Lebanese victims. After the telethons, follow-up coverage and programs continued with focus on the human suffering as well as showing the impact of the funds that were mobilized. In a sense these programs constituted the first real attempt at accountability for donated funds by linking the funding from its source to the end result and its beneficiaries. This is an important contribution of Pan-Arab Satellite TV broadcasting—the sensitization of the ordinary person to the concept of accountability, even though the word itself was not used. This kind of information had a "demonstration effect" that can be used for other situations that require accountability for the use of resources and the term "accountability" is much in use now in GCC countries.

The Social Media Revolution in the Arab Gulf Countries

Social media use in the GCC countries is one of the highest in the world, taking off in 2010 onwards in particular on Facebook, Twitter, YouTube, and also more recently LinkedIn, Instagram, WhatsApp, Snapchat, and others. It has influenced the political, social, and cultural landscape in the GCC countries and beyond in the Arab region (Mourtada and Salem 2012). Social media provided an empowering and safe platform for public debate and new forms of expression that were not possible through other media or societal institutions. It influenced the coverage of humanitarian disasters and the effectiveness and speed of relief efforts. Mobile phones became the eyes of the world through the shared instant images of the damage and the victims on Facebook and Twitter. Often before official assistance arrived, young volunteers and local residents shared images, videos, and calls for help, mobilized support, organized assistance, and distributed much-needed vital supplies. Often, this mobilization through social media saved many lives but it also moved the population to ask difficult questions about the events themselves with the expectation that they will receive answers.

Case Studies Abu Dhabi TV, United Arab Emirates (UAE): Second Intifada September 2000 "Youm Al Quds" (Day for Jerusalem)

As indicated earlier, Abu Dhabi Satellite TV News Channel, launched in 1998, became a leading source of news and current affairs for UAE viewers and those in GCC countries and beyond in the Arab region. Highly experienced TV news editors, presenters, and broadcasting engineers were recruited from within UAE and from other Arab countries, particularly Lebanon, Morocco, Algeria, and Iraq and from the diaspora, in particular from London, which was the home of leading Saudi Pan-Arab media organizations, such as MBC TV and Al Sharq Al Awsat daily newspaper and publishing group.

Abu Dhabi TV launched its news center investing in the latest news broadcast technology and training programs, recruiting highly experienced journalists, as well as opening bureaus in all cities of the Arab region as well as Asia, Europe and the US. It soon won regional and international awards for its leading news coverage of the second Intifada uprising in the Occupied Palestinian Territories of the West Bank and Gaza in 2000 and the Israeli–Lebanon War of 2006. A highlight was the TV fundraiser live telethon "Youm Al Quds" (Day for Jerusalem) in 2001, which raised millions of Emirati Dhirams (AED) for injured victims and for projects that benefited Palestinian children and families and for longer-term infrastructure reconstruction and development. Religious leaders from all major religions, political figures, intellectuals and academics, artists, actors, writers, poets, musicians, singers from across GCC and the Arab region were invited to Abu Dhabi TV and the telethon studio in a roll call that featured discussions, chats, and literary, artistic, and musical contributions.

Follow-up reports on delivery and distribution of funds were featured on news, current affairs, and special programs for the months that followed. Human stories that brought the suffering and challenges of families and communities in Palestinian towns, villages and refugee camps became part of the lives of families in every home in GCC countries and the Arab region. It brought an immediate link and connection between the viewers and Palestine and transformed the abstract stories of Israeli occupation and Palestinian suffering into visual reality and thus heart-felt emotions. It made viewers want to be part of the response and it provided an environment that allowed more empathetic reactions with the Palestinians but also more angry reactions to Israel as an occupier.

Abu Dhabi TV: Israeli–Lebanon War 2006

A vast TV satellite broadcasting operation was set in place linking the news center in TV Headquarters in Abu Dhabi with reporters in the field in Lebanon, including 24/7 live satellite link coverage. It offered courageous frontline war coverage, often with reporters and TV crews taking serious risks, a new experience for the reporters in the region. They documented the aftermath of fighting and bombing and repeatedly focused extensively and graphically on the very high humanitarian cost in terms of lives and infrastructure.

A national fundraising campaign in UAE, "I want to go back to school", was launched by Sheikh Khalifa Bin Zayed Al Nahyan, the UAE President, to rebuild schools in Lebanon after the Israeli withdrawal from South Lebanon. A coordinated public and mass media campaign was launched with promotional videos and public announcement messages. It was an extremely successful campaign that raised awareness, mobilized UAE citizens and expatriate residents of every nationality, volunteers including young people, UAE youth and women organizations, various NGOs, International relief organizations, local offices, and UAE government institutions to mobilize funding across the UAE for one goal: rebuilding every school that was destroyed in the war. It was one of the most successful humanitarian response programs in the GCC countries at the height of the TV Satellite revolution and just before the social media revolution. It was a highly visible campaign with documented and successful outcomes and with visibility of accountability. Building schools and seeing children going back to their classes were a most visible demonstration of use of resources and thus of promises kept.

MBC TV—Second Intifada 2000

Saudi Pan-Arab TV News Satellite broadcaster (MBC) led outstanding coverage of the Palestinian Second Intifada. It worked through its well-established TV news bureau in the West Bank as well as from bureaus in Jerusalem and Gaza. It projected highly professional local journalists and newsgathering operations in around-the-clock coverage of human stories of the uprising and the loss of lives, especially children. In addition, fundraising telethons were used because they proved their successful outreach to the general public. Several were very well organized on a large scale on MBC TV to raise awareness and ensure funding for the relief programs as well as provide financial assistance and moral support to the Palestinians. Many public figures including GCC and Arab government officials, politicians, popular artists, singers, writers, and celebrities joined the telethons, some volunteering their time to receive public pledges on the phones. Millions of Saudi Riyals were raised from MBC TV's viewers in Saudi Arabia and other GCC countries and across the Arab region. People from all socio-economic groups provided donations that ranged from small to larger amounts for Palestinian children and families affected by the conflict. Any amount was most welcome because of the severity of the damage and the greatness of the needs. It also was yet another popular expression of "being part of it" and a demonstration that the issue of Palestine is not only a political issue but an emotional, humanitarian, and cultural one as well.

Al Jazeera TV: Israeli–Lebanon War 2006

Well before the "Al Jazeera effect" became a subject of critical analysis and study in GCC countries and internationally, being compared to CNN and the "CNN effect," Al Jazeera TV news channel had distinguished itself as an important emerging media channel in its 24/7 news coverage of the Israeli–Lebanon War of 2006. It was recognized also for its coverage of the US invasion of Afghanistan after the September 11 attacks, the Second Gulf War and naturally in the "Arab Spring" uprisings. Al Jazeera had distinguished itself like Abu Dhabi Satellite TV news by its highly professional TV News broadcast journalists, in-the-field reporters, producers, news editors, technical crews, and satellite communications capabilities. Al Jazeera news channel brought minute-by-minute developments of the Israeli–Lebanon War of 2006 from the frontlines to all homes, offices, cafés, and anywhere people gathered to watch television in any part of the world, and of course across all of the GCC and Arab region. Also, like Abu Dhabi TV News, Al Jazeera won several regional and International awards for its coverage of the war and the subsequent Israeli army withdrawal from South Lebanon.

Reports and stories on the need for large-scale response to support the local Lebanese population and the Palestinian refugees in the camps played an important role in fundraising and assistance provided by the government and people of Qatar, the home of Al Jazeera TV, as well as from Saudi Arabia, UAE, and the other GCC countries' governments and citizens. Al Jazeera and Abu Dhabi were the two leading TV news channels competing for the first position in terms of viewership in GCC and the Arab region. The channels alternated in occupying the No. 1 spot according to viewership surveys and viewing ratings by well-established GCC and Arab media monitoring and research organizations such as Pan-Arab Research Centre (PARC)[1] among others. Abu Dhabi TV News had the edge initially. Later, however, Al Jazeera in Doha, Qatar, and Al Arabiya News, launched by the Saudi-owned MBC media group in 2002 from Dubai, UAE became the leaders and continue to dominate in GCC and Arab media. It remains the case, however, that UAE, as a host country of many satellite TV news and entertainment channels (including the re-launched and highly successful Dubai TV news and entertainment channels that broadcast in Arabic and English), continues to be the leading satellite TV news broadcasting and media hub in the GCC and Arab region. All the leading TV news broadcasters discussed in this article have added multi-channel offerings, digital media platforms that have been very successful, including live streaming news channels, online news service via smartphones, on-demand viewing of TV news, current affairs and entertainment programs, and highly subscribed social media platforms.

Social Media and Syria's Uprising and Civil War 2011–2016

The popular uprising in Syria, which followed other uprisings in the Arab region in Tunisia and Egypt in 2011 soon developed into a bloody civil war with tragic cost to the people of Syria. The statistics are truly horrific. Now in its sixth year, the war caused loss of life of over 400,000 Syrians according to several estimates including the United Nations and UNHCR,[2] destruction of whole cities, towns, and communities, displacement of populations both within Syria estimated at over two million, and migration to neighboring countries of over four million with women and children making up three-quarters of the refugee population. The world is thus facing what is referred to as the "Syrian refugee crisis." In fact the total number is much higher, should the Syrians who reached Saudi Arabia, UAE, other GCC countries, Egypt, and also Europe be included.

The Syria uprising and civil war is often referred to as the "first social media war." As Patrick Howell said so powerfully in 2013: "This is how we see war in 2013: next to like buttons and view counters" (O'Neill 2013). At the beginning of the uprising, social media or "new media" as it is also called, and SMS messages were used in the Syrian uprising by the various activists to reach out to communities and incentivize them to protest. It was also a powerful tool to reach the outside world to let it know what was really going on, including the human cost of the unfolding conflict. In a contradictory fashion, it was also used as a propaganda tool, and as a safe space for the expression of political views by the competing sides. The role of social media in the uprisings in Egypt and Tunisia had a similar and powerful role, arguably one of the most important factors in the overthrow of both regimes (Shirky 2011). In the case of Syria, as the uprising turned into an armed military conflict and all-out civil war, it was dangerous and often impossible for mainstream regional and international TV news corporations to send reporters to the areas experiencing various forms of violence resulting from a wide range of weapons. Thus, they increasingly relied on online social activists' videos, photos, blogs, and updates from inside Syria, uploaded and shared on the Internet and also shared with TV news organizations. Social media became the main platform and source of information and updates for TV broadcasters, other mass media and the millions of social media followers in GCC, the Arab region and globally. The opposition to the government uploaded immediate, raw, and bloody images and videos of the confrontations between government forces and the uprisings, the shooting of unarmed protestors, the death and human cost, and the destruction of homes, communities and cities. When the conflict escalated, military updates, propaganda images and videos, and death toll statistics from all sides and factions took over TV screens and social media (Ahmad and Hamasaeed 2014). Many uploaded videos were widely circulated and went viral as cameras were mounted on guns during battles, giving viewers on social media a sense of being there and, as some argued, being inside a "real life" war video game. Facebook, Twitter, Tumblr, YouTube, Flickr, and online blogs became political tools in a never-ending escalating bloody and vicious conflict.

In addition, social media in the Syria uprising and subsequent civil war was used and continues to be used today as an emergency humanitarian response tool with various degrees of effectiveness and success. Often, humanitarian relief agencies such as ICRC, UNHCR, and others are unable to reach areas where urgent assistance is needed. Occasionally there are breakthroughs after months of negotiations with the different parties in the conflict. Moreover, these same humanitarian relief agencies rely on online videos, social media updates by local activists, and journalists' reports—if available—for information about ongoing events. In these circumstances, it is very hard to make realistic assessments of humanitarian needs, let alone timely interventions if and when it is possible. However, social media is by far the most effective tool available to report on the humanitarian crisis in Syria and in the wider refugee crisis unfolding.

The Executive Director—and veteran TV news journalist—of leading Pan-Arab Saudi-owned Al Arabiya TV News Channel, Nabil Al Khatib, has described the Syrian situation from the media point of view. He said that "in the case of Syria there is a lost story buried under the daily tallies of those killed," as he explained the challenges faced by mainstream TV news organizations to get the human stories (Ghannam 2016).[3] Some of these include inability to send reporters to the war zones and front lines in Syria, and regional reporters are often reporting on the general events unfolding (even the refugee crises in Europe) rather than telling human stories. "It is in the detail" suggests Nabil Al Khatib "It is the unique individual stories that people want to know about [that] we strive to reach and cover."

Nevertheless, the coverage by mainstream Pan-Arab TV news channels and the multi-digital platforms and online presence of media organizations in GCC countries as well as social media videos, images, and blogs from the war zones on the horrors of the humanitarian crises of the Syria war, have resulted in large-scale national response initiatives in GCC countries to support the Syrian refugees, especially those that fled death and destruction to neighboring countries.

One can only provide a few examples to demonstrate this response. From Saudi Arabia, there were the Saudi Government and Saudi Red Crescent initiatives in Zaatari Refugee Camp in Jordan, which is still ongoing, as well as King Salman Humanitarian and Relief Centre initiatives. The UAE Government and Emirati Red Crescent also embarked on similar humanitarian response initiatives in Jordan and Lebanon. These GCC humanitarian response initiatives include housing units, field hospitals, schools, skills training workshops, and classes including information technology, as well as the distribution of basic necessities such as food, clothes, school books, etc. All the other GCC countries—Kuwait, Qatar, Oman, and Bahrain—have their humanitarian response initiatives to support Syrian refugees.

In addition, community fundraising and collection of emergency items in GCC countries were increased with individuals, social activists as well as NGOs leading such initiatives. Local, regional and international Pan-Arab Satellite News, especially Al Jazeera and Al Arabiya, and regional social media coverage increased people's engagement in humanitarian efforts to assist displaced Syrian refugees in the GCC countries as well as in Syrian refugee camps in Jordan and Lebanon. Again, the emotional impact of these media channels is most obvious in the variety of responses from individuals, communities, and the state. Saudi Arabia for example allowed Syrian "guests" to access national education and health services provided to Saudi nationals, even though it is known that such services are already over-subscribed. However, media reports made the public aware of the importance of providing at least basic opportunities for the Syrians who came into the country as the result of the ongoing conflict. It is interesting to note that what seems to have come about, though based on observations and not documentation, is the non-sectarian humanitarian response to an extremely sectarian internal war among various factions. People who made contributions did not ask about the identity of those being supported—to them, they were all refugees in camps in Arab countries or "guests" in the GCC countries, and they all needed help.

Jeddah Floods—A Unique Example of Natural Disaster Response

I am including one example of response to natural disaster because it was a unique experience that deserves recording and there may be lessons learned from it, especially within the context of climate change, where coastal cities are in danger of being submerged by rising sea level. Jeddah, Saudi Arabia, is such a city, and its encounter with natural disaster came with the floods of 2009, 2010, and 2011. Though the community response was local and national rather than international, it is worth noting as a possible example from which lessons can be learned.

The highlight of the response was the leadership of youth, both women and men, and their use of social media on their smartphones to raise awareness and mobilize relief and rescue efforts. Young "social media activists" set up Facebook pages, uploading photos and videos from victims and their needs. They also became a focal point of response efforts including mobilization of volunteers, coordination and collection of donations and emergency items, and distribution to those affected. Information shared by these young social media activists on Facebook from the affected communities saved many lives; as such they became citizen journalists.

At the same time, mainstream mass media needed social media, which in turn needed mainstream media. It created a symbiotic relationship that allowed feeding information back and forth between the two streams of information providers. As the relief effort developed, a coordination campaign among the various partners took place. Government relief agencies, civil defense resources, NGOs, youth volunteers, locals in the areas—all needed social media to share information, work together, and coordinate humanitarian response. #jeddahfloods and similar hashtags in Arabic constituted a powerful tool to mobilize, get connected, share, participate, and assist in any way possible. Crucial practical information was shared on where to gather in order to deliver, collect, sort, organize, repackage, and distribute food, medicine, clothes, and other much-needed items. Such social media hashtags allowed real-time communication of people's needs and therefore better and timely interventions. It gave birth to a sense of community belonging, pride, and collective giving and sharing. Jeddah came together "as one" for the first time in many years. Other cities in Saudi Arabia including NGOs, voluntary groups, youth and women groups connected with the volunteers on the ground in Jeddah via social media and with government organizations and NGOs and collected donations and emergency items and sent them to the victims through the already established networks in Jeddah.

Naturally, such a disaster requiring immediate and focused response brings challenges to the forefront. One major challenge was to verify the accuracy of the information being shared as well as to discourage rumors and provide accurate, timely, and useful information. Another major challenge was the loss of connectivity in the affected areas of Jeddah. Many of the inhabitants of the flood-affected areas had no access to Internet, though mobile phones and SMS messages were widely used. Young emergency relief volunteers working in the affected areas were crucial in communicating what was going on and guiding the distribution of the emergency supplies through their mobile smart phones and access to the Internet.

The cooperation between youth volunteers, the Civil Defense, Saudi Red Crescent and other NGOs was both unprecedented and effective. This experience illustrated how social media was vital to the effort, resulting in the realization of the right to information, and its use to ensure the rights of communities to life-saving services and compensatory livelihood arrangements. It was also recognized as a critical tool for the organization and the delivery of relief—thus the recognition of it as a management tool in non-office, non-formal work environments.

Conclusion—Ways Forward and Future Trends

As Executive Director of the Internews Center for Innovation and Leadership, Mark Frohardt argues "broadcasting to affected communities with information about the humanitarian services is a one way communication that is outmoded." He adds "We have moved from the broadcast model to the information ecosystem model. It should be imperative to ensure that those who are in need are part of the response" (Frohardt 2010). I would add that this applies to communities affected by natural disasters[4] as well as armed conflict, war, and large-scale displacement of populations. Julia Pitner, Internews Middle East and North Africa Regional Director points to how "user-generated content by a blend of technologies is being used from Gaza to the refugee and migrant crises." But she warns "WhatsApp, Viper, Facebook and Facebook Messenger are used to get and share information in a constant chatter that may not always be accurate." She stresses the need for information to be "accurate and actionable" for effective humanitarian response (Ghannam 2016).[5] Jeffery Ghannam points to the leading role of the members of the Communicating with Disaster Affected Communities Network (CDAC), which includes WHO, ICRC, UN agencies, and others, in building a new humanitarian information ecosystem. Another example he cites is the BBC Action Media program working on preparedness and training of journalists and first respondents with the government and broadcast partner in Nepal, funded by the UK Department for International Development (Ghannam 2016).

Due to the limited amount of published information about the humanitarian response efforts in the GCC countries, it is important to undertake a real assessment of these experiences since much has taken place by groups of people that are not registered or identified. But various formal institutions have also provided experiences, including government, NGOs, established voluntary organizations and voluntary groups, media networks and organizations including TV broadcasting. It is important to evaluate these efforts and the lessons learned through further research and documentation to see what can be scaled-up in media and relief responses to on-going conflicts and natural disasters. I believe this topic is of vital importance and should be undertaken by the well-established and highly experienced humanitarian response institutions. Their assessment would enrich future relief response in the GCC in particular, especially in view of the political complexity of the Arab region and the existing trends of emerging violence within its countries.

It is also vital that special attention be given to the skills related to logistics and coordination among the various actors in response since relief is not just about raising funds but also about volunteering in an organized fashion. This would include ensuring that the most developed and effective communication systems are available and useable at times of crises. It also requires building the skills of community members to effectively use them to help themselves. This could be accomplished by broadcasting professionals at TV channels and media organizations who can impart knowledge and skills through training at the community level.

Finally, two important aspects of relief need to be linked—like the two sides of a coin— volunteerism on one hand, and those affected by disaster on the other, as integral participants in the relief efforts. Experience shows that volunteerism is very much alive and must be nurtured as a living skill in times of war, but also for peace building. Well-established humanitarian response institutions would find much positive resourcefulness in this area. Humanitarianism should always give priority to self-help by the communities themselves as part of the psychological and personal recovery process. Affected communities must be active in providing the relief service to their own people, and telling their stories and expressing their needs in their own voices. The traditional images of refugees, for example, watching as relief agencies provide the services, has been dominant for too long. It should be replaced by real images of communities providing the services themselves. From a recovery perspective, only through such therapeutic actions can the affected population remain dignified and their broken souls be regenerated. And here the media, whether local, mainstream Pan-Arab, or international TV broadcasting, radio, print, and social media platforms with all their various forms of expressions, should play a critical role in transmitting images of affected communities who are working hard to help themselves.

It is important to note that much still needs to be done on the social media front to develop an effective humanitarian response tool as opposed to a political propaganda tool. More-over, media initiatives to provide communities themselves with the means to document their realities, voice their concerns, and articulate their humanitarian needs is a paramount necessity. These could include for example, providing smartphones, cameras, video cameras, as well as other technical equipment and software that incorporates some training and skill development (and potential career) such as sound equipment, editing suites, etc. Moreover, user-generated media by people directly affected by humanitarian disasters needs to reach the relevant humanitarian agencies in time to be distributed over media platforms. This will take much effort. I believe the GCC countries will continue to learn many lessons about humanitarian responses, but much is still needed because the spirit of giving and volunteerism is alive, especially among young people. It is worth investing in them to bring humanitarian response and media access together as tools for saving lives and regenerating self-confidence and self-esteem, and strengthening hope and action.

Notes

1. www.Arabresearch.com/
2. http://data.unhcr.org/syrianrefugees/syria.php, July 2016
3. The interview of Nabil Al Khatib by Jeffrey Ghannam provides an excellent analysis of media coverage of war, displacement, and migration in the Middle East and North Africa.
4. www.ned.org/events/the-role-of-media-in-humanitarian-crises-lessons-learned-from-the-earthquake-in-haiti/
5. Interview of Julia Pitner by Jeffrey Ghannam.

References

Ahmad, A. R., and Hamasaeed, N. H. (2014) "The Role of Social Media in the Syrian Uprising," Paper submitted to the *International Conference on Communication, Media, Technology and Design*, 24–26 April, 2014, Istanbul, Turkey, available at: www.cmdconf.net

Frohardt, M. (2010) "Reporting on Humanitarian Crises: Lessons Learnt from the Earthquake in Haiti," lecture at the *National Endowment for Democracy/Centre for International Media Assistance CIMA*.

Ghannam, J. (2016) "Media as a form of Aid in Humanitarian Crises," *Insights*, Centre for International Media Assistance (CIMA).

Gunter, B., and Dickinson R. (Eds.) (2013) *New Media in the Arab World: A Study of 10 Arab and Muslim Countries*, London: Bloomsbury Publishing.

Gunter, B., Elareshi, M., and Al-Jaber K. (2016) *Social Media in the Arab World—Communication and Public Opinion in the Gulf States*, London and New York: I.B. Tauris.

Mourtada, R. and Salem, F. (2012) "Social Media in the Arab World: Influencing Societal and Cultural Change?" *Arab Social Media Report*, 2 (1): 1–29, available at: www.arabsocialmediareport.com/UserManagement/PDF/ASMR%204%20final%20to%20post.pdf

O'Neill, P. H. (2013) "Why the Syrian Uprising Is the First Social Media War," *The Daily Dot*, 18 September, available at: www.dailydot.com

Robinson, P. (2002) *The CNN Effect: The Myth of News, Foreign Policy and Intervention*, London: Routledge.

Sakr, N. (2001) *Satellite Realms: Transnational Television, Globalization and the Middle East*, London: IB Tauris.

Seib, P. (2008) *The Al Jazeera Effect: How the Global Media Are Reshaping World Politics*, Washington, DC: Potomac Books.

Shirky, C. (2011) "The Political Power of Social Media Technology, the Public Sphere and Political Change," *Foreign Affairs*, 90 (1): 28–41.

28

QUO VADIS? ETHNIC AND CULTURAL GENOCIDE

Chaldean and Assyrian Christians and Yazidis in Northern Iraq and Syria[1]

Purnaka L. de Silva

If we believe in absurdities, we shall commit atrocities
(Voltaire 1694–1778)[2]

Background to Ethnic and Cultural Genocide

In January 2014, Sam David Haddad[3] telephoned me, together with Bishop Mar Bawai Soro, making an impassioned-plea for support to publicize the plight of minority Christians in Iraq. They could see an impending humanitarian catastrophe looming for non-*Takfiri* peoples in Iraq where ethno-religious minorities such as the Chaldean, Assyrian, and Syriac Christians[4] (Namou 2015) and Yazidis (Russell 2014, 39–74) were in the greatest peril. Fighters from the so-called Islamic State (IS or *Daesh*, also ISIS or ISIL) terrorist group had penetrated western Iraq's provincial center Ramadi, and the strategically important city of Fallujah, just 50 miles from the Iraqi capital Baghdad. This emergency was also being documented by the US Commission on International Religious Freedom (2016, 99):

> Iraq's religious freedom climate continued to deteriorate in 2015. . . . ISIL targets anyone who does not espouse its extremist Islamist ideology . . . minority religious and ethnic communities, including the Christian, Yazidi, Shi'a, Turkmen, and Shabak . . . are especially vulnerable.

Daesh's territorial gains came after months of bloody combat against Iraqi government forces in Sunni-majority western Al Anbar governorate (the largest in the country) bordering Syria, Jordan, and the Kingdom of Saudi Arabia. *Daesh* espouses a Sunni-extremist *Takfiri* ideology where all Muslims, Christians, and Jews ("People of the Book"—the Abrahamic faiths) who do not adhere to their misinterpretations of Islamic teachings in the *Holy Qur'an* and *Hadith* (sayings, deeds, and behaviors attributed to the Prophet Mohammed from numerous oral accounts) are labeled apostates or *Kafirs* (unbelievers) who can and should be destroyed at will.

Closer examination of the geopolitical terrain is warranted to understand the ethno-cultural genocide perpetrated by *Daesh*. The radicalism began in 2008 when majority Shi'a Iraqi Prime Minister Nouri al-Maliki backtracked on promises to induct Sunni fighters into the central government armed forces and halted salaries. By 2013, tensions further escalated when al-Maliki used central government anti-terrorism laws to tyrannize and subjugate minority Sunni tribes and politicians. Matters boiled over when peaceful protest camps were violently raided by majority Shi'a, central government-aligned militias. In one incident in April 2013, approximately 50 Sunnis were massacred in Hawija. It all came to a head when Rafih al-Issawi a respected Sunni, and Minister of Finance was targeted, and his personal bodyguards arrested and tortured. He resigned and Sunni tribal elders called for a popular uprising to rearm, defend their legal rights, and resist being crushed by al-Maliki's extrajudicial tactics. Caught up in the uprising were Sunni tribes from the western Al Anbar governorate, the majority of whom belong to the three-million-member Dulemi Tribal Confederation. Other rebel Sunni tribes include the Albu-Rahman tribe from northern Salahuddin governorate, in the provincial center of Tikrit, close to the town of Al-Awja where Saddam Hussein lived (Balaghi 2005). Secular Shi'a parliamentarian and former Iraqi Prime Minister, Ayad Allawi, said that the action of the Sunni tribes was "an uprising of the oppressed." He noted that *Daesh* were exploiting, "the favorable political landscape of sectarianism." Responding to Bloomberg he noted that "Ex-Baathists, ex-army, tribal leaders, academics, ordinary citizens and the old resistance" to the US military were fighting the Iraqi central government.[5]

Al-Maliki's tyranny opened the door for *Daesh* to tap into the resistance movement of disaffected, marginalized Sunnis. It is not surprising that Al Anbar governorate became *Daesh's* base of operations for launching significant military conquests. A multipronged attack by *Daesh* fighters led to the surprisingly quick capture of Iraq's second largest city, Mosul, with a population of two and a half million on June 10, 2014, with little or no resistance from government forces who downed their weapons and fled.[6] It was almost six months since I received the telephone call from Professor Haddad and Bishop Soro, and their worst fears were now playing against the unprotected peoples of the Nineveh plains in northern Iraq.

Daesh, fueled by their military victories, unleashed a reign of terror within their orbit. Sunnis, Kurds,[7] Chaldean and Assyrian Christians, other ethno-religious minorities, and the majority Shi'a alike, were targeted, with Yazidis receiving the most brutal treatment:

> ISIL has committed horrific crimes against the Yazidi community . . . it regards as "devil worshippers"[8] . . . According to the United Nations, at least 16 mass graves have been uncovered around Sinjar, with the remains of likely Yazidi victims. Yazidi women and girls are subject to mass rape, sexual slavery, assault, and forced marriage to ISIL fighters.
> (US Commission on International Religious Freedom (2016, 100–101))

Chaldean and Assyrian Christians and Yazidis

Christianity in Iraq and Syria has been an active presence since apostolic times (Bauer 2010) (Figure 28.1). Throughout centuries of history inhabiting the ancient Mesopotamian region,[9] Christians have been socially prominent in both ecclesial and civil life. Before Islamic

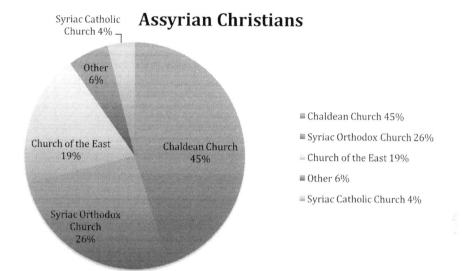

Assyrian Christians

Syriac Catholic Church 4%

Other 6%

Church of the East 19%

Chaldean Church 45%

Syriac Orthodox Church 26%

- Chaldean Church 45%
- Syriac Orthodox Church 26%
- Church of the East 19%
- Other 6%
- Syriac Catholic Church 4%

Figure 28.1 Breakdown of Assyrian Christian Denominations, as Per Expert Advice of Bishop Mar Bawai Soro[10]

Table 28.1 Breakdown of Religious Minorities in Iraq and Syria[11]

Religious Minority Denomination	Iraq	Syria	Total
Chaldeans	850,000	50,000	900,000
Assyrians	200,000	25,000	225,000
Syriac Orthodox	200,000	250,000	450,000
Syriac Catholic	100,000	75,000	175,000
Protestants	50,000	25,000	75,000
Other Christians	50,000	50,000	100,000
Yazidis	25,000	5,000	30,000
Greek Orthodox	—	500,000	500,000
Greek Catholics	—	250,000	250,000
Syriac Catholic Church	—	250,000	250,000
Total	1,475,000	1,480,000	2,955,000

conquests started in 633 AD (Armstrong 1994, 2002), Bishop Soro asserts that Christians made up the majority of peoples (64 percent), whose numbers have since fallen dramatically (presently only 0.04 percent). Now he says "they are a small minority being challenged in the land they so long inhabited."[12]

By the turn of the twenty-first century, as noted in Table 28.1, almost three million non-Muslim religious minorities lived in Iraq and Syria. After the collapse of Saddam Hussein's régime in 2003 and the onset of the Syrian civil war from 2011, minority Christian and Yazidi populations in Iraq and Syria significantly diminished. Bishop Soro estimates two million Christians and Yazidis emigrated from Iraq and Syria to seek safety.

Yazidis constitute a small minority and are close neighbors of Chaldean and Assyrian Christians, and Kurds. Today, their towns and villages straddle northern Iraq (including Nineveh plains) and the Syria–Turkey border region. Yazidis can be defined as an ethno-religious group culturally distinct from Chaldean and Assyrian Christians and Kurds in Iraq. Yazidis are monotheistic, deriving their ancient religious traditions from Zoroastrianism. Yazidi faith is centered in Iraq where their spiritual leader or "Amir" resides. It is also where the tomb of Sheikh Adi, their most revered saint, is situated. In Syria, Yazidis reside around their sacred Sinjar Mountains (Açikyildiz 2014). When *Daesh* launched multiple assaults, capturing Sinjar city and outlying villages on August 3, 2014, around 40,000–50,000 Yazidis escaped to these mountains. Yazidi internally displaced persons (IDPs) were totally unprepared, with little or no shelter in the sweltering heat of northern Iraq, running out of food, water, and medical supplies.

Despite impassioned, desperate appeals, *Daesh*'s onslaught could not be stopped at the time. Sacred Mount Sinjar became a place of carnage with tens of thousands of Yazidi corpses "scattered like leaves." Haji Khedev Haydev stated, "Dogs were eating the bodies of the dead." Iraqi General, Ahmed Ithwany told Jonathan Krohn, "It is death valley. Up to 70 percent of them [Yazidis] are dead." The situation was so desperate that Yazidi parents were throwing their children down from cliffs to end their lives quickly rather than suffering slowly.[13] In response to the plight of Yazidis a multinational airborne rescue effort was launched by the US, UK, Australian, and Iraqi military with airdrops and airlifts, and airstrikes to drive off *Daesh* fighters from Sinjar Mountains. On August 10, Kurdish military opened safe passage off the mountains to Iraqi Kurdistan for around 30,000 Yazidi IDPs, the balance remained trapped with many uncounted casualties.[14] The humanitarian catastrophe, atrocity crimes against humanity, and sexual slavery perpetrated upon defenseless Yazidi women and girls were just unfolding.

> The atrocities committed two years ago in northern Iraq by the so-called Islamic State include the mass slaughter of hundreds, maybe thousands, of Yazidi men; the separation of children away from their mothers and then the mass enslavement to be used as sex slaves of hundreds of Yazidi women,[15] many of who are held in captivity today.[16]

Daesh perceives minority Chaldean and Assyrian Christians, Yazidis, Turkmen and Shabak peoples (Minahan 2016), and majority Shi'a in Iraq and Syria, as "non-Islamic" and "infidels." *Daesh* subjects these peoples to systematic ethno-cultural cleansing tantamount to genocide. "In 2015, USCIRF concluded that ISIL was committing genocide against these groups, and crimes against humanity against these and other groups" (US Commission on International Religious Freedom 2016, 99).

The Case for Indentifying the Situation as Genocide

On August 10, 2016, the US State Department stated that *Daesh* "continued to pursue a brutal strategy of what Secretary (John) Kerry judged to constitute genocide against Yazidis, Christians, Shiites, and other vulnerable groups in the territory it controlled." US Deputy Secretary of State Antony Blinken noted that in March 2016 Secretary Kerry "made clear his judgment that Daesh is responsible for genocide against religious communities in areas under its control." Going on to say, "Daesh kills Yazidis because they are Yazidi, Christians because they are Christian, Shia Muslims because they are Shia," and they are "responsible for crimes against humanity and ethnic cleansing."[17] Secretary Kerry stated on March 17, 2016, that:

[Daesh] is responsible for genocide against groups in areas under its control, including Yazidis, Christians, and Shi'a Muslims [and] for crimes against humanity and ethnic cleansing directed at these same groups and in some cases also against Sunni Muslims, Kurds, and other minorities.

(US Commission in International Religious Freedom 2016, 100)

Secretary Kerry, and Adama Dieng, UN Under-Secretary-General/Special Adviser to the Secretary-General for the Prevention of Genocide, among other high officials have used the term genocide with regard to heinous atrocities and gross violations of human rights carried out by *Daesh* in Iraq and Syria. Dieng officially stated:

The Member States have a duty not to fail the Syrian people yet again and to uphold their pledge to protect populations from genocide, war crimes, crimes against humanity and ethnic cleansing. In this respect, the international community should step up its commitment to end impunity for the perpetrators of the most serious crimes in Syria and thus contribute to preventing new atrocities from being committed. For this reason, I strongly support the Secretary-General's repeated calls to the Security Council to refer the situation in Syria to the International Criminal Court.[18]

Daesh contributed significantly to the destabilization of Iraq and Syria, also affecting trans-national security, causing societal upheaval and a tidal wave of forced migration to Turkey, Lebanon, Jordan, Greece, and other European countries. Evidence is overwhelming and irrefutable, carefully recorded by organizations such as the UN, USCIRF, US Holocaust Memorial Museum, Minority Rights Group, Human Rights Watch, and Amnesty International, in preparation for war crimes trials possibly by the International Criminal Court (ICC) in The Hague. PBS/Frontline on *Daesh* produced a series of documentaries on the topic of the humanitarian crisis and the lack of justice and humanity under the diktat of *Daesh* in northern Iraq and the Syria–Turkey border region.

Article II of the Convention on the Prevention and Punishment of the Crime of Genocide, adopted by the UN General Assembly in 1948, defines *genocide* as follows:

Any of the following acts committed with *intent to destroy*, in whole *or in part*, a national, ethnical, racial or religious group, as such: (a) Killing members of the group; (b) Causing serious bodily or mental harm to members of the group; (c) Deliberately inflicting on the group conditions of life calculated to bring about its physical destruction in whole or in part; (d) Imposing measures intended to prevent births within the group; (e) Forcibly transferring children of the group to another group.[19] (emphasis added)

History shows many examples of these atrocities being committed against various victim groups. The Convention's definition of genocide is very particular, while at the same time it defines various ways and forms that genocide is perpetrated. The definition is contingent on acts committed with "intent to destroy" a particular group. *Daesh*'s atrocity crimes in Iraq and Syria meet more than one criterion and qualify as genocide.

Spectacular Violence, Mimesis, Cultivation of Hatreds and Phobia

In *Fields of Blood* (2015), Karen Armstrong argues that since their earliest manifestations, religions gave meaning to all aspects of life, including warfare, which become intertwined with representations of the "sacred." She surmises that modernity enabled an era of "spectacular violence," little of which can be ascribed directly to any particular religion. With *Daesh*, a false "theology" is being propagandized through social media and graphic videos of atrocities-as-divine-justice, masquerading as "sacred" in the eyes of thousands of impressionable followers and adherents unfamiliar with Islamic sacred texts, precepts, meanings, and practices. Spectacular violence, construction of hatreds and phobia are part of *Daesh*'s modus operandi. Facets of modernity, for example, sophisticated online social media campaigns, are used as tools to disseminate a vitriolic discourse of apocalyptic messages aimed at recruiting new followers. These tools are also used to inspire horrific terrorist attacks across the world on innocent civilians irrespective of nationality, ethnicity or creed.

"Spectacular violence" is choreographed, organized, constructed and reproduced, aligned with culturally embedded representations through symbolic images, narratives, rituals, rumors, and myths, propagating *Daesh*'s strain of *Jihadi-Salafism*. Such representations involve continuously conflicting and competing social realities in deeply divided societies, such as Iraq and Syria, taking place in politically charged and polarized contexts.

Societal fractures and divisions under Saddam Hussein were exacerbated in the aftermath of the ill-advised US invasion of Iraq. The practice of American neoconservative policies on the ground in Iraq—particularly the incompetent "governorship" of L. Paul Bremer (Galbraith 2009)—followed by the despotism of al-Maliki, enabled *Daesh* to simply "go viral" and become a multi-headed hydra.[20] The PBS/Frontline documentary "The Rise of ISIS" by Martin Smith, investigates miscalculations and mistakes behind the brutal rise of ISIS in Iraq. Smith details the country's unraveling after the American withdrawal, and what it means for the US to be fighting there again.[21]

US-led military interventions by the Obama administration in Iraq[22] and Syria[23] have continued to make it easy for *Daesh*'s propaganda–media arm to build upon the Western "crusader" imagery to their target audience of sympathizers. Simplistic and racist "Us versus Them" stereotypes are what strengthen *Daesh* and its cultivation of hatreds and phobias. Such stereotyping also reflects the mirror images in Western, not-so-democratic politics, reflected among others by Donald Trump in the US,[24] and Frauke Petry in Germany,[25] Victor Oban in Hungary,[26] Marine Le Pen in France,[27] and Marian Kotleba in Slovakia who is a neo-Fascist.[28]

Terrorist organizations such as *Daesh* are constantly learning from their military opponents be they US-led multinational or Russian forces or Iraqi and Syrian central government forces or other militaries or militias. Mimesis, or what Paul Ricoeur (1991, 138–139) calls "creative imitation" can be defined as more than copying or replicating. Rather it is a re-production that is adapted to suit particularistic needs of *Daesh*. Mimesis allows *Daesh* to adapt and develop better capabilities with each confrontation to gain knowledge about new weaponry, tactics, strategies, suicide bombing, and asymmetric warfare capabilities. *Daesh* also refines the potent art of terrorism and psychological warfare in tandem with sophisticated use of multimedia messaging aimed at fearful global publics or adoring supporters. *Daesh* learns from hostile environments, irrespective of whether they face conventional battles or urban warfare, for example against Iraqi and Syrian government forces with close air support from Western/Russian airpower; or skirmishes with Western and Russian counter-terrorism forces in the MENA region and worldwide. It remains to be seen whether military defeat and loss of territory in Northern

Iraq and Syria, will end Daesh's reign of terror. Or whether it will morph into "post-Daesh" situated practices of violence and terror unbounded by the need to hold on to territory.

The Making of *Daesh*

Daesh's political raison d'être—i.e. territorial establishment of a "caliphate" with Abu Bakr al-Baghdadi as the caliph[29]—cannot be separated from its "religious" rhetoric, where specific religious communities are targeted for expulsion and destruction simply because they are "apostates" or "devil worshippers." The "theological" roots of such thinking lie in a puritanical Islamist "religious" and political strain, known as *Jihadi-Salafism* (*al-Salafiyya al-Jihadiyya*), which is shared with al-Qaeda (Bergen 2011). It is a combining of two realities, political (*Jihadi*) and "theological" (*Salafism*) and necessitates a deeper look to better understand the making of *Daesh*.

In the late twentieth century, Islamist *jihadi* groups drawing inspiration from heterogeneous *Salafi* ideology emerged with the goal of overthrowing governments and establishing an Islamic state (caliphate). Al Qaeda, one of these groups, started attacking US interests and for a time captured the headlines, impressing radical Islamists globally. In the last 20 years, *Jihadi-Salafism* has gained in currency and captured the imagination of the most violent, extremist elements of Islamist youth, including those marginalized in Western societies. Fast forward to 2015, and Ayman al-Zawahiri the leader of al-Qaeda, criticizes *Daesh*'s "caliphate" and tactics, condemning them for causing splits among the jihadist movements by "attempting to pull jihadists away from other militant organizations to join its self-proclaimed caliphate."[30]

In the case of *Daesh*, it involves a more ambitious project of establishing a transnational power base through terror and military conquest to challenge the hegemony of Western civilization and Russia. In the marketplace of ideas, *Daesh* cherry picks and chooses from disparate Islamist ideologues in fashioning its own brand or strain of perverted *Jihadi-Salafism*, which has in practice led to genocide. As noted by Martin Chulov, al-Baghdadi has the necessary aptitude and background knowledge to contribute to just such a pernicious project; he was:

> Born Ibrahim Awad al-Badari in 1971 near Samarra, a city 50 miles north of Baghdad
> . . . [and] . . . took a master's degree and a PhD in Islamic studies at the University
> of Islamic Sciences in the Baghdad suburb of Adhamiya.[31]

Al-Baghdadi also understands the power of semiotics and symbolism, and the manipulation of multimedia platforms. His most important strategic move, thus far, was a video-broadcast online to his acolytes and global support base from the Grand Mosque in Mosul, immediately after his fighters had captured Iraq's second largest city. He was introduced to the congregation "as your new caliph Ibrahim."

> Clad in black robes that invoked a distant, almost mythical phase of Islamic history,
> Baghdadi gave a half-hour sermon during Friday prayers in Mosul and led worship
> inside one of the most important Islamic sites in Iraq in open defiance of the US
> intelligence officials who have put a $10m bounty on his head. . . . In doing so, he
> laid down a challenge not only to the authorities in Baghdad and the foreign powers,
> . . . but to the radical Islamist mothership from which the Isis movement broke—
> al-Qaida, and its current leader, Ayman al-Zawahiri.[32]

Daesh draws inspiration, on the one hand, from the revolutionary philosopher of the *Jihadi* world, Sayyid Qutb the Egyptian (who belonged to the Shafi'i School of Islamic jurisprudence in Sunni Islam) and from his political manifesto *Milestones* (1991). Qutb wrote this extremely influential book in prison, undergoing torture, during the régime of Gamal Abdel Nasser (Charles River Editors 2014). On the other hand, *Daesh* have appropriated wholesale from the puritanism of one of Qutb's ideological foes, Muhammed ibn 'Abd al-Wahhab (d. 1791). He came from the central Arabian Peninsula (before the existence of the Kingdom of Saudi Arabia) and belonged to the Hanbali School of Islamic jurisprudence.

> Proclaimed the necessity of returning directly to the *Quran* and hadith, rather than relying on medieval interpretations. Denounced as heretical innovations the practices of shrine cults, saint worship, requests for intercession from anyone other than God, and assigning authority to anyone other than God. Promoted strict adherence to traditional Islamic law. Opposed *taqlid* (adherence to tradition). Called for the use of *ijtihad* (independent reasoning through individual study of scripture). Plans for socioreligious reform in society were based on the key doctrine of *tawhid* (oneness of God). Formed an alliance with ibn al-Saud in 1744 that allowed Ibn al-Saud control over military, political, and economic matters and Ibn Abd al-Wahhab responsibility for religious concerns. The alliance resulted in foundation of the first Saudi dynasty and state and remains the basis for Saudi rule today. Many conservatives claim inspiration from the movement he founded.[33]

'Abd al-Wahhab continued the conservative tradition of *Salafism* that embodies different strains, which can be seen worldwide, and is considered today as one of this heterogeneous movement's staunchest pillars. However, he went further, and developed a more strict form of *Salafism*, which is the ultraconservative Wahhabi School of Sunni Islamic Thought that bears his name. It is primarily a Saudi movement that is zealously promoted worldwide by the kingdom's clerics and wealthy donors. In an analysis of Wahhabism, PBS/Frontline notes:

> For more than two centuries, Wahhabism has been Saudi Arabia's dominant faith. It is an austere form of Islam that insists on a literal interpretation of the Koran. Strict Wahhabis believe that all those who don't practice their form of Islam are heathens and enemies. Critics say that Wahhabism's rigidity has led it to misinterpret and distort Islam, pointing to extremists such as Osama bin Laden and the Taliban. Wahhabism's explosive growth began in the 1970s when Saudi charities started funding Wahhabi schools (madrassas) and mosques from Islamabad to Culver City, California.[34]

The heterogeneous *Salafi* movement is primarily theological and aims to "purify the faith." Though it is mainly doctrinal, and not political, its strict theology can and has been expressed violently, including attacks on Christians and the destruction of churches (Høigilt 2011). "It appears that IS has transformed jihad into an official military institution, in the wake of Salafist groups downplaying its spiritual component, turning it into a political tool to fight governments and to implement its expansionist goals."[35]

Considering hagiography and veneration of all shrines, tombs, statues, etc., as idolatrous (*shirk*), and to reaffirm the "Oneness of God," *Daesh* have engaged in the systematic destruction of ancient shrines, tombs, and religious artifacts, including rare icons, books, and manuscripts. The Islamic world was in uproar in early July 2016, with *Daesh* roundly condemned and denounced by all, including even the Taliban and Hezbollah, for the suicide bombing outside Prophet Mohammed's Mosque in Medina (Islam's second holiest site), which incorporates the house he lived in and his tomb; as "Muslims prepared for this week's

Eid al-Fitr festival marking the end of the holy fasting month of Ramadan."[36] In early 2015, *Daesh* bombed the Mosul Public Library burning 8,000 rare books and manuscripts.[37] In July 2014, they blew up what is popularly accepted as the tomb of Prophet Jonah, a key figure in Judaism, Christianity, and Islam, inside the Sunni Mosque of the Prophet Yunus (Jonah) in Mosul.[38] Human Rights Watch quoting local sources reported that in June 2014, *Daesh* destroyed seven Shi'a mosques in the Shi'a Turkmen majority city of Tal Afar, 31 kilometers west of Mosul.[39] The destruction of cultural heritage by *Daesh* is part and parcel of the genocide, war crimes, crimes against humanity, and ethnic cleansing of religious minorities and the Shi'a that is being carried out.

Accuracy in understanding the making of *Daesh* is of great importance for scholars, policy-makers, and humanitarian actors alike. However, there is confusion at times, for example in the Analysis Paper for the Center for Middle East Policy at Brookings, Cole Bunzel states that: "The Islamic State's adoption of this acutely severe version of Jihadi-Salafism is attributable to Abu Mus'ab al-Zarqawi, the founder of al-Qaeda in Iraq who studied theology with the prominent jihadi scholar Abu Muhammad al-Maqdisi" (Bunzel 2015, 9–10). The hint that al-Zarqawi is a "scholar" is contested by Mary Ann Weaver who writes in the *Atlantic Monthly* that "Abu Musab al-Zarqawi, barely forty and barely literate, a Bedouin from the Bani Hassan tribe, was until recently almost unknown outside his native Jordan."[40] Bunzel goes on to comment on doctrinal speeches given by the Islamist ideologue Abu Muhammad al-Maqdisi, and *Daesh*'s first leaders, Abu 'Umar al-Baghdadi and Abu Hamza al-Muhajir, as follows:

> The Islamic State's texts and speeches emphasize a number of doctrinal concepts. The most prominent of these stipulate: all Muslims must associate exclusively with fellow "true" Muslims and dissociate from anyone not fitting this narrow definition; failure to rule in accordance with God's law constitutes unbelief; fighting the Islamic State is tantamount to apostasy; all Shi'a Muslims are apostates deserving of death; and the Muslim Brotherhood and Hamas are traitors against Islam, among many other things. Importantly, the Islamic State anchors these concepts in traditional Salafi literature, and is more dogmatic about their application than al-Qaeda.
>
> (Bunzel 2015, 10)

The paramount question, amidst all of these misinterpretations and distortions of Islam (quintessentially an Abrahamic faith) for humanitarian and human rights organizations (that uphold universally accepted standards and treaties negotiated after the mass genocides of World War Two) is when will the *Jihadi-Salafists* and *Daesh* see reason and regain their lost humanity? What will it take for the killing and mayhem stop?

In the *Holy Qur'an* the very first Verse (*Āyā*) in the Opening Chapter (*Fātiha*) in *Sùra I*, it is stated: "*Bismillah al Rahmān al Rahām*" (In the Name of God, Most Gracious, Most Merciful).

> This verse is placed before every *Sùra* (Chapter) of the Qur'an (except the ninth), and *repeated at the beginning of every act by the Muslim* who dedicates his [sic] life to God, and whose hope is in His Mercy."[41] (emphasis added)

It is generally accepted that the attribute *Rahūm* (Merciful) can be applied to Men [sic]. It is therefore a real travesty that members of *Daesh* (and similar Islamist organizations), and their leaders such as al-Baghdadi, do not pause to reflect on the deep meaning and humanity of the words they utter, especially when dealing with other humans beings and religious minorities. They mimic all the trappings of the sacred, venerated texts and piety (for example al-Baghdadi's carefully choreographed Friday sermon at the Grand Mosque in Mosul), and repeat the very first Verse (Āyā) of the Holy Qur'an *ad infinitum*; however, the praxis of being Merciful is absent in their actions.

Atrocity Crimes in Syria

Select testimony of atrocity crimes provides a more tangible representation of the sheer scale of the ongoing humanitarian catastrophe. Extremist Islamist groups, especially *Daesh*, emerged out of the raging crucible of the Syrian civil war in 2011 and Christians of all denominations were caught up in the maelstrom. George Marlin notes, drawing from a report by Aid to the Church in Need that during the Christmas period of 2011, Christians were being murdered and kidnapped all over Syria; and their homes destroyed, churches burned down, and tens of thousands driven to the mountains outside of the city of Aleppo, which had the second largest population of Christians; where 3,000 were killed and 65 percent forced to leave because Islamist leaders permitted the seizure of Christian homes and property (Marlin 2015). Al-Nusra Front, once in union with *Daesh*, entered Christian homes screaming, "We're here to get you, worshippers of the cross." Marlin reports the findings of a study released in January 2014, which records that: "as many as 600,000 Syrian Christians, a third of the nation's total, fled their homes and were internally displaced within Syrian borders or living as refugees in neighboring countries" (Ibid., 110).

Michael Coren interviewed Sister Hatune Dogan, a Syrian Orthodox nun engaged in humanitarian work who has spoken openly about the persecution of Christians at the hands of Islamists, such as *Daesh*, especially in Iraq and Syria. She tells a story of a man she met, who had as part of his daily routine gone to his field, only to see hundreds of bodies of murdered, decapitated Christians who had suffered the same fate on account of their minority religious identity. In the same interview, she says:

> There are slaughterhouses, many slaughterhouses, in Syria where Christians are taken to be tortured and slaughtered. People who are not political, who do not choose or take sides—forced to deny their faith and then whether they have or not—are killed, often by beheading.
>
> (Ibid.)

Raqqa in northern Syria, near the border with Turkey, which became *Daesh's* "capital," was once home to 3,000 Christians who were given the status of *Dhimmi*.

> Under Islamic rule, Eastern Christians lived as protected people, *dhimmi*: They were subservient and had to pay the *jizya*, but were often allowed to observe practices forbidden by Islam, including eating pork and drinking alcohol. Muslim rulers tended to be more tolerant of minorities than their Christian counterparts, and for 1,500 years, different religions thrived side by side.[42]

In *Daesh's* reinterpretation and gross misrepresentation, it means that Christians are falsely restricted from rebuilding or renovating churches (even ones damaged by acts of violence), publicly displaying crosses or Christian symbols, ringing church bells, publicly exercising their faith, or allowing lectionary (scriptural) readings during church services to reach the ears of Muslims.

Atrocity Crimes in Iraq

Notwithstanding *Daesh*'s territorial gains in northern Syria between 2012 and 2013, making Raqqa the "capital" in August of 2014, etc., al-Baghdadi has openly stated that Iraq is their target (Kikoler 2014). In a fact-finding mission to the region, Kikoler bears witness that in June of 2014, *Daesh* pummeled through Mosul in the Nineveh plains early in the morning, shooting and bombing their way through soldiers, hanging, crucifying, and burning men, women, and children in their goal of conquest. Painting the Arabic letter *nun* (Arabic word for *Nazarene*, a derogatory term used for followers of Jesus of Nazareth). *Daesh* targeted and ethnically cleansed Christians in organized fashion, bringing memories of the Nazi holocaust of Jews, Gypsies and others from 1933–1945 (Megargee and White 2017). Thousands of Christians departed walking or crammed into pickup trucks.

On June 12, 2014, a couple of days after conquering Mosul, *Daesh* issued a decree, ordering women to be sent for the practice of "jihad by sex" or face punishment as per the laws of *sharia* (moral and religious law as per the principles of the Holy Qur'an and *hadith* or the sayings, deeds, and behaviors attributed to the Prophet Mohammed from numerous oral accounts). Considering that no *sharia* source refers to "jihad by sex" this decree is a purely "invented tradition" (Hobsbawm and Ranger 2012) on the part of al-Baghdadi and *Daesh*. It is similar to the use of "comfort women," involving the sexual slavery of women under occupation by the Japanese military during World War Two (Norma 2016). A translation of *Daesh*'s decree in Arabic states thus:[43]

In the Name of God, Most Gracious, Most Merciful

Subject: Mandate   *Daesh* Logo   *Daesh*

The State of Nineveh

In the Name of God, Most Gracious, Most Merciful

After liberation of the State of Nineveh, and the welcome shown by the people of the state to their brotherly mujahideen [those engaged in *jihad*], and after the great conquest, and the defeat of the Safavid [Persian] troops in the State of Nineveh, and its liberation, and Allah willing, it will become the headquarters for the mujahideen. Therefore we request that the people of this state offer their unmarried women so that they can fulfill their duty of jihad by sex to their brotherly mujahideen. Failure to comply with this mandate will result in enforcing the laws of Sharia upon them.

God we have notified, God bear witness.
Sha'ban 13, 1435
June, 12, 2014

In another testimony, the Assyrian International News Agency reported that *Daesh* entered the home of an Assyrian Christian family in Mosul and demanded *jizya*.

> They could either convert or pay the *jizya*, the head tax levied against all "People of the Book": Christians, Zoroastrians and Jews. If they refused, they would be killed, raped or enslaved, their wealth taken as spoils of war.[44]

When the family replied that they did not have the money to make the payment, three *Daesh* fighters raped the man's wife and daughter in front of him; he was so traumatized he committed suicide. In the same news report, four Christian women were shot and killed for not wearing veils, even though no Christian law or cultural norms mandate the wearing of veils.[45] The atrocities committed during the reign of terror in the summer of 2014 motivated the Iraqi Parliament to pass a resolution accusing *Daesh* of genocide.[46] However, this did not stop *Daesh*'s attempts to rid the lands they captured of perceived "infidels," and seize as much as possible, marking the walls of farms and businesses "Property of the Islamic State," as well as women, young girls, and children, notes Eliza Griswold. She reports a harrowing testimony of a young mother:

> It was a searing day. Temperatures reach as high as 110 degrees on the Nineveh Plain in summer. By 9 a.m., ISIS had separated men from women. Seated in the crowd, the local ISIS emir, Saeed Abbas, surveyed the female prisoners. His eyes lit on Aida Hana Noah, 43, who was holding her 3-year-old daughter, Christina. Noah said she felt his gaze and gripped Christina closer. . . . No one was sure where either bus was going. As the jihadists directed the weaker and older to the first of two buses . . . Aida and her blind husband, Khadr, boarded the first bus. The driver, a man they didn't know, walked down the aisle. Without a word, he took Christina from her mother's arms. "Please, in the name of God, give her back," Aida pleaded. The driver carried Christina into the medical center. Then he returned without the child. As the people in the bus prayed to leave town, Aida kept begging for Christina. Finally, the driver went inside again. He came back empty-handed. . . . Rana [a 31-year-old woman abducted by *Daesh* called on a mobile phone] . . . the next day, . . . whispered, in Syriac, [and] . . . said, "I'm taking care of a 3-year-old named Christina."[47]

Cultural Genocide

Daesh has engaged in "cultural genocide" in northern Iraq attempting to destroy its history and culture. In late January 2015, they bombed and shattered the ancient walls of Nineveh, which date back to the eighth century BC. In February 2015, they took sledgehammers to ancient Mesopotamian statues held in the Mosul Museum. *Daesh's* "cultural genocide" has robbed the peoples of northern Iraq of their pride and culture, which has enriched the world.

> The deliberate vandalism and destruction of heritage from Mosul's Library, the Mosul Museum, and the archaeological site of Nineveh at Mosul constitute a moral and cultural outrage that adds to the growing spiral of despair from both Iraq and Syria concerning heritage, looting, and damage due to armed conflict. Without the past, we cannot understand our present, and without understanding our present, we cannot plan for our future. We hope that whatever remnants of this shattered heritage still surviving in Mosul may be salvaged and restored, but it is already clear that so much has been irreparably destroyed or looted. Mosul's heritage is an important part of Mesopotamian civilization and the heritage of the entire world.[48]

The UN's cultural agency, UNESCO, condemned the destruction, which has robbed Nineveh of its great contributions to humanity, and disintegrated the link connecting past with present. Director-General of UNESCO Irina Bokova condemned the destruction of the two historic gates of Mesqa and Adad, and parts of the old ramparts of the archaeological site of Nineveh (Mosul):

> which are new crimes in a long list of attacks against the cultural heritage of Iraq, after the destruction of the winged bull of the Nergal gate, and the destruction at the Mosul Museum in 2015. These deliberate destructions are a war crime against the people of Iraq, whose heritage is a symbol and medium of identity, history and memory. These destructions are linked to the suffering and violence on human lives, and weaken the society over the long term. They are also attacks against the humanity we all share, against the values of openness and diversity of this region, as the cradle of civilizations.[49]

Exodus, Resistance to Genocide and the International Criminal Court

"To stay or not to stay?" is the burning question that religious minorities such as the Chaldean and Assyrian Christians and Yazidis, as well as Sunni Muslims, and the majority Shi'a, have to address when faced with *Daesh*'s brutal genocide, war crimes, crimes against humanity, and ethnic cleansing involving summary extrajudicial executions, torture, sexual violence in conflict, and slavery. The peoples in northern Iraq and Syria from all faith traditions desire to stay in their lands to preserve their ethnic and cultural identities in peace, and live productive and prosperous lives. This is particularly true for the Chaldean and Assyrian Christians and Yazidis who have inhabited these lands for over two millennia. These beleaguered peoples need safe havens in order for them to stay, where law and order and stability govern their lives and future generations. The most realistic place for them to find permanent residence is in Kurdistan, which is a political and economic arrangement that must be negotiated with Kurdish leaders. However, if a majority wish to leave, then they are not to be blamed given that the first instinct of human beings is self-preservation, which they consider a basic human right—the "right to life." The well-being of their children is at stake, and they have nothing left to lose except their lives, which they are not willing to sacrifice.

Such an existential dilemma raises a number of questions. In the face of ethnic and cultural genocide is the depopulation of the ancient religious minorities of northern Iraq and Syria an acceptable solution? From the perspective of humanitarian action, are there genuinely non-military solutions to protect populations from genocide, war crimes, crimes against humanity, and ethnic cleansing? What role can the global media industry play apart from bearing witness? What can the august body of the UN do to make the responsibility to protect (R2P) mandate more effective? These are some of the questions that need to be seriously addressed if sanity and peace are to prevail, while the humanitarian and human rights community with support from the global media continue to record mounting atrocity crimes.

The November 2015, Memorandum to the Foreign Affairs Select Committee with regard to the Extension of Offensive British Military Operations in Syria discusses international strategy as follows:

> The Global Coalition against ISIL comprises 63 countries (see annex). It has a coherent strategy of pressuring ISIL, especially in Syria and Iraq, through military, political and diplomatic action. This has included adopting UN Security Council Resolutions to: sanction ISIL and its affiliates (SCR 2170); to inhibit the use of Foreign Fighters (SCR 2178) and to squeeze ISIL's funding sources (SCR 2199).[50]

A senior French General said in a private dinner conversation (a week before the multiple attacks in Paris on Friday, November 13, 2015)[51] that in the assessment of the national defense establishment, even if *Daesh* is defeated on the battlefields of Iraq, Syria, and Libya, they anticipate terrorist attacks in Western countries to continue for at least another 20 to 30 years. This is a bleak and shocking assessment of generations who are lost to civilization. It means that there is much work to be done for multilateral agencies, governments, and the UN Security Council, which is entrusted with R2P.

> [The] U.N. Security Council met to discuss the plight of Iraq's religious minorities. "If we attend to minority rights only after slaughter has begun, then we have already failed," Zeid Ra'ad al-Hussein, the high commissioner for Human Rights, said. After the conference ended, there was mounting anger at American inaction. Although the airstrikes were effective, since October 2013, the United States has given just $416 million in humanitarian aid, which falls far short of what is needed. "Americans and the West were telling us they came to bring democracy, freedom and prosperity," Louis Sako, the Chaldean Catholic Patriarch of Babylon who addressed the Security Council, wrote to me in a recent email. "What we are living is anarchy, war, death and the plight of three million refugees."[52]

Quo Vadis?

Is military force a workable solution to halt *Daesh*'s ideologically driven, ethno-cultural genocide and atrocity crimes in Syria and Iraq? Do Western military actions impact favorably on *Daesh*'s ability to recruit thousands of new recruits globally, using slick multimedia propaganda campaigns? Can local, regional, and global media networks counter *Daesh*'s murderous narratives? What can faith communities do in this regard? Can the Vatican and similar religious bodies do more to protect their peoples? More questions need to be asked with no easy solutions.

What of the International Criminal Court? How effective is it as an international tool to provide justice for *Daesh*'s victims when it takes years of laborious litigation? How can the ICC become more effective? Examining all the testimonies that have been recorded t hus far it is quite evident that ethnic and cultural genocide is taking place in northern Iraq and Syria, as per the Convention on the Prevention and Punishment on the Crime of Genocide. *Daesh* has stopped at nothing to eradicate the memory of any faith community or culture that does not conform to their criminal reinterpretation and deliberate misinterpretation of Islam. They demonstrate a clear *intent to destroy* ethnic and religious groups, by killing their members, causing serious bodily and mental harm, and deliberately inflicting conditions of life calculated to bring about their destruction and forcibly transferring children. There are the added war crimes of sexual violence in conflict, torture, and slavery. Like all wars and genocide, this too shall end, and the ICC together with the international humanitarian community in partnership with multimedia networks must prepare for such an eventuality.

Notes

1. I am indebted to Bishop Mar Bawai Soro for sharing his intimate knowledge of the subject matter. He has unbounded compassion for members of all religious minorities in Iraq facing existential threats, with whom he is in constant contact, and those in Syria. Born in Ashur Soro, Kirkuk in northern Iraq to an Assyrian Christian

family, Kurdish and Yazidi peoples were his neighbors. He served the Assyrian Church of the East for 20 years as Diocesan Bishop and ecumenical officer of the Assyrian Church Patriarchate. In March 2008 he professed the Catholic faith and on January 11, 2014, His Holiness Pope Francis appointed him Titular Bishop of Foraziana in pastoral service of the Chaldean Catholic Eparchy of Saint Peter the Apostle, San Diego, California.

2. "Voltaire" is the pen name of French philosopher François-Marie Arouet who advocated freedom of religion, and separation of church and state. A diatribe against religion and the Catholic Church accompanies his famous quote. For purposes of this essay it is used in the context of contemporary events in northern Iraq and Syria, and the genocidal actions of *Daesh*.

3. Sam David Haddad is Consulting Professor Electrical Engineering, Stanford University. He is a Chaldean Christian born in Iraq, and inducted to the Silicon Valley Engineering Hall of Fame, available at: www.htcservices.com

4. See Figure 28.1 for breakdown of Assyrian Christian denominations by Bishop Soro.

5. *Bloomberg* news report by Zaid Sabah and Caroline Alexander "Sunni Tribes to Fight Until Iraq's Maliki Goes, Chief Says," available at: www.bloomberg.com/news/articles/2014–07–07/sunni-tribes-to-fight-on-until-iraqs-maliki-goes-leader-says

6. *The Washington Post* news report by Liz Sly and Ahmed Ramadan, "Insurgents seize Iraqi city of Mosul as security forces flee," available at: www.washingtonpost.com/world/insurgents-seize-iraqi-city-of-mosul-as-troops-flee/2014/06/10/21061e87–8fcd-4ed3-bc94–0e309af0a674_story.html

7. Excellent account of Kurdish resistance to *Daesh*—*A Road Unforeseen: Women Fight Islamic State* by Meredith Tax (2016).

8. *The World Post* news report by Brian Glyn Williams "Who Are the Yazidi 'Devil Worshipers' and Why Is ISIS Trying to Slaughter and Enslave This Ancient Minority? Part Two," available at: www.huffingtonpost.com/brian-glyn-williams/who-are-the-yazidi-devil-worshipers_b_9255614.html

9. Mesopotamia refers to the Euphrates and Tigris riparian territory encompassing much of Iraq, Eastern Syria, and the Syria–Turkey border—where *Daesh* operates its murderous campaign—as well as Kuwait and the Iraq–Iran border.

10. In *The Church of the East: Apostolic and Orthodox* (2007), Bishop Soro examines historical record and notes that during the "Classical Era of Eastern Christianity," the Church of Mesopotamia was referred to as Eastern, Nestorian or Syrian. He writes that after devastating Mongolian invasions, between the thirteenth and seventeenth centuries, segments of the Church of Mesopotamia reestablished ecclesial communion with Rome. This union resulted in a collage of denominations with the emergence of the Chaldean Catholic Church (45 percent), Assyrian Church of the East (19 percent), Syrian Orthodox Church (26 percent), and Syrian Catholic Church (4 percent). In the nineteenth century, British Anglican and US Presbyterian missionaries began evangelizing the faithful of these ancient churches, starting in northwestern Iran followed by northern Iraq, which led to the establishment of various evangelical and reformed groups, noted in Figure 28.1 as "Other" (6 percent). For population numbers see Table 28.1.

11. These population figures have been derived from census data recorded by Bishop Soro.

12. Referenced from personal interview with Bishop Mar Bawai Soro, March 2014.

13. *The Telegraph* news report by Jonathan Krohn "Iraq crisis: 'It is death valley. Up to 70 per cent of them are dead,'" available at: www.telegraph.co.uk/news/worldnews/middleeast/iraq/11024037/Iraq-crisis-It-is-death-valley.-Up-to-70-per-cent-of-them-are-dead.html

14. BBC news report "Thousands of Yazidis 'still trapped' on Iraq mountain," available at: www.bbc.com/news/world-middle-east-28756544

15. BBC news report by Paul Wood "Islamic State: Yazidi women tell of sex-slavery trauma," available at: www.bbc.com/news/world-middle-east-30573385

16. BBC news report "Yazidis subjected to 'mass rape' by IS," available at: www.bbc.com/news/world-middle-east-36961355

17. AFP news report by Nicolas Revise "US decries IS 'genocide' of Christians, Shiites, Yazidis," available at: www.yahoo.com/news/us-decries-genocide-christians-shiites-yazidis-142601972.html?ref=gs

18. Statement by Adama Dieng on the situation of civilians in the Syrian Arab Republic, May 19, 2016, available at: www.un.org/en/preventgenocide/adviser/pdf/2016–05–09%20OSAPG%20statement%20on%20the%20situation%20in%20Syria.pdf

19. *Convention on the Prevention and Punishment of the Crime of Genocide*, available at: www.ohchr.org/EN/ProfessionalInterest/Pages/CrimeOfGenocide.aspx

20. PBS/Frontline documentary by Martin Smith "Truth, War and Consequences," available at: www.pbs.org/wgbh/pages/frontline/shows/truth/

21. PBS/Frontline documentary by Martin Smith "The Rise of ISIS," available at: www.pbs.org/wgbh/pages/frontline/shows/truth/

22. ABC news report by Luis Martinez "US Special Operations Forces Expanding in Iraq to Battle ISIS," available at: http://abcnews.go.com/Politics/carter-us-special-operations-forces-expanding-iraq/story?id=35510035

23. *The Guardian* news report by Dan Roberts and Tom McCarthy "Obama orders US special forces to 'assist' fight against Isis in Syria," available at: www.theguardian.com/world/2015/oct/30/syria-us-deployment-troops-obama-special-operations

24. *Time* news report by Daniel White, "50 GOP Security Experts Sign Letter Calling Donald Trump 'Dangerous,'" available at: http://time.com/4444125/trump-gop-security-experts/

25. *The Guardian* news report by Kate Connolly, "Frauke Petry: The acceptable face of Germany's new right?" available at: www.theguardian.com/world/2016/jun/19/frauke-petry-acceptable-face-of-germany-new-right-interview

26. *International Business Times* news report by Tom Porter "Viktor Orban: The 'fascist' Hungarian prime minister at the centre of Europe's refugee crisis," available at: www.ibtimes.co.uk/viktor-orban-fascist-hungarian-prime-minister-centre-europes-refugee-crisis-1518346

27. *The New York Times* news report by Andrew Higgins, "Leader of French Far Right Hopes to Fix Europe From the Inside," available at: www.nytimes.com/2014/05/29/world/europe/leader-marine-le-pen-of-french-far-right-hopes-to-fix-europe.html?_r=0

28. BBC news report by Rob Cameron, "Marian Kotleba and the rise of Slovakia's extreme right," available at: www.bbc.com/news/world-europe-35739551

29. *The Guardian* news report by Martin Chulov, "Abu Bakr al-Baghdadi emerges from shadows to rally Islamist followers," available at: www.theguardian.com/world/2014/jul/06/abu-bakr-al-baghdadi-isis

30. *The Washington Post* news report by Missy Ryan, "Al-Qaeda leader criticizes Islamic State for dividing jihadist ranks," available at: www.washingtonpost.com/world/national-security/al-qaeda-leader-criticizes-islamic-state-for-dividing-jihadist-ranks/2015/09/09/771417a2-5722-11e5-8bb1-b488d231bba2_story.html

31. *The Guardian* news report by Martin Chulov, "Abu Bakr al-Baghdadi emerges from shadows to rally Islamist followers," available at: www.theguardian.com/world/2014/jul/06/abu-bakr-al-baghdadi-isis

32. *The Guardian* news report by Martin Chulov, "Abu Bakr al-Baghdadi emerges from shadows to rally Islamist followers," available at: www.theguardian.com/world/2014/jul/06/abu-bakr-al-baghdadi-isis

33. Oxford Islamic Studies Online report on Muhammed ibn 'Abd al-Wahhab, available at: www.oxford islamicstudies.com/article/opr/t125/e916

34. PBS/Frontline's analysis of Wahabbism, available at: www.pbs.org/wgbh/pages/frontline/shows/saudi/analyses/wahhabism.html

35. *Al Monitor* news report by Ali Mamouri, "Extremist groups transform concept of jihad," available at: www.al-monitor.com/pulse/originals/2015/06/jihad-concept-extremism-isis-qaeda-salafism-wahhabism-sufi.html

36. AFP news report by Ian Timberlake, "Muslim world condemns Saudi holy site bombing," available at: www.yahoo.com/news/multiple-suicide-blasts-hit-saudi-arabia-191235559.html

37. The library was built in 1921, the year modern Iraq was created. It contained eighteenth-century manuscripts, Syriac books printed in Iraq's first printing house in the nineteenth century, Ottoman era books, early twentieth-century Iraqi newspapers, old antiques such an astrolabe and sand glass used by ancient Arabs. It hosted personal libraries of more than 100 notable families from Mosul over the last century. *Daesh* even destroyed drums and other musical instruments for being "un-Islamic." *The Fiscal Times* news report "ISIS Burns 8000 Rare Books and Manuscripts in Mosul," available at: http://finance.yahoo.com/news/isis-burns-8000-rare-books-030900856.html

38. Prophet Jonah has a special connection to Nineveh, which is why his tomb was in Mosul. Bishop Soro notes that in the Bible, Prophet Jonah was sent by God to Nineveh to warn the Ninevites of God's coming wrath on account of their wickedness. Heeding his words the Ninevites fasted and prayed, and God spared them, which is why he has been so devoutly revered for so long in Nineveh, and his shrine attracted devotees over centuries to meditate on God's mercy and justice. Bishop Soro comments that even the despot Saddam Hussein renovated the shrine in the 1990s.

39. CNN news report by Dana Ford and Mohammed Tawfeeq, "Extremists destroy Jonah's tomb, officials say," available at: www.cnn.com/2014/07/24/world/iraq-violence/index.html

40. *The Atlantic* article by Mary Ann Weaver, "The Short, Violent Life of Abu Musab al-Zarqawi: How a video-store clerk and small-time crook reinvented himself as America's nemesis in Iraq," available at: www.the atlantic.com/magazine/archive/2006/07/the-short-violent-life-of-abu-musab-al-zarqawi/304983/

41. Explanation of *Rahīm* (Merciful) is in footnote 19 of *The Holy Qur'an* (1983: 14).

42. *The New York Times Magazine* news report by Eliza Griswold, "Is This the End of Christianity in the Middle East?" available at: www.nytimes.com/2015/07/26/magazine/is-this-the-end-of-christianity-in-the-middle-east.html?_r=0

43. *Assyrian International News Agency* news report, "ISIS in Mosul Orders Unmarried Women to 'Jihad By Sex,'" available at: www.aina.org/news/20140621162728.htm

44. *The New York Times Magazine* news report by Elizas Griswold, "Is This the End of Christianity in the Middle East?", available at: www.nytimes.com/2015/07/26/magazine/is-this-the-end-of-christianity-in-the-middle-east.html?_r=0

45. *Assyrian International News Agency* news report, "ISIS Rape Christian Mother and Daughter, Kill 4 Christian Women for Not Wearing Veil," available at: www.aina.org/news/20140623185542.htm
46. *Assyrian International News Agency* news report, "Iraqi Parliament Resolution Calls ISIS Acts Genocide," available at: www.aina.org/news/20140807164526.htm
47. *The New York Times Magazine* news report by Eliza Griswold, "Is This the End of Christianity in the Middle East?", available at: www.nytimes.com/2015/07/26/magazine/is-this-the-end-of-christianity-in-the-middle-east.html?_r=0
48. Oriental Institute Statement on Cultural Destruction in Iraq, available at: http://oi.uchicago.edu/about/statement-cultural-destruction-iraq
49. Statement of the Director-General of UNESCO, available at: http://whc.unesco.org/en/news/1483
50. Memorandum to the Foreign Affairs Select Committee, "Prime Minister's Response to the Foreign Affairs Select Committee's Second Report of Session 2015–16: The Extension of Offensive British Military Operations to Syria," available at: www.parliament.uk/documents/commons-committees/foreign-affairs/PM-Response-to-FAC-Report-Extension-of-Offensive-British-Military-Operations-to-Syria.pdf
51. Gist of a conversation in the presence of an ISSD Malta associate who requested that the source remain anonymous, as it was an informal comment made in private and not officially sanctioned by the French military.
52. The *New York Times Magazine* news report by Eliza Griswold, "Is This the End of Christianity in the Middle East?", available at: www.nytimes.com/2015/07/26/magazine/is-this-the-end-of-christianity-in-the-middle-east.html?_r=0

References

Açikyildiz, B. (2014) *The Yezidis: The History of a Community, Culture and Religion*, London: I.B. Tauris.

Armstrong, K. (1994) *A History of God: The 4,000-Year Quest of Judaism, Christianity and Islam* (Paperback ed.), New York: Ballantine Books.

Armstrong, K. (2002) *Islam: A Short History* (Revised and Updated ed.), New York: Modern Library Chronicle, Random House.

Armstrong, K. (2015) *Fields of Blood: Religion and the History of Violence* (Reprint ed.), New York: Anchor Books.

Balaghi, S. (2005) *Saddam Hussein: A Biography* (Greenwood Biographies), West Port, CT: Greenwood.

Bauer, S. W. (2010) *The History of the Medieval World: From the Conversion of Constantine to the First Crusade*, New York: W.W. Norton.

Bergen, P. L. (2011) *The Longest War: The Enduring Conflict between America and Al-Qaeda* (Reprint ed.), New York: Free Press.

Bunzel, C. (2015) "From Paper State to Caliphate: The Ideology of the Islamic State," in *The Brookings Project on U.S. Relations with the Islamic World*, No. 19, March, Washington, DC: Center for Middle East Policy at Brookings.

Charles River Editors. (2014) *Gamal Abdel Nasser: The Life and Legacy of Egypt's Second President*, CreateSpace Independent Publishing Platform.

Galbraith, P. W. (2009) *Unintended Consequences: How War in Iraq Strengthened America's Enemies* (Reprint ed.), New York: Simon & Schuster.

Hobsbawm, E. J., and Ranger, T. (Eds.) (2012) *The Invention of Tradition* (20th ed.), Cambridge, UK: Cambridge University Press.

Høigilt, J. (July 2011) "The Salafis Are Coming: But Where Are They Going?" Oslo: Norwegian Peacebuilding Resource Centre, available at: www.peacebuilding.no/

Kikoler, N. (2014) *"Our Generation Is Gone": The Islamic State's Targeting of Iraqi Minorities in Ninewa* (Bearing Witness Trip Report), Washington, DC: United States Holocaust Memorial Museum and the Simon-Skjodt Center for the Prevention of Genocide.

Marlin, G. J. (2015) *Christian Persecutions in the Middle East: A 21st Century Tragedy* (First ed.), South Bend, IN: St. Augustine's Press.

Megargee, G. P., and White, J. (Ed.) (2017) *Encyclopedia of Camps and Ghettos: 1933–1945 (Seven Volumes)*, Washington, DC: United States Holocaust Memorial Museum.

Minahan, J. B. (2016) *Encyclopedia of Stateless Nations: Ethnic and National Groups around the World* (2nd ed.), Santa Barbara, CA: Greenwood.

Namou, W. (2015) *Iraqi Americans: Witnessing A Genocide*, Sterling Heights, MI: Hermiz.

Norma, C. (2016) *The Japanese Comfort Women and Sexual Slavery during the China and Pacific Wars*, London and New York: Bloomsbury Academic.

Qutb, S. (1991) *Milestones*, Delhi: Markazi Maktaba Islami.

Ricoeur, P. (1991) "Mimesis and Representation" in Mario J. Valdés (Ed.), *A Ricoeur Reader: Reflection and Imagination*, New York and London: Harvester Wheatsheaf.

Russell, G. (2014) *Heirs to Forgotten Kingdoms: Journeys Into the Disappearing Religions of the Middle East*, New York: Basic Books.

Soro, M. B. (2007) *The Church of the East: Apostolic & Orthodox*, San Jose, CA: Adiabene Publications.

Tax, M. (2016) *A Road Unforeseen: Women Fight Islamic State*, New York: Bellevue Literary Press.

The Holy Bible: Old and New Testaments (Authorized King James Version) (2001), New York: Thomas Nelson.

The Holy Qur'an (Text, Translation and Commentary A. Yusuf Ali) (1983), Brentwood, MA: Amana Corp.

United States Commission on International Religious Freedom (2016) *United States Commission on International Religious Freedom 2016 Annual Report*, Washington, DC: USCIRF.

29

CHILD PROTECTION AND UNICEF'S COMMUNICATION AND MEDIA STRATEGY

A Conflict-related Study from Mindanao, the Philippines

Priti Vaishnav

Background

The Republic of the Philippines has historically borne the brunt of Maoist insurgencies and faced the consequences of violent extremism meted out by a number of rebel groups in the southern island of Mindanao. The island could be considered one of the world's longest-running armed conflict areas that began with the independence of the Philippines in 1946. Mindanao has a long history of rebellion and resistance against Spain's colonial conquest in the country. Three centuries of Spanish rule failed to conquer Muslim areas in the south of the archipelago. After being defeated militarily by the US in 1898, Spain ceded the Philippines to the Americans and forcibly incorporated the southern Muslim areas.

The Muslim population of the Philippines is concentrated in the Sulu Archipelago, some parts of Western Mindanao and certain mountainous areas in northern Luzon. Central Mindanao is a majority Muslim area but also has a large number of Christian and Indigenous (Lumad) communities. The majority of Christians are "settlers" who migrated from the northern Philippines to relocate in the resource-rich lands of Mindanao. From the 1960s onward successive governments sponsored resettlement programs for Christians to live in Mindanao. These policies were a turning point as native populations felt threatened and were compelled to protect their ancestral lands and culture. It also led to the creation of several separatist movements. Today, Central and Western Mindanao are internally divided not only on religious grounds but on political differences as well. These political differences only served to further exacerbate ethnic and religious cleavages in Mindanao.

There are multiple armed groups active in the region. The Armed Forces of the Philippines (AFP) and the Philippine National Police (PNP) maintain a strong presence and are often supported by paramilitary groups—that are privately funded as well as government/state-backed—such as Citizen Armed Force Geographical Units (CAFGUs) and Civilian Volunteer Organizations (CVOs). CAFGUs are a military-supervised paramilitary group to protect communities against communist insurgency and Islamic separatism. Although the government claims that paramilitary forces are better monitored, trained, and regulated, they often violate human rights and are suspected to have links to organized crime syndicates as stated in several reports by Human Rights Watch and the Department of Justice of the Philippines. Non-state armed groups include the Moro National Liberation Front (MNLF), Moro Islamic Liberation Front (MILF) with its military wing Bangsamoro Islamic Armed Force (BIAF) and women's military wing (mainly engaged in assisting medical, communication and other auxiliary needs), Bangsamoro Islamic Women Auxiliary Brigade (BIWAB), the Bangsamoro Islamic Freedom Fighters (BIFF), also popularly known as Bangsamoro Islamic Freedom Movement (BIFM), the Abu Sayyaf Group (ASG), and the New People's Army (NPA), which is the military wing of the Communist Party of the Philippines (CPP).

Western and Central Mindanao have predominantly been affected by conflicts between the AFP and the Muslim separatist organizations, first the MNLF and in more recent times, the MILF and BIFF. Mindanao is also highly exposed to violence between Christian and Muslim communities, as well as a culture of political warlords whereby political elites exert their domination through private militias and armies, which operate with impunity. An example of this is the November 2009 Maguindanao massacre where 57 people were allegedly murdered by the Ampatuan clan. In addition, rogue "lost commands" from non-state armed groups and armed criminal gangs create a pervading sense of insecurity as the lines between conflicts, politics and criminality are blurred. The potential for violence is exacerbated by an abundance of small arms in the region, which also contribute to local conflicts, knows as "*ridos*" frequently descending into bloodshed. The Central and Western Mindanao regions are therefore vulnerable to various kinds of armed clashes.

The southwestern island of Basilan and Sulu have been famous for Abu Sayyaf extremists. Abu Sayyaf Group (ASG) is a long-established criminal group that has pledged allegiance to the so-called Islamic State (IS—also known as ISIS, ISIL, and Daesh), followed suit by the Maute Group (which is battling the Philippines Marines and AFP in Marawi City). ASG is prone to kidnapping and also the brutal killing of hostages, as witnessed in several kidnapping cases. Notoriously, it is also known that ASG has recruited many children, luring them through drugs and crime.

In 1996, the Government of the Philippines (GPH) signed a peace agreement with MNLF, giving predominantly Muslim areas a degree of self-rule, setting up the Autonomous Region in Muslim Mindanao (ARMM). Autonomy, instead of independence, resulted in ideological and personality clashes and political strategies that led to the breakaway of the bulk of the Maguindanao-based Kutawato Revolutionary Committee, led by its former Chairman for Foreign Affairs, Salamat Hashim in 1977, forming MILF in 1984. Interestingly, at present MILF is in talks with the government for a greater degree of autonomy in the region instead of independence, which again resulted in BIFF breaking away from MILF.

The complex mixture of ethnicities, religions, and social groups in the region heavily influences Mindanao and its neighboring islands, Basilan, Sulu, and Tawi Tawi. Aside from conflicts between these groups on a local level, numerous non-state actors throughout the last half-century have taken up arms to secede from the central government's political control, which has resulted in protracted conflicts that have lasted for more than four decades. Such actions have resulted in humanitarian crises involving heavy displacement of civilians, killings, torture and maiming, recruitment of children by various armed groups, damage to schools and other civilian infrastructure, etc., in turn prompting the government and international community to address these complex emergencies more robustly.

There have been several attempts at peacemaking, given that these conflicts have been a critical issue on every President's table since 1946. At the moment the southern Philippines seems closest to making peace and the current President Rodrigo Duterte—lawyer and seven-term former Mayor of Davao city in Mindanao—has proposed an "enabling law" that brings together members of different southern ethnic, religious and political groups. During my five years of work in Mindanao I had a few opportunities to communicate with and understand Mayor Duterte's point of view on the federalized structure of government. While he may not choose exactly the same path as his predecessor Benigno Aquino, President Duterte was one of the peace deal's biggest supporters, which he made clear during his successfully concluded election campaign to win the presidency.

Child Protection in Mindanao

Based on my five years of fieldwork in Mindanao, child protection is a hard-hitting issue. I worked with Nonviolent Peaceforce, which specializes in Unarmed Civilian Protection. We worked very closely with the United Nations and in particular UNICEF in order to report and respond to Child Protection issues in Mindanao and surrounding islands. The work demanded neutrality, impartiality to the parties in the conflict, an active presence and access to remote conflict-affected areas, and a strong inclination that Humanitarian Action be used to benefit thousands of civilians suffering and being displaced by the conflicts as internally displaced persons (IDPs).

The region is engulfed by heavy recruitment of children by various armed groups and numerous cases of grave child rights violations. The effects of these violent conflicts and the subsequent displacements on children have been extensive. Thousands of children have been killed or wounded during the years of war and many thousands displaced along with their families. Schools were and are still being used as evacuation centers disrupting the education system. These evacuation centers lack sufficient support and supplies. In addition, families that remain displaced face a lack of health and educational facilities, and continuing insecurity in their places of origin. Children have been accidentally caught in the crossfire, but also, alarmingly, been directly targeted and in some cases abducted.

Acts of recruitment and use of child soldiers, killing and maiming of children, rape or other grave sexual violence against children, attacks on schools and hospitals, and abductions by an armed party to conflict triggers an inclusion of their names in the "list of shame." In May 2013, the Secretary-General of the United Nations once again listed parties to the conflicts in the Philippines as those that recruit and use children, specifically the Abu Sayyaf Group, the MILF and the NPA, while noting "credible" reports that the BIFF also recruits minors (Report of the Secretary-General on Children and Armed Conflict, A/67/845–S/2013/245, May 2013). Based on the Report of the Secretary-General to the UN Security Council (A/69/926–S/2015/409) issued on April 20, 2016, the United Nations verified the recruitment and use of 17 children, including 15 children used as human shields, by the BIFF in one incident and two recruited by NPA. Unverified reports indicated that ASG recruited around 30 children in Basilan. The UN also verified the killing of six children and maiming of 25 children, a third of which were attributed to ASG.

Recognizing the critical need to address child protection, the UN has devised various strategies to protect the rights of children and to prevent recruitment and use of child soldiers, with its leading agency for Child Protection—UNICEF. In 2005, following the issuance of UN Security Council Resolution No. 1612, the UN initiated the Monitoring and Reporting Mechanism (MRM) on Grave Child Rights Violations (GCRV) to contribute toward the protection of children affected by armed conflict. The MRM aims to prevent occurrences and trigger immediate responses to GCRVs, as well as enhances the accountability of the perpetrators (whether state or non-state actors). The Philippines along with four other countries were prioritized for the implementation of the MRM in 2007.

Child Protection with the issue of recruitment of children in various existing non-state armed forces in the Philippines is at the heart of UNICEF's work. MILF has been included in the "list of shame" as a non-state actor, which recruits and uses children. Inclusion on the "list of shame" sets into motion concrete steps on the ground, as country level Task Forces negotiate time-bound Action Plans with the relevant parties listed, with the purpose of putting an end to the violation for which they were listed and thereafter eventually delisting them. In December 2008 senior MILF leaders received the UN Secretary-General's Special Representative for Children and Armed Conflict, Radhika Coomaraswamy, to start a process of engagement on the future of "Children of War." This term was dedicated to those children who came under the aegis of MILF after losing their parents in war or living with their parents in the MILF camps. In 2009 MILF signed an Action Plan with the UN as a commitment to ensure that no children under 18 are associated either as combatants or in any supporting roles.

The MILF is currently on the last benchmark of the Action Plan as I write this essay. The Action Plan outlines activities pertaining to the separation of children from MILF ranks, gives unimpeded access for UN verification, and promotes awareness-raising on child rights and protection for those living in MILF communities. All these must be complied with and if successful the MILF would be the first non-state armed group to have complied with the UN requirements on elimination of child soldiers and could be delisted. Incidents of recruitment continue to occur and children remain associated with armed groups, hence monitoring this grave violation against children will continue to be a central issue that requires more attention in light of the advancing process of normalization, as well as ensuring compliance by the MILF to its Action Plan.

I would like to emphasize certain benefits for MILF in showing its support to the UN and adhere to the Action Plan. As we understand, MILF is a non-State armed actor, which may become a legitimate political party with the success of the peace process. MILF has been trying hard to find its supporters in the international community and struggling for the "legitimacy to its cause." MILF is in need of funds, advice, political legitimacy and international recognition. Adhering to the UN Action Plan not only benefits MILF to save their own children but also brings political and financial benefits. For the aging leadership of MILF, the legacy of the successful peace process is a much-needed dividend, and support of the international community as being advocates of the peace process could play a big role. Also, as stated by some MILF leadership it is a tactic that was adopted in order to "knock on the door of the UN" and further their political aspirations by "pleasing the UN" through compliance with international norms—i.e. as a fallback measure, in case the peace process failed to achieve their objectives.

I would like to mention the reprisals MILF leadership faces from some of its associates due to its adherence to the UN MILF Action Plan. Surely, not everyone perceives this development as beneficial to his or her cause. Some even consider this as interference in their culture based on "Islamic notions of puberty" which determine the age children take up their responsibilities. Also, the social fabric is so intertwined that families live within the MILF camps so to separate children from families is not recommended. These children often are not combatants but are working in auxiliary roles such as messengers, porters, cooks, etc., while attending schools. Therefore, creating greater awareness among the community members and establishment of child protection networks with the ownership of community is highly important.

The Government of the Philippines has likewise responded constructively via engagement with UNICEF to recurring issues related to children and armed conflict cited in the Secretary General's reports, establishing a Monitoring, Reporting and Response System (MRRS) to GCRVs. In 2013, Department of Education of the Republic of the Philippines issued *Guidelines on the Protection of Children During Armed Conflict*, which serves as a guide for all members of AFP. The guidelines require AFP to abide by several national (Republic Act No. 7610; Republic Act No. 9851; Executive Order No. 138; etc.) and international laws and agreements (United Nations Conventions on the Rights of the Child and its Optional Protocol on the Involvement of Children in Armed Conflict, United Nations Security Council Resolution Numbers 1539 s. 2004, 1612 s. 2005, 1882 s. 2009, and 1998 s. 2011, etc.).

The Role Social Media and Journalism Play in Mindanao

It is hard to overstate the role played by Social Media and Journalism in today's world. There have been many debates about the impact media can have—positive as well as negative—on any issue. The relationship between media, humanitarian organizations, and government policymakers is very complex. In Mindanao the news media has become a major actor when it comes to influencing the perceptions of Filipinos, which in turn affects the ability of humanitarian actors such as UNICEF and others in the international community to act. Sadly, the most unfortunate aspect of the fighting in Mindanao is the portrayal of the conflict in the mainstream media. For years, national news reports have been one-sided, habitually using terms such as "Muslim rebels," or "Muslim extremists," to explain the complexities of the Moro rebellion and their fight for autonomy or independence. Often MILF has been compared to ASG or other criminal or terror outfits. This lack of understanding of the conflict has altered the perceptions of Mindanao in the rest of the country and has had a highly negative impact on the overall peace process as a consequence.

I have had countless encounters with any number of members of civil society, from taxi-drivers, to sales persons, intellectuals, students, businessmen, restaurant owners, and even streetwalkers, all telling me how scared they are of Mindanao. I have felt the rising mistrust and malignant nature of Manila's intentions toward Muslims in Mindanao. Such negative perceptions are a result of constant media coverage that showcases Mindanao as a "troublesome location" for the rest of the Philippines.

The Manila-based Center for Media Freedom and Responsibility has conducted various studies and published many articles—e.g., "Covering Conflict in Mindanao: Terror and the Press," "Mindanao in the News: Some Minuses and a Few Pluses," and "Media at Work: Beating the War Drums in Mindanao," etc.)—that are based on the limited, narrow, and biased media coverage of the Mindanao conflict. Apart from that, media coverage is a subject often being touted by various international reports and studies. To cite a few examples: a report by the Norwegian Peacebuilding Resource Centre talks about the political economy of the news media in the Philippines and the framing of news stories on the GPH-CNN peace process, Marites Danguilan Vitug "Media and Conflict in the Philippines," Inter Press Service "Press a Casualty in Mindanao Conflict," etc. Press narratives that ignore a rights-based discourse and collapse the long history of struggle for people's aspirations into a simple, dominant frame that simplifies the complexities into religion and ethnicity are certainly diminishing the chances for a peaceful solution of this conflict.

Comparing an On-the-ground Account to Press Reporting

On January 25, 2015, the government's Special Armed Forces (SAF) launched a secret operation to arrest two explosives experts affiliated with Jemaah Islamiyah (JI) named Zulkifli Adhir (alias "Marwan") and Abdul Basit Usman in Mamasapano town of Maguindanao in Mindanao. In this incident 44 SAF, 18 MILF, five civilians, and several BIFF were killed. The two suspects were hiding in a BIFF camp encircled by MILF controlled territory. The MILF was not informed about this operation and as a result when government forces entered the particular territory they were attacked and killed by MILF and BIFF. It is important to note the close family, territory, religious, and cultural ties among members of BIFF and MILF in this conflict. The ties are so close as to make the lines blur between their affiliations, which at times switch from one group to the other group. In many instances one member of a family is BIFF and another MILF. Further complicating the situation is the fact that there are government-recognized MILF camps and territory as part of the ceasefire agreement. The government does not recognize BIFF as they are called "lawless elements." MILF has been accused several times about its "ties" to BIFF, bringing a question mark on its ability to uphold law and order in its own territory.

Undoubtedly, we can say that all the involved parties—government, planners of the operation, MILF, BIFF, and other involved agencies—are partly to blame as they did not respect the ceasefire, and on the side of MILF and BIFF they killed and mutilated all the SAF members they could lay their hands on. Yet the portrayal of this incident in the national media put sole blame on the MILF. I was at that time living in Cotabato city, which is very close to where the incident occurred, and I witnessed the situation. A much-publicized investigation of the incident portrayed MILF as an advocate of extremism and terrorism with headline-grabbing videos that compared MILF to the so-called Islamic State (IS), and further deepened general public fear of violent extremism in the south. The biased national media coverage through the lens of terrorism depicts southern Muslims as the sole perpetrators of the violence, and the biggest threat to Filipinos' survival. This incident derailed the peace process—the painstaking hard work that took decades to accomplish—and certainly multimedia played a large role in that.

Hardline Islamist radicals across the globe such as JI and IS look to expand their franchise in the Philippines. The risk of religious radicalization is limited; however, it could become real if the momentum of peacemaking fails. As we have seen, IS and other similar violent extremist movements have shown a clear ability to capitalize on social vulnerability, disorder, and disillusionment of the young people to find new recruits. For the success of any peace process it is important for the global, regional, national, and local media to report conscientiously and impartially on such complex emergencies.

Instead of blame, fear, and the easy media framing that evokes those feelings, accurate, unbiased coverage that explains the complexities of the island and its conflicts would benefit Mindanao, the Philippines, and the world. Alternative media coverage would open discursive pathways that would allow a peace dialogue. International humanitarian actors and UN agencies such as UNICEF need to support and bolster platforms to promote inclusive dialogue at a national and regional scale, which could help change the long-established negative national narrative. All parties to the conflict need to agree on a strategic communication plan for the peace process that expands public understanding and awareness. All media producers need to be more accountable and constructive to the grievances of the multiethnic, political, and religious groups in the Philippines.

UNICEF's Communication and Advocacy Strategy with Focus on Media

Humanitarian action strategies must be put in place to monitor the general condition of children affected by the conflict in Mindanao. That process would involve working with local partners and communities, facilitating timely responses to address the needs of vulnerable children, and raising awareness of the public at various levels, from the local to the national, regional and global. This process must confront numerous obstacles.

Cases relating to GCRVs often do not come to the attention of relevant agencies and organizations due to the lack of knowledge and public awareness about their rights. In addition, difficulties in accessibility to relevant authorities compound the problem, as does the absence of reporting mechanisms. To address the lack of knowledge and mitigate the adverse and disproportionate effects suffered by children in situations of armed conflict, agencies must work to intensify advocacy, monitor, verify, and report on the six GCRVs as stipulated by UN Security Council Resolution 1612. The creation of the MRM advocacy and communication strategies play a large role.

The Philippines has been affected by many armed conflicts and natural disasters over the years. Based on their longstanding experience, humanitarian organizations have devised several strategies when it comes to communication and media. As in the case of the Philippines, a Humanitarian Communication Group (HCG) is convened before or during a sudden escalation of a conflict or natural disaster to strengthen cooperation in the humanitarian response phase and to increase the media profile of humanitarian needs and activities. Yet few of the main responsibilities of this group seek to develop and promote emergency communication plans, or the creation of joint communications products for communities, donors, and the media. Information sharing and streamlined facts and figures in messaging for key constituencies and stakeholders is also necessary. The purpose of HCG is to coordinate public information and campaigns; nonetheless, in some situations coordination among involved members is difficult and can also either delay or frustrate concerned humanitarian actors and efforts.

Humanitarian organizations put a significant amount of effort into media, advocacy, and communications. Media and advocacy usually are targeted at different levels—global, regional, national, and local. A few of the main objectives for such a broad advocacy are to gather support of the international community or raise awareness on the issues, secure funding, or advocate for timely and coordinated responses. UNICEF has a special communication for development (C4D), mainly designed for advocacy.

UNICEF's Strategic Communication program raises awareness, knowledge, and engagement about existing and emerging issues (early warning) affecting women and children, including child protection issues. This program caters to two broad areas, which are communication for development (C4D) and media relations. C4D is a well planned and evidence-based strategic process to promote positive behavioral and social change. For the UN MILF Action Plan, MILF leadership developed and launched with UN support a communication campaign for MILF troops and for the MILF, as well as non-MILF community, through appropriate media channels for prevention, and to garner response to child recruitment and the use of children.

Advocacy and media relations involve a set of traditional and new styled multimedia that champions children's rights through forums, workshops and symposia. While developing this strategy, the role of local languages, local media, interviews, videos, and plays were emphasized. An effective communication campaign targeted the MILF-BIAF and MILF communities to raise awareness, to influence a positive change in community values, practices, social norms and behaviors attributed to the involvement of children with MILF-BIAF and prevent further child recruitment. The target group for this communication campaign was MILF-BIAF, MILF-BIWAB, children, youth, and families located in MILF Base Command Areas. I would like to cite a few examples of C4D to promote the UN-MILF Action Plan on the Recruitment and Use of Children—"Children NOT Soldiers" Campaign.

Examples of Advocacy, Communication, and Media Activities for C4D

- Orientations/awareness raising/consultations/focus group discussions with children and youth.
- Peace camps with children, and children and youth Recreational and Educational activities.
- Radio Promotion—special radio program with segments on promoting child protection and prevention of involvement of children with armed groups.
- Briefings in study circles and in Islamic symposiums.
- Monthly community gatherings—dissemination of messages through parents, *Mudirs* (directors) and Community Associations.
- Dissemination of messages through *Tahderriyah* (religious) teachers and administrators.
- Dissemination of messages through Rural Health Units.

Tools: Comic book/reading materials, illustrative and functional materials, tarpaulin/streamers, banners, social media messages, and human-interest stories.

Limitations of Media, Communication, and Advocacy

We discussed the role of advocacy, communication and media for humanitarian action in the conflict context with special focus on Mindanao. Interaction between media, government, and humanitarian agencies is complex. The questions remain, can media expand the framing of crises to provide context, help garner public support for peace, and influence public narratives? Media producers are constantly on the lookout for headline-grabbing crises and reporting from conflict sites, thus making media a major humanitarian action influencer. Social media is perceived as the fastest medium to reach multiple audiences (undeniably with countless benefits); however, sometimes things can be blown out of proportion, sensationalized and become viral, as there is no monitoring of the sensitive contents or distortion (or fake news). After the Mamasapano incident, several hypersensitive videos of killings were uploaded that took no time to go viral and resulted in cultivating more hatred.

We also need to keep in mind several constraints faced by humanitarian organizations such as mandates, funding, security, donor responsibility, changing environments and priorities, geographical area, and coordination. Competition to provide response in adherence with their mandate does make them limited in their approaches. As observed in Mindanao and sur-rounding island provinces, southern-western islands are extremely remote with multiple languages, challenging security terrains and extremely low literacy rates. Here, the capacity of media outreach is very limited, making it very challenging to organize large-scale com-munication interventions.

Limitations: Security, Political Will, and Agency Competition

Mainland views and feelings on the Mindanao issues: Consider this as an important issue as it is very important to develop a public communication strategy to prepare the rest of the country for the peace process, civilian and child protection, and other relevant issues. This also applies to MILF and other recognized non-state armed actors to reach out to non-Muslim constituencies in Mindanao as well as to the rest of the country, particularly to Christian and indigenous groups to ensure that they do not feel threatened, and their interests are acknowledged and protected.

Security is one of the major constraints for the communication strategy. As observed, due to lack of security in remote and highly sensitive conflict environments, UNICEF has to partner with existing local NGOs to carry forward its C4D activities. In many cases, local NGOs lack capacity, training and accountability, and also risk having biased staff. UNICEF personnel are not allowed to go to highly sensitive areas due to lack of security permission. Military protection is not always sought, as humanitarian actors tend to be more willing to take risks than have military protection. The association with armed forces may compromise their neutrality and impartiality in the eyes of warring factions or civilian populations. As in the case of Mindanao, usually the security and safe passage to traverse are coordinated with state armed forces as well as non-state armed groups depending on the territory and negotiated agreements.

The combined political will of the Filipino nation, whether it is the ruling party or opposition or rebel groups, their collective support for the peace process, development and humanitarian action are prerequisite for better and timely response. This aspect is very important as the UN cooperates with the national government to carry out its work. Because there are an increased number of players in the humanitarian action field there is much competition among humanitarian agencies. Every agency competes for their "market share." One can see numerous humanitarian organizations in conflict settings operating with almost identical mandates, at times even duplicating efforts. For example, organizations such as Plan, and Save the Children, have carved out their own niche in protecting the lives and rights of children, and they now compete with UNICEF. Media publicity for their work is "the lifeline of fundraising," and as a result every agency strives for media attention. Also, there are no regulations in this regard to make it less competitive and more constructive and collaborative. Such unhealthy competition by humanitarian actors also negatively affects sharing of crucial information, aid distribution, rebuilding efforts and service delivery. Nonetheless, in some cases, we can see cooperation among the agencies and also joint partnerships for programs.

Donor fatigue and changing priorities are also presenting problems for humanitarian assistance globally. There is a rise in conflicts in many parts of the world with "loud emergencies" that result in the diversion of resources and a difficult choice of deploying limited resources. I witnessed huge donor fatigue for the Mindanao conflict in comparison to the louder conflict situations in the Middle East and North Africa. The semi-closure of UNHCR and International Organization for Migration (IOM) offices in Mindanao means that they are operating now only from the capital, Manila. Staff and resources in several other international non-government organizations (INGOs) have been cut due to shifting priorities and limited resources.

Labeling "MILF" as "Muslim extremist" or even "terrorist" in some cases, comparing them with extremist terror outfits such as IS and Al Qaeda, and seeing the conflict more on an ethno-religious setting than an ideological/community-rights based one, compromises the peacemaking process. The realities on the ground and field can be very challenging and different at times with multiethnic, religious, language, and cultural aspects. The fractions within community structures, within rebel groups and their own affiliations are very tricky to navigate impartially. Planning advocacy and communications strategy without proper understanding of such nitty-gritty details can undermine local engagement and results in ineffectiveness.

Conclusion

We can sum up by saying that it is imperative for media professionals to uphold high standards and act responsibly by presenting balanced and even-handed coverage able to augment public understanding of complex conflicts. Such reporting would open a pathway to expand peaceful dialogue and support peacemaking efforts, helping also to stabilize decades-old societal and identity-based conflicts. Humanitarian organizations must continue to develop fruitful relationships with media, as such work is intimately connected to humanitarian action. Sadly, it now often takes sensational or unprecedented violence or tragedy to be featured in "breaking news" or on headlines, when early warning of a potential crisis is needed.

Instead of breaking news, media should feature historical background and political contexts for enhanced and holistic reporting. The long genesis, history, and complexities of local conflicts often bear little resemblance to conflicts framed through the lenses of "Western interests". A situation framed through a Western prism could undermine local institutions and efforts on the ground by overemphasizing the importance of international and Western-led policies and initiatives. Governments and humanitarian agencies need to have mature and sagacious media strategies, so as to avoid making catastrophic mistakes that have huge consequences that affect the lives and livelihoods of peoples, and vulnerable sections of the population especially children.

References

Conde, C. (2016) "Illegitimate Encounters." *Inquirer*, January 28, available at: http://opinion.inquirer.net/92395/illegitimate-encounters#ixzz3yULhiHFz

Human Rights Watch. (2012) "Philippines: Keep Promise to Disband Paramilitaries", March 30, available at: www.hrw.org/news/2012/03/30/philippines-keep-promise-disband-paramilitaries

Human Rights Watch. (2015) "Philippines: Paramilitaries Attack Tribal Villages, School", September 23, available at: www.hrw.org/news/2015/09/23/philippines-paramilitaries-attack-tribal-villages-schools

Lingao, E. (2012) "Media at Work Beating the War Drums in Mindanao". CMFR, January 9, available at: http://cmfr-phil.org/media-ethics-responsibility/ethics/media-at-workbeating-the-war-drums-in-mindanao/

Maslog, C., Tuazon, R. R., Abunales, D., Soriano, J., and Ordenes, L. (2015) "The Political Economy of the News Media in the Philippines and the Framing of News Stories on the GPH-CNN Peace Process", Norwegian Peace-building Resource Centre, September, available at: www.files.ethz.ch/isn/193492/1d2b81d7f85e12c5c832edc8f78d7dff.pdf

Pinlac, M. Y. and Dura, E. V. D-T. (2008) "Mindanao in the News: Some Minuses and a few Pluses", *CMFR*, September 1, available at: http://cmfr-phil.org/uncategorized/campus-journalism/

Punay, E. (2015). "Paramilitary Groups' Hand in Lumad Killings Alarms DOJ." Philstar.com, September 28, available at: www.philstar.com/nation/2015/09/28/1504676/paramilitary-groups-hand-lumad-killings-alarms-doj

Rara, C. (2006) "Covering Conflict in Mindanao: Terror and the Press". CMFR, September 27, available at: http://cmfr-phil.org/media-ethics-responsibility/journalism-review/covering-conflict-in-mindanao-terror-and-the-press/

Tekwani, S. (2008) *Media and Conflict Reporting in Asia*. Singapore: Booksmith.

30

ENVIRONMENTAL DEGRADATION, POVERTY, AND CORRUPTION

Media, Power, Humanitarian Action, and Sustainable Development Goals (SDGs) in Latin America

Rudelmar Bueno de Faria

Latin America is known as a multicultural region and holds many of the world's wonders. Its fortunate location at the center of the equator makes for an ideal climate in most Latin American countries. Latin America is also known for its friendly people, cultural diversity, beautiful natural landscapes, and famous festivals. Nevertheless, Latin America has also a sad history marked by wars, conquests, and atrocities that have shaped its current cultural, social, and political dynamics. In 1494 the Treaty of Tordesillas divided the region between Spain and Portugal and during the colonial and independence periods many events helped to shape how Latin Americans lived and interacted with global and regional processes and dynamics. The cultural concepts of honor and shame played an important role in the history of Latin America, influencing everything from national politics to domestic divisions of labor. Some of these cultural notions reach back to the Mediterranean world in the centuries before the European encounter with the Americas.

The Latin American region faces a number of challenges. It has more than 130 million poor people, pervasive inequality, high levels of violence, and recurrent natural disasters. The region is increasingly affected by climate-related disasters, including the strongest El Niño phenomenon in the past 40 years, which is severely impacting the already drought-prone region. The region also has the highest homicide rates in the world, especially among young people. This state of affairs triggers humanitarian crises, undermines substantive development gains, and boosts chronic poverty, in addition to the recent economic slowdown in the region.

In addition, the region has other features common to many of its countries. These include high proportions of urban populations (almost three-quarters live in urban areas), high ethnic diversity coupled with the existence of native indigenous populations, rapidly expanding agricultural frontiers, national economies that are being or have been subjected to structural adjustment programs, a changing role for the state and its functions, an emerging active civil society, and increasing inequality and poverty.

The region has continued to experience high levels of forced displacement and migration due, in part, to drought, climate change, food insecurity, and violence. Forced displacement and migration are largely related to national policies and political tensions. In Colombia, a peace agreement was achieved after more than 50 years of armed conflict, but its consequences continue to generate human rights violations against the civilian population. The region is also impacted by disease epidemics that pose a threat to the whole region. The Zika Virus and its link to microcephaly in newborn children was declared by the World Health Organization (WHO), as a public health emergency of international concern on February 1, 2016.

Corruption is another big problem in Latin America. The abundance of prominent scandals is setting some new records in countries such as Chile, Brazil, Guatemala, and Mexico. Public distrust has increased to a large degree by the growing understanding that the seemingly endless corruption is directly causing enormous economic problems for almost all citizens, forcing them to exist in degrading levels of poverty. In order to understand the nexus between each factor (environmental degradation, poverty, and corruption) and other leading social phenomena, it is important to have a focused analysis of each factor, recognizing that if there is a change in one of them, that change is accompanied by a corresponding modification of all the rest.

Poverty

Throughout its history, Latin America has struggled to overcome poverty, exclusion, and discrimination. These struggles have been expressed in different forms, from people's revolutionary movements to diplomatic and political processes. However, people have realized that the only way to successfully address poverty, exclusion, and discrimination is to underline that equality must be considered a priority. In the Latin American region, women make up the majority of the poor, a trend that has increased despite the reduction of poverty. This suggests that special attention is urgently required to gender inequality, which is more prevalent among the most vulnerable groups, including indigenous women, Afro-descendants, those living in rural areas, and the elderly. In this context, social protection plays a crucial role, alongside employment and economic growth, in closing these gaps (e.g., social protection systems play a fundamental role in eradicating poverty and reducing inequality). Equality as the objective should include the gender dimension as a main cross-cutting issue, and it is important to consider the impact of gender equality of the different areas and objectives. However, the gender perspective should not be confined to social issues but incorporated in the debate on the sustainable development model and its implementation.

Although global discussions on the 2030 development agenda recognize the need for social protection measures aimed at the poor, vulnerable, and persons with disabilities, as well as to move towards universal health coverage, more decisive commitments are required. The 2030 development agenda should explicitly address social protection as a citizen's right.

Corruption

As Latin American nations work to break out of the middle-income trap, and struggle to grow in the face of global economic headwinds, the ability to take on corruption will increasingly matter. Corruption favors connections over quality, stifles entrepreneurship, and scares away foreign direct investment. This seems to be a lesson Latin America's most open economies have yet to learn. The years 2015 and 2016 were the anti-corruption years for Latin America. After resigning in the face of a growing corruption scandal, Guatemalan President Pérez Molina faced trial. Investigations into government corruption have disrupted politics as usual in Brazil, Chile, and Mexico, while scandals continue to unfold in Argentina and Panama. But there are differences in how the cases are playing out across the region. In Brazil and Guatemala, wide-ranging investigations have led to prosecutions and convictions of many of the most connected political and economic elites. In contrast, in Mexico and in Chile, investigations have taken a different route. The divergent outcomes are due in part to the differing nature of the alleged crimes. In Brazil and Guatemala, officials have been charged with embezzling public funds. Through the use of wiretaps, email monitoring, and financial forensics, Brazilian prosecutors traced the flows of hundreds of millions of dollars that private companies such as the conglomerate Odebrecht overcharged the state-led energy company Petrobras for construction and service work, and then distributed among themselves and into political party coffers. And the Guatemalan president and vice president have been accused of running a customs fraud operation, pocketing tens of millions of dollars in import duties.

The divergent outcomes also reflect the importance of independent and tenacious prosecutors. Brazilian attorney general Rodrigo Janot and his team have gone after dozens of high-profile suspects, including Eduardo Cunha, former head of Brazil's lower house of Congress; construction magnate Marcelo Odebrecht; and former President Lula da Silva, despite pushback from many economic and political leaders. The Judiciary System was also accused of disrupting the democratic order and breaching the rule of law, and a crisis between the Legislative and Executive powers emerged at the end of 2016. The enterprising Guatemalan attorney general Thelma Aldana has found a sophisticated and willing partner in the UN-backed and independent International Commission against Impunity in Guatemala (CICIG), using its ten years of experience building corruption cases to take on the nation's highest ranking officials.

Latin America is also a base for international corruption. The scandal of the Panama Papers case was revealed to the public in 2016. It is an unprecedented leak of 11.5 million files from the database of the world's fourth biggest offshore law firm, Mossack Fonseca, which is a Panama-based law firm whose services include incorporating companies in offshore jurisdictions such as the British Virgin Islands (BVI). The documents show the countless ways in which the rich can exploit secretive offshore tax regimes. Twelve national leaders were among 143 politicians, their families, and close associates from around the world known to have been using offshore tax havens. Corruption in humanitarian assistance has been a big concern in the region. Governmental institutions have in some cases used public and donor funds for other purposes, but this pattern was also present within civil society humanitarian organizations. However, it is important to understand that perceptions of what constitutes corruption vary within and across cultures, and are often limited to financial mismanagement and fraud. "Nonfinancial corruption" such as nepotism/cronyism, sexual exploitation, and the diversion of aid resources to non-target groups are often less understood as corrupt practices, and in some cultures may not be considered corrupt at all.

The worst impact of corruption is the diversion of life-saving resources from the most vulnerable people, caught up in natural disasters and civil conflicts. That this occurs is hardly surprising, as relief is delivered in challenging environments. The injection of large amounts of resources into poor economies, where institutions may have been damaged or destroyed, can exaggerate power imbalances and increase opportunities for corruption. The immense organizational challenges in suddenly expanding the scope and scale of program delivery are often accompanied by pressure to deliver aid rapidly. And many countries in which humanitarian emergencies occur suffer high levels of perceived corruption prior to an emergency, and may present risks of aid being diverted by powerful groups and embedded corrupt networks. Principled humanitarian organizations have advanced in addressing corruption risks as an integral part of quality assurance, accountability, and good management strategies, and not a marginal issue handled separately.

Environmental Degradation

The Latin American region encompasses countries with great economic, social, and environmental diversity. It is not easy to summarize concerns that are common to large and multiecosystem nations such as Brazil and the Andean States. Yet the region also has a number of common environmental characteristics that distinguish it from other regions of the world.

Latin America is also dealing with the issue of lack of access to clean water. In many areas around the world including South America, water is being extracted from the ground at rapid rates, causing dramatic drops in the levels of underground aquifers. Many areas that desperately need water for drinking and irrigation suffer water shortages during times of drought.

Protecting the environment and protecting people from the effects of its degradation are increasingly challenging as a key part of any strategy for overcoming poverty and intragenerational inequality. The quality of the environment depends on how we use land and natural resources. Every human activity, be it industry or farming, creates many kinds of polluting byproducts that for centuries have been dumped on land, into the atmosphere, and into rivers, lakes, and the ocean.

Social organizations have refocused their political agenda towards the formation of a citizenry whose members are increasingly aware of their rights and responsibilities in terms of sustainable development and who have brought the issue of equality into the debate regarding access to natural resources, the right to live in a healthy environment, access to information, the opportunity to participate, and environmental justice. Tropical forests occupy a large portion of the surface in 11 Latin American countries with significant population pressures and low to medium incomes: Mexico, Guatemala, Costa Rica, Panama, Honduras, Colombia, Venezuela, Ecuador, Peru, Bolivia, and Paraguay. The substantial use of these forest lands as timber resources, for growing tropical products, or for cash crop agriculture or cattle grazing, can help alleviate poverty and fulfill the country's need for more foreign exchange and food. Many governments with extensive tropical forest resources, such as Brazil, actually encourage migration of the landless poor to the forest margins to relieve demographic pressures.

For citizens to adopt sustainable and environmentally friendly behavior, reliable and fair legal mechanisms should be created to enforce long-term property rights and other legal obligations. Unfortunately, too often the judicial system in Latin America responds to political pressures when it is not downright corrupt. Legal reforms are also needed to ensure the adoption of environmentally friendly policies by both governments and individuals. Many countries possess adequate environmental legislation; almost all Latin American countries have a cabinet-level environmental official. Yet these ministries are usually without enforcement power. An exception, and a model for Latin America and the world, is Costa Rica.

How Do These Factors Inform Humanitarian Action and the Sustainable Development Goals (SDGs)?

Humanitarian Action

Latin America is located in one of the most disaster-prone regions in the world, particularly exposed to recurrent and severe floods, hurricanes, landslides, earthquakes, and volcanic eruptions. Droughts and floods are also frequent in all Latin American countries and cause significant losses of crops, livestock, and forestry, wiping out livelihoods and threatening the food security of whole populations. Fast population growth and rapid urbanization also increase the poorest communities' vulnerability in the face of disasters. Poverty, environmental degradation, and corruption have a direct connection with humanitarian action in the region. Humanitarian organizations have started to identify and understand the principal changes in policy, practice, and institutional architecture that the humanitarian sector has undergone since the beginning of the twentieth century. The concept of humanitarianism has evolved and been interpreted across the region in a different way. Key disaster events and institutions have shaped the region's management of disasters and disaster risk, especially after hurricane Mitch that hit Central America in 1998, when poverty and environmental degradation were identified as main causes for the extent of the destruction and the number of victims. Also, corruption was identified as a factor that undermined humanitarian action and impeded the provision of fast and effective assistance—putting lives and dignity at risk.

The first World Humanitarian Summit organized by the United Nations in Istanbul in May 2016 addressed the intersections between humanitarian action and the principles related to humanitarian response, reaffirming that it needs to be connected with other actions oriented to deal with root causes that lead to disaster and conflict. Groups of "principled" humanitarian organizations, such as the Steering Committee for Humanitarian Response (SCHR, a voluntary alliance of nine of the world's leading humanitarian organizations), have been promoting the idea of certification for humanitarian organizations, with the purpose of exploring the feasibility and relevance of certification for humanitarian organizations, in order to demonstrate transparency and compliance with humanitarian principles, quality, and accountability standards.

Sustainable Development Goals

In 2012 at the Rio+20 Conference, the international community decided to establish a High-level Political Forum on Sustainable Development to subsequently replace the Commission on Sustainable Development. At this Conference, UN Member States also decided to launch a process to develop a set of Sustainable Development Goals (SDGs) that were to build upon the Millennium Development Goals (MDGs) and converge with the post-2015 development agenda. The process of arriving at the post-2015 development agenda was Member Stateled with broad participation from major groups and other civil society stakeholders. On September 25, 2015, the United Nations General Assembly formally adopted the universal, integrated and transformative 2030 Agenda for Sustainable Development, along with a set of 17 Sustainable Development Goals (SDG) and 169 associated targets.

At the center of concerns in the Latin American region in relation to the 2030 development agenda are the persisting challenges of eradicating poverty and reducing inequality. Countries in the region are striving to advance towards greater equality and poverty eradication within their borders, but the results of these efforts depend to a large extent on the international environment and on a strong global agenda. The new agenda is now putting forward the need to strengthen early warning systems and reduce the risk to the poor caused by economic shocks and natural disasters, including those related to climate change, as well as to integrate biodiversity conservation with national and local strategies for poverty reduction and development. Disasters have significant social repercussions, expressed in various dimensions of human development and poverty. The current discussions represent an improvement over approaches in past decades, which tended to view poverty from a narrower perspective, focusing on the reduction of extreme income poverty and promoting economic growth as the main instrument. The countries in the region are pushed to bring risk management into national policies within the framework of a sustainable development strategy, and improve social and economic resilience in the face of destructive events. Social inclusion provides the progressive compliance and fulfilment of rights critical to attain many of the aspirations of a safe, healthy, and prosperous society within planetary boundaries, with food and nutritional security, health and well-being. Work is seen as the key to social inclusion and greater equality. In current discussions surrounding the 2030 development agenda, the promotion of inclusive and sustainable economic growth with decent work for all has emerged as a high priority.

Another priority area for further poverty eradication is education, with a view to strengthening and matching the people's capabilities to labor market needs in the medium and long term. Easing segmentation of learning and achievement reduces inequality from one generation to the next and allows new generations to enter the labor market, facilitates access to capital, lowers the risks of child malnutrition and adolescent pregnancy, and combats intergenerational exclusion. The Economic Commission for Latin America and the Caribbean (ECLAC) has worked on the concept of a trilogy (i.e., social equality, environmental sustainability, and economic growth with innovation) in the context of the 2030 development agenda (ECLAC 2014). The great challenge to implement this concept is to identify synergies among them. The strategic vision that joins these three areas should be based on three premises, namely: growth for equality, equality as a driver of growth, and both of these embedded in environmental sustainability. Incorporating the contributions of gender, ethnic, and environmental perspectives calls for policies on equality in the distribution of roles (i.e., in the family, at work, and in politics), in the relationship between present and future generations, and in the visibility and affirmation of collective identities.

Poverty is a multidimensional phenomenon with adverse effects on the welfare of people and the full enjoyment of their human rights. Given its links with other priority areas of sustainable development (including decent jobs, energy, sustainable cities, food security and sustainable agriculture, clean water, oceans, and disaster readiness), poverty eradication requires advances in multiple economic and social dimensions. At the same time, reducing poverty has positive synergies with other priority areas of sustainable development.

The current global discussion on the 2030 development agenda is calling for an end to poverty in all its forms. To eradicate extreme poverty and significantly reduce the percentage of people below national income poverty lines, social protection measures need to be implemented at the national level, including the definition of social protection floors, prioritizing the poor and vulnerable, and providing opportunities for men and women through access to land, property rights, financial services, and production assets. Civil society organizations must and need to play an important role in shaping this process along with governments, academia and the private sector.

Power Dynamics and the Role of Media

In addition to the structural factors mentioned above and their intersections with humanitarian action and sustainable development, it is important to keep in mind other elements that have a great influence on how business evolves in Latin America. Within the context of globalization, emerging regional powers have increasingly called for the democratization of the international multilateral arena, and in a number of Latin American countries this demand for international democracy has been accompanied by a shift to left-wing governments. These administrations have opened up new avenues of political participation, formerly reserved exclusively for national and international elites, to segments of the population who were previously marginalized from both national politics and international power relations.

Two examples are Bolivia, where there has been an unprecedented emergence of new democratic institutions adapted to its specific multicultural profile, and Brazil that experienced a decade of economic and social progress (2003–2013) in which over 26 million people were lifted out of poverty and inequality was reduced significantly. Latin America has experienced three decades of uninterrupted democracy. The triumph of democracy in the 1980s and its current day-to-day development are closely linked to the tradition of social mobilization in Latin America. An analysis of events over recent years shows that the regional scene has become punctuated with new dynamics of change. This change is based on the advance of an alternative social or non-political approach associated with the rise of grassroots, community forms of social organization and local development. This phenomenon constitutes a central issue in political developments across Latin America today. However, in the second half of 2016 conservative political parties have taken power in most of the major economies in the region, a phenomenon that needs further analysis to explore the consequences for the region.

The state is a central actor in power negotiations and conflict, but it has a limited capacity to manage and resolve them while maintaining social cohesion and strengthening democracy. The characteristics of states and institutions vary significantly across Latin America. Some countries have greater state capacity to manage conflicts, whereas others have lesser capacities and tend to suffer chronic governance failures. At the same time, there is a tendency for social action to become increasingly polycentric as Latin American conflicts experience "fragmentation" and actors become more diverse and dispersed. New and old actors, both collective and individual, interact in different social and cultural dimensions that the state and institutions have difficulty managing.

The role of the private sector and the churches in Latin America is significant. These two sectors are increasingly playing a more influential role in politics and shaping the discussions between conservative and liberal ideologies. They are contributing, along with social media, to inform a new way of defining politics: right-wing versus left-wing. Clerics, especially from Evangelical/Pentecostal churches are well represented in the parliaments, where they defend more conservative policies and practices, very often reducing rights conferred decades ago.

Brazil plays a role in regional leadership. It is an effective regional leader in the promotion of integration and its future role was viewed with growing hope, although tempered by some mistrust. Brazil is intent on assuming a regional and global political role that corresponds to its growing economic weight. The challenge is finding a regional role compatible with the country's size, which does not create mistrust and which, at the same time, benefits the rest of the region. Consistent with its ambition to gain a permanent seat at the UN Security Council, Brazil has presented itself internationally as fulfilling an extra-regional political role. Brazil has also established international multilateral alliances such as IBSA (India, Brazil, and South Africa) and BRIC (Brazil, Russia, India, and China).

In contrast, other participants expressed doubt about Brazil's effective regional role, pointing to the fragmentary effect caused by the creation of Unasur without Mexico. Viewed from this standpoint, it was felt that what is good for Brazil is not necessarily good for Latin America, and that the institutionalization that benefits Latin America must benefit the whole region, not just one country. A shared leadership between Brazil and other countries was also discussed as an option as none of the region's new strategic partners are capable of filling the hegemonic vacuum left by the United States. China, for example, has no intention of stepping up. EU countries prefer bilateral agreements over regional ones because Latin America is not a strategic region for the European Union. Participants felt that shared leadership on a subregional scale could provide an effective solution that would enhance consensus.

Media Influence

Historically the media have proven highly efficient in molding public opinion. Media paraphernalia and propaganda have created or destroyed social movements, justified wars, tempered financial crises, spurred on some other ideological currents, and even created the phenomenon of media as producers of reality within the collective psyche. Noam Chomsky, the distinguished American philosopher, political activist, and professor emeritus of linguistics at the Massachusetts Institute of Technology (MIT), has exposed some tactics used by powerful elites to establish a manipulation of the population through the media (Chomsky 2002). Encouraging ignorance, promoting a sense of guilt, promoting distraction, or constructing artificial problems and then, magically, solving them are just some of these tactics. It seems to be the case in most Latin American countries.

The mass media are often referred to as a "fourth power," to denote their potentially powerful role in influencing political processes and shaping cultural habits. The media function within the context of structures of concentrated power that are strongly questioned by large segments of society. The mainstream media is the most obvious in its inherent bias and manipulation. The mainstream media is owned directly by large corporations, but typically controlled by wealthy families or individuals with conservative political leanings.

The media are comprised largely of businesses that depend on the market and respond to the interaction of interests and pressures from specific actors. Media companies are never neutral, but nor are they mechanical instruments of power. There is a dialectic between the media and society. The media also construct social reality, actively portraying narratives and views that influence the political system, decision-making processes, and the actions of social actors. Politicians often become owners of the media, using the position to gain broadcasting concessions and then using them as political mouthpieces.

Historically, patterns of media ownership, combined with conservative governments in many countries, have meant that the media often colluded with politically like-minded leaders. More recently, the rise of a "new Left" in Latin America has brought to power presidents who routinely clash with their country's media owners. Where the media might have been complicit in prior abuses of executive power, they now aggressively denounce them. Yet the polarized political climate in these countries complicates the media's watchdog function—journalists are unlikely to investigate malfeasance on their own side of the political divide, and retaliation by authorities or the media owners themselves may silence some critical voices. Elsewhere, conflict between politicians and the press is rampant at the local level, where political bosses can eliminate potential watchdogs through their manipulation of the judicial system or control over local security forces. In such countries, media with national scope may exercise all the functions of a fourth power, but local media remain weak, intimidated, and subject to political control.

Never before has it been so important to have independent, honest voices and sources of information. The society is inundated and overwhelmed with a flood of information from a wide array of sources, but these sources of information, by and large, serve the powerful interests and individuals that own them. The main sources of information, for both public and official consumption, include the mainstream media, alternative media, academia, and think tanks.

The proliferation of low-power community media offers the possibility that new voices might gain access to the airwaves, but all too often, these broadcasters also fall under the sway of powerful politicians. Some countries have started processes to democratize the media, but with strong resistance from corporate media and their allies in the country. Argentina was able to pass a bill reducing the monopoly of mass media companies by providing media licenses to community radio, newspapers, and television. Radio plays an important secondary role in some countries, particularly in Bolivia and Peru, where its penetration rates are somewhat higher. These incipient initiatives have shown positive results in specific countries. Newspapers matter for political information—particularly in Venezuela, where their circulation rates are relatively high—and in some countries they play particularly important roles in breaking scandals and setting the political agenda. Where relevant, therefore, the chapter also examines trends in newspapers and radio.

New actors, such as media communicators, publicists, and non-governmental organizations are decisive elements in the new order of communicational politics in the region. Individuals have increasing space and opportunity to produce information and directly contribute to the creation of narratives and collective perspectives. A broader variety of actors now participate in redefining, differentiating, and/or homogenizing collective notions and perspectives of society. Social media offer public spaces where power relations are reflected, created, and contested, conflicts between opposing parties are recognized, and political and social interests are expressed through different journalistic and editorial lenses.

All these elements contribute to make the situation in Latin America a complex one. However, if structural changes to combat extreme poverty, corruption, and environmental degradation are put in place, the situation may change for the better, contributing to promote a culture of sustainable development based on human rights and human dignity, and hence addressing power dynamics by promoting democratic participation and action.

References

Benedikter, R., and Siepmann, K. (2015) *Chile in Transition, Prospects and Challenges for Latina America's Forerunner of Development*, Switzerland: Springer International Publishing.

Boas, T. C. (2013) "Mass Media and Politics in Latin America" in J. I. Dominguez, M. Shifter (Eds.), *Constructing Democratic Governance in Latin America* (4th ed.), Baltimore, MD: The John Hopkins University Press, pp. 48–77.

Chomsky, N. (2002) *Media Control: The Spectacular Achievements of Propaganda* (2nd ed.), New York: Seven Stories Press.

Dominguez, J. I. and Michael, S. (2013) "Mass Media and Politics in Latin America" in *Constructing Democratic Governance in Latin America* (4th ed.), Baltimore: MD: The John Hopkins University Press, p. 49.

ECLAC. (2014) *Preliminary Reflections on Latin America and the Caribbean in the Post-2015 Agenda Based on the Trilogy of Equality*, limited distribution, reports.

Johnson, B. R. (2012) "Water, Cultural Diversity, and Global Environmental Change: Emerging Trends, Sustainable Futures?" UNESCO.

McTaggart, A. (2012) *Shame and Guilt in Chaucer*, New York: Palgrave Macmillan, pp. 12–13.

Miller, W. I. (1993) *Humiliation: And other Essays on Honor, Social Discomfort, and Violence*, Ithaca, NY: Cornell University Press, pp. 84–85.

O'Neil, S. (2016) "Taking on Corruption in Latin America," *Council on Foreign Relations*, available at: www.cfr.org/blog-post/taking-corruption-latin-america

Sheffield, J. and Wood, E. F. (2011) *Drought: Past problems and Future Scenarios*, Abingdon, UK: Earthscan, p. 123.

UN General Assembly. (2015) *Transforming our World: The 2030 Agenda for Sustainable Development*.

UNDP, UNIR. (2013) *Understanding Social Conflict in Latin America*, Fernando Calderón, report coordinator.

UNEP. (2015) *Latin America and the Caribbean: Major Environmental Concerns*, Global State of Environment Report.

United Nations Research Institute for Social Development. (2010) *Combating Poverty and Inequality: Structural Change, Social Policy and Politics*, Geneva: UNRISD.

Woodrow Wilson International Center for Scholars. (2015) "Brazil as a Regional Power: Views from the Hemisphere", available at: www.wilsoncenter.org/sites/default/files/Brazil-as-a-Regional-Power3.pdf

Part 7

LEGACY MEDIA FROM FICTION TO DOCUMENTARY

Representations of Crisis, Conflict, Humanitarian Assistance, and Peacekeeping

INTRODUCTION
TO PART 7

News Broadcasting and the press have long been thought of as the primary sources for information about humanitarian crises, and certainly they remain essential to public information, awareness, and concerned action. But there are numerous challenges to independent, accurate, knowledge-based reporting in the age of corporate control, fast-paced delivery, reduced resources, and geopolitical nationalism—much is left out, and many stories offer interpretive views often dictated by predetermined frameworks familiar to audiences and readers, but not always reflective of the situation on the ground. In Part 7 we explore other forms of legacy media such as long-form documentary and fictional dramatic realism. We also look at innovative practices, such as a diary format and media designed to promote diplomacy.

In 2005 Hurricane Katrina hit the United States Gulf Coast killing 1,800 people in the worst humanitarian disaster the county had experienced in modern memory. Floodwaters breached the levees that protected New Orleans and 80 percent of the city was flooded, severely damaging 182,000 homes. A total of 90,000 square miles of the Gulf Coast were devastated. Neither New Orleans, the state of Louisiana, nor the Federal Government were prepared for such a disaster, and thousands of people were stranded on roof tops, overpasses, in hot attic rooms, and apartment buildings without water or food supplies. In "HBO's *Treme* and the Evolving Story of Hurricane Katrina: From Mythic News to Fictional Drama," Robin Andersen critiques the news coverage of the disaster and compares it to HBO's series, *Treme*, a fictional rendering of the storm and its aftermath. She argues that the initial news coverage of Katrina was inaccurate, misleading, and sensationalized, dominated by themes of anarchy in which the residents of New Orleans, particularly poor African Americans, were portrayed as criminals. This has been identified as a "disaster myth" frame through which crisis is associated with social chaos, accompanied by looting and deviant behavior. This paper views *Treme*'s narrative as a significant intervention in that discursive trajectory. The program offered a counter-narrative to initial news coverage by recounting the disaster from a humanistic perspective from the point of view of the victims, dramatizing the traumatic consequences to human life. In an age of hybrid genres and media convergence, dramatic events will inevitably be rendered across a broad spectrum that straddles fiction and nonfiction, ultimately influencing memory and understanding. She concludes that the way we memorialize such a disaster has a profound influence on our public responses to future crises.

Half the Sky is an ambitious humanitarian documentary about the global crises in gender discrimination. Based on Nicholas Kristof and Sheryl WuDunn's book (Kristof and WuDunn 2010), the nearly four-hour documentary visits six countries to explore six issues: gender-based violence in Sierra Leone, sex trafficking in Cambodia, education in Vietnam, female genital mutilation in Somaliland, intergenerational prostitution in India, and economic empowerment in Kenya. In "'Shine a Little Light': Celebrities, Humanitarian Documentary, and *Half the Sky*," Heather McIntosh explores the role of celebrity in telling these stories. Six American actresses, each of whom visits a country, meet local activists and survivors, and learn about the situation. Drawing on scholarship about documentary representation and celebrity, McIntosh engages critical perspectives that charge that the appearance of notable personalities simplifies complex issues, and overshadows survivors' voices. She evaluates the success of *Half the Sky* and the film's attempt to cast celebrities as moral agents helping viewers emotionally connect to the issues and the people involved. Ultimately, she questions the film's ability to overcome the tensions between suffering and poverty, and glamour and Western privilege.

On Friday March 11, 2011, an undersea megathrust earthquake of magnitude 9.0 hit the east coast of Japan. The earthquake moved Honshu, the main island of the country, about 8 feet east, and shifted the earth on its axis about 4 inches. It was the biggest earthquake ever to hit the country, and the fourth largest earthquake recorded on the globe since modern record keeping. Images of the tsunami's destruction as it hit Japan's north east coastline constitute a set of stunning visual documents that circulated rapidly around the globe. The earthquake caused level 7 meltdowns at three nuclear reactors within the Fukushima Daiichi Nuclear Power Plant complex and evacuation zones affected hundreds of thousands of people. By 2015, the Japanese Police Agency confirmed about 18,500 dead or missing and thousands more injured in the worst humanitarian disaster since WWII in the country. "*The Record of a Total Power Loss*: First Five Days at the Fukushima Nuclear Power Plant" by Hajime Ozaki, is a first-hand account by staff at the power plant that documents their experience in real time in diary format. It adds a layer of engaging narrative rarely found in humanitarian journalism.

Increasingly strategic communication design is being used as a tool for humanitarian action. In "Media Interventions as Humanitarian Action," Shawn Powers highlights the various ways in which state and intergovernmental actors intervene in foreign environments in times of conflict and crisis to introduce information technologies, institutions, and content for the purpose of providing humanitarian and emergency relief. Building on the work of Metzl (1997) and Price and Thompson (2002), while media interventions are often studied through the lens of propaganda, Powers argues that these strategic communication campaigns can have significant humanitarian import, and impact, while also serving a collective, social good. Highlighting such programs will not only make the case for seeing media policy as a direct part of the humanitarian action tool-kit (as opposed to it being simply a variable in the broader humanitarian action equation), but also calls for an uncolored theoretical approach to studying state-led strategic communication campaigns.

"*Last Station Before Hell*: United Nations Peacekeepers," discusses the film by Pierre-Olivier François. United Nations' Peacekeepers known as the Blue Helmets, are often the subject of criticism and negative press reports. Most notably they have been blamed for transmitting cholera to the victims of the earthquake that struck the island nation of Haiti in 2010. The UN reluctantly admitted its role in bringing the Peacekeepers who brought the disease to the island, and has finally agreed to compensate the people of Haiti. Based on his experience at the United Nations in New York as a press attaché in charge of the General Assembly and the Security Council, filmmaker Pierre-Olivier François was asked to make a film about the United Nations peacekeeping forces for the seventieth anniversary of the world body. In this chapter, François discusses the making of the documentary, *Last Station Before Hell*, and he details the challenges posed by the mostly negative media frames applied to UN Peacekeepers. François introduces an interesting peace keeping device—Radio Okapi. During the regional wars in DRC in the 1990s and 2000s, it was often the only means to connect Eastern and Western Congo. Radio Okapi, which calls itself "the radio of peace," advocates professionalism, democracy, and civic education. In fact, he says, "Radio Okapi is probably one of the most effective, lasting legacies of the UN in DRC." He goes on to identify the faultlines between this complex bureaucracy and the news narratives that tell its story; he also offers an analysis of the interrelated dynamics between the UN and its relationship to the Blue Helmets and to the press.

References

Kristoff, N. D., and WuDunn, S. (2010) *Half the Sky: Turning Oppression into Opportunity for Women Worldwide*. New York: Vintage.

Metzl, J. (1997) "Information Intervention: When Switching Channels Isn't Enough," *Foreign Affairs*, 76 (6), 15–20.

Price, M. and Thompson, M. (2002) *Forging Peace: Intervention, Human Rights, and the Management of Media Space*. Bloomington, IN: Indiana University Press.

31

HBO'S *TREME* AND THE EVOLVING STORY OF HURRICANE KATRINA

From Mythic News to Fictional Drama

Robin Andersen

What hit the Mississippi Gulf Coast was a natural disaster; a hurricane pure and simple. The flooding of New Orleans is a man-made catastrophe, a federal f★★★ up of epic proportion, and decades in the making.

(*Treme*'s Creighton Bernette, played by John Goodman)

Episode 1

When *Treme* debuted on April 11, 2010, foregrounding a storm-damaged New Orleans, the pilot episode was well-received. The program was the second major production by the creative team of David Simon and Eric Overmyer, whose previous series *The Wire*, set in Baltimore, is considered by many to be one of the best serial dramas ever produced for television (Williams 2014). Great fans of visiting New Orleans, the producers' intention was to create a sense of place distinct from the tired media portrayals of the tourist saturated French Quarter, its Spring Break debauchery, and the loud, sloppy caricatures of the city's food and music culture.[1]

Though offered as an entertainment, *Treme* occupies a borderland where lines of historical narrative, fictional drama, performance, art, journalism, and media critique merge. As scripted entertainment, the show features talented actors such as Wendell Pierce and Clarke Peters who had roles in *The Wire*, and many non-actors such as musicians, performers, chefs, residents, and Mardi Gras Indians, who often appear on the series playing themselves. Some characters are based on prominent figures in New Orleans such as civil rights attorney Mary Howell, the inspiration for Toni Burnette (Melissa Leo). City historians and other professionals also served as consultants to the program. Real, composite, or invented (including the more problematic roles of cops or developers), the characters weave through the battered fragments of trauma and memory as they struggle to recover from the disaster. Amidst such hardships, positive emotional moments are found in the artful, liminal spaces that dance onto the screen, propelled by the musical and cultural forces that drive the city.

Treme is as much about place as it is about people. Though a character-centered drama, the people who inhabit the screen must negotiate New Orleans on the unstable ground left as the fetid floodwaters receded. Their experiences correspond to the events that took place in New Orleans in the aftermath of Katrina.

Five Years After the Storm

With *Treme*, the producers breathed new life into a story that, after five years, was no longer major news in the mainstream press. As early as 2006, FAIR noted in a piece titled, "Katrina's Vanishing Victims," that the recovery of New Orleans had lost its news value.[2] After a steady decline, the story was relegated to an "anniversary event," and by 2008 the Tyndall Report found that Katrina was not among the top 20 stories on TV news. There were only six hurricane-related stories on TV in the first seven months of 2009.[3] Brian Williams' admonition to fellow journalists had certainly by then come true:

> If we come out of this crisis and in the next couple of years don't have a national conversation on the following issues: race, class, petroleum, the environment, then we, the news media, will have failed by not keeping people's feet to the fire.[4]

With *Treme*, producers David Simon and Eric Overmyer were stubbornly refusing to let New Orleans fade from collective memory. That April in 2010 *Treme* jumped into the cultural renderings of the story of the storm, offering a new, fictional treatment that would leave an indelible mark on the national narrative. Simon and Overmyer created a unique vision of the city and an alternative view of a humanitarian disaster. To do so, they struggled with the numerous challenges of creating a new televisual narrative, one that takes seriously the representation of place—New Orleans' music, cuisine, and culture—and also attempts to accurately portray, through entertainment, an actual humanitarian crisis.

Building *Treme* from the Media Rubble of the Storm

Treme revived a story many—especially those formerly in "official" positions—would rather have left forgotten. The storm had become a dirty word in politics, used to signify technical failure, corruption, government incompetence, and the overall disappointing performance of George W. Bush and his cabinet.[5] In the immediate aftermath of the storm and in the years that followed, the word Katrina had come to mean political fall from grace and failure in general.[6] The spotlight that *Treme* directed toward the disaster was harsh. From the beginning the program did not mince words of condemnation. The flooding described by the memorable character, Creighton Bernette, as a man-made disaster occurs 19 minute into the first episode. Bernette will not let the story die. The intensity of his on-going blogs, his hilarious profanity, and biting criticisms of the country's ambivalence about bringing back one of its "great cities," indicated from the start that the writers intended to rekindle a national dialogue.

Treme as Media Critique

The program strategy would be more complicated then simply starting from scratch with the story they wanted to tell. Intimately interwoven into *Treme*'s narrative was a critique of previous media narratives. The writers challenged the news coverage of the storm and its aftermath, and what better way to begin such an expose than through the words and actions of Creighton Bernette, patterned after an outspoken New Orleans blogger. As a composite character, he is also a Professor at Tulane University in New Orleans. From the start he is shown as a source for media interviews, from NPR to press journalists, yet with each media encounter Bernette becomes more frustrated by the discursive themes that invariably shape what he considers inane questions. No little bit of cheek is involved in the most dramatic, early scene illustrating Bernette's disgust. In an interview Bernette is shocked by the dismissive tone of the reporter who asserts that the cuisine is unoriginal and the city's music "has seen its day." "Why should American taxpayers take on the expense of rebuilding the city?" he asks. As Bernette grows increasingly agitated, he then grabs the microphone of the British television journalist and throws it into the canal.

Indeed, there was much in the record to set straight. But in truth, corrections to the media narrative of the storm and its aftermath were well underway by the time the writers of *Treme* jumped into the fray. Investigative reporters Jeremy Scahill and A. C. Thompson had been sifting through the historical rubble, and filmmaker Spike Lee had unearthed many holes, distortions, and omissions of post-Katrina news coverage. Such documentation had been constructing alternative views, explanations, and background information; the context needed to understand the complexities of the disaster. The writers of *Treme* made use of these counter-narratives as well. But public perceptions left by initial coverage of extreme events is often hard to alter.

The First Draft of History: Demonizing the Victims

Initial Katrina coverage was an appalling moment in media reportage. It set the tone and interpretive frame, making fundamental assumptions about the city and its residents. News reports from New Orleans during Katrina and in the immediate aftermath of the storm were dominated by stories of looting, and themes of anarchy and chaos in which the residents, particularly poor African Americans, were portrayed as deviants and criminals. Consider *The Washington Post* reporting on August 31, 2005:

> Even as the floodwaters rose, looters roamed the city, sacking department stores and grocery stores and floating their spoils away in plastic garbage cans. . . . In drier areas, looters raced into smashed stores and pharmacies and by nightfall the pillage was widespread.
>
> (Gugliotta and Whoriskey)[7]

The New York Times (September 1, 2005) repeated the same sensationalized themes, "Chaos gripped New Orleans on Wednesday as looters ran wild . . . looters brazenly ripped open gates and ransacked stores for food, clothing, television sets, computers, jewelry, and guns".[8] Who can forget the news images of people waist deep in water trying to negotiate supplies they are floating in large garbage bags. Under the pictures of white people, the caption explains they are "finding supplies," under images of African Americans, the caption identifies them as "looters."[9]

The Disaster Myth

Writing in the Annuls of the American Academy, Tierney, Bevc and Kuligowski (2006) argue that reporting conformed to the conventions of a "disaster myth," a predictable media frame in which crisis is habitually "accompanied by looting, social disorganization, and deviant behavior." The researchers attribute this mythic understanding to past news reporting of crisis. They point out that in covering the storm "the media greatly exaggerated the incidence and severity of looting and lawlessness."[10] The escalating drama of chaos that shaped Katrina coverage descended into greater depths of depravity with each passing day. Consider this exchange, live from New Orleans on September 1, between John Gibson and David Lee Miller of Fox News Channel:

> *Gibson*: "These are pictures of the cops arriving on the scene, armed and ready to take on the armed thugs . . . Thugs shooting at rescue crews."
>
> *Miller*: "Hi, John, as you so rightly point out, there are so many murders taking place. There are rapes, other violent crimes taking place in New Orleans."

By September 3 Maureen Dowd of *The New York Times* concluded that New Orleans was a "a snake pit of anarchy, death, looting, raping, marauding thugs" (Dowd 2005). Even the *Financial Times* of London, not known for sensationalism, offered this September 5 description of the Convention Center, sourced from "*unnamed refugees*": "Girls and boys were raped in the dark and had their throats cut and bodies were stuffed in the kitchens while looters and madmen exchanged fire with weapons they had looted."

By the end of the year, the *American Journalism Review* evaluated press reporting of the storm and found that "media coverage of Hurricane Katrina was marred by the widespread reporting—sometimes attributed to public officials—of murders and rapes that apparently never took place."[11] *New York Times* reporter Jim Dwyer noticed that reporting seemed to have transformed into myth, "I just thought that some of the reports were so garish, so untraceable and always seemed to stop short of having actual witnesses to the atrocities . . . like a galloping mythical nightmare had taken control." Just short of a decade after the storm, in an article reporting on the controversy over trusted NBC news anchor Brian Williams' embellishments of New Orleans reports, *The Guardian* (February 6, 2015) reported that "Public perception of the aftermath of the hurricane has been heavily informed by pictures of devastation in the city and news reports at the time of widespread violence that turned out later to be unfounded." Almost ten years later, Williams was still repeating that he saw a body floating in the water in front of the hotel where he stayed, and also that the hotel was "overrun with gangs."[12] The Ritz-Carlton in the French Quarter where he likely stayed saw very little flooding and never made a claim about gangs. Sources in New Orleans said it was highly unlikely that a body would be seen in that area, as the water was about a food deep at most.[13] And "absolutely hogwash" was how Dr. Brobson Lutz, former director of the New Orleans health department and French Quarter resident who ran an EMS station after the storm, characterized Williams' claims that he was told not to drink bottled water in front of people because they would kill him for it.[14]

Author Rebecca Solnit who writes about humanitarian crisis and media response to disaster says, "many major media outlets repeated rumors of snipers firing on helicopters. These rumors were never substantiated, but they interfered with the rescue operations nonetheless."[15] Portrayals that the city's residents had gone berserk, mostly African Americans who did not have the means or money to leave the city, coincided with punitive disaster responses from those in positions of authority. Mayor Ray Nagin, who together with members of the police department had contributed to spreading the violence myths that so saturated media coverage, ordered 1,500 police officers to leave their search-and-rescue missions and return to the streets of the city to stop the looting. As Solnit puts it:

Only two days after the catastrophe struck, while thousands were still stuck on roofs, in attics, on overpasses, on second and third stories and in isolated buildings on high ground in flooded neighborhoods, the mayor chose protecting property over human life. There was no commerce, no electricity, no way to buy badly needed supplies. Though unnecessary things were taken, much of what got called looting was the stranded foraging for survival by the only means available.[16]

Treme would disrupt, undermine, debunk, and transform the narrative of the storm constructed by the disaster media frame. The writers went about it by establishing their own story logic, one that sought to follow historical sequences within fictional entertainment parameters. They created characters, some of whom lived through the storm, and others, if they were not in New Orleans at the time, were dealing with government corruption and racism in its aftermath. They were telling the story from a humanistic perspective, seeing the disaster through the eyes of its victims.

Establishing Characters and a Sense of Place on Unstable Ground

The series' writers were determined to closely follow events as they actually unfolded in post-Katrina New Orleans. As former *Times-Picayune* journalist Lolis Eric Elie, story editor for the series told me, "We have a time-line of the events as they occurred hanging on the wall of our conference room. We use it as an outline and fill it in with personal stories of people's lives." For example, he offered, "We wanted to describe what it was like to come back and see your flooded house for the first time" (Elie 2015).[17] This skeletal framework structured the story arc, and writers were tasked with creating a human point of view, the disaster as seen through the eyes of people who stubbornly re-inhabit the city. In this sense, the experiences depicted are both fiction and testimony, and those narrative conventions intermingle throughout the series. Take for example the character of Desiree, played by a New Orleans resident who survived the storm, Phyllis Montana-Leblanc. Leblanc came to prominence as one of the voices in Spike Lee's documentary about Katrina *When the Levees Broke* (2006). She gave compelling testimony and stinging analysis as an outraged victim of the storm. She then wrote a memoir of her experiences.[18] When she later joined the cast of *Treme* her words were scripted and she takes on a fictional role as a member of a community she remains part of. As she moves from outspoken resident to a cast member her story is retold and she inhabits a space between non-fiction subjectivity and the fictional characterization created through the rhetorical tropes and conventions of entertainment television. Other residents of the city also crossed media boundaries, such as former *Times-Picayune* reporter, historian, and food writer Lolis Eric Elie, who was the story editor for the series. Local musician and Mardi Gras Indian Cheif Donald Harrison Jr., was a major consultant and appeared several times throughout the series (Elie 2014). In *Treme*, he is a Mardi Gras Indian playing a Mardi Gras Indian in a fictional series.

A Totally Different Narrative

The program challenged past news reporting of the storm and the stereotypes in just about every way: in detail, theme, point of view, and most importantly, when it came to telling the stories of the musicians, culture, and low-income African American communities. Foregrounding the considerable creative and cultural contributions in all of their variety and complexity meant drawing from the city's own cultural community. Residents of New Orleans—authors, musicians, chefs, lawyers—populated the series both on screen and off. Many worked behind the scenes as consultants and writers, and showed up in cameo appearances and as extras, to create a complex, compelling, verité view of New Orleans. Yet the portrait is rendered in the aftermath of a devastating, horrific disaster, and the characters are fictionalized versions of real people and composite personalities.

The look of the series was unique, eerily real, with people and places cinematically embedded in a city clearly in distress. Nowhere is this more apparent than in the opening sequences that are at once beautiful and disturbing. Mold spores on walls visually measure out the high water marks of interior spaces; visual references to those used in Spike Lee's *When the Levees Broke*. Along with the real images of floodwaters that surge into doorways and places where water should never be, the eye of the storm hits viewers week after week.[19]

The Pilot Episode

The first episode introduced a compelling ensemble cast, a diverse set of personalities, many of whom embody a wide range of strengths and flaws. The story lines are introduced as the city is re-inhabited. The search to make sense of the human, emotional, and physical destruction of the storm is often difficult. The main character, trombone player Antoine Batiste (Wendell Pierce), doesn't have the money to pay the cab to get to his playing gig. Another main character, DJ Davis McAlary (Steve Zahn) can't provide hot water for his lover to take a shower before she goes to work. When his lover, Chef Janette Desautel (Kim Dickens) does get to work, she has half the oysters she needs and no staff to set up for opening the restaurant. Only her Sous Chef is there to help. All of this happens in the initial 20 minutes of the first pilot episode.

True to writer and script editor Lolis Elie's words, Mardi Gras Indian Chief Albert Lambreaux (Clarke Peters) is shown opening the door to his storm damaged house for the first time. As he walks slowly through the rubble, he sees walls covered with the round dark mildew stains, the visual icons of the destruction of the flooding and the rot in the aftermath of the storm. As his daughter looks on in distress, he walks over mud-caked floors leaving footprints as he does. The contents of his house are strewn about, at contorted angles, evidence of the wake of receding floodwaters. Lambreaux's daughter has driven him back into town and during their drive back across the bridge from Jefferson parish, she remembers being turned back at gunpoint during the storm. That community refused to allow the city's hurricane victims to enter their county as the city flooded.

Though endearingly portrayed, the city and its residents are also drawn as complex and imperfect in many ways. Chief Lambreaux is a caring father and Mardi Gras Indian Chief who wields respects and authority, yet he beats a young black thief senseless. By the second episode, the cornerstone of the music scene DJ Davis has lost two jobs. Creighton Bernette is at times incandescently angry, and other times inconsolably depressed. As with quality character-driven fiction, these inhabitants of a destroyed city have been set up to undergo dramatic transformations over the course of the series. And they do—some develop in predicable ways, and others take surprising and disturbing turns. But they are all living in what comes to seem like at times, an endless post-disaster limbo of anxiety stress and dysfunction. Tracking the characters and their development reveals the ways in which actual events and fictional convention interweave through the arc of the story and influence the trajectory of the program.

One of the main threads of season 1 has attorney Antoinette "Toni" Bernette (Melissa Leo) attempting to locate LaDonna Batiste-Williams' (Khandi Alexander) missing brother, David "Daymo" Brooks, who has been lost in the criminal justice system since the storm. After a long search that reveals some of the layers of subterfuge involved in the loss of life during and after the storm, and after a number of false leads, Daymo's body is found stored in a container and the season ends with his funeral. In addition, Chief Lambreaux is beaten by the police trying the inhabit public housing untouched by storm damage. Themes of police corruption, racism, murder, and misconduct, as well as the portrayal of the privatization and corruption involved in the city's reconstruction, were on-going themes throughout *Treme*. These and other topics were based on the actual experiences and structural realities of post-Katrina New Orleans. Against this backdrop of struggle, oppression, and injustice in which difficulties often seem insurmountable, the program offers viewers moments of joy, celebration, and camaraderie, set to a musical pace that moves the rebuilding forward.

Treme's New Orleans: Race, Place, and Mardi Gras Indians

Treme the series takes its name from the oldest inhabited African American neighborhood in the country, the Faubourg Treme, where free people of color owned property as early as the 1700s. The low-income neighborhood outside the more well-known locales of the French Quarter or the upscale setting of the Garden District (known from the feature film *Pretty Baby* 1978) was extremely significant. At the center of the neighborhood is Congo Square, a historic center where African slaves drummed and danced and American jazz was born (Evans 2012). One of the show's writers and *Treme* resident (mentioned above) Lolis Eric Elie told NPR (April 8, 2010):

> It's significant that the show features a neighborhood long neglected by the city's elite. . . . To have people like David Simon and Eric Overmyer come here and go to the heart of a community that is emblematically black—and also considered an area of high crime and high blight—is a hell of a statement about what is really important about New Orleans.

Treme's inclusion of this history, its dedication to telling the story of New Orleans from multiple perspectives that include low-income and African American communities and their culture, portray the city in ways rarely viewed. The setting also helps narrate a very different national story of American culture, community, and identity. Such portrayals are significantly divergent from American dramatic TV series, and set a tone recognizably different from previous media narratives of the storm.

The Suits, Culture, and Secret of the Mardi Gras Indians

"Masking Indian" is an African American tradition in New Orleans that pays homage to Native Americans who sheltered runaway slaves in the bayous (Kennedy 2010). In the city, Indians parade on Mardi Gras day and also on "Super Sunday" when over 50 Indian Tribes come out onto the street drumming and chanting in dazzling feathered suits. One of the most important events in post-Katrina New Orleans was Mardi Gras day 2006 when Donald Harrison Jr., Chief of the Indian tribe Congo Nation, emerged from St. Augustine's Church in the neighborhood of Treme. With the storm-damaged steeple in the background, in a stunning newly sewn Indian suit, Harrison led the first second line after the storm through the streets of New Orleans. The day is remembered in the city as an historical event, and is featured in the African American Museum in the Treme neighborhood. It is the day that the Indian tribes became known as *spiritual first responders*, because the culture and rituals of the city had survived the storm. Indian culture, the Treme community, and these events all play a significant role in the series *Treme*.[20]

Music is a Character

Musicians, musical performances, live music clubs, the sound track, a school band, a DJ, and a local radio station, are all part of the musical shafts that form the foundation at the core of this program. The variety of bands and performers, clubs and buskers that appeared on the program was a musical phenomenon in itself. Singer songwriter Steve Earl plays an indigent street musician who teaches the fictional character Annie (violinist Lucia Micarelli) to write songs. *Treme* was filled with guest appearances from local musicians such as Kermit Ruffins, and many others. Elvis Costello appears in episode 2. Music comes to define the city and establish a sense of place. Some of the most stunning sequences in *Treme* were performances shot on location at many of the smaller music venues, most outside of the well-known tourist spots on Bourbon Street. Frenchmen Street outside the French Quarter is currently a vibrant music revue, and the jazz at Snug Harbor and other clubs took the program to creative realms wholly different from the confines of ordinary television.

One of the highlights of a later episode "Can I Change My Mind," is the appearance of Donald Harrison Jr. with Delmond, first at the bar at Domenica, and later at the studio of legendary New Orleans musician, Dr. John. The musicians are dreaming up a collaboration that would mix traditional Mardi Gras Indian chants with modern jazz. They will try to persuade Delmond's father Chief Lambreaux, to do the chanting when they later record in the studio. Here *Treme* merges different musical styles—from modern jazz to traditional New Orleans blues, Indian chants, and well-known songs. The music of *Treme* is a dynamic, potent source of solace, expression, and creativity that nourishes the characters, becoming a significant transformative force on the program. As with any meaningful and complex representation, music is also implicated in troubling sequences and setbacks for the characters. For example, the band Hot 8 Brass Band, appears in season 2, performing a post-storm anthem, "New Orleans." The band had sustained the loss of trombonist Joe Williams, shot by police in 2004, and then the shooting death of snare drummer Dinerral Shavers in 2006, whose funeral would be depicted in "Slip Away."

Treme featured a vast amount of talented local musicians, depicting a culture in practice, presenting a complex view of people and community distinct from the biased and ill-informed news stereotypes of disaster coverage. In doing so, this type of representation creates an opening for public understanding, offering a narrative of inclusion and concern, allowing viewers to empathize with those who experience disaster through no fault of their own.

Television Representations and Production as Historical Force

Treme provides a view into a story about place in which the representation becomes part of the place, its historical flow and the broader understanding of its significance. In many instances, from filming in the streets, to clubs, restaurants, and other venues, the program's embeddedness in New Orleans contributed to the remaking of the city. In some cases, as some scholars have noted, the program's presence in the city was problematic, contributing to congestion, and some argue, encouraging an inherently unequal economic redevelopment model, one primarily based on tourism instead of social justice and economic equality (Mayer 2011; Rathke 2012). But the program and its producers also demonstrated a commitment to and engagement with justice issues as well. For example, in season 3, Chief Albert Lambreaux (Clarke Peters) is sick. Though diagnosed with lymphoma, he refuses to start chemotherapy until after Mardi Gras day. By the fourth episode of the season, his son Delmond (Rob Brown) takes the chief to the Musicians' Clinic, an actual non-profit facility that provides health care to the city's musicians. The cast and producers of *Treme* were involved in fundraising for the clinic, organizing and appearing at an event where the profits were donated to the clinic for medical care. By foregrounding the clinic, the program serves as a source of information about the clinic and, through the dialogue, the program openly argues that access to medical care is a human right.

What Went Wrong, What was Left Out

The last episode of *Treme* aired on December 29, 2013, after three and a half seasons. There were multiple reasons for shortening the series, but a couple weeks before that last episode aired, Simon joked that HBO had an odd idea that their programming needed viewers.[21] As it stands, *Treme* may be destined to become a cult classic, or it may live a long life in syndication. But there is no doubt that we will continue to talk about the unique space the city of New Orleans occupies in American culture in a post-*Treme* television universe.

It is worth exploring some of the televisual challenges of *Treme's* rendering of the story of the storm. Ironically, it can be argued that most notable on the list of difficulties was the producers' dogged dedication to getting the story of post-Katrina New Orleans right. The writers were working within a structure defined by actual events, creating characters and giving voice and emotion to those occurrences. Though the drama was character centered, the characters seemed at times to illustrate the various expressions needed for social positions and identities occupying moments in time; the chef, the musician, the lawyer, the cop, the Indian, the bar owner, etc. As a consequence, the relationships the characters had with one another were sometimes confusing, inconsistent, and even nonexistent. This made it difficult to depict a sense of place and community. This was especially important, given that response to disaster demands a sense of unity and shared community purpose (Cahill 2005; Solnit 2009).

Throughout the series, references to the Danziger Bridge shootings were foregrounded, but the series was not able to depict those events. On September 4, 2005, six days after Katrina, police killed two of the city's residents and wounded others on the Danziger bridge (Burnett 2006). The victims were unarmed and the police covered up the crime (Maggi and McCarthy 2010). Clearly, in order to come to terms with the failures of the public, government, and law enforcement response to Katrina, more media dialogue about such events is required.

The Legacy: Media and Humanitarian Crisis

To understand the broader significance of *Treme*, we must place the program within the larger context of media coverage and humanitarian disaster. The program's critiques of the initial news narratives that depicted Katrina and New Orleans—overtly expressed and implied—constituted a strategy to rewrite the story of the storm. The early "disaster myth" frame that demonized the city's residents gave way in the series to a number of storylines featuring residents as victims of disaster in complex ways. The program foregrounded issues of racism, criminal justice, housing, and the larger issues of the failures of city, state, and federal government policies.[22] Because the fictional program told the story through the eyes of the people who suffered through the hurricane, and experienced the continuing trauma after it, the initial mythic coverage that demonized the city's residence was markedly challenged. After *Treme* began to air, a number of Katrina stories on Public Radio and other media outlets began to recount very different kinds of narratives; notably stories of musicians and how they survived the storm. With the certainty that humanitarian disaster will continue, the need for media representations that evoke empathy for those affected is apparent. Policies, planning and resources, and care and services in the aftermath of disaster depend on credible public witness, dialogue, and a knowledge base. The communication strategies aligned with such an information mandate were expressed in a fictional format.

Treme presented a narrative distinct from previous rendering of humanitarian crisis. Counterbalancing the continuing blows delivered to the city's residents are the dazzling moments of joy and satisfaction evoked through cinematic skill and the sheer force of performance—the music, culture, and food of New Orleans—all the primary markers for the sense of place and identity illuminated in *Treme*. And here *Treme* lives up to the impossible legacy of its predecessor. Like *The Wire*, it expanded the boundaries of contemporary televisual practices and left series television greatly augmented by the effort.

The program has influenced the city, its residents, and the discursive issues that revolve around the city's experience of humanitarian disaster. The *Treme* story expanded the news framework for disaster coverage from voyeuristic blame to humanistic inclusion. The evolving stories of the storm have significance beyond the geography of New Orleans and beyond the historical moment of their origin, especially in an age of climate instability and the demonstrated and growing threat of environmental crisis. In *Treme* the hurricane remains catastrophic, but is now understood as part of an equally forceful historical flow, one defined by the legacy of power, corruption, and racism and the failure of government to deliver basic services in the face of catastrophic events in situations of life and death. HBO's television production of *Treme* will continue to reverberate through media representations and provide a reference point for media coverage of future humanitarian disasters.

Notes

1. These sentiments were the taken-for-granted assumptions of many who worked on the program.
2. Neil deMause (2006) July–August, available at: www.fair.org/index.php?page=2933
3. Media Advisory (2009) "Erasing Katrina: Four Years On, Media Mostly Neglect an Ongoing Disaster, September 2, FAIR, available at: www.fair.org/index.php?page=3891
4. Julie Hollar (2010) "Brian Williams Rehashes Katrina Violence Myth," August 25, FAIR, available at: www.fair.org/blog/2010/08/25/dateline-rehashs-katrina-violence-myth/
5. Donald P. Moynihan, "The Response to Hurricane Katrina," International Risk Governance Council, Geneva 2009.
6. *The Guardian* (2005), "The Week Bush Failed America," September 3, available at: www.theguardian.com/news/2005/sep/04/leaders.hurricanekatrinaed
7. The *Washington Post* report is based on an *Associated Press* news report, available at: http://tdn.com/news/floods-ravage-new-orleans/article_af5f0d1f-3326-511c-9c4f-3dd8a836797e.html
8. R. D. McFadden and R. Blumenthal (2005) "Higher Death Toll Seen: Police Ordered to Stop Looters," *The New York Times*, September 1, available at: www.nytimes.com/2005/09/01/us/nationalspecial/higher-death-toll-seen-police-ordered-to-stop-looters.html?_r=0
9. Van Jones (2005) "Black People 'Loot' Food . . . White People "Find" Food. *Huffington Post* (September 1), available at: www.huffingtonpost.com/van-jones/black-people-loot-food-wh_b_6614.html
10. Kathleen Tierney, Christine Bevc and Erica Kuligowski (2006) "Metaphors Matter: DisTheseaster Myths, Media Frames, and Their Consequences in Hurricane Katrina," *Annals of the American Academy*, March, available at: www.scribd.com/doc/14711012/Metaphors-Matter-Disaster-Myths-Media-Frames-and-their-consequences-in-Hurricane-Katrina

11. Brian Thevenot, (2006) "Myth Making in New Orleans," *American Journalism Review*, December/January, available at: http://ajrarchive.org/article.asp?id=3998
12. The duPont talks: "Tom Brokaw and Brian Williams on Covering Katrina pt 1 of 3." Columbia University Graduate School of Journalism for the Alfred I. duPont-Columbia University series, The duPont Talks. June 26, 2014, available at: www.youtube.com/watch?v=TBoyOGu6Gt8
13. Tom McCarthy (2015) "Brian Williams' Reports on Katrina Called into Question by New Orleans Residents," February 6, *The Guardian*, available at: www.theguardian.com/world/2015/feb/06/brian-williams-hurricane-katrina-new-orleans-residents
14. Ibid., McCarthy.
15. Rebecca Solnit (2010) "Reconstructing the Story of the Storm: Hurricane Katrina at Five," *The Nation*, August 26, available at: www.thenation.com/article/154168/reconstructing-story-storm-hurricane-katrina-five
16. Solnit (2010), Ibid.
17. Interview with the author, March 15, 2011.
18. Phyllis Montana-Leblanc (2008) *Not Just the Levees Broke: My Story During and After Hurricane Katrina*, New York: Atria Paperbacks.
19. With each season, the opening sequences would change to reflect the narrative progression.
20. Personal Communication with Donald Harrison Jr., March 2011.
21. Remarks made at a public forum at the 92 Street Y, New York City, December 13, 2013.
22. For a thorough discussion of the failures of government assistance during the storm and the privatization and corruption during reconstruction of government contracts in post-Katrina New Orleans, see Gratz 2015.

Further Reading

Adams, V. (2013) *Markets of Sorrow, Labors of Faith: New Orleans in the Wake of Katrina*, Durham, NC: Duke University Press.

Andersen, R. (2006) *A Century of Media, A Century of War*, New York: Peter Lang.

Andersen, R. (2011) "Music is a character," antenna, June 15, available at: http://blog.commarts.wisc.edu/2011/06/15/music-is-a-character/

Andersen, R. (2011) "Fiction More Real Than What's Fit to Print: HBO's *Treme* Covers New Orleans Recovery," *EXTRA!* July, available at: http://fair.org/extra-online-articles/fiction-more-real-than-whats-fit-to-print/

Andersen, R. (2011) "HBO's *Treme*: Exposing the Fractured Press Coverage of the Storm and Post-Katrina New Orleans," in M. Huff and Project Censored (Eds.), *Censored 2012: The Top Censored Stories and Media Analysis of 2010–2011*, New York: Seven Stories Press, pp. 423–436, available at: https://books.google.com/books?id=bzwmpHIQWlUC&pg=PT298&lpg=PT298&dq=HBO's+Treme:+Exposing+the+Fractured+Press+Coverage+of+the+Storm+and+Post-Katrina+New+Orleans&source=bl&ots=Bjh4s3prFo&sig=lM40VI5Z9u7h2OmeADepbO34wN4&hl=en&sa=X&ved=0ahUKEwiWzeKep6rTAhUnrVQKHZ5KAfcQ6AEIJDAA#v=onepage&q=HBO's%20Treme%3A%20Exposing%20the%20Fractured%20Press%20Coverage%20of%20the%20Storm%20and%20Post-Katrina%20New%20Orleans&f=false

Andersen, R. (2012 "Mediating the Past: *Treme* and the Stories of the Storm," antenna, November 14, available at: http://blog.commarts.wisc.edu/2012/11/14/mediating-the-past-treme-and-the-stories-of-the-storm/

Banks, J. (2011) "Keepin' it Real," on *Treme* antenna, May 25, available at: http://blog.commarts.wisc.edu/2011/05/25/keepin-it-real-on-treme/

Baum, D. (2010) *Nine Lives: Mystery, Magic, Death, and Life in New Orleans*, New York: Spiegel & Grau.

Bolter, J., and Grusin R. (2000) *Remediation: Understanding New Media*, Cambridge, MA: MIT Press.

Cahill, K. (1999) (Ed.) *A Framework for Survival: Health, Human Rights, and Humanitarian Assistance in Conflicts and Disasters*, New York: Routledge.

Codrescu, A. (2006) *New Orleans, Mon Amour: 20 Years of Writings from the City*, Chapel Hill, NC: Algonquin Books of Chapel Hill.

Crutcher Jr., M. (2010) Treme: Race and Place in a New Orleans Neighborhood (Geographies of Justice and Social Transformation), Athens, GA: University of Georgia Press.

Farmer, P. (1992) *AIDS and Accusations: Haiti and the Geography of Blame*, Berkeley, CA: University of California Press.

Gray, J. (2008) *Entertainment Television*, New York: Routledge.

Jenkins, H. (2006) *Convergence Culture: Where Old and New Media Collide*, New York: New York University Press.

Lemann, N. (2010) "Charm City USA," *The New York Review of Books*. September 30.

Medley, K. W. (2003) *We as Freemen: Plessy v. Ferguson*, Grentna, LA: Pelican.

Medley, K. W. (2014) *Black Life in Old New Orleans*, Grentna, LA: Pelican.

Mitchell, J., Thomas, D., Hill, A., and Cutter, S. (2000) "Catastrophe in Reel Life Versus Real Life: Perpetuating Disaster Myth through Hollywood Films," *International Journal of Mass Emergencies and Disasters*, 18: 383–402.

Negra, D. (2010) *Old and New Media after Katrina*, New York: Palgrave Macmillan.

Ondaatje, M. (1976) *Coming Through Slaughter*, New York: Vintage International.

Pearson, R., and Davies, M. M. (2014) *Star Trek and American Television*, Oakland, CA: University of California Press.

Piazza, T. (2005) *Why New Orleans Matters*, New York: HarperPerennial.

Rose, C. (2007) *1 Dead in Attic after Katrina*, New York: Simon & Schuster.

Sublette, N. (2009) *The Year Before the Flood*, Chicago, IL: Lawrence Hill Books.

Teachout, T. (2009) *Pops: A Life of Louis Armstrong*, Boston, MA: Houghton Mifflin Harcourt.

Vale, L., and Campella, T. (2005) *The Resilient City: How Modern Cities Recover from Disaster*, New York: Oxford University Press.

References

Burnett, J. (2006) "What happened on New Orleans' Danziger Bridge?" *NPR*, September 13, available at: www.npr.org/templates/story/story.php?storyId=6063982

Cahill, K. (2005) *To Bear Witness: A Journey of Healing and Solidarity*, New York: Fordham University Press.

Dowd, M. (2005) "United States of Shame," *New York Times*, September 3, available at: www.nytimes.com/2005/09/03/opinion/03dowd.html?_r=1&

Elie, L. E. (2014) *Treme: Stories and Recipes from the Heart of New Orleans*, San Francisco, CA: Chronicle Books.

Elie, L. E. (2015) "After the Deluge," *Columbia Magazine*, Spring/Summer, pp. 39–45.

Evans, F. W. (2012) *Congo Square: African Roots in New Orleans*, Lafayette, LA: University of Louisiana Press.

Gratz, R. (2015) *We're Still Here Ya Bastards*, New York: Nation Books.

Kennedy, A. (2010) *Big Chief Harrison and the Mardi Gras Indians*, Grentna, LA: Pelican.

Maggi, L., and McCarthy, B. (2010) "Judge in Danziger Case Sickened by 'Raw Brutality of the Shooting and the Craven Lawlessness of the Cover-up'," *Times-Picayune*, April 7, available at: www.nola.com/crime/index.ssf/2010/04/judge_sickened_by_raw_brutalit.html

Mayer, V. (2011) "Film Your Troubles Away," antenna, April 27, available at: http://blog.commarts.wisc.edu/2011/04/27/film-your-troubles-away/

Montana-LeBlanc, P. (2008) *Not Just the Levees Broke: My Story During and After Hurricane Katrina*, New York: Atria Paperbacks.

Rathke, W. (2012) "*Treme* for Tourists: The Music of the City without the Power," *Television & New Media*, 13: 261–267, first published on October 24, 2011.

Solnit, R. (2009) *A Paradise Built in Hell: The Extraordinary Communities that Arise in Disaster*, New York: Viking Press.

Tierney, K., Bevc, C., and Kuligowski, E. (2006) "Metaphors Matter: Disaster Myths, Media Frames, and Their Consequences in Hurricane Katrina," *Annals of the American Academy*, March, available at: www.scribd.com/doc/14711012/Metaphors-Matter-Disaster-Myths-Media-Frames-and-their-consequences-in-Hurricane-Katrina

Williams, L. (2014) *On The Wire*, Durham, NC: Duke University Press.

32

"SHINE A LITTLE LIGHT"

Celebrities, Humanitarian Documentary, and *Half the Sky*

Heather McIntosh

Contemporary documentaries about humanitarian issues face three challenges in representing global crises. First, critics dismiss humanitarian documentaries for their heavy-handed representations that come across as "overtly didactic, ideological, and spectacular" (Härting 2013, 332). Second, these documentaries mute the voices of those suffering in favor of "giving voice to the traumatized Western humanitarian aid worker or peacekeeper" (Härting 2013, 333). Third, these documentaries face the challenge of the "unrepresentability" of these issues because of these issues' extreme spectacle, lack of explanations, and rational denials (Ball 2000, 10).

One of these global crises that humanitarian documentaries struggle to represent is the systemic oppression of women and girls. This oppression manifests as gender-based violence, sex trafficking, forced prostitution, and female genital mutilation. No less pernicious, it also manifests through denials of education, health care, and economic opportunities. While multiple humanitarian documentaries address only one of these issues at a time, *Half the Sky: Turning Oppression into Opportunity for Women Worldwide* (2012) assumes a more ambitious scope in representing six gender-based issues happening in deeply affected countries around the world. The film is based on Nicholas Kristof and Sheryl WuDunn's book by the same name (Kristof and WuDunn 2010). Six segments address gender-based violence in Sierra Leone, sex trafficking in Cambodia, education in Vietnam, female genital mutilation in Somaliland, intergenerational prostitution in India, and economic empowerment in Kenya. Talking-head montages of humanitarian, political, and other leaders appear between the sequences, at episode openings, and at episode closings. The nearly four-hour documentary aired over two nights on US public broadcasting as part of the Independent Lens series in October 2012, and an active social marketing campaign titled Half the Sky Movement accompanied it. Continuing at halftheskymovement.org, the campaign includes information about the issues addressed in the documentary and beyond, an awareness-raising game on Facebook, and opportunities for further involvement such as screening the film, buying female entrepreneurs' goods, sharing personal stories, and even becoming journalists.

Half the Sky attempts to address the three representational challenges in facing humanitarian documentary by incorporating six American actresses as a strategy for avoiding overly didactic criticisms, for offering proxies to those experiencing these issues, and for creating guides to these issues in ways that may make them watchable. One actress appears in each country segment. Eva Mendes visits Sierra Leone, Meg Ryan travels to Cambodia, and Gabrielle Union visits Vietnam in the first part, and Diane Lane visits Somaliland, America Ferrera travels to India, and Olivia Wilde visits Kenya in the second part. While other humanitarian documentaries downplay celebrities' presences, *Half the Sky* addresses their appearances in the opening minutes, and it does so, without irony, using other celebrities. George Clooney offers the first explanation, casting both possibilities and limitations in the same comments: "The celebrity involvement may be able to amplify the story. That's all. That's all we can do." An actress well-known for her activism, Susan Sarandon adds that celebrities should "shine a little light on people that are actually doing the hard lifting." In other words, using celebrities can help raise awareness about these issues.

This chapter analyzes the roles of celebrities within *Half the Sky*. After a brief literature review about documentary representation, celebrity authenticity, and celebrity authority, this chapter examines these actresses through their motivations, their attempted emotional connections, and their observations about the issues and the people involved. Overall, this chapter argues that while the celebrities in *Half the Sky* help make the horrific stories presented more representable or maybe even relatable, they ultimately serve to address the posthumanitarian audience through their replacement of the survivors' voices.

The Celebrity in Humanitarian Documentary

This literature review covers three areas of scholarship within documentary theory and humanitarian studies. The review begins with examining the key questions of documentary representation as they relate to humanitarian campaigns and celebrity appearances. Building on documentary representation, it continues with a section about celebrity authenticity and its relationship to their management of personas. The review then addresses questions about the celebrity's authority within humanitarian issues.

Documentary pursues truth as its ultimate goal, and the social or committed documentary in particular focuses on social problems, raising awareness about those problems and sometimes suggesting potential solutions (Waugh 1984, xi–xxvii). Documentary never simply shows the truth, but instead makes an argument about a truth or multiple truths (Nichols 1991). This argument develops through the representational choices made among archival footage, action footage, talking heads, voiceover narration, on-camera hosts, and musical scores. Not all of these conventions appear in every documentary; they are combined to create the documentary's intended argument both visually and rhetorically. The goals drive both social documentary and humanitarian campaigns, making the form well suited to align with these causes. Contemporary social documentary in particular focuses on making some kind of impact, which moves beyond raising awareness to an active form of participation such as encouraging and guiding action, overturning a prison sentence, or changing policy and regulation.

The people appearing within a documentary, called social actors, provide lived experience, contextual insights, background information, and expert commentary. They also provide an emotional lens through which to read their experiences and circumstances. According to Marquis (2013, 1), "[G]esture, posture, facial expression, word choice, intonation, and the like . . . contribute significantly to observers' understandings of the situations and events at hand." Usually, these social actors are everyday people whose stories represent larger social issues, or they serve as first-hand witnesses to these issues. These people are never neutral. What they represent and how the documentary represents them are culturally constructed.

As documentaries typically focus on "real" people, the appearance of celebrities as social actors requires careful consideration. A celebrity garners public attention through popular culture, politics, scandal, or even personality (Street 2004), and with that attention, the celebrity gains freedom, and potentially power, but also more scrutiny. A celebrity's presence introduces a performative aspect that raises questions about the documentary's representation of the reality and the truth of the celebrity's presence (Marquis 2013). Chouliaraki (2012, 5) defines this performative aspect as a persona, or

> a specific form of public self that articulates "universal" discourses, such as human vulnerability and everyday ordinariness, with aesthetic choices of unique individuality, such as rare talent or beautiful looks, that establish the celebrity as a figure both intimate and distinguished in our public culture.

This persona raises questions whether documentaries show the celebrity as a "real" person or just another facet of the persona.

Documentary offers celebrities an opportunity to appear more everyday, but not all of them see it that way. Even a documentary can be a promotional vehicle and thus requires some degree of image management. Celebrities' negotiation between persona and promotion dates to the 1960s, when American observational documentaries started turning their cameras on celebrities, including politicians, musicians, and sports figures. The observational form, which eschewed voiceover narration, formal interviews, and archival footage in favor of a "fly on the wall" approach, attempted to remove the filmmakers' influence as much as possible and to give seemingly intimate access to these famous figures (Saunders 2007). Yet these celebrities still managed their personas within these observational documentaries. For example, *On the Pole* (Drew Associates, 1960), which is about Indianapolis 500 race car driver Eddie Sachs, shows Sachs after losing a race struggling to decide how to act natural in the face of such disappointment (Pryluck 1976).

While documentary film criticism later cited the cinema verité approach as naive and overly idealistic in its truth-representing claims (Hall 1991; Taylor 2011), the approach does reveal a documentary turn in representing celebrities and the managing of their publicity. Just because the camera attempts to be unobtrusive does not mean that the people appearing in the film were unaware of its presence. Celebrities in particular must remain mindful of their presence within the camera's sights, and these documentaries can serve as promotional vehicles to bolster their images. Former Spice Girl Geri Halliwell decided to make a documentary about her post-girl group life. Throughout the documentary, Halliwell balances her public image with her "true self"—a conundrum Tolson (2001, 444) labels a "paradox." According to Tolson (2001, 444), "Apparently, from Geri's point of view, her self-managed public might be enhanced by ways of 'being herself' in a documentary film." Thus, the appearance within a documentary, either one about them or about something else, offers an opportunity to further the public image in a more "authentic" way through self management.

Authenticity, then, plays an important role in a celebrity's image and publicity, and it is highly constructed, shaped, and managed. Authenticity functions on two levels: the authentic persona and the authentic representative for humanitarian issues. The authentic persona is based on the illusion that the celebrity is just like everyone else. To this end, a celebrity might offer glimpses into her "real life," such as through stories she tells on a talk show (Tolson 2001) or, more commonly, through social networking sites such as Facebook, Twitter, and Instagram, which allow creating parasocial relationships between the star and her followers on those sites (Steele and Shores 2014). Those followers catch glimpses of a star's life much in the same way they catch glimpses of their friends' lives through status updates and photos of lunches, pets, travels, and significant others. The more savvy celebrities choose carefully what they post on these sites, careful to cultivate their personal brand (Huliaras and Tzifakis 2010).

The authentic representative for humanitarian issues builds on the authentic persona. By showing these more personal sides of themselves, they appear to strip away the star persona in favor of a more everyday one. By showing this side of themselves, they seemingly put themselves in service to something larger, such as humanitarian or political causes, or in this case *Half the Sky*. But this construction of authenticity is not completely altruistic in that the celebrities still benefit from becoming representatives: "[T]his 'real' person that is constructed through mediated quasi-interaction is also something to be used" (Tolson 2001, 451). This construction plays into the performative aspect of western values. Yrjölä (2012, 363) explains:

> [T]he performed celebrity identity which projects an exemplary "natural" self that is centrally constructed with the liberal values of individual equality, being true to oneself, conformity and self-actualisation, has rendered celebrities the lingua franca of modern identity and identity politics in western capitalist societies.

These values carry degrees of privilege and power with them. Embodying these values as part of the creation of their authentic self and then using that authentic self within humanitarian causes and documentaries about those causes further these values and their self-interests, sometimes at the expense of the humanitarian efforts they are trying to help.

Questions of celebrity authenticity in humanitarian campaigns, such as appearing in public service announcements, serving as United Nations ambassadors, or promoting issues on their social media accounts, derive from questions of their authority. The idea of celebrities embodying authority draws mixed reactions, as celebrities make both positive and negative impacts within humanitarian campaigns. In terms of policy, for example, Street (2004) cites how celebrities being taken seriously through their involvement in political activities, their attention from politicians, and their support from audiences can put a spotlight on overlooked issues. Celebrities present ideas in ways that engage audiences within the media's soundbite culture. Celebrities can even become the expert-advocate when involved in humanitarian issues (Steele and Shores 2014). The criticisms outstrip the praise, however. While academic and other experts can support their claims with appropriate research, celebrities sometimes present information without verification (Chouliaraki 2012; Steele and Shores 2014; Haynes 2014). Their presentation of information might reduce humanitarian complexities into gross oversimplifications (Yrjölä 2012; Haynes 2014). Their celebrity status might overshadow the issues and the survivors, denying these survivors a right to speak (Chouliaraki 2012).

The idea of authority critiqued above relies on the traditional model of knowledge-based expertise. Moral authority offers an alternative in that celebrities gain an authority "once associated with sages of charismatic leaders" (Cashmore 2006). This authority derives from personal experience, such as with a traumatic situation, with turning the person with the experience into a witness, and their testimony is imbued with cultural value for being real (Sturken 1997). These witnesses give testimony to atrocities such as war, genocide, gendercide, extreme poverty, and other issues.

In addition to first-hand accounts, witnesses also include others involved in traumatic situations though possibly not directly affected by them, such as volunteers, doctors, journalists, and celebrities. Celebrities visit countries affected by crises, and they see first hand the atrocities there. Haynes (2014, 29–30) describes the celebrity presences in these situations as "trauma tourism," which she defines as "the practice of traveling to see or visit with victims of humanitarian disasters or human rights abuses." Through their travels, the celebrities become a witness who offers testimony about what they have seen in public service announcements, in fundraising campaign materials, in documentaries, before non-government organizations, and even before the US Congress. Their witnessing only adds to their moral authority, though sometimes the moral authority gets confused with traditional authority (Haynes 2014).

This testimony arising from traumatic situations complicates the process of bearing witness. Trauma frequently becomes unrepresentable on screen (Ball 2000; Hirsch 2003). Instead of the truth coming from a logical place, which is where many documentaries attempt to pinpoint it using the very same testimony, the truth from traumatic situations emerges through emotion, which provides a way of making sense of a situation that appears to defy a logical framework (White, 1987; LaCapra 1997). By becoming witnesses, celebrities imbued with moral authority offer this emotional viewpoint for understanding a traumatic situation, and that emotion allows for a different kind of truth to be revealed. These emotional connections prove more effective in mobilization than straightforward facts as the focus is on people, not statistics.

Celebrities in *Half the Sky*

Drawing on documentary representation, celebrity authority, and celebrity authenticity, this section examines the roles of the American actresses within *Half the Sky*. The documentary structure facilitates this analysis as each segment follows a similar pattern with each celebrity traveling to the country, meeting Kristof, and interacting with local activists and survivors. Throughout each segment, the actresses offer their observations in interviews, interactions, voiceovers, and diaries. They usually appear onscreen more than the local activists and survivors. To analyze their roles, this section details the celebrities' personal motivations for participating in the project, their attempted emotional connections with the people and their circumstances, and their overall observations about the humanitarian issues and the people involved.

The actresses' motivations for participating in *Half the Sky* are primarily personal, and they share these motivations early in their segments. After reading about *Half the Sky*'s mission in an email, Gabrielle Union states, "Who doesn't care about the oppression of women and girls across the world? And I just wanted to be a part of telling the story." Diane Lane visits Somaliland "as a witness." She states, "I wanted to put my money where my mouth is. I wanted to physically take myself the next step of my belief system and my interest and my curiosity and my compassion and my hope for the world." The book provides the motivation for both Olivia Wilde and America Ferrera. Wilde considers herself an activist ready to learn, and the book motivates her in that direction.

In asserting these motivations, these actresses remain careful to stay within the "appropriate" roles for moral agents as storytellers, witnesses, and inspired participants. For Union, Ferrera, and Wilde, their motivations connect with the *Half the Sky* project, while Lane sees a cosmopolitan opportunity to expand her worldview. Interestingly enough, their motivations make no connections with the specific people or organizations in the destination countries. While this disconnect might appear disingenuous, it actually reinforces their roles as moral agents who remain in their box as designated by the documentary and prevents them from making the expertise claims that can become so problematic. By stating their personal motivations, they need not demonstrate expertise. By asserting these motivations and adopting these roles, they engage in their own form of casting as explorers in a discovery process through their trauma tourism. Their motivations offer a potential emotional connection to the imagined audience and allow a glimpse of the everyday person as well.

In addition to showing their motivations, the actresses also attempt to connect their own experiences with what they witness in their respective countries. They do so in an attempt to process what they see and hear, though arguably the atrocities they witness prove almost beyond understanding. The shifting comments from Eva Mendes demonstrate this point. When traveling to Sierra Leone, Eva Mendes is excited to meet the girls, and she claims, "I relate to struggle, and I relate to meeting challenges." After she meets three-year-old and 14-year-old rape victims, she changes the tone of her comments and repeatedly states how the entire situation remains incomprehensible.

Some of the actresses attempt to connect the girls they meet with themselves and their own experiences. In India America Ferrera meets ten-year-old Monisha, who is likely to be sold into prostitution though the organization and its local representative, Urmi Basu, fight to prevent it. Deeply upset, Ferrera remarks, "When you see these things with your own eyes here, you know, I can't help but see myself in Monisha." She offers no further elaboration, however. Gabrielle Union connects her experiences with Nhi Nu Thi Huynh, a Vietnamese girl who sells lottery tickets to support her family and struggles to continue her education. After a visit to Nhi's home, Union shares the story of her rape and education's role in her recovery:

> I see so much of my own struggle as a, you know, as a teenager, um, and how education, like, plays a role. Um, you know, when I was 19, and I left home, and, um, you know, I-I ended up getting raped on the when I was at-at work at my after-school job. And, um, the thing that I immediately went into was, uh . . . was school. Like, 'cause, you know, when you're . . . when you're raped, it's–it's the absence of control. So the one thing I could control was school. And I just dove into my schoolwork, and I became an amazing student. So I can relate to Nhi being so driven in school, and I just wish for girls who have to go through any kind of adversity that they have education as an outlet for healing.

Despite their differences, Ferrera and Union attempt to close the gaps between themselves and the girls. None of the three speak as experts or authorities in trying to explain what they see. Instead, their comments originate in their own emotions and traumas.

Among the six actresses, Olivia Wilde brings the most enthusiasm and eagerness on her journey. In Kenya, she visits Umoja, a haven village for Samburu women and their children. Samburu traditions allow men to beat and even murder their wives with impunity, so the women seek safety with each other and attempt to sustain themselves through beadmaking. The women experience much resistance, as the men raid the village at night. Despite these and other hardships, Wilde is excited about visiting and even expresses a wish to remain there for the rest of her life. Kristof jokes that Wilde will start the Los Angeles version of Umoja; their local advocate, Rebecca Lollsoli, also laughs at the suggestion. In contrast to Wilde's enthusiasm, Meg Ryan appears emotionally distant, if not removed, from the Cambodia situation. She makes no spontaneous effort to connect her own experiences with the girls there. One of the girls asks Ryan how she feels about hearing all of these stories, and Ryan replies:

Well, it's a very powerful thing to tell your story, to say personally what happen to you, for anyone. . . . It's very far from my experience, and um, to see that you have come out and that you are able to tell your stories in such a dignified way is very, is very moving.

Like the other actresses, Ryan is moved by listening to people's stories. Instead of closing the gaps, however, she separates herself, reinforcing her place as a listener, a witness.

In their own way, both Wilde and Ryan contribute to the complex emotional palette in *Half the Sky*. Wilde's enthusiasm brings levity, such as through her comments about Umoja L.A. and through her observations about "The Vagina Song" and the Samburu women's shyness about singing it for her. She describes the joy and freedom in the song. Ryan represents an unfortunate opposite. Though she struggles with tears at times, Ryan appears mostly overwhelmed with her Cambodian visit.

Overall, their attempts at relating to the women and girls align with the criticisms and possibilities for celebrities in humanitarian campaigns. By focusing emotionally, they offer a way of interpreting the situations that avoids didacticism (Härting 2013). They also offer a way to represent issues by shifting away from the horrors these women and girls embody. It further reinforces the self-cast roles as moral agents. The negatives also appear, however.

Finally, with Kristof accompanying each of them, all of the actresses meet local advocates and survivors. Their encounters provide a framework for introducing not only the humanitarian issues but also the people advocating for, fighting against, or living with them. This framework situates the actresses most firmly as witnesses, which creates an interesting representational turn. Frequently, the local advocates and changemakers explain the systemic, cultural, and sometimes economic issues that enable the practices repressing these women and girls. Some of the advocates are survivors of the very same exploitative practices, which adds another layer to their authority. Through that representational strategy, then, the documentary affords them a more traditional expert role. As moral agents, the celebrities offer support, add encouragement, and express admiration.

The support and encouragement is often directed at the child survivors. For one example, Eva Mendes tells Fahulamatu, a 14-year-old rape survivor, that she is strong, and she should ignore people's criticisms even though in Sierra Leone women and girls are blamed for their own rapes. For another example, Gabrielle Union writes in Nhi's notebook: "To Nhi. You are so beautiful and so smart I know you'll be very successful."

The admiration is directed at the advocates. Mendes expresses a deep reverence for Amie Kandeh, who works with the Rainbo Center and with the International Rescue Committee in Sierra Leone:

She's one of those women that, you know, you're just like . . . you just kind of feel a little bit worse about yourself going, "Really? You do that, too?" Okay, so now I have absolutely no excuse when I go back home because she's done it, and she's doing it, and, um, she's incredibly inspirational. She's beautiful, um, and she still has a lightness about her.

Meg Ryan observes of Somaly Man: "The more you talk to Somaly, she doesn't see an end to this situation in her lifetime. But it doesn't stop her from putting one foot in front of the other." Of Edna Ada, Diane Lang notes, "I just have such reverence at this point in time for people who, like Edna, have the willingness to do the right thing or go out of their comfort zone to help people do the right thing."

The representations of advocates and survivors as experts give them roles of greater authority. In doing so *Half the Sky* reinforces the roles of the actresses as moral agents and legitimizes their uplifting comments. These comments suggest that advocates and survivors deserve admiration for taking on and persevering through such extreme challenges in the face of threats and other obstacles. It is here where the light shines the brightest, for if these women can struggle and prevail, then so can the audience.

Conclusion

Half the Sky uses six female celebrities to "shine a little light" on gender-based issues occurring around the globe. It uses these celebrities to try and avoid the criticisms detailed at the start of this chapter, including the didacticism, the muted voices, and the unrepresentable nature of the issues. In the film celebrities share their motivations, their attempted emotional connections, and their positive observations and encouragements. They serve as moral agents who bring troubling issues to posthumanitarian audiences in seemingly authentic ways, in an active struggle to prevent their celebrity statuses from overshadowing the subjectivity of others.

But despite its being upfront about the celebrities' purposes, *Half the Sky*'s incorporation of them also demonstrates the problems with their appearances in humanitarian campaigns and documentaries. Engaging diplomacy "normally requires listening and taking stock of the complexities" (Tascon 2012, 877), but the complex and multilayered issues undergirding each humanitarian issue become flattened and compressed. The actresses do listen. Diane Lane in particular attempts to understand how women can conscientiously still perform female genital cutting as she learns just how horrifying are the procedure's techniques and effects. Though her discoveries magnify the horror of the procedure, they still attempt a culturally based explanation, but the film stops short of critiquing or condemning the practice. The actresses also ask questions. Mendes, Union, and Ferrera engage the situations through personal motivations and experiences as befitting their roles as moral agents, but they do not attempt to move beyond those roles such as reflecting on their own privileges in these situations.

In addition to flattening these complex issues, the incorporation of celebrities falls squarely into the critiques of Western voices supplanting the local ones. Celebrities sometimes take the spotlight, even speaking before the local advocates. By the time the local advocates do speak, the comments from the celebrities and from Nicholas Kristof and Sheryl WuDunn's book frames them in discourses such as personal strength, dedication, and hard work. As a result, voices of the women who experience such humanitarian trauma are given less time, particularly when they serve as local experts as well. While the celebrities gain opportunities to explain their motivations and roles such as witness and storyteller, the local advocates gain no similar opportunity for themselves.

This approach also glosses over the Western privileges afforded by the actresses. They frequently speak from inside hotels, but these privileges extend beyond accommodation. This disregard occurs particularly in those who attempt to connect their personal experiences with the girls. This is not to downplay the significance of traumas that they have endured and overcome, but it is to say that their experiences are markedly different from those who live in extreme poverty, lacking education, safety, and opportunity. An Umoja village in Los Angles will not face the same challenges as the one in Kenya. Unlike those living in these countries, the celebrities can leave whenever they wish, and the women and girls living there possess little chance of escape even after the documentary brings their stories to viewing screens.

Half the Sky affords these actresses an opportunity to be represented as authentic and with moral authority. In their roles as guides, these actresses do help make these issues more watchable. For some of them, their roles continued beyond the film as their presences created an amplification effect that the film might not otherwise have had. Their presences fueled media coverage of the documentary and its issues. Some actresses, including Olivia Wilde and Meg Ryan, took to their social networking accounts and posted about their involvement with the project. Others deepened their involvement with the *Half the Sky* movement through participating in events. Wilde, for example, attended a high school's screening and spoke with the audience afterward. Overall, their presences demonstrate the changes occurring in celebrity representation in humanitarian documentaries and their accompanying campaigns.

Further Reading

Chouliaraki, L. (2012) "The Theatricality of Humanitarianism: A Critique of Celebrity Advocacy," *Communication and Critical/Cultural Studiesi* 9 (1): 1–21.

Huliaras, A., and Tzifakis, N. (2010) "Celebrity Activism in International Relations: In Search of a Framework for Analysis," *Global Society*, 24 (2): 255–274.

Street, J. (2004) "Celebrity Politicians: Popular Culture and Political Representation," *The British Journal of Politics and International Relations*, 6: 435–452.

Tascon, S. (2012) "Considering Human Rights Films, Representation, and Ethics: Whose Face?" *Human Rights Quarterly*, 34: 864–883.

Tolson, A. (2001) "Being Yourself: The Pursuit of Authentic Celebrity," *Discourse Studies*, 3 (4): 443–457.

References

Ball, K. (2000) "Introduction: Trauma and Its Institutional Destinies," *Cultural Critique*, 46: 1–44.

Cashmore, E. (2006) *Celebrity Culture*, New York and London: Routledge.

Chouliaraki, L. (2012) "The Theatricality of Humanitarianism: A Critique of Celebrity Advocacy," *Communication and Critical/Cultural Studies*, 9 (1): 1–21.

Half the Sky: Turning Oppression into Opportunity for Women Worldwide. (2012) Prod. Joshua Bennett. Perf. Nick Kristof, America Ferrera, Diane Lane, Eva Mendes, Meg Ryan, Gabrielle Union, and Olivia Wilde. Docurama Films.

Hall, J. (1991) "Realism as a Style in Cinema Verite: A Critical Analysis of 'Primary,'" *Cinema Journal*, 30 (4): 24–50.

Härting, H. (2013) "Foreign Encounters: The Political and Visual Aesthetics of Humanitarianism in Contemporary Canadian Film Culture," *University of Toronto Quarterly*, 82 (2): 331–352.

Haynes, D. F. (2014) "The Celebritization of Human Trafficking," *The Annals of the American Academy of Political and Social Science*, 653: 25–45.

Hirsch, J. (2003) *Afterimage: Film, Trauma, and the Holocaust*, Philadelphia, PA: Temple University Press.

Huliaras, A., and Tzifakis, N. (2010) "Celebrity Activism in International Relations: In Search of a Framework for Analysis," Global Society, 24 (2): 255–274.

Kristof, N. D., and WuDunn, S. (2010) *Half the Sky: Turning Oppression into Opportunity for Women Worldwide*. New York: Vintage.

LaCapra, D. (1997) "'Shoah': Here There Is No Why," *Critical Inquiry*, 23 (2): 231–269.

Marquis, E. (2013) "Performance, Persona & the Construction of Documentary Identity," *Post Script* 33 (1): n.p.

Nichols, B. (1991) *Representing Reality: Issues and Concepts in Documentary*, Bloomington: IN: Indiana University Press.

Pryluck, C. (1976) "We Are All Outsiders: The Ethics of Documentary Filmmaking," *Journal of the University Film Association*, 28 (1): 21–29.

Saunders, D. (2007) *Direct Cinema: Observational Documentary and the Politics of the Sixties*, London: Wallflower Press.

Steele, S. L., and Shores, T. (2014) "More Than Just a Famous Face: Exploring the Rise of the Celebrity Expert-Advocate through Anti-Trafficking Action by the Demi and Ashton Foundation," *Crime Media Culture*, 10 (3): 259–272.

Street, J. (2004) "Celebrity Politicians: Popular Culture and Political Representation," *The British Journal of Politics and International Relations*, 6: 435–452.

Sturken, M. (1997) "Reenactment, Fantasy, and the Paranoia of History: Oliver Stone's Docudramas," *History and Theory*, 36 (4):64–79.

Tascon, S. (2012) "Considering Human Rights Films, Representation, and Ethics: Whose Face?" *Human Rights Quarterly*, 34: 864–883.

Taylor, A. (2011) "Angels, Stones, Hunters: Murder, Celebrity, and Direct Cinema," *Studies in Documentary Film*, 5 (1): 45–60.

Tolson, A. (2001) "Being Yourself: The Pursuit of Authentic Celebrity," *Discourse Studies*, 3 (4): 443–457.

Waugh, T. (1984) "Introduction: Why Documentary Filmmakers Keep Trying to Change the World, or Why People Changing the World Keep Making Documentaries," in T. Waugh (Ed.), *"Show Us Life:" Toward a History and Aesthetics of the Committed Documentary*, Metuchen, NJ: Scarecrow Press p. 32.

White, H. (1987) *The Content of the Form: Narrative Discourse and Historical Representation*, Baltimore and London: Johns Hopkins University Press.

Yrjölä, R. (2012) "From Street into the World: Towards a Politicised Reading of Celebrity Humanitarianism." *The British Journal of Politics and International Relations*, 14: 357–374.

33

THE RECORD OF A TOTAL POWER LOSS

First Five Days at the Fukushima Nuclear Power Plant

Hajime Ozaki

Six years has passed since the magnitude 9.0 earthquakes and tsunami hit the northeast coast of Japan on March 11, 2011. More than 15,800 people died and over 2,500 people are still missing. In its aftermath more than 3,300 people died or committed suicide during prolonged evacuation from the affected area. Nearly 200,000 people are still relocated or living in temporary housing, waiting for the day to come when they can go back to where they belonged.

One of the main reasons why the people can't go home is the nuclear disaster at the Fukushima Daiichi (Japanese word for Number One) nuclear power plant. Three of the six generators suffered nuclear reactor core meltdown, and the situation is far from under control after six years of efforts to stabilize the defective generators.

There were fragmented reports, rumors and speculations as to how the engineers on the site, Tokyo Electric Power Co. (TEPCO) officials in their Tokyo headquarters, and the government officials including then prime minister Naoto Kan of the inexperienced Democratic Party of Japan (DPJ) cabinet interacted to avoid the worst scenario. But they did not give a clear picture to the people in and outside of Japan as to what really happened.

In 2014, Kyodo News, a Japanese news wire service, distributed a series of feature stories depicting the critical first five days at the Fukushima Daiichi nuclear power plant, based on interviews with around 100 people, including employees of plant operator TEPCO, politicians and other first responders who actually dealt with the crisis.

The series later became a book in Japanese, titled *The Record of a Total Power Loss*, that reconstructs in chronological order the physical efforts and inner struggles of the workers, identified by their real names, as they fought to regain control of the doomed reactors.

The workers included Fukushima Daiichi plant chief Masao Yoshida and his aides, who were collectively known as the "Fukushima 50" for their heroic determination in risking their lives to remain at the site on the morning of March 15, 2011, facing the threat of a nuclear catastrophe.

The following is an excerpt of the English version of the investigative report. Job titles, ages and company names are as of March 2011.

DAY 1

Tsunami

When the earthquake rattled TEPCO's six-reactor nuclear complex in Fukushima Prefecture, about 220 km north to Tokyo at 2:46 p.m., March 11, 2001, workers at the site did not feel any imminent danger, having no reason to believe at that time that the incident would develop into a triple reactor core meltdown disaster.

Fukushima Daiichi nuclear power plant chief Masao Yoshida entered the emergency response office on the second floor of the plant's quake-resistant building. He was relieved to confirm that the Nos. 1 to 3 reactors, which were in operation at the time, had achieved emergency shutdowns. The Nos. 4 to 6 reactors were under routine maintenance.

The TV news was showing an alert for 3-meter high tsunamis headed for Fukushima. But Yoshida did not anticipate any problem. The earthquake had knocked out external power supply, but emergency diesel generators had been activated to keep powering emergency core cooling pumps, valves and monitoring instruments.

At the main control room for the Nos. 1 and 2 reactors, Mitsuyuki Ono, a TEPCO employee who had been supervising reactor operations, activated No. 2 reactor's Reactor Core Isolation Cooling (RCIC) system. Nuclear fuel rods continue to generate massive amounts of heat even after shutdown. It was the utmost priority to cool them down.

At 2:50 p.m., Ono successfully activated the RCIC. He repeated the action to maintain water levels. The system automatically stops when a certain water level is achieved.

But the situation suddenly changed after Ono's third attempt to activate the RCIC. One operator shouted that the emergency diesel generators had stopped functioning.

As if on cue, the lights on the control panel suddenly went off one after another. Eventually they all went out and the sirens triggered by the earthquake disappeared.

Blackout

The Nos. 1 and 2 reactors had lost all power. The workers were left in the dark. Only the emergency lights were on.

None of them knew then that the tsunami was the reason for the power failure. There was no TV, nor any windows in the control room.

A young reactor operator, soaking wet, barged into the control room to say that seawater was flowing inside the buildings. It meant that the diesel generators located in the basement of the turbine building had been submerged by the tsunami.

The tsunami was more than 10 meters high. It had swamped the buildings of all six reactors, causing the loss of all power sources except for one emergency diesel generator for the No. 6 reactor.

Members at the emergency response office were stunned to hear from the Nos. 1 and 2 reactor control room that operators were facing a "station blackout."

Yoshida later revealed he thought he had to prepare for the worst. "I felt like I was told to operate a plane that lost all the engines with no monitoring instruments," he said.

DAY 2

Suicidal Mission

It was already 4 a.m., on March 12, when the water-spraying operations began at the No. 1 reactor to lower the temperature. Almost 12 hours had passed since the plant lost power.

"The radiation level was very high outside. All of the workers came back contaminated," recalled Hiroyuki Ogawa, the head of TEPCO's firefighting unit.

"The pressure of the No. 1 reactor's containment vessel was rising rapidly. There was a need to reduce the pressure before the vessel broke," said Mitsuyuki Ono. "We all knew that venting was the only way."

Somebody had to go inside the reactor building, where the radiation level was rising, to manually open the valves.

Ikuo Izawa had been instructed by the emergency response headquarters to select members to carry out the job. "Does anybody come with me? I will go first." Izawa looked around.

Venting was considered "suicidal" as it would involve a release of radioactive substances into the environment, an action that operators had been taught to avoid at all costs.

No one spoke a word until senior operators volunteered one after another, while telling Izawa to stay in the control room to manage the operation.

Ono froze. "I was scared. I might die. I thought about my family," he said.

Three teams were organized, each composed of two workers. The first team would open the valve outside the containment vessel. The second would go to the bottom area of the vessel to open another valve, while the third would act as a backup.

It was less than 12 hours after the tsunami hit the Fukushima Daiichi nuclear complex that TEPCO sought government approval for the unprecedented step of releasing radioactive steam from troubled reactors to reduce a dangerous buildup of pressure.

Prime Minister Naoto Kan, however, would soon become increasingly distrustful of TEPCO because of delays in starting the venting operations.

"TEPCO said it wanted to do venting. So I told TEPCO to do it, but they didn't," Kan recalled. "I asked why, but there wasn't a reply. I thought things would go wrong if they kept going on like this."

Frustrated by TEPCO's response, Kan left for Fukushima. The prime minister arrived at the plant shortly after 7 a.m. He had no idea at the time that nuclear fuel was already melting in the No. 1 reactor.

"What is going on?" Kan heatedly asked Yoshida in a meeting room of the emergency response office building.

Yoshida explained that because of the power loss at the No. 1 reactor, the workers would have to operate the valves manually. "We will do the venting. We will do it even if we have to form a suicide corps," Yoshida said.

At 9:04 a.m., the first team headed to the No. 1 reactor building to open a valve. When they returned to the main control room, having completed their job successfully, they had been exposed to up to 25 millisieverts of radiation.

At 9:24 a.m., the second team departed.

After opening the door to the reactor's building, Hideyoshi Endo's radiation meter jumped to 500 millisieverts per hour. When Endo was some 30 meters away from the valve, he saw the radiation meter surpass 1,000 millisieverts.

It meant Endo would have exceeded the 100-millisievert radiation dose limit a nuclear power plant worker is allowed to be exposed to in five years in just six minutes.

Endo decided to return. When the two came back, Endo reported, "It failed. The radiation meter scaled out." During the 8-minute journey, Endo was exposed to 89 millisieverts of radiation, while his colleague was exposed to 95 millisieverts.

Explosions

Yuichi Sato was heading for the Fukushima Daiichi nuclear power plant on a fire engine in the morning of March 12. He was driving through the town of Okuma, Fukushima Prefecture, where the 22-year-old was born. The familiar view was gone—the walls of houses had collapsed, roads were full of bumps and the town looked deserted.

"It was like a ghost town," Sato, of Japan's Ground Self-Defense Force's artillery regiment based in the prefecture, said.

When Sato arrived at the gate of the plant around 7 a.m., he did not know a meltdown was happening. It was only after entering the emergency response office building where the squad members told him what to do.

TEPCO was using only one fire engine to pour water into the No. 1 reactor. The water injection was interrupted with periodical water refills. The GSDF's fire engines were supposed to assist the operation.

Izawa had not given up venting the No. 1 reactor. He decided to give it another try. But only several minutes after two workers had departed for another attempt to vent, the emergency response office alerted Izawa that white smoke was coming from a 120-meter-high stack connected with the reactor's container.

"White smoke," Izawa murmured, and then screamed. "Stop them!"

At 3:36 p.m., the main control room was shaken by a blast. A hydrogen explosion had blown away the roof and walls of the No. 1 reactor building. It was the result of an accumulation of hydrogen generated from overheating fuel rods reacting with steam.

The emergency care room on the first floor of the emergency response office building was soon packed with workers. It was like a field hospital.

Mitsuyuki Ono was in the main control room for the Nos. 1 and 2 reactors. "I later found it was a hydrogen explosion. But at the time, I thought the reactor containment vessel itself had exploded. I thought it was all over."

There were some 40 reactor operators in the room. Everyone was exhausted. Izawa decided to stay with experienced workers and let the others evacuate.

Around ten workers remained. Ono and Kazuhiro Yoshida, whom Ono once worked with to operate the No. 1 reactor were among others.

Ono was thinking how he could let his family know about what he thought might be his final moments.

"Why don't we take a photo at the end," Yoshida proposed cheerfully, as if he had read Ono's mind.

Flashlights lit the dark room. "If the radiation level rises or hot steam comes into the control room, I will probably die. But someone will find the camera some day. Then this picture will be the witness to my life." Ono thought.

Water Injection

TEPCO was running out of freshwater to cool the reactor. The utility decided to use seawater that had been pooled inside a large pit near the No. 3 reactor after the tsunami. They needed the help of GSDF members.

Under the plan, a GSDF fire engine was to pump seawater from the pit and pass it on to another GSDF engine. TEPCO's fire engine would inject the seawater into the reactor.

At 7:04 p.m., seawater injection started at the No. 1 reactor.

Unknown to Sato and Arai, there was another struggle developing between the plant's emergency response office and members at the prime minister's office in Tokyo.

Plant chief Yoshida was surprised when he was ordered to suspend injecting seawater.

"Stop it immediately," Ichiro Takekuro, a senior TEPCO official who had been dispatched to the prime minister's office, ordered Yoshida around 7:20 p.m.

"Why?" asked a defiant Yoshida.

"Shut up! The prime minister's office keeps on pestering me," Takekuro hung up.

About 20 minutes before the call, Takekuro had explained to Prime Minister Kan that it would take more than an hour and a half to switch from freshwater to seawater injection at the No.1 reactor.

He thought he could not tell Kan that reactor cooling with seawater had already commenced.

Yoshida was fuming after the phone conversation. Why a decision by someone who was not at the site was being prioritized? Dissatisfied, he consulted TEPCO's head office in Tokyo. Again, Yoshida was told to stop the injection. Tokyo asked him to pretend that the injection had been done "on a trial basis."

Yoshida approached a TEPCO employee, who was supervising the seawater injection, and whispered, "No matter what happens, do not stop the injection."

At 7:25 p.m., Yoshida said in a teleconference that the ongoing "trial" seawater injection would be temporarily halted on the prime minister's order, but was expected to be resumed soon because Takekuro was negotiating resumption.

Hundreds of people at the plant's emergency response office and senior TEPCO officials in Tokyo believed the injection had been halted. Actually, the operation was never suspended.

"I felt, at the end, it had to be my decision. There was just no time for arguments," Yoshida later told his staff.

DAY 3

Reactor #3

Around 2 a.m., on March 13, the No. 3 reactor pressure began to decrease. The High Pressure Coolant Injection system was supposed to stop automatically when the pressure decreases substantially. But it did not. Fearing a system breakdown and release of steam from the reactor, senior reactor operator Kazumi Takamiya decided to manually suspend the HPCI.

Takamiya ordered workers to open valves to direct the steam inside the reactor pressure vessel to the suppression chamber. "It won't open!" an operator shouted.

Satoru Hayashizaki, an auxiliary equipment operator, was born and raised in a town less than 20 kilometers from the plant. He joined TEPCO six years ago after graduating from a local high school.

At 5:15 a.m., the control room was ordered to prepare to reduce the pressure in the No. 3 reactor's containment vessel.

Hayashizaki had instructions to go to the suppression chamber connected to the container and check if an air-operated vent valve had opened as planned.

Hayashizaki felt intense heat when he opened the door to the room housing the suppression chamber at the basement of the reactor building. "It was like being in a sauna," he said.

Cautiously, he put his right foot down onto the chamber. The rubber sole of his shoe instantly melted, leaving a black smear. He gave up checking on the valve and returned to the control room.

Hayashizaki checked his pocket dosimeter. The figures were unmistakable signs that fuel inside the No. 3 reactor was melting. Hayashizaki thought, for the first time, he could die.

He ripped off a page from his pocket planner and started writing a farewell letter to his parents in the darkness.

"Father, Mother, please forgive me for dying before I could fulfill my duty as a son. After the earthquake, I would have wished to hear your voices even once."

At 9:25 a.m., workers started injecting water into the No. 3 reactor from fire engines. More than six hours had passed since its cooling system had stopped.

DAY 4

The blast happened at 11:01 a.m. March 14 at the No. 3 reactor building. The impact was far larger than that of the previous explosion at the No. 1 reactor building, Mitsuhiro Matsumoto, a TEPCO employee said. A mushroom-like cloud of smoke rose from the building.

Matsumoto was outside at the time of both explosions. With thick dust in the air, he could not see his car about 10 meters away. When he finally reached it, he found the driver's seat had been smashed by a concrete block. "If I had been inside, I would have been killed," Matsumoto recalled.

"I have heard people in the office building saying after the nuclear accident broke out that they were prepared to die," he said, "But I wasn't prepared to die even when I actually came very close to dying. Death had stared me in the face."

Kimio Ikeda who belonged to Matsumoto's team found a time to call his wife for the first time since the nuclear crisis had begun. His wife started crying over the phone. "I cannot believe you are alive even after those explosions. You are alive!" she exclaimed.

Four TEPCO employees, three contracted workers and four GSDF members were injured due to the explosion.

Reactor #2

A cooling system for the No. 2 reactor continued to work for three days despite a power loss. The fact that the Reactor Core Isolation Cooling system lasted that long for the No. 2 reactor was a "blessed relief," plant chief Yoshida later said. Without the RCIC, the three units could have spun out of control at the same time.

But the RCIC finally stopped at 1:25 p.m., on March 14. Workers had to depressurize the reactor pressure vessel to pump in seawater to cool down the reactor. The depressurization finally started at 6:02 p.m., using car batteries to manipulate valves to release steam from the vessel.

About 20 minutes later, however, the main control room for the Nos. 1 and 2 reactors reported that the water level had sunk to 3.7 meters below the top of the fuel, meaning that the fuel was fully exposed above the water surface. There was also no sign that water was entering the reactor.

Just then, a member of TEPCO's firefighting unit returned to the building and said that the fire engines had run out of fuel.

"Didn't I tell you?" Yoshida said, looking up helplessly.

Yoshida later recalled that this felt like a "turning point." "We had run out of all options and I thought I might really die," he said.

At the emergency response office, Toshiko Kogusuri of TEPCO's management team had been secretly ordered by the team head to secure as many buses at the plant site as possible.

Just before 8 p.m., about 700 TEPCO employees and 150 workers from other companies were inside the building. More than 90 minutes had passed since water injection had stopped.

Yoshida thought he should no longer keep contract workers inside the plant site. The contract workers had all left by around 8:30 p.m., leaving only TEPCO employees at the plant.

Yoshida asked the management team head if there was any place people could take refuge. The team head told Yoshida that the Fukushima Daini (Number 2 in Japanese) plant, located about 12 kilometers south of the Daiichi plant, was ready.

At about 8 p.m., seawater injection into the No. 2 reactor started as fire engines were refueled, bringing relief to members in the emergency response office.

But the situation remained tense at the No. 2 reactor as TEPCO then faced the need to vent radioactive steam to prevent a rupture of the reactor's containment vessel, which threatened even more serious consequences.

The pressure inside the containment vessel continued to rise. Water injection had also stopped again due to the high pressure.

DAY 5

Early on March 15, members at the emergency response office were at the end of their tether and had become quiet.

Suddenly, Yoshida stood up from the center table and started staggering around. "It's all over," he murmured.

He was later quoted by his aides as saying that he was thinking about what might happen if the No. 2 reactor containment vessel failed and a massive amount of radioactive substances was released. TEPCO would have to give up handling the situation from inside the Daiichi plant and even have to abandon the plant.

Not only people in Fukushima Prefecture but also people in the area around Tokyo, about 220 kilometers away from Daiichi, might have to evacuate. But Yoshida could not think of any solution to avoid the worst.

Yoshida said afterwards he was calling to mind the faces of each of the staff he had known for a long time. "There were about ten or so. I thought those guys might be willing to die with me."

Yoshida was searching for the right time to let TEPCO employees leave the plant, except for a skeleton force to keep watching the reactors' condition and to continue water injections. There were still women at the site.

Mistrust

"I'm sorry. We are in a situation beyond our control," Susumu Kawamata, the head of TEPCO's Nuclear Quality and Safety Management Department, told industry minister Banri Kaieda before breaking down in Tokyo.

A government nuclear safety panel member who witnessed the scene thought it marked the end of one of the most prestigious companies in Japan.

Shortly after 4 a.m., on March 15, Prime Minister Kan was sitting face to face with TEPCO President Masataka Shimizu, telling him that the utility does not have the option of withdrawing its people from the plant.

It was about eight and a half hours before their meeting that TEPCO's top-level officials started considering the evacuation of its employees from the plant.

At around 7:30 p.m., on March 14, TEPCO's Managing Director Akio Komori, who was at an emergency response center set up about 5 kilometers from the plant, started discussing the situation with the officials in Tokyo.

Executive Vice President Sakae Muto was ordered to craft an evacuation plan, while plant chief Yoshida started arrangements to secure buses.

Shimizu phoned Kaieda and Chief Cabinet Secretary Yukio Edano many times to seek approval for staff withdrawal, which he called an "evacuation."

But Shimizu did not say clearly that TEPCO would keep the minimum necessary number of people inside the plant.

Kaieda thought TEPCO was seeking a "complete withdrawal" from the plant and had turned down Shimizu's request.

At around 3 a.m., on March 15, when the condition of the No. 2 reactor deteriorated, Kaieda decided to ask Kan to make a judgment.

"If they withdraw, the eastern part of Japan will be destroyed," Kan said, rejecting the idea and ordered Shimizu to come over to his office.

As Shimizu arrived, Kan immediately said, "I heard that you are thinking about a withdrawal. That's impossible."

Shimizu said in a thin voice, "We do not have in mind such a thing as withdrawal."

Officials in the prime minister's office had misunderstood TEPCO's intentions, while the utility's president was at fault for making unclear remarks.

The exchanges led Kan to launch an unprecedented accident response task force in which the government and TEPCO would jointly deal with the nuclear crisis inside the utility's head office in Tokyo.

The prime minister told Shimizu he would set up the task force and that he would go to TEPCO's head office right away.

Kan was still furious when he arrived at TEPCO headquarters, unable to conceal his distrust of the company.

"TEPCO will go 100 percent bust if it withdraws. You won't be able to escape even if you try!" Kan yelled at TEPCO Chairman Tsunehisa Katsumata, Shimizu and other executives. "It doesn't matter if senior officials in their 60s go to the site and die. I will also go. Make up your minds!" Kan shouted.

Evacuation

At the Fukushima Daiichi plant, hundreds of people inside the emergency response office were glued to the teleconference monitor showing the angry prime minister.

"We felt being shot in the back," Takeyuki Inagaki, leader of an equipment restoration teams recalled.

Yoshida was about to answer a call from Tokyo when a dull sound reached the emergency response office at about 6:14 a.m. The impact was smaller than the two previous explosions, but it was not an earthquake.

People's blood ran cold as they heard from reactor operators that the pressure inside the No. 2 reactor's suppression chamber had dropped to zero.

If the chamber was not airtight, a massive amount of highly radioactive steam could be released outside.

"The suppression chamber might have got a huge hole. A hell of a lot of radioactive substances could come out," Inagaki told Yoshida.

Yoshida instantly decided it was time for evacuation. He told TEPCO's head office in Tokyo that he had to consider evacuating many of the employees. But people in Tokyo did not share the sense of urgency.

"It doesn't make sense to remain when the radiation level rises!" Yoshida responded angrily.

All the operators overseeing the Nos. 1 to 6 reactors at the main control rooms were told to evacuate to the quake-resistant building where Yoshida was.

Yoshida checked that the wind was blowing from the northwest, meaning that TEPCO's Fukushima Daini nuclear power plant would make a safe shelter.

"Look for a place where the radiation level is low. If there is no such place, head to 2F (the Daini plant). The direction of the wind is OK," Yoshida told the leader of the evacuation team.

At 6:33 a.m., Yoshida ordered team leaders at the emergency response headquarters to decide who should stay.

But what Yoshida said about 10 minutes later, recorded by the teleconference system, was puzzling. "Evacuate to an area within the plant's premises where the radiation level is low," he said. "If the headquarters confirm there is no problem, I want you to come back."

Yoshida's staff thought that Yoshida had given such an instruction on the record for a reason. He might have tried to protect his people from being accused of running away.

Explosion at Reactor #4

Yoshida had initially believed the No. 2 reactor was in deep trouble. But operators in the main control room for the Nos. 3 and 4 reactors saw the situation differently.

At 6:14 a.m., the control room shook to the accompaniment of a booming sound. Judging from where the impact came from, Toshiyuki Tomita, who was the leader of the room at that time, told the emergency response office that "something happened at the No. 4 unit."

But the office insisted that the blast came from the No. 2 reactor.

Tomita could not understand why the sound of an explosion could be heard from the No. 4 unit. There was no fuel inside the reactor core as the unit was under maintenance on March 11.

But as he headed to the emergency response office, he saw the shattered roof and crumbled walls of the No. 4 reactor building.

When he arrived at the office at 6:55 a.m., he found the number of people at headquarters had sharply decreased. The names of the people to stay written on a whiteboard looked like grave markers.

There was no doubt that the fuel meltdown was progressing in the No. 2 reactor, in addition to the Nos. 1 and 3 reactors, as the radiation levels at the plant site were rising.

There was no longer any place inside the plant's premises where radiation level was low. "Let's head to 2F (Fukushima Daini)," the management team leader told the bus drivers.

Early in the morning of March 15, at least 71 TEPCO workers stayed at the Fukushima Daiichi nuclear complex, prepared to sacrifice their lives to bring the doomed reactors under control.

The people were lionized by foreign media as the "Fukushima 50," as TEPCO initially said some 50 workers would stay.

Having sent off the last evacuees from the emergency response office building, Toshiyuki Hayashida, a safety control team member, started writing an email to his wife. "Take care," he typed and sent that one sentence to her. He thought he might not meet his wife again.

Yoshida slowly walked around the office as if he was trying to imprint the face of each person on his mind.

At 9 a.m., the emergency response headquarters received notification that the radiation level at the plant's main gate had reached 11,930 microsieverts per hour, the highest reading measured outdoors in the area since March 11.

But regardless of the radiation level, workers had to continue refueling fire engines and monitor the conditions of the reactors.

Six members from the two equipment restoration teams stayed, including the leaders Inagaki and Shiro Hikita. "We didn't mind being killed. I felt we just could not back down," Inagaki recalled.

When Inagaki went outside for the fueling mission, he saw flames and black smoke coming from the No. 4 reactor building.

A total of 1,535 fuel rod assemblies were placed inside the spent fuel pool inside the No. 4 reactor building. If the pool dried up, exposed fuel would continuously release radiation into the atmosphere. There was no roof or walls to block the radiation because the building was damaged by an explosion that occurred at 6:14 a.m.

"A fire broke out at the No. 4 unit. 1F (Fukushima Daiichi) can't do anything. Please ask the SDF or the US military for help," Yoshida told the head office in Tokyo at 9:39 a.m.

"Is this going to be my graveyard?" Arai thought.

Signs of Stability

But not everything was going badly. The radiation level near the plant's main gate was gradually falling. "The situation is not getting that much worse," Yoshida told Susumu Kunito, who agreed. Inagaki, who joined the conversation, said the radiation level remained high, but it was not impossible to do work around the reactor buildings.

The three were starting to feel the situation might not be as critical as before. If people were brought back, they could prevent the situation from deteriorating, they thought. "Get back several guys we need!" Yoshida ordered.

Kunito, Hikita and others started calling workers who had evacuated to Fukushima Daini nuclear power plant.

Hiraku Isogai, a member of the electricity equipment restoration team, received a call. "We are somehow OK. Would you come back?" his colleague at the Daiichi plant asked. Isogai said he would without hesitation.

Isogai asked other members to come with him. Some refused. He could not blame them. Five or six agreed to go back.

In the morning of March 15, members of the equipment restoration team and others started returning to the Fukushima Daiichi plant. It was yet another beginning of an unprecedented struggle to calm down a man-made monster that is not only not over yet, but would continue for several decades into the future.

Chief's Departure

About nine months after the Fukushima Daiichi nuclear power plant accident occurred, Yoshida retired as plant chief.

He had been diagnosed with esophageal cancer, discovered during a health check in November 2011.

But even before he came to know of his illness, Yoshida had thought about quitting TEPCO to take responsibility for ignoring a government order to suspend injecting seawater into the troubled No. 1 reactor.

Media reported on May 20 that Prime Minister Kan had ordered a halt to the seawater injection. TEPCO said six days later that Yoshida's earlier report was false and that he had actually continued injecting seawater.

"I am thinking about quitting and starting a company," Yoshida said one day in June to Shiro Hikita, his friend and most trusted staff he had worked with to contain the crisis.

Yoshida did not quit after all, and was verbally reprimanded by the utility for giving a false explanation.

In February 2012, Yoshida underwent surgery.

When Yoshida was in the hospital, he sent an e-mail to Hikita. It depicted how Yoshida felt the morning of the evacuation day.

"I was determined to evacuate everyone but you and me if the situation further worsened. We couldn't leave the plant empty, could we? Please apologize to your wife. I'm sorry", the message said.

"Who is willing to die with me?" Yoshida's words came back to Hikita.

Yoshida passed away at the age of 58 on July 9, 2013, after going through three more operations. He was found to have had a recurrence of cancer.

Further Reading

Kadota, R. (2014) *On the Brink: The Inside Story of Fukushima Daiichi* (Translator Simon Varnam), Tokyo: Kurodahan Press.

Lochbaum, D., Lyman, E., Stranahan, S. Q., and the Union of Concerned Scientists. (2015) *Fukushima: The Story of a Nuclear Disaster*, New York: The New Press.

Rissman, R. (2016) *Swept Away: The Story of the 2011 Japanese Tsunami* (Tangled History Series), Mankato, MN: Capstone Press.

34

MEDIA INTERVENTIONS AS HUMANITARIAN ACTION

Shawn Powers

Introduction

This chapter outlines how information interventions—extensive external management, manipulation or seizure of information space in conflict or disaster zones—can be conceived of as humanitarian action. Building on the work of Metzl (1997) and Price and Thompson (2002), I highlight the various ways in which state and intergovernmental actors intervene in foreign environments in times of conflict and crisis to introduce information technologies, institutions, and content for the purpose of providing humanitarian and emergency relief. While media interventions are often studied through the lens of propaganda, I argue that these strategic communication campaigns can have significant humanitarian import, and impact, while also serving a collective, social good. Highlighting such programs will not only make the case of seeing media policy as a direct part of the humanitarian action tool-kit (as opposed to it being simply a variable in the broader humanitarian action equation), but also calls for an uncolored theoretical approach to studying state-led strategic communication campaigns.

Related to information interventions is the study of public diplomacy, defined as "an international actor's attempt to manage the international environment through engagement with a foreign public" (Cull 2009, 12). This broad analytic category describes a variety of ways in which international engagement serves geostrategic purposes, from nation branding to gastro-diplomacy. Public diplomacy programs typically include long-term, broad campaigns, aimed at building relationships or constituencies, and are implemented in coordination (to a certain extent) with the government of the target country. Given the long-term nature of these endeavors, it can be difficult to assess short-term effectiveness. Information interventions, on the other hand, are typically targeted, strategic, limited, tangible, and emphasize achievable goals.

For clarity, I define information interventions as: (a) governmental efforts to (b) disseminate or disrupt media flows or consumption (not merely gathering intelligence), (c) lacking a target government's explicit consent, (d) for the primary purpose of altering an information ecosystem (infrastructure or content). Information interventions typically aim to raise awareness, change opinions, attitudes, and/or behavior favoring domestic reform, regime change, or atrocity and violence prevention.

While information interventions are utilized in a variety of contexts, my focus is on how, why, and to what effect, states use media interventions for the purpose of preventing the escalation of violence, providing crucial information in the immediate aftermath of a humanitarian catastrophe, or offering depoliticized, fact-based news and information in conflict-prone or post-conflict communities. Focusing on the potential for information interventions in the pursuit of conflict cessation is intentional. While it is well known how governments use strategic communication campaigns in pursuit of war and violence, far less attention has been dedicated to the peacebuilding capacities of media interventions. This is not to discount the tremendous work done on the weaponization of information (see Tumber and Webster 2006; Hoskins and Ben O'Loughlin 2010) and media imperialism (see Schiller 1976, 1999; Mattelart 2003; Hill 2007; Winseck and Pike 2007); rather, it aims to restore some balance to the analytic category of propaganda (for example, see Ellul 1973). Put another way, the existence of violent strategic information campaigns does not discount the possibility of strategic communication for the pursuit of conflict resolution and in support of humanitarian action. Indeed, researchers have a responsibility to highlight the potential and real productive capabilities of such programs, as they typically do not receive the media or public attention compared to stories of information and cyber warfare.

The concept of media or information intervention as humanitarian action was brought to the mainstream after the 1996 Rwandan genocide, when Hutu-hardliners used Radio-Télévision Libre des Milles Collines to organize militias and goad youth into killing by "reading lists of enemies to be hunted down and butchered" (Metzl 1997, 15). Despite knowledge of the extremist broadcasts, and evidence of their inciting ethnically targeted violence, the international community refused to jam the radio signals for fear of interfering with another government's right to information sovereignty. The United States, in particular, was concerned with how jamming would impact its efforts to promote unfettered freedom of expression around the world. The decision to not intervene—either by jamming the inciting broadcasts, or with a robust peacekeeping force—meant that the world stood by while 800,000 Tutsis and moderate Hutus were killed. General Romeo Dallaire, Force Commander to the United Nations Assistance Mission for Rwanda (UNAMIR I), argued that simply jamming Hutu broadcasts and replacing them with messages of peace and reconciliation would have significantly altered the course of events, saving hundreds of thousands of lives (Dallaire 2003). The case of Rwanda, as well as the former Yugoslavia, coupled with the emergence of low-cost and mobile connective technologies, has driven policymakers to consider more and more the role of direct information intervention for the purpose of humanitarian action.

Two case studies are explored in empirical detail to investigate how information interventions can serve direct humanitarian and peacebuilding purposes. The first case study explores efforts to re-establish telecommunications services in Haiti in 2010, and the use of the rejuvenated information infrastructure to disseminate crucial, and timely information regarding relief services and aid, as well as coordinate the broader network of relief services operating in the country. The second case study outlines multinational efforts to support local, fact-based and non-sensational news and information programming in Syria between 2011 and 2015, with a particular focus on support for establishing and securing information infrastructures capable of amplifying independent and organic Syrian civil society. Distinct from the traditional tools for strategic influence (i.e., Voice of America, Radio France

International, etc.), foreign governments supported the provision of technical support and training for Syrians eager to gather and disseminate stories not directly crafted for the purpose of spreading a particular ideology or political message.[1] Case studies are drawn from a combination of archival research and interviews with practitioners directly involved in each of the interventions.

Haiti

On January 12, 2010, a 7.0 magnitude earthquake rattled Haiti, destroying approximately 250,000 residences, 30,000 commercial buildings, and affecting at least three million Haitians. Haiti is the poorest country in the Western hemisphere and one in five Haitians were left homeless. The earthquake—including 52 aftershocks that followed—severely damaged the vital infrastructure necessary to respond to the disaster, including all hospitals in the capital city, Port-au-Prince. Air, sea, and land transport facilities, and most major communication systems were also destroyed. Worse, the very actors who would normally lead in coordinating the response were themselves victims of the earthquake. National and municipal government buildings were destroyed and many civil servants died, were injured, or justifiably occupied caring for their own families.

Given the scale of the devastation, and the urgency of the situation, governments around the world moved swiftly. Neighboring Dominican Republic was the first to act, sending water, food and heavy lifting machinery, as well as opening its hospitals and airports to support the relief effort. Iceland and China each sent emergency response teams to Port-au-Prince, landing within 36 hours of the disaster. Qatar sent a strategic transport aircraft (C-17), loaded with 50 tons of relief materials, along with Qatari military, internal security and police forces, as well as personnel from the Hamad Medical Corporation. The Israeli Defense Force set up a field hospital specializing in treating children, the elderly, and women in labor. A Korean International Disaster Relief Team, including 40 rescuers, medical doctors, nurses, and two k-9s was deployed to assist the Haitian Government. All told, governments, intergovernmental organizations, NGOs, and the private sector gave $13 billion towards Haiti's immediate relief and long-term reconstruction.

Crucial to the early stages of the relief effort was restoring Haitians' capacities to impart and receive information. According to Mindal De La Torre, Chief of the Federal Communication Commission's (FCC) International Bureau, after the earthquake, "anything that made the [communications] network work . . . was just completely gone." For example, as a result of the total destruction of major telecommunications facilities, Haiti's wired telephone system was entirely inoperable (International Bureau and Public Safety and Homeland Security Bureau 2010). The only submarine cable providing Haiti direct international wired connectivity was also severely damaged at its landing site near Port-au-Prince. Put simply, Haiti's communications infrastructure was "essentially broken" (Jackson 2010).

This had direct and severe implications for the relief effort. According to International Telecommunications Union official Cosmas Zavazava, "Telecommunications is essentially the basic link to co-ordinate any form of assistance" (Marow 2010). Coordinating relief operations requires basic communications infrastructure, but considering the dozens, and eventually hundreds, of government and non-government actors operating in the space, as well as a crippled physical infrastructure and local government, establishing reliable communications networks was deemed crucial.

Telecommunications support came in three waves: (1) re-establishing the means for real-time communication in order to stand up and implement the relief effort; (2) re-establishing and improving the means for Haitians to impart and receive information about their safety, needs, and where to find help if needed; (3) re-building Haiti's telecommunications infrastructure for long-term safety and expanded use.

The U.S. military spearheaded the initial effort to re-establish reliable lines of communication. The first priority was to get Port-au-Prince International Airport back online so that the international community could land planes with humanitarian and emergency supplies. While the earthquake did not damage the runway, the control tower's communication systems were destroyed. United States Southern Command used a Coast Guard Major Cutter to stand in for air traffic control in the immediate aftermath of the earthquake. The Department of Defense (DoD) was able to repair the control tower and re-establish normal air traffic control operations within two days of the disaster (Fraser 2010). The U.S. Coast Guard also led efforts to restore the Haitian national police's Land Mobile Radio (LMR) network, the backbone of the country's emergency response communications system (e.g., 911) (McClain 2010).

As soon as the Port-au-Prince International Airport was operational, the UN dispatched a cargo plane from Brindisi, Italy, jammed with several thousand mobile phones and a two-ton container-based mini GSM system for mobile communications. Sweden's Ericsson donated the unit capable of supporting data and calls for up to 5000 devices. The International Telecommunications Union (ITU) supplemented the Ericsson unit by setting up a Qualcomm Deployable Base Station (QDBS), a complete cellular system designed to enable vital wireless communications aimed at strengthening response and recovery mechanisms in a disaster zone. The ITU also sent 100 satellite telephone and broadband terminals to help stand up relief efforts in the direct aftermath of the earthquake (ITU 2010).

Telecoms Sans Frontières, a UN-funded international relief organization, was the first entity into Haiti (the day after the earthquake) to provide emergency telecommunications via Broadband Global Area Network (BGAN) terminals. The devices provided a mobile hookup for phone or data communication through the Inmarsat satellite network. China, via its ZTE Corporation, delivered 1500 solar-powered GSM handsets, 300 Global Open Trunking Architecture (GoTa) command and dispatch systems (8900 Series; 800MHz), as well as mobile diesel engines to power the systems directly to the Haitian government. NetHope, an NGO funded primarily by USAID and American technology companies, established a network of VSAT dishes and WiMax wireless networks around Port-au-Prince to expand the speed and range of connectivity, facilitating GIS mapping, FTP for videos and photos, as well as standard voice and data exchange. Combined, these contributions established a basic infrastructure for NGOs and governments to coordinate their relief efforts moving forward.

The insertion of such a variety of communications systems into a foreign context raises various technical and legal questions. Launching self-standing telecommunications services, for example, requires spectrum to operate. Yet, at the same time, the Haitian communications regulatory agency—Conseil National des Télécommunications (CONATEL)—was itself crippled and overwhelmed by the scale of the catastrophe. As a result, the FCC took the lead in assessing, repairing, and improving the legal and technical architecture constituting Haiti's telecommunications infrastructure. A first FCC team from the US deployed to Haiti days after the earthquake to support a FEMA Mobile Emergency Response Team, followed by a larger FCC team that conducted a detailed damage assessment and recommended reconstruction projects. Subsequent teams conducted spectrum assessments and helped to restart broadcasts in northern Haiti (De La Torre 2011). The FCC also eased the procedures for satellite communication providers to increase coverage over the areas affected by the earthquake, including issuing special temporary authorities (STAs) to increase available satellite capacity.[2] This was the first time the FCC had ever participated in a humanitarian disaster outside of the United States.

By the end of January, CONATEL and the FCC signed a "Memorandum of Understanding (MOU) Regarding Communications Regulatory Cooperation," whereby the FCC agreed to assist in ongoing assessment of the needs of the communications sector in Haiti, spectrum management, licensing policies and procedures, human resource capacity building, as well as other regulatory issues as needed (De La Torre 2010).

Despite the attention these new media initiatives received (e.g., Ushahidi), the significance of these initiatives was, in some cases, overstated. This is because, in Haiti, radio is the most utilized means of mass communication. Before the quake, over 250 community and commercial radio stations operated, and radio ownership was nearly universal (Gallup 2012). Thus, "radio [was] the undisputed lifeline for the Haitian public after the earthquake" (Nelson and Patel 2011, 11). As Haiti's radio signals went back online, they became the country's central information network. "Collectively, these groups put together a remarkable range of information and communications responses" (Ibid., 10).

Restoring information systems was just the beginning. With over three million Haitians impacted by the catastrophe, it was also crucial to establish improved lines for direct, multidirectional communications. With damaged mobile telephony systems and a lack of power to charge mobile phones, the relief effort turned to radio-based communications. For example, the U.S. Air Force, working with Joint Task Force Haiti, delivered 50,000 handheld radios to survivors to help in identifying people in need of evacuation, sustenance or medical treatment. The solar-powered and hand-cranked radios were able to charge cell phones through use of a USB port, thus having a broader, layered means of enabling Haitian communications. Internews, a non-profit organization funded primarily by USAID, distributed an additional 9,000 wind-up radios.

With Haitian broadcast infrastructure severely limited, US Air Force Special Operations Command dispatched its EC-130J "Commando Solo" plane to relay news and information to survivors from the skies over Haiti. This modified aircraft broadcast Voice of America call-in shows in Creole, Haiti's national language, over three AM and FM radio frequencies (92.4 FM, 104.1 FM, 1030 AM). During breaks in the live programming, the plane broadcasted public health and safety messages and other information regarding relief efforts.[3] In addition, partnering with the Louisiana Association of Broadcasters, the FCC helped to establish public safety radio stations in two rural cities so that the Government of Haiti could begin relocating displaced citizens from relief camps in Port-au-Prince.

Individual and eyewitness on-the-ground accounts of the devastation were helpful, but painted an incomplete picture of the damage and needs of the Haitian population. Thus, the U.S. military diverted a high-flying spy drone, the RQ-4 Hawk, from Afghanistan, to surveil and assess the damage. The drone took over a thousand photos a day, all of which were unclassified and shared with the broader disaster relief community to assist in coordinating their relief efforts in reaching the worst hit places (Hodge 2010a). The images also provided valuable operational intelligence for relief workers. For example, when drone images showed a large number of people had fled to sports stadiums, relief workers set up food and water delivery hubs nearby. The images were also crucial in helping relief groups determine the most suitable places to set up their headquarters upon arriving in Port-au-Prince.

Crucially, these efforts had impact. According to Commando Solo's Lieutenant Colonel Mike Rice, "it was pretty evident that we were making a difference." When the relief organizations had to change a point of aid delivery, for example, a Commando Solo plane would broadcast the information; and within hours, Haitians would start forming queues at the new distribution point. According to Rice, "Haiti was one of the few times where we got clear feedback" (Hodge 2010b). FCC International Bureau Chief Mindel De La Torre similarly noted the significance in establishing telecommunications provisions for all Haitians. When he first arrived, "people were milling around and there was no hope." As communications systems were established, and connectivity improved, Haitians became more optimistic. Connectivity was seen as fundamental as other elements central to any relief effort. According to De La Torre, "more often than not, when a Haitian victim was asked whether they wanted bread or a phone, they wanted a phone" (Jackson 2010).

Syria

So much attention has been focused on the violence taking place in Syria, and the various geopolitical actors supporting different sides of the civil war. This focus is certainly warranted, as the conflict is fundamentally a political one, driven by desires for resources and power. On the humanitarian side, however, the European and North American governments have been investing heavily in building communications capacities and infrastructure among members of Syria's civil society in order to create an architecture for long-term and lasting peace once there is a negotiated end to the violence. Operating alongside, and in addition to more traditional forms of humanitarian aid, this information intervention is purposefully considered humanitarian in its own right, aiming to help Syria's capacity to hold those guilty of grotesque violence accountable and to cultivate the organs necessary for a healthy democratic society.

Beginning in 2009, the U.S. State Department began investing in its internet freedom agenda, promoting connectivity as a means for economic, political, and social modernization. Grounded in humanitarian discourse and norms, Secretary of State Hillary R. Clinton saw internet freedom as a compelling and pervasive narrative to legitimize a variety of efforts dubbed "21st Century Statecraft," or the geostrategic use of information communication technologies (ICTs) in pursuit of national interests (Powers and Jablonski 2015). While well intentioned, and closely aligned with international protections guarding the right to access to and expression of information, internet freedom programs ranged from supporting privacy protecting applications (e.g., Tor) to smuggling internet-enabled satellites into non-democratic countries to support dissident political movements. One project in particular, Internet in a Suitcase, received media attention in 2011 as having the potential to circumvent governmental efforts to cut off connectivity during political protest or conflict.

The Internet in a Suitcase project was housed at the New America Foundation, based in Washington DC, and had a fairly simple goal: create software that's simple to install and operate, enabling the creation of shared local networks, or mesh networks for short. According to Internet in a Suitcase engineer Brian Duggan:

> The idea is that the system will automatically set itself up. Drop a unit near another unit and they'll start talking to one another and trading data . . . Add a thousand and you can cover a whole city. Then if one of those routers is hooked up to an internet connection, everyone on the network can connect.
>
> (Singel 2011)

By transforming mobile telephones and computers into autonomous networked technologies, Mesh networks allow information to hop directly between the devices, turning each into a mini cell tower, requiring no centralized network hub or static operator.

The State Department funded the Internet in a Suitcase project, and other similar pro-grams, to re-create infrastructures for connectivity among citizens facing information blackouts. There was particular interest in how such programs could help tilt the odds in favor of civil society or opposition actors in conflict-torn regions such as the Middle East. For example, in 2011, faced with a Gadhafi-imposed internet blackout, Libyan rebel groups in Benghazi worked with State Department experts to reestablish internet access in eastern Libya. Re-routed through Egypt's telecommunications infrastructure, opposition groups were able to coordinate and share crucial information while Gadhafi assumed the groups were crippled by their inability to communicate with the outside world. As a result of the State Department's intervention, Gadhafi's forces were caught off guard, thinking that opposition groups remained offline and segregated, and were eventually overwhelmed by a rebel force backed with international air and logistical support (U.S. Department of State, n.d.).[4]

Energized by the significance of ICTs in contributing to political speech and protest during the Arab Spring, the State Department was keen to bring the internet freedom mission to Syria at the outset of its civil war in 2011. Constrained by a commander in chief hesitant to get militarily involved in the conflict, the Department of State was tasked to work with foreign governments and NGOs in providing non-lethal support for Syrian rebel groups and political dissidents. According to Clinton, most of the $500 million nonlethal aid went to equipping and training civil society groups on the latest connective technologies (Miller 2012, Blanchard et al. 2015).[5] To name a few, communications aid included: satellite phones (900 in 2012 alone); Astra 2 portable satellite receivers; laptops; thousands of meters of cable to connect rooftop satellite receivers to laptops; and mobile radio transmitters and receivers. Training was also offered to activists not only on how to use the equipment properly, but also on the importance of using encryption and coded language when communicating over unsecured channels. The true amount of aid provided is, at this juncture, hard to determine, as governments utilized numerous proxy organizations (e.g., Access Research Knowledge, Center for International Private Enterprise, International War and Peace Reporting, International Research and Exchange Board, International Republican Institute, Internews, National Democratic Institute, Freedom House, U.S. Institute of Peace, and others) to assist in resource dissemination and training on the ground within Syria.

At the outset of Syria's civil war, foreign broadcasts were strictly banned, its information infrastructure was highly centralized and vulnerable to governmental controls, and foreign journalists were under severe threats of violence and persecution, placing Syria's media among the least free in the entire world. Thus, substantial aid was also provided to support independent media (radio and television), including mentoring to Arab media experts in Syria, training for networks of citizen journalists and activists to document violence and other atrocities, and technical assistance to support information security among activists and journalists within Syria. This aid built on nearly a decade of assistance from the US Middle East Partnership Initiative (MEPI), which funded Syrian activists and opinion leaders to help build and maintain robust, independent media and civil society organizations (Whitlock 2011). By 2015, the U.S. Department of State's Bureau of Conflict and Stabilization Operations was funding training programs and technological infrastructure support for 12 newly established, independent radio and television stations (Dollet 2015).[6]

ICT training and equipment served two additional purposes. First, it enabled Syrians to coordinate, even during government-imposed internet blackouts, including providing warnings to civilians about approaching Syrian troops or missiles, and sharing locations of medical facilities and available aid. Second, it was used to document the brutality of Bashar

Al-Assad's violent crackdown, and to share news of the violence, to hopefully apply pressure on Assad and, eventually, hold him and his confederates accountable. For example, working with the Syria Justice and Accountability Centre (SJAC), the US and UK have supported efforts to document violations and abuses of international human rights law committed by all sides of the conflict.

US and European technical, logistical, and financial assistance helped build resilience and the capacity for civil society actors to advocate on behalf of their communities, build trust and tolerance, and mitigate the likelihood of prolonged conflict. Specifically, the ICTs enhanced linkages between Syrian activists, human rights organizations, and independent media outlets and empowered women leaders to play a more active role in transition planning. According to US Ambassador to the UN Susan Rice (2012):

> We are proud to help train civil society activists and to provide Syrians with equipment that lets them communicate securely with one another, to reach out to the outside world, and to document the regime's atrocities . . . We will continue to expand and intensify these efforts and we will not rest until the Syrian people are free to realize their aspirations to govern themselves and live without fear.

To elaborate, I will briefly outline several examples of support for media training and information dissemination that stand out as having a lasting value to Syria's citizenry. International Media Support, a non-profit organization based in Copenhagen, Denmark, and funded by the Danish, French, Swedish, and Norwegian Foreign Ministries, launched Radio Rozana (rozana.fm). Radio Rozana is a community-based news organization aiming to provide independent news and unique perspectives from Syria with the help of 70 local journalists across the country, a handful of which defected from Syria's state news and information agencies. Rozana's journalists receive independent and recurring training from Reporters Sans Frontières[7] to ensure professional and independent reporting techniques are utilized throughout their coverage. Available via FM broadcasts, as well as via satellite and the internet, Rozana deviates from opposition and state media by focusing on providing a depoliticized, human-centered news agenda. Programming revolves around Syrians' daily lives, and their stories, with journalists identifying and highlighting successful projects and developments in order to inspire similar initiatives moving forward. The station also provides its listeners with practical advice, including how to illuminate homes without electricity, and keep children warm and well-nourished with limited access to resources (Syria Untold 2013).

Outside of government-controlled areas, intermittent and unreliable access to electricity and the internet elevated radio as an important medium for daily access to reliable news and information (MICT 2014). At the same time, years of escalating violence and shifting alliances and territories have made it incredibly difficult to coordinate the allocation of broadcast spectrum, and nearly impossible to maintain the security of the broadcast infrastructure. In 2013, the German Federal Foreign Office funded the creation of the Syrian Radio Network Initiative (SYRNET), via the Media in Cooperation and Transition (MICT), to coordinate the distribution of radio transmitters and spectrum between independent radio broadcasters and help maintain the integrity of the broadcast system. SYRNET has since helped to "diversify the information sources on the airwaves and help media producers increase their professionalism" by allocating frequencies, negotiating content sharing between news organizations, establishing shared principles for professional journalism, and maintaining the security of broadcast transmitters (Dollet 2015, 8). For example, each of the nine radio stations involved in the project agreed on a code of conduct,[8] including: balanced reporting; respect for privacy and accuracy; and avoiding discrimination on ethnic or sectarian basis, and the glorification of violence.

Arguably, the most significant foreign interventions into Syria's information ecology are not with state-funded programming, but rather initiatives propping up a communications architecture capable of amplifying authentic and organic Syrian voices. For example, central to SYRNET's effectiveness is its installation of mobile and mini-FM transmitters throughout Syria. The broadcast architecture is secured from ISIS (Daesh) and government attacks by the fact that SYRNET's sponsor (MICT) has exclusive knowledge of the location and movement of its mobile and micro antennas.[9] Backed with European Union funding, France's Media Development Agency, Canal France International (CFI) is working with Emirati-based Broadcast Systems Arabia to set-up a similar coordinating agency to strengthen broadcasting in northern Syria, including in ISIS-controlled territories. Related, Dutch-funded Radio Netherlands Worldwide sent a "Radio in a Box" stand-alone, mobile broadcasting unit to Aleppo to assist in maintaining independent broadcasts after local radio infrastructure was damaged.

Foreign donors have also been eager to capitalize on the opportunities that new and mobile media technologies offer in destabilized conflict zones. The Democracy Council,[10] a proxy group funded by the US State Department and tasked to fund local civil society organizations operating in conflict zones, supports the Center for Civil Society and Democracy in Syria (CCSDS). CCDSD launched The Women for the Future of Syria (WFS) program, which in turn created "Lahoon Wa Bas" (*Enough is Enough*), a web portal and application to protest and report the violations of extremist groups against citizens and activists. Lahoon Wa Bas activists use social media to inform other organizations of what is going on, they send information to Syrian civil society abroad who will circulate it and ask for investigation. The Democracy Council also supports a range of independent and opposition broadcast media programs, including Barada TV, which is closely affiliated with the Syrian Exile-led Movement for Justice and Development. In 2011, Barada TV was central to advising Syrians on tactics for filming protests and violence safely, while simultaneously broadcasting citizen-produced content and setting the regional news agenda (Amos 2011).

While it is hard to measure effectiveness given the continued state of Syria's conflict, there are indications that foreign support for information operations inside Syria have been productive. In March 2011, prior to the Syrian uprising, local, independent civil society organizations were virtually non-existent.[11] A 1958 law—no. 93—required that all civil society organizations be approved by the security services, while criminalizing cooperation with foreign governments and the receipt of funds from abroad.[12] Since the beginning of the war, foreign assistance helped build the capacity of a network of more than 3,000 grassroots activists from more than 400 opposition councils and organizations from around the country, linking Syrian citizens with the national and local level Syrian opposition (U.S. Department of State 2014). By 2016, researchers identified over 900 Syrian civil society organizations working in or directly surrounding the country (Citizens for Syria 2016). An independent survey of the state of Syrian civil society conducted in 2014 found that, as a result of growing access to pluralistic information flows

> the one positive phenomenon Syria is experiencing today is the rise of a dynamic, grassroots-based civil society embodying strong potential for positive change inspired by the notions of justice, equality, freedom, democracy and citizenship. The emergence of civil society has already contributed to containing the process of

fragmentation along ethnic, sectarian, political and ideological lines, and continues to do so today despite the prevailing climate of violence.

(Khalaf et al. 2014, 50)

Conclusion

This chapter aims to introduce the concept of an information intervention as an example of humanitarian action. Typically associated negatively with government efforts to incite conflict and tension, two case studies are explored—Haiti and Syria—to better understand how state-led information interventions can contribute to the restoration of normalcy (Haiti) and the development of community-led civil society (Syria). Of course, both Haiti and Syria remain in flux, making it difficult to draw firm conclusions on the efficacy of these efforts. That said, in both cases, there is evidence of effectiveness. Reports from Haiti indicate that the information intervention provided a crucial backbone for additional humanitarian relief, without which Haitians would have faced far worse devastation. In Syria, the emergence of a robust civil society sector, despite the fact that nearly half of Syrians are now internally or externally displaced, speaks to the capacity for open communications mediums and technologies to facilitate productive storytelling and information sharing.

These examples are not meant to combat the fact that many government-initiated strategic communication programs can and do cause harm. Nor are they meant to distract from the fact that dependence on Western media systems and content can have negative impacts on local culture and language preservation. Yet, at the same time, it is important to highlight, and encourage, the positive impact that information interventions can have when structured as humanitarian assistance. Highlighting media interventions as part of the humanitarian action tool-kit should broaden the spectrum of possible approaches to addressing ongoing and future humanitarian disasters.

Given the nature of an intervention as an exception to the rule (e.g., compelling a temporary and limited cessation of sovereignty), to be properly incorporated into the system of laws and norms governing the international system, an information intervention requires justification. Just as a humanitarian intervention is justified by evidence of a government's unwillingness or inability to protect its citizenry from serious harm, an information intervention needs similar evidence if it is to become a recognized and legitimate tool of foreign policy. Put another way, articulating information operations as interventions provides an international legal context for the growing use of information as a weapon of war. Whereas discussions of "propaganda" struggle to move beyond simple questions of definition, the category of intervention provides an analytical tool to provide some definitional and legal clarity to this otherwise muddled area of foreign policy.

Notes

1. This distinction is not meant to indicate that the humanitarian approach to information intervention is devoid of strategic intentions or implications. In general, states fund information interventions, including those of a humanitarian intent, for strategic reasons. See M. Price (2003) *Media and Sovereignty*, Cambridge, MA: MIT Press.
2. Initially, the FCC team deployed prior to establishing contact with the Director General of Haiti's regulator, CONATEL. Contact was established two days after the FCC's arrival in Port-au-Prince, when the FCC team provided the Director General with an Iridium satellite phone which enabled him to stay in contact with FCC staff at headquarters. See Richard Lee (2010). "And Now Haiti, Part One." FCC Blog, February 17, available at: http://reboot.fcc.gov/blog/?entryId=171839
3. Commando Solo has been deployed in a variety of conflict and post-conflict environments; Haiti was its first purely humanitarian mission.

4. When Gaddafi tried to cut Libyan citizens off from the internet during the civil war in 2011, Benghazi-based telecom engineer Khaled el Mufti relied on Alec Ross and his technology and innovation team at the US State Department to negotiate with the Egyptians to provide access to a telecom switch. See S. I. Stirland (2013) "Alec Ross, Leaving State Department for Private Sector, Talks '21st-Century Statecraft,'" *TechPresident*, March 11, available at: http://techpresident.com/news/wegov/23594/alec-ross-qa

5. This is in addition to over US$4.5 billion the US government has provided Syria in the form of direct humanitarian aid. See: USAID Press Office (2015) United Stats Announces Additional Humanitarian Aid for Syria Crisis. September 21, available at: www.usaid.gov/news-information/press-releases/sep-21-2015-united-states-announces-additional-humanitarian-aid-syria-crisis

6. Ten radio stations and two TV stations. Funding provided via U.S. government subcontractors Access Research Knowledge (ARK) and Creative Associates International.

7. Training takes place in Turkey, with new training sessions scheduled about every two months. Reporters Sans Frontières is an international non-profit, non-governmental organization that promotes and defends freedom of information and freedom of the press. See https://rsf.org/en

8. SYRNET Journalistic Code of Ethics states: (a) Unconfirmed reports, rumors or assumptions must be quoted as such; (b) The basic facts of the story must be carefully checked in respect of accuracy in the light of existing circumstances; (c) Refrain from vituperating against religious, ethnic groups, women and refrain from any kind of hate speech; (d) Respect the private life of the person and his/her right to self-determination about personal information and intellectual property; (e) Seeking to an honest, fair and convenient coverage; (f) No call for violence or participation in armed activities; (g) No support for extremists activities and radical thoughts.

9. SYRNET currently broadcasts programs from stations including: Rozana FM, Radio Rooh, Radio Al-Assima, Hara FM, Nasaem Syria, and Sout Raya4. The micro-antennas, or "Pocket FMs," are Raspberry Pi-operated transmitters tasked to rebroadcast content from a satellite feed onto a FM frequency while running on 12 volts electricity, typically via solar power or a car battery. The Pocket FM's are GSM-enabled, and can be controlled via SMS (text) messages. For more information, see www.mict-international.org/projects/syrnet-syrian-radio-network/

10. According to leaked cables from Wikileaks, the State Department funnels money to exile groups via the Democracy Council, a Los Angeles-based nonprofit. The April 2009 cable from the U.S. Embassy in Damascus states that the Democracy Council received US$6.3 million from the State Department to run a Syria-related program called the "Civil Society Strengthening Initiative." That program is described as "a discrete collaborative effort between the Democracy Council and local partners" to produce, among other things, "various broadcast concepts." Other cables make clear that one of those concepts was Barada TV. Our understanding is that the aforementioned Democracy Council grant is used for this purpose and passes the MEPI grant money on to the MJD.

11. This does not include GONGOs (governmental non-governmental organizations), or groups formed under the supervision of the Assad government in an effort to make Syria appear to be embracing democratic reforms.

12. Foreign funds could be accepted under strict conditions, with prior government approval, which rarely was given after the law was enacted in 1958. While some civil society groups emerged in the 1990s, their members were subjected to persecution and arrest by the security services. For example, see: US Department of State (2010) 2010 Human Rights Report: Syria, April 8, Washington, DC, available at: www.state.gov/j/drl/rls/hrrpt/2010/nea/154473.htm

References

Amos, D. (2011) "Barada TV Puts Syria's 'YouTube Revolution' On Air," *All Things Considered* (National Public Radio), June 13, available at: www.npr.org/2011/06/13/137154947/barada-tv-puts-syrias-youtube-revolution-on-air

Blanchard, C., Humud, C., and Mikitin, M. B. (2015) "Armed Conflict in Syria: Overview and U.S. Response," *Congressional Research Service*, 7–5700, October 9, available at: www.fas.org/sgp/crs/mideast/RL33487.pdf

Citizens for Syria. (2016) "Mapping the Syrian Civil Society Actors: Phase One," Berlin, available at: https://citizensforsyria.org/OrgLiterature/CfS-mapping-phase1-EN.pdf

Cull, N. J. (2009) "Public Diplomacy: Lessons from the Past," *CPD Perspectives on Public Diplomacy*, Los Angeles, CA: Figueroa Press.

Dallaire, R. (2003) *Shake Hands with the Devil: The Failure of Humanity in Rwanda*. Toronto: Vintage Canada.

De La Torre, M. (2010) "Helping Haiti: The FCC's Work with Conatel," *FCC Blog*, February 19, available at: www.fcc.gov/news-events/blog/2010/02/19/helping-haiti-fccs-work-conatel

De La Torre, M. (2011) "Haiti's Earthquake: One Year After," *FCC Blog*, January 18, available at: www.fcc.gov/news-events/blog/2011/01/18/haitis-earthquake-one-year-after

Department of State, Bureau of Democracy, Human Rights, and Labor, (2014) Written Testimony for Assistant Secretary Tom Malinowski. Senate Foreign Relations Committee hearing on "ISIL's Reign of Terror: Confronting the Growing Humanitarian Crisis in Iraq and Syria." December 9, Subcommittee on International Operations and Organizations, Human Rights, Democracy, and Global Women's Issues.

Dollet, S. (2015) *The New Syrian Radio Stations: Appraisal, Challenges, and Outlook*, Canal France International, July, available at: www.cfi.fr/sites/default/files/study_on_the_New-Syrian_radios_stations.pdf

Ellul, J. (1973) *Propaganda: The Formation of Men's Attitudes*. New York: Vintage.

Fraser, D. (2010) "Transcript: SOUTHCOM Briefing on Haiti Relief Operations." U.S. Southern Command Public Affairs, Number: NNS100115–08, January 15.

Gallup. (2012) "Analytical Report for Haiti Media Use Survey," International Audience Research Project. October. Commissioned by the Broadcasting Board of Governors.

Hills, J. (2007) *Telecommunications and Empire*, Urbana, IL: University of Illinois Press.

Hodge, N. (2010a) "US Diverts Spy Drone from Afghanistan to Haiti," *Wired*, January 15, available at: www.wired.com/2010/01/pentagon-shares-earthquake-images-from-high-flying-spy-drone/

Hodge, N. (2010b) "Inside the Air Force's Secret Psyops Place," *Wired*, May 27, available at: www.wired.com/2010/05/inside-the-air-forces-secret-psyops-plane/

Hoskins, A. and O'Loughlin, B. (2010) *War and Media*. Cambridge, UK: Polity.

International Bureau and Public Safety and Homeland Security Bureau. (2010) *Haiti Update: Federal Communications Commission Open Meeting*, Washington, DC: Federal Communications Commission, February 18, pp. 1–30, available at: https://apps.fcc.gov/edocs_public/attachmatch/DOC-296380A1.pdf

ITU. (2010) "Haiti: ITU moves to restore telecommunications after earthquake," *ITU Press Release*, January 14.

Jackson, D. (2010) "A Painful Lesson," *Urgent Communications*, June 1, available at: http://urgentcomm.com/networks_and_systems/mag/disaster-communications-201006

Khalaf, R., Ramadan, O., and Stolleis, F. (2014) "Activism in Difficult Times Civil Society Groups in Syria 2011–2014," Badael Project, Beirut, Lebanon.

McClain, J. (2010) "Restoring Communications," *The Coast Guard Journal of Safety and Security at Sea Proceedings of the Marine Safety and Security Council*, 67 (2): 72–73.

Marow, I. (2010) "The Rush to Restore Communications in Haiti," *The Globe and Mail*, January 19.

Mattelart, A. (2003) *The Information Society: An Introduction*. London: Sage.

Metzl, J. (1997) "Information Intervention: When Switching Channels Isn't Enough," *Foreign Affairs*, 76 (6): 15–20.

MICT. (2014) "Syria Audience Research 2014." Media Studies Program at the American University of Beirut, available at: www.mict-international.org/wp-content/uploads/2014/08/syrienstudie_20140813.pdf

Miller, G. (2012) "Syrian Activists Say Pledges of U.S. Communications Aid Are Largely Unfulfilled," *The Washington Post*, August 20.

Nelson, A. and Patel, M., with Zambrano, D. (2011) *Media, Information Systems and Communities: Lessons from Haiti*, Miami: Knight Foundation, Internews, and Communicating with Disaster Affected Communities.

Powers, S., and Jablonski, M. (2015) *The Real Cyber War: The Political Economy of Internet Freedom*, Urbana, IL: University of Illinois Press.

Price, M. (2003) *Media and Sovereignty*. Cambridge, MA: MIT Press.

Price, M., and Thompson, M. (2002) *Forging Peace: Intervention, Human Rights, and the Management of Media Space*. Bloomington: IN: Indiana University Press.

Rice, S. E. (2012) "Remarks by Ambassador Susan E. Rice, U.S. Permanent Representative to the United Nations," U.S. Mission to the United Nations, Security Council Meeting on Syria, New York City, August 30.

Schiller, D. (1999) *Digital Capitalism: Networking the Global Market System*, Cambridge, MA: MIT Press.

Schiller, H. I. (1976) *Communication and Cultural Domination*, White Plains, NY: International Arts and Sciences Press.

Singel, R. (2011) "U.S.-Funded Internet Liberation Project Finds Perfect Test Site: Occupy D.C.," *Wired*, December 15, available at: www.wired.com/2011/12/internet-suitcase-dc/

Syria Untold. (2013) "Radio Rozana," October 27, available at: www.syriauntold.com/en/work_group/radio-rozana/

Tumber, H., and Webster, F. (2006) *Journalists Under Fire: Information War and Journalistic Practices*, London: SAGE.

U.S. Department of State. (n.d.) "21st Century Statecraft," available at: www.state.gov/statecraft/overview/

U.S. Embassy in Damascus. (2009) "Behavior Reform: Next Steps for a Human Rights Strategy," Cable ID 204645, available at: https://assets.documentcloud.org/documents/85633/09damascus306-redacted.pdf

Whitlock, C. (2011) "U.S. Secretly Backed Syrian Opposition Groups, Cables Released by WikiLeaks Show," *The Washington Post*, April 17.

Winseck, D., and Pike, R. (2007) *Communication and Empire: Media, Markets, and Globalization, 1860—1930*, Durham, NC: Duke University Press.

35

LAST STATION BEFORE HELL

United Nations Peacekeepers

Pierre-Olivier François

Peace operations can and have succeeded when they are an expression of strong and unified international political will. They have failed when they are not. To deploy them in the absence of a political strategy for resolving the conflict is to risk lives and money in pursuit of a peace that will likely remain elusive.

(Ban Ki Moon, UN Secretary General)

I know you share my horror and disgust at allegations that troops committed unspeakable acts against those they were sent to protect.

(Ban Ki Moon, UN Secretary General)

In 2014, I was asked by the French–German public television channel ARTE, a kind of European PBS, to work on a one-hour documentary covering the seventieth anniversary of the UN. The subject was the legacy of peacekeeping. This was to be a difficult assignment. UN Peacekeepers have for years been the subject of biting criticism in best-selling books (Polman 2004), films (Kondracki 2010), television dramas (Jackson and Kosminsky 1999), and widely read articles about how the "Blue Helmets", as they are called, are basically useless, ineffectual soldiers who are not getting the job done, and who sometimes even abuse their position.

Why do Blue Helmets get such bad press? In years past they were the "good cops," the guys who rescue orphans and widows, the peaceful units who stand between warring parties. They bravely waved their small blue flags to separate Hezbollah fighters from the Israeli army. They were able to pre-empt post-colonial genocide and possible civil war in Namibia, and received Nobel Peace Prizes for their efforts. But today they have become targets, not only of terrorists and armed groups who have no regard for the UN Charter, but also of many opinion-makers who have read the books and agree with the critiques.

Filming the documentary took me to the Department of Peacekeeping Operations at UN headquarters in New York. I also visited a number of UN missions. The oldest mission was in Lebanon. The United Nations Interim Force in Lebanon (UNIFIL) has 11,500 troops from 38 countries. The biggest and arguably most difficult mission is in the Democratic Republic of Congo where the United Nations Organization Stabilization Mission in the Democratic Republic of the Congo (MONUSCO), with initially 25,000 troops from 52 countries, is now shrinking. The most recent mission was the Central African Republic, United Nations Multidimensional Integrated Stabilization Mission in the Central African Republic (MINUSCA), which has roughly 12,000 troops. We spent days patrolling borders with soldiers from Ireland and New Zealand, disarming local thugs with police units from Portugal, Côte d'Ivoire, or Rwanda. We followed the daily routine of a French UN Under-Secretary General in New York, of Congolese soldiers in the bush, and of those protecting tribunal buildings and organizing elections in failed states. But the most frequent question I got from my journalist colleagues was "Oh, peacekeeping. Your film must be about prostitution and rape, right?" Indeed, some MINUSCA peacekeepers had just been accused of child prostitution, and the Peacekeeping Department was trying to save the reputations of the other 12,000 Blue Helmets. For months, that was the only news about the Blue Helmets that made headlines, and it is far from over. Why was that?

As a journalist, I have tried to understand the complex dynamics of the UN and its relationship to the press in an attempt to identify the faultlines between this complex bureaucracy and media narratives that tell its story. In an interview for this article Lakhdar Brahimi, the former UN special envoy to Afghanistan and Syria shared his insights: "Very few people care to understand what the UN is about, and how it works." To many people, "the UN is the bureaucracy in New York." But, he went on to say, "it is also and much more importantly, a collection of member-states. Most of the time when failure takes place, it is the member-states who are responsible for it." Excellent books and reports have detailed how the failures in Bosnia, Rwanda, Somalia came about (Howard 2008; Saint-Exupery 2009; Guéhenno 2015). In the world's collective memory and often in the media, "the UN" has failed.

Challenges of News Reporting

Professional journalists and media analysts alike understand the constraints of news reporting, especially in attempting to make sense of an increasingly complex globe in crisis. Breaking news suffers from the twin problems of fragmentation and loss of complexity (Bennett 2015). Background is usually not part of the story. Just imagine a newsroom in the times of 24/7 news and Twitter. A new massacre in Syria, Yemen, or Ukraine has just taken place. Most editors' first reaction will be to argue the UN is impotent because there are no peacekeepers there. It is even worse if there were any, as they seem to have failed in their mission, as you can see in Rwanda (Saint-Exupéry 2009) as well as in the Democratic Republic of the Congo. To explain everything would indeed be a little more complicated. One would need to examine the complex mechanism of the UN institutions—the General Assembly where everybody is equal, the Security Council where some are more equal than others. There is no time, space or column inches to explain in the immediacy of the moment, that the veto power of permanent members of the Security Council stems from the desire of the designers of the UN Charter to avoid the weaknesses of the League of Nations; or that in Syria, Yemen, and Ukraine, they have a hard time agreeing. In a focused story, given the "fragmented" nature of disconnected news, there is no way to address the reasons for the failed attempts to reform of the Security Council. And how could all that fit in a tweet of 140 characters or a breaking news slot of 1 minute 30 seconds? These are the pressures every professional journalist has to work within. These are also the challenges every person working in the UN system has to deal with. They have to repeat over and over again that they work within a bureaucratic system designed 70 years ago. UN staff must function within and adapt to a complex, multilateral diplomacy with almost 200 member-states taking part.

What is Peacekeeping?

Another challenge is that it can be tough to explain what peacekeeping is. "It is extremely difficult for a soldier who has been trained to fight, who has been trained to defend, to understand that in peacekeeping, they have another goal," former Secretary General Kofi Annan said in one of our interviews. "They are not there to fight. They are there to make peace. This is where the idea of peacekeeping becomes a bit awkward at times." This is indeed counterintuitive. Many people in front of their TVs, many decision makers, many journalists, expect soldiers to make war, or at least to forcibly impose peace. But who remembers that the last time the UN went to war, it nearly led to World War III? It was in 1950, during the Korean war, and the UN sided with South Korea, the US and 20 other nations against North Korea, China, and the Soviet Union. Thus, there are good reasons behind the UN's desire to remain neutral, or at least independent, from the warring parties. But they are hardly mentioned, or understood, by the public, and the newsmakers.

Stories with complicated, multiple threads are more difficult to pitch to a news editor, or a news audience, than a classic narrative where we know more or less who are the "good guys," and who are the "bad guys." In most of the peacekeeping missions this is seldom the case. Take the Central African Republic. Both the mostly Muslim Seleka militias and the mostly Christian anti-balaka have been accused of human rights violations. Take the Democratic Republic of Congo (DRC). Both the 40 something militias and the official Congolese army—Forces Armées Congolaises (FAC)—have been accused of killings, rapes, and kidnappings in the eastern provinces of Kivu (Guéhenno 2015). Who are supposed to be the good guys? Unravelling the histories, causes, and long genesis of the many global conflicts reveals that the world does not conform to the simple dichotomies of good and evil. Thus, when the UN becomes part of the story of conflict, it emerges on delicate ground with warring factions that occupy many different terrains that are not included within a simple media frame.

Then there are other, very practical questions in every single peacekeeping mission that are not easily answered in a news story: How do you bring peace to the Central African Republic, a country as big as France, with only 12,000 troops? Or to the DRC, a country as big as all of Europe, with only 25,000 troops? How do you help restore a failed state without behaving like an invader, or a colonizer? This is a question MONUSCO is asked quite often these days, after 16 years of active UN presence. And, last but not least, how do peacekeepers make peace when the local parties don't want to stop fighting? A question you can ask at the Israeli–Lebanese border, or in Kashmir, or along the Congo–Rwanda border.

Complexities of Telling a Different Story

Using pictures and interviews, we tried to address these challenges. Many people, including journalists, soldiers, and diplomats, told us after the screenings they had never thought about these issues. They said they had never been told that side of the story. One could blame the press, and how it functions. But maybe the problem also comes from the UN system's inability to influence the discourse, or promote itself in the best possible way, explaining what they do and how they do it. For whatever reason, they have not as yet been able to convey what they can and cannot do, or why they don't want to do certain things.

Another challenge in narrating the story of UN peacekeepers and their missions, is that there is no clear definition of a peacekeeper's job. To the extent that there ever was, their role and what they do have changed significantly over time. Dag Hammarskjöld famously said they should be "diplomats in uniform." During the Cold War that might have been possible. Peacekeepers were used to monitor existing ceasefires. In the early 1990s, they were still (quite successfully) stabilizing countries, protecting vulnerable populations, monitoring elections, and demining—be it in Namibia, Mozambique, El Salvador, or even Cambodia (Howard 2008). In most of these missions, peacekeepers died more often in car accidents than by enemy fire. But during our filming, almost every third day a peacekeeper was killed in Mali, the deadliest of the current UN missions. In Mali, South Sudan, Darfur, in the Golan Heights, Blue Helmets have become the preferred targets of ISIS, Al Qaeda, AQIM, and other terrorist organizations. How does one deal with that? And how does it affect the image and narrative of the UN in the eyes of the public, the local population, and its own troops?

How to Present Yourself

Indeed, since the dramatic bombing of the UN headquarters by Al Qaeda in Iraq in 2003, many peacekeeping contingents have left the villages where they used to live for isolated camps surrounded by high security. "That attack robbed us of our innocence. It made it clear to us that the UN flag does not protect you. It was a deliberate attack on the UN, and its personnel," Kofi Annan said in another interview. "For many years, the blue flag signified peace. No one was going to attack us. But it did happen." So, the UN has good reason to protect its personnel. But this has presented another set of complications, the consequences of which are keenly felt. "It is difficult to behave like a diplomat in uniform when you are racing through villages in over-protected armored cars," said a senior UN officer of UNTSO. UNTSO, created in 1948 in the Middle East, still sends out ground patrols of lightly, sometimes unarmed officers into every Lebanese village to get a sense of the local mood, collect information, and connect with local people. But because of the real danger, or sometimes because of overprotective security measures, many UN personnel we met regretted they had lost their connections with the local populations. One female peacekeeper told us that "it makes a great difference if I come lightly armed, or even unarmed, to have tea with local villagers. Or if we have to drive around with maximal security."

Protection and Overprotection

Which brings us back to the question of the use of force by the UN and how to present it. Timor Goksel, former spokesperson of United Nations Interim Force in Lebanon (UNIFIL) for almost 30 years, remembers a telling anecdote.

> In 2006, after the last war between Israel and Lebanon, the UN Security Council decided to reinforce the UNIFIL troops. So France sent more troops and 16 Leclerc tanks. But who were they trying to impress? The Israelis have 1,600 tanks. Then the French started to patrol by night. The Lebanese villagers complained: "Even the Israelis don't do that to us. Our children get scared."

Goksel says some French arrived directly from war-torn Afghanistan, and had a hard time adapting to a peacekeeping terrain. He adds that in Lebanon, the most popular Blue Helmets are usually the Indonesians. "They smile and wave during their patrols. That's how you built trust, and get information. That's a big part of peacekeeping." In Lebanon, Italian Blue Helmets are popular because they are good soldiers, but also because they are good football players; Koreans because of their Taekwondo talents. All different tools for effectively building relationships. But in an age of proliferating global conflict and parachute journalism

(Vaughn 2008), this story would probably not be covered by a roving news reporter. TV channels want images of war, not images of friendly "peace management." Discrete mediation can prevent the escalation of conflict. But it is not very telegenic.

This doesn't mean it is not effective. In the Central Africa Republic, a local policeman in a remote village told us that even a small battalion of 60 peace-keepers from Congo-Brazzaville, armed with an anti-aircraft tank that was of no use in the jungle villages of the zone, still had a great impact on the local security situation. He added that what really changed the situation was the fact that these Blue Helmets had an ambulance and gasoline—things that the local police and medical institutions could not afford, but that saved the lives of several local villagers after shooting incidents. In southern Lebanon, the local villagers told us as well that the Italian peacekeeping force had a huge medical impact for the poorest part of the population, those who could not afford the prices of local doctors, and the numerous Syrian refugees stranded in that region since the beginning of the Syrian civil war in 2011. In another area of southern Lebanon, a woman heading a local school told us that the French peacekeepers had helped renovate the structure of the building. This had also contributed to strengthening her position as a woman directing a local public institution. Even in regions where the situation is quite stable, such as southern Lebanon, Blue Helmets can have positive direct and collateral effects.

Improving and Defining the Peacekeeping Narrative

Peacekeeping is a very particular job, and should be reported as such. For coverage to improve, the story of UN peacekeeping has to be articulated at many different levels, be it through seminars, best practices, and case studies, or well-made films and interactive games. And it should reach different audiences, both outside the UN and within, for example new troops before they are sent into the field.

Such training and best practices would also contribute to a wider understanding that Blue Helmets have a special mandate, and behave differently than classical soldiers. Especially in countries where other armies with a different mandate are present. In Mali, the French army is conducting the counterterrorism mission known as Barkane alongside the local MINUSMA peacekeeping mission (United Nations Multidimensional Integrated Stabilization mission in Mali). After long and heated debates in New York, the UN has so far (rightly) refused to become another tool of the "global war on terror." As seen before, the UN has to remain independent, and neutral. But because of their different mandate, the Blue Helmets should have a different appearance, and behave differently than traditional soldiers. In the Central African Republic as well, MINUSCA should differentiate itself very clearly from the French army and its Sangaris mission. Light weapons, body language, contact and interaction with the population are all signs that help distinguish between traditional soldiers and those with blue helmets. This is easier said than done. But it is indispensable to defend the legitimacy and autonomy of the UN on the global battlefield.

Women as Peacekeepers

Another way to differentiate the two would be to incorporate more women in peacekeeping missions. If one reads the current advertisement campaigns, it is clear that the UN is desperately looking for female contingents to deploy. In Lebanon, a female Colonel from New Zealand told us that local populations behave very differently towards female soldiers. If she can, she also prefers to walk unarmed, as a clear visual sign that peacekeeping is different.

In Muslim countries, added Under-Secretary General for field support Ameerah Haq, the highest-ranking woman at the UN, women have access to a whole different world—the sphere of the home. Haq told us of her experience in East Timor. At the time, the mission had to deal with widespread domestic violence, a taboo subject in this traditional society. United Nations Transitional Authority in Cambodia (UNTAC) "[built] in every single police station of this new country a separate building on one side of the police compound. There, we would have a female police officer who could understand exactly what the local women were telling. It made a huge difference." The same could be done in the many countries where rape is used as a weapon against civilians. It is all the more difficult to report that kind of war crime if all the local peacekeepers are men. But another woman who worked as UN civilian in Sudan mentioned that, so far, peacekeeping (soldiers, police officers, etc.) was still dominated by men. In her compound, there weren't even separate showers for the few women in the camp.

Accountability and the UN

However, if Blue Helmets themselves are caught raping women and children, these few criminals ruin the legitimacy of peacekeeping in general. In Bangui, both Blue Helmets from several countries and soldiers from the French Sangaris mission were caught sexually abusing children. According to the UN's own investigative report, the response of the UN was slow and weak. Ban Ki-Moon got so angry that he fired the local head of MINUSCA. "Most people do not understand that the UN does not have real command over the peacekeepers from the various countries," Kofi Annan complained.

> What the UN has is operational command. We have had situations where the commander on the ground will give instructions and the national brigade commander will be told from his capital not to do it. When they commit a crime, when they abuse a child or use prostitution, the UN cannot put them on trial. You have to send them home for the national army to put them on trial and discipline them. Some do it, others don't. The UN has no power to enforce it. The only power the UN would have is to say we are not going to take troops from this country anymore. But sometimes the UN needs the troops so desperately that they will take them anyway.

But what local population could understand such a Byzantine system? The complexity of the UN system is not a valid excuse for this kind of disaster. It needs to be improved, and reformed.

Rethinking the Relationship Between Media and Peacekeeping

Given the changing landscapes of peacekeeping in global conflict, it may be time to redefine some of the multiple ways in which peacekeeping interacts with the media. Each element of a peacekeeping force should aspire to raise the bar in the domain it concerns. Radio Okapi, a UN project in the DRC, is a prime example. Created at the beginning of the United Nations Organization Mission in the Democratic Republic of the Congo (MONUC) with the help of Swiss NGO Hirondelle in 2002, Radio Okapi has since become the country's most popular radio station. It offers what many other local radios lack; accurate news in French and the four languages native to the DRC, balanced reporting, interviews and questions from the listeners, and news from all over the country. During the regional wars in the 1990s and 2000s, it was often the only means to connect Eastern and Western Congo. Radio Okapi, which calls itself "the radio of peace," advocates professionalism, democracy, and civic education. It has definitively helped raise the bar for other indigenous TV and radio stations. In fact, Radio Okapi is probably one of the most effective, lasting legacies of the UN in DRC—not to mention the cheapest. And in its own way, it has also been an effective peacekeeping tool.

We tried to show this and much more in the film. It is not a sensationalist documentary. There are no big war scenes, no good or bad guys, no winning strategies or big "hurrahs" at the end. It is a film that conveys a sense of frustration, a frustration that many peacekeepers, UN workers, and local populations have felt while trying to solve a crisis situation. As Jean-Marie Guéhenno (2015) former head of the Department of Peacekeeping, and now head of International Crisis Group, said, "When the UN is called, it is usually almost too late. But for the populations on the ground, many times, it is of vital importance. That's why the UN is often the last station before hell."

This is the title I chose for the film: *UN—Last Station Before Hell* (François 2015).

Further Reading

Report of the High-Level Independent Panel on United Nations Peace Operations (2015) *Uniting Our Strengths for Peace: Politics, Partnership and People* (Lead Authors: Jose Ramos-Horta and Ameerah Haq), New York: United Nations, available at: http://peaceoperationsreview.org/wp-content/uploads/2015/08/HIPPO_Report_1_June_2015.pdf

UN Women (2015) *Preventing Conflict, Transforming Justice, Securing the Peace: A Global Study on the Implementation of United Nations Security Council resolution 1325* (Lead Author: Radhika Coomaraswamy), New York: UN Women, available at: www.europarl.europa.eu/meetdocs/2014_2019/documents/femm/dv/unw-global-study-1325-2015_/unw-global-study-1325-2015_en.pdf

References

Bennett, W. L. (2015) *News the Politics of Illusion* (9th ed.), Chicago, IL: University of Chicago Press.

François, P-O. (2015) *UN—Last Station Before Hell*, Paris: ARTE France, & Alegria productions.

Guéhenno, J-M. (2015) *The Fog of Peace*, New York: Brookings.

Howard, L. M. (2008) *UN Peacekeeping in Civil Wars*, Cambridge, UK: Cambridge University Press.

Jackson, L. (script), and Kominsky, P. (1999) *Warriors*, British television drama serial screened on BBC One about British Peacekeepers of the UNPROFOR in Vitez, Bosnia.

Kondracki, L. (2010) *The Whistleblower*, a thriller inspired by the real story of K. Bolkovac who denounced sex-trafficking at the UN's SFOR in 1999.

Polman, L. (2004) *We Did Nothing: Why the Truth Doesn't Always Come Out When the UN Goes In*, London: Penguin Books.

Saint-Exupéry, P. de, (2009) Complices de l'inavouable: La France au Rwanda, les Arènes.

Vaughn, C. A. (2008) "Parachute Journalism: International News Reporting," in R. Andersen and J. Gray (Eds.), *Battleground the Media, Vol. 1*, Westport, CT: Greenwood Press, pp. 328–332.

Part 8

THE CONTRADICTIONS OF SOCIAL MEDIA AND THE NEW TECHNOLOGIES OF COMMUNICATION

Information, Fake News, and Xenophobia; Activism, and Witness

INTRODUCTION
TO PART 8

This section presents theoretical, practical, and ethical perspectives on the uses of new communications technologies in humanitarian affairs and crisis situations. Papers also explore the intersections between new media and older, legacy media in different contexts. Using a variety of methodologies, these chapters examine the uses of Twitter, Facebook, cell phones, data platforms, and drone technology to understand the importance of new digital formats and their impact on information and imagery. From the emergence of the use of Twitter in a crisis, to Facebook and human rights campaigns, we seek to assess the impact and influences of computer-based digital technologies in the field. When hand-held devices turn those who bear witness into reporters, and terrorists into celebrities, and drones can protect journalists and facilitate newsgathering, what are the potential negative consequences and ethical challenges that must be addressed?

Nowhere have the principles of humanitarianism and the ethics of solidarity come under attack more in recent times than with the election of Donlad J. Trump in the United States. The role played by social media, the "alt-right," and the fake news of *Breitbart* and other right-wing web-based organizations, demonstrate the power of social media to spread and foster xenophobia and hate, and even at times incite violence.

With these complexities in mind, we begin this section with an international research team and a chapter titled, "Key Communicators' Perspectives on the Use of Social Media in Risks and Crises," conducting structured interviews with three different constituencies involved in humanitarian communications. First, they spoke with crisis information managers, and then the professionals who support first responders. Next, they talked to journalists and editors of news organizations about new media and its relationships with newsgathering and information dissemination during a crisis. Interviewees give their views on the current uses of social media during crises, and express their views on the benefits and shortcomings they have encountered. They also reflect on how the use of social media can be further developed to increase awareness of and improve the responses to crises.

In April 2014, Boko Haram, a militant Islamist group, abducted over 200 Nigerian girls from the town of Chibok in Nigeria. The kidnapping caused global outrage and the local community responded by designing an online social media campaign they called "Bring Back Our Girls" that used Facebook and Twitter and quickly went viral. The campaign garnered worldwide attention and as interest grew, celebrity participation increased. In the United States, First Lady Michelle Obama was part of a massive appeal for the terrorist group to return the community's children. In the chapter titled, "Global Activism on Facebook: A Discursive Analysis of 'Bring Back Our Girls' Campaign," Dorothy Njoroge seeks to understand the role of online community activism. Questioning whether such campaigns provide opportunities for global citizenship, her research grapples with the debate over whether social media campaigns should be understood as mere "clicktivism," or if they are able to lead to other forms of political participation and offline involvement. She explores the discursive constructions of the Facebook postings using three action frames drawn from social movement literature—diagnostic, prognostic, and motivational. She concludes that given broad global lack of effective institutionalized leadership, social media campaigns may perhaps speak to the beginnings of a growing people's movement powered by technology.

The growing use of hand-held digital recording devices such as cell phones has certainly altered the landscape of newsgathering and brought issues of injustice to global publics. Consider for example the role of hand-held recording devices in documenting, bearing witness, and disseminating images of police brutality and the disproportionate number of police killings of African Americans in the United States. The Black Lives Matter movement grew up as a consequence of technology that allowed citizens to bear witness, and ultimately define police killings as racial, political, and social issues that challenge human rights covenants. Globally, organizations such as Witness.org, have provided organizational, legal, and technical support to help empower communities that document government oppression, record corporate crimes in their communities, and organize to publicize and apply pressure to stop such crimes in the name of justice and human rights. Empowered by human rights law, UN conventions and humanitarian principles, global campaigns continue to fight for people's rights and alter the global landscape.

Here we offer a chapter on the use of cell phones titled "'Take my Picture': The Media Assemblage of Lone-Wolf Terror Events, Mobile Communication, and the News," that explores the complex interactions between witness and news frames, and terrorism and publicity. Kenzie Burchell examines a lone-wolf terror attack—the 2013 public daytime murder of a British Army Soldier in Woolwich, London—and the role of eyewitness imagery and its use in the news media. The attack became a media event through an *assemblage* of technical and cultural performances—disparate parts that unfolded in real time to form the horrific violent spectacle. This case study helps clarify the mediations that occurred in the immediate aftermath of the attack and investigates the exploitation of reporting conventions as a plausible terror tactic.

Covering crises has long been a challenge to journalists and news reporting because taking compelling images or videos during conflicts in remote areas is an especially hazardous business. In 2012–2014, according to the Committee to Protect Journalists (2015),[1] over 70 journalists and photographers were killed in conflict zones. In "Keeping Reporters Safe: The Ethics of Drone Journalism in a Humanitarian Crisis," researchers Turo Uskali and Epp Lauk analyze several cases of drone journalism in crisis reporting. Drones have been used for news covering since 2011, starting with the street riots in Warsaw. The latest examples are from the conflict zones of Eastern Ukraine, the aftermath of the earthquakes in Nepal, the destruction of Syria, and the migration crisis in Europe. Drone journalism is defined as the use of unmanned aircraft systems (UAS) for journalistic purposes. This chapter lays out some of the ethical guidelines and propositions for good drone journalism in humanitarian crisis reporting. In addition, based on empirical findings and the World Press Freedom Index, the authors develop three scenarios for the future of drone journalism.

The election of Donald J. Trump has presented its own version of a humanitarian crisis for the globe. In the aftermath of the 2016 presidential election in the United States, as media, political operatives, the American public, and the global community began to come to terms with the outcome, it soon became evident that new media had been the key to the resurrection of old hatreds. The chapter by Robin Andersen, "Weaponizing Social Media:

'The Alt-Right,' the Election of Donald J. Trump, and the Rise of Ethno-Nationalism in the United States," analyzes the message content, construction, and dissemination of alt-right themes—misogyny, racism, white supremacy, xenophobia, fear of immigrants, and "white genocide"—employed in the campaign discourses of Donald J. Trump, and outlines how they propelled him into the White House. Online hate groups from alt-right activists to the anti-woman crusaders of Gamergate, together with political activists adept at the creation of propagandized fake news such as Stephen Bannon of *Breitbart*, were key in spreading Islamaphobia and white supremacy over social media platforms, most notably Twitter and Facebook. The effects of these messages are drawn out in an analysis of voting patterns and exit polling data that demonstrate the efficacy of the alt-right influences of pushing Trump over the top in key swing states.

Humanitarian narratives are now more important than ever, and political, grass-roots, legal, and humanitarian organizations, in addition to national and international leaders, and civil society in general, must respond in effective ways to this new landscape of an old hate if we are to reverse these trends.

Note

1. "In 2012–2014, according to the Committee to Protect Journalists (2015), over 70 journalists and photographers were killed in conflict zones," available at: https://cpj.org/killed/2014/in-combat.php

36

KEY COMMUNICATORS' PERSPECTIVES ON THE USE OF SOCIAL MEDIA IN RISKS AND CRISES

Harald Hornmoen, Klas Backholm, Elsebeth Frey, Rune Ottosen, Gudrun Reimerth, and Steen Steensen

This chapter examines how key communicators understand and evaluate opportunities and challenges of using social media in risk and crisis situations. We have conducted semi-structured interviews with several risk and crisis communicators, ranging from crisis information managers for authorities/NGOs and communicators specifically supporting first responders, to journalists and journalist advisors. Our study provides a preliminary understanding of how use of social media may contribute to altering role conceptions among different key crisis communicators and ultimately to changing different actors' communicative practices in risk and crisis situations.

Introduction

Social media play an increasingly important role for members of the public in risks and crises. However, a mismatch has existed between dominant communication strategies employed by communication managers (top-down, unidirectional, emphasis on traditional media) and the role that members of the public are playing. In emergencies, members of the public are using social media to communicate about the situation in different phases of the crises (Sutton et al. 2008), and they bypass traditional information gatekeepers such as organizations and traditional news media. To a considerable extent, users here control the creation and distribution of information. As Coombs (2012) suggests, crisis communicators using social media must adjust their traditional practices if they are to communicate effectively. Rather than one-sidedly controlling and feeding users with information, communicators need to *listen* to what social media users are saying and provide them with *access* to information.

Research into crisis/risk communication using social media (see further literature review below) suggests that communicators using social media need to develop their ability to prepare for, respond to and cope with crisis situations. In addition, a lack of qualitative research into this area is a problem in itself. We have a poor understanding of crisis communicators' perceptions of how they can use social media in the best possible manner to increase their own and the public's situational awareness, that is, a state of understanding what is happening in a crisis situation (Yin et al. 2012). How do key communicators perceive social media communication in risks and crises based on their experiences with such communication?

We see crisis communication managers as key figures in the process of building high professional and ethical standards of crisis communication. Such managers include decision makers, spokespersons, and public information officers in institutions whose roles involve dealing with crises and risks. We are also of the opinion that journalists and the news organizations that employ them have an important role to play in enhancing situational awareness through news reporting on crisis.

Literature Review

Although research on social media in crises is still in its infancy, it is quickly developing to include studies of social interactions and message content. Research has particularly focused on Twitter. In emergencies, some users generate information either by providing first-hand observations or by bringing relevant knowledge from external sources into Twitter. Analyzing tweets that were posted during Australia's worst fire disaster—Black Saturday in 2009—Sinnappan et al. (2010) conclude that Twitter can be approached as an alternative communication tool carrying invaluable information for the public, apart from relaying information from ground level to the authorities. Other studies point to shortcomings in conventional understandings of emergency response. In their study of the use of social media in the 2007 Southern California Wildfires, Sutton et al. (2008) suggest that community information resources and other backchannel communications activities enabled by social media are gaining prominence in the disaster area, despite concern by officials about the legitimacy of information shared through such means.

A problem with crisis communication conveyed by social media is separating reliable information from false rumors. Some studies (e.g. Mendoza et al. 2010; Castillo et al. 2011) indicate that when information from official sources is scarce, rumors can be posted and re-posted on Twitter that contribute to increasing the sense of chaos and insecurity in the local population. However, it is possible to develop methods to assess the credibility of information spread through social media networks. For instance, newsworthy topics tend to include URLs and to have deep propagation trees (Castillo et al. 2011). Another study shows that credible news is propagated through authors that have previously written a large number of messages, originate at a single or a few users in the network, and have many re-posts (Vieweg et al. 2010). Identifying such credible content and sources of information—whether by using online tools or through more traditional verification techniques—may contribute to enhancing situational awareness.[1]

A small-scale study (Kluge 2012) of the use of social media during the Utøya terrorist massacre in Norway in 2011, displays how Twitter became a place where the youth under attack could reach out with vital information and where people who were not directly affected by the terrorist attacks could support each other and share information. Twitter made it easier for the press to gain an understanding of the situation and the actors that were involved in the incident. However, the study also points to differing opinions on the use and reliability of Twitter as a source and information tool in emergencies. This research suggests that there is a need to improve journalists' evaluation criteria for social media (SoMe) and their practice of source criticism.

Research Question

The reviewed research suggests that crisis communication through social media could benefit from improved filtering and validation of SoMe content, as well as from communicators acquiring a better understanding of the opportunities social media provide for more efficient crisis management. However, as indicated above, we lack knowledge of how key crisis communicators view opportunities and desired improvements in SoMe use based on their experiences. To get a better grip on emerging practices and perspectives, we formulated the following research question:

How do key risk and crisis communicators understand and evaluate the opportunities and challenges of using social media in risk and crisis situations?

Method

To achieve a broad understanding of the issue, we have interviewed a range of key communicators working with different communicational tasks and roles in relation to different types of risks or crises. We targeted communicators with social media experience, based on the premise that such experience is a requirement for providing valuable perspectives. We interviewed communicators that we have divided into three groups depending on their tasks and roles in risk and crisis situations. The first group includes communicators supporting authorities'/NGOs' crisis information management. They are key communicators who contribute in their organizations' processes of identifying, understanding, and coping with crises before, during, and after they have occurred. This group also includes persons who communicate *risk* management: how organizations assess potential threats (such as health and terrorist threats) and advise the public on how to avoid such threats. The second group consists of communicators who are more directly involved in supporting first responders, emergency employees who are likely to be among the first people to arrive at the scene of an emergency. The third group includes journalists and journalist advisors, who are involved in a practice of producing and communicating news stories about risks and crises. We present our informants in Table 36.1.

We conducted 15 semi-structured interviews with different communicators between September 2014 and February 2015. We secured a breadth of data by interviewing persons based in four European countries: Norway (8), Austria (4), Finland (3), and the United Kingdom (1). We interviewed eight men and eight women. All the interviewees had experience with Twitter in their professional work and some with Facebook, Instagram, and blogs in addition.

We approached our interviewees through either (a) a focus group interview (semi-structured) conducted in English at a seminar in Oslo and conducted by the authors on September 18, 2014[2] or (b) extensive semi-structured interviews conducted by individual researchers in Norway, Austria and Finland.[3] The focus group interview lasted for 156 minutes and was audio-recorded and transcribed. The interviews conducted by individual researchers lasted from 60 to 90 minutes and were audio-recorded and transcribed.

Researchers involved in the interviews translated study data from interviews conducted in German, Finnish, or Norwegian. We posed the following guiding questions to all the interviewees:

- What do you consider as optimal risk and/or crisis communication in situations in which you have an important role?
- What do you consider as optimal risk/crisis communication involving social media?
- How can the use of social media be further developed to optimize key communicators' awareness of and response to the situation?
- How do you filter and validate risk/crisis information posted on social media during a threat or crisis situation?

Results and Discussion

In this section, we elaborate on and discuss the expressed views of the informants in the three different groups (see Table 36.1) related to (1) optimal risk and/or crisis communication and current shortcomings, and (2) improving social media use in risk and crises situations.

Optimal Risk and/or Crisis Communication and Current Shortcomings

Authority/NGO Crisis Communication Managers

Interviewees connected to national or regional authorities with communication management responsibilities emphasize the importance of providing people with fast, updated, accurate, understandable, and coordinated information. Some of them see optimal communication as reaching an appropriate communicational goal based on an understanding of the nature of the crisis or risk. For example, for the Institute of Public Health (NIPH) in Norway, mitigating unfounded fear in the population was important in the case of Ebola in 2014, whereas getting people to do something (e.g. get vaccinated) was important during the swine flu pandemic of 2009. In addition, the health governance communicators in England and Norway point to the challenge of maintaining a public engagement during health crises that go on for months (e.g. Swine Flu and Ebola) so that people do not lose interest in what the authorities have to say. In the absence of any new development, challenges also include maintaining trust and managing the stories, myths, and rumors that people start to generate.

Optimal communication using social media involves listening to people's concerns. The head of the department for respiratory diseases in England admits that, during the swine flu in 2009, they could have benefited from listening to social media messages about how a genetic disposition among people in Northern Scandinavian countries could cause narcolepsy in vaccinated people. In this way, they might "have had a heads-up at a much earlier stage."

Additionally, the goal of listening by using social media helps get insights into the moods, questions, and rumors that authorities need to handle. According to the communication director at the NIPH, Twitter and Facebook give them a unique opportunity to capture things they need to manage.

Social media is a gift in situations such as when somebody wants to joke about Ebola, spread rumors such as the misconception that Ebola is spread through the air. Social media give us the possibility to pick up such misconceptions and provide

Table 36.1 Interview Subjects

Group/Name	Role
Crisis communication managers representing authorities/NGOs	
Nick Phin	Head of respiratory diseases in Public Health England (PHE)
Christina Rolfheim-Bye	Communications director at the Norwegian Institute of Public Health (NIPH)
Kristina Brekke Jørgensen	Web editor of Kriseinfo.no at the Directorate of Civil Protection and Emergency Planning (DSB) in Norway
Annette Rinne	Communication director at the Regional State Administrative Agency in Western and Mid-Finland
Hannu-Pekka Laiho	Communication director at the Finnish Red Cross
Trond Hugubakken	Communication director at The Norwegian Police Security Service (PST)
Communicators supporting first responders	
Thomas Meier	Head of public relations/press speaker at the state fire brigade association in Styria, Austria
Hermann Kollinger	Public relations officer at the association of the upperaustrian firebrigades and operation officer at the fire brigade Alkoven, Austria
Kari Huseby/Martine Leang	Communication director/officer at Oslo Police, Norway
Mikael Appel	Head of communication of Ostrobothnia Police Department in Finland
Jens Leirvåg	Advisor at Kokom (National Centre on Emergency Communication in Health)
Journalists and journalist advisors	
Werner Müllner	Deputy Editor in Chief and CIO of the Austrian Press Agency (APA)
Verena Leiss	Journalist at Austrian Press Agency (APA), Bureau Linz
Ingeborg Volan	Head of social media at the Norwegian Broadcasting Corporation (NRK)
Hildegunn Fallang	Journalist and survivor of the Utøya terrorist attack in Norway on July 22, 2011

correct information. In this way, we reach many people with the right information. We are not dependent on a journalist having understood what we say.

For NIPH, adapting crisis communication to the different functions of social media implies that Facebook is used for delivering information in individualized stories and advice for the public in general, whereas Twitter is particularly used to reach agenda-setters, decision makers, health professionals, and the press. Other interviewees in this group also emphasize that dialogues with users on Twitter in particular give them an opportunity to convey their information effectively in direct contact with users.

Several of the interviewees emphasize that a lack of understanding of the importance of social media among top-level information managers and authorities is a major hindrance for beneficial use of SoMe in crisis communication. The result, according to some, is a lack of resources allocated to improving coordination and use of social media before, during, and after crises.

In sum: although most of the interviewees emphasize the importance of engaging in dialogical risk and crisis communication facilitated by social media, the real benefits of SoMe for these communicators is apparently to get the right information through to people in a more efficient manner than they could when they had to rely more on traditional mass media. As the communication director of the Norwegian Police Security Service puts it:

> Twitter is first priority for direct communication. We have been quite passive on Facebook, but realized after the terror threats against Norway in 2014 that we have to be more active on Facebook. How can we choose to abstain from arenas where the majority of the people will be in the next decade? We have to communicate with society. We need to be present in social media and influence it.

Communicators Supporting First Responders

Optimal communication is a somewhat different issue for communicators who support first responders. There is pressure coming in from the affected public. The state fire brigade communication officer in Austria called the extreme floods in the summer of 2013 "the first social media crisis." The press spokesperson of the Styrian Fire Brigades points to a limited use of SoMe in the brigades at present. The authorities handle information management for the population, and the use of emergency tactics will not change by the use of social media channels: "Those who need help will get help. As soon as possible." However, he does see how they could improve social media communication in crises if they develop clearer policies ("exact rules") for their use.

Clear conditions are also seen as crucial in the Ostrobothnian Police Department in Finland. They are currently able to monitor trending issues and to some degree respond to rumors, and prefer to post their updates via a static hub web page with links to chosen social media platforms. However, the communication suffers from a lack of understanding of the "new" specific requirements set by social media, e.g. related to the media format, timing of communication, and organizational resources needed:

> It is all about being fast with information, and informing even though we do not have anything to inform about. This is where we do not function well, if we cannot give something new, we choose not to inform at all. We have not understood that it is important to tell the people that we have nothing new to tell them.

The Oslo Police communicators express concern about how the required rapidness of communication in acute situations may lead to inaccurate information, whereas the Austrian fire brigade emphasize how people can easily misinterpret information provided to them through social media. Some of the interviewees in this group see major shortcomings in relation to their needs for swift and reliable information from users involved in or close to unfolding crises, be it verbal or visual information. For the Ostrobothnian Police Department's spokesperson, verification processes for user-generated content are currently too slow. The advisor at the Norwegian Emergency Communication points out a lack of a system to track and validate potentially important visual documentation from crises posted on social media.

Journalists and Journalist Advisors

Interviewees representing journalistic institutions stress the need to maintain principles of ethics and good standards of journalism in crisis communication, not least principles of truthfulness, accuracy, and the need to use several sources and verify information. The APA editor, reporting on a crisis in which you only have from minutes to an hour to publish news, is best served by relying on "traditional sources," whether it is the police, an official, or three or four news agencies. "Professional journalists on a desk have to know the quality of their sources," he claims. When news of a big, sudden crisis breaks, he finds that there is an abundance of information on social media, but that one cannot verify the messages posted on Twitter by someone who is supposedly observing something.

The social media advisor at the NRK also points to the need to maintain established verification routines as a basis for crisis reporting.

> In journalism, when something breaks you want eyes and ears on the ground. This has always been the hallmark of reporting, and journalism is still about determining fact from fiction. We want the same from social media as we always have wanted. We want facts. Preferably, from two minutes ago and from someone we trust. If it is not from someone we trust, we want it to be somewhere where we can verify it. We want several sources. It is still just journalism.

For the NRK advisor, they could strengthen the significance of the media organization's presence in social media if they were able to validate user-generated content through some industry standards, and to apply knowledge acquired at times when a crisis is not unfolding. The APA editor is more doubtful about the possibility of optimizing crisis reporting by using social media sources. He compares searching for valuable information in social media with trying to find gold rings in *Cloaca Máxima* (the sewage system in ancient Rome).

The Utøya survivor among the journalist interviewees points out how victims of violence are unstable, and need to be met with careful and caring language. In such situations, journalists should consider using other sources, such as the police or witnesses that have not been directly affected. She further emphasizes how a beneficial use of social media in such cases may occur in a phase of grief processing after the acute crisis, pointing to the comforting function of a widely shared tweet after the Utøya massacre: "When a man can cause so much evil, think about how much love we can create together."

In the eyes of the journalism interviewees, then, current shortcomings in the use of social media during crises are a lack of competence and routines for verifying user-generated content in crisis reporting, and underdeveloped ethical guidelines.

Improving Social Media Use in Risk and Crises Situations

Authority/NGO Crisis Communication Managers

How can key communicators further develop their use of social media to optimize their own and the public's awareness of and response to risk and crises? Authority/NGO information managers voice different opinions on what is most needed. The PHE head believes that tools to filter and tease out valid information may help them detect important information. The NIPH communication director envisions a good monitoring tool for social media and tools for validating the credibility of sources' information. However, she stresses that one cannot improve use of social media by seeing them in isolation from an overall crisis communication plan of which social media are an important part. Important for development is to arrange more acute emergency exercises to be better prepared for the speed of information needed in such situations.

Other interviewees also view it as vital to develop competence through training. For the Regional State Agency in Finland, an emphasis is on training to create good information strategies to prevent rumors. In the Finnish Red Cross they consider it important to develop a readiness for social media participation during "expected" peaks such as anniversaries, as well as to start using social media as an internal platform for mapping needs in regional areas after disasters. For the web editor at the Norwegian crisis information, having more staff members that are trained in social media is more important than having more tools: "We need people that know how to do this and a crisis communication plan that emphasizes that we are going to prioritize social media."

When questioned about how they currently filter and validate social media messages, interviewees in this group do not necessarily see this as a vital issue in their communication efforts. Presumably, this reflects how these institutions see their role as channeling their information on social media—or correcting user-generated content—rather than using social media as a source of factual information.

Communicators Supporting First Responders

For the communication officers of the Austrian fire brigades, the increasing use of smartphones creates conditions for improving direct communication and activates victims in a crisis so that they can handle the situation in the best possible manner. In the acute crisis phase in which swift action is required, verification of social media is not an issue for them. However, they are concerned about unfortunate consequences of swiftly spreading information. It can stir up emotions and lead to misinterpretations of information, and to people not acting as they should. This fear is shared by the communication director for the Ostrobothnia police, who suggests a need for more unorthodox strategies, such as benefitting from the crowd-sourcing expertise among ordinary users to monitor social media and verify content, but within an ethically acceptable framework.

The Oslo police communicators believe that with more people dedicated to social media, these media could be communication channels more than information channels. In this way they could pick up on information generated from people on SoMe that may be useful to them. On ordinary days, the operational level of the police follows what people tweet, but there is no time for this during a crisis. Their department of communication then takes over tweeting and moderation, sometimes while stationed at the operational center.

Journalists and Journalist Advisors

When pondering the question of how to improve social media use in crises, journalists and journalist advisors express a different view of the possible value of user-generated content as a source of information than the other two groups. Even the APA *editor*, who is currently doubtful about the possibility of verifying Twitter content, sees some ground for improving the use of social media as a news source in acute crisis phases, if one could establish a "social media crisis network of trusted partners." Whereas the *journalist* at APA believes that much can be gained if crisis authorities engage more extensively on Twitter, the NRK advisor sees the challenge mainly as a question of improved training of journalists:

> We need to learn to verify content in a dialogue with users who generated it by asking questions such as: "Are you actually there? When was this picture taken? Where were you standing? Can we have the data so we can verify this?" We need journalists who have that under their skin and their fingers, before something big happens.

446

Table 36.2 Key Crisis Communicators' Perspectives on SoMe Use

	Optimal SoMe crisis communication	Shortcomings in current use of SoMe in crisis situations	How to improve use of SoMe in crisis situations
Authority/NGO crisis communication managers	• Listen to people's concerns • Get a grip of moods, questions, rumors, and myths and engage in dialogue • Distribute information via SoMe	• Lack of good system to monitor SoMe • Lack of understanding of the importance of SoMe/negative attitude • Do not listen enough	• Need better tools to monitor and analyze SoMe-content • Need more people who know how to deal with SoMe • Communicate via mobile devices, must plan for power fall outs
Communicators supporting first responders	• Use one platform for all information (all authorities together) • Rapid, open, and honest sharing of information • To have a system that quickly can track/validate information (especially pictures) from crisis scenes published on SoMe	• A challenge to balance need for info and ensure correct info • Too slow procedures for verifying SoMe content and identities • No system to track and validate SoMe pictures/facts from crisis scenes	• Make SoMe use mandatory for communication officers • Have enough personnel dedicated to SoMe communication in acute crisis • Need training and established routines for how to communicate via SoMe
Journalists and journalist advisors	• Continuous communication in SoMe, especially Twitter • Journalists have know-how on how to monitor, find, and assess relevant SoMe-information • SoMe functions as a channel for alleviating grief	• Lack of competence on how to verify SoMe-content • Lack of ethical guidelines • SoMe are networks of emotions, cannot verify content • Authorities use SoMe poorly—information gathering difficult	• Need journalists who understand the dialogical aspects of SoMe • Develop ethical guidelines • Get authorities to use SoMe more often • Establish a SoMe crisis network of trusted partners

Filtering and validating SoMe messages is partly seen as a question of applying established journalistic verification routines and partly as requiring improved internal coordination between staff members and better routines for handling tools/applications.

The Utoya survivor/journalist, for her part, stresses a need for improved ethical treatment of crisis victims and families, after having experienced "the storm of journalists" contacting Utoya youth by phone or through social media when they were in a state of shock. Practical crisis training emphasizing ethical aspects and ethical guidelines with an outspoken focus on best practices when approaching first-hand victims via SoMe could improve journalistic conduct in such situations.

Conclusions

The question we posed is how key risk and crisis communicators understand and evaluate the opportunities and challenges of using social media in risk and crisis situations. Table 36.2 summarizes the answers we found.

The communicators in our study see much potential in using social media to create improved situational awareness and management of risks and crises. However, they point to several deficiencies in current uses of SoMe in emergencies. Interviewees in both crisis management organizations and journalistic institutions point to the lack of personnel, lack of organizational routines and coordination, and insufficient training as obstacles. A major reason for these current inadequacies is apparently a lack of understanding and interest in social media within the leadership of crisis communication institutions.

We also found some noteworthy differences between the various groups' views on what the benefits and challenges of using social media in crises are. Crisis communication managers tend to view dialogical communication as something that enables correction of the public's misconceptions during crises. The first responder communicators to a larger degree see postings from SoMe users as containing potentially vital information for them in order to act swiftly and effectively in acute situations. The journalist group also sees a potential value of communicating information in their news stories originally acquired from SoMe users that are present at crisis scenes.

We see such differences in the groups' assessment of the potential value of user-generated content in crisis communication as partly reflecting their distinctive professional roles. The roles range from assessing, understanding, and coping with crisis through all its phases (crisis communication managers), to supporting swift and purposeful action in emergency situations (first responder communicators), to producing engaging news stories that report from crisis scenes (journalists and journalist advisors). We believe that communication in all groups—including the communication managers—can benefit from regarding user-generated content as potentially crucial for enhancing situational awareness and advising on establishing "best practices" in crises.

The question remains, however, of how to filter and validate social media messages posted by the public during crises. Our research suggests a need for more knowledge about such competencies and procedures in specific crisis communication contexts. Our interviewees express different views as well as uncertainty about filtering and validation of SoMe content. Some see a potential value in developing tools that could assist them with filtering trustworthy sources and verifying user-generated content. Others emphasize the prevailing need to follow or adjust established verification routines when evaluating social media. It is also worth noting how our interviewees emphasize the need for stronger coordination and training of communicators as a precondition for any sensible use of social media and tools to evaluate their content.

The differing views on validation strategies reflect the current nature of the social media landscape. SoMe platforms, content formats, and uses patterns are dynamic and continuously changing, and, therefore, creating well-functioning information validation strategies and a robust organizational understanding of social media platforms is a challenging task.

Notes

1. There are several online tools available at present that journalists can use for verification. Brandtzaeg et al. (2016) point out that we do not know the extent to which journalists use verification tools such as SocialMention, Storyful, Politifact, Fastfact, Topsy, Sulia, TinEye, FotoForensics, and Trackur.
2. Nick Phin, Kristina Brekke Jørgensen, Werner Müllner, Ingeborg Volan, and Hildegunn Falang were all interviewed in English at this occasion.
3. Harald Hornmoen interviewed Christina Rolfheim Bye (11.19.14) in Norwegian, and Thomas Meier (09.16.14) by mail in English. Klas Backholm interviewed Annette Rinne (11.04.14), Hanna Pekka Laiho by phone (10.31.14), both in Finnish, and Mikael Appel (11.06.14), in Swedish. Gudrun Reimerth interviewed Herman Kollinger (11.04.2014) and Verena Leiss (11.05.14) by phone, both in German. Elsebeth Frey interviewed Kari Huseby and Martine Leang (01.29.15) in Norwegian. Rune Ottosen interviewed Trond Hugubakken (11.07.2014) in Norwegian. Steen Steensen interviewed Jens Leirvåg by phone (12.05.14) in Norwegian. If not otherwise mentioned, interviewees were interviewed face-to-face.

Further Reading

Brandtzaeg, P. B., Lüders, M., Spangenberg J., Rath-Wiggins L., and Følstad, A. (2016) "Emerging Journalistic Verification Practices Concerning Social Media," *Journalism Practice*, 10(3): 323–342, contributes to new knowledge on journalists' social media working practices.

Eriksson, M. (2015) "Managing collective trauma on social media: the role of Twitter after the 2011 Norway attacks". *Media, Culture & Society*: 1–16, is an interesting analysis of the meaning-making discourse on Twitter during the six days following the 2011 terrorist attacks and massacre in Norway.

References

Brandtzaeg, P. B., Lüders, M., Spangenberg J., Rath-Wiggins, L., and Følstad, A. (2016) "Emerging Journalistic Verification Practices Concerning Social Media," *Journalism Practice*, 10 (3): 323–342.

Castillo, C., Mendoza, M., and Poblete, B. (2011) "Information Credibility on Twitter," in S. Srinivasan, K. Ramamritham, A. Kumar, M. P. Ravindra, E. Bertino, and R. Kumar (Eds.), *WWW*, New York: ACM Press, pp. 675–684.

Coombs, T. (2012) *Ongoing Crisis Communication: Planning, Managing and Responding* (3rd ed.), Los Angeles, CA: Sage.

Kluge, A. R. (2012) *Da Twitter gikk fra kos til kaos*. Bacheloroppgave i journalistikk. Institutt for medie-kultur og samfunnsfag, Universitetet i Stavanger.

Mendoza, M., Poblete, B., and Castillo, C. (2010) "Twitter under Crisis: Can We Trust What We RT?" in *Proceedings of the First Workshop on Social Media Analytics (SOMA 10)*, New York: ACM Press, pp. 71–79.

Sinnappan, S., Farrell, C., and Stewart, E. (2010) "Priceless Tweets! A Study on Twitter Messages Posted During Crisis: Black Saturday," *ACIS 2010 Proceedings*. Paper 39.

Sutton, J., Palen, L., and Shklovski I. (2008) "Backchannels on the Front Lines: Emergent Uses of Social Media in the 2007 Southern California Wildfires," in F. Fiedrich and B. Van de Walle (Eds.), *Proceedings of the 5th International ISCRAM Conference—Washington, DC, USA*, May.

Vieweg, S., Hughes A.L., Starbird, K., and Palen, L. (2010) "Microblogging During Two Natural Hazards Events: What Twitter May Contribute to Situational Awareness," in *Proceedings of ACM Conference on Computer Human Interaction (CHI)*, April, pp. 1079–1088.

Yin, J., Lampert, A., Cameron, M., Robinson B, and Power, R. (2012) "Using Social Media to Enhance Emergency Situation Awareness," *IEEE Intelligent Systems*, 27 (6): 52–59.

37

GLOBAL ACTIVISM ON FACEBOOK

A Discursive Analysis of "Bring Back Our Girls" Campaign

Dorothy Njoroge

Introduction

In April 2014, 276 Nigerian girls were abducted in Chibok, Nigeria, by Boko Haram, an extremist Islamist group. At the time of this writing, 219 are still missing. The kidnapping caused global outrage and before long, the "Bring Back our Girls" campaign had gone viral with no less than the US first lady pitching in as well as celebrities and many ordinary people. Nigeria has for the last several years battled the terrorist group whose actions include decapitation of citizens, burning of buildings, bombings of public places, shooting of worshippers in churches among other horrors, all in an effort to make Nigeria a fundamentalist Islamic state.

Boko Haram, which roughly translates to Boko (Western education) is haram (forbidden) in the Hausa language, had been operating in north-eastern Nigeria for some time but was thrust into international limelight following the "Bring Back Our Girls" campaign. Formed in 2002, the insurgency has grown in strength, taking over territory from the Nigerian army and becoming a major opponent of the Nigerian government. According to the Council on Foreign Relations, the group has killed over 10,000 people and displaced 1.5 million since 2009. Many civilians in the region have been killed in fighting between government forces and Boko Haram, and the group has formed alliances with the Islamic State operating in Chad, Cameroon, and Libya. Over 1,000 schools have been destroyed in Nigeria, Chad, Cameroon and Niger, said the United Nations envoy to the area, Toby Lanzer, according to the *Daily Mail* of November 16, 2015.

The atrocities committed by this group largely remained in the margins of global public discourse. But the capture of the young women in a boarding school changed all that. The "Bring Back Our Girls" campaign quickly acquired visibility on social media as it caught the collective imaginary of the global public. To complement protests in cities across the country, the hashtag #BringBackOurGirls was created by parents and activists in Nigeria who were frustrated by the inaction of the Nigerian government following the abductions.

In the streets of Nigeria, parents wearing red bore placards reading "Bring Back Our Girls" while a coordinated campaign on social media had celebrities around the world appealing for the release of the girls carrying a "#BringBackOurGirls" sign in a symbol of global solidarity. The Bring Back Our Girls (BBOG) campaign was an online sensation recording global attention that garnered more than six million tweets. BBOG was a local campaign aiming to expand globally and as parents protested in the Nigerian seat of government in Abuja, similar protests were taking place in Washington DC, Los Angeles, London, and other cities across Europe and North America.

Digital media have become important tools for political action not just in the West but elsewhere; Egypt, Tunisia, North Africa, and the Middle East all bear witness to the so-called Arab Spring uprisings (Howard and Hussain 2013). Subsequent to the uprisings, "digital media use by multiple political actors and interests continue to shape emerging Arab media systems" (Howard and Hussain 2013, 4). However, little attention has been paid to how these tools are also being used in sub-Saharan Africa where internet reach is expanding rapidly due to falling costs of smartphones and increasing investment in internet infrastructure such as undersea and terrestrial fibre-optic cables across the continent.

While many social media activism studies have been carried out, I would argue that this one is different in a significant way from others like them. First, the initiative came from the distraught parents and activists in Nigeria who took their suffering online, thereby attracting global attention and support. As such, this serves as an example of a local campaign gone global. How did this campaign attract such broad support even though it was not fronted by a Western celebrity as is usually the norm? Have the communication technologies, as it were, flattened the world? Second, despite the involvement of celebrities, many ordinary people participated by staging their own protests and crafting their own messages. I address these questions by analysing the discursive constructions of the campaign through messages posted on its Facebook site.

Background

The parents of the girls frustrated by the slow response of the Nigerian government took to the streets to protest the inaction. They also took their frustration online. A former World Bank Official, Dr. Oby Ezekwesili, in a ceremony to mark Port Harcourt as a World Book Capital in 2014 made an impassioned appeal for the release of the girls. During the ceremony, Ibrahim M. Abdullahi, a lawyer in Nigerian's capital, Abuja, sent the first tweet using the hashtag #BringBackOurGirls on April 23 (http://mashable.com/2014/05/06/nigeria-girls-bringbackourgirls/#c2kvqwDBTOqp). This became the catchphrase for the campaign globally, not just for the social media campaign but also for street protests. Other hashtags used include #Chibok and #Nigeria. Nigeria has the highest number of people using the internet in Africa, standing at 70.3 million in the first quarter of 2014 according to www.internetworldstats.com/stats1.htm.

Following the abductions, there was little information forthcoming from the government on the fate of the girls. On April 30, a huge protest was staged in Abuja to protest government "indifference" to the girls' disappearance. On May 4, President Goodluck Jonathan made his first comments about the abduction and called for international help in finding the girls. Soon after, President Obama announced the US would be sending a team of specialists to help the effort. The UK and France followed suit. Meanwhile, Boko Haram released a video of the girls and declared it would sell the girls as slaves. The Nigerian government used a combination of military manoeuvres and negotiations to try and get the girls back. The army offered a reward of £300,000 for information on the girls' whereabouts.

On May 7, #BringBackOurGirls reached a million tweets. Michelle Obama joined the campaign as she posted a picture of herself on Instagram holding a sign with the hashtag and also gave a radio address, on Mother's Day weekend, extolling the girls' courage and calling for their release. Many other prominent people including the British prime minister David Cameron, Hillary Clinton as well as several celebrities and many ordinary people participated in the campaign by posting pictures of themselves holding signs calling for the release of the girls. Nobel Laureate, Malala Yousafzai, became a critical voice of the campaign as she travelled to Nigeria to meet the Chibok girls' parents as well as President Jonathan.

According to BBC Monitoring, the global response to #BringBackOurGirls reached more than five million tweets following its introduction in Nigeria (www.bbc.com/news/world-africa-33446305). A change.com petition started by a Nigerian girl focusing on world leaders and organizations attracted over 1.1 million signatures. Red and white were selected as the colors of the campaign. According to bringbackthegirls.ng, the red colour was chosen to denote the danger the girls were in and the passion to rescue them. White was chosen to represent their innocence. Organizers asked people to stage rallies, protests, school girl marches, vigils, and other activities as well as a "social media march" where supporters were asked to promote the campaign for 200 minutes on May 8 among their friends on social media networks. The campaign headquarters was in Abuja but had satellite branches in other parts of the world, the most active being the one in the US. These Facebook pages were open to people from various parts of the world.

Activism for Africa

Global activism for causes around the world has grown substantially, powered by communication technologies that create connections extending beyond national borders to reach a global audience. Hence, well-orchestrated civil society information campaigns from far-flung corners of the world have gripped world attention from time to time. A campaign may be defined as "a thematically, socially and temporarily interconnected series of interactions that form the viewpoint of the carriers of the campaign, that are geared to a specific goal" (della Porta et al. 2006, 61). Such campaigns provide space for mediatized citizenship through worldwide audience participation. Given its social and economic problems, the African continent has attracted its share of these campaigns: the anti-apartheid campaign, and the campaign against landmines, among others.

Generally, it appears that such campaigns fall roughly into two categories—those organized by international non-governmental organizations (NGOs) such as Oxfam to campaign for various causes, and the more organic ones that erupt spontaneously in a specific locale, in response to some human calamity. Either way they serve the purpose of focusing attention on an issue and pushing for action to resolve the problem. They often cross-pollinate with news agendas mainstreaming the issue albeit for short periods of time.

Global activism has been conceptualized as global cosmopolitanism or cosmopolitan solidarity across borders (Nash 2008; Engelhardt and Jansz 2015). In her study of the Make Poverty History campaign in 2005 on issues of global citizenship and cultural politics, Nash notes how the campaign attempted to build "popular cosmopolitan support" (2008, 168). The Make Poverty History campaign sought to lobby the leaders of the most powerful nations in the world to address the issue of world poverty, particularly in Africa, by cancelling its debt and creating a fairer and more equitable international trading environment.

In 2005, the campaign became a media sensation with the Live 8 concert in London, dubbed as the "concert of the summer" in 2005. Live 8 concerts brought together 100 artists, a million spectators and an estimated billion viewers around the globe for the cause of eliminating world poverty through music. Concerts were held in major cities and were streamed online.

Though it was successful in mobilizing public sentiment and becoming a media success, Nash sees it as a "terrible failure" and identifies three key deficits that doomed the campaign. The first was a *structural deficit* since the campaign worked within existing frameworks of international governance. She labelled the second a *deliberative deficit* as the campaign did not explain what "justice not charity" meant for both the South and the North, and finally she identified a *media deficit* because even as national media in Europe represented globalism, they did not, or could not create a space for discussing equitable social relations at a global level (Nash 2008, 179). While Nash looks at how global citizenship and solidarity manifest in global campaigns and finds deficits, she proposes that transformation to global citizenship can be accomplished through popular media. The BBOG campaign provides a crucible for observing the possibilities and necessities of this dynamic.

First, let us consider the failures and successes of other campaigns. Save Darfur, organized by the Save Darfur Coalition, was a highly visible advocacy movement to stop the genocide going on in the Darfur region of Sudan. This was probably the highest-profile grassroots movement for Africa outside the anti-apartheid campaign (Strom and Polgreen 2007). The conflict received massive mainstream media coverage in the US in 2004 and 2005 with *The New York Times* leading the way. But as Haeri (2008) points out, this was the culmination of on-going advocacy especially from Christian groups on behalf of the Darfuris since the 1990s. Several of these groups came together and the Save Darfur Coalition was born in 2004 (Haeri 2008). While the US had ignored the Rwandan genocide, the Darfur lobby ensured "Americans would write, call, march, divest, and lobby in a coordinated multi-year campaign to change their government's foreign policy" (Sniderman 2011).

At the height of its influence, this lobby shaped American policy and loosened congressional purse-strings (Sniderman 2011). Darfur became a fashionable cause for the young with "not on our watch" wristbands and "million voice for Darfur" postcard campaigns raising millions for the cause. A rally outside the National Mall addressed by George Clooney among other activists brought out impressive crowds. Later the movement became mired in acrimony over the actions some groups were demanding of President Bush, which other groups felt were not informed by realities on the ground. These issues led to the dismissal of the coalition's executive director (Strom and Polgreen 2007). Some of the problems with the advocacy were the exaggeration of the number of casualties, the refusal to step back from characterizing the crisis as genocide even after hostilities on the ground had reduced significantly, and simplifying the conflict to binaries of Arab/African and Christian/Muslim (Haeri 2008).

Another example is Kony 2012, an online video by Invisible Children, an American NGO, calling for the arrest of Joseph Kony, a strongman who had terrorized northern Uganda. Kony became the fastest spreading internet video, accessed more than 100 million times in six days. This campaign caught the attention of researchers Englehardt and Jansz (2014) who wanted to empirically examine popular claims that online engagement is superficial, that is, mere clicktivism. They discovered that such appeals do lead to short-term personal and moral commitment and may help build a propensity for an enduring global cosmopolitanism. This suggests that dismissing such online activism as mere hype is perhaps premature. Kony marked a watershed moment for campaigns for Africa and showed the potential of using digital networked tools to create a visible campaign for causes.

Online Activism

Scholars have begun to debate whether or not online activism should be dismissed as mere slacktivism or clicktivism (Christensen 2011, Drumbl 2012). Slacktivism refers to online engagement in a cause that makes participants feel better about themselves through a lifestyle appeal, rather than reaching them through a more substantive message connected to the suffering of others. Such activities can be expressed by displaying political messages on your person, car, or joining a social media campaign (Christensen 2011). Activities such as hacking for a cause, which require more effort and risk, would not be considered slacktivism. Others see more potential in online social movement campaigns for a cause. Theocharis (2015) argues that the reduced cost of digital participation makes it easier to mobilize large numbers in the virtual domain, and that may translate into a visible impact. Online movements can be effective in setting the agenda on an issue, influencing policy, or getting endorsements on a policy position by influential actors. Seen from this perspective, Facebook and other social media are transforming citizen activism so that virtual activism is not necessarily slacktivism (Christensen 2011).

In social movement studies, online activism is usually characterized as a support structure for offline, grass-roots forms of mobilization. But increasingly, online activism is becoming an important site of study on its own. As Powell posits, it is important to put "the internet at the centre of a transformation in activist practice away from control of media and towards networked practices" (2016, 250). Exploring the effectiveness of networked activism, Lim (2013) analysed why some social media campaigns in Indonesia were successful and others failed to take off by comparing two successful and two failed social media campaigns in the country. One of her observations was that social media activism was successful in mobilizing popular support in cases when the campaigners used a simplified narrative structure, popular symbols, and called for low risk activities. Her study demonstrates that the framing of a message becomes crucial in attracting support.

Debates over whether virtual activism diminishes political engagement continue to be polarized with some holding that it leads to a decline in political involvement, while others believe that the internet simply diversifies the means of political involvement. This differsification is referred to as micro-activism, which consists of "many-to-many forms of politically oriented communication" (Marichal 2013). Bennett and Segerberg (2012) use the term digitally networked action (DNA) to describe the same phenomenon.

Virtual activism and offline engagement are not mutually exclusive, and Christensen (2011) asserts that no clear evidence exists that online activism hinders or enhances real-life political engagement. In fact, Marichal (2013) argues that Facebook groups provide a means for political performance, "through the formation of idealized political identities." Such participation spills over to other forms of online and even offline activities according to findings from a study on Canadian students' social media use (Vissers and Dietlind 2014). As Harlow and Harp observe, "online and offline actions are not dichotomous and should not be considered separately" (2012, 207–208).

Political action on the Internet is affected by the digital divide with parts of the world having unrestricted access while others have inadequate access, reducing the impact of collective virtual activism (Van Laer and Van Aelst, 2010). The fastest growth in mobile phone adoption is in Africa, and this is significant because people in the sub-Saharan region largely access the Internet through their phones for online activities such as social networking. The Swedish technology company, Ericsson, in the Appendix to its June 2014 report, *Sub-Saharan Africa: Ericsson Mobility Report* notes that internet as well as TV and media services are being accessed at increasing levels through mobile telephony, particularly in Kenya, Mozambique and Nigeria.

Collective action through organizational enabled networks is increasingly becoming augmented, and in some cases supplanted, by personalized activist formation employing social media networks (Bennett and Segerberg 2012). Two main forms of mobilization characterize such campaigns. Micromobilization refers to actions of smaller groups and networks at local level operating disparately while mesomobilization refers to the activating of these groups and forming them into a loose network to pool resources and facilitate protest activities (Gerhards and Rucht 1992). Utopia or dystopia about social media is not warranted because as Howard and Hussain's (2013) work on the Arab Spring demonstrates, "social media alone did not cause political upheaval in North Africa. But information technologies—including mobile phones and the internet—altered the capacity of citizens and civil society actors to affect domestic politics" (2013, 66).

Discursive Analysis of the Bring Back Our Girls Campaign

In this exploratory study, I did a discursive analysis of the comments posted on the BBOG campaign's Facebook pages utilizing three action frames drawn from social movement literature—diagnostic, prognostic, and motivational. Diagnostic is the identification of a problem as well as assignment of blame and causality (Gerhards and Rucht 1992). It includes identification of causes, i.e. naming of cause and causal agents (Gerhards and Rucht 1992, 581). Prognostic framing has to with a proposed solution to the situation at hand. Gerhards and Rucht (1992) hypothesize that the higher the alignment between identified problems and proposed solutions, the greater the mobilization capacity. However, the prognostic frame is less important than the diagnostic one. All the same, spelling out the problem and its solutions may not be enough to mobilize—people must be given a reason to care. A motivational frame—a call to arms—to help resolve the issues is therefore needed. Motives for involvement are created by using terms such as injustice that appeal to the general moral code. Gerhards and Rucht (1992) hypothesize that mobilizing capacity of frames increases with motivational cues.

Analyzing the comments will help identify the way Facebook mobilized individuals and networks to join the campaign by examining how the campaigners defined the problem, the solutions they proffered, and the ways in which offline participation was encouraged.

Methodology

The corpus analyzed was comprised of the Facebook page—www.facebook.com/bringbackourgirls—for the campaign focusing on the initial months of the campaign. I conducted a thematic analysis of posts, messages, and interactions on Facebook to identify the common features in discussions. The Facebook page is characterized by discussions, links to other sites with information on the abduction, links to other campaigners for the same cause such as change.org, media stories on the topic, pictures and signs for the campaign, and assorted information. I focused on the first two months of the campaign—April–May 2014—when the campaign gained worldwide attention.

After collecting the data and organizing it according to source, I read and re-read the data, and repeatedly viewed the videos to become thoroughly familiar with them. I coded the material, generating labels for the data. The codes were both theory-generated from the literature review and also emergent themes from the real-life data. Following that, I coded the data and eventually discovered patterns. As recommended by Marshall and Rossman (2011) I wrote down my thoughts as I started to see how the data were forming clusters as I coded.

The next step was to generate categories and themes from the written and visual postings. I continued to immerse myself in the data, challenging the explanations I had developed against the raw data, following Marshall and Rossman's advice to always go over the work, checking the viability of the explanatory frameworks and interpretations to make sure they are consistent. The material was subjected to a discursive analysis designed to identify the narratives told by Nigerian campaigners and their global supporters in describing the situation, in assigning responsibility, and in calling for action.

Findings

Social media networks are typically characterized by brief comments and short attention spans as was the case in this campaign. A lot of what went on the page were requests for information, activity reports, information sharing, likes, and brief comments with emoticons. Nevertheless, some animated interactions regarding politics, religion, race, and other issues was evident throughout the two-month period.

Discussions on the plight of the missing girls happened at two levels—the first dealt with the immediate problem about what needed to be done to put pressure on leaders to do something about the girls' plight. The other was a larger discussion of our world today that addressed the underlying issues and the context of the tragedy, which the kidnapping is symptomatic of. Hence, the story of the missing schoolgirls is an allegory of what's wrong with our world today, who is responsible, what needs to be done and by whom. I will attempt to tell the smaller story to illustrate the larger one. At the diagnostic level, two subthemes emerged: (a) framing the victims and (b) shaming the duty bearers; at the prognostic: forming alternative solutions; and at the motivational level: storming into action.

Framing the Victims

The missing girls are variously described in posts as "babies," "poor innocent little girls," "helpless children", "daughters of the world," "precious Jewells," "beautiful young girls" and "heroes" who were taken from their school dormitories at night by a terrorist group as they pursued their education in defiance of the group's wishes. As such, people could identify with the cause—it was close to home. People could easily imagine losing a female relative— "they're our sisters, our daughters, our future!" said one comment. Speaking of Boko Haram, another wrote, "how would they feel if their daughter(s) had been kidnapped or taken away by someone else because of a religious belief" [sic].

The girls are portrayed as innocent, brave and good, therefore deserving of saving. This evokes a universal human instinct of protecting its young and vulnerable members. An interesting note is that typically African women are represented negatively according to many studies, but the plight of these girls transforms them and engenders a positive evaluation of them. Such framing creates an obligation to act and universalizes the girls' plight.

The reality is not as straightforward. As one post indicates: "This is not a rare situation. Shit like this happens every day. People are so sheltered they think this is absurd and crazy. When this is the norm. Welcome to earth." This speaks to the fact that while the problem is complex, social media users frame issues simply; they prefer to focus on the heart-wrenching story of the missing girls but not the grittiness of the real situation.

Shaming Duty Bearers

The term duty bearer comes from the field of advocacy and refers to those charged with the responsibility and given capacity to secure the rights of members of society and denotes governments and international governance organizations such as the United Nations among others. In the interactions and comments posted, world governments were criticized for failing in their duty to protect their citizens as were the media for their feckless news coverage. But most criticism targeted the Nigerian and the US governments.

> "This terrorist group has crossed the line the entire world should stop what they're doing and bring back these young women this is unacceptable by every government and everybody shame on our government and all the governments around the world."

> "The problem is, Nigeria's been on a downward spiral for 15–17 years or so. Just like with Afghanistan, the world community didn't do anything, or realize things, before it was too late."

All governments are construed to have been negligent leading to this catastrophe. Frustration and ire over the inaction or slow action of the Federal Republic of Nigeria (FRN) aggravates many, both Nigerians and others alike and as would be expected, it is the target of a majority of the criticism from its citizens and others around the world.

> "shame on the Nigerian government for not protecting it's people!"

> "A very very very very big shame hmmmm nig govment ur finish ooo G E j can't u do sometin?" (A very big shame on the Nigerian government. You are finished. Goodluck Ebele Jonathan, can't you do something?)

> "You hav shown the enemy u are scared n they will keep doing what they do. Stand up Nigeria, time to fight against them, tell them what they are doing is not right"

> "Governmet [sic] must protect people, their rights to go to school and live a life with dignity. They are not doing their job well!!! A country threatened by a group of murderers and kidnappers?? a real shame!!"

The irony is that the Nigerian government is portrayed as inept but at the same time urged to go to the rescue of the girls. The US government is at the receiving end too although it does get some commendation when President Obama offers logistical help. Some blame the US government accusing it of arming the insurgents and destabilizing Nigeria for the sake of oil.

> "Why all of a sudden does the media report this atrocity when it has been happening for ages. . . . Thousands of children are sold for the sex trade every year and nobody cares. Why now? I smell a big fat oil rat."

> "We can fight, invade and kill people over oil, but we can't go and rescue some poor innocent little girls? If it were boys would it have been made priority? This needs to stop and we need to stand up for the innocent regardless of race, region or religion!"

"Bring back our girls campaign is just a revamp of the 'Kony 2012' fail. What about all the underage sex slaves right here in America? Wake up folks, just another globalist agenda for African resources. People on here are idiots."

Some Facebook campaigners see the US as interested only in economic ends but uncaring about social problems especially those that concern people of other races. The issue of race crops up regularly in the discussions. For example, the social media team administering the Facebook campaign speculated that the response would have been different had the girls been white. That generated some interesting responses—"I hate to say it but race matters in everything. From news coverage, to the response, to negotiations, and all the way down to how quickly victims are to be saved" posts one member while another pleads "We sudnt [sic] base this on race this is very heartbreaking."

While others castigate the "globalist agenda" to plunder Africa's resources, interestingly, Nigerian members welcome US help. As one writes "Pls don't blame the U.S. and UK govt, they only just got invited to help. My country is sleeping while terror is raging." It seems most people are comfortable lambasting their own governments.

The trope of shame is universal and is used to require accountability over those who fail to perform their duty. The expectation is that a person so shamed will fulfill their responsibilities to save face. The final duty bearer here, the media, are castigated for their delay in highlighting the issue and for insufficient coverage. Several members comment that the media in the US, focused on trivia—this was the period where the scandal of racist comments by Donald Sterling, owner of the Los Angeles Clippers at the time, were making the rounds—while a human tragedy was unfolding.

"Amazingly courageous woman taking a stand by sitting down. Wish they would show this on CNN."

"There is not enough news coverage. The news seems to be concentration on the idiot basketball guy just a few weeks too late."

"If the media hadn't been so obsessed with the clippers they might have noticed this was going on way back in April and help could have gone in sooner."

"Fox news tends to have a lot of BS"

Clearly the role of the media in setting the agenda is widely seen as crucial in humanitarian crises. The CNN effect, though contested, suggests that high media coverage of a humanitarian catastrophe may lead to action under certain circumstances (Gilboa 2005). Comments indicate the expectation that the media should perform its public interest mandate by informing global publics on critical issues, and some felt the media failed the public with regard to this story. In one post, citing similarities between the coverage of the Rwandan genocide and the girls, the perceived lack of media attention is seen as a pattern of media bias against Africa.

In this case, because of the lack of progress in rescuing the girls, governments of the world and the media take the blame for not doing enough in a timely manner to resolve the issue.

Forming Alternative Solutions

Having demonstrated their disenchantment with world leaders and with media responses, new avenues of hope are created. Alternative proposals are offered as strategies for resolving the crisis. A picture of US female Senators showing their support posted by the campaign staff triggered discussion and a call for women to provide leadership.

> "Come on ladies you all could do better than that—never heard you say out loud on any news that you are behind this . . . shout!!!"

> "More proof we need a woman to lead us so that no important issues are ignored."

> "Me and my 3 year old SON DID THIS!!! I NEED YOU LADIES TO SPEAK LOUDER UNFORTUNATELY I DON'T HAVE THE RESOURCES YOU ALL DO!!"

> "Thank you Beautiful First Lady Michelle Obama, Secretary Clinton and all of our congressional leaders for showing your support!"

One woman even called for a "women's kick ass army!!!" On balance, some Facebook users asked Obama to send SEAL 6 to rescue the girls.

The power of motherhood was also invoked.

> "It doesn't matter where we live. It doesn't matter the color of their skin nor their economic standing. We are all mothers, they are our daughter. We all have the same God designed invisible cord wrapped and intertwined connecting heart to heart between mother and child. It does not discriminate between continents. Today may we unite with the mothers and daughters of Nigeria in prayer."

> "I re-posted, in Germany, Where are all the mothers? . . .

> Every single mother on social media should be shouting and taking a stand to support these mothers who's hearts are broken.

> What if this was Your Child?

> This is serious, where are all the mothers, sisters, aunts grandmothers, godmothers"

While the power of motherhood and womanhood is called on to solve an issue involving women, it is also called upon to provide broader global leadership. In an interesting move toward enlisting celebrity backers, one campaign supporter invoked Oprah. On May 6: "Be sure to write Oprah as well—she has the money and the power to help get the girls back!"

Prayer and divine power was another realm mentioned by many as a source of hope. This however elicited a lot of debate. In the eyes of some, prayer and dependence on God was akin to the fanaticism of the Boko Haram that had resulted in so much death and destruction. These terse exchanges illustrate the dynamic:

Sample 1

B—"We can also pray that The Lord of all will rescue these girls"
D—"Warped religion is the reason they were taken."

Sample 2

C—"God's intervention is the only solution to my dear country. The government has failed us!, but God won't."

459

M—"Yes, if you are counting on "God" to fix it, go . . . on . . . and see the destruction. God helps those who ACT on their convictions, in the face of adversity!"

C—"So its a pity that our commander in chief isnt [sic] really strong willed to make decisions and act out hos convictions. So God has to intervene as the last option."

J—"God helps those that help themselves—GET IT ?"

C—"Yea. I get it. And we helps ourselves by HIS grace. Get it?"

While the Facebook page is sprinkled with all kinds of prayer, and calls for prayer, there is a clear rift between those who place faith in divine power and those who prefer to rely on individual, community, and official actions.

People power is the other alternative touted by some Facebook supporters. There are calls for people to step up since all the other institutions and structures have failed.

> "The Nigerian government knew about the attack ahead of time and did nothing about it. We need to stop putting these bastards in power, give them our power, and then wait for them to do something about it! As John Lennon once said POWER TO THE PEOPLE."

> "Power is in numbers . . . let's turn our anger into strength hope and bright light."

> "We'll do what we can. Never under estimate the power of concerned human beings."

> "It is glaring that all is not well with this administration, the best way to help is to make sure the balloting of 2015 is credible and let the wishes of the masses be respected. Our voice and vote will give us a better alternative, We will win."

Facebook users express a need for alternatives to the current global configuration and ideas proposed, include women showing the way, ordinary people acting collectively, and the contested power of prayer or divine help.

Storming into Action

Motivational frames took the form of posts in which Facebook users reported their activities— rallies, protests, marches, prayer vigils, writing to the leaders, wearing red on certain days, recruiting others and so on—and encouraged others to organize or participate. A related sub-theme was requests for information and offers to host events related to the campaign. For example,

> "I just contacted 311 in NYC for a request for a rally on 5/11. I am clueless in this endeavor but determined. Once again my hope is their safe return by then."

> "Let's do it in NC too!!!!!"

> "Happy to assist in Christchurch"

> "Are there any marches planned in Boston, Mass?? Does anyone know or where I can find out??"

> "I can host meetings to organise in my office glasgow city centre."

> "And if you can't make it to a march, google the contact details for your country's embassy and bombard them with phone calls asking them what is being done to find the girls and support their families."

"THIS NEEDS TO STOP! Help these Girls!!"

"WHAT SHALL WE DO? Likes and shares can only do so much- what is the next step?"

Creation of motives was done by making a personal appeal to people's sense of outrage at such injustice. "Just imagine your daughter, sister, neice, [sic] or someone you love being taken?" Such statements demonstrate the ease with which people could identify with the events in far-away Nigeria. This entailed framing BBOG as a familiar story that raises indignation, reaches into people's deepest fears and propels them to act. It appeals to primal fear in humans—that of losing a close family member. It speaks to our collective vulnerability in a world that is increasingly hostile and threatening.

Exhortation about the need to act as it could happen anywhere showed a measure of self-preservation in joining the campaign. "Let everyone help! The whole world should. It could be one of our daughters!" "If they can do this there—they can do it ANYWHERE; these girls are a symbol of all the children [sic] of the world!"

Discussion

The discourse of the campaign's Facebook pages highlights the injustice that has been perpetrated. Girls were kidnapped from school by a terror group and world governments are unwilling or unable to address this menace. When exploring solutions people invoke the power of women as mothers and family members, divine solutions including prayer, and the power of individuals to reach out to their communities and even celebrities. Participants in the social campaign are motivated by their high level of identification with the situation based on the motivational cues created by the campaign at both the mesomobilization and micromobilization levels.

This chapter started by posing the question of how a local campaign from Africa went global. This can be attributed to the framing of the story, especially its universality. As we saw earlier, various descriptors used to portray the girls on Facebook mirrored those used to describe missing children everywhere. It is the familiar tale—innocent children kidnapped by evil forces—found everywhere. As a narrative theme, its universal appeal is unquestionable. Such narratives proliferate in popular culture and Hollywood films but also in fables and folk stories around the world.

The framing of the Bring Back Our Girls campaign follows the same model of a simple narrative that is easy to latch onto. It fits with Lim's observation that "only simple or simplified narratives can usually go viral." He goes on to identify the problems posed by the use of such narratives. "At the same time, simple or simplified narratives are associated with low risk activism and are congruent with ideological meta-narratives, such as nationalism and religiosity" (Lim 2013, 638). In their discussion of online activism Gotham and Krier (2008, 157) cite another drawback to the use of themes derived from popular cultural narratives. Simple narratives show the power of spectacle for they must be "ruled by the dictates of advertising and commodified media culture" (Gotham and Krier 2008, 157). In this sense, political engagement is circumscribed by demands of the entertainment genre and loses steam when the complexities of real life intrude. The simplified narratives of global commercial media offer quick, often product solutions to simplistic consumer problems. So widely dispersed is this entertainment culture that global conversations from diverse parts of the globe such as Africa, North America, Asia, and Europe can converge within this framework. But what happens when easy resolutions to simplified frameworks cannot be achieved? Online activists may swiftly move on to the next campaign.

The literature suggests that online activism can be fickle, nothing more than lazy armchair activism involving mouse clicks. As Lim notes "social media activism has a tendency for being *fast, thin* and *many*. In other words, online campaigns emerge each minute and often quickly disappear without any trace" (Lim 2013, 637). Inevitably the momentum slows down, and indeed as the months passed involvement with Bring Back Our Girls plateaued, showing much less activity on social media. However, the first anniversary of the girls' disappearance offered new hope, as successful events were carried out in several countries. In defense of online campaigns, these activities do not differ greatly from other forms of collective actions. And as Tarrow points out, "collective action can take many forms—brief or sustained, institutionalized or disruptive, humdrum or dramatic" (1988, 7).

The Save Our Girls campaign was no armchair activism. The campaign resulted in offline participation as can be ascertained from the many posts on the detailed activities—social media users posted pictures of themselves participating in rallies, marches, vigils while others reported fundraising activities, writing to leaders, and attending meetings. Requests for information on campaigns in various cities and countries and requests for country-specific petitions were common. As such, "whether we look at PPF, Arab Spring, the indignados, or Occupy, we note surprising success in communicating *simple political messages* [emphasis mine] directly to outside publics using common digital technologies such as Facebook or Twitter" (Bennett and Segerberg 2012, 742). When such stories get traction, they are then picked up by mainstream media. As such, digital activism is a component of modern-day activism that cannot be ignored. True to Harlow's (2011) findings on Guantamelan social movement, this was a networked social movement that started online and triggered offline activities, showing that commitment was beyond fickle clicktivism.

But did it result in a significant concerted global effort to rescue the girls? Several governments offered help but how that panned out is unclear. What is clear is that almost two years on, the girls are still missing. But important gains were made such as putting Boko Haram on the global watch list making it easier for the Nigerian government to appeal for and secure resources needed to tackle the Islamist group. Almost two years later, the Nigerian army has successfully reclaimed territory in eastern Nigeria such as Maiduguri, the birth place of Boko Haram, although by no means has the group being eliminated as a threat (www.bbc.com/news/world-africa-35175244). Yet as the HBO program Vice has reported, Nigerian government forces have also engaged in atrocities when routing out the Islamic extremists. This brings up the question of simple solutions offered in online comments, to bringing back the girls with Seal Team 6. In an age of global blockbuster films that habitually offer militarization and force as resolutions to global problems, diplomacy, and negotiation are often given short shrift. Indeed, the larger question remains as to the effectiveness of continued global weaponization and bombings to end Islamic extremism even as it creates the conditions for its spread.

Conclusion

Rather than demarcating online and offline collective action, activists should create better coordination between online activism and offline activism since it is unlikely that traditional activism will fully migrate online. Indeed, both are mutually beneficial as off-line activism often provides online content and comments able to boost motivations and breathe new life into the digital world. In addition, digitally mediated collective action needs to be harnessed because of its potential for exponential growth characteristics that assure flexibility in tracking political targets and creating connections between various issues (Bennett and Segerberg 2012, 742).

Increasingly, personalized connections through social media networks now address global challenges. A well-structured campaign with a simple narrative can go viral and attain global attention. Despite the digital divide, there is a critical mass of people in Africa active online due to high mobile phone uptake, which makes it possible for users to initiate digital campaigns that spread fast globally. However, even when activism moves off-line and begins to mobilize multiple publics across national boundaries, it is difficult to maintain momentum when the problem is not solved, and the issue is relegated to a frozen atrocity that lingers over time.

The narratives that go viral are the ones that touch on universal themes, and many of those themes comprise what has become global entertainment culture. As such they can now come from any part of the world because our mediatized cultures are increasingly united by the logic of entertainment media. Social media campaigns that resonate with mediated experiences increase their chances of success. Indeed, fears of child abduction, protective motherhood, invoking an international superpower, celebrity, and even divine intervention are all recognizable narrative tropes. Prospects for successful online collective global action therefore, seem to follow what Tarrow (1988, 16) laid out well before the internet, that "solutions to the problem of mobilizing people into campaigns and coalitions of collective action depend on shared understandings, social networks, and connective structures and the use of culturally resonant forms of action."

What does this portend for the future? With governments and international institutions seemingly unable to tackle mounting global poverty, social problems, and especially global terrorism, and as Islamic fundamentalism spreads in the wake of failed militarized foreign policies and invasions, will a people's movement become the next arena for action? Identifying solutions that can resonate across cultures, national boundaries, and ethnic divides are narratives not easily found in commodified global media forms. The Bring Back Our Girls campaign was about young women, and women were at the vanguard of both online and offline organizing. Will women, whose networking abilities are considerable, be at the vanguard of such movements? If so, will they also have to rewrite the narratives that offer solutions to seemingly intractable problems, ones outside global entertainment culture? These are tantalizing prospects that will be revealed with time.

References

Bennett, W. L., and Segerberg A. (2012) "The Logic of Connective Action," *Information, Communication and* Society, 15 (5): 739–768.

Christensen, H. S. (2011) "Political Activities on the Internet: Slacktivism or Political Participation by Other Means?" by *First Monday* 16 (2–7), http://firstmonday.org/ojs/index.php/fm/rt/printerFriendly/3336/2767

Daily Mail. (2015) "More than 1,000 schools destroyed by Boko Haram this year: UN." November 16, available at: www.dailymail.co.uk/wires/afp/article-3320501/More-1-000-schools-destroyed-Boko-Haram-year-UN.html

della Porta, D., Andretta, M, Mosco, L., and Reiter, H. (2006) *Globalization from Below: Transnational Activists and Protest Networks*, Minneapolis, MN: University of Minnesota Press.

Drumbl, M. A. (2012) "Child Soldiers and Clicktivism: Justice, Myths, and Prevention," *Journal of Human Rights Practice*, 4 (3): 481–485.

Engelhardt, J. von, and Jansz, J. (2014) "Challenging Humanitarian Communication: An Empirical Exploration of Kony," *International Communication Gazette*, 76 (6): 464–484.

Engelhardt, J. von, and Jansz, J. (2015) "Distant Suffering: The Mediation of Humanitarian Disaster," in R. E. Anderson, (Ed.), *World Suffering and Quality of Life*, Dordrecht and New York: Springer Science + Business Media, pp. 75–87, available at: http://link.springer.com/book/10.1007/978-94-017-9670-5#page-1

Gerhards, J., and Rucht, D. (1992) "Mesomobilization: Organizing and Framing in Two Protest Campaigns in West Germany," *American Journal of Sociology*, 98: 555–595.

Gilboa, E. (2005) "The CNN Effect: The Search for a Communication Theory of International Relations," *Political Communication*, 22: 27–44.

Gotham, K. F. and Krier, D. A. (2008) "From the Culture Industry to the Society of the Spectacle: Critical Theory and the Situationist International," *No Social Science Without Critical Theory: Current Perspectives in Social Theory*, 25: 155–192, available at: www.soc.iastate.edu/staff/krier/1761652.pdf

Haeri, M. (2008) "Saving Darfur: Does Advocacy Help or Hinder Conflict Resolution?" *PRAXIS The Fletcher Journal of Human Security*, 23: 33–46.

Harlow, S. (2011) "Social media and social movements: Facebook and an online Guatemalan justice movement that moved offline," *New Media and Society*, 14 (2): 225–243.

Harlow, S., and Harp, D. (2012) "Collective Action on The Web," *Information, Communication and Society*, 15 (2): 196–216.

Howard, P. N., and Hussain, M. M. (2013) *Democracy's Fourth Wave? Digital Media and the Arab Spring*, Oxford, UK: Oxford University Press.

Lim, M. (2013) "Many Clicks but Little Sticks: Social Media Activism in Indonesia," *Journal of Contemporary Asia*, 43 (4): 636–657.

Lim, M., and Moufahim, M. (2015) "The Spectacularization of Suffering: An Analysis of the Use of Celebrities in 'Comic Relief' UK's Charity Fundraising Campaigns," *Journal of Marketing Management*, 31 (5–6): 525–545.

Marichal, J. (December 2013) "Political Facebook Groups: Micro-activism and the Digital Front Stage," *First Monday*, 18 (12), available at: http://firstmonday.org/ojs/index.php/fm/article/view/4653/3800

Marshall, C., and Rossman, G. B. (2011) *Designing Qualitative Research*, Thousand Oaks, CA: Sage.

Nash, K. (2008) "Global Citizenship as Show Business: The Cultural Politics of Make Poverty History," *Media Culture Society*, 30 (2): 167–181.

Powell, A. B. (2016) "Network Exceptionalism: Online Action, Discourse and the Opposition to SOPA and ACTA," *Information, Communication and Society*, 19 (2): 249–263.

Sniderman, A. S. (2011) "A Brief History of 'Save Darfur,'" *Columbia Journalism Review*, available at: www.cjr.org/critical_eye/a_brief_history_of_save_darfur.php

Strom, S., and Polgreen L. (2007) "Darfur Advocacy Group Undergoes a Shake-Up," *New York Times*, June 2, available at: www.nytimes.com/2007/06/02/world/africa/02darfur.html?_r=1&

Tarrow, S. (1988) *Power in Movement*, Cambridge, UK: Cambridge University Press.

Theocharis, Y. (2015) "The Conceptualization of Digitally Networked Participation," *Social Media and Society*, July–December: 1–14.

Van Laer, J., and Van Aelst, P. (2010) "Internet and Social Movement Action Repertoires. *Information, Communication & Society*," 13 (8): 1146–1171.

Vissers, S., and Dietlind, S. (2014) "Spill-Over Effects Between Facebook and On/Offline Political Participation? Evidence from a Two-Wave Panel Study," *Journal of Information Technology and Politics*, 11 (3): 259–275.

38

"TAKE MY PICTURE"

The Media Assemblage of Lone-Wolf Terror Events, Mobile Communication, and the News

Kenzie Burchell

The perpetrator of the 2011 attacks in Norway left a manifesto that included strategies for the "live transmission" of such materials online but in it he stressed the best option would be an internet ready mobile phone with a prepared list of email addresses. During the 2014 University of California Santa Barbara killing spree, the shooter distributed his 137-page manifesto by email and uploaded a video entitled "Retribution" to YouTube (O'Hagan 2015, 3, 5, 6). In Virginia, 2015, a former reporter would shoot two journalists who at the time were conducting an interview live on air. He filmed it on his phone and posted it to Twitter as he fled.

On May 22, 2013, Michael Adebolajo spoke calmly and directly to witnesses who had gathered on the street in Woolwich South London—"Take my picture"—and with the others crowded against the windows of a stopped bus looking on as he and his accomplice Michael Adebowale spoke to those nearby—"I just want to talk to you with your camera" (Pettifor and Lines 2013; *The Telegraph* 2013). He was wielding a meat cleaver and his hands were soaked in blood. Their hands held mobile phones, filming videos and snapping pictures that would blanket the news media for days. The public daytime murder and attempted beheading of British Army Soldier, Fusilier Lee Rigby, by two men near the Woolwich barracks in South London represents a frightening calculus of media and witnessing, echoing the ego-driven machinations of American mass shooters but in order to trigger a mediated "monumentalisation" of the act of terror, a spotlight for the underlying extremist ideology (Hutchings and Burchell, forthcoming). This represents a crisis for terror reporting conventions, the potential exploitation of which becomes a threat to public safety.

The crude simplicity of the mass shooting is being echoed in the strategies of its politicized and organized corollary, terror. The evolution of the latter has seen a shift from the spectacular terror attacks on institutions and landmarks towards the coordinated multi-prong attacks on soft targets and the "lone-wolf" attacks carried out by an isolated but radicalized individual or pair of individuals in a very public manner. This chapter seeks to better understand the contemporary matrices of citizen journalism, mobile technology, and news reporting as they are enrolled within an *assemblage* of normally discrete everyday acts and cultural practices, exploited by the "lone-wolf" attack and constitutive of the resulting terror media event.

In presenting a theoretical model for better understanding the role of mobile communication in terror coverage, this chapter borrows from, and redirects, the data and insights accrued from a co-authored study led by Professor Stephen Hutchings entitled *Comparative Approaches to Islam, Security and Television News* (Hutchings & Burchell 2014),[1] a research endeavor that monitored European Public Service Broadcasting to assess the representations of Islam in British, French, and Russian media and the implications for editorial and political policy. The consistent monitoring and qualitative analysis of news broadcasts, alongside discourse and visual imagery analysis of specific case studies has provided the vantage point from which the analysis in this chapter emerged and that of other ongoing collaborations with Prof. Hutchings.

The Media Event as Assemblage

You decided, between you, and in order to advance your extremist cause, to murder a soldier in public in broad daylight and to do so in a way that would generate maximum media coverage.
(From the sentencing verdict of Justice Sweeney, Stubley 2013)

The "media events" framework was originally developed to interrogate those exceptional moments when routines of both daily media coverage and everyday consumption of news are interrupted and replaced by a heightened attention to large-scale often national events such as the Olympics, state funerals, and coronations that are deemed to be historic and enthralling (Dayan and Katz 1992). This framework has been redeveloped for better understanding "live broadcasting of disruptive events of disaster, terror, and armed conflict" (Katz and Liebes 2010, 25). In a further recalibration the institutionalized event, readied media infrastructure, coverage, and expected national if not global audiences can be understood as a "platform" (Price 2011) that presents an opportunity for non-sanctioned actors, such as protestors or terrorists, to "hijack" the event (Dayan 2010). This implies: "the sometimes forceful, but certainly involuntary or antagonistic, seizure of world attention" (Dayan 2005 as cited in Price 2011, 86). The 1972 hostage crisis at the Munich Olympics remains a salient example of such media event hijacking, while the 2013 bombing of the Boston Marathon offers a contemporary example within the framework of "lone-wolf" terror attacks. The Rigby murder, however, was not a hijacking of a sanctioned event and readied platform, it was or rather became the media event itself. What then served as the platform?

The public daytime murder of Lee Rigby became a media event through an *assemblage* of technical and cultural performances—disparate parts that formed the aftermath of a horrific violent spectacle. I use the word performance, because the assemblage is an extraordinary coming together of certain types of practices: the public as eyewitnesses, mobile and networked communication technologies, and the particular conventions of crisis news reporting coalescing around the event itself. This is more than just the routine news production and dissemination, the existing *apparatus* of the news technologies and practices are involved. The assemblage is also different from the temporary but readied *platform* of an organized media event, where numerous aspects of both infrastructure and media coverage are planned and coordinated. The assemblage is a temporary and functional coming together of disparate elements. Reactive rather than spontaneous, it is a "multiplicity of heterogeneous objects, whose unity comes solely from the fact that these items function together, that they 'work' together as a functional entity" (Patton 1994, 158 as cited in Haggerty and Ericson 2000, 608).

The media event as an *assemblage* draws from two dimensions of the term: performativity and connectivity. In his analysis of spatially situated social "performances," Goffman argues for greater attention to the "assemblages of sign-equipment which . . . performers call their own for short periods of time" (Goffman 1956, 14). The "setting" of any given public interaction becomes "equipment" for the performer and these notions can be borrowed from the everyday context of Goffman's analysis to the multiple scales of the media event: the public space within which the perpetrator and witnesses interact and the wider networked spaces of news production and dissemination. In the former, the public and their mobile phones become equipment. In the latter, eyewitness photos and videos, online commentary, social network testimonies become equipment for the performance of the news. The second dimension, connectivity, borrows from notions of both the institutionally oriented "surveillant assemblage" (Haggerty and Ericson 2000) and everyday "monitoring assemblage" of the public's networked sharing practices (Andrejevic 2007, 223). Both denote the convergence of numerous connected but discrete systems of mobile and online communication. From Haggerty and Ericson's notion of assemblage, I am borrowing the notion that bodies and events are abstracted from their territorial setting into "series of discrete flows" of information. These flows, however, are not the data-based flows attached to their concept of the "surveillant assemblage," but the flows of mobile image production, online sharing, and social networking. Such image-laden social networks form the foundation of Andrejevic's "monitoring assemblage," relating to popular aspects of everyday interpersonal communication that can be understood as "lateral" or "peer-to-peer" surveillance between everyday citizens. In this manner, the media event assemblage brings together the citizen as an eyewitness with the capabilities of mobile communication and the reach of news media infrastructure and production practices.

Witnessing and Citizen Journalism

Understanding the role of mobile footage in reporting the Lee Rigby murder involves inquiry into the constituent transformations involved in its production, dissemination, and framing. These intertwined mediations help us understand the media event as an assemblage that enlists the witness, the technology, and the institutional cultures and economies of news journalism. Our analysis will begin with the very act of witnessing a crisis in the contemporary urban context of nearly ubiquitous mobile technology use.

The varying forms of amateur or user-generated media content are often placed under the ambiguous rubric of "citizen journalism" denoting the "ordinary person's capacity to bear witness" having gained currency in the aftermath of relatively recent natural disasters (Allan 2009: 18). Amateur imagery produced in the aftermath of large-scale humanitarian disasters such as Hurricane Katrina in 2005, the 2009 South Asian tsunami and earthquakes in Sichaun 2008, Haiti 2010 and Japan 2011, each demonstrate the intervening role of the imagery produced by everyday citizens within crisis reporting (Wahl-Jorgensen and Pantti 2013, 191). The particular characteristics of its production, in contrast to those of professional journalists often late to the scene of the crisis, contribute to a type of emotional participation by news audiences in the unfolding events. This sense of mediated witnessing underpins the cultural role of the contemporary "global media event" (Couldry and Hepp 2009), which as Cottle writes, serves to "sustain and/or mobilize [some degree] of collective sentiment and solidarities" around the event (2006, 415).

In the use of citizen journalism, the news media rely heavily on visual imagery and for this reason our examination will draw from the traditions of "eyewitness photography" and "eyewitness accounts" (Mortensen 2011, 63, 64). Given the unexpected nature of natural disasters and terror attacks alike, as well as inaccessibility of crisis areas, news organizations are often dependent on amateur material to "tell the story on the ground" (Allan 2013, 93). The 2008 Mumbai attacks demonstrated the facility of mobile communication and online social networks to place eyewitness imagery at the centre of reporting. As the crisis unfolded, videos reached news organizations from those trapped in the Taj Hotel, online Flickr image streams covered the scenes in the streets outside, and minute-to-minute updates were provided from witnesses over Twitter (Ibrahim 2009, 17; Seib and Janbek 2010, 19). Traditional reporting of such attacks evokes an "aesthetics of the aftermath," where the "emergency services, pools of blood, bodies . . . come to stand for the horrors of urban killing" (Chouliaraki 2013, 150). There is also, however, a concomitant aesthetic of mobile eye-witness photography defined by the physical embodied presence of the witness and risk involved.

In his examination of citizen media production and its impact on contemporary journalism, Allan points in particular to its "raw, immediate, independent and unapologetically subjective" nature (Allan 2013, 94). The immediacy mentioned here is not simply the pragmatic notion of being on the scene before journalists; it carries with it the insinuation of a moral, if not civic, imperative to respond to trauma, victimhood, and/or endangerment by bearing witness, an "injunction to care" despite that danger (Allan 2013, 108). Historically, the credibility of witness accounts is derived from this ethical position as victim or survivor. In the case of terror, the witness account is defined in contradistinction to the violence of perpetrators. Though individual witnesses are perceived to be on "the right side of history" (Mortensen 2011, 69, 70) and the production and dissemination of imagery contributes to holding perpetrators to account, this chapter seeks to complicate this assumption by examining the role of, indeed reliance upon, their presence at the terror attack and appropriation of their recorded imagery within the ensuing media event. Mobile imagery of the Woolwich aftermath is defined, rather, by the (literal) proximity to the event and the affective and moral force of being endangered. This stands in direct contrast to the traditional journalistic notion of objective detachment and rational (figurative) distance.

Eyewitness imagery of terror carries with it an assumption of "neutrality and unbiased reporting," not through the emotional detachment of a professional reporter but through an "embodied objectivity" of the unseen producers of the imagery (Blaagaard 2013, 362). Rather than offering a particular individual's subjective interpretation of the scene, the imagery offers an emotional translation of an individual as a body in mortal danger during the production of the imagery. Much of the Woolwich imagery is shot just a few steps away from the murderers, blood soaked hands and meat cleaver are in full view. The perpetrators passed an old 9.44ml KNIL Model 91 Revolver between them (Metropolitan Police 2013). As the judge commented "Each of you had the gun at one point or another and it was used to warn off any male member of the public who looked as though he might intervene" and, though the gun did not function, "those who saw the gun believed that it was real and loaded" (Press Association 2014). The spatially situated presence of the witnesses during the event as well as their proximity to murder and the murderers represent the conditions of media production. These translate into the authenticity of the imagery as representations of the event and also the highly affective force of the imagery. Drawing on Barthes, Blaagaard (2013, 363) argues that such traumatic images suspend language and other layers of connotation; this leaves the viewer with shock and affect at viewing the scene. The affective force of threat is compounded by the presence of Lee Rigby's body, slain in the street behind, visible in some of the Woolwich imagery over the shoulders of the attackers.

The Assumed Automaticity of the Digital Record

The legal investigation that would follow the Rigby murder would at its peak involve over 600 officers, 4,214 exhibits, the searching of 17 addresses and six cars, as well as the statements from 1,456 individuals (Metropolitan Police 2013). From the numerous eyewitness tweets, photos, and videos, only a few would emerge as part of the media event, many of them from the recordings by a single individual. Their iconic representation of the event would overwrite subtle differences between numerous photos and allow for a further removal of the witness, replaced instead by the technology.

Legal traditions of the eyewitness demonstrate successive shifts in determining the authenticity and credibility of witnessing that is instructive for understanding the uptake of amateur eye-witness imagery during a media event: photos or video imagery produced by eyewitnesses stand in for witness accounts and the mobile camera lens has begun to stand in for the witnesses themselves. Frisch reports that in colonial and juridical cultures of early modern France witnessing shifted from a matter of "being here" to bear witness in the presence of others to holding the privileged eyewitness position of having "been there" to witness something as it occurred, which "encourages the possibility of thinking of experiences as detachable from the people who have them" (2004, 114). This cultural re-evaluation places the objective event and access to it as the source of authenticity rather than the credibility of a particular witness.

A similar re-evaluation would contribute to the acceptance of photography and eventually video imagery as evidence. In the 20 years following its invention, photography was valued by the American court for the divergent uses as a transcription of a scene and also to complement human stories, an "appendage to someone's testimony" (Mnookin 1998, 4–6). The perceived facility of its automatic representation of a scene, however, would come to define its legitimacy as evidence, once again shedding the particular subjective associations linked to the image producer (Mnookin 1998, 18). More recently at the International Criminal Tribunal for the former Yugoslavia at The Hague, the legal basis for using video evidence can be seen to similarly emerge from earlier protocols that attached the authenticity of the video to the presence and evaluation of the eyewitness who produced the video (Ristovska 2015).

The Remediation of Witnessing and Removal of the Witnesses Identity

Upon closer inspection of the shifting conditions for producing and sharing content through mobile and networked technologies, the moral imperative to bear witness takes on a new form whereby the use of mobile photography and videos is enrolled in an "ethics of showing," manifest in one's feeling of "personal obligation to engage in—and render publicly available—their own forms of citizen witnessing" (Allan 2014, 145). Beyond the notion of eye-witness accounts as amateur journalism, this impetus draws from the wider inter-personal cultures and existing infrastructures for "lateral surveillance," popularized by mobile and online platforms for sharing and monitoring that are part of everyday social life (Andrejevic 2005). This produces a form of witnessing that is different in quality from the traditional sense of bearing witness: the act of recording and sharing facilitates the mediated participation of others and this is not a personal testimonial but is rather a networking of the emotional impact of presence and viewing but carrying with it the sense of technological representation.

The particular mediations involved in mobile production and communication of eye-witness imagery result in a sense of authenticity by the particular framing of footage and also from the networked proliferation of multiple representations of the same event. The footage is specifically lacking the more polished look of professional journalistic output, framed instead by the shakiness, hesitation, and picture quality indicative of an eyewitness holding a mobile phone amidst the unfolding traumatic scene. Unlike the instrumental look of security and CCTV footage, the familiar quality and angle of mobile footage carries a sense of raw everyday experience, mistaken for an unmediated presentation of a scene. The images and video of Adebolajo taken during his justificatory rant, and the imagery taken from the inside of a nearby bus of the perpetrators talking to a female eyewitness who hoped to help Rigby, all carry that familiar framing of mobile footage. The motion and rhythm of videos, the particularities of the angle and form of the frame are emotionally significant to the viewer. Witnessing cannot be understood in this case as the passive act of observing. It is a discursive act that, in the case of Woolwich mobile-phone-wielding bystanders, becomes an act of media production. Historical contexts of witness testimonies occur in two stages: passive observation and the act of retelling or "bearing witness." In the case of the media-producing eyewitness, these acts are not temporally distinct. In this manner, the experience of the witness and the event itself are themselves mediated by virtue of the camera's presence (Mortensen, 2011, 70).

The Multiplicity and Immediacy of Networked Witnessing

This act of media production by eyewitnesses with their mobile phones, then, is also part of the wider technological context, specifically the ubiquity of mobile technology and the networked connectivity that enables information sharing across social networking and online platforms. When considering the role of eyewitness footage of the Woolwich attack, the ubiquity of mobile photo and video capture technology—quite literally in the hands and pockets of the population at large—points towards a production of multiple witness accounts. The multiple vantage points and sources from which Woolwich imagery, updates, and commentary was produced validate the authenticity of accounts while undermining and partially erasing the particular identity of witnesses that traditionally were crucial for determining credibility or at least neutrality vis-à-vis the event. The ubiquity of mobile image-producing technology introduces a new tension to our understanding of the witness: "When every onlooker, every participant is free to join the ranks of the eyewitness, it is questionable whether the moral claim still holds, since the basic 'who' and 'why' of picture makers often hang in the balance" (Mortensen 2011, 72).

This represents a disruption of individual responsibility for eyewitness records. We must ask then, what are the consequences for journalism when this record and its dissemination are ostensibly the intended outcomes of terror. Amateur coverage of crisis events combines with the "near instant" dissemination of that material, as individuals share commentary and upload imagery to social networking sites. These platforms bypass traditional journalism outlets for breaking coverage (Allan 2014, 134). While the use of eyewitness imagery and social media during the South Asian Tsunami and the 2008 Mumbai Terror Attacks represent prominent thresholds for the breaking coverage of crisis, live-blogging and reporting on social media has now been incorporated into mainstream reporting on a whole range of unfolding events, crises or otherwise (Thurman and Rodgers 2014, 87).

The attack on Lee Rigby involved an attempted beheading of his body, dragged to the middle of the street after being rammed by the perpetrators' car at approximately 14:20 GMT on May 22, 2013. Footage and commentary was shared across social media as the perpetrators spoke to bystanders and awaited, armed, the arrival of the police for a subsequent public confrontation. The broadcaster ITV posted running updates online by quoting tweets from police and emergency services and bystanders and then at 15:31 from the Press Association alert regarding a "serous incident" (ITV News 2013; Ofcom 2014). *The Sun* and ITV both received mobile videos of Michael Adebolajo speaking directly to witnesses in the immediate aftermath of the murder. ITV News first linked to a YouTube video of the arrest and then later followed this with mobile phone videos received from one of the two individuals who had filmed rather than only photographed the immediate aftermath. ITV posted the video online and the site crashed from the viewer traffic. This video would be first aired on ITV *London Tonight* at approximately 18:20 before being broadcast by multiple other broadcasters (Hollander 2013, Ofcom 2014, 23). Eight of the ten major national British newspapers would carry an image of Adebolajo, hands soaked in blood speaking steps away from the eyewitnesses filming him.

The emergence of event coverage over social media challenges the gatekeeping functions of broadcasters and print newspapers, as they find themselves chasing an online flow of information rather than breaking the story themselves (Seib and Janbek 2010, 19). The related consequences for reporting and verification are compounded by competition across traditional media outlets, no longer waiting until the next broadcast or print edition but racing to update their news online. Unlike the classic media events envisioned by Dayan and Katz, the contemporary terror media event does not depend on the pre-planned coordinated live broadcasting of the event: the presence of eyewitnesses with mobile networked devices provides the basis for mediated witnessing.

Imagery produced in and around the scene of the Rigby murder was captured from multiple vantage points, shared over social media and represented in the national news detached from the personal accounts of the individuals. The coverage of multiple accounts by traditional media would eventually bracket out individual voices in the cacophony of raw footage and aftermath coverage. With no identity to be placed under personal or moral scrutiny, the very technology emerges as a mediator of the account. In his unpacking of the traditional role of the witness, Peters suggests that "the ideal human witness would behave like a thing: a mere tablet or recording" (Peters 2009, 33), but the immediate recording and dissemination of multiple accounts further reinforce that very technological frame. If the public accountability of the witness is excluded by this shift, then what about the editorial responsibility of the journalist and media outlet? The framing of the eyewitness coverage adheres to assumed credibility of the technological frame, reinforced by the single camera of an eyewitness and the multiple re-mediations of accounts across different mediums. The automaticity of mediated witnessing emerges from the immediacy involved in both the production of the image and also its dissemination.

Performativity of the News Apparatus

There is a certain disruptive character to the media event, as witness accounts, emergency service reports, public commentary, and updates by wire services and reporters begin to monopolize social media first, then the websites of news outlets, and finally broadcast bulletins and newspaper front pages. Van Loon suggests that a planned media event such as the Olympics involves "a particular constellation of mediators, humans and non-humans, that are invoked to 'make sense' and 'order" experiences' (2010, 120). For the terror media event, however, there is similarly a particular constellation of actors, technologies, and practices that align in response to an attack: this is the media event assemblage of witnessing, mobile communication, and news conventions that comes together to make sense of, and communicate the emotional shock of an attack. The media event assemblage is defined by its relative immediacy and extension across the media practices and platforms of citizens and journalists, thereby providing a useful analytical complement to the successive framing and reframing of the event by journalists that often occurs in the days and weeks following an attack, a sequence of narrative conventions that Flood et al. have identified as the "terror genre" of reporting (2012, 167–175).

UK broadcasters were subject to nearly 680 public complaints, given the graphic and disturbing nature of the videos and stills presented in the initial reporting of the attack (Ofcom 2014). ITV was the first broadcaster to receive mobile video footage from the scene. After ITV assessed the eyewitness as being "not linked to the incident" and "genuinely a member of the public who happened to be there at the time," ITV edited sequences to avoid showing some of the graphic visual content, but also to avoid broadcasting particular aspect of Adebolago's ideological motivations detailed on camera when he spoke to eyewitnesses. They also blurred "images of the victim and the face of one of the alleged attackers" (Ofcom 2014, 23). In the Ofcom report, ITV is quoted as saying:

> [I]t is crucial that . . . the full sense of what has happened is reported—otherwise there is a danger of the event being distorted in "soft focus" and the public not being given a full picture of the truth of what has occurred.
>
> (Ofcom 2014, 39)

The regulator did not find the broadcasters in breach, citing the "the very limited time in which editorial decisions had to be made" and the "high public interest" (Ofcom 2014, 38). The selected clips that were deemed by the regulator of public interest demonstrated the "implied terrorist motive" of the attack, as well as the "British accent" of the perpetrators, and Adebalogo's "demeanor" as he willingly spoke about his motivations. A closer examination of the use of eyewitness imagery by the news media, however, demonstrates the unique reflexivity and attentiveness given to the conditions of its production (Peters 2009, 43). Audiences, journalists, and witnesses alike are drawn to comment on the startling emotional force of the imagery, contributing to its iconicity as it stands in for the event itself. The initial ITV London broadcast of the mobile video was broadcast without sound and looped four times for a duration of 32 seconds:

Presenter's introduction:

> "Well, we can actually show you some video now and I'll explain what it is exactly . . ."

> "We'll take a look at that just now."

Presenter's voice over the imagery:

> "Well, as I repeat—as I said, this is the picture of one of the alleged attackers in today's incident. We do apologize for the graphic nature of these pictures . . . it is important for us to get an understanding of what happened . . ."

"I'll try to—I'll try to figure out what has happened in Woolwich in south east London."

(Ofcom 2014, 25)

In the context of media events, as the extracts above demonstrate, the rhetoric employed by broadcasters provides the viewers with a sense of mediated participation as they watch the video together *with* journalists. The confusion is voiced live and on air, the unknown is in a sense shared as the journalist is trying to make sense of this footage in full view of the audience. It is not the attack that the audience is witnessing but rather the media event being performed on their screens.

Sjovaag (2011, 85) identifies that the broadcasting usage of amateur footage is often "embellished" to distinguish it from professional output, thereby protecting journalistic standards of verification. While BBC and other broadcasters would report on the ITV footage, on the 19:00 ITV National News broadcast the presenter states:

> "Now ITV News has gained exclusive access to pictures of the incident filmed by an eyewitness. Many parts of the video are simply too violent to broadcast but what we can show leaves no doubt as to the horrifically public nature of the attack."

(Ofcom 2014, 28)

This embellished framing focuses, in part, on the providence of the footage, but statements of what can and cannot be shown also serve to reinforce a notion of the editorial authority while projecting emotional reactions onto the audience. Following the shortened audio of Adebolago's rant, the anchor Paul Davis, again reminds us of the video's providence, "These pictures were taken by a man on a bus heading for a job interview," after he narrates and explains what is being seen in the video sequences. At the same time on the BBC News 24 hour rolling news channel, Ben Geoghegan would similarly speak for the nation's reaction: "Well I think that footage as more and more people see it certainly here is going to heighten the sense of shock and bewilderment that some people are expressing tonight at what has gone on there" (Ofcom 2014, 30).

The journalist is witness *with* "us" but also speaks *for* "us," the audience, guiding not only the interpretation of events but leaving "no doubt" as to the emotional reaction expected of the audience. These unspoken conventions are part of the performativity of the media event. While the eyewitness responds to a moral imperative to record and share the traumatic scene, the journalist similarly contributes to the construction of the "shared experience" (Dayan 2010, 26; Hepp 2015, 169) of the media event as it unfolds.

In the reporting of natural disasters, a similar combination of visceral imagery and tone is used, as the journalist's performance suspends the conventions of objectivity and goes on to communicate an emotionalised injunction for the audience to care (Pantti et al. 2012, 94). Liebes (1998, 75) argues that the transparency and subjectivity that is interjected by journalists during a crisis has a legitimizing effect because "all journalistic work is done in full public view." Zelizer points to the synecdoche of such personalized accounts with "telling the story of its T.V. coverage" to "uphold the primacy of reporting" in relation to the spectacle (1992, 39,40).

With a population hungry for details in the aftermath of the event such as the Woolwich murder, amateur footage is framed and presented as if the reporters are viewing it *with* the audience, representing assumed emotions of the audience back to them—speaking *for* a shocked nation, rather than reporting on events that have occurred within the nation.

The elision of Adebolago's speech and the eyewitness accounts as mobile phone recording represent just one of the convergences of perspective—the "witness" and the "villain"—involved in this assemblage (Hutchings and Burchell, forthcoming). In the reporting of the event, however, there is another important convergence, that of the audience and the media. Given the emotional and moral injunctions carried by the reporting as well as the imagery, the distance between the audience and what is captured by the camera collapses (Peters 2009, 34; Allan 2013, 99).

Conclusion

When the assemblage of citizen witnessing, mobile technology, and crisis reporting conventions coalesce around a terror event, eyewitness accounts are often reduced to traumatic images and journalistic conventions of reporting are replaced with emotionalized representations of appropriate reactions. It is this rupture in journalistic conventions that is being exploited. Terror attacks that become media events such as the Woolwich murder, are dependent not on the presence of the media but on the image producing eyewitnesses and the dissemination of those images by the news media. The result leaves media professionals with little more than a reactive, emotionalized role that serves to monumentalize the terror event in national memory (Hutchings and Burchell, forthcoming). When news professionals suspend independence for the sake of a national emotional consensus little space is left for open public dialogue. What is left is a general hostility to any deviance from that consensus.

Hoskins and O'Loughlin argue that in contemporary warfare actors "anticipate and shape media coverage of their actions" (2010, 19) while Kuntsman and Stein (2015) bring our attention to the emerging exploitation of everyday digital platforms and consumer practices—in particular photo-sharing and social networking—as a new theatre for militarized voices. When imagery becomes the object of journalistic analysis it stands in for the victims, for the survivors, and for the events themselves These mediations, constructed as they are from a new technological and cultural assemblage of performance, flatten the content and distract us all from alternative interpretations and perspectives. Such media events constitute a reordering of cultural functions whereby the moral and professional imperatives of citizens and journalists alike become subservient to the imagery that was constructed and planned for by the perpetrators. In this manner, the media assemblage itself can be understood as a motivation for the horrific and politically symbolic murder of Lee Rigby. Adebolago's words to the witnesses of Lee Rigby's murder demonstrate that "lone-wolf" terror has learned these lessons:

"Take my picture."

"I just want to talk to you with your camera."

Note

1. The wider study referred to was funded by the Arts and Humanities Research Council (AHRC) of the United Kingdom.

Further Reading

Stuart Allan's *Citizen Witnessing: Revisioning Journalism in Times of Crisis* (Cambridge, UK: Polity, 2013) provides a detailed exposition of the emergence of citizen journalism in a variety of forms.

N. Couldry, A. Hepp, and F. Krotz's edited collection *Media Events in a Global Age* (Abingdon, UK: Routledge, 2010) provides a series of case studies and theoretical investigations into the forms taken by contemporary media events in a global context.

A. Hoskins, and B. O'Loughlin's *War and Media* (Cambridge, UK: Polity, 2010) examines the use of media in the context of contemporary conflict.

Mortensen, M. (2011) "When citizen photojournalism sets the news agenda: Neda Agha Soltan as a Web 2.0 icon of post-election unrest in Iran," *Global Media and Communication*, 7 (1), 4–16.

References

Allan, S. (2013) *Citizen Witnessing: Revisioning Journalism in Times of Crisis*, Cambridge, UK: Polity.

Allan, S. (2014) "Witnessing in Crisis: Photo-reportage of Terror Attacks in Boston and London," *Media, War and Conflict*, 7 (2): 131–151.

Allan, S. (2009) "Histories of Citizen Journalism," in S. Allan and E. Thorsen (Eds.), *Citizen Journalism: Global Perspectives*, New York: Peter Lang, pp. 17–32.

Andrejevic, M. (2005) "The Work of Watching One Another: Lateral Surveillance, Risk, and Governance," *Surveillance and Society*, 2 (4): 479–497.

Andrejevic, M. B. (2007) *i-Spy: Surveillance and Power in the Interactive Era*, Lawrence, KS: University of Kansas Press.

Blaagaard, B. B. (2013) "Post-human Viewing: A Discussion of the Ethics of Mobile Phone Imagery," *Visual Communication*, 12 (3): 359–374.

Chouliaraki, L. (2013) "Liberal Ethics and the Spectacle of War," in N. Couldry, M. Madianou, and A. Pinchevski (Eds.), *Ethics of Media*, London: Palgrave Macmillan, pp. 136–158.

Cottle, S. (2006) "Mediatized Rituals: Beyond Manufacturing Consent," *Media, Culture and Society*, 28 (3): 411–432.

Couldry, N., and Hepp, A. (2009) "Introduction: Media Events in Globalized Media Cultures," in N. Couldry, A. Hepp, and F. Krotz (Eds.), Media Events in a Global Age, Oxon: Routledge, pp. 1–20.

Dayan, D. (2010) "Beyond Media Events: Disenchantment, Derailment, and Disruption," in N. Couldry, A. Hepp, and F. Krotz (Eds.), *Media Events in a Global Age*, New York: Routledge, pp. 23–32.

Dayan, D., and Katz, E. (1992) *Media Events: The Live Broadcasting of History*. Cambridge, MA: Harvard University Press.

Flood, C., Hutchings, S., Miazhevich, G., and Nickels, H. (2012) *Islam, Security and Television News*, London: Palgrave Macmillan.

Frisch, A. (2004) *The Invention of the Eyewitness: Witnessing and Testimony in Early Modern France*, Chapel Hill, NC: University of North Carolina Press.

Goffman, E. (1956) *The Presentation of Self in Everyday Life*. New York, NY: Doubleday.

Haggerty, K. D., and Ericson, R. V. (2000) "The Surveillant Assemblage," *The British Journal of Sociology*, 51 (4): 605–622.

Hepp, A. (2015) *Transcultural Communication*, Oxford, UK: Wiley Blackwell.

Hollander, G. (2013) "Sun and ITV defend 'public interest' in showing Woolwich terror videoSky judged too 'distressing,'" *Press Gazette*, May 23, available at: www.pressgazette.co.uk/sun-and-itv-defend-public-interest-broadcasting-woolwich-terror-video-which-sky-news-judged-too

Hoskins, A., and O'Loughlin, B. (2010) *War and Media*, Cambridge, UK: Polity.

Hutchings, S., and Burchell, K. (2014) *Comparative approaches to Islam, Security and Television News: Implications for the Editorial Policies and Practices of Public Sector Broadcasters*. Research and Policy Report, University of Manchester. available at: www.alc.manchester.ac.uk/medialibrary/subjects/rees/projects/tvrepresentations/reports/comparative-approaches-to-islam-report.pdf

Hutchings, S., and Burchell, K. (forthcoming) "Media Genre, Disrupted Memory and the Securitisation Chronotope: The Case of the Lee Rigby Murder," in V. Apryschenko and V. Strukov (Eds.), *Memory and Securitisation*.

Ibrahim, Y. (2009) "Social Media and the Mumbai Terror Attack: The Coming of Age of Twitter," in S. Allan and E. Thorsen (Eds.), *Citizen Journalism: Global Perspectives Volume 2*, New York: Peter Lang, pp. 15–26.

ITV News. (2013) "Live Updates: Woolwich Police Incident," *ITV.com*, May 22, available at: www.itv.com/news/story/2013–05–22/woolwich-police-incident/

Katz, E., and Liebes, T. (2010) "'No More Peace!': How Disaster, Terror and War Have Upstaged Media Events," in N. Couldry, A. Hepp, and F. Krotz (Eds.), *Media Events in a Global Age*. London and New York: Routledge, pp. 32–41.

Kuntsman, A., and Stein, R. (2015) *Digital Militarism: Israel's Occupation in the Social Media Age*, Stanford, CA: Stanford University Press.

Liebes, T. (1998) "Television's Disaster Marathons," in T. Liebes, J. Curran, and E. Katz (Eds.), *Media, Ritual, and Identity*. London: Routledge, pp. 71–86.

Metropolitan Police. (2013) "Two Men Found Guilty of Murdering Lee Rigby," Press Release, December 19, available at: http://content.met.police.uk/News/Two-men-found-guilty-of-murdering-Lee-Rigby/14000216 27852/1257246745756

Mnookin, J. L. (1998) "Image of Truth: Photographic Evidence and the Power of Analogy," *Yale Journal of Law and the Humanities*, 10 (1): 1–74.

Mortensen, M. (2011) The Eyewitness in the Age of Digital Transformation," in K. Andén-Papadopoulos and M. Pantti (Eds.), *Amateur Images and Global News*. Bristol, UK: Intellect, pp. 61–75.

O'Hagan, A. (2015, October 22) "Who's the Alpha Male Now? Andrew O'Hagan on the Manifestos Killers Leave Behind," *The London Review of Books*, pp. 3–6.

Ofcom. (2014) *Ofcom Broadcast Bulletin Issue 245*, January 6, available at: http://stakeholders.ofcom.org.uk/binaries/enforcement/broadcast-bulletins/245/obb245.pdf

Pantti, M., Wahl-Jorgensen, K., and Cottle, S. (2012) *Disasters and the Media*, London and New York: Peter Lang.

Peters, J. D. (2009) "Witnessing," in P. Frosh and A. Pinchevski (Eds.), *Media Witnessing: Testimony in the Age of Mass Communication*, Houndmills, UK: Palgrave Macmillan, pp. 23–41.

Pettifor, T., and Lines, A. (2013) "Woolwich Attack: Horrified Witnesses Tell How Beheaded Soldier Was Hacked at 'Like a Piece of Meat,'" *The Mirror*, May 23, available at: www.mirror.co.uk/news/uk-news/woolwich-attack-horrified-witnesses-tell-1904602

Press Association. (2014) "Lee Rigby Murder: The Judge's Sentencing Speech in Full," *The Guardian*, February 26, available at: http://gu.com/p/3n53b/stw

Price, M. E. (2011) "On Seizing the Olympic Platform," in M. E. Price and D. Dayan (Eds.), *Owning the Olympics: Narratives of the New China* (pp. 86–114). Ann Arbor, MI: The University of Michigan Press.

Ristovska, S. (2015) "Visualizing Human Rights: The Role of Citizen Video in International Human Rights Law," Presented at IAMCR Annual Conference, UQAM, Montreal, July 14.

Seib, P., and Janbek, D. M. (2010). *Global Terrorism and New Media: The Post-Al Qaeda Generation*, London and New York: Routledge.

Sjovaag, H. (2011). "Amateur Images and Journalistic Authority," in K. Anden-Papadopoulous and M. Pantti (Eds.), *Amateur Images and Global News*. Bristol, UK: Intellect Books, pp. 80–95.

Stubley, P. (2013) "Lee Rigby Murder Trial," *The Daily Mirror*, December 17, available at: www.mirror.co.uk/news/uk-news/lee-rigby-murder-trial-live-2935951

The Telegraph. (2013) "Woolwich Attack: The Terrorist's Rant", May 23, available at: www.telegraph.co.uk/news/uknews/terrorism-in-the-uk/10075488/Woolwich-attack-the-terrorists-rant.html

Thurman, N., and Rodgers, J. (2014) "Citizen Journalism in Real Time: Live Blogging and Crisis Events," in E. Thorsen and S. Allan (Eds.), *Citizen Journalism: Global Perspectives Volume 2*, New York: Peter Lang, pp. 81–95.

Van Loon, J. (2010) "Modalities of Mediation," in N. Couldry, A. Hepp, and F. Krotz (Eds.), *Media Events in a Global Age*, London and New York: Routledge, pp. 109–123.

Wahl-Jorgensen, K., and Pantti, M. (2013) "Ethics of Global Disaster Reporting: Journalistic Witnessing and Objectivity," in S. J. A. Ward (Ed.), *Global Media Ethics: Problems and Perspectives*, Malden: Wiley-Blackwell, pp. 191–213.

Zelizer, B. (1992) *Covering the Body: The Kennedy Assassination, the Media, and the Shaping of Collective Memory*, Chicago, IL: University of Chicago Press.

39

KEEPING REPORTERS SAFE

The Ethics of Drone Journalism in a Humanitarian Crisis

Turo Uskali and Epp Lauk

Introduction

Covering crises presents major challenges to news reporting, and indeed the shooting of good images or videos in conflict zones is an especially hazardous business. According to the Committee to Protect Journalists (2015) in 2012–2014 altogether over 70 journalists and photographers were killed in crossfire or combat. This chapter presents, in theory, an alternative way of shooting photos and videos aimed at keeping reporters safe. In other words, it suggests the use of camera drones in reporting humanitarian crises.

In doing so, we are following the steps of Australian TV-reporter and producer Mark Corcoran, who in 2006 in south Beirut asked (Corcoran 2014, 2): "If combatants were able to deploy these 'eyes in the sky', could media adopt this technology for news gathering, both improving the coverage and lowering our exposure to risk in a chaotic, highly dangerous environment?" It took five years before drones were first used in crisis journalism.

Camera drones have been used for news coverage since 2011, beginning with the street riots in Warsaw and the events organized by the Occupy Wall Street movement. In these well-documented cases, drones were operated by amateurs or activists instead of journalism professionals (Klimas 2011; Wagstaff 2011). However, in the same year, the first international organization dedicated to drone journalism was created: the Professional Society of Drone Journalists (PSDJ), which was established for discussing the ethical, educational and technological framework of drone journalism. Today, the PSDJ develops small unmanned aerial systems for journalists, and explores best practices to deploy them for reporting needs, especially for investigative, disaster, weather, sports, and environmental reporting (Drone journalism.org 2015).

By "drone journalism" we mean the use of unmanned aircraft systems (UAS) for journalistic purposes. Goldberg (2016, 218) states that, even if "remotely piloted aircraft" (RPA)

is the most used legal term, it can also be substituted by a shorter term, the word "drone."
In similar vein "drone journalism" can be used, because it corresponds to normal usage.
According to Corcoran (2014) drone journalism can also include their use by citizen
journalists.

Goldberg (2016, 222) defined 2011 as a "seminal" year for drone journalism. He refers
to News Corporation's short lived tablet-only publication *The Daily* as using the first drones
to record storm damage in Alabama and flooding in North Dakota. Also in November 2011,
the first educational project, the Drone Journalism Lab, was founded at the University of
Nebraska by Professor Matt Waite.

Another term being used in this discussion is "robot eyewitnesses" (Gynnild 2014a) because
the drone operator can see in real-time what is happening via the drone's control monitor.
"Robot eyewitnessing" is a similar process to that of shooting stills or videos through a
handheld camera lens. Indeed, in order to better understand the content of recordings, drones
enable more precise interpretations of images and videos because operators can freeze and
repeat images several times. Even before the age of camera drones, closed-circuit television
(CCTV), also known as video surveillance cameras, has been used for journalistic purposes
(Gynnild 2014b). Many accidents and crime scenes has been reported with CCTV
documented video material by news organizations including a train accident in Spain in 2013
(Reuters/Youtube 2013).

In a similar vein, the earthquake and tsunami in Japan in 2011 were captured by many
CCTV cameras, and also by weather cameras (Youtube 2011). The largest earthquake in
Japanese history occurred in the Pacific Ocean, off the north-east coast of the country.
Measuring 9.0 on the Richter scale, it triggered a 10-metre tsunami that claimed about 20,000
lives and made at least 500,000 people homeless. According to Fry (2015), almost instantly,
within 90 seconds of the earthquake, Japan's public broadcasting company NHK switched
all of its channels to disaster coverage. In addition to 460 weather cameras, NHK was able
to mobilize 14 helicopters, 70 OB vans (mobile broadcasting units), and 18 portable satellite
transmission units to live reporting. NHK issued tsunami warnings on all eight of its channels
within three minutes of the start of the earthquake. In hindsight, it can be argued that the
quick response and live video coverage by the governmental broadcaster NHK may have
saved many thousands of lives in Japan.

Live video coverage is proven to be an effective method of communication in crisis
journalism. It can be argued that due to the technological developments in ICT and mobile
internet, live video streams can be produced almost everywhere, wherever internet connection
is available. In 2015, 3.2 billion people were using the Internet (ITU 2015). All this can
amplify the importance of drones in journalism, especially when camera drones could be used
as a real-time video source in an acute humanitarian crisis.

Naturally, helicopters have been traditionally used by many big news organizations for
shooting aerial video footages. According to Goldberg (2016, 222) "newscopter" and
"helicopter journalism" were invented by John Silva in 1958 for KTLA, a TV-station based
in Los Angeles. Helicopters, and even small airplanes, are still used in many news events, but
renting aircraft has always been expensive, and is clearly not possible for all newsrooms. Smaller
news organizations have rarely been able to afford to use helicopters. By contrast, camera
drones can be bought cheaply, and also piloted much more easily than "real" aircraft. In this
way camera drones are democratizing aerial photo and video journalism. Still, many obstacles
remain that hinder the use of drones in journalism. We will focus on these issues next.

Misuse of Drones

Goldberg et al. (2013, 28) predict: "Remotely piloted aircraft will be common in the skies of many nations in the near future because they offer distinct opportunities and advantages to journalism." But drones, like any innovative technology, can be misused. They are already used for drug smuggling and carrying explosives. Also, usage of camera drones in journalism involves some risks and disadvantages. The main concern however is related to the possibility that reporting could turn into surveillance, raising real issues for privacy.

Governments already use drone aircraft for observing enemy movements in conflict areas. It is not hard to anticipate that, under certain circumstances, journalists and news organizations could cooperate with the authorities by sharing images. In addition, media organizations could supply data that the authorities could not get without a warrant.

Camera drones may also easily become the tools of paparazzi journalism. In using camera drones, the distinction between private and public becomes even more blurred: it is very easy to use camera drones for invading people's privacy. Camera drones also pose safety problems. Therefore, it is generally not allowed to fly drones above crowds or near airfields. Also, the military sets restrictions for using drones.

Journalists flying drones should also take into consideration that flying a drone is seen by many as a provocative act. It will likely make people uncomfortable until they are more accustomed to seeing them in the air (Weiss 2015). The Professional Society of Drone Journalists (Dronejournalism.org, 2015) emphasizes that drone journalism basically faces the same issues as shooting still or video images on the ground. However, drone journalism involves additional ethical issues.

Ethical Issues and Guidelines

Journalists should be responsible for knowing how to work with various new devices of newsgathering without causing damage. Journalists must always consider the potential damage they could inflict on people or their property if a drone crashes, and take all possible measures to mitigate the consequences of a crash.

In addition to the guidelines of traditional Codes of Ethics, the Professional Society of Drone Journalists has laid down four basic ethical principles for drone journalists: (1) newsworthiness, (2) safety, (3) protection of privacy and 4) sanctity of law and public spaces.

- *Newsworthiness*: Journalists should consider the necessity of using a camera drone from the viewpoints of the importance of the story and alternative possibilities for getting the story. Journalists must be able to demonstrate that there were no other means for getting the information. Public interest of the story is the measure.
- *Safety*: The ethical question is whether the risk is justified. When using camera drones, it is necessary to ensure that the flight is completely controlled and stable, and that the drone pilots are trained in their equipment and are capable of safely flying the drone remotely.
- *Privacy*: The drone must be operated in a fashion that does not needlessly compromise the privacy of non-public figures. For example, the Code of Ethics of Finnish journalists contains three sections that deal with the issues of "private" and "public" in journalistic material. The guidelines also remind the journalists that the free availability of information does not necessarily mean that it always should be freely published.

- *Sanctity of law and public spaces*: Drone operators must abide by the regulations that apply to the airspace where the drone is operated. They must also appreciate the regulations of the particular country when they fly a drone in a country other than their own.

According to Katherine Culver (2012; 2014), news organizations' adoption of drone technologies must be paired with clear articulations of their ethical use and full transparency with the public. Culver's four ethical key issues are somewhat similar to those of the PSDJ, but with slightly different emphasis. In addition to the responsibility of guaranteeing the safety of nearby people when operating a drone, Culver points out the importance of respecting anyone's desire to be left alone, even in public spaces (beaches, parks, etc.). Culver also warns journalists about the possibility of forgetting the context of situations of remote sensing and decision making. Critics argue that soldiers far removed from the horrors of war make decisions to kill or destroy without context. Though far less lethal, the same danger applies to journalistic uses. By relying on a partially autonomous machine, reporters can distance themselves from the human toll of situations, potentially removing critical context (Culver 2012). Thus, bear-bones stories could publish dramatic or sensationalized images lacking explanations, human story lines, and background relevant to humanitarian disasters.

Camera Drones in Crisis Reporting

While drones open up new ways of journalistic reporting by enabling aerial footage, they also bring about serious legal issues, which differ in countries according to whether or not using drones for journalistic purposes (or at all) is legal. As Goldberg et al. (2013, v) mention, "such aerial platforms raise technical, policy, and journalistic issues that need to be comprehended before they are used for news gathering." So far, it seems, the policy questions, including the decisions made by the aviation authorities, have had the strongest influence on the use of camera drones in various countries.

A well-documented case of using drones for recording the aftermath of a catastrophe was the earthquake in Nepal in April 2015. A drone video showing the destruction of old buildings in the capital Kathmandu and elsewhere went viral, and hundreds of news websites published the clip (Youtube 2015a). The local drone operator said in an interview that "out of respect to the victims" he did not take footage of live rescue operations (Shammas 2015).

Many international news organizations tried to use drones in Nepal. They brought small camera drones with them, and tried to operate them along with other video shooting cameras. However, according to drone journalism professor Matt Waite, "within a week, the government of Nepal banned drones." Waite continued in an interview that "many countries are struggling to figure out how to regulate these devices, and many see journalists launching a flying camera as a threat to the government" (Stapp 2015).

In this way, new communication technology always offers a testing area for both the free press, and the freedom of speech. As Waite notes "countries with a less than free press have quickly banned the devices shortly after someone uses them, particularly if they show something the government doesn't want the public to see." Moreover, instead of making rules, the governments simply ban the new devices that could be somehow harmful to or critical of their existence (Stapp 2015).

As a positive example, during autumn 2015 some leading news organizations used drones when covering the escalating European migrant crisis. The BBC News, in particular, broadcast several powerful drone videos of the migrants trying to enter European countries and seeking asylum. One drone footage, for example, was filmed in September and documented migrants arriving at the beaches of Greek islands from Turkey in small boats. Drone footage was used in the beginning of the news story, creating a dramatic opening, that showed pictures of thousands of abandoned lifejackets (BBC News 2015a). Another popular and widely circulated example of drone footage by BBC News showed how migrants prepared to walk to Austria from Hungary (BBC News 2015b). Of course, in these cases the drones helped to cover the stories in remote areas without using helicopters.

Even before 2015, drones were successfully used in documenting many natural and social catastrophes, such as the aftermath of Super Typhoon Haiyan in the Philippines in 2013, and the riots in Taksim Gezi Park in Istanbul, Turkey in 2013. In the latter case, the police shut down with a gun the drone operated by an amateur (Youtube 2013a; Youtube 2013b). Also riots in Thailand in the same year were reported using drones (Waite 2013).

What about drone journalism in war zones? It is as yet almost non-existent. So far, events in eastern Ukraine have produced the majority of drone videos published in the public domain (for example on Youtube), but almost all of them are made by military personnel on both sides of the conflict, and therefore do not represent actual drone journalism. The war zones, indeed, are often totally sealed from journalists, and controlled by the military. However, for example, a drone video showing the destruction of Donetsk airport went viral in January 2015 (Youtube 2015b), and has since been published by many news organizations on their web sites, such as cnn.com, vice.com, bbc.com/news, theguardian.com, dailytelegraph.com, to mention a few. It was recorded by Pro-Kiev volunteer Yuri Kasyanov.

We could detect only one drone journalist who has been using drones in his reporting in the eastern Ukraine war zones. Graham W. Phillips, a British documentarist and freelancer has his own Youtube video news channel (Gwplondon 2015). Phillips has posted several video clips from eastern Ukraine. The segments are a mixture of ground reporting during conflict and sequences documenting the aftermath of military conflict using drone footage to show the damage done to buildings. Phillips has not been totally neutral in his reporting. According to *The Guardian* (2014) he has worked for Kremlin-funded channel Russia Today and was also detained by Ukrainian authorities in 2014.

In February 2016, drone footage taken by Russia Works, which has connections to Russian state broadcaster Russian 1, showed the devastation of Homs in western Syria. Almost all the buildings were destroyed (*The Guardian* 2016.)

Finally, drone videos produced by military or other non-journalistic sources during wars or other conflicts, should be viewed with a critical eye. Censorship, propaganda, disinformation and misinformation are all correlated to war reporting, and though journalists themselves can be biased, the use of drones for military propaganda purposes should be viewed as highly unethical.

Freedom of the Press Issue: Legal or Not

We agree with Goldberg (2016, 220) that using drones "engages a fundamental human right, namely, the general right to freedom of expression and, specifically, the right to receive ideas and information."

However, the legislation in this area is still evolving. One can already detect a whole spectrum of different versions in many countries. According to our research, various national regulations related to the operation of civil drones are now in use in, for example, the Czech Republic, France, Finland, Germany, Norway, Sweden, the Netherlands, and the UK. Finland introduced its aviation regulations regarding the use of unmanned aircraft and flying models in October 2015. According to the Finnish Transport Safety Agency, Finland introduced one of the most liberal aviation regulations in the world. Its basic notion is that the level of regulation depends on how the device is used. For example, the requirements for model aircraft used for recreational purposes are significantly lighter than those for remotely piloted aircraft used professionally. However, professional operators may legally carry out such tasks that are not allowed for recreational flyers. Of course, the new rules will now be tested in practice by many news organizations, which started to use the drones around 2012, initially related to big sports events and floods.

The aviation regulator in the United States, the Federal Aviation Authority, has prohibited the use of drones for commercial purposes. Goldberg (2016, 226) criticizes this by arguing that "it is simply wrong to claim it is a commercial or 'business' use of an RPA" when using drones for journalistic purposes.

In May 2014, more than a dozen US media organizations challenged the government's ban of the use of drones by journalists arguing that the FAA violates First Amendment's protections for newsgathering (Davies 2013; Keller 2014; Lowy 2014). Later, in January 2015, a coalition of ten news companies received permission from the FAA to participate in testing camera drones for newsgathering purposes together with Virginia Polytechnic Institute and State University, Virginia Tech. The partnership between the news media coalition and Virginia Tech is designed to conduct controlled safety testing of a series of real-life scenarios where the news media could use small camera drones to gather the news. However, according to the opinion of several sources, it may still take years before journalists can legally fly drones to shoot videos and photos in the US. The current regulations in the US demand permission from the FAA, which is given only to certified pilots and sport airplane pilots (Lee 2015).

In Britain, the regulations are not as strict as in the USA. For commercial purposes, applicants must take a written pilot's test as well as a flying test specifically adjusted for flying drones. Once licensed, pilots are restricted to flying within the line of sight and no more than 500 meters off the ground. It is also forbidden to fly near airfields. Getting permission to use the drones in heavily populated areas is difficult. Australia is more permissive: use of drones is legal and it is possible to get permits for journalistic use. Fox TV network has used a drone to cover cricket matches (*The Economist* 2014).

It is obvious that several scenarios for the future of drone journalism are in play. Our question here is, how will drone journalism evolve in the near future? We argue that the Press Freedom Index by Reporters Without Borders (2015) can offer a clue to the future of drone journalism in various parts of the world. In other words, which countries will have the easiest and the hardest pathway to drone journalism. We would argue that the top-20 countries on the index have the best opportunities for drone journalism to prosper (Table 39.1).

These countries are not conflict zones, and therefore not the best areas for testing either crisis reporting or war reporting with drones. However, many weather- and climate-related issues such as storms, floods, and drought could be tested in these countries. More recently, the migrant crisis has demonstrated that humanitarian crises can arise everywhere.

By contrast, the bottom-20 countries on the index are conflict areas, and even war zones, and therefore testbeds for humanitarian reporting (Table 39.2). We argue that allowing news organizations and reporters to use drones in these locations and other global conflict areas, would likely result in saving the lives of many journalists in the future (see also Corcoran 2014).

Finally, we will formulate three different scenarios for drone journalism based mainly on the degree of press freedom and the level of restrictive or prohibitive legislation. The first scenario is *innovative drone journalism*. This scenario emphasizes that liberal societies with mild restrictions for drone journalism can be in the forefront of constantly testing in practice the

Table 39.1 TOP-20: The World Press Freedom Index

1.	Finland	7.52
2.	Norway	7.75
3.	Denmark	8.24
4.	Netherlands	9.22
5.	Sweden	9.47
6.	New Zealand	10.06
7.	Austria	10.85
8.	Canada	10.99
9.	Jamaica	11.18
10.	Estonia	11.19
11.	Ireland	11.20
12.	Germany	11.47
13.	Czech Republic	11.62
14.	Slovakia	11.66
15.	Belgium	11.98
16.	Costa Rica	12.26
17.	Namibia	12.50
18.	Poland	12.71
19.	Luxembourg	13.61
20.	Switzerland	13.85

Source: Reporters Without Borders 2015.

Table 39.2 Bottom-20: The World Press Freedom Index

161.	Rwanda	56.57
162.	Azerbaidjan	57.88
163.	Bahrain	58.69
164.	Saudi Arabia	59.41
165.	Sri Lanka	60.28
166.	Uzbekistan	60.14
167.	Equatorial Guinea	66.23
168.	Yemen	66.36
169.	Cuba	70.21
170.	Djibouti	71.04
171.	Lao People's Democratic Republic	71.25
172.	Somalia	72.31
173.	Islamic Republic of Iran	72.32
174.	Sudan	72.34
175.	Vietnam	72.63
176.	China	73.55
177.	Syrian Arabic Republic	77.29
178.	Turkmenistan	80.83
179.	Democratic People's Republic of Korea	83.25
180.	Eritrea	84.86

Source: Reporters Without Borders 2015.

opportunities and challenges of new drone models and applications for journalism. The second is *restricted drone journalism*. This scenario suits those countries that have already in many ways restricted the use of drones for journalism also for journalism education, as in the USA. The third scenario is *no drone journalism*. This refers to those countries that have totally banned the use of drones for journalism. This category consists of many countries with authoritative and non-democratic regimes.

Conclusions and Discussion

This paper discussed the new opportunities for, and limits of, the use of camera drones in journalism, especially in crisis reporting. Since 2011 there have been numerous examples of drone journalism in crisis situations; the earliest being the demonstrations in Warsaw, and the latest being the European migrant crisis.

We also argue that the opportunities and limits of drone journalism are constantly tested around the world. Based on our empirical findings and the World Press Freedom Index, we created three scenarios for the future of drone journalism: (1) *innovative drone journalism*, (2) *restrictive drone journalism*, and (3) *no drone journalism*.

In recent years, authorities have banned the use of drones for journalism in many countries. Therefore, it is valid to claim that practicing drone journalism often leads to questions of freedom of the press, the right to receive ideas and information, and also the freedom of expression. Clearly, the best opportunities for developing drone journalism are in those countries that respect human rights, freedom of the press, and the right to obtain information. There are certainly a great many countries that bear little or no such respect, and also those where legal scholarship, as well as initial practical cases on this subject, are still developing.

The ethical codes are also still under construction. The basics of journalism ethics are, indeed, very valid when practicing drone journalism. In addition, the discussion of drone journalism ethics has so far mainly focused on safety and privacy issues, with more analysis needed of the ways in which background information and context can be included by reporters using drones.

We openly admit that the information we have gathered here is highly fragmented. Therefore, we suggest that more research on drone journalism should be done, and international collaboration is needed. Drone journalism is already global and constantly evolving, not least because of the new generation of cheaper and more effective drone models and applications in the markets. Tiny camera drones could not cause as much damage as the larger models if they were to malfunction and fall from the sky, but ensuring privacy is sacrosanct, particularly with the emergence of insect-size robot cameras.

Acknowledgments

We thank Helsingin Sanomat Foundation and also ViSmedia project at the University of Bergen for partly funding this research project. We also thank Marcus Denton at Derettens.com for proof-reading our text.

Further Reading

Corcoran, M. (2014) "Drone Journalism: Newsgathering Applications of Unmanned Aerial Vehicles (UAVs) in Covering Conflict, Civil Unrest and Disaster," available at: https://cryptome.org/2014/03/drone-journalism.pdf

Goldberg, D., Corcoran, M., and Picard, R. G. (2013) *Remotely Piloted Aircraft Systems and Journalism Opportunities and Challenges of Drones in News Gathering*. Oxford, UK: Reuters Institute Study of Journalism, available at: https://reutersinstitute.politics.ox.ac.uk/sites/default/files/Remotely%20Piloted%20Aircraft%20and%20Journalism.pdf

Goldberg, D. (2016) "Droning on About Journalism: Remotely Piloted Aircraft and Newsgathering," in A. Završnik (Ed.), *Drones and Unmanned Aerial Systems Legal and Social Implications for Security and Surveillance*, New York: Springer, pp. 217–241.

Gynnild, A. (2014a) "The Robot Eye Witness: Extending Visual Journalism through Drone Surveillance," *Digital Journalism*, 2 (3): 333–343.

Waite, M. (2013) The drone age is here, and so are the lawyers, available at: www.niemanlab.org/2013/12/the-drone-age-is-here-and-so-are-the-lawyers/

References

BBC News. (2015a) "Migrant Crisis: Drone Footage Shows Arrivals," BBC News, available at: www.bbc.com/news/world-europe-34333215

BBC News. (2015b) "Migrant crisis: Activist Convoy Drives to Hungary," BBC News, availale at: www.bbc.com/news/world-europe-34166882

Committee to Protect Journalists. (2015) "235 journalists killed in in crossfire/combat since 1992," available at: www.cpj.org/killed/in-combat.php

Corcoran, M. (2014) "Drone journalism: Newsgathering applications of Unmanned Aerial Vehicles (UAVs) in covering conflict, civil unrest and disaster," available at: https://cryptome.org/2014/03/drone-journalism.pdf

Culver, K. (2012) "Ethics Aloft: The Pros and Cons of Journalists Using Drones," Pbs.org/MediaShift, May 20, available at: www.pbs.org/mediashift/2012/12/ethics-aloft-the-pros-and-cons-of-journalists-using-drones340/

Culver, K. (2014) "From Battlefield to Newsroom: Ethical Implications of Drone Technology in Journalism," *Journal of Mass Media Ethics: Exploring Questions of Media Morality*, 29 (1): 52–64.

Davies, A. (2013) "The FAA Has Shut Down 2 Journalism School Drone Programs," *Business Insider*, August 23, available at: www.businessinsider.com/faa-ends-journalism-school-drone-use-2013–8

Dronejournalism.org. (2015) available at: www.dronejournalism.org/

Fry, A. (2015) "NHK's rapid response," Nhk.or.jp, available at: www.nhk.or.jp/japan311/c21–01-nhks.html

Goldberg, D. (2016) "Droning on About Journalism: Remotely Piloted Aircraft and Newsgathering," in A. Završnik (Ed.), *Drones and Unmanned Aerial Systems Legal and Social Implications for Security and Surveillance*, New York: Springer, pp. 217–241.

Goldberg, D., Corcoran, M., and Picard, R. G. (2013) *Remotely Piloted Aircraft Systems and Journalism Opportunities and Challenges of Drones in News Gathering*, Oxford: Reuters Institute Study of Journalism, available at: https://reutersinstitute.politics.ox.ac.uk/sites/default/files/Remotely%20Piloted%20Aircraft%20and%20Journalism.pdf

Gwplondon. (2015) A Youtube channel of Graham W. Phillips, available at: www.youtube.com/user/gwplondon

Gynnild, A. (2014a) "The Robot Eye Witness: Extending Visual Journalism through Drone Surveillance," *Digital Journalism*, 2 (3): 333–343.

Gynnild, A. (2014b) "Surveillance Videos and Visual Transparency in Journalism," *Journalism Studies*, 15(4): 449–463, available at: https://cryptome.org/2014/03/drone-journalism.pdf

ITU. (2015) *World Telecommunication/ICT Indicators database 2015* (19th ed./December 2015), available at: www.itu.int/en/ITU-D/Statistics/Pages/publications/wtid.aspx

Keller, R. (2014) "FAA hampers MU J-School Drone Classes. Program Needs Certificate to Fly," *Columbia Daily Tribune*, August 22, available at: www.columbiatribune.com/news/education/faa-hampers-mu-j-school-drone-classes/article_162d9e8c-0b51–11e3–83d d-10604b9ffe60.html

Klimas, L. (2011) "Here's the 'Robocopter' Drone That Allowed Civilians to Film the Poland Riots," *The Blaze*, November 22, available at: www.theblaze.com/stories/2011/11/22/heres-the-robokopter-drone-that-allowed-civilians-to-film-the-poland-riots

Lee, D. (2015) "Why a Drone Journalism Educator is Getting his Pilot's License," *Columbia Journalism Review*, August 28, available at: www.cjr.org/united_states_project/matt_waite_drone_journalism_lab.php

Lowy, J. (2014) "News Media Challenge Ban on Journalism Drones," AP, June 5, available at: http://bigstory.ap.org/article/news-media-challenges-ban-journalism-drones

Reporters Without Borders. (2015) *World Press Freedom Index*, available at: https://index.rsf.org/#!/

Reuters/Youtube. (2013) "CCTV Video Shows Spain Train Crash," July 25, available at: www.youtube.com/watch?v=qdmwTE-FtDY

Shammas, J. (2015) "Nepal Earthquake: Drone Captures Incredible Footage over Kathmandu Showing Aftermath of Disaster," Mirror.co.uk, available at: www.mirror.co.uk/news/world-news/nepal-earthquake-drone-captures-incredible-5592151

Stapp, K. (2015) "Journalists, Gov'ts Square Off in Game of Drones," IPS News.net, May 6, available at: www.ipsnews.net/2015/06/journalists-govts-square-off-in-game-of-drones/

The Economist. (2014) "Eyes in the Skies," March 29, available at: www.economist.com/news/international/2=

The Guardian. (2014) "British Journalist Graham Phillips Released by Ukraine Forces, Blogger Working as Freelance for Russia Today TV Station Tweets that he is 'Free and Fine' Following Detention on Tuesday," May 21, available at: www.theguardian.com/world/2014/may/21/british-journalist-graham-phillips-detained-east-ukraine

The Guardian. (2016) "Drone Footage of Homs in Syria Shows Utter Devastation," April 2, video, available at: www.theguardian.com/world/video/2016/feb/04/drone-footage-homs-syria-utter-devastation-video

Wagstaff, K. (2011) "Occupy Wall Street's New Drone: 'The Occucopter,'" *The Time,* December 21, available at: http://techland.time.com/2011/12/21/occupy-wall-streets-new-drone-the-occucopter/

Waite, M. (2013) "The Drone Age Is Here, and So Are the Lawyers," available at: www.niemanlab.org/2013/12/the-drone-age-is-here-and-so-are-the-lawyers/

Weiss, J. (2015) "Matt Waite Suggests Guidelines for Drone Journalism," Ijinet International Journalists' Network, available at: https://ijnet.org/en/blog/matt-waite-suggests-guidelines-drone-journalism

Youtube. (2011) "Japan Tsunami Caught on CCTV Cameras," www.youtube.com/watch?v=noq8FYvRqgs

Youtube. (2013a) "Drone Captures Devastation After Super-Typhoon Haiyan," available at: www.youtube.com/watch?v=vh19naTXFuo

Youtube. (2013b) "DRONE FOOTAGE: Police Clash at Taksim Gezi Park," available at: www.youtube.com/watch?v=MQcW9gijs_0

Youtube. (2015a) "Drone Footage Captures Aftermath of Nepal Earthquake," available at: www.youtube.com/watch?v=N52LX1GZYWs&feature=youtu.be

Youtube. (2015b) "Ukraine War—View of Donetsk Airport from Ukraine drone—Ukraine News," available at: www.youtube.com/watch?v=fTK6xKv8gAE

40

WEAPONIZING SOCIAL MEDIA

"The Alt-Right," the Election of Donald J. Trump, and the Rise of Ethno-Nationalism in the United States

Robin Andersen

Nowhere has xenophobia, racism, and misogyny challenged International Human Rights Conventions, humanitarian principles and the core values of Cosmopolitan Solidarity more than in the United States with the election of Donald J. Trump. From the beginning of his campaign when he claimed that Mexican immigrants were murderers and rapists, Donald Trump continually humiliated people of color, denigrated women, claimed that admitting refugees would be a "Trojan Horse" for terrorism, promised to deport millions of immigrants, and ignited white supremacists across the country. But Trump did not design the winning messages or become the President of the United States on his own. He rode into the White House propelled by a wave generated by ultra right wing groups called the "alt-right"—a term used to diminish the extreme nature of their hyper-virulent views. Skilled at creating messages of fear and hate and sending them spinning across social media platforms, in the words of journalist Luke O'Brien (2016), "Most alt-righters are digital natives, and they have weaponized social media." After the election, as mainstream media, a wide spectrum of pundits, and the international humanitarian community tried to come to terms with the reality that a misogynist bigot would be the 45th president of the United States, the country erupted in a plague of bullying, intimidation, and incidents of hate from California to New York. Yet many refused to believe that the vote that carried Donald Trump to the White House was based on, or at least largely due to, racism and xenophobia. Most notably that included filmmaker Michael Moore, who continued to assert that the American electorate was not racist because they had voted for Barak Obama, an African American, over two election cycles. But the outpouring of hate and xenophobia quickly resulted in 200 incidents within the first few days, and then rose to over 300 in the first week after the election, amounting to a greater number than occurred even after 9/11 (Eversley 2016).

Insults, bullying, neo-Nazi graffiti, attacks on women, people of color, and immigrants—the long list included black women and children being told to get to the back of a bus, or go back to Africa, and Latinos being taunted about the wall between Mexico and the United States, incidents of bullying in schools too numerous to list, college students donning black-face, and women threatened by men grabbing at them.

As the global community comes to terms with the 2016 presidential election, there is little doubt that Trump tapped into and fueled a huge uptick of white power in American politics during a campaign in which neo-Nazis knocked on doors for Trump and screamed "Sieg Heil" outside his rallies. Indeed, just days after Trump's victory, the largest Ku Klux Klan chapter in the country, the Loyal White Knights of Pelham, in North Carolina, announced on its website that it would hold a victory parade for Trump on December 3. "TRUMP = TRUMP'S RACE UNITED MY PEOPLE," said the website's front page.

But the Trump campaign's use of social media, its connections to the alt-right and the winning strategies of Stephen Bannon and *Breitbart*, are not discussed in mainstream media in ways that illuminate their significance, or their interrelationships, or reveal the extreme nature of their discursive content, or their connections to the post-election outpouring of hate. The ways in which these forces came together to elect Donald Trump, and their conse-quences for local and global humanitarianism, are the themes we will address below.

The Alt-Right

The alt-right has been defined as a younger, funkier version of American white nationalism that has sprouted online in forms "so deviant that a few years ago they were in danger of extinction" (O'Brien 2016). After spending time with some of the most outspoken and hard-core promoters of the movement, *Huffington Post* journalist Luke O'Brein detailed the ways in which the expressions of neo-Nazi hate groups reverberate online, often boosted by *Breitbart* web-based "news." On the internet and through his Twitter account Trump tapped into far-right elements around the country, which included some of the most hateful online subgroups such as those involved in Gamergate. O'Brien found Trump's behind-the-scenes supporters to be "unabashed racists who think that blacks, Hispanics and Arabs are congenitally stupid and violent. Most are virulently anti-Semitic. Many are self-identified fascists" (O'Brien 2016). These extremists found a purpose and a megaphone in Donald Trump and his campaign, and Trump helped circulate their rhetoric and imagery.

Some of the most racist social media content often originated on neo-Nazi sites such as *The Daily Stormer*, founded by Andrew Anglin. Anglin is shown on the site with a shaved head and a tattoo on his chest of the "Black Sun"—a pagan symbol Himmler tiled on the floor of his occult castle.

Unleashing the Trolls

Readers of *The Daily Stormer* access news filtered through the lens of racism, "alongside images of blacks being burned alive" (O'Brien 2016). O'Brien tells of an incident during the Democratic Primary in California when trolls unleashed an attack on Erin Schrode, a 25-year-old environmental activist from Marin County running for the Second Congressional District. Four days before the Primary, Schrode made a statement supporting the state of Israel. The first email came in at 7 a.m. the following morning. "Get out of my country, kike. Get to Israel where you belong. That or the oven. Take your pick" (O'Brien 2016).

Over the next few days thousands of emails, voicemails, and tweets poured in from neo-Nazi trolls. None of them used their real names, but many were identified as Trump supporters. The FBI told her they'd never seen such venom directed at a political candidate:

They wondered how she could be a vegan, given all the "Negroe [sic] semen she swallows." They talked about laughing as they "gang raped her and then bashed her bagel eating brains in." It was, she told me, the first time she'd experienced anti-Semitism. "It shook me in a really profound, startling way," Schrode said.

(O'Brien 2016)

The FBI found that her contact information had been posted on *The Daily Stormer*.

Black Comedian Leslie Jones was also set upon by trolls in July 2016, for nothing more than her role in the all-female cast of Paul Feig's *Ghostbusters* remake (Silman 2016). After Milo Yiannopoulos—alt-right commenter, professional troll and *Breitbart* operative—posted a negative review on the "news" site charging Jones with "flat-as-a-pancake black stylings," the alt-right troll brigade blasted Jones with sexist, racist comments, and hateful memes. The hate ramped up when Yiannopoulos began tweeting at Jones directly and sharing fake tweets pretending to be from Jones (Silman 2016).

The Message to "Normies"

In addition to the openly vile language of racist character assassination directed at women (and many others including a number of conservative journalists) meant to demean and intimidate, the online alt-right has learned to shape its messages in ways able to reach "normies" (normal people, many with conservative views). A main theme was to convince normies that they live in a country in the throes of a "white genocide" that is driven by "immigration policies." O'Brien describes the messaging that flows back and forth between Trump, *Breitbart* and the alt-right hate-group who promote fake news and anti-immigration memes online. Many of Anglin's hard-core memes originating on *The Daily Stormer* are transferred to *Breitbart*, a top destination for those who leave *The Daily Stormer*. The site scaremongers with fake news stories about "migrant rape gangs" and black crime, and gives hate trollers a free rein in the comments section. Other conservative sites adopted the strategy as well. *The Daily Caller* now runs the same themes, stories of "immigrant knife-attacks" and "Jew-baiting George Soros exposes" (O'Brien 2016).

Alt-right sites have become adept at the creation of anti-black, anti-immigrant fake news stories that circulate widely on the web. In one incident last fall Trump retweeted a false meme that 81 percent of white murder victims are killed by black assailants. The number is actually 15 percent, not 81 percent. Some journalists debunked the meme but when confronted, Trump shrugged it off saying he got it from "the radio." Mainstream media reported the incident as a gaffe, but *Mother Jones* observed that "alt-right" activists saw the retweet "as proof that Trump was squarely on their side" (Posner and Neiwert 2016). And Trump did not retract it. In fact, other than former Klansman David Duke, "Trump has not disavowed a single endorsement from the dozens of neo-Nazis, Klansmen, white nationalists, and militia supporters who backed him" (Posner and Neiwert 2016). These extremist groups now hail him as "Emperor Trump" because he has gone to great lengths to avoid distancing himself from them, and he has amplified their message on social media. Trump's campaign, his family members and staffers provided an unprecedented platform for the ideas and rhetoric of far-right extremists to extend their reach. When challenged on it by the press, Trump's feigned ignorance was left to deflect any informed criticism or exposure of his agreement with extremists or their ideas. After the election, when told on 60 Minutes about the expressions of hate, he downplayed them saying he'd heard of a couple and told his followers mildly, to "stop it."

Coded Language

In addition to denying his affiliations, messaging of the ultra-right are coded to sound less extreme. As they iterate from neo-Nazi sights, they are often toned down, becoming more subtle, transmuted into implication and nuance, becoming more difficult to define as hate speech. Tying less extreme sounding messages to basic conservative values is also the way to reach a broader audience of "normies." Take for example Pepe the cartoon frog, a humorous image on 4chan and 8chan before pro-Trump trolls fashioned the once innocent frog into a Nazi, complete in uniform, on Nazi flags, and depicted Pepe with Swastika eyes. Nazi Pepe occupied a presence on *The Daily Stormer*. In October, Trump retweeted an image of himself with the face of Pepe, but not in Nazi uniform. Though the message is now less explicit, it is coded and the association to white supremacism remains recognizable. The Anti-Defamation League would later declare Pepe to be a hate symbol. Alt-right message designers are keen not to spell out direct storm-trooping content, or violence, as they are well aware that that will invite FBI investigations and get their Twitter accounts blocked.

By August Trump hired Stephen Bannon, whose *Breitbart News Network* is the most significant transmitter of alt-right ideas to a mass public. Now with a direct connection to the Trump campaign, Bannon set a hard right-wing tack and accelerated racist discourse and alt-right trolls. Bannon put the final touches on a campaign that helped white ethnonationalism become a defining feature of the election, and now the nation. Trump's campaign, says O'Brien (2016), was built with "the iconography, language and infrastructure for a millennial version of an old hate."

The Campaign Against Hamdi Ulukaya and *Chobani*

A key to *Breitbart*'s success has long been the fake news modules, misinformation and propagandized narratives that form the content core of the *Breitbart* News website. *Breitbart* has carefully honed an anti-immigration, anti-Muslim online presence in a media universe complete with stories that raise fears of "white genocide." Take for example the way alt-right social media was used to incite and mobilize anti-immigration invective, as it carried out a concerted misinformation campaign against *Chobani* yogurt company and its founder, Hamdi Ulukaya. Ulukaya is a Turkish immigrant of Kurdish descent who has been building a pro-immigrant business model and hiring resettled refugees in up-state New York and Twin Falls, Idaho. Ulukaya relied on a local refugee resettlement center to find new hires. Of the company's 2,000 full-time employees, Ulukaya hired about 300 refugees from Iraq, Afghanistan, Turkey, and other countries. Gelles (2016) notes that in addition, Ulukaya started the Tent Foundation to help migrants and for his efforts:

> he and his company have been targeted with racist attacks on social media and conspiratorial articles on websites including *Breitbart News*. . . . Now there are calls to boycott Chobani. Mr. Ulukaya and the company have been taunted with racist epithets on Twitter and Facebook. Fringe websites have published false stories claiming Mr. Ulukaya wants "to drown the United States in Muslims."
>
> (Gelles 2016)

It started in January 2016 with an opinion piece Ulukaya wrote for *CNN Money*, about his efforts to motivate businesses to help end the refugee crisis. Though Ulukaya never mentioned Muslims, the piece attracted the far-right website *World Net Daily* that published a story titled, "American Yogurt Tycoon Vows to Choke U.S. With Muslims." Later that month he appeared at the Davos economic forum where he called on the multinational corporations to hire more refugees. "The minute a refugee has a job, that's the minute they stop being a refugee," he said at a press conference at Davos.[1]

Ulukaya's activities began to attract right-wing trolls and the attention of *Breitbart*, even before Bannon was hired by Trump. The coverage from *Breitbart* attempted to smear the company—with annual yogurt sales of about $1.5 billion—as a menace to society and scourge on the local community.

> One Breitbart story suggested that Chobani's hiring of refugees caused Idaho's rise in tuberculosis with the headline, "TB spiked 500 percent in Twin Falls during 2012, as Chobani Yogurt Opened Plant." Another titled "Twin Falls refugee rape special report: why are the refugees moving in," attempted to link the company's hiring of refugees with two sexual assault cases in the Idaho town. And a third article claimed Chobani has "deep ties" to a pro-Clinton advocacy group that imposed the refugee crisis in Twin Falls.
>
> (Tefaye 2016)

As the campaign against Ulukaya grew, it became more closely tied to the Trump campaign. In August a pro-Trump white nationalist organization began to send robocalls across Idaho claiming that the "nonwhite invasion of their state and all white areas constitutes white genocide." *The New York Times* (Gelles 2016) reported that as a result of such narrative inventions and fearmongering, the mayor of Twin Falls, Shawn Barigar, and Ulukaya found themselves the target of racist epithets and death threats. *Business Insider* also analyzed the Twitter campaign against Chobani, which used the hashtag "boycott Chobani" and found that many of the threats came from Trump supporters.

Kenneth Roth, executive director of Human Rights Watch, told the *Times* (Gelles 2016) that Ulukaya stands as a perfect rebuke to those who want to scare the United States into shutting its doors to immigrants. "He's the xenophobe's nightmare. Here's an immigrant who isn't competing for jobs, but is creating jobs . . . It runs completely counter to the far-right narrative." Even so, the power of *Breitbart* narratives together with alt-right social media succeeded in clamping a xenophobic narrative onto Chobani.

"Stochastic Terrorism," and the Implied Threat of Violence

To explore another aspect of the messaging tactics of the Donald Trump campaign, let's take a look at an August speech he gave in North Carolina. Trump sparked concern when at a campaign rally, he said "If she gets to pick her judges, nothing you can do, folks. Although the Second Amendment people, maybe there is. I don't know" (Culp-Ressler 2016). Many people understood the statement to be a clear threat of violence. After all, as Law Professor David Cohen (2016) points out, "What can people who rally around guns do that's different than others? Use those guns." Cohen goes on to assert that throughout his campaign Trump has exemplified a rhetorical strategy that mirrors the way extremists incite violence among their followers. Cohen argues that Trump is engaging in what's known as "stochastic terrorism," a term that refers to the use of suggestive language and innuendo to inspire radicals to carry out violent acts. Though most people will not receive the implied meaning as direct instructions, such language can certainly incite some who may interpret the meaning as a call to action. In addition, through the use of social media, Trump's messages are widely circulated, repeated, and amplified. Such language and the potential actions they suggest can spread and become part of an acceptable culture of belligerency, intimidation, and threats. For example, Senator Richard Burr (R-N.C.) joked at a get-out-the-vote meeting that gun rights supporters may want to "put a bull's eye: on Democratic presidential nominee Hillary Clinton" (Rosenmann 2016). At a Trump rally on October 31, 2016, in Florida a supporter was selling target practice sheets of Clinton's face. This type of language offers at least some explanation for what was ultimately over 900 post-election attacks on women, African Americans, Latinos, Muslims, and immigrants in the immediate aftermath of Trump's victory.

The "Freakishly Large" Impact of Twitter and Social Media

As noted above, social media, and the use of coded language have been key to the acceptance of Trump's message. As O'Brien (2016) notes, a small number of alt-right Twitter celebrities have had a "freakishly large impact." He points to @Ricky_Vaughn 99, the most noteworthy, arguing that Vaughn is an effective disseminator of alt-right terms and ideas because "he mixes his hate memes seamlessly with more standard conservative fare." O'Brien sites the influence of Vaughn as measured by researchers at MIT:

> This February, MIT published a study of the top 150 influencers on the election, based on news appearances and social media impact. Vaughn, who had around 62,000 followers at the time, came in at 107, one spot behind Senator Elizabeth Warren and ahead of NBC News, The Drudge Report, Stephen Colbert and Glenn Beck. "He has pulled off a truly an amazing thing," said Keegan Hankes, a data intelligence expert at the SPLC. "He gets retweeted by so many different people and by people who clearly don't know about his connections."

Facebook

After the election, *The New York Times* ran a story about the undue influence of Facebook on the election saying, "Facebook has been in the eye of a postelection storm for the last few days, embroiled in accusations that it helped spread misinformation and fake news stories that influenced how the American electorate voted." *The Times* (Isaac 2016) cited an article published in *New York Magazine* titled, "Donald Trump Won Because of Facebook," that asserts, "The most obvious way in which Facebook enabled a Trump victory has been its inability (or refusal) to address the problem of hoax or fake news" (Reed 2016). Indeed, now 44 percent of adults in the US admit they receive their news from Facebook. The piece discussed the issue of journalism and the power that online platforms have to shape culture, saying that "Some employees are worried about the spread of racist and so-called alt-right memes across the network." Citing the story about Pope Francis is telling. A fake news item claiming that the Pope had endorsed Mr. Trump was shared almost a million times and was likely visible to tens of millions of users. The story went largely unrefuted, even though the Pope is actually an advocate for refugees (Isaac 2016). But neither the *Times* nor *New York Magazine* mentions the origins of such fake news or the way that alt-right trolls deliberately manipulate content. Instead, content just "spreads."

Non-human Bots Supporting Trump and Spreading Misinformation

In a study of social media election messages, an Associate Professor in Information Sciences found that about one in every five election-related tweets from September 16 to October 21 was generated not by a human, but by computer software programs. Humans set the agenda and program the content for "social bots," and computer algorithms do the rest. Very difficult to identify as non-human, bot content is being retweeted at the same rate as human tweets. The problem is that retweeting bots' content without first verifying its accuracy can spread "rumors, conspiracy theories or misinformation." An article in *The New York Review of Books* also noted the mostly hidden power of computer-generated social media posts that are "unleashed into the global conversation" by "untraceable agents, governments, political parties," and individuals (Halpern 2016).

According to Ferarra, bots were able to build a significant influence around the presidential election because the content is automatically produced, fast and continuous.

> For example, Trump-supporting bots systematically produced overwhelmingly positive tweets in support of their candidate. Previous studies showed that this systematic bias alters public perception. *Specifically, it creates the false impression that there is grassroots, positive, sustained support for a certain candidate.*
>
> (Ferarra 2016, emphasis added)

Another example from the Nevada primary last May was documented in *Wired* magazine, which noted that many members of Trump's tweeting supporters had stereotypical Hispanic names. Turns out they were actually bots impersonating Hispanic voters, used by Trump to appeal to Latino voters—the very subgroup he labeled murderers and rapists. Such practices are increasingly able to shape online and offline behaviors such as voting.

New technology and targeted messages have been successful in spreading very old-fashioned sentiments of hate and xenophobia. And these strategies are increasingly used to shape discourse and confirm and incite fear of the "other" in the West.

Breitbart, Nigel Farage, and Brexit

Long before *Breitbart*'s chief took over Donald Trump's campaign, the right-wing news outlet helped shape the Brexit campaign of Nigel Farage's UK Independence Party, using the same xenophobic narratives to push a nationalist agenda in Britain. Bannon launched *Breitbart's* UK offshoot in early 2014. Journalists who worked there in the early days told *BuzzFeed News* that Bannon saw a gap in the UK market for "a news outlet with a populist, nationalist, anti-immigration agenda" (Le Conte 2016). In a move that presaged Brannon's move to Trump's campaign, *Breitbart*'s UK editor-in-chief Raheem Kassam, a 29-year-old right-winger, briefly quit the site to work as Farage's chief of staff, helping push the party further to the right in the process. After the campaign he moved back into "journalism," a phenomenon that reveals the true agenda of *Breitbart* "news." Both Bannon and Kassam design campaign messages and write speeches for politicians, using the same revolving door that Fox News head Roger Ailes used to move from Republican strategist to Fox News chief. Fox was the first to pioneer fake reporting on network broadcasting, packaged in the costume of fact-based, "fair and balanced" journalism. As Sue Halpern writes in *The New York Review of Books*:

much has been made of the migration of "news" to the web—news conveyed via social media, Facebook and Twitter especially, but also through partisan websites that, while devoting little or no resources to fact-based reporting, have followed the *Fox News* playbook of taking on the appearance of traditional news-gathering operations.

(Halpern 2016)

Theirs is not the world of fact, but rather of inventive narrative, carefully constructed to mislead, distract, distort, and incite, the latest in a long historical trajectory from early propagandists who claimed the Germans bayoneted babies and boiled human corpses down for soap. *Breitbart* now holds the premier position in that exalted universe.

During the Brexit election campaign, Farage's style also became more confrontational and openly anti-immigration. One particular example was a debate in April when Farage complained about the cost of treating immigrants with HIV through the National Health Service. Other party leaders were initially stunned by this new discourse, and some reacted with "shock and disgust." Kassam on the other hand, was in the "spin room that evening boasting to journalists that he was the one who'd come up with that line" (Le Conte 2016).

The Effects: Trump, the Campaign and the Vote

As media, politicians, and pundits look for explanations for Trump's win, blame is cast, rightly, in many directions: James Comey for violating FBI rulings and interfering in the last days of the election; voter suppression and the roll-back of voting rights in Republican states was a factor; even corporate media such as CBS are culpable, and CNN has acknowledged its role in giving Trump a platform; others blame WikiLeaks for releasing material critical of Clinton; Hillary Clinton herself, for her refusal to offer an alternative to global trade deals and Wall Street; and the Democratic Party structure for its ties to corporate backers and for blocking Bernie Sanders at every turn. Misogyny and racism are sometimes added to the mix of explanations, but they remain contentious assertions.

Astute commentators blame neoliberalism, such as Naomi Klein noting that "a hell of a lot of people are in pain. Under neoliberal policies of deregulation, privatization, auster-ity and corporate trade, their living standards have declined precipitously." Clinton offered elite neoliberalism or what Klein calls the "Davos class," which did nothing to address that pain. Trump's message on the other hand, offered "bashing immigrants and people of colour, vilifying Muslims, and degrading women" (Klein 2016). While economics is certainly the underlying context explaining the vote, it is necessary to understand how a scapegoating, xenophobic message was successfully mediated by Trump and how it won him the presidency. Many have called Stephen Bannon a racist and anti-Semite, but few have exposed the truly virulent message of hate that characterized the campaign that he managed, and almost none have chosen to draw out its effects. And most in the mainstream, the same ones who predicted confidently that Hillary Clinton would be the next president, have not brought white America into the field of blame for responding to the messages of xenophobia when electing Donald Trump. But when we look through the lens of the campaign and focus on the election results, we see that much of the blame can be attributed to the messages of the alt-right and how they resonated with white, rural voters.

What Exit Polls Reveal

Voter responses to exit polls were early indications of how and why Trump was elected, and the reasons given correlate to the messages and strategies of the Trump campaign. Xenophobia was evident in the exit poll responses given by Trump voters. When asked what should happen to illegal immigrants working in the US, 84 percent of Trump voters told pollsters they should be deported.[2] And a huge 86 percent were in favor of building a wall along the entire US Mexico border. These exit poll results correspond to an Iowa poll conducted by Public Policy Polling in December 2015, which found that nearly half of Trump supporters believed the Japanese internment camps in WWII were a good idea.[3] A national analysis of Trump supporters by *The New York Times* found that 20 percent disagreed with the Emancipation Proclamation.

In addition, as *USA Today* investigative reporter Brad Heath tweeted on the evening of the election, the "Whitest U.S. counties are voting for Trump by an astonishing and un-precedented margin." Trump's message resonated in counties with the highest white-alone populations. Trump won 71 percent of those voters, up from a Republican win of 62 percent in 2012. This corresponds to the desire of the alt-right, who long for an ethno-state where "Europeans only" are welcome (Figure 40.1).

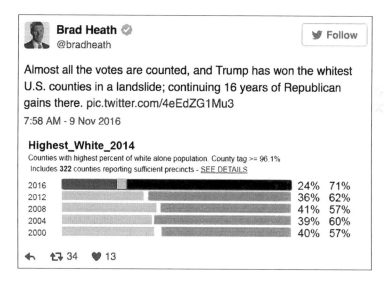

Figure 40.1 @bradheath tweets that "Almost all the votes are counted, and Trump has won the whitest U.S. counties in a landslide."

"Working Class Pain"

Ironically, the poorest Americans voted for Hillary Clinton—those with yearly incomes below $50,000. As Tamara Draut points out on Alternet.org:

> Clinton won the votes of people who are fighting to protect hard-fought gains but still waiting for equity: people of color and women with college degrees. Clinton also won the votes of millennials, those under the age of 30, who more than any

other generation are bearing the burden of our failed economic paradigms. In addition, affluent voters were as likely to vote for Trump as they were for Clinton.

(Draut 2016)

USA Today electoral data also show that a decline in employment does not explain the vote. Trump won twice the number of votes where unemployment has improved (Figure 40.2).

Figure 40.2 @bradheath tweets that "Trump won a two-to-one victory in counties where the unemployment rate has improved the most since 2010."

This number of voters can be explained to a certain extent by the nature of mediated communication. For receivers of Trump's messages in nearly all-white communities, they have little face-to-face interaction with people of color or immigrants, and therefore almost no experiences of their own to compare to the drumbeat of anti-immigrant fake news stories that reverberate over the internet. Therefore, the message is more effective. This confirms the finding of the Brexit vote as well, that the counties that had the highest degree of immigrants voted against the anti-immigration campaign of Farage. It is also telling that in the US, though the poorest voted for Clinton, those that voted for Trump "believed" that the economy was in terrible shape, another prominent Trump campaign theme. In addition, at least part of the efficacious nature of Trump's campaign themes can be attributed to the mainstream media failure to expose their falsity, or Trump's strategies in general, or offer factual, counter reporting about immigrants.

Failing to Expose Trump's Language

In addition to fake news stories that inflamed the internet and were left to stand as truth, mainstream media spent far more time on Clinton's emails than on refuting Trump. A glaring example occurred on October 16, when Trump gave a rousing speech that merged economic issues with the old hatred of "Jewish Bankers." The speech, with its implied language, was written in the signature style of Stephen Bannon. At a rally in West Palm Beach, FL, Trump claimed that there was a "global power structure that is responsible for the economic decisions that have robbed our working class, stripped our country of its wealth and put that money into the pockets of a handful of large corporations and political entities." He also claimed that Clinton "meets in secret with international banks to plot the destruction of U.S. sovereignty in order to enrich these global financial powers" and that the election may be "in fact controlled by a small handful of global special interests rigging the system" (Kaplan 2016). Ironically, there is much truth in these accusations, but Trump is not the candidate to challenge global financial capital. In fact, he is backed by hedge-fund billionaire John Mercer, who also funds *Breitbart*, and it is worth noting that Bannon once worked at Goldman Sachs in the late 1990s.

Whitelash Against Obama's Presidency

Commentator Van Jones called the vote a Whitelash against eight years of an African American president, which was not taken very seriously in media circles. We should note however, that the largest, single issue at the top of the list for Trump voters was criticism of Obama's presidency—a massive 90 percent believed he was a bad president. In the final days of the election the failure of corporate media to grasp the power of Trump and expose his lies became evident with regard to claims he made about the President. On the Friday before the election, Trump falsely asserted over and over again, that President Obama, "screamed and screamed and screamed," at a supporter who heckled him at a campaign rally in Fayetteville, NC. In fact, the opposite had occurred. Obama spoke to the crowd saying,

> Everybody sit down, and be quiet for a second. You've got an older gentleman who is supporting his candidate. . . . First of all, we live in a country that respects free speech. Second of all, it looks like maybe he might have served in our military, and we ought to respect that. Third of all, he was elderly—and we've got to respect our elders.
>
> (Naureckas 2016)

As Jim Naureckas of FAIR points out:

> A search of major US newspapers in the Nexis news database turns up not a single print-edition news story since Friday referencing Trump, Obama and "screaming." Nor does a search of transcripts on Nexis turn up any on-air national stories on ABC, CBS, NBC, PBS, NPR, Fox, CNN or MSNBC.

In addition, FAIR goes on to confirm that overseas outlets recognized it as a significant story. A headline for the London *Independent* read, "Donald Trump Misrepresents Barack Obama's 'Screaming' Response to Protester; Mr. Trump's Version of Events Appears to Differ Significantly from Reality" (Naureckas 2016). But Trump's message would resonate unquestioned with Trump supporters, as he was the original "birther," and scare mongering about the President had been a theme of conservatives and the alt-right for years.

Trump's campaign proved what O'Brien asserts, that a "small group of trolls can poison discourse with violent, racist rhetoric" and help to elevate a candidate who promises to register all Muslim Americans in a database. As news of Trump's pending presidency emerges, it becomes clear that he intends to keep these campaign promises. Kris Kobach (secretary of state of Kansas), the leading architect of drastic anti-immigrant and voter suppression laws, will serve as Donald Trump's immigration advisor. Kobach works through the Immigration Reform Law Institute, the legal arm of the anti-immigration hate group Federation for American Immigration Reform (Blue 2016). Kobach was also responsible for getting the wall into the Republican Party Platform. According to *The Wall Street Journal*, "the transition team includes a unit dedicated to designing the promised wall along the U.S.-Mexico border" (Blue 2016). Kobach, like Trump, has been known to draw on conspiracy theories that bolster fears of "white genocide" in the U.S. In 2014 Kobach took a question from a listener on the radio who wondered if a Hispanic majority in the US would start conducting "ethnic cleansing." Kobach said he thought it was unlikely, but that "things are strange and they are happening" under President Obama (Blue 2016). Drawing out the consequences of Trump's immigration policies, human rights writer Stephen Hopsgood (2016) warned: "if the plan is really to deport millions of undocumented workers, then internment camps, dawn raids by thousands of armed government officials, deaths and killings in custody, border firefights and lacerating misery are almost inevitable."

Conclusion

Many have blamed the election on the failure of the Clinton campaign to reach the significant white working-class male vote, a group that feels left out of the global economy and abandoned by government. Trump directed most, if not all, of his message to that group, in a classic scapegoating strategy that blamed immigrants, people of color and women for the decline of what many white men believe should have been their birthright to white privilege. In the final days of the campaign especially, under the tutelage of Stephen Bannon, Trump drove hard to exploit white working-class angst. One study by Hamilton College political scientist Philip Klinkner found that Trump consistently performed better among voters who feel whites are losing out. Indeed, several recent studies showed that the more resentment a voter has toward minority groups, especially blacks, immigrants and Muslims, the more likely they were to support Trump.[4] Trump succeeded in scapegoating minorities and as it reverberated over the internet, reached Northern rust-belt states. Many made their decision to vote for Trump during and after the month of September, when Bannon's strategies were in full force. Trump voters who said "before that" amounted to 45 percent, and for Clinton it was 52 percent.[5]

As Tamara Draut interprets the election data, she notes that "Not all Trump voters are racist, but they were willing to vote for a racist. Not all Trump voters are sexist, but they were willing to vote for a sexist." In addition, a quarter of Trump voters said he was not qualified to be president, yet still voted for him to lead the country. "That is the definition of privilege" (Draut 2016).

Five days after the election, Trump announced he would hire Stephen Bannon to be the Chief Strategist in his new Trump Administration. Mainstream corporate media was ill-equipped and unprepared to illuminate the very real dangers that such a propagandist poses to democracy. Applying a set of standardized "neutrality frames" (Johnson 2016) to discussions of Bannon, and to Donald Trump himself, the term "normalize" became the word of the week. Amid the fragmented, "balanced" and "unbiased" post-election media chatter, the connections between Donald Trump, *Breitbart* "news," and the influences of the digital natives of the alt-right movement were left to float in a confusing morass as disconnected phenomena, inexplicable in any coherent universe of thought or knowledge-based journalism.

As the country and the international community continue to discuss the election and its consequences, the role of the press to provide information and knowledge, and illuminate the true challenge to democracy posed by xenophobia and white supremacy, is now more important than ever. Trump's campaign spread racism and ethno-nationalism, and his presidency will bring those ideas and actions further into mainstream discourse and acceptance.

Sarah Posner and David Neiwert won the Sidney Journalism award for their *Mother Jones* report, "How Trump Took Hate Groups Mainstream," which offers analysis and context. Journalists should emulate this type of reporting, as Sidney judge Lindsay Beyerstein noted, "*Mother Jones* warned that Trump's win would bring hate groups into the open and normalize their views."

As the world braced for the consequences of a new anti-immigrant, white nationalism, Americans across the country went into the streets to protest the election, its rhetoric and violent acts of hate incited by Trump's campaign. The next four years will prove to be a defining chapter in the formulation of global human rights, the viability of diversity, cosmopolitanism, and the long-held covenant of the humanitarian principle that people, no matter their race, creed, or gender, are equal and entitled to be treated with dignity. Trump is challenging the very foundations of the humanitarian imagination, and the ethics of solidarity that had gained a strong foothold in Western cosmopolitan societies and is currently being rolled back.

Notes

1. Davos 2016-Press Conference: The Refugee and Migration Crisis, available at: www.youtube.com/watch?v=dApJnaaNwQY#action=share
2. *The New York Times 2016 Exit Polls* (November 8, 2016), updated at www.nytimes.com/interactive/2016/11/08/us/politics/election-exit-polls.html?_r=0
3. Public Policy Polling (December 15, 2016), available at: www.publicpolicypolling.com/main/2015/12/trump-edges-cruz-in-iowa-his-supporters-think-japanese-internment-was-good-clinton-still-well-ahead-.html
4. O'Brien, 2016.
5. *The New York Times Exit Polls*, ibid.

References

Blue, M. (2016) "Kris Kobach, Architect of Draconian Anti-Immigrant Policies, Joining Trump's Transition Team," November 12, *Alternet.org*, available at: www.alternet.org/right-wing/kris-kobach-architect-draconian-anti-immigrant-policies-joining-trumps-transition-team?akid=14872.19806.Ww1JCM&rd=1&src=newsletter1067068&t=16

Cohen, D. (2016) "Trump's Assassination Dog-Whistle was Even Scarier than You Think," *Rolling Stone*, August 9, available at: www.rollingstone.com/politics/features/trumps-assassination-dog-whistle-was-scarier-than-you-think-w433615

Culp-Ressler, T. (2016) "The Rhetorical Tool that Allows Trump to Incite Violence without 'Inciting Violence,'" *ThinkProgress*, August 10, available at: https://thinkprogress.org/the-rhetorical-tool-that-allows-trump-to-incite-violence-without-inciting-violence-7fbf7b96d448#.l0mux7sra

Draut, T. (2016) "This Wasn't a Working Class Revolt, It was a White Revolt," *Alternet.org*, November 17, available at: www.alternet.org/election-2016/trumps-election-was-white-revolt?akid=14893.19806.qlzYck&rd=1&src=newsletter1067427&t=14

Eversley, M. (2016) "Post-Election Spat of Hate Crimes Worse than Post 9/11, Experts Say," *USA Today*, November 14, available at: www.usatoday.com/story/news/2016/11/12/post-election-spate-hate-crimes-worse-than-post-911-experts-say/93681294/

Ferrara, E. (2016) "How Twitter Bots Affected the US Election Campaign," *The Conversation*, November 8, available at: http://theconversation.com/how-twitter-bots-affected-the-us-presidential-campaign-68406

Gelles, D. (2016) "For Helping Immigrants, Chobani Founder Draws Threats," *The New York Times*, October 31, available at: www.nytimes.com/2016/11/01/business/for-helping-immigrants-chobanis-founder-draws-threats.html

Halpern, S. (2016) "Facebook, Twitter & Trump," *The New York Review of Books*, November 11, available at: www.nybooks.com/daily/2016/11/11/facebook-twitter-trump-how-internet-changed-election/

Hopsgood, S. (2016) "Fascism Rising," *Alternet.org*, November 12, available at: www.alternet.org/election-2016/fascism-rising?akid=14872.19806.Ww1JCM&rd=1&src=newsletter1067068&t=4

Isaac, M. (2016) "Facebook, in Cross Hairs After Election, Is Said to Question Its Influence," in *The New York Times*, November 12, available at: www.nytimes.com/2016/11/14/technology/facebook-is-said-to-question-its-influence-in-election.html?smid=tw-nytimes&smtyp=cur

Johnson, A. (2016) "Right on Cue, Media Begins to Normalize Trump," *Alternet.org*, November 13, available at: www.alternet.org/election-2016/right-cue-media-begins-normalize-trump

Kaplan, A. (2016) "Trump's Anti-Semitic Speech Came from Breitbart, the Alt-Right, and Alex Jones," *Media Matters*, October 14, available at: http://mediamatters.org/blog/2016/10/14/trumps-anti-semitic-speech-came-breitbart-alt-right-and-alex-jones/213842

Klein, N. (2016) "The Rise of the Davos Class Sealed America's Fate," *Guardian*, November 9, available at: www.theguardian.com/commentisfree/2016/nov/09/rise-of-the-davos-class-sealed-americas-fate

Le Conte, M. (2016) "How a Far-Right US Website Helped Take Nigel Farage to the Heart of the Trump Campaign," *BuzzFeed.com*, August 25, available at: www.buzzfeed.com/marieleconte/how-breitbart-tried-and-failed-to-take-over-ukip?utm_term=.jrMzzWbzNz#.vrz33vP353

Naureckas, J. (2016) "Trump's Unhinged Lie Doesn't Register as News to Corporate Media, November 6, available at: http://fair.org/home/trumps-unhinged-lie-about-obama-doesnt-register-as-news-to-corporate-media/

O'Brien, L. (2016) "My Journey to the Center of the Alt Right," *Huffington Post*, November 2, available at: http://highline.huffingtonpost.com/articles/en/alt-right/

Posner, S. and Neiwert, D. (2016) "How Trump Took Hate Groups Mainstream," *Mother Jones*, October 14, available at: www.motherjones.com/politics/2016/10/donald-trump-hate-groups-neo-nazi-white-supremacist-racism

Reed, M. (2016) "Donald Trump Won Because of Facebook," in *New York Magazine*, November 9, available at: http://nymag.com/selectall/2016/11/donald-trump-won-because-of-facebook.html

Rosenmann, A. (2016) "GOP Senator's Private Jokes About Gun Owners Shooting Hillary Clinton Draw Secret Service Scrutiny," Alternet.org, November 1, available at: www.alternet.org/election-2016/gop-senators-private-jokes-about-gun-owners-shooting-hillary-clinton-draw-secret?akid=14838.19806.Mi9vB2&rd=1&src=newsletter 1066389&t=6

Silman, A. (2016) "A Timeline of Leslie Jones Horrific Online Abuse," *New York Magazine*, available at: http://nymag.com/thecut/2016/08/a-timeline-of-leslie-joness-horrific-online-abuse.html

Tefaye, S. (2016) "Breitbart and Donald Trump's Alt-Right Troll Brigade Attacked Chobano Yogurt Because Its Founder Likes Immigrants," *Salon*, November 3, available at: www.salon.com/2016/11/03/breitbart-and-donald-trumps-alt-right-troll-brigade-attacked-chobani-yogurt-because-its-founder-likes-immigrants/

Part 9

MEDIA INDUSTRY AND GOVERNMENT INFLUENCES ON POLICY AND HUMANITARIAN AFFAIRS

The Propaganda of Warmaking

INTRODUCTION
TO PART 9

The Bill & Melinda Gates Foundation among other major power players in the humanitarian world has helped the term *philanthrocapitalism* become a central concept in humanitarian giving. This new strategy for doing philanthropy takes business thinking from the for-profit capitalist world and applies it to social projects and programs. In the first chapter in this section, titled "The Philanthrocapitalist and the Humanitarian Agenda: Motivations, Measurements and Media Power," Garrett Broad explores the intersections between philanthrocapitalism and media, describing how philanthrocapitalists have leveraged communication technology and media storytelling to amplify their global influence well beyond the force of their monetary donations alone. From the use of celebrity partnerships to the funding of specific filmmaking and journalistic endeavors, philanthrocapitalists have worked hard to set the media and policy agendas in a way that matches their social concerns and aligns with their metrics-oriented and technologically savvy styles. Some scholars and activists have argued that the approach undermines democracy and prevents the development of more systemic social change strategies. After laying out a few of the practical contradictions of such strategies, Broad concludes by saying that the philosophies and practices of these new donors deserve a higher level of scrutiny and interrogation than has thus far occurred in media and the public sphere.

Along with Hillary Clinton, well-known humanitarian author Samantha Powers who ran the Office of Multilateral Affairs and Human Rights in Obama's National Security Council, together with United Nations ambassador Susan Rice, made the case forcefully that Qaddafi was murdering his own people and that if the United Sates military did not intervene in Libya there would be a bloodbath. In "The Impossibility of Humanitarian War: Libya and Beyond," Robin Andersen examines such claims, which were often repeated in the mainstream Western press. This chapter revisits the arguments that called for intervention, details the persuasions that justified it, looks at the UN Resolution that allowed it (to determine what it actual permitted), and examines the role the media played in articulating it. Andersen compares the case made for a "humanitarian" intervention in Libya with the actual situation that was taking place on the ground, the false documentation that drove it, how the war was prosecuted, and offers an assessment questioning, in retrospect, if it was "the right thing to do." Libya merits a closer look because the NATO bombing that destroyed the government and left the country in chaos was promoted by "liberal interventionists" as a "humanitarian war," which Andersen argues is a grave misdirection of the United Nation's humanitarian mission.

In "The CNN Effect and Humanitarian Crisis," Piers Robinson revisits the debates over what has been called the "CNN effect," a term that assumes media coverage of crises invariably leads to instigating humanitarian responses. While many claimed that interventions during humanitarian crises were influenced by media reporting of suffering people, early research indicated that influence was more conditional and dependent upon factors such as policy uncertainty, the political risks, and costs associated with the intervention. Since 9/11, the emergence of the "war on terror" has seen humanitarianism exploited in order to justify invasions of Iraq and Afghanistan and the co-optation of humanitarian organizations as part of winning "hearts and minds." Even though new communication technologies appear to offer the potential for more effective humanitarian responses, the overall space for genuine humanitarian action would appear to have shrunk by the use of it for manipulative organized persuasive communication (propaganda) purposes in the context of the "war on terror" and the aggressive pursuit of perceived Western interests.

41

PHILANTHRO-CAPITALISTS AND THE HUMANITARIAN AGENDA

Motivations, Metrics, and Media Power

Garrett M. Broad

Introduction

"Dear Max," a December 2015 Facebook post, entitled "A letter to our daughter," began simply enough. What followed, however, was hardly typical of most online status updates, given that the author happened to be Mark Zuckerberg, the co-founder and CEO of Facebook, writing along with his wife, the pediatrician Priscilla Chan. Inspired by the birth of their newborn, the couple proceeded to outline their plan to donate 99 percent of their Facebook shares over the course of their lifetimes—estimated to be worth $45 billion—to create and fund the Chan Zuckerberg Initiative (CZI). As the letter explained, the CZI would aim to "advance human potential and promote equality for all children in the next generation," with an initial set of focus areas related to "personalized learning, curing disease, connecting people and building strong communities" (Zuckerberg 2015, par. 65–66). With billions of dollars to be doled out in installments over time, the CZI would take the form not of a traditional foundation, but rather of a more nimble limited liability corporation, allowing them the flexibility to engage in not only philanthropic grant-making, but also direct policy advocacy, a variety of media and communications activities, and investments in for-profit companies.

And with that, another philanthrocapitalist plan was set in motion.

Philanthrocapitalism has been conceptualized as a new way of doing philanthropy, a strategy that takes business thinking from the for-profit capitalist world and applies it to social projects and programs, spurring innovation and scaling-up solutions to global challenges along the way. The concept was described in-depth by Matthew Bishop, a longtime writer and editor at *The Economist*, along with Michael Green, an economist and author, in their 2008 book *Philanthrocapitalism: How the Rich Can Save the World* (following the Great Recession, subsequent editions were titled *Philanthrocapitalism: How Giving Can Save the World*). In that book and elsewhere, the authors outlined their hope and expectation that the actions of several leading philanthrocapitalists would usher in a broader cultural shift, encouraging wealthy capitalists everywhere to become influential humanitarians. As former President Bill Clinton put it in his foreword to the book's 2009 edition, Bishop and Green show "the remarkable extent to which private wealth can advance public good by applying entrepreneurial skills, speed, and score-keeping to our most persistent challenges," adding, "the twenty-first century has given people with wealth unprecedented opportunities, and commensurate responsibilities, to advance the public good" (Bishop and Green 2009, vii–viii).

This chapter aims to explore the intersections between philanthrocapitalism and humanitarian action, focusing specifically on the role of communication technology and media storytelling as central to its current place in global society. In so doing, the chapter first outlines the basic contours of the philanthrocapitalism approach, tracing its roots back to the philanthropy of the Gilded Age and exploring how today's philanthrocapitalists embody the unique personalities and principles of the digital economy. From there, the chapter delves into the ways that strategic communication has been used as a force to leverage and amplify philanthrocapitalists' influence beyond their monetary donations alone. From the use of celebrity partnerships to the funding of specific filmmaking and journalistic endeavors, philanthrocapitalists have worked hard to set the media and policy agendas in a way that matches their fiscal and social concerns. The work concludes with reflections on the media narratives that have taken shape as a result, arguing that incisive critical perspectives have been limited within mostly niche academic and advocacy audiences, while, in some cases, opposition to philanthrocapitalism has veered toward unfounded conspiracy. Ultimately, given the increasing power of philanthrocapitalists in the humanitarian landscape, their philosophies and practices deserve a higher level of interrogation than has thus far occurred in media and the public sphere.

The Principles of Philanthrocapitalism

Zuckerberg might be the most recent super-rich corporate leader to offer up his wealth to charitable causes, but he is hardly the first. There is a long history of voluntary and civic action, philanthropic donation, and religious charity around the world, extending back to the days of the ancients and up through the present day. However, it was in the late nineteenth and early twentieth centuries that a new style of giving emerged in the United States. Championed by some of the wealthiest industrial capitalists of the Gilded Age, the effort was led by the Scottish-American steel magnate Andrew Carnegie. At the time, Carnegie was faced with public and political pressure regarding growing wealth inequality in society. Confident in the ability of men of means like himself to skillfully guide the allocation of public investments voluntarily, in 1889 he penned "The Gospel of Wealth," declaring in that article that, "The man who dies thus rich dies disgraced" (Carnegie 1900, 19). After selling his company to J. P. Morgan in 1901, Carnegie spent the final 18 years of his life donating upwards of $350 million to charitable causes in the United States and Scotland, giving away the vast majority of his fortune. In the coming decades, he would be joined in this philanthropic quest by other leading American capitalists, including Standard Oil founder John D. Rockefeller and later Henry Ford, each of whom created multiple foundations and gave away hundreds of millions of dollars. Together, this boom in charitable giving helped to create and support local arts institutions, libraries, research and educational facilities, hospitals, and public health centers.

Through the twentieth century, the number of philanthropic organizations and the volume of their spending proliferated in both domestic and global contexts. By 1960, US-based foundation assets were estimated at $11 billion, with annual grants totaling $625 million—that number would rise to approximately $385 billion in assets and $19.5 billion in grants by 1998 (Frumkin 2005; The Foundation Center 2009). The increasing influence of foundations over the course of the century, however, did not proceed without controversy. As the scholar Linsey McGoey (2015, 58) has documented, "The freedom to fund whatever areas foundation staff wished to invest in was seen as an unquestionable right." This left donors open to criticism from across the political spectrum—those on the left often argued that philanthropic fortunes were created through exploitative means, and that their programmatic rigidity constrained the work of the non-profit groups they funded; those on the right were concerned about anti-capitalist leanings within funded programs, an anxiety that contributed to the development of right-wing political think tanks that served as an ideological counterforce.

Yet, starting in the 1980s, and with increasing force through the 1990s and into the 2000s, a novel concern about the proper functioning of philanthropic foundations began to take shape. As McGoey (2015, 62) continued, for much of the twentieth century, many critics suggested that philanthropy was *too* powerful and worked *too* well. However, a new set of management scholars insisted that philanthropy had been fundamentally *ineffective* over time, and was dominated by foundations that demonstrated a "failure to meet or even clearly state objectives, to adopt clear performance measures, or to reduce operating overheads." What foundations needed instead, they argued, was the introduction of evidence-based decision-making strategies from the business world that would lead philanthropy into an era of greater innovation, quicker results, and broader social impact. Enter philanthro-capitalism.

Philanthrocapitalism is one term among several that describes an outcomes-oriented approach to philanthropic action in the contemporary moment—concepts such as strategic philanthropy, venture philanthropy, impact investing, effective altruism, and others exist as overlapping approaches within this broader landscape of business-minded giving. And while anyone interested in using money to promote social good can put these ideas to work, there is no doubt that the agenda for philanthrocapitalism has been set by those individuals who have ascended to the greatest heights of capitalist society. Just as the likes of Carnegie, Rockefeller, and Ford led the philanthropic way in the twentieth century, today it is the likes of Gates, Buffet, and Zuckerberg who demonstrate what it means to be a philanthro-capitalist in the twenty-first.

As Bishop and Green tell the tale, the modern era of philanthrocapitalism began in 1997, when another billionaire—CNN founder Ted Turner—pledged to give $1 billion to support United Nations causes. At the same time, he publicly chastised fellow tycoons of the emerging digital age—Bill Gates and Warren Buffet, chief among them—for not doing the same (Bishop and Green 2009, 5). Within a few years, the Bill & Melinda Gates Foundation—named for the Microsoft co-founder and his wife Melinda, formerly a product manager at Microsoft—was well on its way to becoming the largest and most influential foundation in the world. Its philanthropic largesse was bolstered when Warren Buffet—the chairman and CEO of the American multinational conglomerate holding company Berkshire Hathaway Inc., often considered the most successful investor in the world—pledged to give away 99 percent of his fortune to philanthropic causes, most of that directed through the Gates Foundation.

With Bill Gates, Melinda Gates, and Warren Buffet operating as the three trustees of the Gates Foundation (Bill's father William Gates Sr. serves as a Foundation co-chair, while

Bill and Melinda serve as the only two trustees of the Bill & Melinda Gates Foundation Trust, which manages their collective assets), they set out to tackle four primary focus areas. At the Gates Foundation, the Global Development Division focuses on hunger and poverty, the Global Health Division aims to save lives in developing countries, the United States Division works to improve education and support vulnerable families in Gates' home state of Washington, and the Global Policy & Advocacy Division builds relationships and promotes policies in the Foundation's interest. At the end of 2015, the Gates Foundation Trust endowment was listed at just under $40 billion and the Foundation had allocated nearly $37 billion in grants since its inception, including over $4 billion in 2015 alone. And the giving would show no signs of stopping, as stipulated in the Gates Foundation's by-laws:

> The decision to use all of the foundation's resources in this century underscores our optimism for progress and determination to do as much as possible, as soon as possible, to address the comparatively narrow set of issues we've chosen to focus on.
>
> (Gates Foundation n.d.)

Perhaps having learned a lesson from Ted Turner, Buffet, and the Gateses also unleashed the power of billionaire peer pressure when they launched the Giving Pledge in 2006. Described as an effort to address society's most pressing problems by inviting the world's wealthiest individuals and families to pledge at least half of their wealth to philanthropy or charitable causes, they were initially able to secure the commitment of 40 families from the United States. At the time of this writing, there are now 144 current pledges, primarily from Americans but with a growing number of signees from abroad and even a few from developing nations.

An analysis of these Giving Pledge members demonstrates one of the first fundamental intersections between philanthrocapitalism, on one hand, and communication and media technology, on the other. That is, the wealth that is being pledged was largely created through the affordances of digital information technology and the global information economy. These are key components of what the scholar Manuel Castells famously declared the Network Society, an ever-more capitalist world that depends upon the information technology revolution to proceed, without which "it could not be such a comprehensive, pervasive social form, able to link up, or de-link, the entire realm of human activity" (Castells 1997, 15).

The Giving Pledge is populated by those capitalists who have proved most adept at navigating the Network Society, whether through success in globally linked infrastructural endeavors such as real estate and energy production, through informational capitalism operations such as venture capital and hedge funds, through the creation of transformative media and technology platforms put to use by businesses and consumers, or simply through prudent investing in global markets on top of previous family riches accrued during the industrial age. As the inventor and futurist Peter Diamandis, working with journalist and entrepreneur Steven Kotler, wrote in their book *Abundance: The Future is Better Than You Think*, what seems to unify them is "a high level of optimism, a magnanimous sphere of caring, and a hearty appetite for the big and bold," something that should be expected, the authors argue, from captains of the digital age who have seen their work transform technology, economics, and society "with the stroke of HTML code" (Diamandis and Kotler 2012, 132).

Another common interest among many (although hardly all) philanthrocapitalists is a desire to use their wealth to promote global—not just local—action. Diamandis and Kotler (2012, 135) explored this perspective in conversation with Jeff Skoll, the first president of eBay, who now runs the Skoll Foundation and signed onto the Giving Pledge in 2010. "While the industrial revolution focused philanthropy locally, the high-tech revolution inverted the equation," Skoll argued. "Everything from climate change to pandemics have roots in different parts of the world, but they affect everybody. In this way, global has become the new local."

In the eyes of philanthrocapitalists, though, what truly sets them apart is a simple commitment to evidence-based decision making in the process of their philanthropic giving. Bishop and Green (2009) echo a number of philanthrocapitalists when they assert that the lack of good data in the philanthropic world is a huge problem, applauding those who work to apply cutting-edge management theories and rigorously analyze performance data to create more effective social investments. As evidence, in 2013, Bill Gates dedicated his annual letter as co-chair of the Gates Foundation to the topic of "Measuring Progress." In an accompanying video, he offered examples of anti-malarial bed net allocation, vaccinations, and farmer productivity, arguing that the Gates Foundation adopts programs such as these that can be measured to show whether or not they are working. "You can constantly see, where are you making mistakes, what do you need to change?" Gates explained. "So, in contrast to several decades ago, where it was equally well-meaning, now it's more like a business, where you know the numbers, you often see what you have to adjust, and that's letting us make huge progress" (Gates 2013).

One need not have signed onto the Giving Pledge, explicitly, to share these philanthrocapitalist assumptions. In a 2015 editorial for the *Wall Street Journal*, Sean Parker—the co-founder of the early file-sharing service Napster, the first president of Facebook, and chairman of the Parker Foundation—outlined the perspectives of self-described hackers, like himself, who have turned their eye toward philanthropy. "These budding philanthropists want metrics and analytic tools comparable to the dashboards, like Mixpanel, that power their software products. They want to interact directly with scientists, field workers and academics whose ideas power the philanthropic world," he explained (Parker 2015, par. 13). In this manifesto, Parker also pointed to another key component of the philanthrocapitalist approach, one that goes beyond the traditional model of funding specific programs with actionable outcomes. "The trouble for hackers venturing into the field of philanthropy is one of scale," he wrote. "How do these individuals, accustomed to unleashing massive social changes that span the globe, make a lasting contribution in their charitable lives and find satisfaction in doing so?" (Parker 2015, par. 34). Parker's answer? Get political.

Setting the Agenda: Policy, Celebrity, Media, and Journalism

Today's philanthrocapitalists have an awful lot of money, and thanks to initiatives such as the Giving Pledge, they are eager to give a whole lot of it away. Yet, in purely economic terms, even the Gates Foundation's assets pale in comparison to the budgets of major governments or even major corporations from around the world. In order to make the type of transformative impacts they hope to achieve, philanthrocapitalists must become what Bishop and Green (2009, 263) call "hyperagents." Free from the demands of electioneering, fundraising, or shareholder complaints, philanthrocapitalists can go against conventional wisdom, take big risks, and apply pressure on other major decision makers to chart a new course. By leveraging their status and cultural clout, philanthrocapitalists have the ability to put their money to work, strategically setting the agenda for philanthropic and government action to reflect their interests and priorities.

As the media and communication scholars Dearing and Rogers (1997, 6) outlined, the agenda-setting process can be understood as an "ongoing competition among the proponents of a set of issues to gain the attention of media professionals, the public, and policy elites." Philanthrocapitalists have demonstrated a keen understanding of the dynamic relationship between these fields of action, establishing themselves as some of the most effective issue proponents in the Network Society. Indeed, a year before Gates and Buffet created the Giving Pledge, they convened a meeting of the Good Club, a gathering of super-elite billionaires—including Ted Turner, Michael Bloomberg, and George Soros—to discuss the domestic and global problems that should be the focus of their philanthropic giving and advocacy efforts. It is this interest in concerted and coordinated philanthro-policymaking, as the sociologist Robin Rogers (2015) has termed it, that allows philanthrocapitalists to do much more than simply fund humanitarian programs—instead, they shape the very contours of what is considered worthwhile and effective humanitarian action.

No entity has been more assertive in setting the agenda than the Gates Foundation, which has spurred the development of countless public–private partnerships in the global health, disease prevention, agricultural, and educational arenas. Bringing together US and multi-national health and economic institutions, governments, universities, private corporations, and non-governmental organizations, the Gates Foundation has proven to be the premier hyperagent. Its seed money has been leveraged into exponentially higher sums of matching contributions, it has taken influential seats on the boards of newly created multinational institutions (like the Alliance for a Green Revolution in Africa, and Gavi, the Vaccine Alliance), and key Gates allies have become chief executives across the many public and private organizations that are linked through this networked action. With the philosophical and pragmatic perspectives of the Gates Foundation looming large, its issues priorities, preferred technological solutions, and strategies for measuring programmatic success have become deeply engrained within the broader humanitarian landscape (Birn 2014).

Several key philanthrocapitalists have also recognized that the policy agenda is not only shaped behind closed doors, but also in the court of public opinion. It was a reality that occurred to Bill Gates himself after some of his early philanthropic initiatives in the United States—focused on Internet access at public libraries and education reform—floundered when community reinvestment and political support did not pan out as planned. From there, the Gates Foundation took seriously the need to actively persuade the public and to shape the broader media narratives that surround its priority issues (Bishop and Green 2009). Figures such as Bill Gates and Mark Zuckerberg have proved effective at telling their stories, using their own online platforms and garnering coverage in traditional media to make their philanthropic cases. But why make Gates or Zuckerberg the face of a campaign when a rock star is willing to take their place?

Indeed, celebrities have become key players in the advocacy and campaigning practices of philanthrocapitalism, and no celebrity has been more central to this process than U2 front-man Bono. Long engaged in humanitarian issues, in 2004 Bono and American activist Bobby Shriver co-founded ONE, an international advocacy organization that aims to raise awareness and encourage action to end extreme poverty and preventable disease, particularly in Africa. An important division of ONE is (RED), a cause-related marketing program that partners with leading corporations—including Apple, Bank of America, Gap, Coca Cola, and Starbucks—using sales to trigger donations to the Global Fund to Fight AIDS, Tuberculosis, and Malaria. Funded primarily by the Bill & Melinda Gates Foundation, ONE is not a grant-making organization nor does it develop programs on the ground, focusing instead on high-profile digital media campaigns and media events. ONE's "Poverty is Sexist" campaign, for instance, enlisted the support of Beyoncé, Meryl Streep, Elton John, and dozens of other celebrity activists to pressure world leaders to support measures that address female economic empowerment.

Just as Bono is not the only celebrity involved in philanthrocapitalist humanitarianism, the issue-focused ONE campaign is not the only way that philanthrocapitalists have used media to advocate for their concern. In 2004, Jeff Skoll bankrolled the creation of Participant Media, a for-profit film and television production company with a social conscience. With a mission statement declaring that, "A story well told can change the world," at the time of this writing, Participant had produced more than 70 films, earning 50 Academy Award nominations and 11 wins—including Best Documentary for *An Inconvenient Truth* (2006) and Best Picture for *Spotlight* (2015). Each Participant project is accompanied by a social action campaign, with the online platform TakePart serving as the digital hub for news and activism. And, consistent with the measurement-oriented concerns of philanthrocapitalism, the company has launched the Participant Index, a research initiative that conducts surveys to determine whether watching its films actually leads to taking social or political action. Notably, several other philanthropic organizations, including the Gates Foundation, have funded similar media impact measurement initiatives in recent years, trying to develop best practices to capture media's influence in a world of increasing digital saturation (Schiffrin and Zuckerman 2015).

Further, at a time when traditional journalism has faced existential threats to its business model, philanthrocapitalists have also stepped in as major supporters of the news. In 2013, eBay founder and Giving Pledger Pierre Omidyar launched First Look Media, a venue for original journalism. Initially intended to support multiple online platforms, several years in, only its adversarial investigative outlet *The Intercept* has proved viable. The Gates Foundation's support for journalism has been somewhat under-the-radar, but perhaps even more consequential. Grants from the Gates Foundation have supported education coverage on NPR, the "Poverty Matters" global development blog on *The Guardian*, global health reporting on the ABC network, general programming on the PBS Newshour, and much more. Funding has also been used to support trainings and conferences with strategic media partners, as the Gates Foundation has promoted a model of "solutions journalism" that highlights stories of progress and innovation to counter the media's tendency to focus only on problems and mistakes.

All told, the Gates Foundation has established itself as the top foundation funder of news and journalism, using tens of millions of dollars from within its overall budget of over $1 billion allocated specifically to advocacy and policy initiatives (Doughton and Heim 2011; Janssen 2015). As Dan Green, director of Program Advocacy and Communications for the Gates Foundation, explained, "Ideas, research, personal stories, thoughtful conversation, and fostering engaging communities who want to affect change are all critical to making progress on our issues," adding, "Media plays an important role at each and every turn of the process" (Green 2012, par. 5).

The Story of Philanthrocapitalism

In November of 2013, the esteemed television news magazine *60 Minutes* aired a segment entitled "The Giving Pledge: A New Club For Billionaires." In the introduction, correspondent Charlie Rose expressed some concern that the richest 400 Americans own as much wealth as the bottom half of all American households combined, but suggested there may be a silver lining to this inequality: "It turns out a lot of those rich people are giving staggering sums of money away, in what is being called a golden age of philanthropy." The segment—

which was also rebroadcast in 2014 and 2016—featured Rose in conversation with several key Giving Pledgers and their spouses, painting a glowing picture of their commitment to charitable giving and social change. Toward the end of the segment, however, Rose raised a critical question: Is it a good idea for people with enormous wealth to have so much influence? The suggestion was quickly rebuffed, with Warren Buffet remarking that it was a far better option than dynastic wealth or obscenely high living among the rich. Jean Case, CEO of the Case Foundation and wife of AOL co-founder Steve Case, offered a different counterpoint:

> Bill and Melinda's work in polio. I mean, they're close to eradicating polio on the face of the Earth. I think when we have a couple of examples like that, people will see, that's not power being used for personal purposes.
>
> (Rose 2013)

The *60 Minutes* report is illustrative of the media and social narratives that have come to dominate conversations about philanthrocapitalists and their humanitarian action. Awed by their business success, impressed by their selflessness, and appreciative of their documented successes in global health and development, policymakers, journalists, and the public at large have proved extremely receptive to the story of philanthrocapitalism. A gentle nudging about undue influence, like the one offered by Charlie Rose, is consistently rationalized as a noble concern that is outweighed by the good work being done.

More incisive critiques of philanthrocapitalists do exist, however, often relegated to niche academic and intellectual audiences, with other concerns expressed (quietly) by on-the-ground activists and health and education practitioners themselves. Given its scope and impact, the Gates Foundation has taken the brunt of this criticism, and a handful of media exposés, journal articles, investigative reports, and book-length treatments have levied a number of central complaints. Mirroring a political economic critique from the Gilded Age, these opponents have argued that philanthrocapitalist wealth was created through exploitative and monopolistic practices to begin with, and that these major donations operate as a tax-dodge that takes money away from democratically elected governments. Further, the critics have insisted that the preferred solutions of philanthrocapitalists are too market-driven and technology-focused, while their track record in the health and education sectors includes just as many outright failures as it does clear successes (Edwards 2010; Birn 2014).

The Gates Foundation's $40 billion endowment offers one case in point. Over the course of a decade, investigative journalists have uncovered a series of egregious contradictions between its investment portfolio, on one hand, and its stated social change goals, on the other. Donations to prevent polio and measles in the Niger Delta have been countered by holdings in polluting oil companies that sicken children in the very same region, while other investments in pharmaceutical corporations, predatory lenders, military weapons manufacturers, and fossil fuel companies appear directly counter to the Foundation's stated global health and development mission (Piller 2014). A parallel critique has been levied against the Gates Foundation's efforts to advance a new Green Revolution to end hunger in Africa. "What the Gates Foundation is doing is using its private money to fund activities that once were in the public domain and were, albeit imperfectly, under democratic control," scholar-activists Raj Patel, Eric Holt-Gimenez, and Annie Shattuck editorialized. As major agricultural biotechnology projects have commenced, they argue, hundreds of millions of dollars in grants have been awarded to organizations connected to Monsanto and other corporate agriculture behemoths, while little to no attention has been paid to "addressing both the technical and sociopolitical reasons for hunger in Africa" (Patel et al. 2009, par. 12 and 36). In the context of education reform, the charter school advocacy of the Gates Foundation has been critiqued for being ineffective, inconsistent, and overly focused on high-stakes standardized testing and teacher evaluation (McGoey 2015, 115). Indeed, charter schools have emerged as a preferred site of charitable action for many philanthrocapitalists in the United States, who often offer up "disruptive" educational models as the pathway to prosperity for the generationally impoverished—although the results have not backed up such magnanimous claims. Quite the contrary, as the education historian Diane Ravitch has argued, "The charter industry is flourishing and attracting investors and entrepreneurs because it is almost completely unregulated, allowing non-educators to open schools with little financial accountability or transparency and a secure source of funding from the government" (quoted in Joseph 2016, par. 11).

Taken as a whole, the central oppositional argument to this philanthrocapitalist action is that the agenda-setting power of groups such as the Gates Foundation has foreclosed the possibility of more systemic social change strategies, those that tackle the root causes of inequality rather than treat its symptoms. Under the veneer of skillful, technologically savvy, metrics-oriented management, these efforts have actually undermined democracy by allowing unaccountable philanthrocapitalists to shift government priorities and funnel major sums of money from the public to the private sector. All the while, philanthrocapitalist influence has had a chilling effect that mutes the voices of grassroots and media advocates who would otherwise be able to offer viable alternative approaches

Not all critiques of philanthrocapitalists, however, have been as grounded in evidence and reasoned thinking. For instance, in a report by the UK-based campaign organization Global Justice Now, the author highlighted the standard complaints about the Gates Foundation, focusing on its promotion of corporate interests in the global health and agricultural domains. Yet, woven through the report were unsubstantiated claims about forced vaccination campaigns and widespread illnesses and deaths resulting from Gates-led vaccine administration. The authors hedged, insisting that Global Justice Now had been unable to validate these claims and calling for further investigation and media scrutiny (Curtis 2016). The websites used to support the accusations they floated—such as Vactruth.com—as well as other online sources full of anti-Gates Foundation invective, however, tend to be much less careful. Popular conspiracy theorist Alex Jones, for instance, has argued that several key philanthropists are a driving force for global population and mind control initiatives—his Infowars.com website covered the Giving Pledge by stating that, "Billionaire funds all to be diverted to Eugenics at the hands of the Gates Foundation" (Infowars 2010).

Conclusion

This chapter has outlined the philosophical motivations and strategic practices of philanthrocapitalists, interrogating the key place of communication technology and media storytelling within their humanitarian activities. It also explored the central critiques of philanthrocapital-ism that have emerged in response, suggesting that oppositional narratives have played only a minor role in public sphere debates. Fundamentally, philanthrocapitalists have recognized the key role that advocacy plays in setting the agenda of media, policymakers, and the public, cultivating a number of powerful tools to ensure that the stories that get the most attention are those that reflect their own priorities and strategies for humanitarian action. Indeed, at a time when approximately 63 percent of Americans get their news from Facebook (Barthel et al. 2015), the philanthrocapitalist agenda of the newly created

Chan-Zuckerberg Initiative might have the best media platform yet to shape and measure the perspectives of the public. Looking forward, it seems that some balance is needed between recognizing the good work that these philanthrocapitalists can achieve, on one hand, while having opportunities to hold them accountable and propose alternative solutions, on the other. In evaluating the work of the philanthrocapitalists, the ultimate question seems to be whether they can truly promote global well-being when the origins of their wealth, as well as their strategies for social and technological change, remain embedded in the structures of global inequity that have helped to shape the very suffering they hope to alleviate.

References

Barthel, M., Shearer, E., Gottfried, J., and Mitchell, A. (2015) *The Evolving Role of News on Twitter and Facebook*. Pew Research Center, available at: www.journalism.org/files/2015/07/Twitter-and-News-Survey-Report-FINAL2.pdf.

Birn, A. E. (2014) "Philanthrocapitalism, Past and Present: The Rockefeller Foundation, the Gates Foundation, and the Setting(s) of the International/Global Health Agenda," *Hypothesis*, 12 (1):1–27.

Bishop, M., and Green, M. (2009) *Philanthrocapitalism: How Giving Can Save the World*, New York: Bloomsbury.

Carnegie, A. (1900) *The Gospel of Wealth and Other Timely Essays*, New York: The Century Co.

Castells, M. (1997) "An Introduction to the Information Age," *City*, 2 (7): 6–16.

Curtis, M. (2016). "Gated Development: Is the Gates Foundation Always a Force for Good?" Global Justice Now, available at: www.globaljustice.org.uk/sites/default/files/files/resources/gated-development-global-justice-now.pdf.

Dearing, J. W., and Rogers, E. (1997) *Agenda-setting*, Thousand Oaks, CA: Sage.

Diamandis, P. H., and Kotler, S. (2012) *Abundance: The Future is Better Than You Think*. New York: Simon & Schuster.

Doughton, S., and Heim, K. (2011) "Does Gates Funding of Media Taint Objectivity," *Seattle Times*, February 19, available at: www.seattletimes.com/seattle-news/does-gates-funding-of-media-taint-objectivity/

Edwards, M. (2010) *Small Change: Why Business Won't Save the World*, San Francisco, CA: Berrett-Koehler.

Frumkin, P. (2005) "American Foundations and Overseas Funding: New Challenges in the Era of Globalization," in H. Soma and D. Stapleton (Eds.), *Globalization, Philanthropy, and Civil Society: Toward a New Political Culture in the Twenty-First Century*, New York: Springer, pp. 99–116.

Gates, B. (2013) "Annual Letter 2013. The Bill & Melinda Gates Foundation," available at: www.gatesfoundation.org/Who-We-Are/Resources-and-Media/Annual-Letters-List/Annual-Letter-2013

Gates Foundation. (n.d.) *Foundation Trust: Financials*, available at: www.gatesfoundation.org/Who-We-Are/GeneralInformation/Financials/ Foundation-Trust

Green, D. (2012) "Storytelling Matters: A Look at the Gates Foundation's Media Grantmaking," The Bill & Melinda Gates Foundation Impatient Optimists Blog, February 1, available at: www.impatientoptimists.org/Posts/2012/02/Storytelling-Matters-A-Look-at-the-Gates-Foundations-Media-Grantmaking#.VzUMfvkrK00

Infowars. (2010) "40 US Billionaires Pledge Half of Wealth to Charity," August 4, available at: www.infowars.com/40-us-billionaires-pledge-half-of-wealth-to-charity/

Janssen, M. (2015) "Foundation Support for Media: A Boon with Strings Attached," *Society*, 52 (6): 561–564.

Joseph, G. (2016). "Will Trump and Charter Schools Be Another Scam? Just Look at Pal Carl Icahn's Lucrative School 'Charity,'" *Alternet*, June 8, available at: www.alternet.org/right-wing/carl-icahn-used-charity-profit-massive-tax-savings?akid=14333.19806.PVC2T2&rd=1&src=newsletter1057952&t=2

McGoey, L. (2015). *No Such Thing as a Free Gift: The Gates Foundation and the Price of Philanthropy*. New York: Verso.

Parker, S. (2015). "Philanthropy for Hackers," *The Wall Street Journal*, June 26, available at: www.wsj.com/articles/sean-parker-philanthropy-for-hackers-1435345787

Patel, R., Holt-Gimenez, E., and Shattuck, A. (2009) "Ending Africa's Hunger," *The Nation*, , September 2, available at: www.thenation.com/article/ending-africas-hunger/

Piller, C. (2014) "How the Gates Foundation's Investments Are Undermining Its Own Good Works," *The Nation*, August 22, available at: www.thenation.com/article/how-gates-foundations-investments-are-undermining-its-own-good-works/

Rogers, R. (2015) "Why the Social Sciences Should Take Philanthropy Seriously," *Society*, 52 (6): 533–540.

Rose, C. (2013) "The Giving Pledge: A New Club for Billionaires," *60 Minutes*, November 17, available at: www.cbsnews.com/news/giving-pledge-new-billionaires-club/

Schiffrin A., and Zuckerman, E. (2015) "Can We Measure Media Impact? Surveying the Field," *Stanford Social Innovation Review*, available at: http://ssir.org/articles/entry/can_we_measure_media_impact_surveying_the_field

The Foundation Center. (2009) *Foundation Growth and Giving Estimates*, available at: http://foundationcenter.org/gainknowledge/research/pdf/fgge09.pdf

Zuckerberg, M. (2015) "A Letter to Our Daughter," December 1, available at: www.facebook.com/notes/mark-zuckerberg/a-letter-to-our-daughter/10153375081581634/

42

THE IMPOSSIBILITY OF HUMANITARIAN WAR

Libya and Beyond

Robin Andersen

Libyan Regime Change as a "Humanitarian" Intervention

At the end of February 2016, five years after the NATO bombing of Libya, *The New York Times* published two lengthy articles detailing Hillary Clinton's role in ousting Col. Muammar el-Qaddafi. The second one opened with "The fall of Col. Muammar el-Qaddafi seemed to vindicate Hillary Clinton. Then militias refused to disarm, neighbors fanned a civil war, and the Islamic State found refuge" (Shane and Becker 2016).

One month later in an interview with *The Atlantic*, President Obama said he regretted what happened in the aftermath of the Libyan intervention (Ferguson 2016). It was widely repeated in the press. But as the BBC noted, even the apparent display of humility from the President, "given as he considered his legacy, was qualified by his belief the intervention was 'the right thing to do.'"[1]

Writing in Salon.com, Ben Norton (2016) observed that the *Times*' reports, a total of 13,000 words in length, are important contributions to the historical record, and quite critical of Clinton and her leadership in the conflict. In addition to the print story, the *Times* website features a short video that points to some of the consequences of the intervention including a map with arrows showing the flow of weapons into Nigeria, Syria, Mali and other countries as a consequence of regime change. But Norton argues that the *Times* reporting leaves out the most pressing details by failing to acknowledge the crimes of US-backed rebel groups and the extent of the humanitarian disaster that has ravaged Libya since. Overall, they downplay how disastrous the war was, and the significance it has for the future of the United States, and world, and for Libya's suffering people. This chapter will revisit the arguments that called for intervention, detail the persuasions that justified it, look at the UN Resolution that allowed it (to determine what it actual permitted) and examine the role the media played in articulating interventionist talking points. We will compare the case made for a "humanitarian" intervention in Libya with the actual situation that was taking place on the ground, the false documentation that drove it, how the war was prosecuted, and offer an assessment questioning, in retrospect, if it was "the right thing to do."

Libya merits a closer look because the seven months of NATO bombing that destroyed the government and left the country in chaos was promoted by "liberal interventionists" as a "humanitarian war." Along with Hillary Clinton, well-known humanitarian author Samantha Powers[2] who ran the Office of Multilateral Affairs and Human Rights in Obama's National Security Council, together with United Nations ambassador Susan Rice, made the case forcefully to the President, that if the United Sates military did not intervene there would be a bloodbath in Libya. The charge that Qaddafi was "murdering his own people," was a talking point often repeated in the mainstream Western press. Now, five years later, the United States is once again engaged militarily in the country, dropping bombs on ISIS rebels in Sirte, the town where Muammar Qaddafi once lived.

Who Started the Violence?

We will begin with the first claims that started the momentum toward intervention, the charge that Mummar al-Qaddafi's regime was indiscriminately targeting peaceful demonstrators who were part of the Arab Spring uprising. This narrative was the basis for the UN authorized NATO intervention. Admonitions that a "bloodbath" was imminent were also discussed. However, justifications were not based on what was actually happening in Libya at the time. In "Lessons from Libya: How Not to Intervene," a policy brief prepared for the Belfer Center for Science and International Affairs at the Harvard Kennedy School, author Allan Kuperman (2013b) writes, "First, contrary to Western media reports, Qaddafi did not initiate Libya's violence by targeting peaceful protesters." In fact, both the United Nations and Amnesty International documented that in the four cities that experienced civil conflict in February 2011—Benghazi, Al Bayda, Tripoli, and Misrata—the violence in Libya was actually started by the protesters.

On the first day of reporting the demonstrations, February 15, 2011, most Western news outlets incorrectly said that Qaddafi's forces had fired live ammunition at peaceful protesters. This false claim was based on video posted on the Internet. The British Broadcasting Corporation was one of the only media outlets to correct that claim, which they did the next day, admitting, "subsequent inquiries suggested this was footage originally uploaded more than a year ago."[3] But as Kuperman (2013a, 109) notes, "few other Western media corrected the error or acknowledged that they had fallen victim to antigovernment propaganda." This claim remained standard fare and was habitually repeated in opening paragraphs of news reports, as in this *New York Times* piece from February 25, on the freezing of Qaddafi's assets:

> The United States closed its embassy in Tripoli on Friday and imposed unilateral sanctions against Libya including the freezing of billions in government assets, as the Obama administration made its most aggressive move against Col. Muammar el-Qaddafi since his security forces opened fire on protesters.
>
> (Cooper and Landler 2011)

Genocide, Atrocities, and Targeting Civilians

Another key claim repeated in Western media, also inaccurate, was the charge that as Qaddafi's troops battled protesters they targeted civilians. In fact, Qaddafi's troops:

> responded to the rebels militarily but never intentionally targeted civilians or resorted to "indiscriminate" force, as claimed. Early press accounts exaggerated the death toll

by a factor of ten, citing "more than 2,000 deaths" in Benghazi during the initial days of the uprising, whereas Human Rights Watch (HRW) later documented only 233 deaths across all of Libya in that period.

(Kuperman 2013a, 110)

The origin of this error likely comes from an interview in *Agence France-Presse*, and *Le Point*, of a French doctor working in Benghazi, who "extrapolated wildly from the tiny sample in his hospital" (Kuperman 2013a, 110).

Further evidence that Qaddafi avoided targeting civilians is included in another HRW report from Misrata, the Libyan city most affected by the early fighting:

of the 949 people wounded there in the rebellion's initial seven weeks, only 30 were women or children, meaning that Qaddafi's forces focused narrowly on combatants. During that same period, only 257 people were killed among the city's population of 400,000—a fraction less than 0.0006—providing additional proof that the government avoided using force indiscriminately.

(Kuperman 2013b)

Indeed, in discussions about the use of force, Clinton argued that Qaddafi was about to engage in a genocide against civilians in rebel-held Benghazi, but defense intelligence officials could "not corroborate those concerns" and in fact assessed that Qaddafi "was unlikely to risk world outrage by inflicting mass casualties" (Shapiro and Riddell 2015). Clinton's push to war was not based on intelligence reports. As a consequence, Mike Mullen, chairman of the Joint Chiefs of Staff and Defense Secretary Robert M. Gates opposed the use of force. Though the trio called for a humanitarian intervention to forestall a "genocide," Human Rights Watch did not see it that way either. "At that point, we did not see the imminence of massacres that would rise to genocidelike levels," said Sarah Leah Whitson, executive director of the Middle East and North Africa division for Human Rights Watch (Shapiro and Riddell 2015). Writing in *Jacobin* in 2016, Mizner confirms that claims that Qaddafi was on the verge of carrying out genocide against his people were largely baseless (Mizner 2015). Also in 2016 *The New York Times* reported that Human Rights Watch later showed that media claims about Qaddafi's repression of protesters, which were used to sell the war to the public, were grossly exaggerated, by an order of magnitude.[4]

Humanitarian Intervention or Regime Change

The United Nations charter forbids countries from going to war except in response to an attack by another country, but in 2005 the Responsibility to Protect (R2P) provision was endorsed at the UN World Summit in New York. The R2P was a response to the 1994 massacre of some 800,000 people in Rwanda, and the policy says that member states have a responsibility to protect people from genocide, ethnic cleansing, war crimes, and other crimes against humanity. On the basis of R2P, on March 17, 2011, the United Nations Security Council passed Resolution 1973 by a vote of ten in favor and five abstentions, authorizing a No-Fly Zone and member states "to take all necessary measures . . . to protect civilians and civilian populations under threat of attack," while also "excluding a foreign occupation force of any form."[5]

But there are indications that throughout the bombing campaign regime change, if not the original intent, quickly became the military objective early on. According to Kuperman's (2013b) assessment of the documentation:

NATO attacked Libyan forces indiscriminately, including some in retreat and others in Qaddafi's hometown of Sirte, where they posed no threat to civilians. Moreover, NATO continued to aid the rebels even when they repeatedly rejected government cease-fire offers that could have ended the violence and spared civilians. Such military assistance included weapons, training, and covert deployment of hundreds of troops from Qatar, eventually enabling the rebels to capture and summarily execute Qaddafi and seize power in October 2011.

In his 2014 memoir, *Worthy Fights*, Leon Panetta then head of the CIA acknowledged that regime change was always the goal. "I said what everyone in Washington knew but we couldn't officially acknowledge: that our goal in Libya was regime change."[6]

Negotiations Denied

An important requirement of the Responsibility to Protect is that member states must first, "seek a solution by negotiation, enquiry, mediation, conciliation, arbitration, judicial arrangement . . . or other peaceful means of their own choice." As Conn Hallinan (2011) argues, "there was no effort to negotiate anything before the French started bombing Qaddafi's forces. Thus in strictly legal terms, UN Resolution 1973 is a little shaky." In fact, the day the resolution was passed, Clinton ordered a general to refuse a call from Qaddafi's son Seif as he tried to negotiate a resolution (Shapiro and Riddell 2015).

As mentioned above, NATO forces aided the rebels, even after they rejected government ceasefire offers that could have spared civilians. As the NATO bombing carried on, there were numerous indications that Qaddafi and his son Seif were willing to engage in diplomacy to end the conflict. Yet as President Obama had said, Hillary Clinton was directing the Libya operation, and she rebuffed documented efforts to stop the conflict, even when it came from members of her own party. Rep. Dennis Kucinich actively tried to end the belligerencies but his pleas were ignored. He wrote a letter to Clinton and Obama on August 24, 2011 stating "I have been contacted by an intermediary in Libya who has indicated that President Muammar Gadhafi is willing to negotiate an end to the conflict under conditions which would seem to favor Administration policy" (Norton 2016). Ben Norton (2016) also refers to a secret audio recording released in early 2015 that reveals how top Pentagon officials continued to attempt to correspond with the Qaddafi regime "in hopes of pursuing some form of diplomacy." Norton writes that Qaddafi's son Seif wanted to negotiate a ceasefire and began a dialogue with the Joint Chiefs of Staff, but Clinton intervened and asked the Pentagon to stop talking to the Qaddafi regime. At that point Seif Qaddafi also argued that, "many of the U.S.-supported armed rebels were not freedom fighters" but rather jihadists whom he described as "gangsters and terrorists. And now you have NATO supporting them with ships, with airplanes, helicopters, arms, training, communication," he said in one recorded conversation with US officials. "We ask the American government send a fact-finding mission to Libya. I want you to see everything with your own eyes" (Shapiro and Riddell 2015). But a Pentagon intelligence official told Seif Qaddafi that his messages were "falling on deaf ears. Everything I am getting from the State Department is that they do not care about being part of this" (Norton 2016).

Norton points out that most journalists have been uninterested in reporting on the secret tapes, and the trove of material they contain. The fact that Clinton refused to even open a discussion that might have resolved the conflict and led to fewer civilian deaths makes her remarks to CBS about the brutal killing of Qaddafi—reportedly sodomized with a bayonet by rebels—even more chilling "We came, we saw, he died!" she said (Daly 2011).

During the fighting, it had already become clear that Qaddafi, in spite of some bombastic rhetoric, did not perpetrate a "bloodbath" in any of the cities that his forces recaptured from rebels prior to the NATO intervention. In the cities that had been taken by rebel forces there was no "revenge violence." Those cities included Ajdabiya, Bani Walid, Brega, Ras Lanuf, Zawiya, and much of Misrata—so there was no documented risk of such an outcome if he had been permitted to recapture the last rebel stronghold of Benghazi. Kuperman (2013b) concludes, "The conventional wisdom is also wrong in asserting that NATO's main goal in Libya was to protect civilians. Evidence reveals that NATO's primary aim was to overthrow Qaddafi's regime, even at the expense of increasing the harm to Libyans."

Cluster Bombing in Misrata

By April 15, claims that Qaddafi's troops used cluster bombs in civilian neighborhoods became front page and first item news in print and on the television around the world. As *The New York Times* reported, "Qaddafi Troops Fire Cluster Bombs into Civilian Areas" (Chivers 2011). It opens:

> Military forces loyal to Col. Muammar el-Qaddafi have been firing into residential neighborhoods in this embattled city with heavy weapons, including cluster bombs that have been banned by much of the world and ground-to-ground rockets, according to witnesses and survivors, as well as physical evidence.

The report that cluster bombs hit close to a hospital, in the town of Misrata, was certainly true. *Times* reporter C. J. Chivers, and HRW staff were on the ground and saw the destruction. Photographs also show the damage. But both HRW personnel and Chivers immediately blamed the attacks on the Qaddafi regime. Canadian based Human Rights Investigations (HRI) wondered why journalists were so quick to blame Qaddafi's troops. Why, they asked the BBC's Fred Abrahams (2011), whose report also assigned responsibility to Libya, assume the munitions that form part of NATO's arsenal were fired by Libyan rather than NATO forces? Abrahams replied "Because the MAT-120 is mortar-fired and NATO has no troops on the ground." As it turned out, NATO was able to launch such munitions from ships and vessels stationed in the area and admitted to being involved in the fighting (Human Rights Investigation 2011). Among a list of demands by HRI was:

> An end to the ongoing bombing of Libya which is against the spirit and intent of UN Resolution 1973 which was intended to protect civilians, not justify bombing of civilian areas, never mind justify war crimes and the cluster bombing of Libyan cities.
>
> (Human Rights Investigation 2011)

Who Were the Protesters?

There was evidence that Clinton should have been cautious about believing the claims of an imminent genocide that came from rebel groups. Earlier, Qaddafi had identified his opponents in eastern Libya as Al Qaeda, though the charge was not taken seriously. But accounts from two sources bolster this claim. The first comes from a 2008 cable from the US Embassy in Tripoli released by WikiLeaks. The secret cable to the State Department entitled "Extremists in Eastern Lybia," revealed that eastern Libya was rife with anti-American, pro-jihad sentiment. The most revealing aspect of the cable:

is the pride that many eastern Libyans, particularly those in and around Dernah, appear to take in the role their native sons have played in the insurgency in Iraq . . . [and the] ability of radical imams to propagate messages urging support for and participation in jihad.

(St. Clair and Cockburn 2016)

The second is a set of documents—the so-called Sinjar Records—captured Al Qaeda documents that fell into American hands in 2007, which were analyzed by the Combating Terrorism Center at the U.S. Military Academy at West Point. Al Qaeda is known as a bureaucratic outfit and the Records contain precise details on personnel, including those who fought in Iraq and who committed suicide bombings on American and Coalition forces. "The West Point analysts' statistical study of the al-Qaeda personnel records concludes that one country provided 'far more' foreign fighters in per capita terms than any other: namely, Libya."[7] As former CIA operations officer Brian Fairchild noted "it is appropriate to ask our policymakers how American military intervention in support of this revolt in any way serves vital U.S. strategic interests."

As military and academic sources told *The Washington Times* in 2015, Clinton ignored the Pentagon's warnings that no US interests were at stake and regional stability could be threatened. Instead, Clinton relied heavily on the word of the Libyan rebels (Shapiro and Riddell 2015).

The extent to which jihadists were involved in the protests, and today in the Libyan territory in general, remains a matter of debate. We do know that jihadists were brought into Libya from other countries as provocateurs before the demonstrations started. It is safe to say that, given the complexity of the country's political makeup and governance, and the power-sharing structures between tribal leaders that Qaddafi had managed for 40 years, the aftermath of regime change would not be easily managed. There were policy discussions that detailed possible scenarios of how many ways chaos in Libya would fuel jihadists and result in arming extremists in the region. For example, Scott Stewart writing for Stratfor, the geopolitical intelligence firm noted, "Certainly, at the very least the weapons looted in Libya could easily be sold or given to jihadists in places like Egypt, Tunisia and Algeria, turning militancy in Libya into a larger regional problem" (Stewart 2011). Following in the steps of George W. Bush, the United States seemed to have learned nothing from the invasion of Iraq eight years earlier. At the very least, as Jeff Sachs observed about Clinton's role in the Libyan intervention, it demonstrates a "stunning lack of judgment" (Sachs 2016).

Human Right Abuses by US-backed Rebels

As early as October 2011, Seumas Milne, in an opinion piece in *The Guardian* wrote, "it is now absolutely clear that, if the purpose of western intervention in Libya's civil war was to 'protect civilians' and save lives, it has been a catastrophic failure." While most media hailed the Libyan intervention as a "liberation," including *The New York Times* that gave voice to boasting NATO commanders on its opinion page (Daalder and Stavridis 2011), it became clear early on that the brutal death of Muammar el-Qaddafi was only a reflection of a bigger picture and a harbinger of things to come. Human Rights Watch reported the discovery of 53 bodies in Sirte, military and civilian with their hands tied execution style by former rebel militia. HRW investigator in Libya, Peter Bouckaert, said more bodies were continuing to be discovered there. They found evidence that about 500 people, civilians and fighters, were killed in the last ten days alone by shooting, shelling, and NATO bombing (Norton 2016).

Amnesty International has now produced compendious evidence of mass abduction and detention, beating and routine torture, killings and atrocities by the rebels that Britain, France, and the US backed—supposedly to stop exactly those kinds of crimes being committed by the Qaddafi regime.

It is very clear that, in the wake of war, real human rights abuses did take place in Libya that verged on genocide, comitted by the rebels. Few media reports covered the abuses. In addition, in 2013 Human Rights Watch reported "serious and ongoing human rights violations against inhabitants of the town of Tawergha, mostly descendants of black slaves and very poor; they were viewed as having supported Muammar Qaddafi." In these "revenge killings" Libyan rebels targeted dark-skinned, sub-Saharan Africans in Tawergha and "ethnically cleansed" the city of the black Libyans. Human Rights Watch reported that militant groups carried out "forced displacement of roughly 40,000 people, arbitrary detentions, torture, and killings are widespread, systematic, and sufficiently organized to be crimes against humanity" (Norton 2016). For example, rebels put black Libyans, whom they accused of being mercenaries for Qaddafi, in cages, forcing them to eat flags and calling them "dogs." But these racist crimes were not included in *The New York Times* pieces on Clinton's leadership spearheading the "humanitarian" war in Libya.

Libya Today

For loyal Democrats and liberal ironists, including many who supported the US war on Libya, "Benghazi" is a joke about GOP obsession. For Libyans, Benghazi is a ravaged city in a ravaged country.

(David Mizner, *Jacobin* 2015)

Of course, the GOP obsession to which Mizner refers is the lengthy Congressional investigations and hearings into whether or not Hillary Clinton, as Secretary of State, was responsible for the deaths of US Ambassador J. Christopher Stevens and US Foreign Service Information Management Officer Sean Smith. The two were killed on September 11, 2012, just one year after Qaddafi was ousted, when Islamic militants attacked the American diplomatic compound in Benghazi. Stevens was the first US Ambassador killed while on duty since 1979. A second assault several hours later targeted a different compound about one mile away, and killed CIA contractors Tyrone S. Woods and Glen Doherty. The politically motivated hearings, as Clinton was beginning a run for president, and the media spectacle they produced, only served to further discredit the US electoral process and vindicate Hillary Clinton, who did well under questioning.

Today Libya, especially downtown Benghazi, a once thriving city, is in ruins. Millions of Libyans live without a formal government, as the internationally recognized government only controls the eastern part of the country. Rival extremist Islamist groups control large swaths of territory. Ansar al-Sharia, a fundamentalist Salafi militia—designated a terrorist organization by the US—now also controls large chunks of Libya. Thousands of Libyans have been killed, and hundreds of thousands of civilians have fled the violent chaos, sparking a flood of refugees. Hundreds of thousands more have been displaced. A disjointed UN mediated peace process drags on, with no signs of success.

The hearings demonstrate more than anything, the continuing refusal of US officials to come to terms with US war policies and recognize their failures. Compare the GOP focus on investigations into the deaths of US diplomats and CIA agents, to the call made by Human Rights Investigations. HRI called on the United States, the United Nations authorities, and each of the nations that participated to carry out full investigations into the violations of UN Resolution 1973. HRI also called for all members of the coalition, including the USA, Qatar, and the United Arab Emirates to declare their use of cluster munitions and to sign the Convention on Cluster Munitions. They recognize that the bombing of Libya was against the spirit and intent of UN Resolution 1973, which was intended to protect civilians, not justify the bombing of civilian areas, use of cluster bombs, and war crimes.

Clinton's war in Libya is the real Benghazi scandal. As Salon.com has previously reported mere hours after Clinton's day-long Benghazi interrogation by Republicans in October, 2014, at least "six Libyans were killed and dozens more were wounded when militants in Benghazi fired rockets at a protest against a U.N. proposal for a unity government" (Norton 2015).

Double Standards

Even in the face of much evidence against the narrative trope, in many quarters the war in Libya is still promoted as an act of American benevolence. But official investigations into civilian deaths would go a long way to dispel such fantastical thinking. One telling way to assess foreign policy justifications by nation states is to compare the consistency of state actions. The United States is currently aligned with some of the most authoritarian and repressive countries in the Middle East and the world, in neighboring Saudi Arabia, Bahrain, Qatar, Oman, Kuwait, and the United Arab Emirates. In fact, even as Clinton was requesting that Bahrain join the fight in Libya, she was also telling that country to stop the brutal repression of a democracy movement there. That must have been an awkward conversation. As The Real News Network reported on April 15, 2011, "Saudi troops are in Bahrain helping the police there suppress the democracy movement." Killings detentions and torture were reported.[8] As Ben Norton (2015) asked, "If the U.S. was truly so concerned with overthrowing a dictatorship and bringing democracy to the Middle East, why doesn't it start with the planet's most dictatorial nations? That is to say, its own allies in the Gulf?"

War and the Humanitarian Imaginary

Writing about humanitarianism, Gourevich (2010) noted, wars fought in its name have "hardly made war less cruel." As humanitarian interventions have proliferated in this century, so has the brutality they are supposed to alleviate. Chouliaraki (2013, 12) draws out this point, "more recently the resort to moral argument for the use of military violence in new humanitarian wars for instance in Yugoslavia, Afghanistan and Iraq has further profoundly challenged the integrity of humanitarian ethics." The "humanitarian" war in Libya represents yet another signpost along the path of moral challenges to humanitarianism posed by military violence.

The Media

The way operation Odyssey Dawn was framed in news reports and on television did not go unnoticed by media analysts or HRI, which called for: "An end to the 'information war' and military distortion of the public debate." The justification for military intervention in Libya under the so-called Responsibility to Protect Doctrine could not have been accomplished without a dominant media narrative confirming the humanitarian frame. As Piers Robinson observed in this volume, "In this context, mediated humanitarianism starts to look disturbingly like a form of propagandistic organized persuasive communication in which self interested geostrategic goals are facilitated by media narratives that help promote and justify wars as acts of humanitarian protection and democracy building." There are striking aspects of media reporting of Odyssey Dawn that confirm Robinson's assertion that coverage looked like propaganda. Highly standardized content repeated by a number of outlets usually demonstrates a unified frame, something certainly operative with the theme of "targeting civilians."

Writing for the media watch group FAIR in a piece titled, "Libya's Lousy PR," Peter Hart (2011a) noticed another theme, a perennial favorite of slanted conflict coverage, most notable in early reporting, when media is eager to promote war—the *enemy propaganda* frame (Andersen 2006). Reports of civilian casualties by governments under attack are discredited and discarded for some reason, usually having to do with inaccurate numbers of dead, something very hard to calculate on the ground during conflict. Hart (2011a) noted that it was somewhat jarring to see all the same coverage in the space of two days, just when NATO bombing had intensified, "making these 'no dead civilians here' pieces seem curiously timed": *The New York Times* (6/7/11): "Libya Stokes Its Machine Generating Propaganda," *The Wall Street Journal* (6/7/11): "Libya's PR Efforts Are Falling Short," *The Los Angeles Times* (6/7/11): "Libya Officials Put a Spin on Conflict" and *The Washington Post* (6/6/11): "Libya Government Fails to Prove Claims of NATO Casualties."

Indeed, *The New York Times* editorial page of July 1, 2011 that argued against negotiation, now reads like the worst kind of irresponsible war promotion:

> President Obama was wrong to ignore the War Powers Act, but . . . there has been recent talk by all sides about a possible political deal between the rebels and the government. We are eager to see an end to the fighting. But Washington and NATO must stand firmly with the rebels and reject any solution that does not involve the swift ouster of Colonel Qaddafi and real freedom for Libyans.

Of course, in the aftermath of war, in the bloody path left in the wake of deadly weapons and belligerent force, investigators in these same newspapers finally report on what actually happened on the ground. In, *Now It Can Be Told: Libyan Civilian Deaths*, Peter Hart (2011b) describes investigations by C. J. Chivers and the *Times*, of civilian casualties resulting from NATO strikes in Libya. But NATO officials continue to refuse to admit the casualties to Chivers, even though there is evidence of civilian casualties. Reports of the aftermath serve to correct the historical record, but they are almost never repeated, and seem not to affect coverage of the next conflict. They also serve to assure the public that media are independent and not simply mouthpieces of military intervention. As we have seen, criticism and accurate information by human rights organizations and alternative media are fairly easily found in the age of the Internet, but the dominant force of mainstream media persists, and often fails a democratic public.

Militarism or Humanitarianism

Given its failures, there has been much speculation about the true reasons and motivations for Clinton's insistence on the use of military force in Libya. Some talk about the lasting effects of the Rwandan genocide under her husband's administration, others point to the Arab Spring and democracy movements that contributed to ousting dictatorship in countries such as Tunisia—the US just wanted to be on the right side this time. Then there are US geopolitical and strategic interests; Libya's enormous oil reserves, its billions of dollars in gold reserves, or the residual resentment of Qaddafi's history of supporting militant left-wing and anti-imperialist movements. But specific geopolitical interests are questionable (though probably formed a "deep" foundation for antagonisms), because the intervention was not "intelligence driven," and many were against it. The Libyan intervention reveals a profound irrationality behind the prosecution of what has turned out to be a devastating "humanitarian" war.

One argument less often proposed is a simple, but far more likely one. As many journalists and academics analyzed the documents leading up to the war, Hillary's "outrageous war mongering" became apparent. Hillary Clinton has long held hawkish views, evident in her admiration of Henry Kissinger as a friend and mentor. She fundamentally believes in the power of military force. The fact that she refused to negotiate in any way with Libya, even when Qaddafi proposed to step down as long as he and his family could leave the country unharmed, are not the actions and attitudes of a humanitarian. As one journalist pointed out, she would not be satisfied until he was dead.

Clinton had few avenues to justify a Libyan intervention. It could be argued that Qaddafi was a brutal dictator, but he had come in from the cold and back into the American embrace after he denounced nuclear weapons and helped fight Al Qaeda. After all, as late as 2009 his son was welcomed to the White House by Clinton herself. In addition, according to the US constitution, only Congress can declare war unless the United States, or its armed forces are under attack. Because Obama did not consult Congress, nor did he claim the US was under attack by Libya, in essence, the UN R2P provision allowed the Obama administration to bypass the US constitution and the 1973 War Powers Act. The charge that Qaddafi was attacking civilians was really the only path to intervention, and it has opened up yet another door to a far more dangerous world.

Kuperman argues that the lesson we should learn from Libya is that humanitarian interventions can backfire. He offers a long analysis, saying substate groups believe that by violently provoking state retaliation, they can attract such intervention—including regime change; that magnifies the threat to noncombatants; ergo the prospect of humanitarian intervention instead imperils civilians via a moral hazard dynamic. He concludes "To mitigate this pathology, it is essential to avoid intervening on humanitarian grounds in ways that reward rebels, unless the state is targeting noncombatants" (Kuperman 2013b). All this simply confirms what many have long known, and what history, especially recent history, has repeatedly demonstrated—escalating violence leads to more violence. What Libya has also illustrated is that Kuperman's (2013b) last caveat, "unless the state is targeting noncombatants," in an age of nationalist ideologies and official media manipulation, is nearly impossible to determine.

Conclusion

The discussions and actions of humanitarianism in the post-Rwanda era have resulted in an acceptance of military intervention in the field of humanitarianism. This together with the massive build-up and use of US military force, and the loss of a public dialogue or framework for diplomacy and peace building, have all led to the overwhelming dominance of the role of belligerency and war as the model to solve global problems. What we are finding is the actual limits of this post-9/11 war doctrine and its penetration into the field of humanitarianism. It becomes increasingly clear as many parts of the world descend into chaos, that war, and the constant bombing campaigns that inevitably hit civilians and civilian infrastructures, cannot solve political, social, or economic problems. Nor can it create a stable and peaceful world. Arial bombardment serves primarily to increase anti-US sentiment and perpetuate a cycle of violence that forces civilians to flee. This in turn has created displaced persons and contributed greatly to the migrant crisis. When those in power, at the helm wielding great force, fail to recognize this, it is up to the humanitarian community to serve as a countervailing force of reason. In addition, media must return to a time when the practice of journalism was independent from military operations before they can regain their legitimacy and serve democratic publics.

Notes

1. www.bbc.com/news/world-us-canada-36018223
2. Powers made her name during the Bush years with her book, *A Problem from Hell*, a study of the US foreign policy response to genocide, and the failure of the Clinton administration to intervene in the Rwandan genocide.
3. "Libya Protests: Second City Benghazi Hit by Violence," British Broadcasting Corporation (BBC), February 16, 2011, available at: www.bbc.co.uk/news/world-africa-12477275
4. This information was included in the February 26, 2016 pieces by Becker and Shane.
5. Security Council, "Security Council Approves 'No-Fly Zone' over Libya, Authorizing 'All Necessary Measures' to Protect Civilians, by Vote of 10 in Favour with 5 Abstentions," March 11, 2011, available at: www.un.org/press/en/2011/sc10200.doc.htm
6. Quoted in Stephen Weissman, "Lessons from Tonkin and Libya: We Need a President Who Won't Trick Us into War. *In These Times*, August 4, 2015, available at: http://inthesetimes.com/article/18268/military-secrecy-from-the-tonkin-gulf-to-the-battlefields-of-syria
7. In her book *Queen of Chaos*, Diana Johnstone offers a detailed account of the Libyan operation.
8. The Real News Network, "The US, Gulf Kings and Brutal Repression in Bahrain," April 15, 2011, available at: http://therealnews.com/t2/index.php?option=com_content&task=view&id=31&Itemid=74&jumival=6620

References

Abrahams, F. (2011) "Cluster Munitions 'Used in Misrata,'" BBC Radio 4 *Today*, April 16, available at: http://news.bbc.co.uk/today/hi/today/newsid_9459000/9459825.stm

Andersen, R. (2006) *A Century of Media, A Century of War*, New York: Peter Lang.

Chivers, C. J. (2011) "Qaddafi Troops Fire Cluster Bombs into Civilian Areas," *The New York Times*, April 15, available at: www.nytimes.com/2011/04/16/world/africa/16libya.html?pagewanted=all&_r=0

Chouliaraki, L. (2013) *The Ironic Spectator: Solidarity in the Age of Post-Humanitarianism*, Cambridge, UK: Polity.

Cooper, H., and Landler, M. (2011) "US Imposes Sanctions on Libya in Wake of Crackdown," *The New York Times*, February 25, available at: *www.nytimes.com/2011/02/26/world/middleeast/26diplomacy.html?_r=0*

Daalder, I. H., and Stavridis, J. G. (2011) "NATOs Success in Libya," *The New York Times*, October 30, available at: www.nytimes.com/2011/10/31/opinion/31iht-eddaalder31.html?_r=0

Daly, C. (2011) "Clinton on Qaddafi: We Came, We Saw, He Died," CBS.com, October 20, available at: www.cbsnews.com/news/clinton-on-qaddafi-we-came-we-saw-he-died/

Ferguson, N. (2016) "Barak Obama's Revolution in Foreign Policy," *The Atlantic*, March 13, available at: www.theatlantic.com/international/archive/2016/03/obama-doctrine-revolution/473481/

Gourevitch, P. (2010) "Alms Dealers: Can You Provide Humanitarian Aid without Facilitating Conflicts?" *The New Yorker*, October 11, available at: www.newyorker.com/magazine/2010/10/11/alms-dealers

Hallinan, C. (2011) "How the 'Humanitarian' Intervention in Libya Made Our World Infinitely More Dangerous," *Alternet.org*, April 26, available at: www.alternet.org/story/150754/how_the_%27humanitarian%27_intervention_in_libya_made_our_world_infinitely_more_dangerous

Hart, P. (2011a) "Libya's Lousy PR," *FAIR*, June 11, available at: http://fair.org/uncategorized/libyas-lousy-pr/

Hart, P. (2011b) "Now It Can Be Told: Libyan Civilian Deaths," *FAIR*, December 19, available at: http://fair.org/uncategorized/now-it-can-be-told-libyan-civilian-deaths/

Human Rights Investigation. (2011) "Cluster Bombing of Misrata Committed by US Naval Forces, Not Qadhafi," *Global Research*, May 27, available at: www.globalresearch.ca/cluster-bombing-of-misrata-committed-by-us-naval-forces-not-qadhafi/25004

Johnstone, D. (2015) *Queen of Chaos*, Petrolia, CA: Counterpunch Books.

Kuperman, A. (2013a) "A Model Humanitarian Intervention? Reassigning NATO's Libya Campaign," *International Security*, 38 (1): 105–136, available at: www.mitpressjournals.org/toc/isec/38/1

Kuperman, A. (2013b) "Lessons from Libya: How Not to Intervene," a policy brief prepared for the Belfer Center for Science and International Affairs at the Harvard Kennedy School (September), available at: http://belfercenter.ksg.harvard.edu/publication/23387/lessons_from_libya.html

Milne, S. (2011) "If the Libyan War Was about Saving Lives, It Was a Catastrophic Failure, *The Guardian*, October 26, available at: www.theguardian.com/commentisfree/2011/oct/26/libya-war-saving-lives-catastrophic-failure

Mizner, D. (2015) "Worse Than Benghazi," *Jacobin*, July 17, available at: www.jacobinmag.com/2015/07/hillary-libya-nato-qaddafi-obama/

The New York Times. (2011) "The Libya Campaign," July 1, available at: www.nytimes.com/2011/07/01/opinion/01fri2.html

Norton, B. (2015) "The Real Benghazi Scandal that Is Ignored: How Hillary Clinton, the Obama admin. and NATO destroyed Libya," *Salon*, October 26, available at: www.salon.com/2015/10/26/the_real_benghazi_scandal_that_is_being_ignored_how_hillary_clinton_and_the_obama_administration_destroyed_libya/

Norton, B. (2016) "Even Critics Underestimate How Catastrophically Bad the Hillary Clinton Led NATO Bombing of Libya Was," *Salon*, March 2, available at: www.salon.com/2016/03/02/even_critics_understate_how_catastrophically_bad_the_hillary_clinton_led_nato_bombing_of_libya_was/

Sachs, J. (2016) "Hillary Clinton is the Candidate of the 'War Machine,'" *Huffington Post*, February 5, available at: www.huffingtonpost.com/jeffrey-sachs/hillary-is-the-candidate_b_9168938.html

Shapiro, J. S., and Riddell, K. (2015) "Exclusive: Secret Tapes Undermine Hillary Clinton on Libyan War," *The Washington Times*, January 28, available at: www.washingtontimes.com/news/2015/jan/28/hillary-clinton-undercut-on-libya-war-by-pentagon-/

Shane, S., and Becker, J. (2016) "The Libyan Gable Part 2: A New Libya with 'Very Little Times left,'" *The New York Times*, February 27, available at: www.nytimes.com/2016/02/28/us/politics/libya-isis-hillary-clinton.html

Stewart, S. (2011) "Jihadist Opportunities in Libya," Stratfor, February 24, available at: www.stratfor.com/weekly/20110223-jihadist-opportunities-libya

St. Clair, J., and Cockburn, A. (2016) "The Libyan Enterprise: Hillary's Imperial Massacre," *Counterpunch*, April 1, available at: www.counterpunch.org/author/f3e2aguc/

Weissman, S. (2015) "Lessons from Tonkin and Libya: We Need a President Who Won't Trick Us into War. *In These Times*, August 4, 2015, available at: http://inthesetimes.com/article/18268/military-secrecy-from-the-tonkin-gulf-to-the-battlefields-of-syria

43

THE CNN EFFECT AND HUMANITARIAN CRISIS

Piers Robinson[1]

Introduction

The CNN effect was a popular term during the 1990s and, along with its association with instances of intervention during humanitarian crises in Northern Iraq (1991), Somalia (1992–93), Bosnia (1992–1995), and Kosovo (1999), came to epitomize the idea that mainstream news media possessed the power to shape government policy (Hoge 1994). The working assumption back then was that empathetic media reporting of suffering people was influencing Western governments to intervene in order to protect human rights and prevent suffering. Since that era, largely because of the combination of a new geopolitical era dominated by the "war on terror" and rapid developments in communications technology including the Internet, web 2.0, social media, mobile phones etc., new labels have emerged all of which attempt to capture the power and influence of media to shape political processes. These include "diffuse war" (Hoskins and O'Loughlin, 2010), the "Al Jazeera Effect" (Seib 2008) and the "Youtube effect" (Naím 2007). At the same time, notions of humanitarian intervention have been strengthened by the establishment of the Responsibility to Protect (R2P), whereby humanitarian intervention is now a fully legitimated international norm involving the potential for UN-authorized humanitarian intervention, but simultaneously blurred by their incorporation into the Western warfare doctrine whereby humanitarian action is seen as part of helping win hearts and minds (Barnett 2005). This was true during "war on terror" operations in Afghanistan, Iraq, and a whole host of other nations.

From the vantage point of 2016, after 25 years of further usage, it is possible to conduct a fruitful stock-taking exercise with respect to the CNN effect debate and the associated notion of media's role in facilitating humanitarian responses. The chapter starts with a brief review of the arguments emerging from scholarly debate about the reality of the so-called CNN effect before then mapping critical perspectives regarding media-driven humanitarianism. The latter part of the chapter engages directly with the contemporary geopolitical and technological contexts and considers precisely how we should theorize and research the question of media power, influence, and the issue of humanitarianism.

The Original Debate

Debate over the CNN effect emerged in the early days of 24-hour news coverage, made famous by the emergence of Ted Turner's Cable News Network (CNN), and the associated surge in attention to 24-hour live news coverage. To a large extent the debate was anchored around the emerging doctrine of "humanitarian intervention." For many commentators the interventions in Northern Iraq 1991 to create "safe havens" for Iraqi Kurds fleeing Saddam Hussein's forces, Operation Restore Hope in Somalia (1992–93) and various responses to the war in Bosnia (1992–95), were being driven by emotive and empathizing coverage of suffering people which was, in turn, pressuring policymakers to respond through armed intervention (Cohen 1994). Debate revolved around the idea that uncertainty in the political context of post Cold War policy had combined with developments in communications technology (portable live satellite editing and broadcasting equipment) so as to create a more powerful and influential news media that was capable of influencing foreign policy formulation and in a way that seemed to reverse Cold War patterns of media deference to political elites (Hallin 1986; Herman and Chomsky 1988; Bennett 1990). For humanitarian actors and those supportive of a doctrine of humanitarian intervention, these developments were viewed positively and as evidence that media were becoming critical humanitarian actors in their own right.

Researched that focused on the CNN effect and humanitarian intervention during the 1990s tended, as a whole, to offer a more circumspect assessment of the role media played during responses to humanitarian crisis. For example, Livingston and Eachus (1995) concluded the intervention in Somalia (1992) was better understood as an example of media following official cues to cover Somalia rather than *pushing* officials to respond. Robinson (2002) concluded, in line with Livingston's appraisal (1997), that media were unlikely to be driving substantial armed intervention during humanitarian crises but that there might well be a greater effect with respect to less costly responses such as limited airstrikes and non-coercive responses supporting aid agencies. Overall, the major message from early research was a cautionary one: while media might at times influence humanitarian responses, it was by no means the major determinant and, when it came to the major cases of armed intervention, geostrategic concerns and national interest seemed to be playing a greater role with respect to decision making.

The "Dark Side" of Media and Humanitarianism

At the same time as these more modest assessments of the CNN effect were emerging there was also a more critical consideration with respect to the negative dimensions of media-driven humanitarianism. First and foremost, even if media were at times influencing humanitarian responses, it was also apparent that there was a great deal of selectivity going on: some crises were being covered by the media and others not. Moreover, as Hawkins (2008; 2011) argued, many of the world's most serious humanitarian crises were receiving hardly any attention at all. Perhaps the most notable of these absences was that of the war in the DRC, arguably the biggest war in the world across the late 1990s and early new millennium with millions of people being killed and murdered. And yet, despite this, as Hawkins shows, media paid scant attention. On a different track, Jakobsen (2000) insightfully pointed out that media coverage tended to focus on the "hot" phases of a conflict and ignore pre-conflict stages and post conflict rebuilding. As a result, he argues, international responses were being skewed away from the more important tasks of preventing conflict and rebuilding societies after war and towards a short-term fire-fighting approach. In short, the media acted as a fickle and inconsistent force for humanitarian action.

Second, another body of literature identified the problematic ways in which media coverage framed humanitarian crises. While, at best, coverage was able to induce empathy for suffering people, it also tended to frame them in a way that emphasized their inferiority, victimhood and, ultimately reinforced ethnocentric and racist cultural stereotypes (van der Gaag and Nash 1987; Benthall 1993). At worst, coverage framed crises in a "distancing" (Robinson 2002) way whereby conflicts were portrayed as intractable and inevitable and in which all parties to a conflict were seen as being equally to blame. For example, in their analysis of media coverage of the 1994 Rwandan Genocide, Myers et al. (1996) highlight this particular dynamic in which the conflict, and the genocide itself, was presented as a "regular round of tribal bloodletting" emanating from Africa's "heart of darkness" (see also Robinson 2002, 110–116). Aside from the simplifications and racisms underpinning these various modes of representation, their most important consequence was to de-politicize conflicts especially with regard to the power politics of external actors as well as the politics of Western humanitarianism.

This brings us to the third substantive critique of the debate over media-driven humanitarianism. De Waal argued that, to a large extent, media representation was part of an unproductive relationship whereby media representations of suffering people was the fuel that drove aid agencies to deliver "visible relief to suffering" as opposed to ending famine.

In his critique of the aid business, *Famine Crimes* (1997), De Waal presents a critical alternative analysis of the relationship between media, crises, and aid agency responses with respect to famine. Here, he argues that aid agencies, media, and Western publics are linked together in a mutually beneficial relationship that, inadvertently, inhibits effective responses to crises. Aid agencies seek money and resources while news media representation of suffering people provides both a key route to these resources and newsworthy material for journalists and editors: The more dramatic and emotive the coverage, the more resources are likely to flow from concerned publics. These resources are then directed to high-profile famine and crisis relief activities. This in turn provides further publicity and legitimacy to the aid agencies (De Waal 1997, 82–85). For De Waal, this arrangement serves to obscure the political causes of famine, some of which lie in neoliberal international structural adjustment policies, and also replaces local-level government accountability for preventing famine by making people dependent on international aid. He concludes:

> Contemporary international humanitarianism works, but not for famine-vulnerable people in Africa. High-profile 'debased' humanitarianism works to extend the institutional reach of relief agencies, to create an attractive narrative for the media and to provide a political alibi for Western governments.
>
> (De Waal 1997, 217)

Similar analyses are advanced by scholars such as Muller (2013), Terry (2002) and Tester (2010).

Changing Contexts: The New Media Environment, the "War on Terror" and Humanitarianism as a Form of Propaganda

In the 20 years since the CNN effect became a popular term, we have witnessed dramatic transformations with respect to the information environment and a profound reorientation of Western foreign policy around the "war on terror." These developments are set against the backdrop of an emerging global crisis concerning resources and the environment, and major shifts in the global balance of power as the relative preponderance of US power has reduced with the rise of China, India, and other potential and actual global competitors. What does all this mean for the CNN effect and the notion of media-driven humanitarianism?

Media, Humanitarianism, and the New Media Environment

On the one hand, some have seized upon the apparent empowering potential of the new communication technologies as having a force multiplying effect with respect to humanitarianism. So, for example, Allan (2013) describes how people in war zones can now quickly communicate humanitarian suffering and human rights abuses. Other scholars have argued the importance of social media platforms as potential early warnings of humanitarian crisis and their role in coordinating responses (Meier and Leaning 2009; Asimakopoula and Bessis 2010), while some describe the growing significance of transnational advocacy networks, underpinned by digital communication and the Internet, as strengthening humanitarian actors at the national and international governmental levels (e.g. Livingston 2011; Livingston and Klinkworth 2010). Finally, some maintain that the emergence of a variety of global news media providers such as Al Jazeera and BBC World, have complemented and expanded upon the role of CNN as deliverers of cosmopolitan global values and a sense of solidarity (Cottle 2011 88). At the same time, it is also the case that the existing body of research on the CNN effect and humanitarianism can be significantly expanded upon through a more focused engagement with the complex ways in which local actors (i.e. within conflict zones) seek to communicate with and influence international and global actors and how new communications technologies may facilitate more of a bottom-up process (Gilboa et al. 2016). As Gilboa et al. (2016) argue, much of the existing CNN-effect literature has focused primarily upon how Western media coverage of conflicts has at times influenced Western governments to respond to humanitarian crises while ignoring both local-level actors and the role of international and transnational humanitarian actors. Future work in this area needs greater theoretical engagement with an approach that comprehends the multilevel reality of media–conflict dynamics.

Less optimistically, it is also a possibility that the new media environment has actually had a fundamentally disempowering effect upon the ability of humanitarian actors to facilitate substantial responses to humanitarian crises (Gilboa et al. 2016). On the one hand, while the above-mentioned scholars are surely correct to identify the *potential* of new communication technology to enable actors within conflict zones to communicate more readily with global media and distant audiences, it is not entirely clear how the panoply of voices and initiatives actually translates into a cohesive and politically influential message. The problem here is principally one of the possible fragmentation of public spheres, both global and national, in which innumerable voices are all calling for attention but none of which become "loud" enough to be heard; in IT terms, a problem of poor signal-to-noise ratio. This problem is possibly being further hampered by the kinds of pressures that are now being placed upon traditional mainstream media: here there has been a steady decline in the number of high-quality foreign correspondents who possess in-depth understanding of a country or region and, as Otto and Meyer (2012) argue, this tendency undermines the ability of mainstream media to act as an early warning for impending crises. Furthermore, today's media are less well resourced and financed than in previous eras with declining audiences and ever-greater commercial pressures, while many people choose today to receive their news via telling glimpses of *Facebook* and *Twitter*.

Overall, future research needs to engage directly with trying to understand better both the empowering and the disempowering potentials of the new media environment.

Humanitarianism as a Form of Contemporary Propaganda and Organized Persuasive Communication

While debate and research will inevitably continue with regard to the potential, or lack thereof, of media to shape humanitarian responses, the last 15 years have witnessed the co-optation of the humanitarian agenda by the military. Since 9/11, Western foreign policy has been orientated around the "war on terror" and, as a part of this, humanitarianism has become enmeshed with strategic goals. *Propaganda* (Miller et al. 2016) and *organized persuasive communication* (Robinson 2014) are terms used to describe coordinated approaches to influencing beliefs and behavior. Organized persuasive communication (OPC), or organized political communication (Herring and Robinson 2014), refers to all activities aimed at influencing opinions and behavior; propaganda is a sub-set of organized persuasive communication and is normally used to denote organized persuasive communication that involves clearly manipulative strategies, for example involving deception, coercion, or incentivization.

The problem in recent years is that, rather than media being a driving force for humanitarian action, it has become just as common for humanitarianism to function as a way of justifying war and intervention for purposes other than humanitarian ones. For example, Western military action in Afghanistan and Iraq was, to a significant extent, promoted through reference to Western concerns over humanitarianism. For example, as Robinson et al. (2010) document, the British government successfully promoted the invasion of Iraq as a way of resolving humanitarian problems in Iraq and as part of a morally justified act to remove a brutal dictator from power. This was despite the fact that there was no current humanitarian crisis directly attributable to the Iraqi regime and the declaration by the British Attorney General that there was no humanitarian crisis there that would authorize humanitarian intervention (Robinson et al. 2010, 102–104). The war in Afghanistan, now in its fifteenth year, has been regularly framed by Western media, politicians, and academics as an exercise in peace building or democracy building, as opposed to a security-based conflict. However, with respect to the early phase of the post 9/11 "war on terror," the recent British inquiry into the Iraq War has confirmed the deceptive and propagandistic aspect of the "war on terror." The report quotes a British embassy report dated September 15, 2001, which states that "The 'regime-change hawks' in Washington were arguing that a coalition put together for one purpose (against international terrorism) could be used to clear up other problems in the region."[2] The report then cites British Prime Minister Blair's considerations with respect to the emerging "war on terror" strategy:

> [I]n order to give ourselves space that we say: "Phase 1 is the military action focused on Afghanistan because it's there that the perpetrators of 11 September hide.
>
> "Phase 2 is the medium and longer term campaign against terrorism in all its forms. Of course we will discuss that . . . This kicks it away for the moment but leaves all options open. We just don't need it debated freely in public until we know what exactly we want to do; and how we can do it."[3]

Mr. Blair concluded that a "dedicated tightly knit propaganda unit" was required, and suggested that he and President Bush should "talk soon."[4] In light of this revelation from the

British inquiry, humanitarian narratives that have underpinned war in Iraq and Afghanistan start to look like part of the "propaganda" to which Blair referred and with the objective of "clearing up problems." There has also been a growing awareness of the linkage between humanitarianism and Western military action, especially in the context of the "war on terror" since 9/11. Here humanitarianism has also formed part of Western coercive and incentivising OPC during recent conflicts. Specifically, with respect to military strategy, humanitarian actors are part of so-called "counter-insurgency operations" (Barnett 2005; Counter Insurgency Operations 2009). Michael Barnett (2005, 731) points out that these developments have frequently and increasingly compromised the neutrality and independence of humanitarian organizations. Finally, in the last five years we have seen the justification of military intervention in Libya under the so-called Responsibility to Protect doctrine that justified initial Western intervention as an act of humanitarian protection. The intervention then extended to helping topple the Gaddafi regime and facilitated the country's transition to a failed state wracked by violence.

Conclusions and Future Directions

The CNN effect debate research topic has always attracted researchers who are optimistic with regard to the progressive potential of news media to facilitate humanitarian action. During the 1990s, there were grounds for optimism that the *realpolitik* of the Cold War was being replaced by doctrines and practices, underpinned by international law and the United Nations, which could point toward a more rule-governed world and one in which humanitarian and human rights concerns might start to prevail. As noted at the start of this chapter, there was some evidence of media playing a part in this establishing phase of greater humanitarian action. Even back then, however, there were ample grounds to question the inherent goodness and righteousness of media-driven intervention.

For researchers, events of the last 15 years paint a much bleaker picture. While new communication technology in some ways appears to enhance the ability of media to facilitate effective humanitarian responses, there are also grounds to argue that the mobilizing potential of media has been dissipated due to the fragmented and diffused nature of the way in which information is assimilated and disseminated. Theoretical and empirical research is necessary to get a better handle on these developments. At the same time, the "war on terror," which has become the north star of Western foreign policy since 9/11, appears to have shrunk the space for both independent and autonomous humanitarian action and increased the importance of mediated humanitarian crises as a way of underpinning and supporting Western geostrategic goals. In this context, mediated humanitarianism starts to look disturbingly like a form of propagandistic organized persuasive communication in which self-interested geostrategic goals are facilitated by media narratives that help promote and justify wars as acts of humanitarian protection and democracy building. Much more extensive and critical engagement with the issue of humanitarianism as a form of propaganda is essential if scholars are to reveal and critique these kinds of abuses and prevent further shrinkage of the space for genuine humanitarian action.

Notes

1. Thanks to Robin Andersen and Stefanie Haueis for feedback on earlier drafts. This chapter draws upon and develops ideas published in "The CNN Effect and Humanitarian Action," in R. MacGinty and J. Peterson (Eds.), *The Routledge Handbook of Humanitarian Action* (London and New York: 2015) and "The CNN Effect and Humanitarian Action" in P. Robinson, R. Frohlich, and P. Seib (Eds.), *The Routledge Handbook of Media, Conflict and Security* (London and New York: 2017).

2. *Chilcot Report*, section 3.1, p. 324.
3. Ibid.
4. *Chilcot Report*, section 3.1, p. 338.

References

Allan, S. (2013) *Citizen Witnessing: Revisioning Journalism in Times of Crisis*, Cambridge, UK: Polity.

Asimakopoula, E., and Bessis, N. (Eds.) (2010) *Advanced ICTs for Disaster Management and Threat Detection: Collaborative and Distributed Frameworks*, Hershey, PA: Information Science Reference.

Barnett, M. C. (2005) "Humanitarianism Transformed," *Perspectives on Politics*, 3 (4): 723–740.

Bennett, L. W. (1990) "Toward a Theory of Press-State Relations in the United States," Journal of Communication, 40(2): 103–125.

Benthall, J. (1993) *Disasters, Relief and the Media*, London: I.B. Tauris.

Cohen, B. (1994) "The View from the Academy," in W. L. Bennett and D. L. Paletz (Eds.), *Taken by Storm: The Media, Public Opinion and US Foreign Policy in the Gulf War*, Chicago, IL: University of Chicago Press, pp. 8–11.

Cottle, S. (2011) "Taking Global Crises in the News Seriously: Notes from the Dark Side of Globalization," *Global Media and Communication*, 7 (2), 77–95.

De Waal, A. (1997) *Famine Crimes: Politics and the Disaster Relief Industry in Africa*, Oxford, UK: James Currey.

Counter Insurgency Operations, Joint Publication 3–24, October 9, 2009, US Department of Defense, available at: www.dtic.mil/doctrine/new_pubs/jp3_24.pdf

Gilboa, E., Jumper, M. J., Miklian, J., and Robinson, P. (2016) "Moving Studies Beyond the CNN Effect," *Review of International Studies*, 93 (1), 87–111.

Hallin, D. (1986) *The Uncensored War: The Media and Vietnam*, Berkeley, CA: California.

Hawkins, V. (2008) *Stealth Conflicts: How the World's Worst Violence is Ignored*, Aldershot, UK and Burlington, VT: Ashgate, UK and New York: Routledge.

Hawkins, V. (2011) "Media Selectivity and the Other Side of the CNN Effect: The Consequences of Not Paying Attention to Conflict," Special Issue on the CNN Effect edited by P. Robinson, *Media, War and Conflict*, 4 (1), 55–68.

Herman, E., and Chomsky, N. (1988) *Manufacturing Consent: The Political Economy of the Media*, New York: Pantheon.

Herring, E., and Robinson, P. (2014–15) "Report X Marks the Spot: The British Government's Deceptive Dossier on Iraq and WMD," *Political Science Quarterly*, 129 (4), 551–584.

Hoge, J. (1994) "Media Pervasiveness," *Foreign Affairs*, 73, 136–144.

Hoskins, A., and O'Loughlin, B. (2010) *War and Media: The Emergence of Diffused War*, Cambridge, UK: Polity.

Jakobsen, P. V. (2000) "Focus on the CNN Effect Misses the Point: The Real Impact of Media on Conflict Management Is Invisible and Indirect," *Journal of Peace Research*, 37 (2), 131–143.

Livingston, S. (1997) "Clarifying the CNN Effect: An examination of Media Effects According to Type of Military Intervention," research paper R-18, June, Cambridge, MA: The Joan Shorenstein Barone Center on the Press, Politics and Public Policy at Harvard University.

Livingston, S., and Eachus, T. (1995) "Humanitarian Crises and US Foreign Policy," *Political Communication*, 12, 413–29.

Livingston, S. and Klinkworth, K. (2010) "Narrative Power Shifts: Exploring the Role of ICTs and Informational Politics in Transnational Advocacy," *The International Journal of Technology, Knowledge, and Society*, 6 (5), 43–64.

Livingston, S. (2011) "The CNN effect reconsidered (again): problematizing ICT and global governance in the CNN effect research agenda," *Media, War & Conflict*, 4: 20–36. doi:10.1177/1750635210396127, available at: www.newpolcom.rhul.ac.uk/npcu-blog/2011/4/13/cnn-effect-revisited-media-war-conflict-special-issue-out.html

Meier, P., and Leaning., J. (2009) "Applying Technology to Crisis Mapping and Early Warning in Humanitarian Settings," Working Paper Series, Harvard Humanitarian Initiative.

Miller, D., Robinson, P., and Bakir, V. (2016) "Propaganda and Persuasion in Contemporary Conflict," in P. Robinson, P. Seib, and R. Frohlich (Eds.) *The Routledge Handbook of Media, Conflict and Security*, London and New York: Routledge, pp. 308–320.

Muller, T. R. (2013) "The Long Shadow of Band Aid Humanitarianism: Revisiting the Dynamics between Famine and Celebrity," *Third World Quarterly*, 34 (3), 470–484.

Myers, G., Klak, T., and Koehl, T. (1996) "The Inscription of Difference: News Coverage of the Conflicts in Rwanda and Bosnia," *Political Geography*, 15 (1), 21–46.

Naím, M. (2007) "The YouTube Effect: How a Technology for Teenagers Became a Force for Political and Social Change," *Foreign Policy*, 158, 103–104.

Otto, F. and Meyer, C. O. (2012) "Missing the Story? Changes in Foreign News Reporting and Their Implications for Conflict Prevention," in *Media, War & Conflict*, 5 (3): 205–221.

Robinson, P. (2002) *The CNN Effect: The Myth of News, Foreign Policy and Intervention*, New York and London: Routledge.

Robinson, P. (2014) "Media Empowerment vs. Strategies of Control: Theorizing News Media and War in the 21st Century," *Zeitschrift fur Politik*, 61 (4), 461–479.

Robinson P., Goddard P., Parry K., Murray C. and Taylor P. M. (2010) Pockets of Resistance: *British News Media, War and Theroy in the 2003 Invasion of Iraq*. Manchester, UK: Manchester University Press.

Seib, P. (2008) *The Al Jazeera Effect: How the New Global Media Are Reshaping World Politics*, Washington, DC: Potomac Books.

Terry, F. (2002) *Condemned to Repeat: The Paradox of Humanitarian Action*, New York: Cornell University Press.

Tester, K. (2010) *Humanitarianism and Modern Culture*, University Park, PA: Pennslyvania State University Press.

Van der Gaag, N., and Nash, C. (1987) *Images of Africa: The UK Report*, Oxford, UK: Oxfam.

CONCLUSION

Assessing the Media and Humanitarian Landscape: Amidst Complexities, Global Peace and Prosperity Require New Directions and New Expressions of Solidarity

Robin Andersen

When we started this project we felt knowledgeable about the extent and complexities involved in the interconnections between media—their representations and technologies—and the field of humanitarian action. But we found that the topic covers far more territory than we first imagined. First, the humanitarian community is vast, comprised of thousands of organizations globally, with smaller ones founded seemingly every day, all involved in programs such as offering aid, saving lives, pressing for human rights, prosecuting criminals, and designing sustainable development models. As their reach has extended and their numbers proliferated, so too has the need for media and communications technologies. The role media now play constitutes an integral part of most humanitarian organizations. Here are a few examples.

The on-going campaigns that fight contagious diseases and epidemics all demand global and local information and education to understand the science and sort fact from fiction, a feat that also includes countering sensational media reports that play on public fears and prejudice. Of course, new media and digital technologies are also required to communicate and implement action plans, and acquire feedback for programs.

The many relief agencies, International Organizations (IO), and International Non-governmental Organizations (INGO), provide food, water, medicine, shelter, and sanitation to the victims of natural disasters, war, conflict, and complex emergencies, from Oxfam to Doctors Without Borders, Save the Children, UNICEF, just to name a handful. All of these organizations depend on media to tell their stories and garner public support for their efforts. They must compete for donors, funding and recognition as well. In addition, social media has come to play a unique and often contradictory role during crises—sometimes relaying important information not found elsewhere, but it also can serve to spread rumors and inaccuracies. As citizens themselves become more important in reporting crises, their interactions with journalists, aid agencies, and beneficiaries become all the more important.

Other NGOs such as Human Rights Watch, Amnesty International, and so many more, focus on what can only be called global justice campaigns, working on issues such as child exploitation, slavery and kidnapping, and conflict documentation. Many partner with journalists and legislative campaigns working to halt the brutality of "conflict minerals," bring war criminals to justice, and many other global rights issues. Those campaigns are often long term, taking years of hard work that involves in-field research gathering testimonials, documentation, and often serve as information hubs, reaching out to freelance journalists, photojournalists, and news organizations. Campaign organizers must also knock on official doors, lobby lawmakers, and engage the public in legislative work, compel them to sign online petitions, attend an exhibition or a policy forum.

Under the auspices of the United Nations or independent NGOs, development organizations are also key to the humanitarian community, and those agencies, often in partnership with others, require structured long-term media strategies that tell the stories of the people they serve in communities and regions that struggle to combat the legacies of conflict, abuse, displacement, and globalization. So many of these organizations and agencies use strategic media design to focus their message, often requiring professional public affairs staff, or official spokespeople. Multipronged campaigns use a combination of media tactics, including celebrity spokespersons, advertising, online appeals, and outreach to news and media outlets to shape their message and influence public debate on the issues. The professionals working in public affairs units of humanitarian organizations have become the voices of the people they serve, and are increasingly featured on broadcast news programs, in documentaries, and in the press. They provide information, access, and even at times logistical support, especially during complex emergencies. In all of these communication formats, the question also remains—do they reinforce in the public a humanitarian imagination, or do they transform the desire to help those in need in unexpected negative ways? And that question must also apply to news reporting in general, on migration, immigrants, refugees, and those in need.

Such complex interrelationships between media and humanitarian organizations also have consequences. Critics have called into question the role strategic design plays in shaping the messages of aid agencies. In addition, as with all established relationships between sources and the press, they improve information flow through access, but they also present challenges to journalistic independence and the news frame.

In an age identified by increasing conflict and the global chaos that will be caused by massive environmental migrations, every experience presents a learning curve as new, more extensive or unexpected contingencies present themselves. Mistakes are made. But when a humanitarian organization missteps, there are many logistical and ethical ramifications, all of which must be examined, reassessed, and corrected. Like all risk-averse bureaucracies, those can be painful processes involving damage control and denial, but ultimately they must come to light and be subject to public discussion. Independent journalism is therefore an essential part of the growth and development process of humanitarianism.

In this summary we consider these issues and reassess the interrelationships between media and humanitarian actors, drawing out some implications and consequences that have presented themselves in the pages of this volume. We evaluate what we've learned about the history of humanitarian media and global solidarity with those who suffer, and move on to the role humanitarian communication must play in the twenty-first century. We draw out the tensions and contradictions inherent in the sometimes delicate relationships that exist between the press, the public, those who suffer, and aid organizations. In our final pages, we make the case that the current path toward militarization taken by the United Nations has itself become a major obstacle to global peace. We argue that it has contributed greatly to the humanitarian crises unfolding in the Middle East. We hope that by indentifying the fissures that threaten to dismantle the mandate of the world body to promote peace and stability, the UN will seek out new ways to alleviate the suffering of people around the globe.

The Legacy of the Historical Frame

As we found in the early reporting of African famine, images of starving bodies shocked the conscience of the West and led to an outpouring of aid, but they also shaped news reports. The reasons for the famine and the complexities of the situation were lost in the drive to fund the relief effort, thereby extending the war. As Frederick Forsyth noted then, "People who couldn't fathom the political complexities of the war could easily grasp the wrong in a picture of a child dying of starvation" (quoted in Harrison and Palmer 1986, 33). The legacy of that type of reporting is felt today. Writing about a relief effort is quite distinct from explaining the global causes of a situation that results in human suffering. Many times it is easier for journalists to report, or critique, an aid response than detail why it is happening.

Humanitarian Actors as Press Liaisons

The role the Holy Ghost Fathers played in the reporting of Biafra was also significant. They directed the press to the story and as noted by Ken Waters (2004) it forever changed "the nature of the journalist–source relationship in the reporting on international disasters." (It is also worth noting that in Ethiopia, Buerk was able to take advantage of a World Vision plane that flew him into Korem.) Presently the press–agency relationship is highly developed, and often results in expanding the news frame to include humanitarian stories that would otherwise be ignored. Many times it also shapes reporting.

Today's mainstream media, owned and managed by corporate CEOs who must profit from news, especially in the United States, have become far more dependent on press releases and agency staff who have done the research and leg-work for reporting. Because of the dismantling of many of the once well-funded news units, sharing information is now standard procedure between journalists and aid agencies and humanitarian organizations. Reed Brody, counsel and spokesperson for Human Rights Watch explained the need for this relationship. "For example, the *Los Angeles Times* and the *Washington Post*, each have one bureau for all of sub-Saharan Africa." Brody played a critical role in bringing Hissène Habré, the former US-backed dictator of Chad to justice. On May 30, 2016, Habré, accused of killing as many as 40,000 people during his eight years in power in the 1980s, was convicted in a special African Union-backed court in Senegal.[1] It is the first time the leader of one African country has been prosecuted in another African country's domestic court system for human rights abuses. Habré was convicted of rape, sexual slavery, and ordering killings, and was sentenced to life in prison. When Brody took journalists to Senegal and Chad to report on the case against Hissène Habré he raised the money to pay for their trip. "I applied for grant money from the Soros Foundation and Humanity United. Media organizations don't have the money to do those types of trips." He added, "Everybody is doing that now."

Brody went on to explain:

at HRW we do our own content—media style. If a mainstream journalist can't go there, we provide them with footage, and multi-media content. When Habré was arrested, we did two different reports with targeted content, one for France and one for the US. The story made front page news in France, but not the US.

It takes constant work to get stories into the news, then there is no guarantee they will have an effect. In the midst of the humanitarian crisis caused by the US-backed Saudi Arabia bombing of Yemen, a story without much traction in the US media, Amnesty International and HRW called for Saudi Arabia to be expelled from the UN Human Rights Council. As Brody explained, "It was an effective strategy and we got some good media coverage, but of course Saudi Arabia is still on the council."

Shaping the Media Discussion

When aid agencies design their own messages, and serve as press liaisons and sources they help shape the media interpretation of events and the news frames. At times this can hamper independent journalism, especially when media seek to explain the causes of a crisis. As Richard Rowley, co-founder of Big Noise Films and documentary producer (whose shorts and news reports have been featured on leading outlets including Al Jazeera, BBC, CBC, CNN International, *Democracy Now!* and PBS), explained:

> In the work I do I make a distinction between strategic and tactical media. If I'm covering a famine in Mali, I'll need to film inside the Action Contre La Faim/Action Against Hunger (ACF) camp. But I'm not doing it to compel people to give a donation. I'm doing it to provide context so I'm going to cover the IMF and the other reasons why Mali is in this situation.[2]

Influence over the Press

But when close relationships exist between agencies and the media, it affords the largest international bodies influence over the press. This dynamic between journalists and their sources has long been understood, and it becomes more prevalent the bigger the organization and the more influential. Take for example the media failure to provide adequate coverage of the cholera epidemic in Haiti.

Haiti

A cholera epidemic took hold in Haiti after the earthquake that shook the island nation on January 12, 2010. Roughly 10,000 Haitians have died from this very preventable disease, and many more have been sickened by it. In spite of "overwhelming medical evidence" that UN Peacekeepers from Nepal brought the disease to the island,[3] the United Nations did not take responsibility until late 2016. Instead, the UN chose to employ the principle of diplomatic immunity, a position reinforced by a New York Federal Appeals Court. The world body also fought legal efforts that sought to secure compensation for the victims. Cholera spreads easily in places with poor sanitation. To bring the epidemic to an end, Haiti's water and sanitation systems would need to be rebuilt at an estimated cost of about $2.2 billion. But the UN showed no sign of willingness to help solve the problem until activists and alternative media coverage incited the mainstream press to pick up the story.

There was little coverage of the disease in the US media. Kim Ives, publisher of Haiti Liberte explains the silence:

The media is happy to swarm Haiti and even play act—Anderson Cooper carrying cases of water to earthquake victims comes to mind—but if the U.S. and UN don't green-light a crisis, like Haiti's cholera epidemic, they ignore it—until now, thanks to grassroots pressure.[4]

Finally in June, 2016, after the US Congress sent a letter to John Kerry urging him to pressure the UN, *The New York Times*[5] and *The Boston Globe* ran strong pieces about the epidemic. According to Ives, "Now the Times and the Globe as well as Congress, have started to take notice, due to persistent badgering from activists."[6] And in August, 2016, *The New York Times, CNN* and *NPR* all reported that the UN had taken responsibility for the disease outbreak. By October the UN announced a plan to pay victims and finance a health program (Sengupta and Katz 2016). This decision will make a huge difference in Haiti, especially since in the aftermath of Hurricane Matthew that devastated southern Haiti, the epidemic began to spread even more quickly.

Investigative Journalism Takes an Adversarial Role

When journalists investigate aid organizations by taking a critical look at claims about the "good works" accomplished by humanitarian actors, the situation can be difficult but is vital to the progress of humanitarianism. Such was the case, again in Haiti, after the earthquake killed hundreds of thousands and wounded many more. By 2012, The UN estimated that over $1.6 billion in relief aid was given to Haiti by international donors, about $155 per Haitian, and over $2 billion in recovery aid, about $173 per Haitian. Yet two years after the earthquake over half a million people remained homeless in hundreds of informal camps. As *Haïti Liberté* reported:

> It turns out that almost none of the money that the general public thought was going to Haiti actually went directly to Haiti. The international community chose to bypass the Haitian people, Haitian non-governmental organizations and the Haitian government. Funds were instead diverted to other governments, international non-governmental organizations (NGOs), and private companies.
>
> (Quigley and Ramanauskas 2012)

Investigating The Red Cross

The Red Cross alone raised nearly half a billion dollars for earthquake relief, more than any other nonprofit organization. But a joint investigation done by *ProPublica* and *NPR* found that, for example, an extensive plan to build housing resulted in only six permanent homes (Elliott and Sullivan 2015). The detailed report cites internal documents that quote Red Cross staff and Haitian employees, all that paint a picture of mismanagement, lack of accountability, and an utter loss of ethical practices. Keep in mind that this venerable organization is the favored agency of choice for most Americans. A congressional investigation followed the media coverage, resulting in a 300-page document. The investigation led to further coverage and press reports, but it took a long time. Kim Ives discussed the way the scandal finally came to light:

> This issue was spearheaded by progressive media like *Haiti Liberté*, NGO activists, and independent films, such as *Where Did the Money Go?* until it was finally picked up by *NPR* and *ProPublica*, which did an expose that got the congress involved.[7]

Ives also points to other types of humanitarian stories rarely covered by US media—the role played by other countries in crisis relief.

> Mainstream media rarely ever tell the story of the valiant role played by the Cubans[8] and other Latin Americans, a role that is almost always minimized and ignored in press reporting. They are the true unsung heroes of humanitarian efforts in Haiti.

After the failure of the major aid organizations in Haiti in 2010, local women's groups in the country are taking a major role in providing food and security to women and children in the face of the devastation caused by Hurricane Matthew. Writing for *Foreign Policy in Focus*, Anna Tenuta (2016) reports that women are at the forefront of recovery efforts. This new development bodes well for local, ground-up participation in meeting the needs of the people of Haiti and rebuilding the country's infrastructure through local partnerships.

A Different Kind of Documentary

Contemporary new media technologies and innovations have expanded online content and distribution, as well as the number of media producers and makers. In turn, such changes have led to new formats and creative productions, some of which were detailed in this volume. These developments have also inspired innovations in legacy media where the once distinct roles played by presenters and humanitarians can sometimes merge. Such was the case when humanitarian doctor and educator, Alexander van Tulleken, and his twin brother Christoffer, worked with the BBC on *Frontline Doctors*, shot in the early winter of 2016. The film benefits from the professional journalistic practices of this legacy media, especially with regard to the "conflict of interest" issues. The brothers were required by the BBC and indeed went to some lengths to insure there would be no issues with bias, or undue prominence for any particular charity.[9] This protected the independent point of view presented in the film, which documents the journey of Dr. van Tulleken as he follows the migrants who have crossed the Mediterranean and moved into Europe, and on to "the jungle" in Calais, France. The doctor helps treat many of the migrants and evaluates their health and humanitarian needs. Dr. van Tulleken is also the on-camera host, and the "presenter" of the film. "Dr. Xand" speaks directly to the camera, telling viewers they've gotten about 70 people out of one boat and treated a few for hypothermia. He goes on to say, "I feel elated and extremely sad at the same time. It's a very confusing feeling. But you look out and you say oh, these people are safe, and there's another boat right there."[10]

There were times when the different values and practices between the role of humanitarian doctor and journalist clashed. Dr. van Tulleken noted in a forum at Fordham University that when shooting the film at one location they were asked by the authorities to move:

> At first I thought like a humanitarian doctor: oh he's right we probably shouldn't be here. But then the cameraman told the official, "No we're staying. We have a right to be here." I thought yes, that's right we do. How liberating it was to be a journalist.

The film was well-received by the public and the media, with one commentator noting, "The doctors are good guides, naturally articulate enough to describe what we see and how they feel without being overschooled in the affectless media soundbitery that habitually interferes with both presenters' and viewers' responses to the stories being told." This assessment of the film is accurate, and at the same time offers an astute critique that raises an important point about most journalistic reporting on refugees. In this case the doctors' humanitarian sensibility overcomes the often problematic "affectless" stance of on-camera presenters. The doctors have found a way to mediate the story to the public through the eyes of humanitarian aid workers, a legitimate, alternative perspective able to overcome the forced neutrality of most news reporting. Their perspective also serves to nurture a sense of humanitarian solidarity among the public.

High-Tech Storytelling

Consider another development in visual storytelling about Syrian refugees. It is an 8-minute virtual reality film titled *Clouds over Sidra* that immerses the viewer (who must wear Google Cardboard and Samsung Gear headsets) in the day-to-day life of a 12-year-old Syrian girl who lives at the Za'atari refugee camp in the Jordanian desert. The film debuted at the World Economic Forum in Davos, Switzerland in 2015, where 120 diplomats had to wait in line to see the film. Filmmaker Chris Milk teamed with the United Nations to make the film and UN Secretary-General Ban Ki-Moon had it screened at a major reception of the Humanitarian Pledging Conference for Syria. The conference generated $3.8 billion, after it was projected to raise $2.3 billion. The UN clearly uses the film with impact in mind, bringing it to high-level meetings where policymakers, philanthropists, and big donors are present.[11] *Clouds Over Sidra* went on to screen at Sundance, TEDx in Vancouver, and South by Southwest. Chris Milk explains the VR film this way: it "allows us to feel compassion for people who are very different from us."[12]

However, this new format raises questions about the nature of journalism and the role it should play in democratic societies. This type of visual immersion collapses the space between the subject and viewers, and disrupts the cognitive connection between information and action based on knowledge and understanding. Instead, it presents the tendency to act on powerful persuasions, purely at an emotional level, one that bypasses the reasons and causes of suffering and conflict, and therefore citizen-based participation in policy discussions. As VR comes to be utilized as a format for news reporting, such as the special reporting for the *Huffington Post*, these issues will raise further questions as to the use of technology and its effects on citizenship in the future.

Aid Worker as Analyst

At times the mutually beneficial partnerships between reporters and aid workers, and news organizations and agencies, breaks down and shifts from a friendly to an adversarial role. This can happen with aid workers in the field. Just as the foot soldiers experiencing the horrors of the Western Front in the Great War, after reading the propagandistic reports published in the press, called the journalists to account (Andersen 2006). At times, aid-workers on the ground in a conflict or crisis find that media coverage of their situation bears little resemblance to what they have experienced. In this case aid workers become media critics. This was the case with the UNICEF staff member working on the conflict-torn island in the Philippines. She found the national press reported the conflict through the "international Muslim terrorist" frame, when the long-entrenched local conflict bore little resemblance to that interpretation. The point of view of the aid worker, gained through experience on the ground, is not only perceptually astute, many times it is able to offer an analysis for policy solutions, and a critique of policy justifications. Whether staff will be able to offer such context and analysis often depends on the policies of the organization.

Journalistic Independence

Throughout this volume, we have expanded our view of the humanitarian imagination to include the role of the citizen in a democratic process. Citizenship requires an informed public, and the role of media is to provide the knowledge needed for the public to participate in political discussions, and ultimately humanitarian policies. The ability of a news outlet to provide the public with accurate information can be challenged if news media rely too closely on the narratives of aid agencies. But in the case of *Al-Jazeera*, a network that seems to excel in its coverage of war and its human toll, and also partners with humanitarian organizations, there are indications that it has maintained its journalistic mandate, at least in countries not of geopolitical importance to Qatar. For example, the network aired a r eport that questioned the policies Intel put in place to stop them from sourcing conflict mine- ral from DRC (Herrman and Kamat 2015). In addition, unlike mainstream US media outlets, the network published extensively on the humanitarian crisis that the indigenous Wayuu people have been experiencing in Columbia, including a striking photo essay (Rosso 2016). However, Chicago-based writer Stephen Lendman (2011) has pointed out that after Qatar joined the NATO intervention of Libya, *Al-Jazeera* lost much of its critical edge reporting on the consequences of the NATO bombing on civilians in Libya. This confirms what many news analysts have long known, that nationalism and official foreign policy decisions taken by nation states heavily influence the press coverage of global events in the country of origin.

Poverty, NGOs, and Aid Agencies

When the press follows the media messaging from aid agencies it can have consequences for news reporting. As we have seen in the past, when news focused on agency-driven relief efforts, the result was a lack of reporting on the context and causes of famine. Lugo-Ocando (2015) has recently asserted that Western aid agencies have dominated news reporting of poverty as well, especially in coverage outside Europe and the US and this has affected reporting in negative ways. In *Blaming the Victim*, Lugo-Ocando notes that global journalism relies heavily on sources that are "white, male and from elite institutions," when reporting on poverty and the poor (27). Especially when covering Africa and Latin America the voices of the poor are marginalized, and stories frequently fail to include "a single source from the affected country itself." He concludes that, "the whole story is articulated through the voices of Westerners" (62). Lugo-Ocando confirms what we have noted above, that because of cuts by news organizations in the number of correspondents and bureaus, NGO communi- cation operations are a major source of information about developing countries. This holds true for reporting on poverty as well. As we know, NGO public relations campaigns seek to raise awareness that furthers their fundraising efforts, but they benefit from media coverage in other ways. In the competitive universe of proliferating NGOs, press reporting also provides "power and influence to the bureaucracies that deploy them" (128). As a consequence, and not surprisingly given the arguments detailed in Chouliaraki (2013), Lugo-Ocando also finds that NGO media campaigns imitate corporate public relations practices and "poverty is managed like any other topic, by spin doctors who deliver both media attention and tone, while media becomes more and more embedded in supporting organizations' narratives, subsequently embracing their discourses on poverty in their own news" (132). Just as stories about famine focus on food relief and fail to explain the root causes of famine, poverty coverage fails to explain the structural causes of economic inequality. Lugo-Ocando asserts that aid agencies are concerned that such coverage would alienate potential Western donors. Ultimately, the lack of information or context about poverty has many consequences. Global publics are prevented from understanding and therefore acting on economic and political levels that could address the root causes of global structural inequality. They become targets of message manipulations (PR), compelled through modes of persuasion to donate, instead of being addressed as global citizens who are compelled to participate in political and economic policy level discussions. This prevents global publics from acting in solidarity with the poor in meaningful ways, ways that could address structural economic injustice at the root of deprivation. Chouliaraki (2013) calls this revolutionary solidarity. As Lugo-Ocando concludes, the NGOs' "anti-poverty propaganda tends to reinforce current trends on reporting poverty rather than helping to create an alternative matrix to foster critical thinking and action" (2015, 144).

Such an alternative matrix that could result in revolutionary solidarity also depends on alternative narratives, explanations, and knowledge-based reporting not found in mainstream corporate news outlets. Take for example an exposé of market-driven global economic policies that the journalists argue lead to further impoverishment in Cambodia, even though they are promoted by the World Bank as solutions for the country's poverty levels.

Investigative Journalism, the World Bank, and Human Rights

Special Economic Zones

Matt Kennard and Claire Provost (2016) are investigative reporters who wrote a first-hand account of the mistreatment of workers in Special Economic Zones (SEZ) in Cambodia and China. Published in *In These Times* in a piece titled, "Inside The Corporate Utopias Where Capitalism Rules and Labor Laws Don't Apply," the journalists documented labor violations by corporations benefiting from the special laws applied only in SEZ. Kennard was interviewed on *The Real News Network* on August 22, 2016.

Special Economic Zones are places with a different set of business laws than the states in which they operate. Designed by the World Bank, and other development banks, they are promoted as ideal models—the best way to overcome obstacles to development and facilitate a country's entry into the global market. But Matt Kennard calls them "corporate utopias" where investors are sold on the idea that corporations will have more control over business regulations. For example, in Cambodia major independent unions are legal, and they have organized for better pay and working conditions. In 2013 there was an uprising of organized labor and a mass strike supported by civil society groups. After that the minimum wage was raised to $140 a month, or 81 cents an hour. Before then it was as low as $18 a month. The current struggle is to raise it to $200 a month.

But that struggle cannot be carried out in SEZ. These places are walled off, "built in the middle of nowhere," away from the prying eyes of journalists and labor organizers who cannot get inside because of guards and physical security. Unions therefore can't organize. Workers inside told Kennard, "if we try to organize independently, we'll be fired, we'll be disciplined" (*Real News Network* 2016). SEZ get around the law mandating a unionized labor force by creating "yellow" unions, controlled by government and employers. But as Kennard explains, these unions don't represent workers. When they actually have grievances they can't take it to the union or the shop steward.

Violating Core Labor Standards

The International Labor Organization, (ILO), an agency of the United Nations has worked with member states to ratify Core Labor Standards (CLS). CLS are recognized as important to Human Rights, and are employed globally as an International Human Rights Instrument, including the Rights of the Child. They are widely ratified by the international community, and Cambodia is a signatory. The first Core Labor Standard is freedom of association, the provision whereby workers are able to join trade unions that are independent of government and employer influence.[13] Clearly SEZ violate Core Labor Standards, yet SEZ are promoted by the World Bank and sold to investors interested in high returns. As part of the United Nation's structure, the mission of the World Bank is to end poverty, however it is also mandated to "help developing countries achieve sustainable growth" through financing investment and "mobilizing capital in international financial markets." According to its Articles of Agreement, policy decisions prioritize the facilitation of capital investment and international trade.

Here the contradictions between market capitalism's need for profits and the needs of a poor country are glaring, and those contradictions are reflected in the very structure of the United Nation and its affiliated units. As one of the poorest countries in the region, cheap labor is the main attraction for investment in Cambodia, but Kennard says, "there are no real economic benefits here for Cambodia" (*Real New Network* 2016). However, bankers tell him that if they don't promise low wages investors will pull out. Here the demands of high-yield market investment require that national laws protecting workers be bypassed. Increasing wages, however, is the primary way to lift Cambodians out of poverty.

The journalist Matt Kennard sums up the situation, saying what we have created is:

> a system whereby you will be more successful in attracting an investment if you are the most uncivilized country possible in terms of workers rights, environmental regulations [and] taxation. Everything that we think is good about civilized societies, you have to do away with to attach investment.
>
> (*Real News Network* 2016)

Alternatives?

Cambodia is a rural economy. Matt Kennard proposes a development model to support small agriculture, but that is not compatible with integrating the country into the global market economy, as mandated by the World Bank's articles of incorporation. "This model is founded on a very unjust idea where we just have to create a wasteland which is good for corporations." The singular demand for profits will not result in "ideas that are going to benefit the people of Cambodia" in the long term, but obviously they will "make some people very, very rich" (*Real News Network* 2016). Such global economic injustice is structural, and is at the root of poverty and the unequal distribution of wealth—the explanatory "alternative matrix" identified by Lugo-Ocando (2016).

Since the mid 1980s, 3,000 SEZs have been created worldwide. They employ over 65 million people and can be found in half the world's countries. What has become clear to many development groups, economists, and environmentalists is that financial markets have been successful in helping money gravitate to the top globally, but such zones violate human rights and lead to social and economic inequality, deepening the North/South global economic divide. Here we find that the inherent contradictions within the large bureaucracy that is the United Nations lead to policies that work at cross purposes. Labor rights and SEZ are incompatible. In this case, human rights standards are violated by the practices mandated by the articles of agreement adopted at the World Bank.

Countries such as Cambodia will remain poor while the causes of those conditions remain hidden from most of the public, and therefore outside of significant international policy debates. Poverty remains a root cause of humanitarian disasters of all sorts, yet the failure of the media prevents publics from understanding those causes—a prerequisite for revolutionary solidarity. Knowledge-based journalism is most often published on alternative sources—such exposés are not usually found on mainstream media, especially in the United States. Matt Kennard is also a Deputy Director at the Centre for Investigative Journalism, which provides funding and support for independent, critical journalism that informs the public.

Market-based solutions to poverty have been the preferred strategies in the era of neoliberal globalization, and are taken for granted as legitimate development practices in media, but just as SEZ have failed to lift countries out of poverty, so too have other forms of market-based solutions failed to reduce global poverty.

Microfinance (MF) and Women's Empowerment

Microfinance was once all the rage, but for a decade it has been seriously challenged. From its roots in Bangladesh in the early 1970s undertaken by Dr. Muhammad Yunus, the practice has been increasingly supported by the World Bank and the UN, and Yunus was given the Nobel Peace Prize in 2006. Its appeal is based on the assumption that offering microcredit to the poor will result in sustainable economic and social development motivated by the people themselves. But Duncan Green (2009) of Oxfam sees serious ideological overtones to MF. The emphasis on individual entrepreneurship over all other forms of state or cooperative development funding, carries within it a preference for neoliberal market strategies for development.

Citing two comprehensive studies done in India and the Philippines that found that MF did *not* reduce poverty, Green argues that successful development is much more complex than single market solutions. He cites Qazi Ahmad, the President of the Bangladesh Economic Association, who surveyed 2,500 borrowers (99 percent of them women) and concluded that microfinance failed. "They take out credit, and give it back. That's all they do," he said (Green 2009). In his book, Qazi Ahmad (2007) criticized MF for its limited approach to poverty alleviation, arguing that it ignores such crucial issues as existing power relations in society.

Often promoted as a solution to gender inequalities in developing countries, Green found little evidence that women micro-borrowers have been empowered by it. "Often, they are simply the conduit for some money coming into the family." Only a small proportion of women say they are in full control of the management of economic activities undertaken with micro-credit. "A large majority of the micro-credit households have remained condemned to a lowly and subservient state of living" (Green 2009).

Development researchers Bateman and Chang (2012) agree, saying ultimately MF constitutes a "new and very powerful institutional barrier to sustainable local economic and social development, and thus also to sustainable poverty reduction." They add that continued support for MF in economic development policy "cannot be divorced from its supreme serviceability to the neoliberal/globalisation agenda."

Well-meaning NGOs continue to offer MF as the solution to any number of problems women face around the globe, such as the MF solutions offered by *Half the Sky*. If we look at the complexity of the problem of Female Genital Mutilation and Cutting for example, we find that individualized entrepreneurial strategy cannot address the complexities of the processes needed to end the practice—social, cultural and community interrelationship must be considerations. An interagency report published by the World Health Organization (2008, 13) understands that the decision to abandon FGM "must be collective and explicit so that each family will have the confidence that others are also abandoning the practice." In addition, the decision must be "widespread within the practicing community in order to be sustained." They also identify the larger issues of patriarchy that are embedded structurally within the larger societies, meaning that women and girls are also actively involved many times in sustaining the practice.

Celebrity discussions in such complex issues have been charged with flattening and simplifying such complexities. Interestingly, the WHO suggests the use of celebrities, or "public personalities," but in very different roles, suggesting they serve as "champions" against FGM, playing an informational role. It states, "Community-based educational activities can also build on and expand their work with the mass media such as drama, video and local radio" (WHO 2008, 14).

Humanitarian Organizations and the Extractive Industries

Another set of discussions left largely outside of dominant media agendas are policy debates within and between the many international bodies, relief organizations, and NGOs, that often address the central issues of global inequities. For example, the analysis by Philippe Calain (2012) of Doctors Without Borders argues for a policy of non-engagement with extractive industries. He points out that extraction often expands through remote territories, regardless of the land rights of the resident populations, the unique biodiversity, or the presence of historical assets. Fossil fuel extraction often leads to "land seizures, destitution, imposed industrialisation and urbanisation, population displacements, gender disparities, child labour, and the unequal distribution of profits from geological wealth." Because of these factors, extractive industries often generate or perpetuate forms of violence, putting extractive companies on a par with the parties to armed conflicts. He argues that collaborations with such industries could be seen as "an implicit endorsement of a dominant development paradigm based on rapid economic growth and market productivity," and run the risk of co-opting the medical providers who provide mitigation measures when they are brought in to treat the many health conditions caused by pollution, resource depletion, and community disintegration.

The United Nations and the Security Council

In another, possibly more urgent set of contradictions within the UN, are the decisions made by the Security Council that violate every humanitarian standard that the international body has worked so long to establish and implement around the globe. This is the final example we will explore in this volume, and it is possibly the most deplorable—the vast humanitarian crisis in Yemen—and the inadequate media coverage of the suffering of the people of Yemen.

The Humanitarian Disaster in Yemen

This is one of the worst crises in the world and is continuing to get worse.
(Jamie McGoldrick, UN Humanitarian Coordinator for Yemen)[14]

On April 14, 2015, The Security Council Passed S/Res 2216 that allowed what came to be known as the Saudi Coalition to carry out airstrikes and blockade the ports of Yemen. The resolution allowed the Saudis and their Gulf State allies "to immediately provide support, by all necessary means and measures, including military intervention, to protect Yemen and its people from the continuing aggression by the Houthis."[15] A full year and half later, by early October 2016, in an article titled, "Yemen Crisis: Who is Fighting Whom?" the BBC reported:

> At least 4,125 civilians had been killed and 7,207 others injured, according to the United Nations. With just under half of the population under the age of 18, children constituted a third of all civilian deaths during the first year of the conflict.
>
> The destruction of civilian infrastructure and restrictions on food and fuel imports have also led to 21 million people being deprived of life-sustaining commodities and basic services. The UN says 3.1 million Yemenis are internally displaced, while 14 million people are suffering from food insecurity and 370,000 children under the age of five are at risk of starving to death. More than 1,900 of the country's 3,500 health facilities are also currently either not functioning or partially functioning, leaving half the population without adequate healthcare.[16]

The BBC notes that the conflict finds its roots in the failure of the political transition, following an uprising that forced its longtime authoritarian president, Ali Abdullah Saleh, to hand over power to Mr Hadi in November 2011.[17] The piece goes on to acknowledge that the conflict is part of a regional power struggle between Shia-ruled Iran and Sunni-ruled Saudi Arabia.

What is sadly fascinating is that a full year and half after the Saudis began bombing Yemen, the BBC finds it necessary to explain the very basics of the conflict to its readers. The lack of information in the United States is even more extreme. During the presidential election, no mention was made of the dire situation in Yemen by any candidate, nor did one journalist ask the presidential contenders about the conflict—*one of the worst humanitarian disasters on the globe.* Indeed, coverage of the civilian suffering has been virtually absent in the mainstream press.

The near total media blackout has allowed the suffering of the people of Yemen, the poorest country in the region, to continue. In the alternative press, a handful of writers have been documenting the siege. Indeed, they have also charged that the United States and the failure of the media to cover the devastation have contributed to the suffering. For example, on January 18, 2016, Salon.com published a piece written by Sharif Abdel Kouddous, headlined "America has Blood On its Hands: Yemen is Now the World's Worst Humanitarian Crisis." Kouddous (2016) noted that "As the conflict grinds on into its nine month, the level of suffering in Yemen has garnered relatively little attention in the international press." This long piece details the effects of the airstrikes on the country, which have devastated Yemen, "hitting civilian targets like weddings and hospitals with disturbing regularity. The blockade, meanwhile, is having a quieter, slower, but ultimately more deadly impact." Saudi Arabia says the blockade prevents arms from reaching the Houthis, but it has also blocked humanitarian aid. "Effectively, Yemenis are being strangled to death. Every day that passes they lose more and more of the essentials: food, water, shelter, fuel and health care" (Kouddous 2016).

The piece also explains the details of the blockade. The Security Council consisting of five permanent members; the United States, Russia, the UK, China, and France, passed the resolution drafted largely by the Gulf States currently waging the war. The resolution imposed a strict arms embargo on the Houthi leadership and their allies. The United States strongly supported the resolution, and all members except Russia voted in favor. Russia lobbied for the inclusion of language mandating "humanitarian pauses" in the bombing, but Gulf countries vigorously opposed that. Critics charge that "the measure amounts to an endorsement of the siege that is choking supply lines and killing Yemenis who have little or nothing to do with the war" (Kouddous 2016).

Because Yemen relied heavily on imports for basic goods, including 90 percent of its food supply, the blockade has been devastating. The impoverished country also imports fuel and medicine. By September 2015, the UN Office for Coordination of Humanitarian Affairs (OCHA) said that fuel imports fell to just 1 percent of monthly requirements. "Over 21 million people—or more than 80 percent of the population—now require some kind of humanitarian assistance to meet their basic needs." Trond Jensen, the head of OCHA in Yemen said, "we are seeing an enormous impact on civilian populations" because of the blockade. The World Food Program lists ten of Yemen's 22 provinces in dire need of emergency food assistance. As WFP Deputy Regional Director Matthew Hollingworth said in December, "Half of the country is now just one step away from famine." Internally displaced persons attempting to escape "relentless coalition bombardment," now amount to 2.2 million people, or about a tenth of the population, the majority women and children. The piece goes on the quote some displaced persons experiencing starvation, "My life is all hunger and fatigue," says Mariam Ahmed, a gnarled and frail grandmother who says she hasn't eaten for two days. She speaks haltingly, wheezing out short sentences. "There is nothing here. I've cried until I couldn't cry anymore." The piece also includes pictures of rubble and the people experiencing the hardships (Kouddous 2016).

As the situation continued to deteriorate, in July 2016, the *Huffington Post* ran a piece with the headline, "Yemen: The Forgotten Famine." Under the feature image of a despondent-looking child receiving food aid the captions reads:

> The UN World Food Programme warns "Global Acute Malnutrition (GAM) is at an alarming stage in most of the country's governorates, reaching levels of 25.1 percent in Taiz Lowland and 21.7 in Al Hodeidah." Only international food aid can save war victims from starvation.
>
> (Lambers 2016)

Lambers acknowledges that Yemen was in the news that week after an Al Qaeda attack on a military base in the southern part of the country, and notes the chaos created by the civil war—now that both Al Qaeda and ISIS are operating in Yemen. But he goes on to point out that "what has not made the news is the biggest threat of all to Yemen: famine."

It would take an increase in the indiscriminate bombing of civilian infrastructures by the Saudis for *The New York Times* to run an editorial with the headline "America is Complicit in the Carnage in Yemen.[18] On August 17, 2016, after the Saudi-led coalition killed over 40 civilians in airstrikes targeting a school, a potato chip factory and a hospital associated with Doctors Without Borders, the *Times* warned, "Under international law, those facilities in Yemen are not legitimate military targets."[19] The editors detailed the ways the United States was "complicit in the carnage." First on the list were arms sales to the Saudis "to mollify them after the nuclear deal with Iran." Voicing international outrage expressed by the bombing of the hospital, which alone killed 15 people, the *Times* points out that it "was the fourth attack on a facility supported by Doctors Without Borders in the past year even though all parties to the conflict were told exactly where the hospitals were located." The United Nations and human rights groups said war crimes may have been committed. The *Times* charged that the Saudis bear "the heaviest responsibility for inflaming the conflict with the Houthis, an indigenous Shiite group with loose connections to Iran." Pointing out that Yemen is caught in the middle of a regional power struggle, the Saudis believed Tehran was gaining too much influence in the region:

> Although many experts believe the threat to be overstated, Mr. Obama agreed to support the Yemen intervention—without formal authorization from Congress—and sell the Saudis even more weapons in part to appease Riyadh's anger over the Iran nuclear deal. All told, since taking office, Mr. Obama has sold the Saudis $110 billion in arms, including Apache helicopters and missiles.
>
> Mr. Obama has also supplied the coalition such indispensable assistance as intelligence, in-flight refueling of aircraft and help in identifying appropriate targets. Experts say the coalition would be grounded if Washington withheld its support. Instead, the State Department last week approved the potential sale of $1.15 billion more in tanks and other equipment to Saudi Arabia to replace items destroyed in the war.

The *Times* then calls on Congress to oppose the arms deals, quoting Senator Chris Murphy (D-Conn) who told CNN "There's an American imprint on every civilian life lost in Yemen."

One of the very few network news pieces that mentions civilian casualties in Yemen was published on August 15, 2016, and discussed the attempt on the part of US Congressional representatives to block US weapons sales to Saudi Arabia.

In the ABC news piece, Congressman Liu (D-California) frames his words within the discourse of US National Security, saying that Saudi conduct in Yemen that is killing civilians with US-made weapons has "harmed our national security interests." Here the discussion that follows immediately moves away from the loss of life and the humanitarian crisis, and instead stays within the narrow parameters of debate framed by security interests and weaponry. First, the denial by a "State Department spokesman" that downplays "concerns that the weapons transferred to Saudi Arabia could be used to harm civilians in Yemen" (Thorbecke 2015). The source goes on to assert that the "sale is aimed toward strengthening Saudi Arabia's *future defense capabilities* (emphasis added)." It will refurbish "some existing tanks" and these types of "weapons systems are not currently being used for offensive operations in Yemen." After all, these arms sales are for "land force equipment, while most of the civilian casualties have been a result of airstrikes." The ABC journalist offers no response to these assertions, nor do they document the types of weapons being shipped to the Saudis. Many more words are dedicated to Saudi future security than to the people being decimated in Yemen.

The killing of civilians is not mentioned until the twelfth and thirteenth paragraphs, which report that a school was struck in Northern Yemen that killed ten children and injured dozens more. Also, Doctors Without Borders reported on Twitter that one of its hospitals had been hit in an airstrike. United Nations Secretary-General and UNICEF said the children killed were between 6 and 14 years old.

No photographs of injured or hungry children or the rubble that is now Yemen where the country's infrastructure once stood are included. A soldier behind a barricade in front of an automatic rifle serves as visual confirmation of the claim that that weapons sales secure Saudi ground defenses, and a file photo of Ban Ki-Moon is set toward the bottom of the report.

The ABC report illustrates the way mainstream foreign news discourse is framed by US geopolitical policies, especially when those policies are directing active military engagement. A congressional investigation provides an opening for critical discussion, and journalists can report on newsworthy actions and statements by government officials within Washington circles. However, as we have seen, reporting remains framed within the parameters of debate set by military belligerencies and national security. This type of reporting distances the reader from civilian suffering, and proscribes the potential for the public to respond in solidarity with the humanitarian consequences of war (Andersen 2006).

By October 27, 2016, Ben Norton, whose consistent reporting documents the wars in the Middle East for alternative online publications, wrote that the Saudi coalition had been targeting food production facilities just three months into the air war, after airstrikes failed to displace the rebels. Yemen continues to spiral downward, closer each day to the brink of famine where he writers, "'An entire generation could be crippled by hunger,' a World Food Program official warned this week. At least 14 million Yemenis, more than half of the country's population, are going hungry" (Norton 2016). Referencing a research paper by Martha Mundy, a professor emeritus at the London School of Economics, Norton notes that the Saudi coalition is "deliberately targeting Yemen's tiny agricultural sector in a campaign which, if successful, would lead a post-war Yemeni nation not just into starvation but total reliance on food imports for survival." Repeating what the UN and various human rights organizations have been documenting for months, the Saudi-led forces are accused of numerous war crimes for coalition attacks on a wide array of civilian areas, including hospitals, schools, homes, bridges, and refugee camps. The United Nations estimates that the US-backed, Saudi-led coalition is "responsible for two-thirds of civilian deaths, whereas Houthi rebels and allied militias loyal to former Yemeni president Ali Abdullah Saleh have been responsible for less than one-fourth of civilian deaths. Extremist groups such as al-Qaida and ISIS, which have been strengthened by the war, were responsible for the rest. Yet the deaths caused by warring parties could pale in comparison to the numbers that might die from starvation. Norton also includes reports from Amnesty International, noting that the US could be held accountable for war crimes, as it has conducted more than 1,000 refueling sorties, providing tens of millions of pounds of fuel for Saudi warplanes, offered intelligence and has even had "officers physically in the room with Saudi command officers" (Norton 2016). Citing the US-made bomb that the Saudi-led coalition dropped on October 8 on a funeral group in Sanaa that killed more than 140 people and wounded 600 more, Norton also notes that recent atrocities have brought attention to the war, which previously had "received little coverage in U.S. media outlets" (Norton 2016). Human Rights Watch identified the killing as an apparent war crime, and the British government's Middle East minister, Tobias Ellwood, referred to the massacre as a case of "deliberate error." Labour Party leader Jeremy Corbyn asked for an "opposition day" to speak out in Parliament against the continuing UK support for the bombing campaign.

> Scores of similar atrocities have been carried out. Amnesty International and Human Rights Watch have documented more than 70 unlawful coalition airstrikes, as a conservative estimate. These rights groups have also documented the coalition's use

of widely banned cluster munitions, weapons made by the U.S. and U.K., in Civilian areas in Yemen.

(Norton 2016)

Reuters reported that on October 29, 2016, the UN recognized the Yemeni government in exile, headed by Abd-Rabbu Mansour Hadi, now living in Saudi Arabia, who rejected a UN peace proposal. The plan was delivered by UN envoy Ismail Ould Cheickh Ahmed in Riyadh. According to Reuters, the plan would have sidelined Hadi by forming a government comprised of less divisive figures.[20]

Here we see the refusal to halt belligerencies even under a UN peace proposal, and the triumph of sheer military might employed in a strategic regional power struggle devastating millions of innocent civilians, and even challenging the continued existence of the country and its people.

The war in Yemen has only strengthened the rise of al-Qaida and ISIS there, and yet the Saudi bombings continue. Indeed, even in the face of growing humanitarian disaster, the UN Security Council renewed the resolution, signing it on February 24, 2016. These actions have been taken in spite of the documentation and dire warnings from a coalition of UN relief agencies including the UN's Food and Agriculture Organization, the IPC, a partnership of UN agencies, including UNICEF and WFP, and NGOs under the leadership of the European Union-funded Food Security Information Systems (FSIS) programme and the Food Security Technical Secretariat of the Yemeni government's Ministry of Planning and International Cooperation. The UN High Commissioner for Human Rights has also openly contradicted Saudi generals on the ground claiming that they have allowed humanitarian supplies into the port of Yemen saying, "Severe import restrictions, caused mainly by the naval blockade imposed by the coalition forces have aggravated the humanitarian situation" (Kouddous 2016).

As we have seen with the so-called humanitarian war in Libya, in Yemen as well, the United Nations has been acting as a de facto militarized body, calling for and condoning belligerencies through the Security Council and militarizing the diplomatic process, actions that stand well outside of its mandate for global peace and stability through international law and negotiation. In doing so, the United Nations itself has succumbed to a dominant militarized, global superpower and its allies, and created one of the most dire humanitarian crises in the world, even as its own agencies fight to save the people dying in Yemen as a consequence of its actions. The UN must not and cannot continue down this path, for it belies every legitimate claim it has to international solidarity, and must create, through mutual understanding and dialogue, a more peaceful and just world.

In these pages we have sought to identify the tensions and challenges, failures and successes of press reports, media portrayals, and social media discussions of global humanitarian crises, and the general media framing of humanitarian affairs. We have considered the relationships between the press and relief agencies, and the content of humanitarian communication. Amid this complex geography, we have discovered highly positive messages that undergird and nurture a humanitarian imagination. We have also sought to document cases in which xenophobic terms and discourses, and the media outlets used for their dissemination, address publics in the most destructive ways that block the pathways of the empathy and generosity, knowledge and understanding needed for global justice and security. We hope the analyses offered in this volume can bring us closer to negotiating this increasingly vast media environment, pointing to ways in which the interrelationships between media and humanitarian action can be nurtured and developed, while avoiding the pitfalls of the past.

We have come to understand that the humanitarian imagination must be nurtured with the language of solidarity that ties the world's people together as a unified humanity, across borders and boundaries. We also realize, as the globe inches closer to crises of our making, from human-generated to the ultimate consequences of environmental destruction, that information, documentation, understanding, and knowledge are the primary way that global publics will be able to participate in the decisions needed to redirect the earth's resources in ways that nurture humanity and humanitarian sensibilities. Global citizens must be able to participate in the essential discussions about the economic transformations needed to right the imbalances between the Global North and South. Warring states, superpowers, and the market forces that drive hyper-corporate exploitation of the earth's remaining resources will only be halted when global publics understand the need to redirect the world's sentiments and actions. Only then will media and humanitarian action forge the bonds needed to end humanitarian disasters of all sorts.

Notes

1. *Democracy Now*, "From U.S. Ally to Convicted War Criminal: Inside Chad's Hissène Habré's Close Ties to Reagan Administration," May 31, 2015, available at: www.democracynow.org/2016/5/31/from_us_ally_to_convicted_war
2. Interview with the author, July 2, 2016.
3. *New York Times* Editorial, "The Cholora Epidemic the US left Behind in Haiti," available at: www.nytimes.com/2016/07/06/opinion/the-cholera-epidemic-the-un-left-behind-in-haiti.html?smprod=nytcore-iphone&smid=nytcore-iphone-share&_r=1. See Also, "State Dept. Should Demand UN Take Responsibility in Haiti," Opinion, *Boston Globe*, July 12, 2016, available at: www.bostonglobe.com/opinion/editorials/2016/07/11/state-dept-should-demand-take-responsibility-haiti/cXOG9u8hxdSlxwIBR53U0L/story.html
4. Email from Kim Ives to the author, July 2016.
5. *New York Times* Editorial (2016), ibid.
6. *The Boston Globe* ran an earlier editorial calling for UN action in Haiti, but on February 28, 2013, the paper ran a piece titled, "UN's Cold, But Correct, Call on Haiti," available at: www.bostonglobe.com/opinion/columns/2013/02/28/decision-claim-diplomatic-immunity-for-cholera-outbreak-haiti-was-cold-but-correct/MxeER5UM6aWzZB2WNJtjgI/story.html
7. Internet communication with the author, July 21, 2016.
8. Gamma International, "Cuba Will Remain in Haiti for as Long as Needed," available at: www.usmlo.org/arch2010/2010–02/VR100201.htm#04
9. Email communication from Alexander van Tulleken with the author, August 6, 2016. In fact, Xand and Chris resigned form the board of MDM Médecins du Monde/Doctors of the World, prior to the start of filming.
10. For a clip of this sequence see, "A scramble to help freezing migrants," March 3, 2016. Available from the BBC: www.bbc.co.uk/programmes/p03lc9q7
11. www.fastcompany.com/3051672/tech-forecast/how-the-united-nations-is-using-virtual-reality-to-tackle-real-world-problems
12. www.geekwire.com/2015/how-technology-is-turning-humanitarian-workers-into-journalists-and-filmmakers/
13. www.ilo.org/dyn/normlex/en/f?p=1000:11200:0::NO:11200:P11200_COUNTRY_ID:103055
14. Press TV-UN "UN Agencies Warn of 'Food Emergency in Yemen," available at: www.presstv.com/Detail/2016/06/22/471548/UN-alarm-Yemen-food-shortages-hunger-crisis-FAO-World-Food-Programme-Saudi-aggression-Lahij-Ansarullah
15. www.securitycouncilreport.org/un-documents/yemen/
16. "Yemen Crisis: Who is Fighting Whom?" BBC News, October 14, 2016, available at: www.bbc.com/news/world-middle-east-29319423
17. BBC, ibid.
18. Editorial, "America is Complicit in the Carnage in Yemen," *The New York Times*, August 17, 2016, available at: www.nytimes.com/2016/08/17/opinion/stop-saudi-arms-sales-until-carnage-in-yemen-ends.html
19. *The New York Times*, ibid.
20. Reuters, "Air Strike Kills 17 in Yemen, Exiled President Rejects Peace Plan," available at: http://mobile.reuters.com/article/idUSKCN12T0EF. After the Kuwait peace talks failed, special envoy Cheickh told the UN Security Council:

I call on all groups to uphold their obligations under international humanitarian and human rights law to protect civilian life and infrastructure. The military escalation will continue to provide opportunities for the spread of terrorist groups. Al Qaeda and the Islamic State continue to wreak havoc in significant parts of Yemen.

(www.un.org/undpa/en/speeches-statements/31082016/yemen)

References

Ahmad, Q. K. (2007) (Ed.) *Socio-Economic and Indebtedness-Related Impact of Micro-Credit in Bangladesh*, Dhaka, Bangladesh: University Press.

Andersen, R. (2006) *A Century of Media, A Century of War*, New York: Peter Lang.

Bateman, M. and Chang, H-J. (2012) "Microfinance and the Illusion of Development: From Hubris to Nemesis in Thirty Years," *World Economic Review*, 1, 13–36.

Calain, P. (2012) "The Interaction between Humanitarian Non-Governmental Organisations and Extractive Industries: A Perspective from Médecins Sans Frontières," *International Review of the Red Cross*, 887, September 30, available at: www.icrc.org/eng/resources/documents/article/review-2012/irrc-887-calain.htm

Chouliaraki, L. (2013) *The Ironic Spectator: Solidarity in the Age of Post-Humanitarianism*, Cambridge, UK: Polity Press.

Elliott, J., and Sullivan, L. (2015) "How the Red Cross Raised Half a Billion Dollars for Haiti and Built Six Homes," *ProPublica* and *NPR*, June 3, available at: www.propublica.org/article/how-the-red-cross-raised-half-a-billion-dollars-for-haiti-and-built-6-homes

Green, D. (2009) "The Backlash Against Microfinance," available at: https://oxfamblogs.org/fp2p/whats-wrong-with-microfinance/

Herrman, C., and Kamat, A. (2015) "Are Intel's Microprocessors Really Conflict Free," *Al Jazeera*, November 14, available at: http://america.aljazeera.com/watch/shows/fault-lines/articles/2015/11/14/are-intels-microprocessors-really-conflict-free.html

Harrison, P., and Palmer, R. (1986) *New Out of Africa: Biafra to Band Aid*, London: Hilary Shipman.

Kennard, M. and Provost, C. (2016) "Inside the Corporate Utopias Where Capitalism Rules and Labor Laws Don't Apply," *In These Times*, July 25, available at: http://inthesetimes.com/features/special-economic-zones-corporate-utopia-capitalism.html

Kouddous, S. A. (2016) "America has Blood On Its Hands: Yemen Is Now the World's Worst Humanitarian Crisis," *Salon.com*, January 18, available at: www.salon.com/2016/01/18/yemen_is_now_the_worlds_worst_humanitarian_crisis_partner/

Lambers, W. (2016) "Yemen: The Forgotten Famine," *Huffington Post*, July 8, available at: www.huffingtonpost.com/william-lambers/yemen-the-forgotten-famin_b_10864754.html

Lendman, S. (2011) "War Propaganda: Western Media Promotes NATO Terror Bombing of Libya," *Global Research*, July 3, available at: www.globalresearch.ca/war-propaganda-western-media-promotes-nato-terror-bombing-of-libya/25492

Lugo-Ocando, J. (2015) *Blaming the Victim: How Global Journalism Fails Those in Poverty*, London: Pluto Press.

Norton, B. (2016) "Famine Looms in Yemen as US-backed Saudi Bombing Intentionally Target Food Production," *Salon.com*, October 27, available at: www.salon.com/2016/10/27/famine-looms-in-yemen-as-u-s-backed-saudi-bombing-intentionally-targets-food-production/

Quigley, B., and Ramanauskas, A. (2012) "Seven Places Where Haiti's Earthquake Money Did and Did Not Go," *Haïti Liberté*, January 10, available at: http://haiti-liberte.com/archives/volume5–25/Seven%20Places.asp

Real News Network. (2016) "Labor Rights Brazenly Violated in Global 'Corporate Utopias,'" August 22, available at: http://therealnews.com/t2/index.php?option=com_content&task=view&id=31&Itemid=74&jumival=17053

Rosso, N. F. (2016) "Colombia's Abandoned Wayuu People," *Al Jazeera*, February 3, available at: www.aljazeera.com/indepth/inpictures/2016/02/colombia-abandoned-wayuu-people-160201070235052.html

Sengupta, S. and Katz, J. M. (2016) "U.N. Plans to Pay Victims of Cholera Outbreak it Caused in Haiti," *The New York Times*, October 24, available at: www.nytimes.com/2016/10/25/world/americas/haiti-united-nations-cholera.html?mabReward=A1&recp=0&moduleDetail=recommendations-0&action=click&contentCollection=Opinion&region=Footer&module=WhatsNext&version=WhatsNext&contentID=WhatsNext&src=recg&pgtype=article

Tenuta, A. (2016) "After Hurricane, Haitian Women Ready to Lead," *Foreign Policy in Focus*, October 18, available at: http://fpif.org/hurricane-haitian-women-ready-lead/

Thorbecke, C. (2015) "Lawmakers Push to Block Saudi Arms Sales as Casualties Mount in Yemen," *ABC News*, August 15, available at: http://abcnews.go.com/International/lawmakers-push-block-saudi-arms-sale-casualties-mount/story?id=41392840

Waters, K. (2004) "Influencing the Message: The Role of Catholic Missionaries in Media Coverage of the Nigerian Civil War," *The Catholic Historical Review.* 90(4): 697–718

World Health Organization. (2008) "Eliminating Female Genital Mutilation: An Interagency Report, OHCHR, UNAIDS, UNDP, UNECA, UNESCO, UNFPA, UNHCR, UNICEF, UNIFEM, WHO," available at: www.who.int/reproductivehealth/publications/fgm/9789241596442/en/

INDEX